*Fifth Edition*

# CRIMINAL PROCEDURE
## FROM FIRST CONTACT TO APPEAL

**John L. Worrall**
*University of Texas at Dallas*

**PEARSON**

Boston  Columbus  Indianapolis  New York  San Francisco  Upper Saddle River
Amsterdam  Cape Town  Dubai  London  Madrid  Milan  Munich  Paris  Montréal  Toronto
Delhi  Mexico City  São Paulo  Sydney  Hong Kong  Seoul  Singapore  Taipei  Tokyo

**Editorial Director:** Vernon R. Anthony
**Executive Editor:** Gary Bauer
**Program Manager:** Megan Moffo
**Editorial Assistant:** Lynda Kramer
**Director of Marketing:** David Gesell
**Marketing Manager:** Mary Salzman
**Senior Marketing Coordinator:** Alicia Wozniak
**Marketing Assistant:** Les Roberts
**Team Lead for Project Management:** JoEllen Gohr
**Senior Project Manager:** Steve Robb
**Procurement Specialist:** Deidra M. Skahill

**Creative Director:** Andrea Nix
**Art Director:** Jayne Conte
**Cover Image:** © bbourdages/Fotolia
**Media Project Manager:** Leslie Brado
**Media Project Coordinator:** April Cleland
**Full-Service Project Management:** Revathi Viswanathan, PreMediaGlobal
**Composition:** PreMediaGlobal
**Printer/Binder:** LSC Communications
**Cover Printer:** LSC Communications
**Text Font:** 10/12, Minion Pro

Credits and acknowledgments for content borrowed from other sources and reproduced, with permission, in this textbook appear on the appropriate page within text.

**Library of Congress Cataloging-in-Publication Data**
Worrall, John L., author.
 Criminal procedure : from first contact to appeal / John L. Worrall, University of Texas at Dallas. — Fifth edition.
   pages   cm
 Includes index.
 ISBN-13: 978-0-13-349495-2
 ISBN-10: 0-13-349495-0
 1. Criminal procedure—United States.   2. Appellate procedure—United States.   I. Title.
 KF9619.W67 2013
 345.73'05—dc23

                                                                                              2013036878

8

ISBN 10: 0-13-349495-0
ISBN 13: 978-0-13-349495-2

To Dylan
*for never letting life get boring.*

# CONTENTS

# PART 5   Trial, Conviction, and Beyond

## CHAPTER 13   Rights at Trial   374

# PREFACE

I decided to write this book, *Criminal Procedure: From First Contact to Appeal*, after I had taught criminal procedure for several years. During each course, my students typically asked a litany of "what if" questions and became curious about the rules of criminal procedure after the police arrest and book a suspect. Students also expressed frustration with the fact that many of the leading books on criminal procedure presupposed a certain degree of familiarity with the criminal process, including an understanding of basic terminology. Students came to loathe these books' excessive use of legalese and obtuse descriptions of criminal procedure topics that had no real-life applications.

In addition, students frequently pointed out, as did I, that there are often significant differences between what the courts require and what happens in the real world of criminal justice. For instance, consider the definition of a *seizure* for the purposes of the Fourth Amendment. A seizure occurs when a reasonable person would believe he or she is not free to leave. Yet many times, students find this definition wanting and ask, "If a person is not seized according to this definition, is he or she really free to leave?" This question highlights the differences between what this book calls *theory* and *reality*. It and countless other similar questions prompted me to write a criminal procedure book of my own, one that takes a comprehensive yet basic approach to criminal procedure and that connects the material to the real world with examples and exercises.

By way of preview, then, this book presents an introduction to criminal procedure, from the point at which an individual first comes into contact with the police all the way through the appeals process. Approximately half of the book is devoted to traditional criminal procedure topics—notably, search-and-seizure as well as interrogation and identification procedures. The remainder of the book moves beyond these topics and discusses the pretrial process; the roles of defense attorneys, prosecutors, and grand juries; plea bargaining and guilty pleas; rights of criminal defendants at trial; and appeals and *habeas corpus*.

## ▶ Presentation

The material in *Criminal Procedure* is covered, in large part, by focusing on the constitutional rights of criminal defendants, as interpreted by the U.S. Supreme Court. To this end, many leading Supreme Court decisions are discussed; however, lengthy excerpts from the actual decisions have been reduced to relevant remarks in order to avoid distracting from the many important concepts introduced. In order to maintain a real-world focus, the book also incorporates many actual legal documents and excerpts from official policy manuals of police departments and other criminal justice agencies around the United States.

*Criminal procedure* should not be confused with *evidence procedure* or *trial procedure*. Evidence procedure concerns the rules for presenting evidence to prove guilt (or the lack thereof); thus, evidence courses cover such topics as types of evidence, rules for presenting witness testimony, hearsay, and the like. This book touches on evidence only tangentially—by discussing witness questioning and the police actions used to secure evidence through search and seizure. But the focus on evidence does not move beyond these two issues. Likewise, this book is not about trial procedure. That is, it does not address the nuances of criminal trials, including the order of events at trial, what objections can be raised, instructions to the jury, and so on. Trial procedure is a topic typically covered in law school.

Instead, this book presents a comprehensive introduction to criminal procedure, thoroughly presenting basic legal concepts and issues in a conversational written style and tone. Given this content coverage and the frequent use of examples from actual legal documents and policy guides, readers who are pursuing careers in criminal justice will find this book especially useful. Individuals who are already employed in criminal justice will find the book useful as well. Moreover, because the book constitutes more than a general overview of criminal procedure, it should prove beneficial to aspiring law students. But, it should not be over the heads of students with little or no background in criminal justice.

# ▶ Features

*Criminal Procedure* has a number of pedagogical features that will benefit readers. Each chapter begins with learning objectives and an outline of the topics covered, giving readers an at-a-glance preview of the content. Lists of key terms and key cases are also included at the end of each chapter. Each term is defined in a glossary appearing at the end of the book, and each key case is then highlighted in the margins near where it is discussed in the chapter text. Each chapter ends with a set of Review Questions, which cover the basic content and also ask readers to correlate what they have learned. Summaries are also provided at the end of the chapter with each heading aligning with learning objectives. Other key features are as follows:

- Decision-Making Exercises are scattered throughout each chapter. Each exercise places the reader in the position of judge, asking him or her to decide a case based on the facts presented. The answers to the exercises are available to instructors. They explain what was decided in the actual case on which a given exercise was based or what likely would be decided given precedent in the area.

- The book makes extensive use of actual legal forms, calls attention to important rules (such as those spelled out in the *Federal Rules of Criminal Procedure*), and reprints police department policy manual excerpts. Presented as figures, these materials show how professionals working in the field of criminal justice deal with the concepts and issues covered throughout the book.

- Web links and Exercises. Each chapter concludes with a few Web links and exercises designed to elaborate on and reinforce key issues and points raised in the chapter.

- Further Exploration. Each chapter also concludes with an examination of various controversial and unsettled issues in criminal procedure, some that have barely even been conceived of at this point. The objective is to take readers beyond the text and have them entertain ideas that are likely to come up in the not-too-distant future.

In short, this book is intended to move beyond the basic introductory approach to criminal procedure that many of the competing books have taken but not to a level that presupposes any knowledge about the criminal process. Many competing texts focus overwhelmingly on search-and-seizure and on interrogation and confession procedures. This book covers these topics as well, and in great detail, but it also covers many more topics. This is because criminal procedure consists of much more than interactions between the police and criminal suspects.

# ▶ New to the Fifth Edition

The fifth edition has been revised in several ways:

- All chapters have been extensively revised and rewritten for clarity and simplicity.
- The art program has been improved throughout and now includes shorter, clearer figures as well as key case timelines.
- All the latest Supreme Court decisions are included, through the 2012–2013 term.
- New "Further Exploration" exercises appear at the end of each chapter. These can be used to stimulate discussions and serve as the basis for additional assignments/papers.
- Case law presentation has been improved, with more discussion of case facts/details as appropriate.
- Full discussion of the facts from *Terry v. Ohio* now appears in Chapter 6, along with a new section on sources giving rise to reasonable suspicion.
- In Chapter 8, the discussion of confessions and interrogations has been completely revamped and improved.
- A reorganized and expanded section on effective assistance of counsel appears in Chapter 11 (in light of recent Supreme Court decisions).
- A new section on venue changes has been added to Chapter 13.

# ▶ Content

*Criminal Procedure* continues to be divided into five parts: (1) Introduction; (2) Search and Seizure; (3) Interrogations, Confessions, and Identification Procedures; (4) The Beginnings of Formal Proceedings; and (5) Trial, Conviction, and Beyond. The latter two topics are rarely covered in conventional criminal procedure books, particularly at the level of detail found in this text. In contrast, the traditional approach to criminal procedure rarely moves beyond the material covered in the first three parts of this text.

Part 1 contains two chapters. Chapter 1 is introductory and provides readers with the information necessary to begin studying criminal procedure. In particular, it defines criminal procedure; highlights the due process/crime control dilemma, which is at the heart of all controversies in criminal procedure; discusses the relationship among the courts, including a brief section on how to do legal research; and introduces several issues and trends in criminal procedure. Chapter 1 ends with a detailed overview of the text. Chapter 2 begins by discussing the exclusionary rule, then it considers criminal, civil, and nonjudicial remedies. Remedies are presented early in the text so readers will become aware of how people's rights can be enforced in the U.S. courts.

Part 2 covers standard search-and-seizure topics. Chapter 3 provides a framework for studying the Fourth Amendment; specifically, it defines Fourth Amendment terminology and specifies when searches and seizures occur. This chapter also covers the doctrine of justification, focusing on the definitions of probable cause, reasonable suspicion, and what this book calls *administrative justification*. Chapters 4 and 5 go on to cover searches and seizures *with* warrants and *without* warrants, respectively. Chapter 6 covers actions based on reasonable suspicion, including stops and frisks and investigative detentions, and Chapter 7 covers actions based on administrative justification and consent, including inventories, inspections, checkpoints, school and office searches, drug and alcohol testing, and the like.

Part 3 covers interrogations, confessions, and identification procedures. To this end, Chapter 8 focuses heavily on the Fifth Amendment's self-incrimination clause and then summarizes the proper procedures for conducting interrogations and obtaining valid confessions. Further, it also examines how the Sixth and Fourteenth Amendments govern interrogations and confessions. Chapter 9 discusses identification procedures, including the guidelines for proper pretrial identifications, and also introduces identification procedures used during trial, including the proper questioning of witnesses to assist in valid in-court identifications.

The information in Part 4 is pretrial in nature. Chapter 10 begins by discussing booking, the initial appearance, the probable cause hearing, pretrial release, the preliminary hearing, and the arraignment. This chapter also introduces the rules surrounding discovery. While discovery can occur well into a trial, most often discovery is pretrial in nature; thus, it is appropriate to discuss discovery in this context. Chapter 11 covers prosecutors, grand juries, and defense attorneys, including the constitutional guidelines by which each must abide. Of course, the actions of prosecutors, defense attorneys, and even grand juries matter outside the pretrial context, but readers should be familiar with these important actors before moving into the adjudication section. Finally, Chapter 12 covers plea bargaining and guilty pleas. Again, both can occur well into a trial, but most plea bargains and guilty pleas are undertaken in an effort to avoid trial.

Part 5 is titled "Trial, Conviction, and Beyond." Chapter 13, the first of two chapters about the defendant's rights at trial, examines the right to a speedy trial and the right to an impartial judge and jury. Chapter 14 continues the focus on rights at trial, discussing openness, confrontation, compulsory process, double jeopardy, and entrapment. Lastly, Chapter 15 covers important topics in sentencing as well as appeals and *habeas corpus*.

As noted earlier, most texts on criminal procedure give only limited coverage to the topics in Parts 4 and 5, so readers should benefit by the material presented. Once again, the purpose of this book is to present a comprehensive look at criminal procedure, demonstrating that the Constitution affects much more than the actions of law enforcement personnel.

## ▶ Supplements

Several supplements are available for this book. A test bank for the fifth edition is available. Accompanying the test bank are answers to the book's decision-making exercises. These are available for instructors. The fifth edition is also accompanied by PowerPoint slides to assist instructors with the classroom presentations.

## ▶ Acknowledgments

I would like to thank those individuals who reviewed the fifth edition: Beth Bjerregaard, University of North Carolina, Charlotte; James Blair, South Texas Community College; Amy Carrino, KCTCS Gateway Community and Technical College, Covington; Brett Curry, Georgia Southern University; Brian Donnelly, Raritan Valley Community College; Michelle Estis-Sumerel, Itawamba Community College, Tupelo; Soraya Kawucha, University of North Texas; Colin Lau, Chaminade University of Honolulu; Thomas Lawrence, TriCounty Technical College; Mike Martinez, University of South Dakota; Greg Plumb, Park University; Leslie Ridge, Waynesburg University; Louis Roy, West Virginia University at Parkersburg; Kurt Siedschlaw, University of Nebraska; and Margaret Swearingen, Santa Rosa Community College.

I would also like to thank the reviewers of the first four editions: Scott Belshaw, University of North Texas; Robert Boyer, Luzerne County Community College; Jack E. Call, Radford University; Brett Curry, Georgia Southern University; Kevin Daugherty, Albuquerque TVI Community College; Charles Dreveskracht, Northeastern State University; Russell A. Hunt, Dodge City Community College; Mark Jones, Community College of Philadelphia; David Kramer, Bergen Community College; Patrick Massaro, Butler County Community College; Donna Nicholson, Manchester Community College; Kathleen Nicolaides, University of North Carolina–Charlotte; Caryl Anne Poteete, Southern Illinois University at Carbondale; Larry Salinger, Arkansas State University; Philip E. Secret,

University of Nebraska at Omaha; Constance St. Germain-Driscoll, American Public University System; and Carol Lynn Tebben, University of Wisconsin–Parkside.

Special thanks go to the following organizations (including their staff and others who responded to my many queries): San Bernardino, California, Police Department; Portland Police Bureau, Strategic Services Division; Abilene, Texas, Police Department; Alameda County (California) District Attorney's Office; Claremont, California, Police Department; Gallatin, Tennessee, Police Department; Pine Bluff, Arkansas, Police Department; Sage Publications; and the Texas Municipal Court Education Center.

I would also like to thank Craig Hemmens, Washington State University, for fielding many of my questions. My students throughout the years deserve special thanks as well. Their "what if" questions and frustration with the traditional, heavy-on-case-law approach to teaching criminal procedure contributed in no small part to this, the fifth edition. And thanks, as always, to the wonderful people at Pearson and everyone else involved in bringing the book to press, including Gary Bauer, Tiffany Bitzel, Steve Robb, and project manager Revathi Viswanathan at PreMediaGlobal. I am also indebted to development editor extraordinaire, Evan Voboril. His attention to detail brought more improvements to this text than I could imagine. Finally, special thanks go to my family, especially my wife, Sabrina, for her unending support.

# ABOUT THE AUTHOR

John L. Worrall is Professor and Criminology Program Head at the University of Texas at Dallas. He received a Ph.D. in Political Science from Washington State University in 1999. His areas of interest and expertise include policing, courts, and crime control policy, but he has also published research on correctional matters, legal issues, and a range of other criminal justice/criminology topics. His research has focused primarily on identifying successful programs, policies, and interventions aimed at preventing and controlling crime. In this vein, he has also authored a number of best-selling criminal justice books, including the popular *Crime Control in America: What Works?* (3rd edition, Pearson, forthcoming). He also currently serves as editor of the journal *Police Quarterly*.

# 1 Introduction to Criminal Procedure

**LEARNING OBJECTIVES**

When you complete this chapter, you should be able to:

**1** *Summarize the constitutional basis for criminal procedure.*

**2** *Explain the importance of precedent.*

**3** *Compare the theory of criminal procedure to the reality.*

**4** *Describe how the interests of public order (crime control) and individual rights (due process) influence criminal justice and how criminal procedure balances these two interests.*

**5** *Outline the structure of the court system, and describe the responsibilities and jurisdictions of each level.*

**6** *Summarize important issues and trends in criminal procedure.*

**7** *Provide an overview of the process of criminal justice.*

## OUTLINE

# Introduction: What Is Criminal Procedure?

American **criminal procedure** consists of a vast set of rules and guidelines that determine how suspected and accused criminals are to be handled and processed by the justice system. A significant part of this system governs the relationship between the police and the people suspected of criminal activity. Criminal procedure provides law enforcement officials with the guidance necessary to preserve the rights of individuals who are seized, searched, arrested, and otherwise inconvenienced by those officials. It also provides other justice system professionals—such as judges, prosecutors, and defense attorneys—with the necessary guidance to preserve the rights of individuals accused of criminal activity. Criminal procedure begins when the police first contact a suspect and ends well after his or her conviction.

At least three important themes run throughout criminal procedure. First, there is a concern with the constitutional rights of accused persons. The bulk of criminal procedure is governed by what the U.S. Constitution says—as it is interpreted by the U.S. Supreme Court. Second, procedure is closely linked to history, because it is guided by *precedent*, or past decisions by the courts. In making decisions, courts look to how sensitive legal issues have been approached in the past, and will often follow the previous decisions made in similar cases. A third recurring theme is the collision between the world of the courts and the world of law enforcement. The requirements of the courts do not always harmonize with the needs of law enforcement, and court decisions may not always be as relevant in the real world as might be expected.

## ▶ Sources of Rights in Criminal Procedure

The U.S. Constitution is the most important source of rights applying to criminal procedure. In addition to the Constitution, important sources of rights include court decisions, statutes, and state constitutions.

In addition, criminal procedure cannot be understood without attention to the interplay between federal and states' rights. The two-tiered system of government in the United States creates a unique relationship between the federal and state levels.

### The U.S. Constitution

The Preamble to the U.S. Constitution states:

> We the People of the United States, in Order to form a more perfect Union, establish Justice, insure domestic Tranquility, provide for the common defence, promote the general Welfare, and secure the Blessings of Liberty to ourselves and our Posterity, do ordain and establish this Constitution for the United States of America.

Of particular relevance to criminal procedure are the terms *justice* and *liberty*. The Constitution helps ensure justice and liberty by defining the various roles of government and protecting the rights of people within the nation's borders. Throughout the nation's history, the courts have devoted a great amount of energy to interpreting the Constitution and specifying what rights are important and when they apply.

### Court Decisions

Whenever a court makes a decision interpreting the Constitution, it effectively makes an announcement concerning people's rights. For example, the Fourth Amendment states that unreasonable searches and seizures are impermissible. The term *unreasonable* is not self-explanatory, however. In *Wilson v. Layne*, 526 U.S. 603 (1999), the Court decided that it is unreasonable for the police to bring reporters along when serving a warrant, unless the reporters are there to serve a legitimate law enforcement objective.

Most of the court decisions in this text are decisions of the U.S. Supreme Court, although state courts, as well as lower federal courts, also may make decisions interpreting the Constitution.

## Statutes

The Constitution and the courts cannot be expected to protect all the interests and concerns that people may have. Statutes attempt to fill the gaps by establishing that certain rights exist in areas not specifically covered by the Constitution. An example is Title VII of the 1964 Civil Rights Act, which, among other things, prohibits discrimination in employment. Another important statute regarding citizens' rights is Section 1983 of the 1871 Civil Right Act, which allows private citizens to sue local law enforcement officials for violations of federally protected rights.

## State Constitutions

States have their own constitutions, which are another important source of rights. Although the U.S. Constitution is the supreme law of the land that all states as well as the federal government must follow, nothing in the U.S. Constitution precludes individual states from adopting greater protections than federal law. In general, if a state constitution gives *less* protection than the federal Constitution, such a limitation is unconstitutional. But a provision in a state constitution that gives *greater* protection than the U.S. Constitution will be permissible. For example, the Supreme Court has interpreted the Fifth Amendment in such a way that it requires police to advise a suspect of his or her so-called *Miranda* rights when the suspect is subjected to custodial interrogation—an action that does not necessarily rise to the level of an arrest. A *state*, however, could require that *Miranda* rights be read whenever a person is arrested, regardless of whether he or she is interrogated.

Finally, although it is not a source of rights *per se*, the **Federal Rules of Criminal Procedure** are related to protecting the rights of the accused.[1] Excerpts from the *Federal Rules* are reprinted throughout this book because they sometimes clarify important rulings handed down by the U.S. Supreme Court. Additionally, the *Federal Rules* set forth the criminal procedure guidelines by which federal criminal justice practitioners are required to abide.

## ▶ Rights That Are Relevant to Criminal Procedure

Of the many rights specified in the U.S. Constitution, the rights stemming from five amendments are of special importance in criminal procedure. Four of these—the Fourth, Fifth, Sixth, and Eighth Amendments—can be found in the Bill of Rights. In addition to the Bill of Rights, the Fourteenth Amendment is often relevant in criminal procedure. Sometimes the First Amendment, which protects individual rights to assembly and speech, and the Second Amendment, which protects the right to bear arms, are relevant in criminal procedure, but only rarely. Figure 1.1 lists the constitutional amendments that are of particular importance in criminal procedure.

---

[1]*Federal Rules of Criminal Procedure*, http://www.law.cornell.edu/rules/frcrmp accessed date: September 20, 2013.

**FIGURE 1.1 Constitutional Amendments Important to Criminal Procedure and Their Relevant Provisions**

## The Fourth Amendment

The Fourth Amendment is perhaps the most often-cited source of rights in criminal procedure. In fact, it is viewed to be so important that many books on criminal procedure devote the overwhelming majority of their chapters to it. The Fourth Amendment states:

> The right of the people to be secure in their persons, houses, papers, and effects, against unreasonable searches and seizures, shall not be violated, and no Warrants shall issue, but upon probable cause, supported by Oath or affirmation and particularly describing the place to be searched, and the persons or things to be seized.

Several rights can be discerned by reading the text of the Fourth Amendment. It refers to the right of people to be free from unreasonable searches and seizures, and establishes specific requirements for obtaining a warrant—it must be issued by a magistrate or judge, supported by probable cause, and sufficiently specific as to what is to be searched or seized.

## The Fifth Amendment

The Fifth Amendment is applicable in a number of issues in criminal procedure. It states:

> No person shall be held to answer for a capital, or otherwise infamous crime, unless on a presentment or indictment of a Grand Jury, except in cases arising in the land or naval forces, or in the Militia, when in actual service in time of War or public danger; nor shall any person be subject for the same offense to be twice put in jeopardy of life or limb; nor shall be compelled in any criminal case to be a witness against himself, nor be deprived of life, liberty, or property, without due process of law; nor shall private property be taken for public use, without just compensation.

This book focuses in particular on the role of the grand jury, the requirement that no person shall be "twice put in jeopardy of life or limb" (known as the *double-jeopardy* clause), the requirement that no one can be compelled "to be a witness against himself" (also known as the *self-incrimination* clause), and, perhaps most important of all, the requirement that an individual cannot be deprived of life, liberty, or property without due process of law.

## The Sixth Amendment

The Sixth Amendment focuses on court proceedings in criminal trials. It states:

> In all criminal prosecutions, the accused shall enjoy the right to a speedy and public trial, by an impartial jury of the State and district wherein the crime shall have been committed, which district shall have been previously ascertained by law, and to be informed of

the nature and cause of the accusation; to be confronted with the witnesses against him; to have compulsory process for obtaining witnesses in his favor, and to have the Assistance of Counsel for his defence.

Of relevance to criminal procedure is the Sixth Amendment's language concerning speedy and public trials, impartial juries, confrontation, and compulsory process. The Sixth Amendment also suggests that in addition to being public, trials should be open, not closed, proceedings. The Supreme Court has interpreted the Sixth Amendment as providing the right of the accused to be present at his or her trial and to be able to put on a defense.

## The Eighth Amendment

The **Eighth Amendment** deals with bail, as well as sentences imposed in criminal cases. It states:

Excessive bail shall not be required, nor excessive fines imposed, nor cruel and unusual punishments inflicted.

## The Fourteenth Amendment

A small but critical portion of **Fourteenth Amendment** is relevant to the handling and treatment of criminal suspects. That portion states:

All persons born or naturalized in the United States, and subject to the jurisdiction thereof, are citizens of the United States and of the State wherein they reside. No State shall make or enforce any law which shall abridge the privileges or immunities of citizens of the United States, nor shall any State deprive any person of life, liberty, or property, without due process of law; nor deny to any person within its jurisdiction the equal protection of the laws.

The key phrase applicable to criminal procedure is "due process of law." This language mirrors a similar phrase in the Fifth Amendment. However, because the Fifth Amendment is part of the Bill of Rights, it is only binding on the federal government. However, the due process clause of the Fourteenth Amendment has been used by the Supreme Court to *incorporate*, or make applicable to the states, several of the rights provided for in the Bill of Rights.

The Fourteenth Amendment's due process clause, as interpreted by the Supreme Court, consists of two types of due process: (1) **substantive due process** and (2) **procedural due process**. The essence of substantive due process is protection from arbitrary and unreasonable action on the part of state officials. By contrast, a procedural due process violation is one in which a violation of a significant life, liberty, or property interest occurs (See *Geddes v. Northwest Missouri State College*, 49 F.3d 426 [8th Cir. 1995]). Procedural due process is akin to procedural fairness.

Although many of the rights provided for in the Bill of Rights are incorporated and therefore binding on the states, certain rights provided for in each amendment may not be incorporated. Also, even though a particular amendment may provide a particular right, the Supreme Court may have interpreted that amendment to apply only in certain circumstances.

It should also be noted that the Bill of Rights—and indeed the Constitution—are only binding on government officials. Private persons are exempt from having to comply with constitutional restrictions. This is very important and often overlooked. We look more carefully in Section 2 of the book at this issue as it arrives in the search and seizure context.

**THE FIRST AMENDMENT AND CRIMINAL PROCEDURE**

The First Amendment to the U.S. Constitution provides that "Congress shall make no law respecting an establishment of religion, or prohibiting the free exercise thereof; or abridging the freedom of speech, or of the press; or the right of the people peaceably to assemble, and to petition the Government for a redress of grievances." Given what you have read so far, how might the First Amendment be relevant to criminal procedure?

## The Incorporation Controversy

The Bill of Rights, consisting of the first 10 amendments to the U.S. Constitution, places limitations on the powers of the federal government. It does *not* limit the power of the states. In other words, the first 10 amendments place no limitations on state and local governments and their agencies. Government power at the state and local levels is expressly limited by state constitutions.

Even though the Bill of Rights does not limit the powers of state and local governments, the Supreme Court has found a way to do so through the Fourteenth Amendment. It has used the Fourteenth Amendment's due process clause, which holds that no state shall "deprive any person of life, liberty, or property, without due process of law," to make certain protections specified in the Bill of Rights applicable to the states. This is known as **incorporation**.

The extent to which the Fourteenth Amendment should regulate state and local government power has been the subject of some disagreement—hence, this issue is often referred to as the "incorporation controversy." The controversy has centered around the question of to what degree the Fourteenth Amendment's due process clause incorporates the various provisions of the Bill of Rights. In other words, does the Bill of Rights restrict state and local law enforcement to the same extent that it restricts federal law enforcement?

### Significance of the Debate

The incorporation debate is significant because of three concerns. First, since most contact between citizens and the police occurs at the state and local levels, it is critical to determine the role of the federal Constitution at those levels. Comparatively few people have contact with federal law enforcement, so the Bill of Rights actually regulates a limited number of contacts between police and citizens at the federal level. Second, incorporation may threaten the doctrine of *federalism*. Under this doctrine, states have the authority to develop their own rules and laws of criminal procedure. However, if the Fourteenth Amendment incorporates the Bill of Rights, this authority may be compromised. Third, the incorporation debate raises important concerns about the separation of powers among the legislative and judicial branches. If the Supreme Court decides which rights should be incorporated, it is actually performing a legislative function. Many believe that this function is better reserved for Congress.

### Views on Incorporation

There are four leading views on the incorporation debate.[2]

The *total incorporation* view holds that the Fourteenth Amendment's due process clause incorporates the entire Bill of Rights. In other words, all protections specified in the Bill of Rights should be binding on the states. The primary proponent of this view was Supreme Court Justice Hugo Black (see *Adamson v. California*, 332 U.S. 46 [1947]).

The second leading view on incorporation is that of *selective incorporation*, or the *fundamental rights* view. It favors incorporation of certain protections enumerated in the Bill

---

[2]J. Dressler, *Law Outlines: Criminal Procedure* (Santa Monica, CA: Casenotes Publishing, 1997), pp. 2-3–2-4.

of Rights, not all of them. Further, this view deems certain rights as being more critical, or fundamental, than others. The Supreme Court's decision in *Snyder v. Massachusetts*, 291 U.S. 97 (1934) advocates this view, stating that the due process clause prohibits state encroachment on those "principle[s] of justice so rooted in the traditions and consciences of our people as to be ranked as fundamental."

The third view on incorporation is often referred to as *total incorporation plus*. This view holds that the Fourteenth Amendment's due process clause incorporates the whole Bill of Rights as well as additional rights *not* specified in the Constitution, such as the "right to privacy." This view can be found in such Supreme Court cases as *Poe v. Ullman*, 367 U.S. 497 (1961).

Finally, some believe that incorporation should be decided case by case. This means that the facts and circumstances of each individual case should be weighed in order to determine if any protections listed in the Bill of Rights should apply at the state or local level.

## Outcome of the Debate

Arguably, selective incorporation, or the fundamental rights view, is now the prevailing view. The Supreme Court has consistently held that some protections listed in the Bill of Rights are more applicable to the states than others. The Fourth Amendment, it has held, contains several *fundamental rights*. By contrast, the Fifth Amendment's grand jury clause has not been deemed fundamental and is not binding on the states (*Hurtado v. California*, 110 U.S. 516 [1884]).

To some extent, the "total incorporation plus" view has also prevailed. The Supreme Court has repeatedly emphasized that Americans have a fundamental right to privacy, despite the fact that the Constitution makes no mention of privacy. It is often said (as will be noted in the section on the Fourth Amendment) that although people do not enjoy an *expectation of privacy* in public places, they do have a right to privacy in their homes and their bodies. It would seem, then, that certain rights not listed in the Constitution have been identified as well as incorporated.

Figure 1.2 lists the rights that have been deemed fundamental by the Supreme Court and, as a result, incorporated to the states.[3] The Supreme Court cases responsible for these incorporation decisions are listed as well.

| Right | Deciding Case |
|---|---|
| First Amendment freedom of religion, speech, and assembly and the right to petition for redress of grievances | *Fiske v. Kansas*, 274 U.S. 380 (1927) |
| Fourth Amendment prohibition of unreasonable searches and seizures | *Wolf v. Colorado*, 338 U.S. 25 (1949) |
| Fifth Amendment protection against compelled self-incrimination | *Malloy v. Hogan*, 378 U.S. 1 (1964) |
| Fifth Amendment protection from double jeopardy | *Benton v. Maryland*, 395 U.S. 784 (1969) |
| Sixth Amendment right to counsel | *Gideon v. Wainwright*, 372 U.S. 335 (1963) |
| Sixth Amendment right to a speedy trial | *Klopfer v. North Carolina*, 386 U.S. 213 (1967) |
| Sixth Amendment right to a public trial | *In re Oliver*, 333 U.S. 257 (1948) |
| Sixth Amendment right to confrontation | *Pointer v. Texas*, 380 U.S. 400 (1965) |
| Sixth Amendment right to an impartial jury | *Duncan v. Louisiana*, 391 U.S. 145 (1968) |
| Sixth Amendment right to compulsory process | *Washington v. Texas*, 388 U.S. 14 (1967) |
| Eighth Amendment prohibition of cruel and unusual punishment | *Robinson v. California*, 370 U.S. 660 (1962) |

**FIGURE 1.2 Rights Incorporated to the States**

---

[3]Some scholars believe that the Ninth Amendment to the U.S. Constitution (also referred to as the *penumbra clause*) implies that all of the rights not specifically spelled out in the Constitution are automatically protected nonetheless. But to demonstrate this, a court would have to recognize a particular right as fundamental in case law. Privacy could be considered one such right.

# ▶ The Importance of Precedent

A **precedent** is a rule of case law (a decision by a court) that is binding on all lower courts and the court that issued it. The courts will defer to prior decisions based on a similar set of facts and legal questions. This is the doctrine of *stare decisis*.

## Stare Decisis

**Stare decisis** is a Latin term that means to abide by or to adhere to decided cases. Most courts adhere to this principle. When a court has handed down a decision on a specific set of facts or legal questions, future court decisions that involve similar facts or questions will follow the previous decision or precedent.

*Stare decisis* is an important principle in the U.S. court system because it promotes consistency. It is now well established that accused criminals enjoy the right to counsel (see *Gideon v. Wainwright*, 372 U.S. 335 [1963]). But what if from one year to the next, the Supreme Court vacillated on whether this right was constitutionally guaranteed? The criminal process, not to mention the rights of the accused, would be unpredictable and vary from one case to the next.

It is important to note that the practice of following precedent is not always possible or desirable in every case. For example, *stare decisis* usually only applies to courts within a single jurisdiction. Suppose, for example, that a federal circuit appeals court handed down a decision. All the district courts within that circuit must abide by the appeals court decision. Courts outside that circuit are *not* bound to adhere to that decision. However, some courts outside of the jurisdiction may be persuaded by the reasoning in the case, and decide accordingly. Perhaps more important, if a case coming before a court is unique and does not resemble one decided in the past, the court may *distinguish* it.

## Distinguishing Cases

When a previous decision does not apply to the current facts, a court will **distinguish** the case, saying, in effect, that because the facts of the present case are different, the case cannot be decided the same way. In other words, the present set of facts are unique, and therefore the case should be decided differently.

Since only a handful of cases make it to the appellate level, and even fewer still arrive at the Supreme Court, only a very limited set of fact patterns have been considered by appellate courts. This is a critical point. The case law in place currently addresses only a minute quantity of possible constitutional questions. Countless contacts occur between the police and citizens. Many of these contacts may give rise to important constitutional questions, yet they may never see the inside of a courtroom. While the body of case law may appear to be very large, it is important to recognize that there is a nearly infinite number of possible factual circumstances that could arise in the criminal process.

An example of how a case can be distinguished is *Terry v. Ohio*, 392 U.S. 1 (1968). In that case, the Supreme Court held that police officers only need to have reasonable suspicion to stop and frisk a suspect, and do not need to have probable cause as required for a search or a seizure under the Fourth Amendment. The Court felt that a stop-and-frisk is different from a search or a seizure and, as such, should be governed by a different set of standards. Had the Supreme Court *not* decided *Terry*, or any case like it, stop-and-frisk encounters would probably still be considered "seizures" and therefore subject to the Fourth Amendment's requirement for probable cause.

In nearly every class on criminal procedure, students often ask, "What if . . . ?" The "what-if" questions sometimes concern factual circumstances that can be distinguished in some way from the actual cases discussed in classroom text. The best approach to answering such a question is to look to the past and find a decision that closely resembles the hypothetical scenario. However, many factual scenarios have not yet been fully addressed by any court. In order for such questions to be answered, a court must render a decision that distinguishes that specific set of facts.

In this vein, every case discussed throughout this text should be thought of as a "distinguished" case. Every decision was based on some unique set of factual circumstances and was deemed by the reviewing court as worthy of a new decision. Were it not for distinguished cases, criminal procedure case law could be adequately covered in a short amount of time.

# ▶ Theory Versus Reality

Criminal procedure consists mostly of rules and guidelines that have been handed down by the courts to dictate how the criminal process should play out. In some circumstances, however, court decisions may not really have a great deal of influence. That is, some court decisions are made in the **theoretical world**, which is somewhat disconnected from the day-to-day operations of law enforcement within the **real world**. Understandably, there can be differences, even tensions, between the worlds of theory and reality.

Americans are taught that the courts—and the Supreme Court, in particular—are charged with interpreting the Constitution and the laws of the United States. They are further taught that law enforcement should accept such interpretations uncritically and without much reflection. While these understandings are mostly true, theory and reality can still differ. Some Supreme Court decisions have little influence in the real world, and in some cases may even be flatly ignored. There are four reasons for this:

First, the Supreme Court sometimes makes decisions on excruciatingly detailed matters that have almost no applicability to most law enforcement officers, most of the time. A good example is the Supreme Court's recent decision in *Atwater v. City of Lago Vista*, 533 U.S. 924 (2001). The Court decided that the Fourth Amendment does not prohibit the police from arresting people for seatbelt violations. To the parties involved in the actual case, this decision may have been significant. But in most jurisdictions, how many police officers are going to arrest people for seatbelt violations? The case probably has little relevance to most police officers because they usually have more important matters to address.

Second, the Supreme Court frequently hands down decisions that would seem to have dramatic effects on the nature of law enforcement, but actually involve issues that are already being addressed by many police agencies. For example, the Supreme Court's decision in *Tennessee v. Garner*, 471 U.S. 1 (1985) made it a violation of the Fourth Amendment for the police to use deadly force to apprehend an unarmed and nondangerous fleeing felon. However, prior to *Garner*, many police agencies had already adopted restrictive deadly force policies—policies that, in many instances, were more restrictive than the ruling handed down in *Garner*. Police agency policy, therefore, can differ from, and even be more restrictive than, decisions reached by the Supreme Court. To illustrate this, several

---

**DECISION-MAKING EXERCISE 1.2**

### TRADITIONAL LEGAL DOCTRINE MEETS HIGH-TECH CRIME

In *Katz v. United States*, 389 U.S. 347 (1967), the Supreme Court decided that searches occur when a government actor infringes on a person's reasonable expectation of privacy. Assume federal agents have a trained drug dog sniff passengers' luggage on a baggage carousel in an airport. Does this constitute a search? Is *Katz* equipped to deal with a situation such as this, or is the situation such that it calls for a distinguished case?

## THEORY AND REALITY COLLIDE

In *Miranda v. Arizona*, 384 U.S. 436 (1966), the U.S. Supreme Court decided that unless criminal suspects who are interrogated while under custody are advised of their Fifth Amendment privilege against self-incrimination, any evidence subsequently obtained will be inadmissible in court. This case illustrates that (1) *custody* occurs when a reasonable person would believe the suspect is not free to leave (an arrest being a prime example of such action) and (2) *interrogation* refers to actions by the police that are reasonably likely to elicit a response from the suspect. Assume that the police arrest a man but do not interrogate him. Assume further that the man confesses to a crime. Does *Miranda* apply?

excerpts from police agency manuals and guidelines are reprinted throughout subsequent chapters.

The third reason for the gap between theory and reality is that the courts sometimes hand down decisions that can be effectively circumvented or ignored by the police. Clearly, it is not in the best interest of law enforcement to ignore the courts, and probably quite rare that the police do so, but it does occur. For example, in *Kyllo v. United States*, 533 U.S. 27 (2001), the Supreme Court held that a search occurs when the police scan a private residence with an infrared thermal imager without first obtaining a warrant. The consequence of conducting such a scan without a warrant is that any evidence subsequently obtained will not be admissible in court. However, in reality, what is to prevent the police from scanning someone's house if there is no intent to obtain evidence?

Finally, what the courts say and the police do can differ simply as a consequence of some aspects of the U.S. legal system. It is well known, for example, that a police officer cannot stop a motorist without some level of justification. On how many occasions, though, are motorists stopped without justification? That is, how many people are pulled over every day simply because a police officer is suspicious of them? This cannot be established for certain, but it does happen. It *can* happen because the legal system cannot do much to prevent it. Someone who is wrongfully stopped can file a complaint, but research shows that many such complaints are resolved in favor of the police.[4] A lawsuit can be filed, but such suits are rarely successful. And if nothing is discovered that leads to arresting the motorist, then it is doubtful that the illegal stop will draw attention in court.

In fairness to the law enforcement community, the police (or other criminal justice officials) do not regularly trample people's constitutional rights. Most law enforcement officials are responsible, professional, and upstanding enforcers of the law, as are most judges and prosecutors. But the fact cannot be ignored that certain court decisions are somewhat distant from the reality of everyday law enforcement. It is for this reason that distinctions between theory and reality are pointed out throughout this text. Excerpts from police department policy manual are also given to help bridge the gap between theory and reality. They illustrate the procedures that law enforcement officials must follow in addition to those laid out by the Supreme Court.

---

[4]For an informative review, see J. L. Worrall, "If You Build It, They Will Come: Consequences of Improved Citizen Complaint Review Procedures," *Crime and Delinquency* 48 (2002): 355–379.

# ► Competing Concerns in Criminal Procedure

Criminal procedure is an exciting topic because of the inherent tension between two competing sets of priorities. On the one hand, there is a serious interest in controlling crime, with some Americans advocating doing whatever it takes to keep criminals off the streets. On the other hand, Americans value their rights and become angry when those rights are compromised or threatened. These two competing sets of values have been referred to as the *crime control* and *due process* perspectives.[5]

These differing perspectives are probably familiar to many readers because the debate recurs throughout the study of criminal justice. Almost without exception, whenever there is disagreement as to how best to approach the problem of crime—be it through court decisions or legislative measures—the debate between due process and crime control rears its head. A delicate balance must be achieved between the two perspectives.

On its surface, the due process perspective is more closely aligned with a liberal political orientation. Liberals are often viewed as favoring protection of people's rights and liberties to a higher degree than their conservative counterparts. By contrast, the crime control perspective seems to be more frequently subscribed to by conservatives. Of course, in reality, there can be a great deal of overlap between the two orientations, and although the two groups frequently stand in stark contrast to each other, they do sometimes meet in the middle. Liberals occasionally favor conservative crime control policies, and conservatives may be concerned with protecting the rights of American citizens. Regardless, the values espoused by each group—be it an interest in crime control, an interest in civil rights, or an interest in both—continue to influence criminal procedure. It is important to carefully consider each perspective, focusing special attention on the implications for criminal procedure.

## The Due Process Perspective

The **due process perspective** is, first and foremost, concerned with people's rights and liberties. Due process advocates believe that the government's primary job is not only to control crime but also to maximize human freedom, which includes protecting citizens from undue government influence. According to Herbert L. Packer, a leading scholar in the administration of criminal justice, the proponents of due process favor minimizing the potential for mistakes. As he explains:

> People are notoriously poor observers of disturbing events. . . . [C]onfessions and admissions by persons in police custody may be induced by physical or psychological coercion so that the police end up hearing what the suspect thinks they want to hear rather than the truth; witnesses may be animated by a bias or interest that no one would trouble to discover except one specially charged with protecting the interests of the accused (as the police are not).[6]

Due process advocates also strongly support the idea that a suspect is innocent until proven guilty. In addition, they place greater emphasis on *legal guilt* (whether a person is guilty according to the law) rather than *factual guilt* (whether a person actually committed the crime with which he or she is charged).

There appear to be four concepts underlying the due process perspective: (1) The criminal process looks, or should look, something like an "obstacle course"; (2) Quality is better than quantity; (3) Formality is preferred over informality; and (4) A great deal of faith is put in the courts.

---

[5]H. L. Packer, *The Limits of the Criminal Sanction* (Palo Alto, CA: Stanford University Press, 1968).
[6]Ibid., p. 163.

### The Obstacle Course

Advocates of the due process perspective maintain that the criminal process resembles an "obstacle course" that is complex and must be navigated by skilled legal professionals. Further, it is one that is somewhat difficult to operate in a predictable fashion. It is not a process that prides itself on speed and efficiency—values of great importance in the crime control perspective. In fact, the opposite could be said. The obstacle course metaphor also stresses that each case must pass through several complicated twists and turns before a verdict can be rendered.

### Quality over Quantity

The due process and crime control perspectives may also be distinguished in terms of quantity and quality. The due process view favors quality—that is, a fair and accurate decision should be reached at every stage of the criminal process. It stresses that each case should be handled on an individual basis and that special attention should be paid to the facts and circumstances surrounding the event. In addition, the concern with quality is one that minimizes the potential for error. For example, due process advocates are in favor of allowing several death penalty appeals because the possibility of executing the wrong person should be avoided at all costs.

### Insistence on Formality

Due process advocates do not favor informal processes. Because of the potential for human error and bias, they favor a rigorous adversarial criminal process. They also believe that early intervention by judges and other presumptively objective parties (besides, say, the police) is in the best interest of people accused of breaking the law.

### Faith in the Courts

Another value inherent in the due process perspective is intense faith in the courts as opposed to law enforcement officials. Due process advocates correctly point out that a duty of a judge is to interpret the U.S. Constitution. The courts, they argue, will provide a measure of protection to people charged with crimes. Faith in the courts also corresponds with the insistence on formality. When guilt or innocence is determined in court, an air of fairness and objectivity must be maintained.

## The Crime Control Perspective

In contrast to the due process perspective, the **crime control perspective** emphasizes the importance of controlling crime, perhaps to the detriment of civil liberties. From a cost/benefit standpoint, crime control advocates believe that the benefit to society of controlling outweighs the cost of infringing on the rights and liberties of some individuals. Another way to distinguish between the due process and crime control perspectives is to consider the distinction between *means* and *ends*: Crime control is more concerned with the *ends*—wiping out crime, or at a minimum, mitigating its harmful effects. By contrast, due process is concerned with the *means*—the methods by which people are treated by criminal justice officials. The result—either crime or the absence of it—is not of the greatest concern to due process advocates.

Additional differences between the due process and crime control perspectives are illustrated in Figure 1.3.

### The Assembly Line

The crime control view of criminal procedure can be described through the metaphor of an "Assembly Line." It suggests that the criminal process should be automatic, predictable, and uniform. In other words, every criminal should be treated the same, with minimal variations in terms of charges and sentences. The assembly-line metaphor further suggests that the criminal process should be quick and efficient. The goal of crime control advocates is

| Crime Control Values | Due Process Values |
|---|---|
| • Follows "assembly line" metaphor | • Follows "obstacle course" metaphor |
| • Emphasizes quantity over quality | • Emphasizes quality over quantity |
| • Favors informality | • Prefers formality |
| • Has faith in the police | • Has faith in the courts |
| • Makes presumption of guilt | • Makes presumption of innocence |
| • Seeks to benefit society | • Seeks to benefit suspects |
| • Is concerned with ends, not means | • Is concerned with means, not ends |
| • Seeks to maximize police authority | • Seeks to maximize human freedom |
| • Seeks to control crime at all costs | • Seeks to protect people's rights at all costs |
| • Puts emphasis on factual guilt | • Puts emphasis on legal guilt |

**FIGURE 1.3 The Values of Due Process versus Crime Control**

to move criminals through the justice process as swiftly as possible. A rigorous adversarial criminal process, replete with hearings and other delays that serve the interests of the accused, is anathema to the crime control view.

## Quantity over Quality

As just mentioned, the due process model stresses quality over quantity. The crime control model, by contrast, favors quantity over quality, a view that is consistent with the assembly-line metaphor. The goal is to move as many offenders as possible through the criminal justice system with as little delay as possible. If mistakes are made along the way and someone is wrongfully charged or convicted, so be it. That is, the *overall* goal of ensuring that as many criminals are dealt with as possible is superior to protecting any individual's constitutional rights.

## Insistence on Informality

Whereas the due process perspective favors the formality of the criminal process, with particular emphasis on the courts, the crime control perspective favors informality. The courts are to be avoided. Instead, justice should be meted out beyond the walls of a courtroom. Plea bargaining, for instance, is favored because of its swift, behind-the-scenes nature (not to mention that it eliminates the need to go to trial). An insistence on informality suggests further that the law enforcement establishment should be more involved in making determinations of guilt, not the courts.

## Faith in Police

Finally, whereas the due process perspective places a great deal of faith in the courts, the crime control perspective puts a high degree of trust in the police. All Americans are taught that each suspect is innocent until proven guilty in a court of law. Obviously, the courts are charged with making the final decision. However, crime control advocates often favor so-called "street justice," giving the police vast discretion in deciding how to deal with people suspected of being involved in criminal activity.

### DECISION-MAKING EXERCISE 1.4

#### DUE PROCESS OR CRIME CONTROL

How should the *Miranda* decision from Exercise 1.3 be characterized: as due process-oriented or crime control-oriented? In other words, does *Miranda* prioritize the suspect's due process rights or the interest of society in controlling crime? What about the Supreme Court's decision in *Kyllo v. United States*, mentioned in the "Theory versus Reality" section?

## DUE PROCESS OR CRIME CONTROL

In two decisions, *United States v. Leon*, 468 U.S. 897 (1984) and *Massachusetts v. Sheppard*, 468 U.S. 981 (1984), the Supreme Court created what is known as the "good faith" exception to the exclusionary rule. Essentially, both cases are important in that they acknowledge that police make honest mistakes, and hold that violations of people's constitutional rights are permissible, under limited circumstances, as long as the police acted in "good faith." For example, if a police officer relies on a search warrant that was obtained on the basis of a reasonable mistake, he or she could serve the warrant, search for evidence, and seize it, even if these actions violated the rights of the person searched. The key is that the mistake must be a *reasonable* one. How, then, would you characterize both the *Leon* and *Sheppard* decisions: as prioritizing crime control or due process?

# ▶ Finding Court Cases and Tracing Their Progress

Criminal procedure can be complex not only because of the many factual questions that arise in day-to-day encounters between citizens and police, but also because of the two-tiered structure of the U.S. court system. This two-tiered structure reflects the idea of *dual sovereignty*: that the federal and state governments are considered separate, or *sovereign*, in their own right. Each state, as well as the federal government, has its own court structure.

There is no way to succinctly describe all the variations in state court structures, but, generally, they share many features. Typically, the lowest-level courts in a given state are **courts of limited jurisdiction**, which have jurisdiction over relatively minor offenses and infractions. A traffic court fits in this category. Next are the trial courts—also called **courts of general jurisdiction**—which try several types of cases. Courts of general jurisdiction are often county-level courts, and are frequently called **superior courts**. At the next highest level are the **intermediate appellate courts**. Verdicts from courts of general jurisdiction are appealed to these courts. Finally, each state has its own **state supreme court**, the highest court in the state. Figure 1.4 shows a typical state court structure, from the state of Washington. Importantly, state courts try cases involving state laws (and, depending on the level of the court, some county, city, and other local ordinances).

The *federal* court structure, for the purposes of criminal procedure, consists of three specific types of courts. Federal courts try cases involving federal law. The lowest courts at the federal level are the **district courts**. There are 94 federal district courts in the United States (as of this writing), including 89 district courts in the 50 states and 1 each in Puerto Rico, the Virgin Islands, the District of Columbia, Guam, and the Northern Mariana Islands. At the next level are the **U.S. courts of appeals**. There are 13 circuit courts of appeals: 12 regional courts and 1 for the federal circuit. Each is charged with hearing appeals from several of the district courts that fall within its circuit. Finally, the **U.S. Supreme Court** is the highest court in the federal system. As will be discussed, however, the Supreme Court does not only hear federal appeals.[7] Figure 1.5 shows the structure of the federal court system. The courts relevant to criminal procedure are highlighted. Figure 1.6 presents a map of the geographic boundaries of the U.S. courts of appeals and the U.S. district courts.

---

[7]Note that references to the federal-level supreme courts are always capitalized (e.g., *the U.S. Supreme Court, the Supreme Court*, and even *the Court*), whereas those to state-level supreme courts are not (i.e., except in citing a particular state court, such as the *Florida Supreme Court*).

**WASHINGTON COURT STRUCTURE**

**SUPREME COURT**

9 justices sit en banc and in panels*

CSP** case types:
- Mandatory jurisdiction in civil, capital criminal, criminal, administrative agency, juvenile, certified questions from federal court cases.
- Discretionary jurisdiction in civil, noncapital criminal, administrative agency, juvenile, disciplinary, original proceeding, interlocutory decision cases.

Court of last resort

**COURT OF APPEALS** (3 courts/divisions)

22 judges sit in panels

CSP case types:
- Mandatory jurisdiction in civil, noncapital criminal, administrative agency, juvenile, original proceeding cases.
- Discretionary jurisdiction in administrative agency, interlocutory decision cases.

Intermediate appellate court

**SUPERIOR COURT** (31 districts in 39 counties)          A

179 judges

CSP case types:
- Tort, contract ($0/no maximum). Exclusive real property rights ($0/no maximum), estate, mental health, civil appeals, miscellaneous civil jurisdiction.
- Exclusive domestic relations jurisdiction.
- Exclusive felony, criminal appeals jurisdiction.
- Exclusive juvenile jurisdiction.

Court of general jurisdiction

**MUNICIPAL COURT** (125 courts)

98 judges

CSP case types:
- Misdemeanor, DWI/DUI, domestic violence.
- Moving traffic, parking, miscellaneous traffic, ordinance violation.

Jury trials except in infractions and parking.

**DISTRICT COURT*** (44 courts in 56 locations for 39 counties)

109 judges

CSP case types:
- Tort, contract ($0/$50,000). Exclusive small claims jurisdiction ($4,000).
- Misdemeanor, DWI/DUI, domestic violence.
- Moving traffic, parking, miscellaneous (nontraffic) violations.
- Preliminary hearings.

Jury trials except in traffic and parking.

Courts of limited jurisdiction

* "en banc" means all justices/judges hear the case at once. "In panels" means only some of the justices/judges hear the case.
** Court Statistics Project.
*** District court provides services to municipalities that do not have a municipal court.

*Source*: Bureau of Justice Statistics, *State Court Organization, 2004* (Washington, DC: U.S. Department of Justice, 2006), p. 316. Available online: http://bjs.ojp.usdoj.gov/content/pub/pdf/sco04.pdf (accessed May 1, 2013).

**FIGURE 1.4 Structure of a State Court System (Washington)**

The federal government and each of the 50 states are each considered a sovereign entity. That is why each has a court system of its own. The Native American tribes are also considered sovereign entities, so they have separate tribal courts. These tribal courts will receive no further attention in this book because, in general, they do not have to follow the same constitutional requirements as state and federal courts. Rather, they come under the Indian Civil Rights Act of 1968. The U.S. military also has its own structure, in which the rules of criminal procedure differ markedly from those covered here. Because of the complexity of

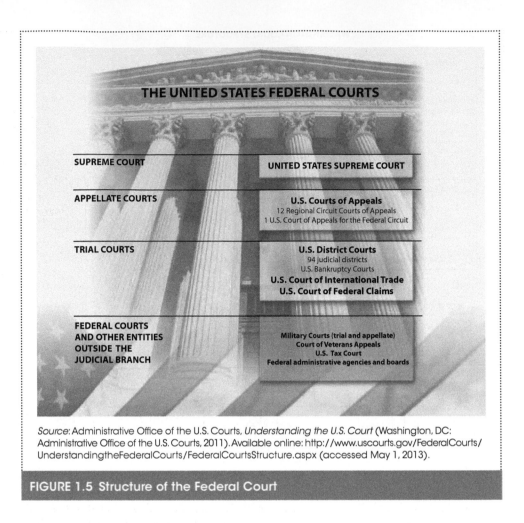

THE UNITED STATES FEDERAL COURTS

| SUPREME COURT | UNITED STATES SUPREME COURT |
|---|---|
| APPELLATE COURTS | **U.S. Courts of Appeals**<br>12 Regional Circuit Courts of Appeals<br>1 U.S. Court of Appeals for the Federal Circuit |
| TRIAL COURTS | **U.S. District Courts**<br>94 judicial districts<br>U.S. Bankruptcy Courts<br>**U.S. Court of International Trade**<br>**U.S. Court of Federal Claims** |
| FEDERAL COURTS AND OTHER ENTITIES OUTSIDE THE JUDICIAL BRANCH | Military Courts (trial and appellate)<br>Court of Veterans Appeals<br>U.S. Tax Court<br>Federal administrative agencies and boards |

*Source:* Administrative Office of the U.S. Courts, *Understanding the U.S. Court* (Washington, DC: Administrative Office of the U.S. Courts, 2011). Available online: http://www.uscourts.gov/FederalCourts/UnderstandingtheFederalCourts/FederalCourtsStructure.aspx (accessed May 1, 2013).

**FIGURE 1.5 Structure of the Federal Court**

the Uniform Code of Military Justice, military courts and criminal procedure will also not be covered in this book.

Generally, if the case involves federal law, it will be tried in federal court. If, however, it involves state law, it will be heard in state court. Certain crimes—such as kidnapping, transportation of illegal narcotics across state lines, and robbing a federally insured bank—may be tried in both federal and state courts, if the prosecutors agree. As will be discussed later, such a dual prosecution does not violate the Fifth Amendment's double-jeopardy clause.

If a prosecution originates in state court, there is rarely a federal prosecution to follow, absent a compelling federal interest. Indeed, the U.S. Justice Department's so-called "petite policy" is responsible for this convention.

This text will focus almost exclusively on U.S. Supreme Court decisions, rather than *state* supreme court decisions. This is because many important cases move from the state supreme courts to the U.S. Supreme Court, which is the court of last resort. Decisions of the U.S. Supreme Court are, therefore, important because they represent the last word on what conduct is constitutional and what is not.

To understand the relationship between the federal and state courts, it is necessary to understand first where to find criminal cases and then how to trace the progress of criminal cases as they move from the trial to the appellate level. Attention will then turn to what types of cases are decided by the U.S. Supreme Court and how state-level court decisions arrive at the nation's highest court.

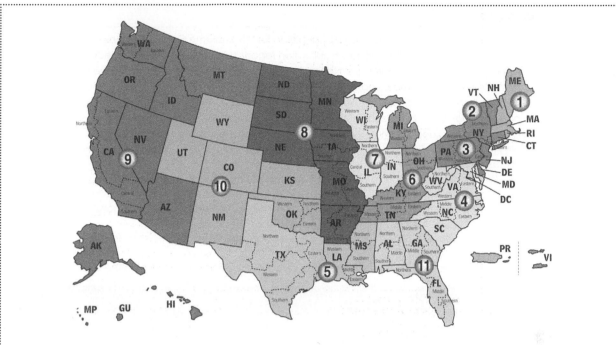

*Source*: Administrative Office of the U.S. Courts, *Court Locator* (Washington, DC: Administrative Office of the U.S. Courts, 2011). Available online: http://www.uscourts.gov/Court_Locator.aspx (accessed May 1, 2013).

**FIGURE 1.6 Geographic Boundaries of the U.S. Courts of Appeals and the U.S. District Courts**

## Finding Cases

Being able to find court cases requires that readers be familiar with legal citations as well as the publications in which cases can be found. Legal citations are somewhat cryptic but can be deciphered with relative ease. The following is the citation format used throughout this text:

### Miranda v. Arizona, 384 U.S. 436 (1966)

*Miranda* and *Arizona* refer to the parties to the case. Importantly, the party listed first is the one initiating the action in that court. In this case, *Miranda* appealed his conviction to the U.S. Supreme Court, which is why he is listed first in the Supreme Court case. The legal citation format that follows the parties is interpreted as follows: The first part, *384*, is the volume; the second part, *U.S.*, is the publication in which the case can be found; the third part, *436*, is the page on which the case starts; and the fourth, *1966*, is the year the decision was published. See Figure 1.7 for a listing of publications in which court cases can be found.

After becoming familiar with case citations, it is necessary to learn where the cases can actually be found. Most university law libraries have several sets of books called reporters, listed in Figure 1.7. They can be found in bound form on the library shelves. Online research is also an option. Cases can be found at such Web sites as www.findlaw.com. U.S. Supreme Court cases can be found at www.supremecourtus.gov. Another Web site, maintained by Cornell University, is helpful for finding Supreme Court cases: http://www.law.cornell.edu/supct/.

Many university libraries also have access to subscription databases, such as LexisNexis, which contain cases from nearly all courts across the country. Both Lexis and West have a feature known as *Sheppard's Citations*, which allows researchers to enter a case citation and

| Abbreviation | Description |
|---|---|
| U.S. | *United States Reports*: This is the official publication for U.S. Supreme Court decisions. |
| S.Ct. | *Supreme Court Reporter*: This Westlaw publication reports U.S. Supreme Court decisions. |
| CrL | *Criminal Law Reporter*: This Bureau of National Affairs publication reports U.S. Supreme Court decisions. |
| L.W. | *United States Law Week*: This Bureau of National Affairs publication reports U.S. Supreme Court decisions. |
| F.2d | *Federal Reports*, Second Series: This Westlaw publication reports decisions of the Federal Courts of Appeals. |
| P.2d | *Pacific Reporter*, Second Series: This Westlaw publication reports decisions from the Pacific states. |
| A.2d | *Atlantic Reporter*, Second Series: This Westlaw publication reports decisions from the Atlantic states. |
| N.E.2d | *North Eastern Reporter*, Second Series: This Westlaw publication reports decisions from the northeastern states. |
| N.W.2d. | *North Western Reporter*, Second Series: This Westlaw publication reports decisions from the northwestern states. |
| S.E.2d | *South Eastern Reporter*, Second Series: This Westlaw publication reports decisions from the southeastern states. |
| S.W.2d | *South Western Reporter*, Second Series: This Westlaw publication reports decisions from the southwestern states. |
| S.2d | *Southern Reporter*, Second Series: This Westlaw publication reports decisions from the southern states. |

**FIGURE 1.7 Publications Containing Court Cases**

retrieve every other case that has cited it. Doing a Sheppard's search is useful for tracing the history and current status of an important decision.

For those who do not have the time to read and study actual court decisions, other sources of legal information may be useful to provide an overview of the law in various areas. For example, legal dictionaries and encyclopedias offer clarification of important legal concepts. Legal digests identify and consolidate legal issues, provide commentary on and interpret cases, and otherwise "digest" complex material. Finally, law reviews are useful places to find discussions of various aspects of the law as well as opinions and interpretations of court cases. Databases such as LexisNexis contain full-text articles from nearly all law reviews. The Web links listed at the end of this chapter include some legal research sites with information on how to find cases, statutes, and other relevant information.

## Tracing the Progress of a Criminal Case

One of the more frustrating aspects of criminal procedure, especially for those who have little familiarity with the law or legal jargon, is the sometimes laborious task of tracing the progress of a criminal case. If final decisions were reached in a single court, then criminal procedure would be vastly simplified. In reality, though, a single case can bounce back and forth between trial and appellate courts, sometimes for years. Indeed, many U.S. Supreme Court decisions concern events that occurred a decade or more ago. Thus, it is of particular importance for students of criminal procedure to learn how to trace a criminal case.

There are several essential steps to tracing the progress of a criminal case. First, it is necessary to have a basic understanding of the nation's court structure. This requires knowing where the criminal trial in question took place. If it took place in a federal circuit court, then tracing the progress of the case will be fairly easy. There are only three possible courts—district court, circuit appellate court, and the Supreme Court—that may have handed down decisions on the matter. If the case originated in state court, however, it can be decidedly more difficult to trace the case over time. Familiarity with the state court structure is needed, as well as an understanding of how cases can jump back and forth between the state and federal courts, which will be discussed later in this section.

Second, to adequately follow the progress of a criminal case, it is also necessary to understand the legal jargon. The *parties* to the case are the people involved who will be bound by the court's decision. At the trial level, the parties of interest are the **defendant**, or the person charged with the crime in question, and the government (the "state" in state court cases, or the United States in federal court cases). The **prosecutor** is the official representing the government in the case. At the appellate level, these parties are no longer called *defendant* and *state*, but rather **appellant** and **appellee**. The *appellant* is the party that appeals; either the state or the defendant can appeal, but the defendant appeals more often than the state. The *appellee* (sometimes called the *respondent*) is the party appealed against. The term **petitioner** is also used at times, namely, when a prisoner files a *habeas corpus* petition. A petitioner is one who petitions an appellate court to hear his or her case.

Next, to follow a criminal case, it is essential to have an understanding of how cases are decided and what possible decisions can be reached. At the trial level, two decisions can result: guilty or not guilty. At the appellate level, however, the decision becomes more complex. Assume, for example, that a defendant is found guilty in a federal district court and appeals to one of the circuit courts of appeals. Assuming that the court agrees to hear the case, it can hand down one of several types of decision. It could **reverse** the lower court's decision, which is akin to nullifying or setting it aside. Sometimes the appellate court **vacates** the lower court's decision, which is basically the same as reversing it. A reversal does *not* always have the effect of setting the defendant free, however. The appellate court could also **remand** the case back to the lower court. When a case is remanded, it is sent back to the lower court for further action consistent with the appellate court's decision. Cases can also be reversed and remanded together. The appellate court can also **affirm** the lower court's decision, in which case it agrees with the lower court.

If there was only one appellate court, tracing the progress of a case would be fairly simple. Unfortunately, multiple appellate courts exist, which means the decisions from court to court can change. This is a very important point. Assume, for example, that a defendant is found guilty in a state trial court. He or she could appeal to the state's intermediate appellate court, which could reverse the defendant's conviction. The case could then go to the state's supreme court, which could reverse the appellate court's decision and basically uphold the defendant's conviction. Finally, the case could go to the U.S. Supreme Court, which could again reverse the defendant's conviction. Believe it or not, this is a fairly simple progression. Nothing prevents a single case from going from the trial court to the appellate court, back to the trial court, up to the appellate court again, then up to the state supreme court, back to the intermediate appellate court, and so on.

It is essential to understand what has happened with a criminal case before making any claims as to its importance or influence. In other words, doing incomplete legal research can be a recipe for disaster. If, for instance, a researcher finds a state supreme court decision that supports a point he or she wants to make, but that decision was later reversed by the U.S. Supreme Court, whatever argument he or she makes in reliance on that state supreme court case will be inaccurate. Thus, in tracing the progress of a criminal case, it is necessary to understand whether the issue in question has been resolved or may currently be on the docket of an appellate court, which could render an altogether different decision.

In tracing a criminal case, especially when interpreting one decided at the appellate level, it is important to understand the components of a published decision. An appellate court often consists of a panel of judges who may not always agree with one another, even though the court reaches a single decision. For example, a 5 to 4 decision by the U.S. Supreme Court is one in which the Court reached a single decision because of a majority, but four of the justices disagreed. The **opinion** is the voice of the five justices, although one or more of the five may opt to write a **concurring opinion**, which supports the majority's decision but for different reasons. The four remaining justices will probably write a **dissent**, in which they argue why they disagree with the majority's decision. If they wanted to, each of the four minority justices could write his or her own individual dissent. Either way, it is important to distinguish between a given court's opinion and possible concurring and dissenting opinions.

There is much more to tracing the progress of a criminal case than understanding the terminology encountered along the way. How is it that certain cases are appealed and others are not? Under what circumstances may the defendant appeal, but not the prosecution, and vice versa? Why do some defendants file several appeals and others do not? Answers to these questions are presented in the last chapter of this text, where special attention is given to the appellate process and other methods for challenging the verdicts of trial courts throughout the United States.

## How Cases Reach the Supreme Court

Most criminal cases originate at the state level. This should be obvious because there are 50 state court structures and only one federal court system. Also, the number of state laws criminalizing certain types of conduct vastly exceeds the number of federal laws with the same objective. However, many cases are also heard at the federal level, and under some circumstances, state-level cases can eventually arrive at the U.S. Supreme Court.

A state-level case can reach the Supreme Court if it raises a federal question, which is usually a question concerning the U.S. Constitution. First, however, such a case must proceed through several steps. It must move all the way to the state supreme court. That is, a case cannot jump from a state-level intermediate appellate court to the U.S. Supreme Court.

Next, like many appellate courts, the U.S. Supreme Court must decide whether it wants to hear the case. The party seeking a decision must file documents with the Court, asking to be heard. If the Supreme Court agrees the case is worth deciding, it issues what is known as a **writ of certiorari**. This is an order by the Court, requiring the lower court to send the case and a record of its proceedings to the U.S. Supreme Court for review. Four of the nine U.S. Supreme Court justices must agree to hear a case before a *writ of certiorari* will be issued. This is known as the **rule of four**.

If four justices do not agree to hear the case, that is the end of the legal process. When tracing the progress of a case, encountering a statement such as "cert. denied" will indicate this result. The case was denied a hearing by the Supreme Court. Figure 1.8 summarizes how cases arrive at the Supreme Court.

It cannot be overemphasized that only a small fraction of cases ever reach the U.S. Supreme Court. It is not uncommon for the Supreme Court to review thousands of petitions, yet grant less than 100 *writs of certiorari* in a year. Most cases that are appealed stop

---

### DECISION-MAKING EXERCISE 1.6

**INTERPRETING A SUPREME COURT HOLDING**

Assume that John Smith was subjected to a search that was not supported by probable cause. Assume further that he was convicted in a federal district court based on evidence obtained from the search. He appealed his conviction to the U.S. court of appeals, which remanded his case back to the district court to determine if the search to which Smith was subjected required probable cause. (Some searches, as will be discussed later, do not require probable cause.) The district court concluded that the search did not require probable cause. The case was then appealed again to the U.S. court of appeals, which reversed the district court's decision, holding that the search *did* need to be supported by probable cause. The U.S. Supreme Court then granted *certiorari* and reversed the U.S. court of appeals decision, holding that the search did not need to be supported by probable cause. In plain English, what happened here? What is the practical effect of this convoluted case progression?

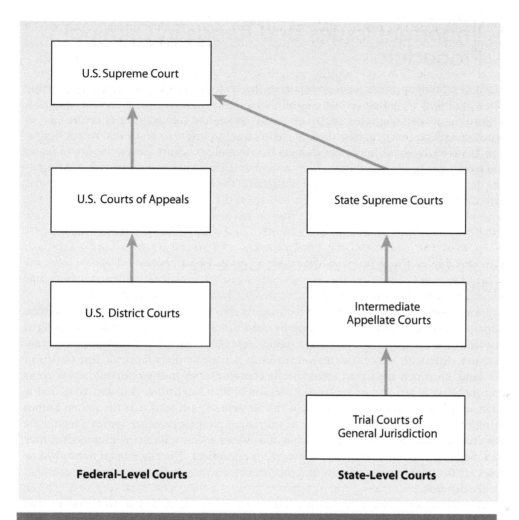

U.S. Supreme Court

U.S. Courts of Appeals

State Supreme Courts

U.S. District Courts

Intermediate
Appellate Courts

Trial Courts of
General Jurisdiction

**Federal-Level Courts**

**State-Level Courts**

FIGURE 1.8 How Cases Arrive at the U.S. Supreme Court

short of reaching the Supreme Court, so it is necessary to find out at what level the final decision was reached. Not tracing a case to its final decision can be fatal to a legal argument. In other words, if a researcher wants to argue a specific point with reference to a previously decided case, he or she must be sure that the decision is, if only for the time being, a final one.

## DECISION-MAKING EXERCISE 1.7

### WOULD THE SUPREME COURT HEAR THIS CASE?

Assume that a state supreme court heard an appeal from one of the state's intermediate appellate courts. In the appeal, the defendant argued that her conviction should be overturned, because the judge should have ruled that certain testimony by the government's lead witness was inadmissible according to the state's rules of evidence. The appellate court sided with the government, and upheld the defendant's conviction. Would the U.S. Supreme Court likely hear this case? What if, instead, the defendant argued that the original judge mistakenly permitted the prosecutor to comment to the jury concerning the defendant's refusal to take the stand and testify? Would that issue likely get a hearing from the Court?

# ▶ Important Issues and Trends in Criminal Procedure

Much of criminal procedure, as presented in this text, involves interpreting U.S. Supreme Court decisions regarding certain constitutional rights. In interpreting those decisions, it is worth understanding some important terms, issues, and trends in the Supreme Court's decision-making practices over the years. Also, it is important to know that recent legislation has brought about important changes in criminal procedure. Seven important issues and trends can be identified in the way the Supreme Court makes its decisions: (1) bright-line decisions versus case-by-case adjudication; (2) the distinction between *subjectivity* and *objectivity*; (3) an increased faith in the police; (4) the notion of judicial restraint; (5) the issue of personal privacy; (6) how the war on terror has influenced criminal procedure; and (7) whether the Constitution is equipped to deal with rapidly advancing technology.

## Bright-Line Decisions versus Case-by-Case Adjudication

Supreme Court decisions can be divided roughly into two categories: (1) **bright-line decisions** and (2) decisions requiring **case-by-case adjudication**. A bright-line decision is one in which the Court hands down a *specific rule* that is meant to be applied uniformly in every case, with very little interpretation. It is like the metaphorical "line drawn in the sand" in which the Court emphatically communicates to the criminal justice community what it can and cannot do. An example of a bright-line decision is *Wilson v. Layne*, mentioned previously, in which the Supreme Court said that the police cannot bring the media along on the service of warrants unless its presence serves a legitimate law enforcement objective. Exactly what constitutes a "law enforcement objective" may be somewhat vague, but otherwise, this rule is quite clear. The advantages of bright-line rules are that they promote clarity and consistency, and are easily understood by criminal justice officials.

A decision requiring case-by-case adjudication is quite different. In these types of rulings, the Supreme Court often refers to the concept of **totality of circumstances**. This means that all the facts and circumstances surrounding the case must be examined in order to determine whether a constitutional rights violation has taken place. Deciding whether the totality of circumstances supports the action in question requires looking at each case *individually*. There is no established "recipe" specifying exactly what authorities should or should not do in every case. For example, in the case of *Manson v. Braithwaite*, 432 U.S. 98 (1977), the Supreme Court held that the totality of circumstances determines whether eyewitness identification is admissible at trial. The Court noted a number of variables to be examined, including the passage of time, the accuracy of the witness's description, and the witness's level of certainty. A case-by-case decision is preferable in some cases because it is rarely possible to know in advance all the possible twists and turns in a criminal case. Case-by-case decisions promote flexibility, leaving it up to the lower courts (usually, the trial court) to decide if the action in question conforms to constitutional guidelines. However, this approach can also create uncertainty for law enforcement officials.

*Manson v. Braithwaite*
*(432 U.S. 98 [1977])*

## Subjectivity versus Objectivity

The terms *subjective* and *objective* are sometimes used to describe the thought process used in Supreme Court decisions. Although these terms are well understood in everyday use, what they mean in the language of criminal procedure is not necessarily so well defined. Part of the confusion stems from the fact that *subjective* and *objective* are sometimes used with the term *reasonable*. It is not uncommon to read a Supreme Court opinion referring to *objective reasonableness* or *subjective reasonableness*. Usually, phrases such as these are considered in the context of the Fourth Amendment because of its explicit prohibition of "unreasonable" searches and seizures.

Police conduct that is deemed subjectively reasonable, or characterized by **subjective reasonableness**, is conduct that would be considered reasonable by the police officer engaged in the conduct. For example, if a police officer arrests a person without probable cause but he personally believes that probable cause was present, his or her actions can be considered subjectively reasonable. **Objective reasonableness**, by contrast, refers to what a reasonable person (usually, a reasonable police officer) would do or feel under the circumstances. It is meant to reflect what society at large is prepared to accept as reasonable. For example, an arrest based on probable cause is considered objectively reasonable if a reasonable police officer observing the situation would believe that probable cause existed to make the arrest.

Objective and subjective language can also be found in the Supreme Court's references to people's privacy interests. For example, in deciding whether a person enjoys a reasonable expectation of privacy when engaging in some sort of activity, that expectation may be described as subjective or objective. In such cases, the Court decides whether individuals should be trusted to identify their own privacy interests (subjective), or whether society at large determines whether a reasonable expectation of privacy exists in a given situation (objective).

In the past few decades, the Supreme Court has moved from subjective analyses to objective analyses in many of its decisions. The reason for this shift is that a subjective analysis puts a high degree of faith in the individual police officer, citizen, or other person. Assume that a man has a marijuana field on his property, and it is observed by the police in a helicopter flyover. He will probably argue that he should be able to enjoy privacy in his backyard and that the police should not be able to spy on him. Such an argument is quite predictable in a case like this because it requires the suspect to assert a privacy interest. However, what the suspect believes and what a "reasonable person" may believe could be two entirely different things. Indeed, the Supreme Court has moved to an objective analysis in many scenarios such as this for the simple reason that individuals are not entirely without bias in making such determinations. The Court now prefers to defer to an objective analysis of privacy interests.

In some ways, the term *objective*, as used in court decisions, mirrors its meaning in everyday use. It suggests a more or less unbiased view of a particular matter. By comparison, the term *subjective* suggests more of an individually based determination. Unfortunately, it is not always easy to identify what a "reasonable person" would believe. The notion of a reasonable person is, in fact, a hypothetical construct. For this reason, the Court usually must provide guidance as to what can be considered an objectively reasonable belief.

The distinction between objective and subjective reasonableness has been illustrated in the landmark case of *Graham v. Connor*, 490 U.S. 386 (1989), the leading case on the use of nondeadly force to date. The Supreme Court declared emphatically that all claims involving allegations of excessive, nondeadly force against police officers must be analyzed under the Fourth Amendment's reasonableness requirement. As the court stated:

"[A]ll claims that law enforcement officers have used excessive force—deadly or not—in the course of an arrest, investigatory stop, or other 'seizure' of a free citizen should be analyzed under the Fourth Amendment and its 'reasonableness' standard."

Similarly, in *Tennessee v. Garner*, 471 U.S. 1 (1985), the Court adopted a test of objective reasonableness to decide whether excessive force has been used. The Court held that the test must focus on what a *reasonable* police officer would do "without regard to [the officer's] underlying intent or motivation." In trying to decide what a reasonable police officer

## A BRIGHT-LINE DECISION OR CASE-BY-CASE ADJUDICATION

In *Garner*, a Memphis police officer shot and killed an unarmed 15-year-old boy who was fleeing the scene of a residential burglary. The officer called to the boy, Garner, to stop, but he did not. When Garner was about to climb a fence, the officer shot him in the back of the head, fatally wounding him. Garner's surviving family members filed a Section 1983 lawsuit, claiming the level of force used was excessive.

The Supreme Court agreed, ruling that deadly force may be used only when two criteria are present: (1) It is necessary to prevent the suspect's escape, and (2) the officer has probable cause to believe the suspect poses a serious threat of death or serious physical injury to other people or police officers. Can the Court's decision in *Garner* be characterized as bright line in nature?

would do, the Court looked to three factors: (1) the severity of the crime; (2) whether the suspect posed a threat; and (3) whether the suspect was resisting and/or attempting to flee the scene. Courts must, in focusing on these three factors, allow "for the fact that police officers are often forced to make split-second judgments—about the amount of force that is necessary in a particular situation." Note that the Court was not concerned with what the individual officer felt with regard to these three factors. Rather, the preferred focus was on what a reasonable officer would believe.

## Increased Faith in the Police

Earl Warren was appointed chief justice of the U.S. Supreme Court in 1953, and his judicial opinions were highly influential in shaping criminal procedure. References to the "**Warren Court**" refer the time from 1953 to 1969, during which Warren was chief justice. The Warren Court handed down a number of decisions, particularly during the 1960s, that established extensive constitutional protections for criminal defendants. To use the words of Herbert Packer, the Court was highly concerned with "due process" during this period. Others describe the Court as being extremely liberal during the Warren era. In general, the Court did not place a great deal of trust in the police, much less other criminal justice officials. Rather, it was concerned primarily with individual rights.

From 1969 to 1986, the position of chief justice was held by Warren E. Burger. During his tenure, the Court moved closer to the center of judicial and political thought and away from the liberal stance of the Warren Court. This movement toward conservatism gained significant momentum with the appointment of William H. Rehnquist as chief justice in 1987. The decisions handed down by the Court in the area of criminal procedure began to take on a different orientation, one that placed a great deal of faith in the police. In practice, many of the Court's decisions of late have increased the power of law enforcement as well as granted the police extensive latitude with regard to controlling crime. For example, the Court created the well-known "good faith" exception to the exclusionary rule. Also, many decisions have carved out exceptions to the Fourth Amendment's warrant requirement, suggesting that judicially authorized search and arrest warrants are not of particular use or importance much of the time.

The reader is encouraged to take note of the dates of the many Supreme Court decisions discussed throughout this text. With only a handful of exceptions, the decisions of the Warren Court in the 1960s were concerned with the rights of criminal suspects, and placed significant restrictions on the authority of criminal justice officials. Many of the decisions handed down since approximately the 1980s reflect something of a change in priorities, favoring increased law enforcement authority and a concern with effective crime control, as opposed to due process.

## Judicial Restraint

The term **judicial restraint** refers to the philosophy of limiting decisions to the facts of each case, and deciding only the issue or issues that need to be resolved in a particular situation. The practice of judicial restraint also entails avoiding unnecessary decisions on constitutional questions that have yet to be posed. In the area of criminal procedure, a judicially restrained judge will look to the language of the Constitution for guidance. Should the wording of the Constitution not be entirely clear, he or she will attempt to understand the framers' original intent. Another way to think of judicial restraint is that it is *interpretive*, seeking only to interpret the Constitution itself. Another aspect of judicial restraint is the reliance on *precedent*. A judge who is exercising judicial restraint will defer to precedent as much as possible, and avoid setting new guidelines and rules.

In *Silverman v. United States*, 365 U.S. 505 (1961), the Supreme Court elaborated on the notion of judicial restraint when it was deciding a Fourth Amendment case:

> [T]he facts of the present case . . . do not require us to consider the large questions which have been argued. We need not here contemplate the Fourth Amendment implications of these and other frightening paraphernalia which the vaunted marvels of an electronic age may visit upon human society.

The Court basically stated only the specific question before the Court should be decided, and larger questions should be left unanswered.

On the spectrum of judicial philosophies, judicial restraint is the opposite of **judicial activism**. A judicially active judge is one who sees his or her role as more than simply interpreting the Constitution. A judicially active judge is not hesitant to hand down decisions that have sweeping implications for the future. Cases handed down by judicially active judges are often referred to as "judge-made" law, since they create new rules rather than upholding established ones.

## Personal Privacy

The Supreme Court has repeatedly emphasized that people should enjoy protection of their privacy beyond physical intrusions into their property. The Supreme Court's landmark decision in *Katz v. United States*, 389 U.S. 347 (1967), reflects this high degree of respect for people's privacy. The Court stated that "the Fourth Amendment protects people, not places," emphasizing that the scope of the "Amendment cannot turn upon the presence or absence of physical intrusion." This has to be known as the *privacy doctrine*.

Prior to *Katz*, the Court held that the Fourth Amendment only protected against physical intrusion by authorities into a person's private property. This was known as the **trespass doctrine**. People did not enjoy protection of their privacy unless the police or other government officials physically trespassed on their property. Today, fortunately, the Fourth Amendment's protection of privacy has been extended to encompass more than personal

## THE ISSUE OF PERSONAL PRIVACY

In *Kyllo v. United States*, 533 U.S. 27 (2001), the Supreme Court decided that law enforcement's use of a thermal imaging (infrared) device constitutes a search. The Court stated, "Where, as here, the Government uses a device that is not in *general public use*, to explore *details of the home* that would previously have been unknowable without physical intrusion, the surveillance is a 'search' and is presumptively unreasonable without a warrant." Did the Court exercise judicial restraint in its decision? Why or why not?

property. What people say in private telephone conversations (as in *Katz*), for instance, is subject to intense constitutional protection:

> We conclude . . . that the "trespass" doctrine . . . can no longer be regarded as controlling. The Government's activities in electronically listening to and recording the petitioner's words violated the privacy upon which he justifiably relied while using the telephone booth and thus constituted a "search and seizure" within the meaning of the Fourth Amendment. The fact that the electronic device employed to achieve that end did not happen to penetrate the wall of the booth can have no constitutional significance. (*Katz*, 389 U.S. 347)

The privacy doctrine has been reaffirmed over the years in many court decisions and by prominent academics. Sam Ervin

> The oldest and deepest hunger in the human heart is for a place where one may dwell in peace and security and keep inviolate from public scrutiny one's innermost aspirations and thoughts, one's most intimate associations and communications, and one's most private activities. This truth was documented by Micah, the prophet, 2,700 years ago when he described the Mountain of the Lord as a place where "they shall sit every man under his own vine and fig tree and none shall make them afraid."[8]

The increasing trend in applying the Fourth Amendment to personal privacy is interesting because there is no explicit mention of the word "privacy" in the entire Bill of Rights. Nevertheless, the Supreme Court has held that a right to privacy can be inferred from the wording of its various amendments.. As such, privacy is something of a judicially created right.

## Criminal Procedure and the War on Terror

Criminal procedure is sometimes altered in significant ways by federal and state legislation. One example of such legislation is the Antiterrorism and Effective Death Penalty Act of 1996, which was passed following the 1995 bombing of the Oklahoma City federal building. This legislation has altered the federal law of *habeas corpus*, by limiting the power of federal judges to grant this form of relief.

An arguably more important piece of legislation, one that has affected several aspects of criminal procedure, was signed into law in response to the September 11, 2001, attacks on the Pentagon and the World Trade Center towers. In order to empower the Department of Justice to combat terrorism, Congress passed the PATRIOT Act on October 26, 2001.[9] This legislation made several important changes to past law and practice. First, it centralized federal

---

[8]S. J. Ervin, "The Exclusionary Rule: An Essential Ingredient of the Fourth Amendment," *Supreme Court Review* (1983): 283, 288–289, 296–297.

[9]On March 9, 2006, President Bush signed a law that made the PATRIOT Act permanent. Certain provisions were changed and some civil liberties protections were added, but most of the original act remains intact.

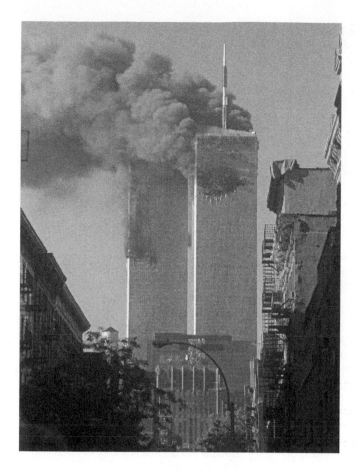

A fiery blast rocked the World Trade Center in New York City after both towers were hit by hijacked passenger planes on September 11, 2001. This attack, along with a similar attack on the Pentagon in Washington, DC, prompted passage of the PATRIOT Act.

law enforcement authority in the U.S. Department of Justice. For example, Section 808 of the Act reassigned the authority for investigating several federal crimes of violence from law enforcement agencies, such as the Secret Service and the Bureau of Alcohol, Tobacco, and Firearms, to the attorney general. The act also provided for Central Intelligence Agency (CIA) oversight of all domestic intelligence gathering. Prior to the PATRIOT Act, the CIA's role was primarily concerned with foreign intelligence gathering. The act also expanded the definition of the terms *terrorism* and *domestic terrorism* to include activities that

(A) involve acts dangerous to human life that are a violation of the criminal laws of the United States or of any state; (B) appear to be intended (i) to intimidate or coerce a civilian population; (ii) to influence the policy of a government by mass destruction, assassination, or kidnapping; or (iii) to effect the conduct of a government by mass destruction, assassination, or kidnapping; and (C) occur primarily within the territorial jurisdiction of the United States.[10]

Many major changes in criminal procedure are attributable to the PATRIOT Act. First, the PATRIOT Act alters and even abolishes constitutional protections historically available to legal and illegal aliens. The Supreme Court has traditionally held that the Fifth and Sixth Amendments' rights of due process and access to jury trials apply to *all persons*, not just citizens of the United States (*United States v. Verdugo-Urquidez*, 494 U.S. 259 [1990]). In addition, the Supreme Court has held that all undocumented aliens living inside U.S. borders are entitled to the protections enunciated in the Bill of Rights (*Mathews v. Diaz*, 426 U.S. 67 [1976]). Specifically, the Court has stated that "the Fifth Amendment, as well as

---

[10]USA PATRIOT ACT, Public Law 107–56, Section 802.

the Fourteenth Amendment, protects every one of these persons from deprivation of life, liberty, or property without due process of law. Even one whose presence in this country is unlawful, involuntary, or transitory is entitled to constitutional protection." These rights have also applied to the removal of aliens from within U.S. borders. That is, proceedings for the deportation of aliens have had to conform to constitutional requirements, especially due process (*Shaughnessy v. United States ex rel. Mezei*, 345 U.S. 206 [1953]). In short, legal, illegal, resident, and temporary aliens have *all* historically enjoyed the same constitutional protections as ordinary U.S. citizens. But with the passage of the PATRIOT Act, that is no longer the case.

The legislation prompted by the war on terror has had far-reaching implications for criminal procedure. To illustrate, Figure 1.9 summarizes a number of key Supreme Court cases pertaining to terrorism and the primary holdings from each. Notice how some decisions favor the suspect and others favor the government.

| Case | Question before the Court* | Decision |
|---|---|---|
| *Ex Parte Milligan* (1866) | Is it constitutional to try U.S. citizens before military tribunals when civilian courts are available? | No. It is unconstitutional to try U.S. citizens before military tribunals when civilian courts are available. |
| *Hamdi v. Rumsfeld* (2004) | Can U.S. citizens arrested abroad and detained on suspected involvement in terrorism challenge in court the government's justification for detaining them? | Yes. Detained U.S. citizens enjoy the right to challenge their detentions before an impartial judge. |
| *Rumsfeld v. Padilla* (2004) | Can U.S. citizens arrested domestically and detained as "enemy combatants" on suspected involvement in terrorism challenge in court the government's justification for detaining them? | Not answered. The case was remanded. The principal issue in this case remains unresolved. |
| *Rasul v. Bush* (2004) | Can noncitizen detainees at Guantanamo Bay challenge the constitutionality of their confinement? | Yes. The federal courts have jurisdiction to decide the constitutionality of detaining foreign nationals. |
| *Hamdan v. Rumsfeld* (2006) | Is it within the authority of Congress and the President to try suspected terrorists before military tribunals? | No. Bush-era military tribunals violate the Uniform Code of Military Justice and the Geneva Conventions. |
| *Boumediene v. Bush* (2008) | Are parts of the Military Commissions Act of 2006 that strip federal courts of jurisdiction to hear habeas corpus petitions from foreign citizens illegal? | Yes. Parts of the Military Commissions Act of 2006 that strip federal courts of habeas corpus jurisdiction in cases involving Guantanamo Bay detainees are unconstitutional. |
| *Holder v. Humanitarian Law Project* (2010) | Are parts of the AEDPA prohibiting "any . . . service, . . . training, [or] other specialized knowledge" to designated terrorist organizations unconstitutionally vague? | No. The Court decided that the kind of support the Humanitarian Law Project wished to provide was clearly prohibited in the statute. |
| *Ashcroft v. al-Kidd* (2011) | Does the attorney general have qualified immunity for his involvement in the arrest of a person as a material witness? Can a validly obtained warrant be challenged on the motive that the arresting authority had an improper motive? | Yes. The attorney general enjoys qualified immunity in such cases.<br>No. Detaining al-Kidd as a material witness was constitutionally reasonable, even if the government's motive to hold him was based on a belief that he was a terrorist. |
| *Clapper v. Amnesty International USA* (2013) | Do "United States Persons" have standing to challenge the Foreign Intelligence Surveillance Act of 1978 and the FISA Amendments Act of 2008? | No. The respondents asserted that their foreign contacts will be targeted for surveillance, but the Court said they had no knowledge of the government's "targeting practices." |

*The case may have dealt with more than one question. The key question with relevance to criminal procedure is presented here.

**FIGURE 1.9 Key Supreme Court Cases in the War on Terrorism**

▼

## Criminal Procedure and Technology

Technology continues its relentless march. New devices are constantly being invented to help law enforcement officials detect crime and catch criminals. However, many of these technological innovations raise constitutional questions. In addition, many Supreme Court decisions were rendered years ago before many of today's technologies were conceived of. Is our Constitution and the resulting court decisions equipped to deal with these advances in technology? Only time will tell. This book thus contains several references in upcoming chapters to technological innovations that have implications for criminal procedure.

# ▶ The Criminal Process: An Overview

There is no easy or concise way to describe the criminal process. Figure 1.10 presents only one example of the process, but there are countless variations at both the federal and state levels in how criminal cases are handled. The criminal process may also assume different forms depending on the seriousness of a case.

It should be noted that this section is only an overview of the criminal process. However, because of the variations from one jurisdiction to the next, readers should take steps to familiarize themselves with the criminal processes in the areas in which they reside.

## Pretrial

A typical criminal case begins with a *complaint.* It may come in the form of a 911 call from a citizen, a report to the police that someone has been victimized, or a report from a law enforcement officer who observes a crime in progress. If a citizen reports the crime, the police will usually follow up on the complaint by performing an investigation, and take steps to confirm the observations of the citizen. If a police officer observes the crime, less investigative scrutiny will be necessary. In fact, when an officer observes a crime in progress, he or she will probably attempt to arrest the suspect on the spot. This arrest will then be subjected to judicial scrutiny in a court hearing, in which a judge will decide if there was probable cause to arrest the suspect.

If a crime is reported by a citizen, and the police have identified a suspect, they will approach a judge and seek either an arrest or a search warrant. In either case, the police must be able to show probable cause that the evidence they seek will be found in the place to be searched or that the suspect to be arrested was the one who committed the crime. If this burden is met, an arrest, a search warrant, or both, will be issued and the police will arrest the suspect or search the premises named in the search warrant. The burden of probable cause that is required for search and arrest warrants is not to be taken lightly and has spawned a great deal of debate in the courts.

The role of the police during the pretrial process cannot be overemphasized. In the period from the first contact between an officer and suspect up to the point when the suspect is arrested and detained, the role of the police is complex and multifaceted. The Constitution, particularly the Fourth Amendment, places significant restrictions on what the police can and cannot do when they investigate crimes and handle suspects. This is why the role of the police in the criminal process deserves extensive attention. *Criminal* procedure is, in many ways, *police* procedure.

If a police officer arrests a suspect for a crime committed in his or her presence, no warrant is necessary. But even when arresting a suspect or searching his or her residence based on a citizen complaint, a warrant is not always required. Many situations arise in which the police are permitted to arrest or to search without a warrant. Suspects who evade authorities, seek to destroy evidence, or are likely to inflict harm on others create circumstances in which the police must act quickly. Indeed, in many other areas of law

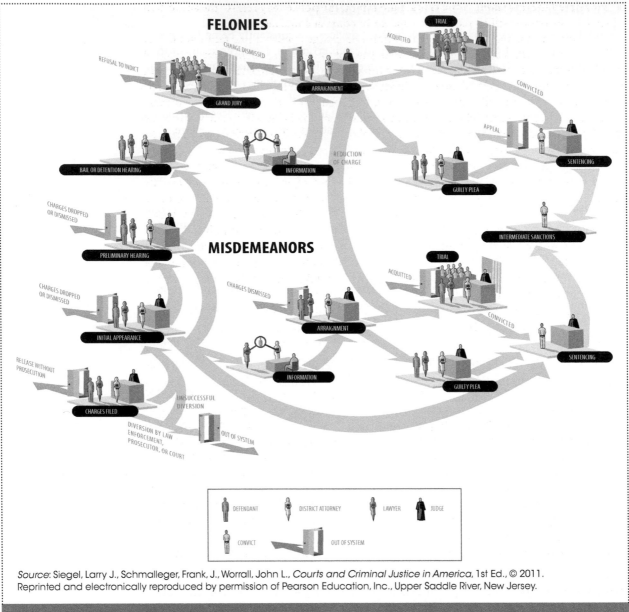

**FELONIES**

TRIAL

ACQUITTED

CHARGE DISMISSED

REFUSAL TO INDICT

GRAND JURY

ARRAIGNMENT

CONVICTED

APPEAL

SENTENCING

BAIL OR DETENTION HEARING

INFORMATION

REDUCTION OF CHARGE

GUILTY PLEA

INTERMEDIATE SANCTIONS

CHARGES DROPPED OR DISMISSED

PRELIMINARY HEARING

**MISDEMEANORS**

TRIAL

ACQUITTED

CHARGES DISMISSED

CHARGES DROPPED OR DISMISSED

INITIAL APPEARANCE

ARRAIGNMENT

CONVICTED

SENTENCING

RELEASE WITHOUT PROSECUTION

INFORMATION

GUILTY PLEA

CHARGES FILED

UNSUCCESSFUL DIVERSION

DIVERSION BY LAW ENFORCEMENT, PROSECUTOR, OR COURT

OUT OF SYSTEM

DEFENDANT          DISTRICT ATTORNEY          LAWYER          JUDGE

CONVICT          OUT OF SYSTEM

*Source*: Siegel, Larry J., Schmalleger, Frank, J., Worrall, John L., *Courts and Criminal Justice in America*, 1st Ed., © 2011. Reprinted and electronically reproduced by permission of Pearson Education, Inc., Upper Saddle River, New Jersey.

**FIGURE 1.10 Sequence of Events in the Criminal Justice System**

enforcement, the police may be forced to make split-second decisions, whether to arrest or search, without the protection of a warrant.

Once a suspect is arrested—whether pursuant to an arrest warrant, a warrant to search his or her residence, or another method—he or she will be searched to protect the police and to discover contraband that may be in the suspect's possession. Then, the suspect will be transported to the police station and booked. *Booking* is the process in which the suspect is fingerprinted, processed, photographed, and probably placed in a holding cell. The suspect may also be required to submit to testing (such as a Breathalyzer) and possibly be required to participate in a lineup for identification by a witness to the crime.

After booking, the police will present their case to the prosecutor, and if the prosecutor believes the evidence is persuasive enough, he or she will bring charges against the suspect, subject to certain restrictions identified by the U.S. Supreme Court. The suspect will now be considered the *defendant*. If the charges are minor, the police may release the suspect, in which case he or she will be required to appear in court at some later date.

Suspects who are booked, placed in detention, and charged with a crime face a number of different court hearings, depending on the seriousness of the crime. Misdemeanors, because of their less serious nature, tend to be fast-tracked through the courts. A misdemeanor defendant may appear at only one court hearing, in which the judge will decide guilt or innocence. Felony defendants, by contrast, face a longer legal road. If the suspect is arrested without a warrant, he or she will be granted a probable cause hearing, in which the judge will decide whether the arresting officer had appropriate justification to make the arrest. (This hearing may, in fact, be merged with other hearings, but for clarity, it is treated here as a separate event.)

The next step in the criminal process is the *arraignment*, at which the suspect comes before a judge and is, at a minimum, informed of the charges against him or her. The defendant will also be notified of the right to counsel, the right to remain silent, and other important rights. He or she will also be allowed to enter a *plea*. Common pleas are guilty, not guilty, and *nolo contendere* (which is akin to a plea of "no contest"). A public defender may be assigned at this stage if the defendant is unable to afford his or her own representation. Probable cause may also be determined at this stage, if a separate hearing is not required. Finally, for a misdemeanor charge, a trial may take place at the arraignment. In more serious cases, a bail determination could be made as well.

If the bail determination is not made at the arraignment, a separate hearing may be warranted (for clarity, the bail determination is treated here as a separate hearing.) In deciding whether bail should be granted, the judge will take such factors into account as the seriousness of the crime as well as the defendant's prior record, likelihood of flight, and level of dangerousness. The defendant's financial status may also be considered.

It is important to note that the prosecutor's method of filing charges varies from one state to the next. Some states require that the prosecutor proceed by *information*, a document that describes the charges the prosecutor is filing. Other states require that the prosecutor proceed by a *grand jury indictment*. That is, a grand jury decides whether charges should be filed, usually with the advice and assistance of the prosecutor. Some states require or allow both methods of filing charges, depending on the nature of the case. In jurisdictions in which the prosecutor proceeds by information, he or she is usually required to show that the charging decision is appropriate. This is accomplished in a so-called *preliminary hearing*, during which the prosecutor makes out what is known as a *prima facie case* of the defendant's guilt. A preliminary hearing can also be required in a grand jury jurisdiction, requiring the prosecutor to present his or her case before seeking a grand jury indictment.

## Adjudication

Once the pretrial process has concluded and the charges have stood, a trial may or may not take place. If, at arraignment, the defendant pleads guilty, then a trial is not necessary. In such an instance, special steps must be taken to ensure that the defendant's guilty plea is valid. The defendant may also agree to a *plea bargain* agreement, in which in exchange for leniency from the prosecutor or the court, he or she pleads guilty to the crime with which he or she is charged. Plea bargaining of this nature can occur at any stage of the criminal process, however. That is, a suspect can reach a plea agreement with the prosecutor as early as the pretrial stage, during the trial, or well into jury deliberations. In any case, the plea bargain, if there is one, must be accepted by the judge.

If the defendant pleads not guilty, the case is set for trial. The trial is usually scheduled for some date well after the arraignment. This allows both sides—the prosecution and the defense—to prepare their respective cases. A balance needs to be achieved between providing enough time for both sides to present effective arguments and protecting the defendant's Sixth Amendment right to a speedy trial. During this preparation process, the *discovery* process takes place, in which each side learns what evidence the other side will present. Information that is attorney work product or reveals an attorney's legal strategy is off limits, but the identities of witnesses who will testify, the physical evidence in possession of both parties, and other items must all be made available in the discovery process.

At trial, the prosecutor bears the burden of proving that the defendant is guilty beyond a reasonable doubt. After the prosecution has presented its case, the defense steps in and presents its case in which it seeks to cast doubt on the prosecution's evidence. A criminal trial may move back and forth in this fashion until both sides rest. At this point, a verdict must be reached. Depending on the seriousness of the offense, the verdict is decided by either a judge or a jury. A "bench trial," in which a judge decides the defendant's fate, is only allowed for an offense that is likely to result in less than six months' imprisonment. A jury decides the verdict when the alleged offense is more serious. Special steps must be taken in either instance to ensure the impartiality of the judge or the jury.

## Beyond Conviction

The criminal process does not necessarily end once the verdict has been read. *Sentencing* usually takes place at a separate hearing. The guilty party may be sentenced to death (for a capital crime), committed to prison, fined, placed on probation, or subjected to a host of other possible sanctions. After a person is committed to prison or sentenced to death, the appeals process may drag on for years beyond the criminal trial.

Appeals come in two varieties: automatic and discretionary. Most convicted criminals are entitled to at least one *automatic appeal* (also known as an *appeal of right*). An automatic appeal must be heard by an appellate court. If an appeal is discretionary, however, it is up to the appellate court to decide whether the appeal will be heard. The right of a convicted criminal to file excessive discretionary appeals is deplored by supporters of the death penalty and other serious sanctions.

An appeal is not the only method of challenging a guilty verdict. The right of *habeas corpus*—also commonly referred to as a *collateral attack*—is guaranteed in the Constitution. Every convicted criminal has the right to petition a court to decide on the constitutionality of his or her confinement. All that is granted, however, is the right to *file* a petition, or to *request* to be heard. The decision whether to grant a prisoner's *habeas* petition is up to the reviewing court. If a prisoner exhausts all available appellate mechanisms and is denied *habeas* review, he or she will remain in prison for the full term of his or her sentence.

# Summary

## 1. Summarize the constitutional basis for criminal procedure.

Criminal procedure is mostly about constitutional rights. What's more, it is about constitutional rights as primarily interpreted by the U.S. Supreme Court. State laws, agency policies, time-honored practices, and the like also set forth rules and guidelines, but the focus here is almost exclusively on rights spelled out in the U.S. Constitution—notably, those found in the Fourth, Fifth, Sixth, Eighth, and Fourteenth Amendments.

## 2. Explain the importance of precedent.

Criminal procedure is closely linked to history because of the importance of precedent. Before making decisions, courts almost always look to the past for the purpose of determining whether a case with similar facts has already been decided. If one has not, the court will distinguish the present case and hand down a decision that may be relied on by some other court, at some later date.

## 3. Compare the theory of criminal procedure to the reality.

Even though criminal procedure, as presented in this text, is mostly about court decisions, it would be a crucial mistake to become hopelessly mired in the world of judicial decision making. In the real world, the police and other criminal justice officials must act, and what they do does not always agree with decisions handed down by the courts. That is, the theoretical world of the courts can differ in important ways from the real world of law enforcement. Understanding that these two different worlds exist and that they can be at odds with one another will allow us to look at court decisions with a critical eye and a dose of reality.

## 4. Describe the public order (crime control) and individual rights (due process) perspectives of criminal justice and how criminal procedure balances the two.

Throughout criminal procedure—indeed, throughout all of criminal justice—two competing perspectives can almost always be seen. The crime control perspective emphasizes controlling crime, often at the expense of people's rights. The due process perspective is concerned primarily with protecting people's rights. Every court decision, policy, and action of the criminal justice system in response to the threat of crime must balance both of these concerns. Some decisions and policies lean too far in the direction of crime control and, for that reason, become quite controversial. The same holds true for decisions and policies that cater to due process. For the justice process to flow smoothly, a balance needs to be achieved.

## 5. Outline the structure of the court system, including the responsibilities and jurisdictions of each level.

The United States has a two-tiered court structure consisting of federal and state courts. At the federal level, three types of courts are relevant: district courts, circuit courts of appeals, and the U.S. Supreme Court. The district courts try cases involving violations of federal laws. The decisions of district courts are appealed to circuit courts of appeals and then to the U.S. Supreme Court. State court structures vary from one state to the next but generally consist of courts of limited jurisdiction, trial courts of general jurisdiction, intermediate appellate courts, and supreme courts. Most criminal cases originate in trial courts of general jurisdiction. The decisions of these courts are appealed to intermediate appellate courts and then to the state supreme court. A state supreme court decision can be appealed to the U.S. Supreme Court but will only be heard if it raises a constitutional question. This is usually true for federal cases, as well.

## 6. Summarize important issues and trends in criminal procedure.

Several important topics, issues, and trends need to be understood in order to fully understand court decisions. First, some decisions consist of specific bright-line rules, whereas others favor case-by-case adjudication. Next, the courts—in particular, the U.S. Supreme Court—have moved from a subjective to an objective focus, meaning that they are now more concerned with how a reasonable person would act under the circumstances. Third, Supreme Court decisions of late have reflected an increased faith in the police to make judgments. Fourth, one must understand the notion of judicial restraint—the practice of deciding only the specific legal question before the court. Fifth, throughout criminal procedure there is a concern with *people's privacy* (even though the Constitution contains no mention of the term). Finally, it is important to have an appreciation for how the war on terror and technology have altered criminal procedure.

## 7. Provide an overview of the criminal process.

There is no single way to describe the criminal process because there are simply too many variations from state to state. Even so, a more or less accurate overview can be given. The description followed throughout this book begins with encounters between police and citizens and then moves into arrest, booking, pretrial hearings, trial, and appeals. Along the way, special attention is given to constitutional rights stemming from several amendments to the Constitution and to the four important actors—the police, prosecutors, defense attorneys, and judges—whose decisions affect the whole of the criminal process. Because of the variations in jurisdictions, the reader is strongly encouraged to become familiar with the details of the criminal process in his or her area of residence.

## Key Terms

affirm *21*
appellant *21*
appellee *21*
bright-line decisions *24*
case-by-case adjudication *24*
concurring opinion *21*
courts of general jurisdiction *16*
courts of limited jurisdiction *16*
crime control perspective *14*
criminal procedure *4*
defendant *21*
dissent *21*
distinguish *10*
district courts *16*
due process perspective *13*
Eighth Amendment *7*
Federal Rules of Criminal Procedure *5*

Fifth Amendment *6*
Fourteenth Amendment *7*
Fourth Amendment *6*
incorporation *8*
intermediate appellate courts *16*
judicial activism *27*
judicial restraint *27*
objective reasonableness *25*
opinion *21*
PATRIOT Act *28*
petitioner *21*
precedent *10*
procedural due process *7*
prosecutor *21*
real world *11*
remand *21*
reverse *21*

right to privacy *28*
rule of four *22*
Sixth Amendment *6*
*stare decisis 10*
state supreme courts *16*
subjective reasonableness *25*
substantive due process *7*
superior courts *16*
theoretical world *11*
totality of circumstances *24*
trespass doctrine *27*
U.S. courts of appeals *16*
U.S. Supreme Court *16*
vacate *21*
Warren Court *26*
writ of certiorari *22*

## Key Cases

* *Manson v. Braithwaite*, 432 U.S. 98 (1977)

## Further Exploration

1. Your local police department is testing a new gun detection device that utilizes "terahertz imaging detection." It functions similar to night vision, but rather than detecting heat, it detects radiation emanating from a person's body. When that radiation is impeded, the object blocking it stands out. The shape of a gun stands out clearly

from a distance. Is this technology beneficial or harmful to privacy rights? Why or why not?

2. The Supreme Court decided in *Florida v. Jardines* (569 U.S.____[2013]) that a drug dog sniffing a person's front porch constitutes a search, requiring a

warrant. In other words, the warrantless action was "unreasonable" from a Fourth Amendment standpoint. Explain this decision in terms of the distinction between theory and reality introduced in this chapter. Will the Supreme Court's decision dramatically alter law enforcement behavior? Why or why not?

3. In the landmark case of *Katz v. United States*, 389 U.S. 347 (1967), the Supreme Court defined a *search* as government action that infringes on a "reasonable expectation of privacy." This decision was binding on all courts in the United States, federal, state, and local. Is the decision "bright line" in nature? Why or why not? If not, how are lower courts supposed to follow a higher court's decision if the definition of a key case concept is not clear?

4. Are available Supreme Court decisions equipped to deal with emerging (and as yet undiscovered) technological advances? This is a difficult question to answer. It may be interpreted loosely—"technological" doesn't need to be electronic and/or computer-related. Here are some suggestions: (a) focus on specific technologies, such as "gun detectors;" (b) focus on warrant requirements for searches/seizures in cyberspace; or (c) think about high-tech search technologies, such as surveillance drones.

# Review Questions

1. Identify several sources of rights.
2. What is the incorporation controversy? What are the leading perspectives in conflict within this controversy?
3. What rights have been incorporated? What rights have not?
4. In what ways can *theory* differ from *reality* in criminal procedure?
5. Compare and contrast the *due process* and *crime control* perspectives.
6. Describe the federal court structure, as it applies to criminal procedure.
7. How does a case arrive at the U.S. Supreme Court?
8. Distinguish between a *bright-line* decision and *case-by-case* adjudication.
9. How are the terms *subjective* and *objective* used in criminal procedure?
10. In what ways have recent Supreme Court decisions shown increased faith in the police?
11. What is judicial restraint? How does it compare to judicial activism?
12. Is privacy a right? If not, why is it so important in many Supreme Court opinions?
13. What happens, briefly, during the pretrial phase?
14. What happens, briefly, during the adjudication phase?
15. What happens, briefly, beyond conviction?

# Web Links and Exercises

1. Finding the law: Search the U.S. Code for "search and seizure" (put "search and seizure" in quotes in the "Search Word[s]:" box), then find and discuss a statute with implications for criminal procedure.
Suggested URL: http://uscode.house.gov/search/criteria.shtml (accessed May 1, 2013)

2. State court organization: Compare and contrast your state court system's organization to that of another state.
Suggested URL: http://bjs.ojp.usdoj.gov/content/pub/pdf/sco04.pdf (accessed May 1, 2013)

3. Federal court organization: Explain the relationship between the federal courts and the other branches of government.
Suggested URL: http://www.uscourts.gov/FederalCourts.aspx (accessed May 1, 2013)

4. Legal research: Find a recent U.S. Supreme Court case (one that did not make it into this edition of *Criminal Procedure*) with implications for criminal procedure.
Suggested URL: http://www.supremecourtus.gov/ (accessed May 1, 2013)

5. PATRIOT Act: Discuss the pros and cons associated with the PATRIOT Act.
Suggested URL (pro): http://www.proconservative.net/PCVol5Is293WrayTerrorism.shtml (accessed May 1, 2013)
Suggested URL (con): http://www.aclu.org/reform-patriot-act (accessed May 1, 2013)

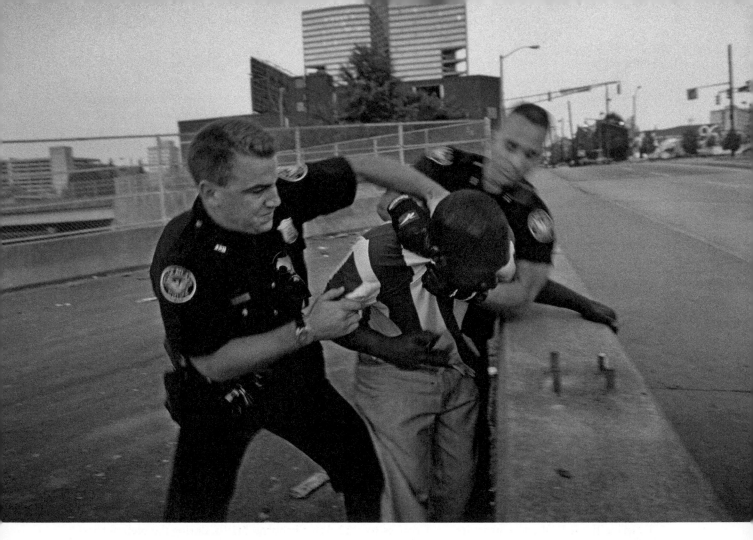

# 2 Remedies

## LEARNING OBJECTIVES

When you complete this chapter, you should be able to:

**1** *Summarize the exclusionary rule and the issues associated with it.*

**2** *Summarize the "fruit of the poisonous tree" doctrine and the exceptions to it.*

**3** *Describe criminal prosecution and civil remedies for constitutional rights violations.*

**4** *Describe nonjudicial remedies for constitutional rights violations.*

**OUTLINE**

. . . . . . . . . . . . . . . . . . . . . . . . . . . . . . . . . . . . . . . . . . . . . . . . . . .

# Introduction: Remedies for Constitutional Rights Violations

A **remedy** is a method of rectifying wrongdoing. When a person believes he or she has been harmed in some way, that person may seek relief from the harm, or make the person who caused the harm "pay" for the damage done. For example, if Sandy is unjustifiably assaulted by Jim, an on-duty police officer, she may seek a remedy for the wrong inflicted on her. A remedy is thus an enforcement mechanism for violations of people's rights. Criminal procedure cannot be fully appreciated without some discussion of the remedies that may be used to cure constitutional rights violations.

Remedies may be legal or extralegal in nature. **Extralegal remedies** are those conducted outside the legal process. An example of an extralegal remedy is vigilantism. If one man is assaulted by another, the assaulted individual may seek revenge and opt to solve the perceived injustice with his fists. **Legal remedies** are remedies made available by the law, by court decisions, or by a police policy or procedure.

As you know by now, the bulk of criminal procedure concerns *constitutional* procedure. It focuses on whether various forms of government action are permitted or not permitted by the U.S. Constitution. Accordingly, the bulk of the discussion in this chapter is on remedies for constitutional rights violations. The most frequently discussed remedy in criminal procedure is the *exclusionary rule*. This rule is a creation of the courts, and is not found in any statutes. Although it is frequently discussed, it only applies in limited contexts in which a person's *constitutional* rights have been violated. In cases in which a person's constitutional rights have not been violated, other remedies are available. These include state tort litigation, disciplinary procedures, civilian review, mediation, and the criminal law.

The first section of this chapter discusses the exclusionary rule and the so-called "fruit of the poisonous tree" doctrine. The second section touches on criminal remedies other than the exclusionary rule, notably state and federal law. The third section looks at *civil remedies* that are sought by filing lawsuits. The chapter closes with a discussion of *nonjudicial remedies*, including internal review, civilian review, and mediation.

• • • • • • • • • • • • • • • • • • • • • • • • • • • • • • • • • • • • • • • • • • • • • • • • • • • •

# ▶ The Exclusionary Rule

The most significant remedy in criminal procedure is the **exclusionary rule**. It requires that evidence obtained in violation of the Constitution cannot be used in a criminal trial to prove guilt. This rule is not found anywhere in the wording of the Constitution—it was created by the Supreme Court.

## The Rule and Its History

Surprisingly, the U.S. Constitution contains no provisions for enforcing the protections spelled out in the Bill of Rights. For example, even though people enjoy the right to be free from unreasonable searches and seizures, the Constitution does not specify how this right is to be enforced.

For a time, then, the Bill of Rights was more or less a sham, especially when it came to criminal procedure. Without a means for remedying an unlawful search, improperly obtained confession, or similar violation, evidence obtained in flagrant violation of the Constitution could be admissible at trial.

Fortunately, as early as 1886, the U.S. Supreme Court began to suggest that improperly obtained evidence be excluded. In *Boyd v. United States*, 116 U.S. 616 (1886), the Court held that business records should have been excluded because

> a compulsory production of the private books and papers of the owner of goods . . . is compelling him to be a witness against himself, within the meaning of the Fifth Amendment to the Constitution, and is the equivalent of a search-and-seizure—and an unreasonable search-and-seizure—within the meaning of the Fourth Amendment.

*Weeks v. United States*
*(232 U.S. 383 [1914])*

Then, in *Weeks v. United States*, 232 U.S. 383 (1914), the Court relied solely on the Fourth Amendment as a basis for exclusion. Without a warrant, police entered the home of Fremont Weeks and seized documents that tied him to criminal activity. The Court held that the documents were seized in violation of the Fourth Amendment and should have been returned to Weeks, rather than used in a criminal trial against the petitioner.

In *Silverthorne Lumber Co. v. United States*, 251 U.S. 385 (1920), a similar set of circumstances was presented. Silverthorne allegedly avoided paying taxes. Without a warrant, federal agents seized documents from him and made copies. The Court declared that authorizing such activities would encourage law enforcement to circumvent the Constitution. Justice Holmes stated that without an enforcement mechanism, "the Fourth Amendment [is reduced] to a form of words" and little else.

It is important to note that *Boyd*, *Weeks*, and *Silverthorne Lumber* were all *federal* cases. Following these decisions, the Supreme Court continued for several years to apply the exclusionary rule only in federal cases (see *Agnello v. United States*, 269 U.S. 20 [1925]). Then, in 1949, the Court began to turn its attention to constitutional rights violations occurring at the *state* level. In *Wolf v. Colorado*, 338 U.S. 25 (1949), a man was convicted of conspiring to perform abortions, based in part on evidence that was obtained improperly and without a warrant. The Supreme Court decided that the Fourth Amendment is applicable to the states under the due process clause of the Fourteenth Amendment, but it stopped short of mandating exclusion:

> Granting that in practice the exclusion of evidence may be an effective way to deterring unreasonable searches, it is not for this Court to condemn as falling below the minimal standards assured by the Due Process Clause a State's reliance upon other methods which, if consistently enforced, would be equally effective. . . . We cannot brush aside the experience of the States which deem the incidence of such conduct by the police too slight to call for a deterrent remedy not by way of disciplinary measure but by overriding the relevant rules of evidence.

Even though the Court was hesitant to mandate exclusion of improperly obtained evidence in state courts, at the time of the *Wolf* decision, many states had already adopted their own versions of the exclusionary rule. By 1960, 26 states had adopted exclusionary rules.

In *Elkins v. United States*, 364 U.S. 206 (1960), the Court denounced the so-called "silver platter" doctrine, which permitted the use of evidence in *federal* court that had been obtained illegally by *state* officials. For example, federal officials could not expect illegally obtained evidence to be admissible if they seized it themselves (as decided in *Weeks*). But under the silver platter doctrine, if they asked state law enforcement officials to seize the evidence, even in violation of the Constitution, it would be admissible in federal court. The silver platter doctrine was thus a convenient means of circumventing the *Weeks* decision. The Supreme Court caught on to this practice and scrapped the doctrine.

## A Turning Point: Mapp v. Ohio

The year 1961 marked a watershed in criminal procedure, as it was the year the Supreme Court decided the landmark case of *Mapp v. Ohio*, 367 U.S. 643 (1961). Arguably, this was, and continues to be, one of the most significant criminal procedure cases the Supreme Court has decided.

*Mapp v. Ohio*
*(367 U.S. 643 (1961)*

On May 23, 1957, three Cleveland police officers arrived at Dollree Mapp's residence to search for a suspect whom they thought was hiding there. The officers demanded entrance, but they were not allowed in. Ms. Mapp called her attorney and was advised not to let the officers in. The officers once again sought entrance three hours later. Ultimately, they forced entry and confronted Ms. Mapp in the entryway, who demanded to see a warrant. A paper claimed to be a warrant was held up by one of the officers. Ms. Mapp took it and placed it in her bosom. A struggle ensued, and Ms. Mapp was handcuffed and taken upstairs to her bedroom where officers searched a dresser, a closet, and some suitcases. The search fanned out from there. The officers eventually found obscene materials, which formed the basis of the conviction and ultimately were at issue in the case.

In a 5-to-4 decision, the Supreme Court decided that the exclusionary rule applied to the states. It concluded that other remedies, such as reliance on the due process clause to enforce Fourth Amendment violations, had proven "worthless and futile." It also noted that " . . . the State, by admitting evidence unlawfully seized, serves to encourage disobedience to the Federal Constitution which it is bound to uphold."

In *Ker v. California*, 374 U.S. 23 (1963), the Court extended the ruling in *Mapp* to state cases that were in violation of *federal* standards of Constitutional law, even if the *state* court had upheld the search or seizure. In *Ker*, the California Supreme Court ruled that a search conducted by the police was lawful, and evidence seized in that search was admissible. The U.S. Supreme Court overruled the California court, holding that the search was in violation of the Fourth Amendment, and the evidence obtained should be excluded. The Court noted that it had no "supervisory authority over state courts, . . . and, consequently, [*Mapp*] implied no *total* obliteration of state laws relating to arrests and searches in favor

**Timeline of Key Exclusionary Rule Cases**

| 1886 | 1914 | 1920 | 1949 |
|------|------|------|------|
| ***Boyd* v. United States, 116 U.S. 616** Evidence obtained in violation of the Fourth and Fifth Amendments should be excluded. | ***Weeks* v. *United States*, 232 U.S. 383** Evidence obtained in violation of the Fourth Amendment should be excluded. | ***Silverthorne Lumber Co.* v. *United States*, 251 U.S. 385** The decision establishing the "fruit of the poisonous" tree doctrine, but it is important in exclusionary rule development because of Justice Holmes's observation that without an enforcement mechanism, the "Fourth Amendment [is reduced] to a form of words" (p. 392). | ***Wolf* v. *Colorado*, 338 U.S. 25** Evidence obtained in violation of the constitution *may* be excluded from state proceedings under the Fourteenth Amendment's due process clause, but it need not be. |

**FIGURE 2.1**

of federal law." In essence, the Court must defer to the states to decide what made up a reasonable search or seizure, but only to the extent such decisions are "consistent with federal constitutional guarantees." Thus, whenever determining the reasonableness of a questionable Fourth Amendment action, federal standards must be applied. However, if a state adopts procedures that are *more restrictive* than federal standards, doing so complies with the *Mapp* decision.

One final limitation of *Mapp* is that it only mandates exclusion of evidence obtained in violation of the federal Constitution. If, instead, evidence is obtained in violation of a rule or state law, but is not a constitutional violation, exclusion is not required under *Mapp* (*Cady v. Dombrowski*, 413 U.S. 433 [1973]). Such evidence may be excluded, however, on some other basis in case law. For a summary of all key exclusionary rule cases in a timeline format, see Figure 2.1.

### Applicability of the Exclusionary Rule beyond the Fourth Amendment

There has been some debate concerning the applicability of the exclusionary rule to violations of constitutional rights besides those stemming from the Fourth Amendment. As a general rule, evidence obtained in violation of either the Fifth or Sixth Amendment will be excluded at a criminal trial. However, some issues remain unresolved regarding the applicability of the exclusionary rule to these amendments.

Some have argued that because the Fourth Amendment contains no specific reference to what should happen when an improper search or seizure takes place, the sole purpose of the exclusionary rule is to enforce the Fourth Amendment. They argue, furthermore, that because the exclusionary rule operates differently outside the Fourth Amendment context, it was not meant to apply to Fifth and Sixth Amendment violations. For example, just because a confession is improperly obtained does not mean that any subsequently obtained physical evidence will be excluded.

On the other hand, some observers argue that evidence can still be excluded because of Fifth, Sixth, and even Fourteenth Amendment violations. They have pointed out that evidence can technically be excluded when any constitutional provision giving rise to such evidence is violated. Improperly obtained confessions can be excluded from a criminal trial. Coerced confessions can be excluded under the Fourteenth Amendment's due process clause, as well as identifications stemming from Sixth Amendment violations.

The view adopted in this book is that the exclusionary rule applies across the board. Any constitutional provision that governs law enforcement's efforts to secure evidence that could be used in a criminal prosecution falls under the purview of the exclusionary rule. That is, whenever law enforcement violates one or more of the Fourth, Fifth, Sixth, and Fourteenth Amendments—the evidence resulting from such a violation will not be admissible in a court of law. It is important to note, however, that the exclusionary rule and its

TIMELINE

**Timeline of Key Exclusionary Rule Cases,** *continued*

| 1960 | 1961 | 1963 | 1973 |
|------|------|------|------|
| ***Elkins* v. *United States*, 364 U.S. 206** The Supreme Court denounced the "silver platter doctrine," the practice of using in federal court evidence unconstitutionally obtained by state officials. | ***Mapp* v. *Ohio*, 367 U.S. 643** The exclusionary rule applies to the states through the due process clause of the Fourteenth Amendment. | ***Ker* v. *California*, 374 U.S. 23** Federal standards must be applied when determining whether the exclusionary rule should apply. States can also apply more restrictive procedures for evaluating admissibility of evidence, but they cannot relax the *Mapp* standard. | ***Cady* v. *Dombrowski*, 413 U.S. 433** Evidence obtained in violation of a state rule or law that is not of a constitutional dimension need not be excluded under *Mapp*. It may, however, be excluded under state law. |

**FIGURE 2.1** *(continued)*

close cousin—the "fruit of the poisonous tree" doctrine (discussed later in this chapter)—do not always operate in the same manner outside the context of the Fourth Amendment.

## Arguments for and against the Rule

The debate over the exclusionary rule centers on three important issues: (1) whether the rule deters police misconduct; (2) whether the rule imposes unnecessary costs on society; and (3) whether alternative remedies would be effective and should be pursued.

• Critics of the exclusionary rule argue that the rule does very little to deter police misconduct. They claim that most constitutional rights violations are unintentional and the potential for exclusion of evidence will not prevent such accidental violations. They further argue that even in cases where the police act in bad faith, the officers will often commit perjury to mask a constitutional rights violation. Supporters of the exclusionary rule respond that the rule is not intended to deter individual officers (*specific deterrence*) but is intended to have a broader, systemic deterrent effect (*general deterrence*). This is supported by that fact that many police departments have amended their policies in the wake of the *Mapp* decision and encouraged their officers to adhere to constitutional safeguards.

• Critics also claim that any possible benefit of the exclusionary rule is outweighed by its social costs. First, they believe that the exclusionary rule requires throwing out some of the most reliable forms of evidence (such as confessions), freeing criminals who would have been easily convicted. Second, critics believe that innocent people have nothing to gain from the exclusionary rule because they have nothing to be seized by law enforcement officers who would infringe on constitutional protections. Critics also believe that the exclusionary rule creates public cynicism because it allows some individuals to escape prosecution. Finally, critics believe that the exclusionary rule is too extreme, in that a relatively trivial violation by a police officer may result in the exclusion of significant evidence.

Supporters of the exclusionary rule, by contrast, believe its benefits outweigh the costs. For example, they argue, quite persuasively, that the exclusionary rule is rarely applied. Motions to exclude evidence based on alleged constitutional rights violations are relatively rare, and they succeed even more rarely. Second, supporters believe the rule is beneficial because it *does* help innocent people. Since *Mapp* and other significant decisions, innocent people have been subjected to fewer unconstitutional searches, not only because the police fear the exclusion of evidence, but because of the potential for civil liability, citizen complaints, and the like. Supporters of the exclusionary rule also argue that public cynicism, to the extent it exists, should be directed at wayward government officials, not the exclusionary rule. Finally, supporters argue that the exclusionary rule is not disproportionate in terms of its consequences, but rather is intended to serve as a general deterrent.

- Critics of the exclusionary rule further claim that alternative remedies such as civil litigation, criminal prosecution, and discipline within police departments are effective and should be pursued. It is argued that overzealous law enforcement officers can be deterred from violating the Constitution by these enforcement mechanisms. Proponents of the exclusionary rules counter that these alternatives are not likely to prove effective. They claim, for example, that juries are more likely to favor police officers in civil trials, that immunity is often extended to police officers in civil litigation cases, and that internal police discipline is something of a sham. Within police departments, disciplinary decisions tend to favor the officer, not the citizen filing the complaint.

Both sides to the debate have presented persuasive arguments for and against the exclusionary rule. However, the rule is probably more beneficial than it is harmful. There have been a relatively small number of cases in which serious criminals have gone free as a result of the application of the rule. In addition, the fact that some evidence may be excluded because of police misconduct does always mean the defendant will "walk." In many cases, the prosecutor possesses other evidence sufficient to convict. For example, if a defendant's confession is excluded, but several witnesses are still willing to testify that the defendant committed the crime, he or she will, in all likelihood, be convicted.

## When the Exclusionary Rule Does Not Apply

The exclusionary rule applies primarily in criminal trials. But it may also be applied in some circumstances in other proceedings, both criminal and noncriminal. Its application in other situations depends on whether the rule will serve the objective of deterrence. In other words, if in a particular circumstance, the exclusion of evidence would not in theory deter misconduct, the rule will not apply. With a handful of exceptions, the exclusionary rule does not apply in following four situations: grand jury investigations, *habeas corpus* proceedings, parole revocation hearings, and civil proceedings.

First, it has been held that the exclusionary rule does not apply in the context of grand jury investigations. In *United States v. Calandra*, 414 U.S. 338 (1974), a witness called before a grand jury refused to answer questions that were based on evidence obtained from him during an unlawful search. Worried that enforcement of the exclusionary rule would impede grand jury investigations, the Court held that it did not apply in those proceedings. The Court noted that "[a]ny incremental deterrent effect which might be achieved by extending the rule to grand jury proceedings is uncertain at best." Because grand juries serve investigative functions, it is unlikely that the exclusionary rule would have any deterrent effect on law enforcement. In addition, the evidence would still be excluded at trial.

The exclusionary rule also does not apply in *habeas corpus* proceedings. Every state or federal prisoner in the United States enjoys the constitutional right to challenge his or her conviction in federal court through a *habeas corpus* petition alleging that his or her constitutional rights were violated. *Habeas corpus* is not an appeal—it is known as a *collateral attack*. Since a *habeas corpus* petition always *follows* a criminal trial, the Court removed Fourth Amendment issues from the list of violations that can be raised in such a petition, assuming the petitioner had a "full and fair" opportunity to challenge such violations at trial. In other words, the Court reasoned that since the exclusionary rule applies at trial, any deterrent effect is most likely served there. Deterrence *after* the trial would essentially be pointless. In the Court's words:

The view that the deterrence of Fourth Amendment violations would be furthered rests on the dubious assumption that law enforcement authorities would fear that federal habeas review might reveal flaws in a search or seizure that went undetected at trial and on appeal (*Stone v. Powell*, 428 U.S. 465 [1976]).

Another type of criminal proceeding in which the exclusionary rule does not apply is a parole revocation hearing. This was the decision reached in *Pennsylvania v. Scott*, 524 U.S. 357 (1998), in which the majority argued that application of the exclusionary rule in a parole revocation hearing "would both hinder the function of state parole systems and alter the traditionally flexible administrative nature of parole revocation proceedings." The Court further noted that the relationship between a *parole officer* and a *parolee* (as opposed to the relationship between a *police officer* and a *suspect*) is supervisory rather than adversarial, so it would be "unfair to assume that the parole officer bears hostility against the parolee that destroys his neutrality." Although this view is clearly debatable, it is one of the main reasons the Court offered for its decision not to apply the exclusionary rule in parole revocation proceedings.

In area of civil proceedings, it has been held that the exclusionary rule does not apply in civil actions brought by the Internal Revenue Service (IRS) to collect taxes. This decision was reached in *United States v. Janis*, 428 U.S. 433 (1976). Janis had successfully excluded evidence in his prior criminal trial, citing officer misconduct, and then moved to have the same evidence excluded in a civil action brought against him by the IRS. The Court held that the IRS case fell "outside the offending officer's zone of primary interest." Thus, excluding the evidence a second time would not deter the officer's misconduct, which was remedied at the criminal trial in which the evidence was first excluded.

## Exceptions to the Exclusionary Rule

Critics of the exclusionary rule routinely argue that it constitutes a loophole in the criminal justice process that allows guilty criminals going free. On the whole, this argument is somewhat deceptive, in part because it ignores the broad exceptions to the exclusionary rule that mitigate its effects. Over the years, the Supreme Court has seen fit to allow evidence in cases involving honest mistakes as well as other circumstances. There are two exceptions to the exclusionary rule: (1) the "good faith" exception and (2) the impeachment exception.

*Good Faith Exception.* As a general rule, when an honest mistake is made during the course of a search or seizure, any subsequently obtained evidence will be considered admissible. The "good faith" exception was announced in two related cases: *United States v. Leon*, 468 U.S. 897 (1984) and *Massachusetts v. Sheppard*, 468 U.S. 981 (1984).

*United States v. Leon (468 U.S. 897 [1984])*

In *Leon*, police relied on a search warrant that was later declared invalid because it was not supported by probable cause. The Court upheld the search because the officers acted in good faith.

In *Sheppard*, officers had a difficult time finding a warrant form because it was the weekend, so they settled on a form previously used in another search for controlled substances. They made some changes to the form and presented it to a judge at his residence. The judge signed off on the warrant after making some changes of his own. But the references to controlled substances remained in the warrant, even though that was not what the officers set out to search for. A trial judge declared the warrant invalid, but the Supreme Court disagreed.

In both *Leon* and *Sheppard*, the Supreme Court concluded that evidence obtained in reasonable (good faith) reliance on a defective warrant was admissible:

> [W]e cannot conclude that admitting evidence obtained pursuant to a warrant while at the same time declaring that the warrant was somehow defective will in any way reduce judicial officers' professional incentives to comply with the Fourth Amendment, encourage them to repeat their mistakes, or lead to the granting of all colorable warrant requests. (*Leon*, 468 U.S. 897).

The good faith exception enunciated in *Leon* and *Sheppard* is not unqualified, however. If, for example, a warrant is "so lacking in indicia of probable cause as to render official belief in its existence entirely unreasonable, then evidence obtained following its service will not be admissible" (*United States v. Hove*, 848 F.2d 137 [9th Cir. 1988]).

Similarly, if a warrant is "so facially deficient—that is, in failing to particularize the place to be searched or things to be seized—that the executing officers cannot reasonably presume it to be valid, then the exception does not apply" (*United States v. Leary*, 846 F.2d 592 [10th Cir. 1988]). Furthermore, if the judge issuing the warrant is deliberately misled by information in the affidavit, as when a police officer acts in *bad* faith, then the good faith exception will not apply (*Lo-Ji v. State of New York*, 442 U.S. 319 [1979]). Also, if the judge issues a search warrant without sufficient consideration, then good faith cannot later be asserted.

The good faith exception was most recently applied in *Davis v. United States*, 564 U.S. ___ (2011). Officers arrested a vehicle passenger for giving a false name. When he was handcuffed in the back of the patrol car, the officers searched his jacket, which had been left in the car, and found a gun. The search was technically impermissible because of another Supreme Court decision decided soon after the time of the incident (*Arizona v. Gant*, 556 U.S. 332 [2009]). But the Supreme Court held that the officers acted on what they thought at the time was good law and thus the good faith exception applied.

Not long after *Gant*, the Court decided *Davis v. United States*, 564 U.S. ___ (2011). In that case, the court held that in conducting a warrantless search, police may act in objectively reasonable reliance on an existing appellate decision, even if that decision is later overruled. Davis was a passenger in a vehicle that was pulled over. He was arrested for giving police a false name. While he was seated in the back of the patrol car, officers searched the jacket he left in the vehicle. They found a gun, which Davis was not legally permitted to carry. The incident took place before the ruling in *Gant*, and under that decision, the officers would not be permitted to search the jacket because the search was not related to the arrest. But the Supreme Court sided with the police because at the time of the search (before the *Gant* decision was issued), their actions did not violate the Fourth Amendment case law in effect at that time. In other words, they acted in good faith, relying on case law existing at that time.

Critics believe that the good faith exception gives police officers an incentive to "forum shop" or to find judges who will be quick to sign off on a warrant. This point was made by Justice Brennan in his *Leon* dissent:

> Creation of this new exception for good faith reliance upon a warrant implicitly tells magistrates that they need not take much care in reviewing warrant applications, since their mistakes will from now on have virtually no consequence: If their decision to issue a warrant is correct, the evidence will be admitted; if their decision was incorrect but [not "entirely unreasonable" and] the police rely in good faith on the warrant, the evidence will also be admitted. Inevitably, the care and attention devoted to such an inconsequential chore will dwindle.

The good faith exception has been extended to other situations besides searches and seizures based on defective warrants. Typically, such cases arise where police reasonably rely on information later determined to be incorrect. For example, if a police officer acts in reasonable reliance on a statute that is later found to be unconstitutional, then the good faith exception will not apply (see *Michigan v. DeFillippo*, 443 U.S. 31 [1979]). If evidence is obtained following a search or seizure that is conducted in reasonable reliance on computer records that turn out to be inaccurate, then the exception will not apply. For example, in *Arizona v. Evans*, 514 U.S. 1 (1995), a defendant was arrested during a traffic stop because the officer's computer showed an outstanding warrant that, unknown to the officer, had been quashed 17 days earlier. Evidence obtained from a search of the vehicle was admissible because, according to the Court, "there is no basis for believing that application of the exclusionary rule in these circumstances will have a significant effect on court employees responsible for informing the police that a warrant has been quashed."

Similarly, police arrested an individual and found contraband in a search incident to arrest, yet unbeknownst to the officers, the arrest warrant had been recalled months

**WHEN DOES THE EXCLUSIONARY RULE NOT APPLY?**

Two officers from the state liquor control board, acting without a warrant, stopped and searched an automobile. They found that the car contained many cases of liquor not bearing state tax seals. The driver was arrested, and his car was seized. The government sought to forfeit the automobile, but the trial judge, concluding that the officers had acted without probable cause, did not permit it on the grounds that doing so depended on the admission of evidence illegally obtained in violation of the Fourth Amendment. Should the exclusionary rule apply in a civil forfeiture case, such as that described here?

earlier. The search was upheld, because the officers' reliance on the warrant was reasonable (*Herring v. United States*, 555 U.S. 135 [2009]).

*Impeachment Exception.* In some cases, evidence that has been excluded as direct evidence of guilt may be used for the purpose of impeachment (attacking the credibility) of a witness. This is known as the **impeachment exception**.

The impeachment exception was upheld in *Walder v. United States*, 347 U.S. 62 (1954). Walder was indicted for possession of narcotics, but heroin that had been seized by the government was excluded because the search and seizure was unlawful. As a result, the indictment against Walder for possession was dismissed. However, in a later trial for a different incident involving the sale of narcotics, Walder testified he had never purchased, sold, or possessed narcotics. To impeach Walder's testimony, the prosecution introduced the testimony of an officer who had participated in the illegal search leading up to the earlier indictment. This testimony was sanctioned, as it was solely used for the purpose of impeaching Walder's statements.

*Walder v. United States (347 U.S. 62 [1954])*

An important limit on the impeachment exception is that it applies only to the impeachment of criminal defendants, not other witnesses. This restriction was established in *James v. Illinois*, (493 U.S. 307 [1990]). James was arrested for the murder of another adolescent. While under arrest, James was questioned in violation of his *Miranda* rights. During this questioning, James made certain statements about his hair color the day of the murder. During trial, a witness testified about James' appearance the night of the crime. The testimony contradicted statements James provided during the illegal questioning. The prosecution sought to introduce the out-of-court statements to reveal the in-court witness's supposed perjured testimony. The Supreme Court refused to sanction this application of the impeachment exception to third-party witnesses.

## The "Fruit of the Poisonous Tree" Doctrine

The expression "fruit of the poisonous tree" can be traced to the biblical story of the Garden of Eden. As the story goes, Adam and Eve ate the apple, the forbidden fruit, from the tree, bringing original sin into the world. In the **"fruit of the poisonous tree" doctrine**[1], the "poisonous tree" is the initial unconstitutional search or seizure. Anything obtained from the tree is considered "forbidden fruit" that should be excluded.

The doctrine was first announced by the Supreme Court in *Silverthorne Lumber Co. v. United States*, 251 U.S. 385 (1920). In that case, Silverthorne Lumber Company was convicted on contempt charges for failing to produce documents that were learned of during the course of an illegal search. The Court reversed the conviction, ruling the company should not be forced to produce documents that were learned of strictly through an illegal search.

*Silverthorne Lumber Co. v. United States (251 U.S. 385 [1920])*

---

[1]Courts often use the term *derivative evidence* in lieu of "fruit of the poisonous tree." The former refers simply to evidence *derived* from a previous unconstitutional search or seizure.

## AN ACT OF GOOD FAITH?

County Deputy Smith learned from an informant that some businesses had been broken into during the previous night. Without making any effort to corroborate the information supplied by the informant, the deputy signed a complaint naming Mark Laurel and Carl Rogers as the persons who had broken into the buildings. After receiving this complaint, a judge issued a warrant for the arrests of Laurel and Rogers. Deputy Smith then sent out a police radio bulletin describing both suspects, the car they were likely to be driving, and items that had been taken from the buildings.

Police Officer Wesson, who was employed by the city, stopped a car that met the description in the radio bulletin. Wesson observed that the car had two men in it and that one of the men met Laurel's description in the radio bulletin. Officer Wesson arrested both occupants and searched the car. He found items in the interior of the car that had been described in the radio bulletin, and burglars' tools in the trunk. Assuming the warrant is invalid (because it lacks any corroboration), should Officer Wesson's arrest of the car occupants fall under the good faith exception to the exclusionary rule?

The *Silverthorne* holding was reaffirmed in the case of *Nardone v. United States*, 308 U.S. 338 (1939), a case in which illegally intercepted phone messages formed a vital component of the prosecution's case. The Supreme Court noted that it should be left to the discretion of "experienced trial judges" to determine whether "a substantial portion of the case against [the accused] was a fruit of the poisonous tree."

Here are some examples of how the fruit of the poisonous tree doctrine would work in other situations:

- A suspect is coerced to confess and alerts police to where evidence can be found. The evidence would be inadmissible because it is fruit of an unconstitutional confession.
- Police arrest a suspect without probable cause, and he confesses. The confession would be inadmissible as fruit of the unconstitutional arrest.
- Police arrest a suspect without probable cause. The suspect rats out two co-conspirators who the police then arrest. The second set of arrests would be considered fruit of the poisonous tree, assuming the police had no other basis for arresting the co-conspirators.

## THE IMPEACHMENT EXCEPTION

Dewey and Rodriguez boarded a flight from Lima, Peru to Miami, Florida. In Miami, a customs officer searched Rodriguez and found cocaine sewn into makeshift pockets in the T-shirt he was wearing under his clothing. After Rodriguez was arrested, he claimed that Dewey, who had cleared customs, was also carrying cocaine. Dewey was located and arrested. His luggage was then seized and searched without a warrant. The officers found no drugs but seized a T-shirt from which pieces had been cut that matched the pieces sewn to Rodriguez's T-shirt.

Because Dewey's luggage had been searched without a warrant, the T-shirt and other evidence were suppressed prior to trial. At trial, Rodriguez, who had pleaded guilty, testified as a witness for the prosecution that Dewey had supplied him with the altered T-shirt and had sewn the makeshift pockets shut. Dewey, the defendant, then took the stand in his own defense and denied Rodriguez's claims. On cross-examination, the prosecutor introduced the shirt into evidence. Could the introduction of the shirt be permissible for any reason?

In short, the exclusionary rule applies not only to evidence obtained as a direct result of a constitutional rights violation but also to evidence *indirectly* derived from a constitutional rights violation. In many ways, the fruit of the poisonous tree doctrine resembles a "but for" test, in which the courts have to ask: "But for the unconstitutional police conduct, would the evidence have been obtained regardless?" If the answer is no, then the evidence will be excluded. If the answer is yes, then the issue becomes more complicated, and certain exceptions to the doctrine may apply.

## Exceptions to Fruit of the Poisonous Tree

The Supreme Court has carved out three important exceptions to the fruit of the poisonous tree doctrine: purged taint, independent source, and inevitable discovery.

*Purged Taint.* The "purged taint" exception to the fruit of the poisonous tree doctrine is also known as the *attenuation exception*. In *Nardone*, Justice Frankfurter observed that in some cases, "sophisticated argument may prove a causal link obtained through [illegality] and the government's proof. As a matter of good sense, however, such a connection may have become so attenuated as to dissipate the taint." In *Nardone*, the Court did not actually admit evidence because of attenuation. However, Justice Frankfurter's observation was somewhat prophetic because several years later, in the case of *Wong Sun v. United States*, 371 U.S. 471 (1963), the Court did admit evidence because of attenuation.

*Wong Sun v. United States (371 U.S. 471 [1963])*

In making an attenuation analysis, the court must decide whether the derivative evidence was obtained by exploitating the initial unconstitutional act, or by other means that purged the taint of the unconstitutional act. In *Wong Sun*, the defendant was illegally arrested and released, but later returned to the police stationhouse on his own initiative. The Court held that his statements were admissible because they did not result from the illegal arrest. Instead, the defendant made the statements when he decided to come back *later*, following his release. The Court noted that his statement had become attenuated to the extent that it dissipated the taint of the initial unconstitutional act.

In *Brown v. Illinois*, 422 U.S. 590 (1975), the Supreme Court listed several factors that should be considered in determining whether the purged taint exception applies: (1) whether the *Miranda* warnings were given prior to a voluntary confession; (2) the "temporal proximity" of the illegal police conduct to verbal statements made by a suspect; (3) the presence of intervening events or circumstances; and (4) the "purpose and flagrancy of the official misconduct." Several later cases focused on these four factors to varying degrees.

For example, in *Dunaway v. New York*, 442 U.S. 200 (1979), the Court decided whether a confession obtained following a questionable stationhouse detention was admissible. The *Miranda* warnings had been given, but the Court still held that the stationhouse detention intruded "so severely on interests protected by the Fourth Amendment as necessarily to trigger the traditional safeguards against illegal arrest." The Court then held that despite the *Miranda* warnings, Dunaway's statements should not be admissible. To hold differently would allow "law enforcement officers to violate the Fourth Amendment with impunity, safe in the knowledge that they could wash their hands in the 'procedural safeguards' of the Fifth."

In another case, *Taylor v. Alabama*, 457 U.S. 687 (1982), the Court held that the purged taint exception should not apply even under these circumstances: (1) the defendant had been advised of his *Miranda* rights; (2) six hours had elapsed between the defendant's illegal arrest and confession; and (3) the defendant had been permitted to visit with friends before making his confession.

Contrast *Taylor* with *Rawlings v. Kentucky*, 448 U.S. 98 (1980), in which the Court held that statements made 45 minutes after an illegal arrest *were* admissible because the defendant (1) had been advised of his *Miranda* rights just before making an incriminating statement; (2) had been in a house instead of a police station; and (3) had made spontaneous statements that did not result from direct questioning. Furthermore, the Court noted that

## THE "PURGED TAINT" EXCEPTION

Officer Lewis was taking a break and conversing with an employee in a flower shop when she noticed an envelope with money protruding from it lying on the cash register. Lewis examined the envelope and found that it contained not only money but betting slips. She placed the envelope back on the register, and without telling the employee what she had found, she asked who it belonged to. The employee told Lewis that the envelope belonged to Steve Stevens, the store's owner.

The officer reported this information to local detectives, who interviewed Stevens some four months later without referring to the incident at the flower shop. About six months after that incident, Stevens was summoned before a grand jury, where he testified that he had never taken bets at his flower shop. However, the store employee testified to the contrary. Stevens was then indicted for perjury. Should the employee's statement be ruled inadmissible at trial?

the illegal arrest was not flagrant and that the defendant never argued that his admission was an involuntary product of police questioning.

*Segura v. United States*
*(468 U.S. 796 [1984])*

*Independent Source.* The **independent source** exception was first established in *Segura v. United States*, 468 U.S. 796 (1984). In that case, police requested a search warrant to search an apartment based on information they received from a suspect about a drug sale. While waiting for the search warrant to be issued, they entered the apartment illegally and observed drug paraphernalia. The police later returned with the search warrant and legally searched the apartment. The Court held that even though the police had entered the apartment illegally *prior* to serving the search warrant, the evidence found in the apartment pursuant to the search warrant was admissible because the warrant was based on information totally disconnected with the initial illegal search. In other words, even though the police first entered the apartment illegally, the warrant they later served was based on information independent from that search, and therefore evidence obtained was not excluded as fruit of the poisonous tree.

*Nix v. Williams*
*(467 U.S. 431 [1984])*

*Inevitable Discovery.* The **inevitable discovery** exception states that if evidence would be found regardless of unconstitutional police conduct, then it is admissible. This exception was first recognized by the Supreme Court in *Nix v. Williams*, 467 U.S. 431 (1984). In that case, the evidence was the body of a young girl, which was discovered after the police had illegally questioned the defendant concerning the body's whereabouts. Under ordinary circumstances, the body would not have been considered admissible, but the prosecution was able to prove that at the time of the illegal questioning, a search party looking for the girl's body had narrowed in on its target and would have "inevitably discovered" the body. The Iowa Supreme Court approved admission of the body into evidence because "(1) the police did not act in bad faith for the purpose of hastening discovery of the evidence in question,

## THE INDEPENDENT SOURCE

Suspecting that people were storing marijuana in a warehouse, several police officers entered the building without obtaining a warrant to do so. (Later, they argued that they were concerned that evidence would be destroyed or that the people would escape if they had waited to obtain a warrant.) The search revealed

bales of marijuana, but no people. The police then applied for a warrant to search the building, deliberately failing to mention their previous search. The warrant was granted, the search was conducted, and the police "discovered" the marijuana. Should the marijuana be considered admissible at trial?

**Exceptions to the Exclusionary Rule and Fruit of the Poisonous Tree**

| Exclusionary Rule | Fruit of the Poisonous Tree |
|---|---|
| Good Faith | Purged Taint |
| Impeachment | Independent Source |
| | Inevitable Discovery |

**FIGURE 2.2 Exceptions to the Exclusionary Rule and Fruit of the Poisonous Tree Doctrine**

and (2) ... the evidence in question would have been discovered by lawful means" (*Iowa v. Williams*, 285 N.W.2d 248 [Iowa 1979]). The U.S. Supreme Court agreed.

The inevitable discovery exception bears striking resemblance to the independent source exception. For all practical purposes, information leading to evidence that would be inevitably discovered usually comes from an independent source. The search that was underway in *Nix v. Williams*, for example, was totally disconnected from the questioning of the defendant. In light of the similarities between these two exceptions to the fruit of the poisonous tree doctrine, some courts have simply opted to call the inevitable discovery exception the *hypothetical independent source* exception (see *Nix*, 467 U.S. 431). See Figure 2.2 for a summary of the exclusionary rule and fruit of the poisonous tree.

# ▶ Criminal Remedies for Constitutional Rights Violations

Various statutes at the federal and local levels provide criminal remedies for police violations of constitutional rights. Some states make it a criminal offense for police officers to trespass or to falsely arrest people. In fact, most criminal sanctions that apply to ordinary citizens also apply to police officers. Likewise, various statutes at the federal level make it not only improper but also criminal for police officers to engage in certain types of conduct.

## Federal Law

At the federal level, the most common statute for holding police officers criminally liable is **18 U.S.C. Section 242**. Section 242 is to criminal liability what Section 1983 (discussed below) is to civil liability. It can be used to prosecute either a state or a federal law enforcement officer. Section 242 states,

> Whoever, under color of any law, statute, ordinance, regulation, or custom, willfully subjects any inhabitant of any State, Territory, or District to the deprivation of any rights, privileges, or immunities secured or protected by the Constitution or laws of the United States, or to different punishments, pains, or penalties, on account of such inhabitant being an alien, or by reason of his color, or race, than are prescribed for the punishment of citizens, shall be fined not more than $1,000 or imprisoned not more than one year, or both; and if death results shall be subject to imprisonment for any term of years or for life.

To be held liable under Section 242, a law enforcement officer must act with specific intent to deprive a person of important constitutional (or other federal) rights (*Screws v. United States*, 325 U.S. 91 [1945]). Also, for criminal liability to be imposed under Section 242, a constitutional right must be clearly established (*United States v. Lanier*, 520 U.S. 259 [1997]). Because of these restrictions, relatively few Section 242 cases have been filed. In fact, criminal liability under Section 242 is reserved for the most egregious forms of police misconduct.

Despite its relatively infrequent application, there is a handful of noteworthy cases invoking Section 242. For example, in *Miller v. United States*, 404 F.2d 611 (5th Cir. 1968), a police officer was held criminally liable for allowing his canine unit to bite a suspect. In *Williams v. United States* (341 U.S. 97 [1951]), a defendant had been beaten, threatened, and physically punished for several hours, and a police officer was held criminally liable for those actions. And in *Lynch v. United States*, 189 F.2d 476 (5th Cir. 1951), Section 242 was applied as a result of the assault and battery of several criminal defendants.

Additional federal statutes make it a criminal act to unlawfully search and seize individuals (18 U.S.C. Section 2236), although applications of this statute are rare, as well. 18 U.S.C. Section 2235 makes it a criminal offense to maliciously procure a warrant, and Section 2234 makes it a criminal offense to exceed the authority of a warrant.

Regardless of which criminal statute applies, an important distinction must be made between the various criminal statutes and 42 U.S.C. Section 1983. An officer who is held *criminally* liable will receive a criminal conviction and may go to prison. Section 1983, by contrast, is *civil*, meaning that it is used independently of the criminal process. A successful Section 1983 lawsuit will never result in imprisonment of the defendant.

## State Law

The same laws that apply to ordinary citizens also apply to police officers. For example, if a police officer knowingly and intentionally kills someone and is not legally justified in doing so (such as using deadly force to prevent injury to a third party), that officer can be held criminally liable for murder. Similarly, if a police officer trespasses on private property without appropriate justification, he or she can be held criminally liable. Criminal liability can extend to a police officer for virtually any conceivable offense.

Some crimes are committed by police officers more often than other crimes. Michael L. Birzer, a noted expert on criminal justice, has indicated that the most common crimes committed by police officers are crimes involving violence, sexual misconduct, and illegal drugs.[2] With respect to violent crimes, a notable example is the case in which the so-called Miami River Cops were charged with murdering drug smugglers. As for sex crimes, a

New York City Police Officer Sean Carroll becomes emotional during testimony about his suspected involvement in the Amadou Diallo shooting, one of the most infamous cases of criminal behavior by police.

---

[2]M. L. Birzer, "Crimes Committed by Police Officers," in M. J. Palmiotto (Ed.), *Police Misconduct* (Upper Saddle River, NJ: Prentice Hall, 2001), pp. 171–178.

**USE OF DEADLY FORCE**

Officers responded to a call that a woman in an isolated cabin was shooting at people who were camped out on her property. On arriving at the scene, officers heard loud music coming from inside the cabin. They knocked on the door and said they wanted the woman to identify herself and to ask her some questions about what happened earlier that night. After hearing nothing, one of the officers shined his flashlight into a window and observed the woman lying on her bed with a rifle next to her. Shortly thereafter, the woman left her room, apparently without the rifle, and knelt on her couch with her hands behind it. Still not receiving a response from the woman, the officers kicked in the locked front door and entered. Once inside, the woman pointed a rifle at one of the officers. They ordered her to put down the gun, but when she did not do so, she was fatally shot. Was deadly force justified?

police officer in Fort Myers, Florida, was charged with sexual assault against a 19-year-old female. These examples are not offered to suggest that police officers frequently engage in criminal activity, but only that it happens. No one is above the law, even police officers.

Police officers often engage in many actions that would be crimes if performed by ordinary citizens. However, they enjoy immunity from criminal liability for these actions, if the actions are committed (justifiably) as part of their official duties. On these occasions, police officers are shielded from criminal liability by the law enforcement or **public duty defense** to criminal liability.

Beyond the public duty defense, police officers do not have much in the way of defense against criminal liability. If a police officer who committed burglary for his or her own personal gain attempted to assert a public duty defense, he or she would almost certainly fail. Similarly, if a police officer shoots and kills a person, not for the purpose of preventing a crime or effecting an arrest, but for vengeance, that officer will almost certainly be convicted of some degree of homicide and probably sentenced to prison.

## ▶ Civil Remedies for Constitutional Rights Violations

When a person's constitutional or other federal civil rights are violated, that person can bring a lawsuit in civil court. Even if a person merely *believes* his or her rights have been violated, litigation is still an option. The worst (or best) that can happen is that the lawsuit will be dismissed. Indeed, it is not a stretch to say that anyone can be sued for anything. This can put law enforcement officials in something of a difficult position. And while civil liability may be an effective remedy for people whose rights are violated, litigation may come with a high price tag.

What is the purpose of **civil litigation**? Aside from sometimes being the only remedy available, civil lawsuits are attractive because money can be awarded. The *plaintiff*, or the person filing the lawsuit, seeks payment for injuries or perceived injuries suffered, known as **damages**. In addition to damages, the plaintiff can also seek **injunctive relief**, which basically means he or she wants the court to bring the injurious or offensive action to a halt. Figure 2.3 provides an overview of the stages of a typical civil lawsuit.

Why should we care about civil remedies in a book about criminal procedure? One reason is that criminal remedies do not always apply to every case. Also, the exclusionary rule does not apply if there are no criminal charges. Likewise, criminal remedies made available by state and federal law will only in cases of the most egregious police misconduct. It should also be noted that several important decisions in criminal procedure (which we will explore later) began as civil lawsuits.

1.  *Citizen complaint:* The first step in filing a lawsuit normally involves a citizen complaint. In a citizen complaint, the aggrieved party can do one of two things: call attention to inappropriate police conduct or demand some form of remedial action (e.g., injunctive relief or monetary damages). This latter form of citizen complaint is considered a *demand.*

2.  *Demand:* If the complaint filed with the police by a citizen (the *complainant*) requests some action on the part of the police, then the complainant will make a more or less informal demand of the police, who will then send a *response.* This may lead to informal discussions between the two sides. The complainant may retain the services of an attorney, but the procedure remains largely informal at this early juncture.

3.  *Citizen complaint board:* In some jurisdictions (e.g., Spokane, WA), the complainant can further file a complaint with a local citizen complaint board if the police agency in question fails to take satisfactory action. Citizen complaint boards vary considerably in use, authority, and terminology, so they are only mentioned here in passing as one mechanism for dispute resolution. Other avenues of dispute resolution may well be in place.

4.  *Lawyer's letter:* If the complainant and the police cannot work things out informally, the complainant usually brings in an attorney. The attorney will send a so-called lawyer's letter to the police agency, the officer(s) in question, and/or the city or county. While this letter may not have any legal significance, it usually gets a serious response.

5.  *Prelitigation settlement discussion:* An informal prelitigation settlement discussion is often held, in which the police and/or their representatives and the complainant and/or his or her representatives work together to try to reach a settlement. If no settlement is reached, the complaint/demand will likely evolve into a full-blown lawsuit.

6.  *Claim with city/county clerk:* Before being able to proceed with a lawsuit, the citizens in some states and counties are first required to file a claim with the city or county against which the complaint is made or to give the police agency a chance to respond to a formal complaint or a request for damages. This *claim* should be distinguished from a *citizen complaint,* discussed above. This claim is an explicit prerequisite that must be completed before a lawsuit can move forward; it is mandated by law. The purpose of such a claim is primarily to inform officials of what is about to transpire. Often, a lawsuit cannot be filed until the parties in question are given the opportunity to respond to a claim.

7.  *Lawsuit:* A citizen complaint/demand evolves into a full-blown lawsuit when none of the informal proceedings discussed satisfy the complainant. To reach the stage of a lawsuit, two actions must occur: First, a *complaint* must be filed with the clerk of the court in which the lawsuit will be heard. (This complaint is a legal requirement and differs from the citizen complaint already filed.) Second, the court or an attorney must issue a *summons* to be served on the agencies or people named in the complaint. Sometimes, the summons is personally delivered; other times, it is sent by registered or certified mail. The parties named in the complaint (e.g., the police, their agencies, municipalities) are now known as the *defendants,* and the aggrieved party or parties filing the lawsuit are now known as the *plaintiffs.*

**FIGURE 2.3 Stages of a Civil Lawsuit**

# 42 U.S.C. Section 1983: Liability of State Officials

**42 U.S.C. Section 1983** provides a remedy in federal court for the "deprivation of any rights . . . secured by the Constitution and laws" of the United States. Specifically, Section 1983 states:

> Every person who, under color of any statute, ordinance, regulation, custom, or usage, of any State or Territory, subjects, or causes to be subjected, any citizen of the United States or

other persons within the jurisdiction thereof to the deprivation of any rights, privileges, or immunities secured by the Constitution and laws, shall be liable to the party injured in an action at law, suit in equity, or other proper proceeding for redress.

Section 1983 was originally enacted as part of the Ku Klux Klan Act of April 20, 1871 (also known as Section 1 of the Civil Rights Act of 1871). The act was designed to address atrocities being committed by Klan members in the wake of the Civil War, but it did not target Klan members as such. Instead, Section 1983 imposed liability on state representatives who failed to enforce state laws against illegal Klan activities. The statute was rarely used, however, and remained effectively dormant for some 90 years after it was signed into law.

Section 1983 was revived in *Monroe v. Pape*, 365 U.S. 167 (1961). In that case, a group of police officers allegedly entered the home of James Monroe without warning and then forced the occupants to stand naked in the living room while the house was searched and ransacked. Monroe brought a Section 1983 action against the police officers and the City of Chicago. The case eventually reached the U.S. Supreme Court, where eight justices held that the alleged misuse of authority could support a Section 1983 action against the police officers. That is, the Supreme Court held that Section 1983 could be used as a vehicle to sue the police.

*Monroe v. Pape (365 U.S. 167 [1961])*

Since *Monroe*, Section 1983 litigation has become quite popular. The reasons for this increase are many, but the Supreme Court's decision in *Monroe* had the greatest influence. Former Supreme Court Chief Justice William Rehnquist referred to *Monroe* as "the fountainhead of the torrent of civil rights litigation of the last 17 years."[3]

The next four subsections focus carefully on Section 1983. The first discusses the concept of *color of law*, a requirement for any successful Section 1983 claim. Second, the types of actions that amount to constitutional rights violations are considered. Third, theories of liability under Section 1983 are reviewed. Finally, qualified immunity, the main defense available to defendants in Section 1983 actions, is introduced.

## Color of Law

One of the requirements for a successful Section 1983 lawsuit is that the defendant, the person being sued, acted under color of law. The Supreme Court has stated that someone acts under color of law when he or she acts in an official capacity (*Lugar v. Edmondson Oil Co.*, 457 U.S. 922 [1982]). For example, a police officer who appears to be acting within his or her authority while on duty acts under color of law. By contrast, someone who appears to be acting only in a private capacity, such as that of an ordinary citizen, cannot be said to have acted under color of law.

Offering further clarification, two authorities on criminal justice, Michael S. Vaughn and Lisa F. Coomes, have stated that police officers act under color of law when one or more of the following conditions are satisfied:

- They have identified themselves as officers.
- They are performing a criminal investigation.
- They have filed official police documents.
- They are making an arrest.
- They are invoking police powers in or outside their jurisdiction.
- They are settling a personal vendetta with police power.
- They are displaying weapons or police equipment.[4]

---

[3]J. K. Lieberman, *The Litigious Society* (New York: Basic Books, 1983), p. 152.
[4]M. S. Vaughn and L. F. Coomes, "Police Civil Liability under Section 1983: When Do Police Officers Act under Color of Law?" *Journal of Criminal Justice* 23 (1995): 395–415, 409.

## COLOR OF LAW

One night, while off duty at a local bar, Officer Webster got into a fight, drew his gun, and shot and killed James Ramos. Ramos's heirs filed a Section 1983 lawsuit against the city for which Webster worked, alleging that it failed to adequately train him as to whether and how to react during off-duty altercations. Furthermore, Ramos's heirs alleged that this failure caused Webster, acting under color of law, to deprive Ramos of his constitutional rights. Will this lawsuit succeed?

Interestingly, plaintiffs *can* sue private parties under Section 1983 when private parties conspire with state officers. With regard to these suits, the Supreme Court has held that a state normally can be held responsible for a private decision only when it has exercised coercive power or has provided such significant encouragement, either overt or covert, that the choice must in law be deemed to be that of the state (*Blum v. Yaretsky*, 457 U.S. 991 [1982]).

### Constitutional Violation

The second requirement for a successful Section 1983 lawsuit is that a constitutional rights violation has taken place. The plaintiff must establish that the defendant's conduct violated a specific constitutional provision, such as the Fourth Amendment. As noted in *Daniels v. Williams*, 474 U.S. 327 (1986), "[I]n any given Section 1983 suit, the plaintiff must still prove a violation of the underlying constitutional right."

Not all constitutional rights violations are (or should be) actionable under Section 1983. Recently, the courts have required that constitutional rights violations alleged under Section 1983 be committed with a certain level of **culpability**. That is, the plaintiff generally has to prove that the defendant officer intended for the violation to occur. In other words, Section 1983 is generally reserved for the most egregious of civil rights violations. The level of culpability required for a constitutional rights violation varies, depending on the type of unconstitutional conduct alleged by the plaintiff.[5]

### Theories of Liability

The term **theory of liability** is the legal premise upon which a case rests. It is the legal argument on who should be held accountable—and why. Typically, in Section 1983 cases, the plaintiff's lawsuit will target an individual officer, that officer's supervisor, the city or municipality for which the officer works, or any combination of each. While the individual officer responsible for inflicting harm should arguably be held liable, it is often attractive to plaintiffs to go after the "bigger fish" because that is the party likely to have the funds to pay damages. For this reason, governmental entities are often attractive targets for civil litigation. The three most common theories of liability under Section 1983 attempt to hold the government accountable for the plaintiff's alleged injuries.

*Supervisory Liability.* The theory of supervisory liability attempts to hold a manager or supervisor responsible for the actions of the police officer working under them. The only Supreme Court case concerning **supervisory liability** in the Section 1983 context is *Rizzo v. Goode*, 423 U.S. 362 (1976). In *Rizzo*, the plaintiffs sued the mayor of Philadelphia, the city's managing director, the police commissioner, and two other police department supervisors, alleging a "pervasive pattern of illegal and unconstitutional mistreatment by police officers . . . directed against minority citizens in particular and against all Philadelphia residents in general." The plaintiffs further charged supervisors with "conduct ranging from

*Rizzo v. Goode*
*(423 U.S. 362 [1976])*

---

[5]J. L. Worrall, "Culpability Standards in Section 1983 Litigation against Criminal Justice Officials: When and Why Mental State Matters," *Crime and Delinquency* 47 (2001): 28–59.

express authorization or encouragement of this mistreatment to failure to act in a manner so as to assure that it would not recur in the future." The lower federal courts found in favor of the plaintiffs, but the Supreme Court disagreed, stating that "there was no *affirmative link* between the occurrence of the various incidents of police misconduct and the adoption of any plan or policy by [the supervisors]—express or otherwise—showing their authorization or approval of such misconduct" (emphasis added). In other words, for a Section 1983 lawsuit to succeed against a supervisor, there must be a clear link between the supervisor and the constitutional violation committed by a subordinate.

*Municipal/County Liability.* Cities and counties can be held liable under Section 1983 if they adopt and implement policies or adopt customs that result in constitutional rights violations (see *Monell v. Department of Social Services*, 436 U.S. 658 [1978]). In general, a plaintiff will not succeed with a Section 1983 municipal/county liability claim if lower-ranking officials engage in a common practice, but have no authority to make policy in the traditional sense. For example, if a group of police officers regularly use excessive force, but do so on their own, with no authorization from the city or county, then the city or county cannot be held liable for these officers' actions.

*Monell v. Department of Social Services* (436 U.S. 658 [1978])

In another city/county liability case, *City of Canton v. Harris*, 489 U.S. 378 (1989), the Supreme Court held that counties (and, by extension, cities) can be held liable for inadequately training their law enforcement officers. In *Canton*, Harris was arrested and brought to the police station in a patrol wagon. On arrival, the officers found Harris lying on the floor of the wagon. She was asked if she needed medical attention, but she responded incoherently. After she was brought into the station, she slumped to the floor on two occasions. Eventually, she was left lying on the floor and no medical attention was summoned for her. Harris later sued, seeking to hold the city liable for a violation of her Fourteenth Amendment right, under the due process clause, to receive medical attention while in police custody. However, the Court held that "only where a municipality's failure to train its employees in a relevant respect evidences a 'deliberate indifference' to the rights of its inhabitants can such a shortcoming be properly thought of as a city 'policy or custom' that is actionable under [Section] 1983." A similar standard has been applied to cases regarding the conduct of prosecutors—a single failure to disclose exculpatory evidence to the defendant does not mean the district attorney's office should be held liable under Section 1983 (*Connick v. Thompson*, 563 U.S. ___ [2011]).

*City of Canton v. Harris* (489 U.S. 378 [1989])

In *Board of Commissioners of Bryan County v. Brown*, 520 U.S. 397 (1997), the Supreme Court revisited the city/county liability issue. In particular, the question before the Court was whether a single hiring decision by a municipality's policy maker could give rise to an inadequate hiring claim under Section 1983. Brown's claim was based on the injuries she suffered at the hands of Bryan County Reserve Deputy Stacy Burns during a high-speed pursuit, and the fact that Burns had two previous misdemeanor convictions for assault and battery (both of which were overlooked during the preemployment screening process). Brown seemed to have a good case, but the Court felt otherwise, finding for Bryan County and setting a high standard for claims against a municipality for inadequate hiring. Specifically, the Court held that

> [e]ven assuming without deciding that proof of a single instance of inadequate screening could ever trigger municipal liability, [the county commissioners'] failure to scrutinize Burns's record cannot constitute 'deliberate indifference' to [the] respondent's federally protected right to be free from the use of excessive force.

*Individual Liability.* For a finding of individual liability, Section 1983 requires a plaintiff to demonstrate that his or her constitutional rights were violated by someone acting under color of state law. Accordingly, numerous constitutional amendments have been implicated in Section 1983 cases. The amendments most commonly invoked, however, have been the Fourth, Eighth, and Fourteenth.

**MUNICIPAL LIABILITY**

Danny Koller, 17 years old, stole a van from a car lot by driving it through a showroom window. Almost immediately, members of the local police department began to pursue him. After a dangerous, lengthy, high-speed chase, the van was forced to stop. Danny emerged from the van unarmed. When the pursuing officers approached him, they hit him and pulled his hair. In the scuffle, one of the officer's pistol discharged. The bullet struck Danny in the head and he died as a result of the wound. Danny's parents brought suit under 42 U.S.C. Section 1983, seeking damages from the city. They argued that the city maintained a formal policy of using excessive police force that caused Danny's death. Assuming this tragedy was an isolated event, will the plaintiffs succeed with their lawsuit?

## Bivens Claims against Federal Officials

*Bivens v. Six Unknown Named Agents* (403 U.S. 388 [1971])

Prior to 1971, it was not clear whether federal officials could be sued in civil court for civil rights violations. In *Bivens v. Six Unknown Named Agents*, 403 U.S. 388 (1971), however, the Supreme Court held that federal law enforcement officers can be sued for Fourth Amendment violations. *Bivens* claims must meet two essential requirements, which are effectively the same requirements as for a Section 1983 lawsuit against state officials; namely, (1) the official acted under color of state law and (2) the official deprived someone of his or her constitutional rights. *Bivens* claims are not limited to the Fourth Amendment, however.

A *Bivens* claim is primarily limited to law enforcement officers. Other federal officials enjoy **absolute immunity,** meaning that the official cannot be sued under any circumstances—at least as far as their official duties are concerned. Federal officials who enjoy absolute immunity include federal judges (*Bradley v. Fisher*, 80 U.S. 335 [1871]) and federal prosecutors (*Yaselli v. Goff*, 275 U.S. 503 [1927]).

## The Qualified Immunity Defense

Qualified immunity is a judicially created defense to a Section 1983 suit, much like the exclusionary rule has been created through judicial decisions. In some cases, qualified immunity is more than a defense; it may afford immunity from suit.

Qualified immunity was developed to accommodate two conflicting policy concerns: effective crime control, and the protection of people's civil liberties. While the Supreme Court has clearly upheld Section 1983 as a deterrent to official misconduct, the Court has

**INDIVIDUAL LIABILITY**

A police officer was in pursuit of a motorcycle carrying a passenger. During the pursuit, the motorcycle crashed directly in front of the police cruiser. Despite his attempt to stop his cruiser in time, it slid into the back of the motorcycle, killing the passenger. The passenger's family members brought a Section 1983 lawsuit against the officer, alleging that the passenger's substantive due process rights were violated. The case worked its way up to a federal circuit court, where it was decided that the appropriate standard for Section 1983 civil liability for a substantive due process violation is deliberate indifference, and that the officer acted in a deliberately indifferent manner. Finally, the case reached the U.S. Supreme Court. As a Justice of that Court, would you affirm or reverse?

also recognized that it is not fair to hold officials liable for lapses in judgment and honest mistakes.

Similar to the Fourth Amendment's test for reasonableness, an objective reasonableness standard has been applied in order to determine if qualified immunity should be extended to criminal justice officials who are defendants. For the purposes of qualified immunity, a defendant is said to have acted in an objectively reasonable fashion if he or she does not violate clearly established rights about which a reasonable person would have known (*Harlow v. Fitzgerald*, 457 U.S. 800 [1982]).

*Malley v. Briggs*, 475 U.S. 335 (1986), further clarifies the standard to be applied to qualified immunity. In that case, the plaintiffs filed a Section 1983 suit alleging that a police officer applied for and obtained a warrant that failed to establish probable cause. Rather than focus on the probable cause issue, the Supreme Court stated that the "question in this case is whether a reasonably well-trained officer in petitioner's position would have known that his affidavit failed to establish probable cause and that he should not have applied for the warrant." It went on to note that "[o]nly where the warrant application is so lacking in indicia of probable cause as to render official belief in its existence unreasonable will the shield of immunity be lost."

*Malley v. Briggs*
*(475 U.S. 335 [1986])*

Qualified immunity was strengthened in *Messerschmidt v. Millender*, 565 U.S. ___ (2012). Police were seeking a sawed-off shotgun in connection with a gang shooting, but the search warrant authorized the officers to search for *all* firearms. The warrant was challenged as overbroad and not in compliance with the Fourth Amendment's particularity requirement. The Ninth Circuit Court of Appeals refused to grant the officers qualified immunity in the Section 1983 lawsuit that followed the search, but the Supreme Court sided with the officers, holding in part that the officers " . . . reasonably believed they had a fair probability of finding illegal firearms and other evidence relevant to the crime."

In some Section 1983 cases, defendants have benefited from qualified immunity even for violating clearly established constitutional rights, provided that the defendants' mistaken belief was objectively reasonable. *Ryburn v. Huff*, 565 U.S. ___ (2012) illustrates this trend. Officers visited the home of a boy who had allegedly threatened to "shoot up" his school. The officers spoke to the boy and his mother after they opened the front door at the officers' request. When the officers asked if there were any guns in the house, the mother turned and retreated into the interior of the house. Fearing for their safety and others who may have been inside, the officers entered the house. The conversation continued and it was determined that the rumor implicating the boy was false. The officers were later sued under Section 1983 on the theory that they entered the home without a warrant. The Supreme Court decided they enjoyed qualified immunity for their actions because ". . . reasonable police officers in the petitioners' position could have come to the conclusion that the Fourth Amendment permitted them to enter the Huff residence if there was an objectively reasonable basis for fearing that violence was imminent," which there was.

Qualified immunity thus affords protection to defendant criminal justice officials not just for reasonably mistaken beliefs, but for any number of actions that are objectively reasonable under the circumstances—viewed from "the perspective of a reasonable officer at the scene, rather than with the 20/20 vision of hindsight" (*Ryburn*, 565 U.S. ___ [2012]).

# ▶ Nonjudicial Remedies

Three nonjudicial remedies are available for police misconduct. First, an *internal review* is a process by which a police department investigates complaints against its own officers. Typically, an internal affairs division takes up this task. The second remedy, *civilian review*,

**THE FOURTH AMENDMENT AND QUALIFIED IMMUNITY**

In a recent case, *Wilson v. Layne*, 526 U.S. 603 (1999), the Supreme Court considered (1) whether law enforcement officers violated the Fourth Amendment by allowing members of the media to accompany them on the service of warrants and (2) whether the officers were nonetheless entitled to qualified immunity if such activity violates the Fourth Amendment. The Court decided that "a media 'ride-along' in a home violates the Fourth Amendment, but because the state of the law was not clearly established at the time the entry in this case took place, respondent officers are entitled to qualified immunity." Do you see any problems with this decision?

is a mechanism by which private citizens serve in some capacity to review complaints of police misconduct. Not to be confused with civilian review, *mediation* asks an objective third party, such as an ombudsman, to resolve a grievance between a police officer and a citizen who complains of wrongdoing.

Nonjudicial remedies are important because they are available for situations where neither the exclusionary rule nor civil liability are viable options. Consider the hypothetical case of a motorist who is stopped without proper justification. Assume the motorist is released. To be sure, he or she has suffered an inconvenience, but if no contraband was found and there was no egregious misconduct on the officer's part, what can this person do? About the only choice available is to file a written complaint. A Complaint/Commendation Form from the Abilene, Texas, Police Department is shown in Figure 2.4.

## Internal Review

Many police agencies have developed innovative and highly respected internal review mechanisms. In its model police misconduct policy, the Police Executive Research Forum listed three ways that the police themselves can implement effective complaint procedures:

> (1) [T]hrough the provision of meaningful and effective complaint procedures, citizen confidence in the integrity of police increases and this engenders community support and confidence in the police department; (2) through disciplinary procedures that permit police officials to monitor officers' compliance with departmental procedures; and (3) by clarifying rights and ensuring due process protection to citizens and officers alike.[6]

Figure 2.5 shows the District of Columbia Metropolitan Police Department's complaint review process, depicting one agency's approach to internal discipline.

William A. Geller, a prominent defender of internal review, has argued that civilian input into the process of investigating complaints against the police suffers from a number of drawbacks:

- They ignore existing legal resources at citizens' disposal.
- It is difficult for people disconnected from the police department to have an adequate understanding of the internal operations of a civilian review board.

---

[6]Police Executive Research Forum, *Police Agency Handling of Officer Misconduct: A Model Policy Statement* (Washington, DC: Author, 1981), p. 1.

## Abilene Police Department
## Citizen Complaint/Commendation Form

CITY OF ABILENE

File complaints or commendations about Police Department employees on this form. Return the completed form to the desk duty officer, 1st floor at the Police Department, 450 Pecan or hand deliver to the City Manager's Office, 555 Walnut, Room 203 or by mail to P.O. Box 60 Abilene, Texas 79604. Complaints will not be investigated until a Police Supervisor has contacted the Complaining Party.

**Involved Officer/Employee(s) Information:**

| Name: | |
|---|---|
| Name: | |

**Person Making the Complaint/Commendation:**

| Name: | | Phone: | |
|---|---|---|---|
| Address: | | Phone: | |

**Information:**
Please provide as much information about the reason you were contacted by the officer/employee. Specific information about the date, time and location will help in locating computer-based information if you do not know the officer/employee's name.

| Date of Contact: | | Approximate Time: | | AM/PM |
|---|---|---|---|---|
| Location Contacted: | | | | |

**Reason For The Complaint/Commendation:** (attach additional pages if needed)

 

**Witness Information:**

| Name: | | Phone: | |
|---|---|---|---|
| Address: | | Phone: | |

| Name: | | Phone: | |
|---|---|---|---|
| Address: | | Phone: | |

Submitted by_____Date_____

*Source:* Abilene (Texas) Police Department. Reprinted by permission. Available online at http://www.abilenetx.com/index/doc/ APDcomplaintcommentform.pdf (accessed May 2, 2013).

**FIGURE 2.4** Citizen Complaint Form

**MPD Complaint Investigation Process**

A complaint may be submitted to either the MPD or Office of Police Complaints (OPC). The following flowcharts detail the complaint review processes.

**Step 1**

The complaint is filed with the MPD.

**Step 2**

The MPD official responsible for investigating the complaint contacts you to let you know he or she is investigating it. If necessary, the official will obtain additional information.

**Step 3**

The complaint is investigated–witnesses and the officer against whom the complaint is filed are interviewed. The officer is entitled to know the complainant's name, if it is known, and the nature of the complaint. However, the MPD will not reveal the complainant's name if the complainant requests to remain anonymous.

**Step 4**

- Investigation is completed and one of the following conclusions is made:
- Sustained – where the person's allegation is supported by sufficient evidence to determine that the incident occurred and the actions of the officer were improper.
- Insufficient Facts – where there are insufficient facts to decide whether the alleged misconduct occurred.
- Exonerated – where a preponderance of the evidence shows that the alleged conduct did occur but did not violate MPD policies, procedures, or training.
- Unfounded – where the investigation determined no facts to support that the incident complained of actually occurred.

**Step 5**

You are notified of the outcome of the investigation. If you do not agree with it, you may appeal the decision in writing by sending a letter to the Chief of Police at 300 Indiana Ave., NW, Rm. 5080, Washington, DC 20001.

*Source*: District of Columbia Metropolitan Police Department, http://mpdc.dc.gov/page/mpd-complaint-investigation-process (accessed May 2, 2013).

**FIGURE 2.5 Complaint Investigation Process**

- Citizen review damages morale.
- Civilian review invites abdication of authority by line supervisors.
- Such boards weaken the ability of top management to achieve conformity through discipline.
- They are tantamount to admitting that the police are incapable of policing themselves.[7]

## Civilian Review

There has been a marked increase in the number of cities involving citizens at some stage of the complaint review process.[8] This has occurred because of the demand for some form of external input in the investigation of police. It has also increased due to rising

---

[7]W. A. Geller, *Police Leadership in America* (New York: Praeger, 1985), pp. 157–198.
[8]S. Walker and V. W. Bumphus, *Civilian Review of the Police: A National Survey of the 50 Largest Cities* (Omaha, NE: University of Nebraska at Omaha, 1992).

sentiment that citizens can investigate the police better than the police themselves. As one study has noted:

> Citizen involvement in the complaint process will produce (1) more objective and more thorough investigations; (2) a higher rate of sustained complaints and more disciplinary actions against guilty officers; (3) greater deterrence of police misconduct (through both general and specific deterrence); and (4) higher levels of satisfaction on the part of both individual complainants and the general public.[9]

A study of citizen complaints against police has identified three distinct forms of the process: (1) civilian review; (2) civilian input; and (3) civilian monitor.[10] Pure **civilian review** is the strongest form—a civilian panel investigates, adjudicates, and recommends punishment to the police chief. The second strongest form is **civilian input**. In this form, a civilian panel receives and investigates a complaint, leaving adjudication and discipline to the department itself. The weakest of the three, the **civilian monitor** form, leaves investigation, adjudication, and discipline to the department, but a civilian is allowed to review the adequacy and impartiality of the process. The research reported in the study focused only on the first two forms: civilian review and civilian input. Both place investigative authority with an independent body and are arguably more satisfactory to disgruntled citizens than the third form, a civilian monitor.

## Mediation

Some have argued that **mediation**, or relying on a neutral third party to render decisions, is the most desirable approach to address the problem of police misconduct. In a mediation, a neutral third party, or **ombudsman** (sometimes called a "mediator" or "arbitrator"), recommends a decision.[11] As another text on criminal procedure has observed,

> [Another] remedial system which, like the civilian review board, operates outside the judicial and internal police spheres, is the Scand[i]navian ombudsman system. The ombudsman is, most simply, an external critic of administration. His goal is improvement of administration rather than punishment of administrators or redress of individual grievances. Thus, instead of conducting formal hearings associated with adjudicating individual complaints, he relies primarily on his own investigations to gather information. On the basis of his findings, he may recommend corrective measure to the department, although he cannot compel an official to do anything.[12]

A key characteristic of the ombudsman system is that it is independent of the complainant and the person being complained against. The ombudsman should be a person to whom people may feel comfortable bringing grievances connected with the government. The ombudsman stands between the citizen and the government, acting as something of an intermediary.

---

[9]S. Walker and B. Wright, "Varieties of Citizen Review: The Relationship of Mission, Structure, and Procedures to Police Accountability," in R. G. Dunham and G. P. Alpert (Eds.), *Critical Issues in Policing: Contemporary Readings*, 3rd ed. (Prospect Heights, IL: Waveland, 1997), pp. 319–336, 322.

[10]P. West, *Investigations of Complaints against the Police: Summary Findings* (Washington, DC: Police Executive Research Forum, 1987).

[11]Technically, there is a difference between the terms *arbitration* and *mediation*, but for our purposes it is safe to treat them as more or less identical.

[12]C. H. Whitebread and C. Slobogin, *Criminal Procedure*, 4th ed. (New York: Foundation Press, 2000), p. 65.

As another alternative, Chief Justice Burger suggested in *Bivens* that a quasi-judicial body be appointed for the purpose of recovering damages against the government. Under his plan, if damages are awarded, the record of what transpired will become part of the offending officer's permanent file. Such a system has not gained widespread acceptance, much less adoption.

## Summary

### 1. Summarize the exclusionary rule and the issues associated with it.

A number of legal remedies are available for addressing violations of people's rights, including those provided by the law, court decisions, and police policy and procedures. The most common remedies in criminal procedure are (1) the exclusionary rule; (2) criminal liability; (3) civil litigation; and (4) nonjudicial remedies.

The exclusionary rule is the main remedy that will be focused on throughout the remainder of this book. It requires that evidence obtained in violation of certain constitutional amendments (notably the Fourth, Fifth, Sixth, and Fourteenth) be excluded from the criminal trial. Exceptions to the exclusionary rule have been recognized in cases in which (1) the police acted in good faith but nonetheless violated the Constitution and (2) the prosecutor sought to impeach a witness at trial by pointing to contradictions in his or her out-of-court statements, even if such statements were obtained in an unconstitutional manner.

### 2. Summarize the "fruit of the poisonous tree" doctrine and the exceptions to it.

The exclusionary rule has been extended to require that derivative evidence obtained from a constitutional rights violation also be excluded. This is known as the "fruit of the poisonous tree" doctrine. Exceptions to this doctrine include inevitable discovery, independent source, and purged taint. That is, if evidence would have been discovered inevitably, if it was arrived at by means of an independent source, or if the taint of an initial unconstitutional act has been purged, then derivative evidence will be considered admissible at trial.

### 3. Describe criminal prosecution and civil remedies for constitutional rights violations.

Police can be held *criminally* liable, as well. For instance, both state and federal law enforcement officers can be held criminally liable for violating certain federal laws. Officers are also bound by the criminal law at the state level. They may, of course, be permitted to engage in certain authorized conduct that would be a crime if committed by regular citizens (such as the use of deadly force in appropriate circumstances).

Civil lawsuits against government officials—the police, mainly—can be filed when neither the exclusionary rule nor other criminal remedies apply. Section 1983 litigation requires the plaintiff to show that a constitutional rights violation was committed by an official acting under color of state law. Section 1983 lawsuits can be filed against individual police officers, supervisors, and municipalities/counties. *Bivens* claims are virtually identical to Section 1983 claims but are intended to target federal, instead of state, officials.

## 4. Describe nonjudicial remedies for constitutional rights violations.

Nonjudicial remedies include internal review, civilian review, and mediation. Internal review, the most common of these remedies, refers to a police agency investigating its own for allegations of misconduct. Internal affairs divisions engage in this sort of activity. Civilian review occurs when citizens get involved in the investigation process. Numerous forms of citizen review are in place around the United States. A less common method of rectifying constitutional rights violations is mediation, in which a neutral third party decides on the issues in dispute.

# Key Terms

18 U.S.C. Section 242 *51*
42 U.S.C. Section 1983 *54*
absolute immunity *58*
*Bivens* claim *58*
civil litigation *53*
civilian input *63*
civilian monitor *63*
civilian review *63*
culpability *56*
damages *53*
exclusionary rule *40*

extralegal remedies *39*
"fruit of the poisonous tree"
   doctrine *47*
"good faith" exception *45*
impeachment exception *47*
independent source *50*
individual liability *57*
inevitable discovery *50*
injunctive relief *53*
internal review *60*
legal remedies *39*

mediation *63*
municipal/county liability *57*
ombudsman *63*
public duty defense *53*
"purged taint" exception *49*
remedy *39*
"silver platter" doctrine *41*
supervisory liability *56*
theory of liability *56*

# Key Cases

## Exclusionary Rule

- *Weeks v. United States*, 232 U.S. 383 (1914)
- *Mapp v. Ohio*, 367 U.S. 643 (1961)
- *United States v. Leon*, 468 U.S. 897 (1984)
- *Walder v. United States*, 347 U.S. 62 (1954)
- *Silverthorne Lumber Co. v. United States*, 251 U.S. 385 (1920)
- *Wong Sun v. United States*, 371 U.S. 471 (1963)
- *Segura v. United States*, 468 U.S. 796 (1984)
- *Nix v. Williams*, 467 U.S. 431 (1984)

## Criminal Remedies

- *Screws v. United States*, 325 U.S. 91 (1945)

## Civil Remedies

- *Monroe v. Pape*, 365 U.S. 167 (1961)
- *Rizzo v. Goode*, 423 U.S. 362 (1976)
- *Monell v. Department of Social Services*, 436 U.S. 658 (1978)
- *City of Canton v. Harris*, 489 U.S. 378 (1989)
- *Bivens v. Six Unknown Named Agents*, 403 U.S. 388 (1971)
- *Malley v. Briggs*, 475 U.S. 335 (1986)

# Further Exploration

1. The police suspect that Scott Henders is a serial murderer. They obtain enough evidence to convince a judge to issue a search warrant. When the warrant is executed at Henders' residence, the officers find no evidence of his involvement in criminal activity. While conducting the search, another victim was killed, thus giving Henders an airtight alibi. Since Henders is innocent, is there anything he can or should do? What are the barriers or difficulties he might encounter should he seek to pursue one or more of the remedies introduced in this chapter?

2. In *Bivens v. Six Unknown Agents*, Chief Justice Burger dissented, arguing that the exclusionary rule does nothing to punish officials for wrongdoing. It may, however, reduce the number of wrongdoing defendants. He proposed an alternative scheme:

   For example, Congress could enact a statute along the following lines: (a) a waiver of sovereign immunity as to the illegal acts of law enforcement officials committed in the performance of assigned duties; (b) the creation of a cause of action for damages sustained by any person aggrieved by conduct of governmental agents in violation of the Fourth Amendment or statutes regulating official conduct; (c) the creation of a tribunal, quasijudicial in nature or perhaps patterned after the United States Court of Claims to adjudicate all claims under the statute; (d) a provision that this statutory remedy is in lieu of the exclusion of evidence secured for use in criminal cases in violation of the Fourth Amendment; and (e) a provision directing that no evidence, otherwise admissible, shall be excluded from any criminal proceeding because of violation of the Fourth Amendment.

   Discuss the pros and cons of this proposed arrangement.

3. A number of states have rejected the good faith exception to the exclusionary rule under their own constitutions, which they are permitted to do (states are free to interpret their own state constitutional rights more broadly than the federal government does with analogous guarantees, and a rejection of good faith essentially *expands* a person's rights). For example, in *State v. Novembrino*, 519 A.2d 820 (1987), the New Jersey Supreme Court held in part that the good-faith exception will inevitably and inexorably diminish the quality of evidence presented in search-warrant applications. By eliminating any cost for noncompliance with the constitutional requirement of probable cause, the good-faith exception assures us that the constitutional standard will be diluted. Do you agree with this decision? Why or why not?

4. Several states have refused to accept certain exceptions to the fruit of the poisonous tree doctrine. Here is how the Washington State Supreme Court explained the incompatibility of the inevitable discovery exception with its constitution:

   It is well-established that article I, section 7 [of the Washington State Constitution] provides greater protection of privacy rights than the Fourth Amendment. It differs from its federal counterpart in that article I, section 7 'clearly recognizes an individual's right to privacy with no express limitations.' Based on the intent of the framers of the Washington Constitution, we have held that the choice of their language 'mandate[s] that the right of privacy shall not be diminished by the judicial gloss of a selectively applied exclusionary remedy.' Because the intent was to protect personal rights rather than curb government actions, we recognized that 'whenever the right is unreasonably violated, the remedy must follow.' The constitutionally mandated exclusionary rule provides a remedy for individuals whose rights have been violated and protects the integrity of the judicial system by not tainting the proceedings with illegally obtained evidence. Because of textual differences, state action may be valid under the Fourth Amendment but violate article I, section 7.

   (*State v. Winterstein*, 220 P.3d 1226 [Wa. 2009]). Compare this logic with the U.S. Supreme Court's logic in recognizing the inevitable discovery exception. Look up the *Winterstein* case and familiarize yourself with the facts. Which case is more convincing?

5. Find and read this important article by Barry Latzer: "Four Half-Truths About State Constitutional Law," published in the *Temple University Law Review* (65 Temple L. Rev. 1123 [1992]). Pay particular attention to the practices of "lockstepping" and "disincorporation." What is meant by these concepts? Provide examples.

6. One Christmas eve, a police officer observed a motorist traveling in excess of the posted speed limit. The officer pulled in behind the vehicle, turned on his lights, and attempted to stop the motorist. Unbeknownst to the officer, he was traveling on a road just outside the city limits. The driver did not stop and increased his speed, eventually running a stop sign. When the officer was finally able to stop the

motorist, it quickly became apparent the driver was under the influence of alcohol. The officer arrested the driver, but the motorist claims that the evidence of his failed field sobriety test should be inadmissible because the officer did not have jurisdiction in the city where the arrest was made. What do you think? Read *Delker v. State*, 50 So.3d 300 (Miss. 2010) to explore further.

## Review Questions

1. Define the term *remedy*, and distinguish between two types of remedies.
2. What is the exclusionary rule? Explain circumstances in which it is applicable beyond the Fourth Amendment.
3. Explain the arguments for and against the exclusionary rule.
4. When does the exclusionary rule *not* apply?
5. What are the two exceptions to the exclusionary rule?
6. Define the "fruit of the poisonous tree" doctrine, and explain the three exceptions to it.
7. How does the criminal law operate as a remedy?
8. How does civil litigation act as a remedy?
9. What are the requirements for a successful Section 1983 lawsuit against an individual police officer? A supervisor? A city or county?
10. What is a *Bivens* claim?
11. What defense is available to a law enforcement officer charged in a Section 1983 lawsuit?
12. Distinguish among three types of nonjudicial remedies.
13. What are the varieties of civilian review? How do they differ from one another?

## Web Links and Exercises

1. Taking sides on the exclusionary rule, weigh the pros and cons of the exclusionary rule.
Suggested URL: http://www.wadsworth.com/criminaljustice_d/templates/student_resources/0534616232_gaines/debates/ex_rules.html (accessed May 2, 2013).

2. Police criminal liability: Discuss the incidents surrounding the shooting of Sean Bell. How does the case fit with this chapter's section on "Criminal Remedies Besides the Exclusionary Rule"?
Suggested URL: http://www.msnbc.msn.com/id/24305660 (accessed May 2, 2013).

3. Find a case: Go to the website of Americans for Effective Law Enforcement and browse back issues of the Law Enforcement Liability Reporter. You can find them under the "Free Law Library and Publications" link on the main page. Find and write about the facts/decisions of five civil liability cases.
URL: http://www.aele.org (accessed May 2, 2013).

5. Alternative dispute resolution: Read about mediation and other forms of alternative dispute resolution. How does mediation differ from arbitration?
Suggested URL: http://www.adr.org/ (accessed May 2, 2013).

# 3 Introduction to Search and Seizure

## LEARNING OBJECTIVES

When you complete this chapter, you should be able to:

**1** *Summarize the Fourth Amendment's basic terminology.*

**2** *Define* search *within the context of the Fourth Amendment.*

**3** *Define* seizure *within the context of the Fourth Amendment.*

**4** *Distinguish between three levels of justification.*

## OUTLINE

. . . . . . . . . . . . . . . . . . . . . . . . . . . . . . . . . . . . . . . . . . . . . . . . . . . . .

# Introduction: The Core Purpose and Elements of the Fourth Amendment

The Fourth Amendment to the U.S. Constitution was written to address one of the primary grievances early American colonists had toward the Crown. The British Parliament, intent on rooting out smuggling activities taking place in the American colonies, issued writs of assistance, which permitted unlimited searches. Officials needed no justification to obtain writs of assistance, and there was no judicial supervision designed to limit the scope of the searches authorized by the writs. The practice was not well received in the American colonies. By adopting the Fourth Amendment, the framers of the U.S. Constitution placed significant restrictions on searches conducted by government officials. The Fourth Amendment continues to fulfill an important role in restricting government intrusions into the private lives of citizens.

Despite the Fourth Amendment's seemingly simple language, the 54 words that make up its text have been subjected to incredible amounts of scrutiny and interpretation. There are literally millions of pages of text—in the forms of case opinions, law review articles, and legal treatises—devoted to interpreting the language of the Fourth Amendment. The Supreme Court alone has added several layers of interpretation to the Fourth Amendment through hundreds of significant decisions over the years. As a result,

▼

a complete understanding of Fourth Amendment rules and procedures comes with considerable difficulty. In fact, it is probably impossible to fully understand the scope, reach, and language of the Fourth Amendment because of its continued evolution. Almost without exception, the Supreme Court will decide a Fourth Amendment case during every term.

The Fourth Amendment contains two basic clauses: The **reasonableness clause**, which proscribes unreasonable searches and seizures, followed by the **warrant clause**, which says that "no Warrants shall issue, but upon probable cause, supported by Oath or affirmation, and particularly describing the place to be searched, and the persons or things to be seized."

A fundamental question has been raised about these two clauses. They are joined in the text of the Fourth Amendment by the conjunction *and*, which has led to a great deal of debate over whether the two clauses are related or separate. Some have argued that the warrant clause gives meaning to the reasonableness clause, so that *any* search conducted without a warrant is deemed unreasonable, and therefore unconstitutional. Justice Frankfurter took this position in *United States v. Rabinowitz*, 339 U.S. 56 (1950): "What is the test of reason which makes a search reasonable?...There must be a warrant to permit search, barring only inherent limitations upon that requirement when there is a good excuse for not getting a search warrant." This is the *warrant requirement* interpretation, which prefers that a neutral magistrate come between the officer conducting the search and the citizen targeted by the search.

Others have argued that the reasonableness clause and the warrant clause should be read separately. Their position is that the reasonableness of a search should not depend on whether a warrant was obtained or on whether there was a good excuse for not obtaining a warrant. Instead, they believe that the courts should focus on the factual circumstances justifying the search. They also believe, specifically, that the courts should consider the manner in which the search was executed, not whether a warrant was secured. The main protection offered by the Fourth Amendment should lie, then, not with a judge *prior* to the search but with the courts *after* the search. In this view, the courts should reflect on what occurred and seek to determine whether the search was reasonable at the time it was actually conducted.

A third view, known as the *warrant preference view*, has come to the forefront in recent years. As a result, much of the confusion surrounding the nexus of the reasonableness clause and the warrant clause has been cleared up. As the Supreme Court stated in *Mincey v. Arizona*, 437 U.S. 385(1978), "The Fourth Amendment proscribes all unreasonable searches and seizures, and it is a cardinal principle that searches conducted outside the judicial process, without prior approval by judge or magistrate, are per se unreasonable under the Fourth Amendment, subject to a few specifically established and well delineated exceptions." Basically, the rule of thumb is that a warrant should be obtained whenever practical. If, however, there is an emergency or other such exception, such as a significant risk to public safety, a warrant may not be necessary. This third view prevails today.

· · · · · · · · · · · · · · · · · · · · · · · · · · · · · · · · · · · · · · · · · · · · · · · · · · · ·

## ▶ Basic Terminology

The Fourth Amendment protects *persons*, *houses*, *papers*, and *effects* from unreasonable searches and seizures. Few court cases have turned on the meanings of these terms, but it is still important to define them.

The term **person** encompasses the individual as a whole, both internally and externally. An arrest, for example, is a seizure of a person. If a police officer pulls up the sleeves of a suspected drug user to look for needle tracks, this is a search of a *person* within the meaning of the Fourth Amendment.

In the early twentieth century, the Supreme Court ruled that the Fourth Amendment applied only to searches and seizures of tangible items (*Olmstead v. United States*, 277 U.S. 438 [1928]). Oral communications fell outside the scope of the Fourth Amendment, so surveillance of conversations, regardless of how it was pursued, did not enjoy constitutional protections. Today, however, in the wake of *Katz v. United States*, 389 U.S. 347 (1967), the Supreme Court stated emphatically that oral communications trigger the protections of the Fourth Amendment. Thus, the definition of *person* for purposes of the Fourth Amendment not only includes the person's internal and external physical body but also (most) oral communications made by people.

**House** is a term that is broadly construed to mean any structure that a person uses as a residence (and frequently a business) on either a temporary or long-term basis. A hotel room or its equivalent is considered a "house," as it is a temporary residence that enjoys Fourth Amendment protection. Also, a garage or other structure not connected to a house can also fall within the meaning of a "house" under the Fourth Amendment. Whether a garage is actually a house, though, depends on a number of considerations, which we examine later in this chapter. An open field, by contrast, does not trigger the protection of the Fourth Amendment because it is not a house. (Open fields and curtilage are defined later on in this chapter.)

**Papers and effects** include nearly all personal items. Business records, letters, diaries, memos, and countless other forms of tangible evidence can be defined as *papers*. *Effects* is the catch-all category. Anything that is not a person, house, or paper is probably an effect. Effects can include cars, luggage, clothing, weapons, contraband, and the fruits of criminal activity. If the police activity in question does not involve a person, house, paper, or effect, no Fourth Amendment protections exist. In reality, though, almost any conceivable tangible item or form of communication falls within the protection of the Fourth Amendment. What becomes important, then, is determining precisely when the Fourth Amendment applies and when a search or seizure can be considered reasonable.

## ▶ A Framework for Analyzing the Fourth Amendment

This book approaches the Fourth Amendment in a series of specific steps. It begins in this chapter by introducing basic Fourth Amendment terminology, focusing in particular on (1) which police activities trigger the protections of the Fourth Amendment and (2) what justification is required for the police to engage in certain types of activities. Later chapters focus on the types of law enforcement activity authorized (and not authorized) by the Fourth Amendment as well as on relevant procedures.

In determining when the Fourth Amendment is triggered, it is important to draw a distinction between a **search** and a **seizure**. Each action triggers the protections of the Fourth Amendment, but each is distinctly different. In addition, the law that governs searches is not the same as the law that governs seizures.

A *search* is an activity geared toward finding evidence to be used in a criminal prosecution. To define when a search takes place, two important factors need to be considered: (1) whether the presumed search is a product of **government action** and (2) whether the intrusion violates a person's **reasonable expectation of privacy.**

The term *seizure* has a dual meaning in criminal procedure. First, *property* can be seized. Often, the result of a search is a seizure of property to be used as evidence. For example, if the police successfully serve a search warrant to look for illegal weapons at 345 Oak Street, the weapons they find will be seized. Second, *people* can also be seized. Seizures of people can occur almost anywhere and at any time. An arrest, for example, is considered a seizure within the meaning of the Fourth Amendment.

The second stage in Fourth Amendment analysis focuses on the **reasonableness** of the search or seizure. In other words, once the protections of the Fourth Amendment are triggered, did the police act in line with Fourth Amendment requirements? For example, if a person is arrested, did the police have adequate reason to believe the person arrested in fact committed the crime? When the courts focus on the reasonableness of a search or seizure, they speak in terms of *justification*. If the police (or other government actors) engage in a search or seizure without justification, they violate the Fourth Amendment.

The only justification mentioned in the Fourth Amendment is *probable cause*. Over time, however, the Supreme Court has carved out exceptions to the Fourth Amendment's probable cause requirement by ruling that there are certain situations in which the police can seize people and/or look for evidence with a lesser degree of certainty than probable cause.

Think of this chapter as being almost pre–Fourth Amendment in its orientation. It is designed to supply the reader with the tools for approaching any situation resembling a search or a seizure. Without an understanding of (1) when the Fourth Amendment applies and (2) what justification is required for the police to act, it will be impossible to judge the constitutionality of the police conduct.

# ▶ When Does a "Search" Occur?

Not every act of looking for evidence is considered a "search" *within the meaning of the Fourth Amendment.* Thus, one requirement in determining when a search occurs is to ascertain *who* is looking for evidence. For example, a private citizen may look for evidence, but because private citizens are not government actors, their actions are not bound by the Fourth Amendment. The Fourth Amendment protects citizens from *government* action.

Whether a "search" occurs within the meaning of the Fourth Amendment also depends on *where* it occurs. A search only takes place where a person has a *reasonable expectation of privacy*. For example, if police look for evidence in an open field, they have conducted a nonsearch.

## Government Action, Not Private Action

The Fourth Amendment is limited to conduct that is governmental in nature. Thus, when a private individual seizes evidence or otherwise conducts a search, the protections of the Fourth Amendment are not triggered. For example, if Angela knows that her neighbor Larry has a large supply of stolen stereo equipment in the garage behind his house, she could conceivably enter his garage, seize the evidence, and turn it over to the police. The police, in turn, could use the evidence to arrest Larry. Angela could be found guilty of criminal trespass, but as far as the Fourth Amendment is concerned, she committed no constitutional violations. Angela acted in a private capacity.

*Burdeau v. McDowell*
*(256 U.S. 465 [1921])*

In *Burdeau v. McDowell*, 256 U.S. 465 (1921), the Supreme Court first recognized that the Fourth Amendment does not apply to private individuals. In that case, some private individuals illegally entered McDowell's business office and seized records that contained incriminating evidence against him. The records were later turned over to the Attorney General of the United States, who planned to use them against McDowell in court. The Supreme Court ruled that the records were admissible, and stated that the Fourth Amendment's "origin and history clearly show that it was intended as a restraint upon the activities of sovereign authority, and was not intended to be a limitation upon other than governmental agencies" (*Id.* at 475).

The Court's decision in *Burdeau* has been reiterated in one way or another in several subsequent decisions. For example, in *Coolidge v. New Hampshire*, 403 U.S. 443 (1971), the Court stated that if a private person "wholly on [his] own initiative" turns over evidence to authorities, "[t]here can be no doubt under existing law that the articles would later [be] admissible in evidence." Similarly, in *Walter v. United States*, 447 U.S. 649 (1980), the Court ruled that "a wrongful search and seizure conducted by a private party does not violate the Fourth Amendment and . . . does not deprive the government of the right to use evidence that it has acquired [from the third party] lawfully."

Three key questions have come before the Supreme Court in seeking to further distinguish between governmental and nongovernmental actors: (1) Who is a government actor? (2) When is a private person *not* acting wholly on his or her own initiative considered a government actor for the purposes of the Fourth Amendment? and (3) Once it is clear that a search is private in nature, what later government action does the private search authorize?

## What Are Government Officials?

A uniformed police officer acting in his or her official capacity is a *government official* within the meaning of the Fourth Amendment. However, the police officers are only a small percentage of the government officials responsible for enforcing the law.

Even individuals who are not directly involved in criminal investigations are bound by Fourth Amendment restrictions. For example, in the case of *Camara v. Municipal Court*, 387 U.S. 523 (1967), the Court held that regulatory officials conducting health and safety inspections can be considered government actors for purposes of the Fourth Amendment. This ruling has been expanded, in fact, to apply to numerous other government officials, including

- fire inspectors, *Michigan v. Tyler*, 436 U.S. 499 (1978),
- Occupational Safety and Health Administration (OSHA) inspectors, *Marshall v. Barlow's, Inc.*, 436 U.S. 307 (1978),
- federal mine inspectors, *Donovan v. Dewey*, 452 U.S. 594 (1981), and
- public school teachers, *New Jersey v. T.L.O.*, 469 U.S. 325 (1985).

The situation is decidedly less clear for individuals who perform clear law enforcement functions but are not employed by the government per se. This includes store detectives, security guards, and insurance inspectors, among others. At the risk of over-simplification, the rule is this: When a private source is used deliberately in place of the police, Fourth Amendment protections are triggered. That is, the officials are said to be acting in a government capacity (see *People v. Mangiefico*, 25 Cal.App.3d 1041 [1972]).

## When Do Private Individuals Become Government Agents?

An otherwise private person can be treated like a government official if he or she acts at the behest of a government official. In *Coolidge v. New Hampshire*, 403 U.S. 443 (1971), the Supreme Court stated that "[t]he test . . . is whether [the private person] in light of all the circumstances of the case, must be regarded as having acted as an 'instrument' or agent of the state." Simply put, when government officials join in on a private search or instruct a private individual to conduct a search, the private individual can be viewed as a government actor within the meaning of the Fourth Amendment.

A variation on this line of cases involves the situation in which a government official does not actively participate in or order a search or seizure but instead merely provides information that leads to a private search or seizure. For example, in *People v. Boettner*, 80 Misc.2d 3 (1974), a New York court upheld a search conducted by private university officials based on information supplied to them by the police. In support of its decision, the court noted that the private search was carried out without the knowledge of the police, who, at the time, were proceeding with their own investigation of the incident.

---

### DECISION-MAKING EXERCISE 3.1

#### A "MOONLIGHTING" SCENARIO

Officer Clark is a sworn policeman by day and a private security guard by night. One night, while on duty as a security guard in the parking lot outside a major retail store, Clark witnessed Lenore Rand, a patron whom he suspected of shoplifting, leaving the store. Clark confronted Rand, seized her bag, and discovered several items that she had not paid for. The incident was reported and the evidence was turned over to the police. May Rand mount a Fourth Amendment challenge to Clark's actions?

---

### A PRIVATE OR GOVERNMENT SEARCH?

A meter reader for the local electric company was making her usual rounds and approached the house of Michael Cramer. While reading the meter, she looked through the window just above the meter and observed a significant number of marijuana plants growing under several rows of bright lights. The meter reader returned to her vehicle and reported her observations to the police. Armed with this new information, as well as information from an ongoing investigation, the police obtained a warrant, searched Cramer's house, and seized the plants. The plants were then entered as evidence against Cramer at trial. May Cramer move to have the plants excluded on the grounds that the meter reader was a government actor, whose actions triggered the protections of the Fourth Amendment?

### When Does a Private Search Become Governmental?

An otherwise private search may become a government search when a government official receives items that were seized by the private party and subjects the items to additional scrutiny. An illustrative case is *Walter v. United States*, 447 U.S. 649 (1980). In that case, sealed film canisters containing pornographic images were mistakenly sent to a private company. The company's employees noticed the suggestive labels on the canisters and opened them, but were unable to ascertain what was on the film. They turned the canisters over to the Federal Bureau of Investigation (FBI), who subsequently opened the canisters and viewed the film. The Court ruled that the FBI's actions turned the private search into a government search. Because the Fourth Amendment came into play, the Court declared that the FBI agents should have obtained a warrant before viewing the contents of the film canisters.

*United States v. Jacobsen*
*(466 U.S. 109 [1984])*

In *United States v. Jacobsen*, 466 U.S. 109 (1984), the Supreme Court modified its *Walter* decision and ruled that the subsequent government search must be *substantially more intrusive* in order for the Fourth Amendment to be triggered. In that case, Federal Express employees opened a damaged package and found several smaller packages containing a suspicious white powder. They closed the package and then summoned federal agents, who reopened the packages and conducted a field test on the substances. The Court held that "[t]he agent's viewing of what a private party had freely made available for his inspection did not violate the Fourth Amendment" and the field test had nothing more than a "*de minimus* [minimal] impact on any protected property interest."

## Infringement on a Reasonable Expectation of Privacy

Government action alone is not enough to implicate the Fourth Amendment. The law enforcement activity must also infringe on a person's reasonable expectation of privacy. In other words, there are times when police officers and other government officials look for evidence (as in an public place, for instance) but do not act intrusively enough so as to trigger the Fourth Amendment.

Prior to 1967, the definition of a *search* was closely tied to a person's physical and tangible property interests. Police action would only be deemed a search if it physically infringed on an individual's property. The activity basically had to amount to trespassing before it would be considered a search. Any police activity that was not trespassory in nature was not considered a search. This definition became outdated in the landmark decision of *Katz v. United States*, 389 U.S. 347 (1967).

*Katz v. United States*
*(389 U.S. 347 [1967])*

In *Katz*, federal agents placed a listening device outside a phone booth in which Katz was having a conversation. Katz made incriminating statements during the course of his conversation, and the FBI sought to use the statements against him at trial. The lower court ruled that the FBI's activities did not amount to a search because there was no physical entry into the phone booth. The Supreme Court reversed that decision, holding that the Fourth Amendment "protects people, not places," and so its reach "cannot turn upon the presence or absence of a physical intrusion into any given enclosure." Instead, the Fourth Amendment definition of a *search* turns on the concept of privacy. In the Court's words, "The Government's activities in electronically listening to and recording words violated the privacy upon which [Katz] justifiably relied while using the telephone booth and thus constituted a 'search and seizure' within the meaning of the Fourth Amendment."

Despite the dramatic change in the definition of a "search" in *Katz*, several subsequent decisions have interpreted the *Katz* ruling rather narrowly. For instance, in *California v. Greenwood*, 486 U.S. 35 (1988), the Supreme Court ruled that a Fourth Amendment search or seizure occurs only when (1) the citizen has a manifested subjective expectation of privacy and (2) the expectation of privacy is one that society (through the eyes of a court) is willing to accept as objectively reasonable.

*California v. Greenwood*
*(486 U.S. 35 [1988])*

Recall from the discussion in Chapter 1 that a *subjective* interest focuses on what one individual thinks (such as the person presumably being subjected to a search) and that an *objective* interest focuses either on what society thinks or what a reasonable person would think. Just because someone *feels* he or she should enjoy privacy in a particular activity is not enough to trigger the Fourth Amendment. His or her activity needs to be one that society perceives as reasonable, as well. In other words, it is not enough for someone to believe his or her rights have been infringed upon; his or her belief must also be an objectively reasonable one.

Today, the courts rarely view cases from the *subjective* point of view, and focus almost exclusively on the *objective* expectation of privacy. The reason for this approach is that it is pointless to dwell on an individual's subjective expectation of privacy because if the seizure is questionable at all, the defendant will almost certainly proclaim he or she expected privacy in the place being searched. Focusing only on an objective (instead of a subjective) expectation of privacy seems eminently more sensible.

Another important point announced in *Katz* involves *knowing exposure*. The Court stated that "[w]hat a person knowingly exposes to the public, even in his own home or office, is not subject to Fourth Amendment protection." Protection is only afforded for "what he seeks to preserve as private" (*Katz*, 389 U.S. 347).

A number of Supreme Court cases have attempted to define the vague concepts of *reasonableness* and *knowing exposure*. These cases can be placed into at least five categories: (1) the undercover agent/false friend cases; (2) the abandoned property cases; (3) the physical characteristics cases; (4) the open fields and curtilage cases; and (5) the enhancement device cases.

---

## DECISION-MAKING EXERCISE 3.3

### THE SCOPE OF A PRIVATE SEARCH

Glen Olson is accused of poisoning dogs in his neighborhood by feeding them dog biscuits laced with a harmful chemical. Olson's girlfriend, in a desperate attempt to end her boyfriend's cruelty, turned a bag of dog biscuits, presumably containing the chemical used to poison the helpless animals, over to the police. Since the police were not sure what the substance in the biscuits was, they took the biscuits to a laboratory and subjected them to a chemical analysis. Laboratory technicians found that the substance was a chemical known to bring about violent illness. May Olson move to suppress the evidence on the grounds that the laboratory analysis triggered the protections of the Fourth Amendment?

## Undercover Agents and False Friends

*Hoffa v. United States*
*(385 U.S. 293 [1966])*

Many government investigations are conducted by undercover agents or "false friends" posing as others. Generally, whether the search is illegal turns on whether the target of the investigation *voluntarily* disclosed information or turned over materials. This issue came up in *Hoffa v. United States*, 385 U.S. 293 (1966). The defendant, Hoffa, had a conversation with a union official who was in Hoffa's private suite by invitation but who was, in fact, a government informant. The informant reported what Hoffa said to government officials, and Hoffa sought to have the evidence excluded on the grounds that it was an illegal search. The Supreme Court did not buy the argument, noting that the informant "was not a surreptitious eavesdropper," but a person who "was in the suite by invitation and every conversation which he heard was either directed to him or knowingly carried on in his presence."

*United States v. On Lee*
*(343 U.S. 747 [1952])*

A more difficult question arose in *United States v. On Lee*, 343 U.S. 747 (1952). *On Lee* addressed the issue of whether an undercover agent could wear a recording device during a conversation with a suspected criminal. The majority ruled that this activity did not constitute a search, again, because the informant was invited into the area where the conversation took place. Justice Burton dissented, however, noting that the recorder "amount[s] to [the agent] surreptitiously bringing [the police] with him." The majority countered by arguing that the listening device was simply designed to improve the accuracy of the evidence obtained by the informant.

At a glance, it may seem that *On Lee* and *Katz* are at odds with one another. After all, both involved surreptitious recordings. How do we draw a distinction? In *On Lee*, the information was conveyed voluntarily to a false friend. In *Katz*, the information was *not* voluntarily surrendered to the authorities who were listening in on the conversation. Also, in *On Lee* the recording was just that. It was not an intercepted communication, as was the case in *Katz*. Generally speaking, then, when people voluntarily convey information or provide material to third parties, they cannot have a reasonable expectation of privacy (even if those third parties are best friends) because the third parties could easily turn the information over to authorities.

## Abandoned Property

Whether property is abandoned also has important implications for a person's reasonable expectation of privacy. In *California v. Greenwood*, the Supreme Court reached the following decision:

> [G]arbage bags left on or at the side of a public street are readily accessible to animals, children, scavengers, snoops, and other members of the public. Moreover, respondents placed their refuse at the curb for the express purpose of conveying it to a third party, the trash collector, who might himself have sorted through respondents' trash or permitted others, such as the police, to do so. Accordingly, having deposited their garbage in an area particularly suited for public inspection and, in a manner of speaking, public consumption, for the express purpose of having strangers take it, respondents could have no reasonable expectation of privacy in the inculpatory items they discarded.

While the holding in *Greenwood* dealt specifically with discarded trash, it has been extended to other types of abandonment. For example, if a murder suspect discarded a gun on public property, it would be considered abandoned, because a person cannot have a reasonable expectation of privacy in a public place or an "open field" (see Open Fields and Curtilage section below).

## Privacy in One's Physical Characteristics

The Supreme Court has also held that people's physical characteristics, including their voices, are knowingly exposed to the public and are thus outside the scope of the Fourth

Amendment. As noted in *United States v. Dionisio*, 410 U.S. 1 (1973), for example, "No person can have a reasonable expectation that others will not know the sound of his voice, any more than he can reasonably expect that his face will be a mystery to the world." In that case, individuals were subpoenaed by a grand jury to provide voice samples as part of an investigation (voice samples, not confessions). They claimed Fourth Amendment protection, but the Supreme Court disagreed. In light of the *Dionisio* decision, the government can require not only handwriting samples, but also other forms of physical evidence, such as locks of hair and even fingerprints.

Physical attributes not on public display, however, generally fall within the protection of the Fourth Amendment. For example, in *Skinner v. Railway Labor Executives' Association*, 489 U.S. 602 (1989), the Court ruled that blood, urine, and breath analysis all amount to searches because "they intrude upon expectations of privacy as to medical information."

Finally, the fact that external physical characteristics are knowingly exposed does not mean that the police are not restricted in other ways by the Fourth Amendment. For example, if a suspect is at home in his or her private residence and the police wish to obtain his or her fingerprints, in almost all circumstances, they will need appropriate justification to do so. The search could be accomplished by demonstrating probable cause and obtaining a warrant. In other words, a person may not enjoy a reasonable expectation of privacy with regard to his or her physical characteristics that are on public display, but he or she will *always* enjoy a reasonable expectation of privacy in his or her residence, provided the police attempt to find him or her at that location.

## Open Fields and Curtilage

The physical setting in which police activity takes place is also important in determining whether the Fourth Amendment applies. Clearly, the inside of a residence is protected by the Fourth Amendment, but what about the outside? And if the outside is protected, how far beyond the residence can the Fourth Amendment be expected to apply?

In addressing searches of residences, the courts often refer to the term *curtilage*. According to the Supreme Court, **curtilage** is the "area to which extends the intimate activity associated with the sanctity of a man's home and the privacies of life" (*Oliver v. United States*, 466 U.S. 170, 225 [1984]). By contrast, an **open field** is any unoccupied or undeveloped real property falling outside the curtilage of a home. Open fields do not enjoy Fourth Amendment protection, but homes and curtilage do. Figure 3.1 distinguishes between a house, curtilage, and an open field.

*Oliver v. United States*
*(466 U.S. 170, 225 [1984])*

## DECISION-MAKING EXERCISE 3.4

### A "FALSE FRIEND" SCENARIO

John Quinn was put in jail after being arrested as a homicide suspect. The prosecutor did not think she had enough evidence to proceed to trial, so she asked a police officer to dress in street clothes, pose as a jail inmate, and strike up a conversation with Quinn. The officer was placed in the same cell with Quinn and began to make small talk with him. Eventually, Quinn mentioned that he was involved in the murder of Valerie Hutton but that he was not the "trigger man." The police officer reported this conversation to the prosecutor, who then sought to use Quinn's incriminating statements against him at trial. Quinn's attorney moved to have the statements suppressed on the grounds that a Fourth Amendment violation took place. In particular, the defense attorney argued that Quinn had a reasonable expectation of privacy that his conversation would not be shared with or repeated to other individuals. Is the defense attorney correct?

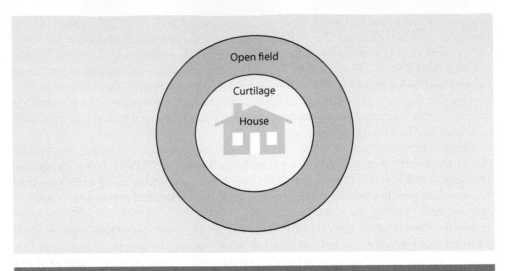

**FIGURE 3.1 Relationship between a House, Curtilage, and Open Field**

Note, however, that open fields need not be *open* or *fields* to fall beyond the reach of the Fourth Amendment. If a barn that is located 50 yards from a house is not used for "intimate activities," it *can* be considered an open field, even though it is located on private property. In *United States v. Dunn*, 480 U.S. 294 (1987), police entered the defendant's property without a warrant, climbed over several fences, and peered inside his barn. They eventually obtained a warrant to search the barn, but the Court ruled that their earlier activity was a search within the meaning of the Fourth Amendment. How did they reach this decision? The following factors were considered:

- the proximity of the area to the house;
- whether the area is included within a fence or another enclosure surrounding the house;
- the nature of the use to which the land/property is being put; and
- the steps taken by the resident to protect the area from observation.

The main issue was the officers' decision to climb the fence, which was put up to preserve a certain element of privacy.

Aerial surveillance from a fixed-wing aircraft and/or helicopter also raises Fourth Amendment questions. In *California v. Ciraolo*, 476 U.S. 207 (1986), the Supreme Court ruled that naked-eye observation of a fenced-in backyard from a height of 1,000 feet did not constitute a search. The logic offered by the Court was that in "an age where private and commercial flight in the public airways is routine, it is unreasonable for respondent to expect that his marijuana plants were constitutionally protected" from such observation.

Similarly, in *Florida v. Riley*, 488 U.S. 445 (1989), the Court held that the Fourth Amendment was not implicated when the police flew a helicopter at an altitude of 400 feet over the defendant's partially covered greenhouse, which was found to contain marijuana. The Court stated: "Riley no doubt intended and expected that his greenhouse would not be open to public inspection, and the precautions he took [including placing a wire fence around the greenhouse and a Do Not Enter sign] protected against ground-level observation." Since any person could position himself or herself over the greenhouse in a helicopter, the surveillance did not amount to a Fourth Amendment violation. The Court supported its position by noting that the helicopter's altitude was within legal parameters and Federal Aviation Administration (FAA) guidelines.

1. Is the area close to a house or residence?
2. Is the area contained by a fence or similar enclosure?
3. To what use is the area being put?
4. What steps have been taken to protect the area from observation?

**FIGURE 3.2 Factors Used to Distinguish between a Curtilage and Open Field**

A similar decision was reached in *Dow Chemical Co. v. United States*, 476 U.S. 227 (1986), a case in which the Environmental Protection Agency (EPA) hired an aerial photographer to take pictures of the defendant's plant. Despite the photographer's use of a camera to take pictures (as opposed to simple, naked-eye observation), the Supreme Court ruled that aerial photography of the type used in *Dow Chemical* did not amount to a search, thereby triggering Fourth Amendment protections.

In a 2013 case, *Florida v. Jardines*, 569 U.S. ___ (2013), the Supreme Court was confronted with the question of whether an officer's decision to let a narcotics-sniffing dog sniff around the front door of a man's house constituted a search. The Court decided it was, and based its reasoning on the concept of curtilage. Had the officer entered the house, a search would have undoubtedly occurred. In contrast, had the dog detected the narcotics from a public sidewalk, a search *would not* have occurred. But was the porch considered curtilage? Indeed it was. The Court applied this creative logic:

To find a visitor knocking on the door is routine (even if sometimes unwelcome); to spot that same visitor exploring the front path with a metal detector, or marching his bloodhound into the garden before saying hello and asking permission, would inspire most of us to—well, call the police.

To further grasp the distinction between open fields and curtilage, see Figure 3.2 for a list of factors the courts often consider.

## Enhancement Devices

The rules become significantly more complicated when law enforcement officials use so-called *enhancement devices* to look for evidence. Enhancement devices can include flashlights, drug dogs, satellite photography, thermal imagery, and so on. Whatever their form, the devices are designed to enhance or replace the sensory abilities of the police, usually when police are operating from an otherwise lawful vantage point.

In determining what level of sensory enhancement is appropriate, the courts generally give consideration to six specific factors:

- the nature of the place surveilled,
- the nature of the activity surveilled,
- the care taken to ensure privacy,
- the lawfulness of the vantage point,

### DECISION-MAKING EXERCISE 3.5

**IS A PUBLIC STREET AN OPEN FIELD?**

Officer Perez suspects that a local man is growing marijuana in his backyard but cannot tell for certain because of the large fence surrounding the house. To find out, Perez places a stepladder on a nearby public sidewalk, climbs up to the top, peers over the fence, and observes several dozen marijuana plants growing in the man's garden. Has a search occurred in this situation?

- the availability of sophisticated technology, and
- the extent to which the technology used enhances or replaces the natural senses.[1]

The Court addressed the first factor in *United States v. Knotts*, 460 U.S. 276 (1983). The case involved the constitutionality of federal agents' placement of a "beeper" (a tracking device) in a container and tracking the container to the defendant's cabin. The Court concluded that "[a] person travelling in an automobile on public thoroughfares has no reasonable expectation of privacy in his movements from one place to another." The determinative factor in that case was that the beeper was placed in the container *before* Knotts took possession of it—and with the permission of its then owner.

In 2012, the Supreme Court was confronted with a similar scenario, this time involving GPS monitoring. The government obtained a warrant to install a GPS tracking device on a woman's car. It authorized the device to be placed on the vehicle within 10 days, and within the District of Columbia. The device was actually placed on the vehicle on the 11th day, and in Maryland, in violation of the warrant. Thus, the device was put on the vehicle without a warrant. The government tracked the vehicle for 28 days and used information thereby obtained to bring a case against the woman's husband. The Supreme Court held that "[t]he Government's attachment of the GPS device to the vehicle, and its use of that device to monitor the vehicle's movements, constitutes a search under the Fourth Amendment" (*United States v. Jones*, 565 U.S. ___ [2012]).

*United States v. Jones*
*(565 U.S. ___ [2012])*

If the police are not in a lawful vantage point but continue to look for evidence, a search occurs. Examples of lawful vantage points include sidewalks, streets, and, of course, public airways. The police can take up positions anywhere outside the home or the curtilage of the home and still be in a lawful vantage point. In fact, even if the police find themselves in curtilage that is open to the public, they may still find themselves in a lawful vantage point.

The availability of sophisticated technology to the public is also an important factor in deciding which sensory enhancement devices the police can use. In *Dow Chemical*, the use of a camera from a publicly navigable airspace was beyond the scope of the Fourth Amendment because the camera equipment was available on the open market. However, the Court also pointed out that "using highly sophisticated surveillance equipment *not* generally available to the public, such as satellite technology, might be constitutionally proscribed absent a warrant" (emphasis added). Moreover, the use of "an electronic device to penetrate walls or windows so as to hear and record confidential discussions of chemical formulae or other trade secrets would raise very different and far more serious questions."

*Kyllo v. United States*, 533 U.S. 27 (2001) provides a good example. In that case, law enforcement officials were suspicious that marijuana was being grown in Kyllo's home. Agents scanned his home using a thermal imaging device (also known as FLIR, for Forward Looking Infrared). The scan revealed that Kyllo's garage roof and side wall were relatively hot compared to the rest of his home. Based in part on the results from the thermal imager, a federal magistrate issued a warrant to search Kyllo's home. However, the Supreme Court declared that "[w]here . . . the Government uses a device that is not in general public use, to explore details of a private home that would previously have been unknowable without physical intrusion, the surveillance is a Fourth Amendment 'search,' and is presumptively unreasonable without a warrant."

The courts will also consider the extent to which a sensory enhancement device actually enhances the natural senses. In doing this, several courts have distinguished between devices that *enhance* the senses versus those that *replace* the senses. Generally, an enhancement device that is used to assist the senses (as binoculars do, for instance) is less likely

---

[1]C. H. Whitebread and C. Slobogin, *Criminal Procedure*, 4th ed. (New York: Foundation Press, 2000), pp. 120–125.

**DRUG DOGS AS SENSORY ENHANCEMENT DEVICES**

A female traveler paid for a plane ticket to Miami. When she checked in at the airport, the ticket agent took her luggage and placed it on a conveyor belt so it could be loaded onto the plane. As the luggage was traveling along the conveyor, it passed a narcotics agent, whose dog sniffs every bag in an attempt to find drugs. The dog was alerted to the woman's bag, so the narcotics officer grabbed it and opened it. Several kilogram packages of cocaine were inside. Before the woman could board her flight, she was arrested. Has a search occurred?

to violate the Fourth Amendment than a device that replaces the senses (as some satellites do). The use of binoculars is often permitted because courts recognize that police officers need to avoid detection. Flashlights are clearly devices that enhance the natural senses, and courts have ruled that, when used, they do not trigger the Fourth Amendment.

A slightly more controversial law enforcement tool is the drug-sniffing dog. Some courts have ruled that their use does not trigger the Fourth Amendment under certain circumstances (see *United States v. Place*, 462 U.S. 696 [1983]). However, it has been argued that they do implicate the Fourth Amendment because a drug dog's senses are used to *replace* an officer's senses. In *Commonwealth v. Johnston*, 515 Pa. 454 (1987), a court ruled that law enforcement officers' use of drug dogs violated the state constitution, stating that "a free society will not remain free if police may use this, or any other crime detection device, at random and without reason."

*United States v. Place*
*(462 U.S. 696 [1983])*

# ▶ When Does a "Seizure" Occur?

Like the term *search*, the definition of *seizure* has a very specific meaning in criminal procedure. An object need not be physically grasped for a seizure to take place. Indeed, the police can stop short of actually touching a person, but their actions can still constitute a seizure. At the other extreme, though, there are certain things the police may do to inconvenience people without triggering the Fourth Amendment. It is also important to distinguish between two types of seizures: (1) seizures of property and (2) seizures of persons. Different rules apply to each of these types of seizures.

## Seizures of Property

As the Supreme Court declared in *United States v. Jacobsen*, 466 U.S. 109 (1984), a **seizure of property** occurs "when there is some meaningful interference with an individual's possessory interest in that property."

In determining if a piece of property is "seized," courts often refer to *actual* and *constructive* possessions. A piece of property is in a person's actual possession if he or she is physically holding or grasping the property. Constructive possession, by comparison, refers to possession of property without physical contact. An example is a bag that is next to a person on the ground but not in his or her hands. A piece of property is seized, therefore, if the police remove it from a person's actual or constructive possession, such as when they take a person's luggage at an airport and move it into another room to be searched (see *United States v. Place*, 462 U.S. 696 [1983]).

Relatively few cases are encountered concerning the constitutionality of seizures of property. Usually, property is seized *after* a search occurs. When a search is declared unlawful, the seizure of the property that follows is generally unconstitutional because of the exclusionary rule (see Chapter 2). However, there are certain cases in which seizure occurs without a search. For example, in *Soldal v. Cook County*, 506 U.S. 56 (1992), the

*Soldal v. Cook County*
*(506 U.S. 56 [1992])*

question before the Supreme Court was whether the Fourth Amendment applied when a family's trailer was removed from a trailer park. The Court held that the Fourth Amendment applied, meaning a seizure occurred. There was no search *per se*.

## Seizures of Persons

A **seizure of a person** occurs when a police officer—by means of physical force or show of authority—intentionally restrains an individual's liberty in such a manner that a reasonable person would believe that he or she is not free to leave (see *Terry v. Ohio*, 392 U.S. 1 [1968]; *United States v. Mendenhall*, 446 U.S. 544 [1980]). One way to determine if a Fourth Amendment seizure has occurred is to ask if a reasonable person would believe that he or she is free to decline the officer's requests or otherwise terminate the encounter.

The seizure of a person can take place in a number of ways. For example, a person is seized when he or she is arrested and taken to the police station for questioning (*Dunaway v. New York*, 442 U.S. 200 [1979]). A person is also seized if he or she is physically restrained on the street so that he or she may be frisked (as in *Terry v. Ohio*) or if he or she is pulled over by the police in his or her car.

The seizure of a person does not have to be *physical* for the Fourth Amendment to be implicated. For example, a seizure can occur when a police officer simply questions a person. However, the Supreme Court stated in *Terry v. Ohio* that "not all personal intercourse between policemen and citizens involves 'seizures' of persons" (392 U.S. 1 [1968]). Nevertheless, a seizure has occurred if the officer's conduct in conjunction with the questioning would convince a reasonable person that he or she is not free to leave.

A seizure can also occur by *pursuit*, even if the person sought by the police is never caught. However, it is not always clear whether a pursuit constitutes a seizure. This is important because if the pursuit of a suspect is *not* a seizure, then the police may lawfully chase people without justification. Moreover, if the person discards anything during the chase, the police may lawfully seize the item because the Fourth Amendment does not apply. In fact, as the Supreme Court noted in *California v. Hodari D.*, 499 U.S. 621 (1991), when an officer chases a suspect but does not lay hands on him or her, a seizure does not occur until which point the suspect submits to police authority.

*California v. Hodari D.*
*(499 U.S. 621 [1991])*

In *Hodari D.*, a police officer chased a suspect on foot. The officer did not have justification to stop or arrest the suspect. The suspect discarded an item during the chase, which the officer stopped to pick up. The Supreme Court upheld the officer's action because the suspect was still in flight at the time the officer picked up the object. The Supreme Court did state in *Hodari D.*, however, that a seizure *does* occur the instant a police officer lays hands on a suspect during a chase, even if the suspect is able to break away from the officer's grasp.

The definitions of seizure offered in this section are general. The cases on which they are based will be encountered in the next three chapters as the topics of stop-and-frisk and arrest are considered. For now, remember that there are different types of seizures. An arrest, for example, is a type of seizure, but a seizure does not have to rise to the level of an arrest for the Fourth Amendment to be implicated. The following chapters will take care to ensure that the reader will be able to distinguish among different types of seizures.

## ▶ Justification

To this point, only the threshold question of whether the Fourth Amendment applies has been addressed—that is, has a search or seizure occurred? If the answer is no, then the issue will go no further, and justification will not matter because a search or seizure did not occur. However, if the government's action constitutes a search or seizure, the next issue involves deciding whether the police acted within the limits of the Fourth Amendment.

If they did not, then any evidence they obtained during the course of such an illegal search or seizure cannot be used in a criminal proceeding to determine guilt.

Once it has been determined *whether* the Fourth Amendment applies, it is then necessary to consider *what else* the Fourth Amendment requires. The first and most fundamental inquiry in terms of Fourth Amendment requirements concerns the doctrine of justification. The police need to have **justification,** or cause, before they can conduct a search or a seizure. Justification needs to be in place *a priori*—that is, before a person or evidence is sought in an area protected by the Fourth Amendment. The police cannot conduct an illegal search to obtain evidence and then argue *after the fact* that what they did was appropriate.

Probable cause is the only standard of justification mentioned in the Fourth Amendment, but the Supreme Court has invoked the amendment's reasonableness clause to carve out exceptions to the probable cause requirement. Some law enforcement investigation techniques are sanctioned nowadays on less than probable cause. We examine some of them in Chapters 6 and 7.

Justification can be viewed as something of a sliding scale that hinges on the type of intrusion the police make. Generally, the more intrusive the police action, the higher the level of justification required. Conversely, the lower the level of intrusion, the lower the justification needed. Three primary levels of justification recognized by the courts will be considered throughout the remainder of this chapter: (1) probable cause, the standard for searches and seizures; (2) reasonable suspicion, the standard for stop-and-frisk; and (3) administrative justification, the standard for administrative searches.

## Probable Cause

Probable cause refers to the basis for believing that an offense has occurred or will occur. If there is not sufficient basis for this belief, any resulting search or seizure will violate the Fourth Amendment. **Probable cause** was formally defined in *Beck v. Ohio*, 379 U.S. 89 (1964) as more than bare suspicion; it exists when "the facts and circumstances within [the officers'] knowledge and of which they [have] reasonably trustworthy information [are] sufficient to warrant a prudent man in believing that the [suspect] had committed or was committing an offense." In *Brinegar v. United* States, 338 U.S. 160 (1949), the Court added, "The substance of all the definitions of probable cause is a reasonable ground for belief of guilt."

*Beck v. Ohio*
*(379 U.S. 89 (1964))*

*Brinegar v. United States*
*(338 U.S. 160 [1949])*

Unfortunately, these legal definitions are of little use to those on the frontlines of law enforcement. A more practical definition of probable cause is *more than 50 percent certainty*. As such, it lies somewhere below absolute certainty and proof beyond a reasonable doubt (the latter of which is necessary to obtain a criminal conviction) and somewhere above a hunch or reasonable suspicion (which is required to conduct a stop-and-frisk).

The notion of a *prudent man* is akin to the idea of "objective reasonableness" previously discussed. Basically, it means that courts consider what the average person on the street would believe, not what a person who has received special training in the identification and apprehension of lawbreakers (such as a police officer, judge, etc.) would believe. This is not to say, however, that the experience of a police officer is not relevant to a determination of probable cause. On the contrary, in *United States v. Ortiz*, 422 U.S. 891 (1975), the Court ruled that "officers are entitled to draw reasonable inferences from these facts in light of their knowledge of the area and their prior experience with aliens and smugglers" and, by extension, other people suspected of criminal activity.

Figure 3.3 lists a number of the ingredients in the "recipe" for probable cause as well as examples of each ingredient. Each in isolation is rarely, if ever, enough. Rather, a combination of the factors listed in Figure 3.3 is necessary for probable cause to be established.

**1.** Prior record
   *Examples*
   - prior conviction for same activity
   - offender known to have committed similar offense in the past

**2.** Flight from the scene
   *Examples*
   - suspect sees police and runs away
   - flight from an apartment known for drug dealing

**3.** Suspicious conduct
   *Examples*
   - failure to make eye contact with officers
   - extreme inattention to police
   - suspect appears startled by police and turns quickly away
   - "casing" a jewelry store

**4.** Admissions
   *Examples*
   - suspect tells informant that he committed a crime
   - officer overhears two men talking about their involvement in a crime
   - officer hears one suspect tell another, "I told you not to do it"

**5.** Incriminating evidence
   *Examples*
   - suspect found in possession of drug paraphernalia
   - burglary suspect found with pillowcase full of loot
   - sack of cash and ski mask in robbery suspect's car

**6.** Unusual hour
   *Examples*
   - At 2:30 A.M., an officer sees a man depart a darkened property where valuables were kept
   - At 3:30 A.M., an officer observed two men walking in a business area who then fled at the sight of the officer

**7.** Suspect resembles the perpetrator
   *Examples*
   - suspect wears clothes similar to the perpetrator of a crime
   - suspect is an occupant of the same car thought to flee the scene of a robbery
   - the number of suspects in the car is the same as the number of suspects reportedly involved in the crime

**8.** Evasive and untruthful responses to questions
   *Examples*
   - suspect caught in a lie about where she was coming from
   - suspect gives false name and/or identification
   - use of an alias
   - suspect denies owning a car that is registered to him
   - suspect gives vague and confusing answers to an officer's questions

**9.** Obvious attempt to hide something
   *Examples*
   - officers hear a toilet flush when arriving to serve a search warrant
   - officer observes a suspect push something under the seat of his car
   - suspect is looking into the trunk of a vehicle but slams it quickly on seeing a police officer

**10.** Presence in a high-crime area and/or near a crime scene
   *Examples*
   - officer observes a vehicle leave the scene of a burglary at which no other people or vehicles were located

**FIGURE 3.3 Ingredients in the Probable Cause Recipe**

**FIGURE 3.3** (*continued*)

Probable cause is always required in the following scenarios:

- arrests with warrants;

- arrests without warrants;

- searches and seizures of property with warrants; and

- searches and seizures of property without warrants.

When a warrant is required, the probable cause determination is made by the magistrate charged with issuing the warrant; when a warrant is not used, the police officer makes the probable cause determination.

The courts sometimes treat the probable cause requirement differently, depending on the conduct in which the police engage. When the police make an *arrest*, the probable cause determination concerns whether there is a reasonable belief that an offense has been committed and whether the suspect did, in fact, commit the offense. In the case of a search, however, the probable cause issue concerns whether there is a reasonable belief that the items to be seized are connected with criminal activity and whether they can be found in the place to be searched.

The fact that an officer has probable cause to search a suspect does not necessarily mean the officer has probable cause to arrest the person. Alternatively, probable cause to arrest does not necessarily create probable cause to search. Consider this hypothetical situation: Police officers pursue a drug suspect into her residence and arrest her in her living room. Assuming they had probable cause to pursue the suspect, the police do not possess unfettered latitude once in the house to search the place up and down. The courts have placed restrictions on what can be done in a situation such as this—that is, on how far the police can go with a search following, or "incident" to arrest. This example illustrates that the ingredients in the probable cause recipe are not always the same for arrests as they are for searches.

In several arrest cases, the courts have considered what sources of information meet the probable cause burden. Three main sources of information have been examined: (1) informants and other third parties; (2) firsthand knowledge; and (3) information that turns out, after the fact, to be mistaken but is reasonably relied on.[2] Other information may help establish probable cause to arrest, but the courts have been most vocal about these three sources.

---

[2]C. H. Whitebread and C. Slobogin, *Criminal Procedure: An Analysis of Cases and Concepts*, 5th ed. (New York: Foundation Press, 2008). pp. 84–96.

## Informants and Other Third Parties

The police routinely rely on information supplied to them by a sophisticated network of *informants*. Informants are not necessarily shady characters connected to the criminal lifestyle—they can also be victims of crime, witnesses of crime, and other police officers.

The courts have attempted to create tests to ensure that information supplied by informants is credible. In *Aguilar v. Texas*, 378 U.S. 108 (1964), the Supreme Court ruled that an affidavit based on a tip from an informant must show (1) sufficient information to demonstrate how the informant reached his or her conclusion and (2) sufficient information to establish the reliability of the informant. Stated differently, the first prong asks, "Why should the police believe this person?" and the second prong asks, "How does the informant know what he or she claims to know?"

For both prongs of the *Aguilar* test to be satisfied, the police need to supply specific information in their affidavit. A statement to the effect that "this informant has provided reliable information in the past" is not enough. More appropriate is a statement such as "This informant has supplied information in the past that led to the conviction of John Doe" (see also *United States v. Freitas*, 716 F.2d 1216 [9th Cir. 1983]).

In *Spinelli v. United States*, 393 U.S. 410 (1969), the Supreme Court clarified the meaning of the first prong. It concluded that insufficient knowledge of the details of the reported criminal activity can be overcome if "the tip describe[s] the accused's criminal activity in sufficient detail that the magistrate knows that he is relying on something more substantial than a casual rumor . . . or an accusation based merely on a individual's general reputation" (p. 416). Similarly, in *Draper v. United States*, 358 U.S. 307 (1959), the Court ruled that the first prong—the credibility prong—may also be satisfied even though the informant implicates himself or herself in criminal activity, provided that such a statement is against self-interest. An example of a self-interested admission of criminal activity would be one in which the informant seeks to curry favor with the police and/or prosecutors in exchange for supplying information.

The *Aguilar* and *Spinelli* tests were heavily modified in *Illinois v. Gates*, 462 U.S. 213 (1983), when the Supreme Court basically abandoned the two-pronged probable cause analysis and replaced it with a *totality of circumstances* test. Thus, if "a particular informant is known for the unusual reliability of his predictions of certain types of criminal activities in a locality, his failure, in a particular case, to thoroughly set forth the basis of his knowledge surely should not serve as an absolute bar to a finding of probable cause based on his tip" (p. 233). In other words, a deficiency in one prong can be compensated for with an abundant supply of information in the other.

*Aguilar*, *Spinelli*, and *Gates* were all search cases, which would seem to limit their applicability in the arrest context, but the *Illinois v. Gates* totality of circumstances test is now used for determining probable cause based on information from informants in both the arrest and search/seizure contexts. The courts will give consideration to five factors in determining whether the totality of circumstances creates probable cause:

- when the informant describes how he or she found out about the criminal activity;
- when the informant gives a detailed description of that activity;
- when evidence for the informant's reliability exists;
- when the informant predicts criminal activity that is later corroborated by the police; and
- when the informant implicates himself or herself in criminal activity.

In cases where the informant is not implicated in some criminal activity, but is a victim or eyewitness, the Supreme Court has relaxed the *Aguilar/Spinelli/Gates* tests. For example, in *Jaben v. United States*, 381 U.S. 214 (1965), the Court held that "whereas some supporting information concerning the credibility of informants in narcotics cases or other common garden varieties of crime may be required, such information is not so necessary in

*Aguilar v. Texas*
*(378 U.S. 108 [1964])*

*Spinelli v. United States*
*(393 U.S. 410 [1969])*

*Illinois v. Gates*
*(462 U.S. 213 [1983])*

▼

the context of the case before us." Similar rulings have been applied when the informants have been other police officers. For example, in *United States v. Ventresca*, 380 U.S. 102, 111 (1965), the Supreme Court ruled that "[o]bservations of fellow officers of the Government engaged in a common investigation are plainly a reliable basis for a warrant applied for by one of their number." Of course, probable cause is still required. When probable cause is found lacking, the arrest will most likely be deemed unconstitutional.

## Firsthand Knowledge

The second major category of probable cause cases hinges on information that results from *firsthand knowledge*. The courts usually do not worry about the truthfulness or accuracy of the arresting officer's observations but, instead, whether probable cause to arrest was in place. In particular, the courts have required that probable cause *to* arrest must be determined independently from the arrest itself, meaning that probable cause to arrest must be required *before* the arrest. This means that police cannot search people and illegally seize evidence simply for the purpose of establishing probable cause to arrest. Stated differently, probable cause cannot be established in hindsight. It should be pointed out, though, that evidence encountered during law enforcement activity that does not constitute an arrest or a search (a patdown, for instance) can create or be used to establish probable cause to arrest or conduct a further search, depending on the circumstances.

In many cases the officer does not actually observe criminal behavior, but he or she knows the suspect is in close proximity to criminal conduct. In such cases, proximity to criminal conduct does not, by itself, give probable cause to arrest (*United States v. Di Re*, 332 U.S. 581 [1948]). Officers arrested Di Re from the front seat of a car on the grounds that there were two other men in the car passing counterfeit ration coupons between one another. The Court noted that had Di Re even seen the activity, "it would not follow that he knew they were ration coupons, and if he saw that they were ration coupons, it would not follow that he would know them to be counterfeit." In other words, proximity to criminal activity does not create probable cause to arrest.

In *Ybarra v. Illinois*, 444 U.S. 85 (1979), the police had a valid warrant authorizing them to search a tavern, but the Court held that the search warrant did not give them permission to search the patrons of the bar, including the petitioner, because they were not named in the warrant. If, however, the arresting officer were armed with additional

---

### DECISION-MAKING EXERCISE 3.7

#### INFORMANTS AND PROBABLE CAUSE

In *Chambers v. Maroney*, 399 U.S. 42 (1970), the Supreme Court considered the following facts:

> . . . a Gulf service station in North Braddock, Pennsylvania, was robbed by two men, each of whom carried and displayed a gun. The robbers took the currency from the cash register; the service station attendant, one Stephen Kovacich, was directed to place the coins in his right-hand glove, which was then taken by the robbers. Two teenagers, who had earlier noticed a blue compact station wagon circling the block in the vicinity of the Gulf station, then saw the station wagon speed away from a parking lot close to the Gulf station. About the same

time, they learned that the Gulf station had been robbed. They reported to police, who arrived immediately, that four men were in the station wagon and one was wearing a green sweater. Kovacich told the police that one of the men who robbed him was wearing a green sweater and the other was wearing a trench coat. A description of the car and the two robbers was broadcast over the police radio.

A vehicle fitting the description was stopped. The occupants were arrested and the car was driven to the police station and searched. Was the stop justified? In other words, did the officers have probable cause to arrest the occupants of the car?

▼

### HAVING PROBABLE CAUSE TO ARREST

An observant police officer was on foot patrol and noticed a suspicious person standing at the counter in a convenience store. The person, who had one hand in his coat pocket, appeared to be carrying on a conversation with the clerk, who was reaching into the cash register and appeared to be very nervous. On a hunch that she was witnessing a robbery in progress, the officer quickly entered the store, surprised the person talking to the clerk, arrested him, and upon searching him incident to the arrest, found a handgun in his coat pocket. His attorney moved to suppress the handgun on the grounds that the police officer did not have probable cause to arrest. What should the courts decide?

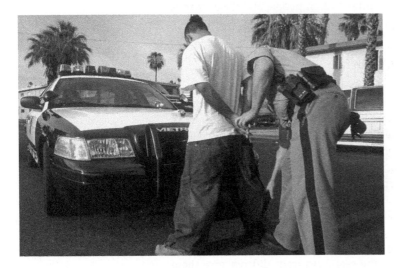

Probable cause is required to make an arrest. Here an officer searches a suspect pursuant to an arrest.

information (from a third-party informant, for example), then probable cause would be easier to establish.

### Reasonable Reliance on Mistaken Information

If information supplied by an informant or by an officer's firsthand observations later proves to be false, the courts will uphold the arrest or search, so long as the mistake was a reasonable one (*Franks v. Delaware*, 438 U.S. 154 [1978]). When such a mistake is deemed *unreasonable*, however, the courts will almost always reach a different conclusion. An example of an unreasonable mistake is a police officer's reliance on an informant who had provided false information on 50 previous occasions (*Albright v. Oliver*, 510 U.S. 266 [1994]).

## Reasonable Suspicion

Much police activity is not as intrusive as a search or a seizure. For example, the police routinely have to confront people on the street in order to question them, or pull over automobiles to enforce traffic laws. If probable cause were required under such circumstances, the police could do little in terms of investigating suspicious activity.

Recognizing how essential these lesser intrusions are to the police mission, the Supreme Court established in *Terry v. Ohio*, 392 U.S. 1 (1968) a different level of justification for such activities, namely, reasonable suspicion. In *Terry*, an officer's attention was drawn to two men on a street corner who appeared to the officer to be "casing" a store for a robbery.

*Terry v. Ohio*
*(392 U.S. 1 [1968])*

The officer approached the men and asked them to identify themselves. The officer then proceeded to pat down the men and found a gun on each one. The men were placed under arrest. They tried to suppress the guns, but the Supreme Court eventually held the officer's actions valid in the interest of "effective crime prevention and detection."

There is no clear definition of *reasonable suspicion*, just as there is no clear definition of *probable cause*. As the Supreme Court has stated:

> Courts have used a variety of terms to capture the elusive concept of what cause is sufficient to authorize police to stop a person. Terms like "articulable reasons" and "founded suspicion" are not self-defining; they fall short of providing clear guidance dispositive of the myriad factual situations that arise. But the essence of all that has been written is that the totality of circumstances—the whole picture—must be taken into account. Based upon that whole picture the detaining officers must have a particularized and objective basis for suspecting the particular person stopped of criminal activity (*United States v. Cortez*, 449 U.S. 411 [1981]).

Reasonable suspicion is a level of justification lying below probable cause, and is "considerably less than proof of wrongdoing by a preponderance of evidence" (*United States v. Sokolow*, 490 U.S. 1 [1989]). However, it is more than a vague hunch. Figure 3.4 contains a list of specific factors that can contribute to reasonable suspicion—as well as some types of information that *cannot* give rise to reasonable suspicion.

Like probable cause, reasonable suspicion can be based on a number of different sources, including informants. But because the reasonable suspicion standard falls below the standard for probable cause, less information is required. For example, in *Adams v. Williams*, 407 U.S. 143 (1972), the Supreme Court held that reasonable suspicion may be based on an anonymous telephone tip, so long as the police can corroborate certain details from the informant. Likewise, in *Alabama v. White*, 496 U.S. 325, 330 (1990), the Supreme Court observed that

*Alabama v. White*
*(496 U.S. 325, 330 [1990])*

> [r]easonable suspicion is a less demanding standard than probable cause not only in the sense that reasonable suspicion can be established with information that is different but also in the sense that reasonable suspicion can arise from information that is less reliable than that required to show probable cause.

In short, reasonable suspicion must be based on articulable facts that connect the suspect to criminal activity. The key factor is knowledge of **articulable facts**. An articulable fact is an event that is witnessed and can be explained, as opposed to a gut reaction or a mere hunch. For example, in *Sibron v. New York*, 392 U.S. 40 (1968), the Court held that talking to known addicts and reaching into their pockets does not produce reasonable suspicion that criminal activity is afoot. Another good example is *Brown v. Texas*, 443 U.S. 47 (1979), in which two police officers observed Brown and another man walking away from one another. One of the officers later testified that he thought the officers' arrival broke

| Factors That *May* Give Rise to Reasonable Suspicion | Factors That *Will* Not Give Rise to Reasonable Suspicion |
|---|---|
| Suspect in high-crime area at unusual hour | Hunch |
| Suspect flees from officers | Rumor |
| Suspect appears to receive cash in exchange for two small envelopes | Intuition |
| Suspect puts television in the trunk of a car in an area where most businesses are closed | Instinct |
| Suspect appears to be "casing" a convenience store | Curiosity |

**FIGURE 3.4 Factors That May and Do Not Give Rise to Reasonable Suspicion**

up some suspicious activity. Officer Venegas approached Brown and asked him to identify himself. Brown refused and was later convicted under a statute that made it illegal to refuse to give an officer one's name and address. According to the Court:

> There is no indication in the record that it was unusual for people to be in the alley. The fact that the appellant was in a neighborhood frequented by drug users, standing alone, is not a basis for concluding that the appellant himself was engaged in criminal conduct. In short, the appellant's activity was no different from the activity of other pedestrians in that neighborhood.

Contrast *Brown v. Texas* with the Supreme Court's decision in *Illinois v. Wardlow*, 528 U.S. 119 (2000), in which Chicago police officers were patrolling an area known for narcotics traffic. Upon seeing the officers, Wardlow ran and was chased down by the police. When he was patted down, the officers found a Colt .38 pistol and arrested him. Wardlow appealed his conviction, arguing that the stop-and-frisk was illegal because the officers did not have reasonable suspicion. The Court disagreed, noting that "a location's characteristics are relevant in determining whether the circumstances are sufficiently suspicious to warrant further investigation." In addition, the Court noted that "it was Wardlow's unprovoked flight that aroused the officers' suspicion" and that "nervous, evasive behavior is another pertinent factor in determining reasonable suspicion, and headlong flight is the consummate act of evasion." Thus, in the Court's view, the officers *did* have reasonable suspicion to stop and frisk Wardlow.

More recently, the Supreme Court has highlighted the importance of the totality of circumstances as well as officers' experience in making a determination of reasonable suspicion. In *United States v. Arvizu*, 534 U.S. 266 (2002), a border patrol agent in a remote part of Arizona became suspicious of a van when it slowed upon seeing him. The driver also failed to acknowledge the agent. The Supreme Court upheld the agent's decision to stop the van, stating that the agent was "entitled to make an assessment of the situation in light of his specialized training and familiarity with the customs of the area's inhabitants."

## Administrative Justification

Government entities occasionally conduct searches in circumstances that are not criminal investigations. Because these types of searches involve different considerations than criminal investigations, courts have applied a third level of justification in such cases. Instead of the test of "reasonableness," the **administrative justification** adopts a balancing approach, weighing the privacy interests of individuals with the interests of society in preserving public safety.

The administrative form of justification was first adopted in *Camara v. Municipal Court*, 387 U.S. 523 (1967), which involved a health code inspection of residential dwelling units. The Supreme Court held that such inspections were subject to Fourth Amendment protection. However, the Court rejected the argument that probable cause (or reasonable suspicion) needed to be shown. Instead, the Court balanced the public interest in enforcing safety codes with the "relatively limited invasion of the urban citizen's privacy," given that "the inspections are neither personal in nature nor aimed at the discovery of evidence

---

**DECISION-MAKING EXERCISE 3.9**

**IS THERE REASONABLE SUSPICION?**

Officer Hopper was on patrol in a high-crime area at 3:00 A.M. and was waved over to the curb by a woman on the sidewalk. She told Hopper that there was a person sitting in a car nearby who had illegal narcotics and a gun on his lap. Officer Hopper approached the car and asked the driver to open the door. Instead, the driver started to roll down the window. Hopper quickly reached into the window and grabbed the gun from the driver's lap. Was the officer's conduct justified?

of crime." The Court further noted that such searches are permissible, so long as "reasonable legislative or administrative standards for conducting an area inspection are satisfied with respect to a particular dwelling." In other words, administrative searches should not be conducted arbitrarily or with selective enforcement. More recently, the Supreme Court has stated that the

> standard of probable cause is peculiarly related to criminal investigations, not routine, non-criminal procedures. . . . The probable-cause approach is unhelpful when analysis centers upon the reasonableness of routine administrative caretaking functions, particularly when no claim is made that the protective procedures are a subterfuge for criminal investigations[.] (*South Dakota v. Opperman*, 428 U.S. 364, 367 [1976]).

Accordingly, the courts have required that administrative searches be conducted according to objective, standardized procedures. It is also important to note that authorities cannot use an administrative search as a pretext for a full-blown search.

A good example of the balancing approach taken in administrative searches is *Vernonia School District v. Acton*, 515 U.S. 646 (1995). In that case, the Court considered a school policy that required athletes to submit to random urinalysis for drugs. The Court allowed the search because it was not geared toward any particular individual. Further, the Court reasoned that athletes in public schools enjoy a lesser expectation of privacy because they must participate in other examinations, they dress together in the locker room, and they participate in the sports *voluntarily*. In reaching its decision, the Court cited the government interest in preventing "drug use by our Nation's school children." This was a controversial decision, as it seemed to reduce the need for justification set forth explicitly in the Fourth Amendment.

The administrative search rationale has been applied in a number of related situations. For example, the courts have been rather liberal in terms of upholding questionable searches of highly regulated business establishments. In *New York v. Burger*, 482 U.S. 691 (1987), for instance, the Supreme Court authorized a warrantless search of an automobile junkyard. In *Donovan v. Dewey*, 452 U.S. 594 (1981), the Court upheld the warrantless inspection of mines. And the same logic carried over to a case involving the inspection of a gun dealership (*United States v. Biswell*, 406 U.S. 311 [1972]). In support of its decisions, the Court argued that people who choose to conduct business in highly regulated environments enjoy a reduced expectation of privacy.

The administrative rationale has also been applied in a number of other situations, including arson investigations (*Michigan v. Clifford*, 464 U.S. 286 [1984]; *Michigan v. Tyler*, 436 U.S. 499 [1978]); border checkpoints to stop vehicles in an effort to detect illegal aliens (*United States v. Martinez-Fuerte*, 428 U.S. 543 [1976]); searches of impounded vehicles (*Colorado v. Bertine*) and other personal items in need of inventorying (*Illinois v. Lafayette*, 462 U.S. 640 [1983]); and mandatory drug testing of public and private employees (*National Treasury Employees Union v. Von Raah*, 489 U.S. 656 [1989]; *Skinner v. Railway Labor Executives' Association*, 489 U.S. 602 [1989]). In *Skinner*, the Court observed:

> In light of the limited discretion exercised by the railroad employers under the [drug testing] regulations, the surpassing safety interest served by toxicological tests in this context, and the diminished expectation of privacy that attaches to information pertaining to the fitness of covered employees, we believe it is reasonable to conduct such tests in the absence of a warrant or reasonable suspicion that any particular employee may be impaired.

It should be noted that the courts have placed significant restrictions on the scope of these so-called "administrative searches." For example, in *Marshall v. Barlow's, Inc.*, 436 U.S. 307 (1978), the Court ruled that a search under the Occupational Safety and Health Act is unconstitutional if a business has not been heavily regulated in the past.

At the same time, however, administrative searches can be given great latitude in seizing contraband and evidence of a crime, regardless of who conducts the search. As

▼

## ADVENTURE ON THE SEAS

U.S. Customs and Border Protection agents used a drug dog to search the staterooms of 10 passengers aboard the *Adventure of the Seas* cruise ship while it was in port in St. Thomas, a U.S. territory. One of the passengers, James Whitted, was selected for the search because he purchased his ticket at the last minute, had traveled in and through various "source cities," and had a criminal record. During the search of his stateroom, the drug dog alerted the agents to a certain bag. Nothing suspicious was found in the bag, so it was X-rayed. At that point, the agents noticed pebbles inside a shaving cream can. Through field tests, the pebbles were determined to contain heroin. Whitted was arrested and charged with possession with intent to distribute a controlled substance. He now moves to have the drugs excluded from his trial due to an alleged Fourth Amendment violation. Will he succeed?

stated in *New York v. Burger*, "The discovery of evidence of crimes in the course of an otherwise proper administrative inspection does not render that search illegal or the administrative scheme suspect." Further, if the purpose of an administrative search is to detect evidence of criminal activity, probable cause is required. This was the decision reached in *City of Indianapolis v. Edmond*, 531 U.S. 32 (2000). The Supreme Court decided whether a city's checkpoints for detecting illegal drugs were constitutional. The Court held that stops such as those conducted during checkpoint operations require individualized suspicion. In addition, "because the checkpoint program's primary purpose [was] indistinguishable from the general interest in crime control," it violated the Fourth Amendment.

The administrative search justification has also been applied to situations involving "special needs beyond the normal need for law enforcement" (*Skinner*, 489 U.S. 602). In *New Jersey v. TLO*, 469 U.S. 325 (1985), a student's purse was searched by an assistant principal, who suspected that the student was violating the school's policy against smoking. The search turned up marijuana. The Supreme Court sanctioned its seizure, noting that the school's " . . . legitimate need to maintain an environment in which learning can take place" (p. 340) did not require a warrant or even probable cause. Similarly, in *Griffin v. Wisconsin*, 483 U.S. 868 (1987), a case in which a probation officer searched the home of a probationer under the officer's supervision, the Court invoked the logic of special needs beyond normal law enforcement to dispense with the warrant requirement. The Court noted that a probationer enjoys a lesser expectation of privacy than an ordinary citizen.

# Summary

## 1. Summarize the Fourth Amendment's Basic Terminology.

The Fourth Amendment protects *persons*, *houses*, *papers*, and *effects* from unreasonable searches and seizures. The term ***person*** encompasses the individual as a whole, both internally and externally. ***House*** is a term that is broadly construed to mean any structure that a person uses as a residence (and frequently a business) on either a temporary or long-term basis. A hotel room is a prime example of a short-term "house." **Papers and effects** include nearly all personal items. Business records, letters, diaries, memos, and countless other forms of tangible evidence can be defined as *papers*. *Effects* is the catch-all category, including almost any other personal items that are not "papers".

## 2. Define *Search* Within the Context of the Fourth Amendment.

Not every act of looking for evidence is considered a "search" *within the meaning of the Fourth Amendment*. The Fourth Amendment protects citizens from *government* action. Whether a "search" occurs within the meaning of the Fourth Amendment also depends on *where* it occurs. A search only takes place where a person has a *reasonable expectation of privacy*. For example, if police look for evidence in an open field, they have conducted a nonsearch.

## 3. Define *Seizure* Within the Context of the Fourth Amendment.

Seizures of property occur when a meaningful possessory interest is interfered with. Seizures of persons occur when a reasonable person would believe he or she is not free to leave. A search or seizure is unreasonable when it is not supported by proper justification (such as probable cause).

## 4. Distinguish Between the Three Levels of Justification.

*Justification* requires that police have a valid reason for conducting a search or a seizure. There are three standards of justification necessary for searches and seizures. Only one of them, *probable cause*, is spelled out in the Fourth Amendment. Probable cause can be described as a certainty of between 51 and 100 percent, and is required for arrests and searches with and without warrants.

Reasonable suspicion, which can be defined as a certainty of below 51 percent, but greater than a hunch, is required for stops and investigative detentions that fall short of arrests. Administrative justification is required in administrative searches and searches that serve "special needs beyond law enforcement." The constitutionality of a search based on administrative justification is determined by balancing the interests of society with the privacy interests of the individual. Both reasonable suspicion and administrative justification are lower standards than probable cause.

Figure 3.5 summarizes this chapter's Fourth Amendment introduction in question-and-answer form. Figure 3.6 summarizes the levels of proof discussed in this chapter and situates them within other popular levels of proof, such as proof beyond a reasonable doubt (note that most of the probabilities listed in Figure 3.6 are the author's approximations based on the case law).

---

1. Did a search or seizure take place?
    a. For a search, did a government actor violate a reasonable expectation of privacy?
    b. For a seizure, would a reasonable person have believed that he or she was not free to leave?
       *If either of these questions can be answered no, then the Fourth Amendment does not apply.*
       *If either can be answered yes, continue with item 2.*
2. Was the search or seizure justified?
    a. Identify the level of the intrusion: seizure, stop, nonstop, and so on.
    b. Identify the level of justification appropriate to the intrusion.
       *If the justification was not appropriate, the search or seizure was not reasonable.*
3. Was the search or seizure conducted in accordance with constitutional guidelines?
   *See Chapters 4–7 to answer this question.*

**FIGURE 3.5 Fourth Amendment Checklist**

| | |
|---|---|
| Proof beyond a reasonable doubt | around 95 percent certainty |
| Probable cause | more than 50 percent certainty |
| Preponderance of the evidence | civil equivalent of probable cause |
| Reasonable suspicion | between 1 and 50 percent certainty |
| Administrative justification | balancing approach |
| Hunch | no justification at all |

**FIGURE 3.6 Levels of Proof and Their Approximate Degrees of Certainty**

# Key Terms

articulable facts *89*
administrative justification *90*
curtilage *77*
government action *71*
house *71*
justification *83*
open field *77*

person *70*
papers and effects *71*
probable cause *83*
reasonableness clause *70*
reasonableness *71*
reasonable expectation of
 privacy *71*

reasonable suspicion *88*
search *71*
seizure *71*
seizure of property *81*
seizure of a person *82*
warrant clause *70*

# Key Cases

## Searches

- *Burdeau v. McDowell*, 256 U.S. 465 (1921)
- *United States v. Jacobsen*, 466 U.S. 109 (1984)
- *Katz v. United States*, 389 U.S. 347 (1967)
- *Hoffa v. United States*, 385 U.S. 293 (1966)
- *United States v. On Lee*, 343 U.S. 747 (1952)
- *California v. Greenwood*, 486 U.S. 35 (1988)
- *Oliver v. United States*, 466 U.S. 170 (1984)
- *United States v. Jones*, 565 U.S. ___ (2012)
- *United States v. Place*, 462 U.S. 696 (1983)

## Seizures

- *Soldal v. Cook County*, 506 U.S. 56 (1992)
- *California v. Hodari D.*, 499 U.S. 621 (1991)

## Justification

- *Beck v. Ohio*, 379 U.S. 89 (1964)
- *Brinegar v. United States*, 338 U.S. 160 (1949)
- *Aguilar v. Texas*, 378 U.S. 108 (1964)
- *Spinelli v. United States*, 393 U.S. 410 (1969)
- *Illinois v. Gates*, 462 U.S. 213 (1983)
- *Terry v. Ohio*, 392 U.S. 1 (1968)
- *Alabama v. White*, 496 U.S. 330 (1990)

# Further Exploration

1. Had *Katz v. United States* involved cell phones, would the Supreme Court have reached the same decision? Why or why not?
2. Drones and other unmanned aerial surveillance devices are beginning to be used in domestic law enforcement. What are the Fourth Amendment implications and how does available precedent apply? For example, would *Katz v. United States* be helpful in terms of deciding when drones can and cannot be used?
3. What if the federal government announced on national television that "all homes will now be subject to warrantless entry," would that alter the meaning of "reasonable expectation of privacy"? In other words, could the government actively manipulate the privacy expectations of

its citizens through such an announcement or are those expectations more or less set in stone and timeless?

4. Bob Smith, a wealthy land owner, enjoys hunting for protected species on his 1,000-acre ranch. Suspecting that he may be violating the law, agents place a motion-activated camera in an area on Smith's property (hundreds of feet away from his house) where he is presumed to do most of his hunting. They obtain video evidence of Smith killing a protected animal. Have the agents infringed on Smith's reasonable expectation of privacy? Why or why not?

5. *California v. Greenwood* dealt with whether a homeowner enjoys a reasonable expectation of privacy in trash placed curbside. What if rather than placing trash curbside for pickup, the trash is left accessible for trash collectors in the back of a driveway away from the street? How would this "twist" in the facts alter the *Greenwood* decision, if at all?

6. Is there a reasonable expectation of privacy in information stored in a cloud data facility?

7. What if police use canines to sniff for contraband outside of locked self-storage units? Would this activity implicate any Fourth Amendment protections?

8. If a police officer stood on a public street and used a parabolic microphone (listening enhancement device) to hear conversations inside private residences, would that activity implicate the Fourth Amendment? Why or why not? Cite specific case examples.

## Review Questions

1. Summarize the conflicting perspectives on the relationship between the warrant and reasonableness clauses of the Fourth Amendment.

2. Define *person*, *house*, *paper*, and *effect*, as used under the Fourth Amendment.

3. Under what specific circumstances does the Fourth Amendment apply?

4. When does a search take place under the Fourth Amendment? Explain both elements of a search, and discuss pertinent cases.

5. When can private parties be considered "government actors" for the purposes of the Fourth Amendment?

6. What can authorities *not* do following a private-party search?

7. Explain the notion of "reasonable expectation of privacy." When does a person *not* enjoy an expectation of privacy? Cite relevant cases.

8. What is a seizure? Distinguish between seizures of persons and seizures of property.

9. What is the doctrine of justification? Why is it important?

10. Explain probable cause as well as acceptable sources of information for the establishment of probable cause.

11. How can a mistake serve as a legitimate source of information in determining probable cause?

12. What is the procedure for challenging a probable cause determination?

13. What is "reasonable suspicion"? How does it differ from probable cause and other standards of justification?

14. What is "administrative justification"? How does it differ from reasonable suspicion and probable cause?

15. Explain the balancing of interests associated with administrative justification.

## Web Links and Exercises

1. High-tech searches: Browse recent issues of *Law Enforcement Technology* and discuss the Fourth Amendment implications of one or more of the technologies you identify.
URL: http://www.officer.com/magazine (accessed April 18, 2013).

2. Confidential informants: Read about the requirements for the use of confidential informants in federal law enforcement investigations. To what extent can confidential informants participate in criminal activity?

Suggested URL: http://www.fas.org/irp/agency/doj/fbi/dojguidelines.pdf (accessed April 18, 2013).

3. Anonymous tips: Visit the site of Cornell University Law Schools' Legal Information Institute. Enter "anonymous tip" in the sitewide search box and discuss the facts and decisions of at least two cases decided in the lower courts (courts other than the U.S. Supreme Court).
URL: http://www.law.cornell.edu (accessed April 18, 2013).

# 4 Searches and Arrests with Warrants

## LEARNING OBJECTIVES

When you complete this chapter, you should be able to:

**1** *Outline the components of search and arrest warrants.*

**2** *Describe how search and arrest warrants are executed.*

**3** *Explain how bodily intrusions and electronic surveillance create "special circumstances" for Fourth Amendment purposes.*

## OUTLINE

# Introduction: Provisions of the Fourth Amendment

Five types of activities are governed by the Fourth Amendment:

- arrests with warrants,
- arrests without warrants,
- searches with warrants,
- searches without warrants, and
- the seizure of evidence.

This chapter's primary focus is on arrests and searches *with warrants*. Warrantless actions are discussed in the next three chapters.

The Fourth Amendment seems fairly clear with respect to warrants: "and no Warrants shall issue, but upon probable cause, supported by Oath or affirmation, and particularly describing the place to be searched, and the persons or things to be seized." Despite this seemingly simple language, the Fourth Amendment's warrant requirement has been litigated extensively in the courts. As indicated in

Chapter 3, the courts have focused on the meaning of *probable cause* as well as acceptable sources of information used to determine the existence of probable cause. Many decisions have also focused on the Fourth Amendment's requirement that warrants be supported by "Oath or affirmation" and on the particularity requirement. This chapter turns attention to these latter issues.

Although much of the law of search and seizure is very complex, the law is very clear with respect to *when* a warrant is required. Generally, a search warrant is required for *any* type of search, regardless of where it is conducted, provided that (1) there are no exigent (emergency) circumstances and (2) the search is not one justified on administrative/special needs grounds. Even searches pursuant to arrest and searches under the automobile exception are justified in terms of exigencies. Arrest warrants, by contrast, are required for arrests in private places, provided exigent circumstances are absent.

# ► Components of Warrants

An **arrest warrant** or a **search warrant** (see Figures 4.1 and 4.2 for examples) has three essential components. First, it must be issued by a neutral and detached magistrate. Second, a showing of probable cause is required. Finally, it must conform to the Fourth Amendment's particularity requirement. The first requirement—a neutral and detached magistrate—is the same regardless of the type of warrant. The probable cause and particularity requirements differ depending on the type of warrant in question. These requirements are considered in the following subsections.

## A Neutral and Detached Magistrate

The logic for requiring a **neutral and detached magistrate** in the issuance of an arrest or a search warrant was explained by the Supreme Court in *Johnson v. United States*, 333 U.S. 10 (1948):

> The point of the Fourth Amendment . . . is not that it denies law enforcement the support of the usual inferences reasonable men draw from evidence. Its protection consists in requiring that those inferences be drawn by a neutral and detached magistrate instead of being judged by the officer engaged in the often competitive enterprise of ferreting out crime.

---

**WARRANT OF ARREST ON COMPLAINT**

(RCr 2.04,2.06)
(Caption)

**TO ALL PEACE OFFICERS**

You are hereby commanded to arrest _____

                                    (Name of defendant)

and bring him forthwith before judge of the District Court (or, if he be absent or unable to act, before the nearest available magistrate) to answer a complaint made by _____ charging him with the offense of reckless driving.

Issued this _____ day of _____, 19_____.

                                              _____
                                              Judge

(Indorsement as to bail)

The defendant may give bail in the amount of $_____.

                                              _____
                                              Judge

(Amended October 14, 20__, effective January 1, 20__.)

**FIGURE 4.1 Sample Arrest Warrant**

IN THE SUPERIOR COURT DISTRICT, EAST DESERT DIVISION COUNTY OF SAN BERNARDINO, STATE OF CALIFORNIA

## SEARCH WARRANT
### (PENAL CODE 1529)

**THE PEOPLE OF THE STATE OF CALIFORNIA:** To any Sheriff, Constable, Peace Officer or Policeman in the County of San Bernardino:

Proof, by Affidavit, having been this day made before me by:

**ROGER PEREZ**
**Deputy Sheriff**
**San Bernardino County Sheriff's Department**
**Morongo Basin Station**

**THAT THERE IS PROBABLE CAUSE FOR BELIEVING THAT:**

There are narcotics, controlled substances and restricted substances records and documents which tend to show that a felony to wit, Transportation of Controlled Substances, in violation of Health and Safety Code Section 11379, Possession for Sales of Controlled Substances, in violation of Health and Safety Code Section 11378, Sales of Controlled Substances, in violation of Health and Safety Code Section 11379, is being committed in the County of San Bernardino, State of California.

**YOU ARE THEREFORE COMMANDED** at any time of the day or night _____ to make a search of:

**PREMISES TO BE SEARCHED:**

The premises located at:

**2400 MAIN STREET, #12**
**TOWN OF PLEASANTVILLE COUNTY OF SAN BERNARDINO**
**STATE OF CALIFORNIA**

The location is further described as a multi-unit apartment complex located on the east side of Main Street south of Oak Dr. The complex consists of numerous two-story buildings with each building having multiple apartments. Apartment 12 is located in building "C," which is located at the northwest corner of the complex. The exterior is tan stucco with grayish/blue trim and a gray composite shingle roof. Apartment 12 has the numbers "12" which are black and approximately 4 inches tall, affixed to the wood trim to the right of the front door, which faces north.

And all rooms, attics, basements, cellars, safes, vaults, closed or locked containers, trash receptacles and other parts therein, surrounding grounds, garages, sheds, storage rooms, vehicles, campers, trailers and outbuildings of any kind located thereon.

And all persons located on or at the premises. And all vehicles belonging to or in the control of said persons.

And you are hereby authorized to answer all incoming telephone calls received at the premises and the vehicles to be searched and to further seize and record all the incoming telephonic pager numbers and messages received at the premises and the vehicles to be searched and to seize all telephonic "fax" messages received at the premises and the vehicles to be searched. And to determine if the aforementioned telephone calls, telephonic messages, or "faxed" messages are related to illegal activities.

**FOR THE FOLLOWING PROPERTY:**

Methamphetamine and paraphernalia commonly associated with the possession, packaging, and sale of methamphetamine such as scales, weighing devices and measuring devices; packaging materials including paper bindles, glass vials, plastic baggies, foil; processing materials including sifters, filters, screens and cutting agents; recordation of the purchase and/or sales of methamphetamine including ledgers,

**FIGURE 4.2 Example of a Search Warrant That Meets the Particularity Requirement**

notebooks, pay/owe sheets, customer lists, video tapes and phone answering machine tape recordings, personal phone books; personal photographs which document the possession, sales and/or possession for sales of methamphetamine; and proceeds from the sales of methamphetamine consisting of currency.

Financial records including expenses incurred in obtaining chemicals and apparatus and income derived from sales of narcotics and other controlled substances as well as records showing legitimate income or the lack thereof and general living expenses.

Serial numbers, model numbers, identifying marks and descriptions of all personal property including, but not limited to, televisions, radios, stereo equipment, and other electrical devices, appliances, hand and power tools, firearms, bicycles, items of jewelry, silver, gold and coins which can be identified as stolen and/or evidence of the crime of Burglary and/or Possession of Stolen Property or property which is readily traded for narcotics in lieu of cash.

All articles of personal property which will identify persons in control of the premises, storage areas or containers where controlled substances may be found, including keys to those areas that may be locked, rental agreements and receipts, deeds of trust, documents or papers bearing names, canceled mail, paycheck stubs and other employment records, tax documents and personal identification.

**AND IF YOU FIND THE SAME OR ANY PART THEREOF**, to bring it forthwith before me at my courtroom

**GIVEN UNDER MY HAND**, and dated this *17*th day of September 2002.

*James D. Franklin*

Judge of the Superior Court
East Desert Division
County of San Bernardino
State of California

**FIGURE 4.2** (*continued*)

Most judges meet the requirement of "neutral and detached," but what about other officials? In *Coolidge v. New Hampshire*, 403 U.S. 443 (1971), the Court declared that a state attorney general cannot issue a search warrant. State attorneys general are chief prosecutors and thus inclined to side with law enforcement officers. Similarly, in *United States v. United States District Court*, 407 U.S. 297 (1972), the Court decided that the president, acting through the attorney general of the United States, cannot authorize electronic surveillance without judicial approval. Justice Powell observed,

*Coolidge v. New Hampshire*
*(403 U.S. 443 [1971])*

> The Fourth Amendment does not contemplate the executive officers of Government as neutral and detached magistrates. Their duty and responsibility is to enforce the laws, to investigate and to prosecute. . . . [T]hose charged with this investigative and prosecutorial duty should not be the sole judges of when to utilize constitutionally sensitive means in pursuing their tasks. The historical judgment, which the Fourth Amendment accepts, is that unreviewed executive discretion may yield too readily to pressures to obtain incriminating evidence and overlook potential invasions of privacy and protected speech.

*Lo-Ji Sales, Inc. v. New York*
*(442 U.S. 319 [1979])*

There have also been some cases in which the Court has focused on the extent to which magistrates can be viewed as neutral and detached. For example, in *Lo-Ji Sales, Inc. v. New York*, 442 U.S. 319 (1979), a magistrate issued a warrant for two items believed to violate an obscenity law, but he also authorized the police to seize any other items that he might find obscene upon searching the location specified in the warrant. The magistrate then accompanied the officers on the search, discovered items that he deemed to be obscene, and added them to the initial warrant. The items were then admitted into evidence against the defendants. The Supreme Court declared that the magistrate was not acting in a neutral and detached capacity: "[H]e was not acting as a judicial officer but as an adjunct law-enforcement officer."

Moreover, if a magistrate has a financial interest in the issuance of warrants, he or she cannot be considered neutral and detached. This issue was presented to the Supreme Court in *Connally v. Georgia*, 429 U.S. 245 (1977). A Georgia statute authorized unsalaried magistrates to receive five dollars for each warrant issued but no money for warrant applications that were denied. The Court unanimously held that the statute violated the Constitution, citing that "judicial action by an officer of a court who has 'a direct, personal, substantial, pecuniary interest' in his conclusion to issue or to deny the warrant" cannot possibly be considered neutral and detached.

## A Showing of Probable Cause

Probable cause (defined in Chapter 3) is a necessary component of a valid warrant. However, the meaning of "probable cause" varies, depending on whether warrant is issued for an arrest or a search. However, it is important to point out that probable cause is required as a component of a valid warrant. Also, the meaning of probable cause—as opposed to the sources of information that give rise to it—differs, depending on whether an arrest or a search warrant is issued.

### Showing of Probable Cause in an Arrest Warrant

It is not difficult for an officer to show probable cause for the issuance of an arrest warrant. The officer is not required to show probable cause that the suspect will be found at a particular location. All that is necessary is for the officer to show that the person sought may have committed the crime in question.

### Showing of Probable Cause in a Search Warrant

The showing of probable cause for a search warrant is twofold. First, the officer applying for the search warrant must show probable cause that the items to be seized are connected with criminal activity. Second, the officer must show probable cause that the items to be seized are in the location to be searched. Note that this second requirement does not apply to an arrest warrant.

## Particularity

The Fourth Amendment expressly states that warrants particularly describe the "place to be searched, and the persons or things to be seized." Not surprisingly, the **particularity** requirement differs, depending on the type of warrant issued. For an arrest warrant, the particularity requirement is easily satisfied. The particularity requirement for a search warrant, however, is far more complex.

### Particularity in an Arrest Warrant

There are two ways to satisfy the Fourth Amendment's particularity requirement with regard to an arrest warrant. First, if the suspect's name is known, then simply supplying his or her name is enough to meet the particularity requirement. In some situations, however, the suspect's name is *not* known. Then, a specific description of the suspect is sufficient and a "John Doe" warrant will be issued. As long as other officers may locate the suspect with reasonable effort, the suspect's name is not required.

An arrest warrant without the suspect's name is rarely issued. This is not to suggest, however, that the police almost always know the suspect's name. There are many occasions in which an arrest can be made without knowledge of the suspect's name (such as an arrest after a suspect is caught fleeing the bank he or she just robbed). As long as probable cause exists, the name of the suspect is not essential, regardless of whether a warrant is issued.

### WHO WAS THAT BALD MAN?

The police have in their possession the video from a security camera at a bank that was recently robbed. The suspect is a white male who is six feet tall and has a mustache, a bald head, a scar on his left cheek, and a tattoo of a skull and crossbones on his neck. May the police apply for an arrest warrant based on this information, even if they never learned of the suspect's name prior to applying for the warrant?

## Particularity in a Search Warrant

The particularity requirement for a search warrant has two elements. First, the warrant must specify the *place* to be searched. Next, the warrant must specify the *items* to be seized. The reason for this particularity requirement stems from the framers' concerns with so-called "general warrants" issued by the English Crown. These warrants basically permitted limitless searches for evidence of treason.

Contrary to popular belief, a search warrant does not need to state with absolute precision the place to be searched. It "is enough if the description is such that the officer with a search warrant can, with reasonable effort, ascertain and identify the place intended." (*Steele v. United States*, 267 U.S. 498 [1925]). However, the items mentioned in the warrant should be described with sufficient specificity that a reasonable officer would know where to look for them.

*Maryland v. Garrison (480 U.S. 79 [1987])*

In situations where the warrant incorrectly specifies the place to be searched, the courts may still find the warrant to be valid if the officer's error was reasonable. For example, in *Maryland v. Garrison*, 480 U.S. 79 (1987), police officers obtained a warrant to search the person of Lawrence McWebb and the premises known as "2036 Park Avenue, third-floor apartment." They believed that McWebb's apartment occupied the entire third floor when, in fact, there were two apartments on that floor—one of which belonged to another person named Garrison. Nevertheless, the Court held that the warrant was valid because it was based on information by a trusted informant, and the police had inquired with the local utility company and were given the impression that there was only one apartment on the third floor.

The warrant must also clearly specify what the police wish to seize. The case of *Lo-Ji Sales, Inc. v. New York* provides a clear example of this requirement. The magistrate issued a warrant that named two specific items, but also permitted the police to seize anything the magistrate considered obscene. The Court unanimously held that the warrant failed to "particularly describe . . . the things to be seized."

*Andresen v. Maryland (427 U.S. 463, 479 [1976])*

Contrast *Lo-Ji Sales* with *Andresen v. Maryland*, 427 U.S. 463, 479 (1976), in which the Court upheld a warrant that authorized the seizure of several items "together with other fruits, instrumentalities and evidence of crime at this [time] known." The Court noted that the crime in question was particularly complex and "could be proved only by piecing together many bits of evidence." This was a controversial decision because it suggested that, under certain circumstances, the police can circumvent the Fourth Amendment's particularity requirement.

### THE FOURTH AMENDMENT'S PARTICULARITY REQUIREMENT

A police officer obtained a search warrant from a judge that authorized the seizure of "numerous marijuana plants and growing equipment" at 123 Main Street. Does this warrant comply with the Fourth Amendment's particularity requirement? What if the warrant also authorized the seizure of "stolen stereo equipment"?

Also, the fact that an item is not listed in a warrant does not mean that it cannot be seized. If the police only have a hunch that an item is in a place to be searched, but do not include the item in the application for a warrant, the item can be seized under the doctrine of "plain view," as long as the police are legally authorized (by obtaining a warrant) to be on the premises. *Plain view* is discussed in further detail in the next chapter. Also, if a warrant does not particularly describe the items to be seized (or the place to be searched), then it is not automatically deemed in violation of the Fourth Amendment. If there is an objectively reasonable basis for the officers' mistaken belief, then the warrant will most likely be upheld (see *Massachusetts v. Sheppard*, 468 U.S. 981 [1981]).

# ▶ Arrests with Warrants

As Justice Powell once stated, "A search may cause only an annoyance and temporary inconvenience to the law-abiding citizen, assuming more serious dimensions only when it turns up evidence of criminality [but an] arrest . . . is a serious personal intrusion regardless of whether the person seized is guilty or innocent" (*United States v. Watson*, 423 U.S. 411 [1976]). Yet an unconstitutional arrest has little significance by itself in criminal procedure. The reason for this is that the remedy for an illegal arrest is simply a release from custody. It is possible that a person unlawfully arrested may sue, but little recourse is generally available to a person who is unlawfully arrested. Why, then, focus attention on the constitutionality of arrests? The answer is that the constitutionality of an arrest is frequently critical in determining whether evidence seized in connection with the arrest is admissible in court.

Consider this example: Assume that a police officer arrests a defendant without probable cause. Such an arrest is automatically unconstitutional. Assume further that the officer finds an illegal firearm on the defendant and turns it over to the prosecutor, who decides to use it against the defendant at his trial on firearm charges. The defendant will almost certainly seek to have the firearm excluded as evidence on the grounds that it resulted from an unlawful arrest. In other words, the defendant will argue that the firearm is "fruit of the poisonous tree," as discussed in Chapter 2.

This hypothetical situation is the main reason it is important to study the law of arrest. It is not that the legality of an arrest matters by itself. What is important is that an unconstitutional arrest can lead to the exclusion of evidence. Virtually all arrest cases that make it to the Supreme Court have something in common: A convicted defendant is seeking to have his or her *arrest* declared unconstitutional so the evidence that led to his or her conviction will be suppressed and/or the conviction reversed.

## The Definition of *Arrest*

Criminal procedure can become confusing when terms like *seizure*, *stop*, and *arrest* are used without reference to their legal definitions. It is important to understand that these terms, as they are used in connection with the Fourth Amendment, have a very different meaning than how they are used in everyday language. **Stops** and **arrests** should be thought of as specific types of seizures. Additionally, each type of seizure can be placed along a scale of seriousness—an arrest is the most intrusive type of seizure, and a stop is the next most intrusive.

Another important distinction between a stop and an arrest is the level of justification required. Arrests require probable cause; stops only require reasonable suspicion. If the circumstances surrounding a stop are such that it evolves into an arrest, then the arrest will be declared unconstitutional and the evidence will be thrown out, assuming the officer did not have probable cause.

### Restricted Liberty of Movement and Beyond

At one time, the Supreme Court suggested that anything the police did to restrict a person's movement constituted an arrest. For example, in *Henry v. United States*, 361 U.S. 98 (1959), the Court found that an arrest occurred when the police stopped a car whose occupants were suspected of transporting illegal alcohol. According to the Court, "When the officers interrupted the two men and restricted their liberty of movement, the arrest, for purposes of this case, was complete." Since the police in *Henry* did not have probable cause to stop the men, the so-called arrest was deemed unconstitutional.

More recently, however, the Supreme Court has held that the police must do more than restrict a person's movement for an arrest to occur. In *Terry v. Ohio*, 392 U.S. 1 (1968), a key case in defining the meaning of "arrest," the Court ruled that a suspect's movements can be restricted without such activity being considered an arrest. The Court distinguished between arrests that "eventuate in a trip to the station house and prosecution for crime" and lesser intrusions that can occur "whenever a police officer accosts an individual and restrains his freedom to walk away."

## Distinguishing between a Stop and an Arrest

In some cases, distinguishing between an arrest and a lesser type of intrusion is easy. For example, when a suspect is handcuffed, placed in the back of a patrol car, and driven to the police station for booking, an arrest has clearly occurred. By contrast, if a person is confronted by a single police officer and asked general questions about his or her suspected involvement in a crime, an arrest has not occurred. However, there are many encounters between citizens and police that fall between these two extremes. A stop can develop into an arrest if the circumstances dictate. A seizure that is technically not a formal arrest may be so intrusive as to constitute a *de facto* arrest. In this situation, probable cause, rather than reasonable suspicion, would be required to make the encounter constitutional.

Generally, the courts will weigh (1) the duration of a stop and (2) the degree of the intrusion in assessing whether a stop evolved into an arrest. Sometimes, the courts also refer to the officers' intentions and the manner in which the stop took place. The importance of these issues—particularly, degree and duration—is evidenced by the Supreme Court's opinion in *Florida v. Royer*, 460 U.S. 491 (1983):

> The predicate permitting seizures on suspicion short of probable cause is that law enforcement interests warrant a limited intrusion on the personal security of the suspect. The scope of the intrusion permitted will vary to some extent with the particular facts and circumstances of each case. *This much, however, is clear: an investigative detention must be temporary and last no longer than is necessary to effectuate the purpose of the stop. Similarly, the investigative methods employed should be the least intrusive means reasonably available to verify or dispel the officer's suspicion in a short period of time.* (emphasis added)

Several additional Supreme Court cases help illustrate how a stop can be treated as an arrest. These cases can be placed in four categories: (1) cases involving detention in a stationhouse or similar structure, such as the investigation room in an airport; (2) cases involving an encounter between police and citizens on the street; (3) cases involving a border detention; and (4) cases involving detention in the home. Each category is briefly considered in the paragraphs that follow.

*Davis v. Mississippi*
*(394 U.S. 721 [1969])*

*Davis v. Mississippi*, 394 U.S. 721 (1969), is a leading example of a stationhouse detention. Several youths, including Davis, were taken into custody and fingerprinted as part of a rape investigation. The officers did not have probable cause to detain Davis, and he was held for two days and interrogated throughout his detention. On the basis of his fingerprints and confession, Davis was charged, convicted, and sentenced to death. The Supreme Court reversed Davis's conviction on the grounds that detention was too long, too intrusive, and unsupported by probable cause. The Court did not explicitly address the distinction between a stop and an arrest, but it intimated that because probable cause was required to detain Davis, the police officers had effectively arrested him.

In a similar case, *Dunaway v. New York*, 442 U.S. 200 (1979), police officers took a person into custody during the course of a robbery and murder investigation. They read him the

*Miranda* warnings and subjected him to questioning—without probable cause. The Supreme Court reversed the man's subsequent conviction. The Court did not expressly define "arrest," but it did declare that a custodial interrogation (questioning of a person while in custody), such as that in *Dunaway*, must be supported by probable cause. The Court further declared that *Terry* was inapplicable because it permits only a "limited violation of individual privacy" while ensuring "interests in both crime prevention and detection and in the police officer's safety."

Other forms of detention that are not a formal arrest may also require probable cause, rather than reasonable suspicion. In *Royer*, officers in an airport asked a man to accompany them into a room because he was suspected of carrying narcotics. The officers found drugs in the man's luggage, and he was arrested. The Court declared that the detention, which lasted 15 minutes, constituted an arrest, which required probable cause. As Justice White stated, "What had begun as a consensual inquiry in a public place had escalated into an investigatory procedure in a police interrogation room, where the police, unsatisfied with previous explanations, sought to confirm their suspicions" (*Royer*, 460 U.S. 491). What is important in this case, as well as the preceding two, was that the detention was not consensual. If a person consents to the detention, he or she is not considered under arrest.

It is important to note, also, that not all *nonconsensual* encounters between police and citizens amount to arrests. As will be addressed later, detentions at the national borders and in other locations are permissible under certain circumstances. In addition, there are situations in which the courts have declared that holding a person for investigative purposes may not rise to the level of an arrest, and therefore not require probable cause. For example, even though the Court reversed a defendant's conviction in *Davis v. Mississippi*, it did state that "because of the unique nature of the fingerprinting process, [detentions for the purpose of obtaining fingerprints] might, under narrowly defined circumstances, be found to comply with the Fourth Amendment even though there is no probable cause in the traditional sense" (*Davis*, 394 U.S. 721).

There are also situations in which encounters on the street (as opposed to questioning in a stationhouse or its equivalent) can evolve into arrests. In *Terry*, the Supreme Court noted that a stop must be *brief*, suggesting that any stop that is not brief may require probable cause. While the Supreme Court has been hesitant to put a precise time limit on the length of a stop, it has stated that the purposes of law enforcement should be taken into account. As the Court noted in *United States v. Sharpe*, 470 U.S. 675 (1985):

> While it is clear that "the brevity of the invasion of the individual's Fourth Amendment interests is an important factor in determining whether the seizure is so minimally intrusive as to be justifiable on reasonable suspicion," we have emphasized the need to consider the law enforcement purposes to be served by the stop as well as the time reasonably needed to effectuate these purposes. . . . Much as a "bright line" rule would be desirable in evaluating whether an investigative detention is unreasonable, common sense and ordinary human experience must govern over rigid criteria.

A handful of cases have involved detentions in the home, focusing, in particular, on the extent to which detention of a person (such as an owner, renter, or guest) in a home can develop into a full-blown arrest. Somewhat surprisingly, nonconsensual encounters in the home between residents and the police do not always rise to the level of an arrest. For example, in *Beckwith v. United States*, 425 U.S. 341 (1976), the Supreme Court ruled that questioning by Internal Revenue Service (IRS) agents of a defendant in his living room was not an arrest or even custodial in nature. Contrast this decision with that of *Rawlings v. Kentucky*, 448 U.S. 98 (1980), in which several individuals were detained at a house where officers had served an arrest warrant but had failed to find the person named in the warrant. The Court declared that this type of detention amounted to an arrest because there was no probable cause to detain the individuals not named in the warrant. In addition, the detention lasted 45 minutes, which was unnecessarily long, under the circumstances (though not as long as some detentions that the Supreme Court has upheld).

## WHAT TYPE OF SEIZURE?

A recent investigation of a burglary and rape led police to a particular suspect who was also responsible for another incident of burglary and rape. Without a warrant and without probable cause, the police went to the suspect's home to obtain fingerprints. Arriving at the home, the police spoke to the suspect on his front porch, and when he expressed reluctance to accompany them to the stationhouse, one officer said that they would arrest him. The suspect then replied that he would rather go to the station than be arrested. He was then taken to the station and fingerprinted. Does the police action constitute an arrest?

The Supreme Court seemed to backpedal on the *Rawlings* decision in *Michigan v. Summers*, 452 U.S. 692 (1981), decided a year later. In *Summers*, the Court held that an individual *can* be detained during a search of his or her house, without such activity rising to the level of an arrest, as long as the police have a search warrant and even if there is no probable cause to arrest him or her. In support, the Court noted that (1) such detentions are not as embarrassing or stigmatizing as public detentions and (2) when there is probable cause to search for evidence of criminal activity, it is reasonable to assume that the person who lives on the premises is involved. See Figure 4.3 for a summary of this discussion.

### Distinguishing between a Stop and a Nonstop

As emphasized above, it is important to distinguish not just between a stop and an arrest but between a stop and a **nonstop**. A stop occurs when a reasonable person *would not* believe that he or she is free to leave. A nonstop occurs when a reasonable person *would* believe that he or she is free to leave. A nonstop requires no justification at all because it is not considered a seizure within the meaning of the Fourth Amendment. As will be discussed in Chapter 6, police officers are free to confront people and ask questions of them, as long as the people are free to leave. However, reasonable suspicion is required to "stop" a person. Probable cause is required to justify an arrest.

All four of these criteria should be considered together. For example, if a police/citizen encounter occurs at the stationhouse, the encounter may not be considered an arrest. However, if the encounter is overly lengthy and the citizen is not free to leave, then an arrest has taken place.

1. Purpose
   a. Intent to arrest = Arrest
   b. No intent to arrest = *Terry* stop or nonstop
2. Manner
   a. Person not free to leave = Arrest or *Terry* stop
   b. Person free to leave = Nonstop
3. Location
   a. At police station or in private = Arrest or *Terry* stop
   b. Public = Arrest, *Terry* stop, or nonstop
4. Duration
   a. Lengthy = Arrest
   b. Short = *Terry* stop or nonstop

**FIGURE 4.3 Factors Used to Distinguish between a Stop and an Arrest**

## Summary: Distinguishing between Arrests, Stops, and Nonstops

Distinguishing between arrests and lesser intrusions, such as investigative stops, can be confusing. At one extreme, a seizure that is accompanied by handcuffs, or words to the effect that the person is "under arrest," is always considered an arrest. At the other extreme, when a person is confronted by a police officer and is not free to leave, but nevertheless briefly detained and not interrogated, an arrest has not occurred. Where the distinction is confusing is in the gray area between a stop and an arrest. A stop can evolve into a *de facto* arrest in a number of circumstances. The courts will give weight to four factors in making their decision: (1) the purpose of the stop (such as to question or interrogate a person); (2) the manner in which the stop takes place (such as whether the person was stopped by one officer or several); (3) the location in which the stop takes place (such as stationhouse, street, or home); and (4) the duration of the stop. No single factor is necessarily determinative. If, however, a person is detained by several officers in a stationhouse for several days so as to be interrogated, then the courts will almost certainly consider such police activity tantamount to an arrest.

Although this text has endeavored to provide guidance in defining an *arrest*, in fact, no clear definition really exists in the case law. The courts will weigh each case individually based on a number of factors it has identified in its decisions. However, when the police take a person into custody with the intent of making a formal arrest, it is usually clear that an arrest has been made.

# When Is an Arrest Warrant Required?

At one time, the case law held that if an arresting officer had probable cause to believe that (1) a person was committing or had committed a felony or (2) a person was committing a certain misdemeanor in the officer's presence, then an arrest warrant was not required. This held true regardless of where the arrest took place, even if it was effected in someone's private home. The only real situation in which an arrest warrant *was* required was for a misdemeanor committed out of view of the arresting officer. The logic for this was set forth by the Supreme Court in *Carroll v. United States*, 267 U.S. 132 (1925):

> The reason for arrest for misdemeanors without warrant at common law was to promptly suppress breaches of the peace . . . while the reason for arrest without a warrant on a reliable report of a felony was because the public safety and the due apprehension of criminals charged with heinous offenses required that such arrests should be made at once without warrant.

Since 1925, the Supreme Court has adhered to the rule set forth in *Carroll*, subject to two exceptions. First, an arrest in someone's private home cannot be made without a warrant, unless exigent circumstances are present. Second, an arrest in the home of a third party is impermissible without a warrant, again providing no exigent circumstances are in place. An example of a third-party situation is one in which the police seek to arrest a person who is visiting a friend's house. One additional restriction was recognized in *Gerstein v. Pugh*, 420 U.S. 103 (1975)—namely, a judicial determination of probable cause is required when an arrest is made without a warrant. With rare exceptions, an arrest warrant is only required in two situations: (1) arrests in the home and (2) arrests in third-party homes.

## Arrests in the Home

In the landmark decision of *Payton v. New York*, 445 U.S. 573 (1980), the Supreme Court held that the Fourth Amendment prohibits a warrantless, nonconsensual entry into a private home for the purpose of making an arrest. In that case, police officers, after two days of investigation, had assembled enough evidence to establish probable cause to believe that Payton had murdered the manager of a gas station. The officers went to Payton's apartment to arrest him. When no one answered the door, they used a crowbar to open the door and enter the apartment. They did not find Payton, but they did find, in plain view, a .30 caliber shell casing lying on the floor. They seized it and admitted it into evidence at Payton's trial. Payton ultimately surrendered to the police and was indicted for murder. The lower court

*Payton v. New York*
*(445 U.S. 573 [1980])*

admitted the shell casing into evidence, but the Supreme Court reversed, stating, "In terms that apply equally to seizures of property and to seizures of persons, the Fourth Amendment has drawn a firm line at the entrance to the house. Absent exigent circumstances, that threshold may not reasonably be crossed without a warrant." Justice Stevens also stated that "physical entry of the home is the chief evil against which the wording of the Fourth Amendment is directed." In *Payton*, then, the Court established a bright-line rule: an arrest in the home must be accompanied by a warrant in the absence of exigent circumstances.

### Arrests in Third-Party Homes

*Steagald v. United States*
*(451 U.S. 204 [1981])*

Not long after *Payton*, the Supreme Court decided *Steagald v. United States*, 451 U.S. 204 (1981). Justice Marshall expressed concern that although an arrest warrant may protect a person "from an unreasonable seizure, it [does] absolutely nothing to protect [a third party's] privacy interest in being free from an unreasonable invasion and search of his home." Accordingly, the Court decided that in such situations, the police must obtain not only an arrest warrant for the person they seek but also a *separate* warrant to search the third-party residence for the arrestee.

The facts in *Steagald* were as follows: Acting on an arrest warrant issued for a person by the name of Lyons, Drug Enforcement Administration (DEA) agents entered the home of Steagald. This entry was made without a warrant. While searching Steagald's home for Lyons, the agents found cocaine and other incriminating evidence, but they did not find Lyons. Steagald was arrested and convicted on federal drug charges. He appealed, and the Supreme Court eventually reversed Steagald's conviction. The Court offered the following in support of its position:

> Two distinct interests were implicated by the search in this case—Ricky Lyons' interest in being free from an unreasonable seizure and petitioner's [Steagald's] interest in being free from an unreasonable search of his home. Because the arrest warrant for Lyons addressed only the former interest, the search of petitioner's home was no more reasonable from petitioner's perspective that it would have been if conducted in the absence of any warrant.

The Court's decision in *Steagald* was not without opposition. Justices Rehnquist and White dissented, arguing that the police and judges "will, in their various capacities, have to weigh the time during which a suspect for whom there is an outstanding arrest warrant has been in the building, whether the dwelling is the suspect's home, how long he has lived there, whether he is likely to leave immediately, and a number of related and equally imponderable questions." The majority countered by pointing out that if the police did not need warrants to enter third-party residences, "[a]rmed solely with an arrest warrant for a single person, [the police] . . . could search all the homes of that individual's friends and acquaintances."

---

**DECISION-MAKING EXERCISE 4.4**

### A PUBLIC OR PRIVATE ARREST?

Federal drug agents had probable cause to arrest John Crook. They knew he was staying at the local motel, but they did not know what room he was in. The agents asked hotel personnel to supply the room number, which they did, and then the agents went to that room. Standing in the hall, one of the agents identified himself to a housekeeping employee and asked him to knock on the door of the room and check whether anyone was in it. The employee knocked and called out, "Housekeeping." Crook opened the door. The agents recognized him immediately, at which point one of the agents drew his weapon, pointed it at Crook, and ordered him to raise his hands. Crook immediately raised his hands and said to the agents, "I won't give you guys any trouble. I've got a gun in my right pocket." Both agents, with their weapons drawn, entered the room. Crook's gun was removed, and he was advised that he was under arrest. Was a warrant required in this situation? Or, in other words, could this be considered a public arrest? Note that based on the facts supplied, there are no exigent circumstances in place.

1. When an arrest warrant is required:
   a. In a home/residence absent exigent circumstances
   b. In a third-party home; a separate search warrant is also required
2. When an arrest warrant is not required:
   a. The arrest is made in public (see Chapter 5)
   b. Exigent circumstances exist (see Chapter 5)
   c. Consent is given (see Chapter 7)

**FIGURE 4.4 Summary of Arrest Warrant Requirements**

Simply put, having an arrest warrant does *not* allow authorities to enter a third-party residence. A warrantless entry into a third-party residence violates the third party's rights. There are two exceptions to this rule, however. First, if the third party consents to a request by police, a search warrant won't be necessary (but the arrest warrant will still be necessary). Second, if there is an emergency, or "exigent circumstances," a warrant may not be required. See Figure 4.4 for a summary of situations in which an arrest warrant is required/not required.

# Executing an Arrest Warrant

Assuming a valid warrant is in place, the police cannot use any means available to effect the arrest. For example, they cannot kick in a door without having any reason to do so. Similarly, they cannot use deadly force unless absolutely necessary, and for the most dangerous of criminal offenders. In almost all cases, the procedures for executing an arrest warrant are laid out in police department policy manuals.

There are four important issues to be considered with regard to the service of arrest warrants:

- when the police are required to "knock and announce" their presence,
- whether property damage is acceptable,
- when deadly force can be used, and
- the consequences of arresting the wrong person.

## The "Knock-and-Announce" Rule

Under common law, the police were entitled to break into a house to make an arrest after announcing their presence and their reason for being there. Today, the method of entry the police can use to serve warrants (either arrest or search warrants) is usually set forth in legislation. With regard to federal law enforcement, for example, 18 U.S.C. Section 3109 states that an officer "may break open any outer or inner door or window of a house . . . to execute a search warrant, if, after notice of his authority and purpose, he is refused admittance."

The law also generally requires that police officers announce their presence and state their authority (such as, "Police officers! Search warrant!"). Doing so is important for several reasons: (1) it helps avoid needless destruction of property; (2) it helps prevent violence resulting from unnecessary surprise; and (3) it helps preserve people's dignity and privacy. However, in certain situations, the "knock-and-announce" requirement does not serve its intended purposes. In fact, regarding the second reason, the requirement can have the opposite effect than intended. If the police announce their presence in some situations, such an announcement could *result* in violence, rather than reduce the possibility of it. Because of this and other issues, the Supreme Court has established criteria for determining when "knock-and-announce" is not required.

The first case in which the Court addressed the constitutionality of the common-law knock-and-announce rule was *Wilson v. Arkansas*, 514 U.S. 927 (1995). In that case, Wilson had conducted several narcotics transactions with an informant over a period of several months. Based on the informant's information about those transactions, police officers obtained an arrest warrant for Wilson as well as a search warrant for her home. When the officers arrived at Wilson's residence, they identified themselves and declared that they had a warrant *as they entered the home through an unlocked door*. They did not knock and wait for an answer. In addition to finding evidence, the officers found Wilson in the bathroom, flushing marijuana down the toilet. At her trial, Wilson moved to suppress the evidence collected by the officers on the grounds that the search was invalid because the officers did not follow the common-law knock-and-announce rule before entering her home to serve the warrants. The Supreme Court ruled that the officers *were* required to follow the knock-and-announce rule: "An examination of the common law of search and seizure . . . leaves no doubt that the reasonableness of a search of a dwelling may depend in part on whether law enforcement officers announce their presence and authority prior to entering."

The Supreme Court later clarified its position in the case of *Richards v. Wisconsin*, 520 U.S. 385 (1997), holding that police can dispense with the knock-and-announce rule if they have *reasonable suspicion* that such a requirement "would be dangerous or futile, or that it would inhibit the effective investigation of the crime by, for example, allowing the destruction of evidence." In other words, if the police have reasonable suspicion to believe that exigent circumstances are present, they do not necessarily have to knock on the door and announce their presence.

It is critical that when an announcement is required, police officers announce their authority *and* their intentions. This came to light in *Miller v. United States*, 357 U.S. 301 (1958). In that case, police officers arrived at Miller's apartment at 3:45 a.m. without a warrant but for the purpose of arresting Miller. One of the officers knocked on Miller's door. When Miller asked who it was, the officers did nothing more than answer "Police." Miller then opened the door slightly, as it was secured by a chain, and inquired as to the officers' intentions. At that point, Miller attempted to close the door, but one of the officers reached through the opening and disconnected the chain. The officers then entered the apartment and arrested Miller. The Supreme Court ultimately reversed Miller's conviction on the grounds that the officers never adequately announced their intention to arrest Miller.

In some circumstances, police are required to wait for a period of time between knocking and announcing, and entering the premises. In *United States v. Banks*, 540 U.S. 31 (2003), the Supreme Court considered how long the police should wait after announcing their presence and intentions. The police had served a warrant by first knocking on the door and then calling out "Police, search warrant." They waited 15–20 seconds and, after getting no response, broke down the door with a battering ram. The Supreme Court upheld this action, arguing that the 15–20-second wait—coupled with the announcement—was sufficient. The Court did *not*, however, require that police always wait 15–20 seconds before entering.

*Hudson v. Michigan*
*(547 U.S. 586 [2006])*

Most recently, in *Hudson v. Michigan*, 547 U.S. 586 (2006), the Supreme Court decided that a violation of the knock-and-announce rule need not lead to exclusion of evidence. In that case, officers had a search warrant but failed to follow the knock-and-announce rule. Evidence was seized and a trial court judge ruled that it could not be used. A Michigan appeals court reversed and the Supreme Court affirmed. In a 5 to 4 decision, the Court held that evidence need not be excluded simply because the police violated the knock-and-announce rule. In support of its decision, the Court summarized the basic purposes of the knock-and-announce rule:

> The interests protected by the knock-and-announce rule include human life and limb (because an unannounced entry may provoke violence from a surprised resident), property (because citizens presumably would open the door upon an announcement, whereas a forcible entry may destroy it), and privacy and dignity of the sort that can be offended by a sudden entrance. But the rule has never protected one's interest in preventing the government from seeing or taking evidence described in a warrant. Since the interests violated here have nothing to do with the seizure of the evidence, the exclusionary rule is inapplicable.

## Property Damage

*Sabbath v. United States*
*(391 U.S. 585 [1968])*

In *Sabbath v. United States*, 391 U.S. 585 (1968), the Supreme Court focused on the extent to which police officers can *break and enter* for the purpose of serving a warrant. In

## SERVING A SEARCH WARRANT IN A THIRD-PARTY RESIDENCE

Sue Lyons leases an apartment and lives by herself. However, when she found out that her old boyfriend, Fred Taber, had been on the run from authorities for several months, she offered to let him stay at her apartment. She gave him a key so he could come and go at will. After eight weeks, during which time Fred continued to live with Sue, the police were alerted as to his presence by a vigilant neighbor. Officers then entered Sue's apartment without a warrant and arrested Fred. Will the arrest hold up?

particular, the Court focused on the part of 18 U.S.C. Section 3109 that permits officers to "break open an outer door or window." In *Sabbath*, police officers enlisted the help of a man named Jones, whom they had caught trying to smuggle drugs into the country, to apprehend Sabbath, the man who was to receive the shipment of drugs. Jones agreed to deliver the drugs to Sabbath while the police looked on. After Jones entered the apartment, the officers knocked on the door. Not hearing a response, the officers opened the unlocked door, entered the apartment with guns drawn, and arrested Sabbath. The court of appeals affirmed Sabbath's conviction on the grounds that because the officers did not enter by force, the knock-and-announce rule of Section 3109 was not triggered.

The Supreme Court disagreed with this reasoning, however, and reversed Sabbath's conviction. According to the Court, "An unannounced intrusion into a dwelling—what Section 3109 basically proscribes—is no less an unannounced intrusion whether officers break down a door, force open a chain lock on a partially open door, open a locked door by use of a passkey, or, as here, open a closed but unlocked door." This case seems to suggest that whether physical damage inflicted to the premises is immaterial. Instead, what is important is merely that officers knock and announce their presence.

In cases in which physical damage to the premises *is* significant or excessive, the Fourteenth Amendment's due process clause enters in because it protects citizens from arbitrary government action. If property damage "shocks the conscience," then the police may be liable under the due process clause to reimburse owners for their damaged property. There is no easy way to define what conduct "shocks the conscience." At least one case has suggested that when police officers show "deliberate or reckless indifference," their conduct can be seen as conscience shocking (see *Estelle v. Gamble*, 429 U.S. 97 [1976]).

## Permissible Degree of Force

Although it is accepted that police must often use force to arrest suspects, there are limits on the level of force that may be used against people who are the targets of arrest warrants. Almost every state has a law or regulation concerning police use of force. The American Law Institute adopted just one such regulation, which resembles many others in place around the United States. Section 120.7 states that a police officer "may use such force as is reasonably necessary to effect the arrest, to enter premises to effect the arrest, or to prevent the escape from custody of an arrested person." Further, **deadly force** is authorized when the crime in question is a felony and when such force "creates no substantial risk to innocent persons," and the officer reasonably believes that there is a substantial risk that the fleeing felon will inflict harm on other people or police officers.

In *Tennessee v. Garner*, 471 U.S. 1 (1985)—which involved the shooting death of a young, unarmed, fleeing felon—the Supreme Court adopted a rule similar to the American Law Institute's formulation. The result was the leading Supreme Court precedent concerning the use of deadly force to apprehend fleeing felons. The *Garner* decision declared unconstitutional a Tennessee statute that authorized police officers who give notice of the intent to arrest to "use all the necessary means to effect the arrest" if the suspect flees or resists.

*Tennessee v. Garner*
*(471 U.S. 1 [1985])*

## A PROPERLY SERVED ARREST WARRANT?

DEA agents and county police officers executed a search warrant at a drug dealer's house. In executing the warrant, the agents and officers gathered on the back porch of the house, knocked on the back door, yelled "Police, arrest warrant!" several times, and then broke down the door. During the search that followed, the officers seized a fully loaded revolver, 150 vials of cocaine, and cash in excess of $27,000. Did this action comport with the federal knock-and-announce rule enunciated in 18 U.S.C. Section 3109, which states that officers "may break open any outer or inner door or window of a house . . . to execute a search warrant, if, after notice of his authority and purpose, he is refused admittance"?

The Court ruled that deadly force may be used when (1) it is necessary to prevent the suspect's escape and (2) the officer has probable cause to believe the suspect poses a serious threat of death or causes serious physical injury to other people or police officers. Somewhat surprisingly, three justices dissented, noting that the statute struck down by the majority "assist[s] the police in apprehending suspected perpetrators of serious crimes and provide[s] notice that a lawful police order to stop and submit to arrest may not be ignored with impunity."

*Graham v. Connor*
*(490 U.S. 386 [1989])*

Four years after *Garner*, the Supreme Court decided the landmark case of *Graham v. Connor*, 490 U.S. 386 (1989), which set the standard for **nondeadly force**. The Court declared emphatically that *all* claims involving allegations of excessive force against police officers must be analyzed under the Fourth Amendment's reasonableness requirement. Further, the Court adopted a test of objective reasonableness to decide when excessive force is used. This requires focusing on what a *reasonable* police officer would do "without regard to [the officer's] underlying intent or motivation." In determining what a reasonable police officer would do, the Court looked to three factors: (1) the severity of the crime; (2) whether the suspect posed a threat; and (3) whether the suspect was resisting and/or attempting to flee the scene. Courts must, in focusing on these three factors, allow "for the fact that police officers are often forced to make split-second judgments—about the amount of force that is necessary in a particular situation." Generally, then, if the crime in question is a serious one and the suspect is dangerous and resists arrest, then he or she will have difficulty succeeding with an excessive force claim.

Incidentally, both the *Garner* and *Graham* decisions resulted from Section 1983 lawsuits. Garner's surviving family members and Graham himself both sued on the grounds that their constitutional rights were violated. Whereas many of the cases examined in this book focus on the evidence of crimes (e.g., weapons, drugs, confessions), *Garner* and *Graham* do not. How evidence was obtained was not at issue because there was none. Thus, the only remedy available to Garner's family and Graham was *civil litigation*.

*Garner* and *Graham* set very minimum standards under the constitution, but local laws have set more restrictive rules. States, cities, and counties around the country have adopted more restrictive guidelines for their officers concerning the use of force. To illustrate, portions of the San Bernardino, California, Police Department's use of force policy are reprinted in Figure 4.5.

### Arresting the Wrong Person

On occasion, the police mistakenly arrest someone other than the person intended by the warrant. Although the person is eventually released, the arrest sometimes leads to evidence that may be relevant to a criminal case. This leads to the issue of whether the evidence resulting from the wrongful arrest will be admissible at trial. An example of such a situation would be one in which the police serve an arrest warrant at the wrong house and, during the course of arresting the wrong person, discover evidence of another crime. To what extent would such evidence be admissible? Ultimately, it will often depend on the reasonableness of the police action.

STANDARD OPERATING PROCEDURE     CHAPTER #35     PROCEDURE #1
USE OF FORCE     Revised     12-22-04

PURPOSE

To provide guidelines and parameters for police personnel concerning their use of force to accomplish their lawful duties and objectives.

POLICY

Police personnel have the legal authority to use the appropriate amount of force to protect themselves and the public from assaultive criminal behavior. However, the amount of force used must be both necessary and reasonable. Personnel shall use only that amount of force that reasonably appears necessary based upon articulable facts and the totality of circumstances known to the officer at the time of the event. Personnel should choose the appropriate force response to overcome active resistance or aggressive behavior. Therefore, personnel should be reasonable in their actions and demonstrate common sense when employing force.

The primary objective in the application of force is to ensure control of resistant or combative suspect(s) with the minimal amount of force necessary. No specific guidelines or policies can apply to all situations; therefore, personnel should constantly evaluate all use of force applications or options. The use of force will either escalate or de-escalate based upon the totality of circumstances during the course of an arrest or detention.

This policy will also include the use of force on combative subject(s) who do not rise to the level of being criminal suspects, such as W&I 5150.

The scale of force options in order of increasing severity are: verbal persuasion, compliance control techniques, intermediate force (chemical agents, lateral vascular neck restraint, or electronic disabling devices), and impact weapons. It is not necessary for personnel to exercise each option before escalating to the next level of force but flexibility is essential to maintain control during the dynamics of a physical confrontation.

When choosing a particular force option, these factors should be taken into consideration:

1. The severity of the crime(s) involved or subjected.
2. The conduct/behavior of the suspect(s).
3. Whether the suspect(s) poses an immediate threat to the officer(s) or others.
4. Whether the suspect(s) has, used, or displayed a weapon.
5. The proximity of weapons.
6. Officer/suspect factors (age, physical size, relative strength, skill level, injury/exhaustion, number of officer(s) versus number of suspect(s)).
7. Influence of drugs or alcohol.
8. Potential for injury to bystanders.
9. Availability of other options.
10. Other exigent circumstances.

PROCEDURE

Personnel shall only possess that equipment authorized or issued by the department. Only those defensive tactics or arrest control techniques authorized by or instructed by department personnel or other authorized persons are permitted excluding exigent circumstances. The level of force utilized should be that level which would quickly, safely, and humanely bring resisting subject under physical control. Personnel should employ escalating scale of force options in order of increasing severity to overcome the suspect(s) resistance.

1. Scale of Force

   A. Persuasion
      The presence of a confident uniformed police officer displaying professional demeanor coupled with good verbal communication will generally convince

**FIGURE 4.5 Use of Force Policy (San Bernardino, CA, Police Department)**

a resistant subject to submit to your authority without the necessity of an escalation in force. Good verbalization may be advising, admonishing, warning, or persuading a subject to submit to your authority without the use of profanity or derogatory language. Officers should use their verbal techniques to de-escalate confrontations.

**B.** Compliance Control Techniques

Compliance techniques consist of the physical application of force in the form of joint manipulations, blocks, pain compliance, and takedowns. These empty handed techniques should be coupled with a police officer's verbal commands.

**C.** Intermediate Force

**1.** *Chemical Agents*

Police personnel may use chemical agents as an intermediate level of force for controlling or subduing combative persons. Chemical agents are defensive control weapons used to control or subdue subjects who are physically resisting arrest. Chemical agents should not be used indiscriminately and shall not be used against non-combative persons. It should not be used against a subject who is under restraint unless that subject is physically assaulting officers or others.

**2.** *Lateral Vascular Neck Restraint*

The lateral vascular neck restraint (LVNR) is a means of subduing physically combative persons. This technique is a method which permits personnel to apprehend violent subjects who cannot be controlled or restrained with compliance or control holds.

**3.** *Taser*

The electronic disabling device (taser) is a device, which may be used to subdue physically combative person/s in violent or potentially violent situations lessening the injury to the subject/s or officers involved. The taser may be used if other apprehension methods or restraints have failed or are deemed impractical and there is a reasonable expectation that it would be hazardous for personnel to approach and physically contact the subject/s.

**D.** Impact Weapons

Impact weapons are methods of subduing physically combative persons or immediately impeding the threatening actions of a violently resistant subject with physical strikes to the subject's body. These physical strikes shall be directed to those areas which are easily accessible, effective for quickly subduing the subject/s, and unlikely to cause serious injury. Other self defense techniques, kicks or arm strikes, can be used if the officer's baton is unavailable. Other authorized police equipment may be used as an impact weapon in exigent circumstances.

*Source:* Chapter 35, Procedure I, "Use of Force," from *Standard Operating Procedure*, San Bernardino, California, Police Department (rev. December 22, 2004). Reprinted with permission.

**FIGURE 4.5** *(continued)*

In *Hill v. California*, 401 U.S. 797 (1971), the police arrived at Hill's apartment to arrest him, but Miller answered the door. Since Miller fit Hill's description, the police arrested Miller. Although Miller provided identification to prove that he was not Hill, the Court dismissed this fact, stating that "aliases and false identifications are not uncommon." A pistol and ammunition clip were in plain view. These were admitted into evidence, and the Supreme Court focused on their admissibility. The Court ruled that the police could have reasonably believed that Miller was Hill. Furthermore, the Court pointed out that "sufficient probability, not certainty, is the touchstone of reasonableness under the Fourth Amendment and on the record before us the officers' mistake was understandable and the arrest a reasonable response to the situation facing them at the time."

**DEADLY FORCE BEYOND PRESENT DANGEROUSNESS**

*Garner* seems to be concerned with *present dangerousness*. That is, police officers contemplating the use of deadly force have to consider, among other factors, how dangerous the suspect is before resorting to deadly force. But what if the suspect committed the crime days or even months earlier? Can the police use deadly force to apprehend, say, an unarmed, fleeing individual who is the suspect in a weeks-old robbery?

# ► Searches with Warrants

Searches with warrants are subjected to many of the same restrictions as arrests with warrants. However, because the purpose of obtaining a search warrant is to search for things, as opposed to seizing a person, the courts have placed significant restrictions on what the police can do when searching for evidence with warrants. The fact that a warrant has been obtained does not mean that the police can look anywhere and take unlimited time to search for the items named in the warrant.

## Executing a Search Warrant

The knock-and-announce rule discussed earlier carries over to the service of search warrants. As indicated before, the police do not have to announce their presence if they have reasonable suspicion that exigent circumstances are present. Moreover, even if police do not "knock and announce," the evidence seized cannot be excluded for that reason, as held in *Hudson* (547 U.S. 586).

Use of force is rarely an issue during the service of a search warrant because, strictly speaking, a search warrant only authorizes the police to look for evidence. However, if a person gets in the way during the service of a search warrant, he or she may be arrested and force may be applied, if necessary (subject to the restrictions discussed earlier).

If the police mistakenly search the wrong residence, the search will not automatically be declared invalid. As pointed out earlier, as long as the mistake is a reasonable one, any evidence seized during a search of the wrong residence may be admissible in a criminal trial, subject to the rules of evidence or other procedural rules. The key, however, is that the mistake must be an *objectively reasonable* one, gauged from the standpoint of a reasonable officer.

Four other issues are relevant to the service of a search warrant. These do not necessarily apply in the case of arrest warrants. They are: (1) time restrictions, both for when the warrant can be served and for how long the police can look for evidence; (2) the scope and manner of the search; (3) the procedure after the service of the search warrant; and (4) the presence of the media during the service of a search warrant. To illustrate the complexity inherent in search warrant procedure, portions of the Portland (Oregon) Police Bureau's search warrant policy are reprinted in Figure 4.6.

It is important to note that the police can sometimes request a search warrant with special instructions, which can include night service, no-knock authorization, and the like. An example of the face sheet for a special instructions warrant from the state of California is reprinted in Figure 4.7.

### Time Constraints

There are three restrictions imposed on the police regarding the timing of search warrants. First, the service of a search warrant should take place promptly after its issuance. The probable cause that formed the basis for the warrant could dissipate if an excessive amount of time elapses between the time the warrant is issued and the time it is served. To avoid

**Execution of the Warrant (652.00)**

a. Only a police officer may serve a search warrant. Generally, execution of a search warrant is restricted to between 0700 and 2200 hours unless it is otherwise endorsed on the warrant by the issuing magistrate.

b. A warrant is generally valid for five days after the date of its issuance. If the warrant is not executed within this period, it is void. A new affidavit must be filed and new search warrant issued. The issuing magistrate may, however, authorize execution of the warrant for up to ten days after its issuance. This authorization must be specified on the face of the warrant. Before entering any premises, the executing member will knock and give appropriate notice of identity, authority and purpose to the person to be searched or to the person in apparent control of the premises to be searched. If the member is not admitted after such notification, force may be used to enter the premises. In emergency situations, a no-knock entry may be performed (e.g., where members or others are at risk of bodily harm or where evidence may be destroyed). If such entry occurs, the circumstances leading to the entry will be clearly articulated in the incident report form. If it is determined that no one is at the residence, members have the authority to forcibly enter (see DIR 631.60). Before undertaking any search or seizure pursuant to the warrant, the executing member will:

   1. Read and give a copy of the warrant (not the affidavit) to the person to be searched, or to the person in apparent control of the premises to be searched.

   2. Affix a copy of the warrant to the premises if the premises are unoccupied, or there is no one in apparent control.

c. In the course of executing a search warrant, the member may take reasonable precautions to ensure that property will not be removed while the search is being conducted and to prevent interference with the search. Members have the same power and authority in all respects to break open any door or window and to use all necessary and proper means to overcome any forcible resistance as they do in executing or serving a warrant of arrest. In securing the premises to be searched, the member may seek out all persons on the premises and bring them to a central location for observation during the search.

d. Members of the media will not be allowed to enter private property without the consent of the property owner or individual in charge of the involved property.

*Source:* Portland Police Bureau, *Manual of Policy and Procedure* (January 2007). Reprinted with permission of the Portland Police Bureau.

**FIGURE 4.6 Search Warrant Policy (Portland, OR, Police Bureau)**

this potential problem, a warrant will sometimes specify that the search be conducted within a certain period of time.

A second time restriction that is occasionally imposed pertains to the time of day. Judges commonly restrict the service of warrants to the daytime hours, or at least favor daytime service. The *Federal Rules of Criminal Procedure*, for example, restrict the service of warrants to daytime hours, unless the issuing judge specifically authorizes execution at another time. *Daytime hours*, according to the *Federal Rules*, are between the hours of 6:00 A.M. and 10:00 P.M.

The third time restriction concerns how long the police can search for evidence. The general rule is that a search cannot last indefinitely. Once the item in the warrant has been discovered, the search must be terminated. If the police have difficulty finding the item or items named in the warrant, they can take as long as necessary to find them. If the police do not succeed in finding the evidence named in the warrant, leave the location, and then come back later, they will be required to obtain another warrant. Steps should always be taken to avoid the appearance of arbitrariness, and people's Fourth Amendment privacy interests should always be respected.

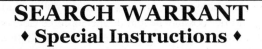

## SUPERIOR COURT OF CALIFORNIA
### County of _____

### SEARCH WARRANT
### ◆ Special Instructions ◆

**THE PEOPLE OF THE STATE OF CALIFORNIA to:**          **Warrant No.** _____

**Any peace officer in** _____ **County**

The affidavit filed herewith by _____, sworn to and subscribed before me, has established probable cause for this warrant which you are ordered to execute as follows:

    **Place(s) to be searched:** Described in Exhibit 1A, *attached* hereto and incorporated by reference.

    **Property to be seized:** Described in Exhibit 1B, attached hereto and incorporated by reference.

    **Disposition of property:** All property seized pursuant to this search warrant shall be retained in the affiant's custody pending further court order pursuant to Penal Code §§ 1528(a), 1536.

### ◆ SPECIAL INSTRUCTIONS ◆

The Statement of Probable Cause, filed herewith, has demonstrated legal justification for the following special procedures which are authorized if checked:

☐ **Night Service:** This warrant may be served at any hour of the day or night.

☐ **No Knock Authorization:** Compliance with Penal Code § 1531 is excused *unless* a change in circumstances negates the need for non-compliance.

☐ **Special Master:** The search shall be conducted by a Special Master pursuant to Penal Code §§ 1524(c)-(g). The Special Master shall be _____.

☐ **Sealing Order:** The following documents shall be sealed and delivered into the custody of the Clerk of the Superior Court pending further court order: ☐ All documents filed herewith. ☐ Documents listed in Exhibit 2. Grounds for sealing: ☐ Informant protection (Evid. Code § 1041) ☐ Official information (Evid. Code § 1040)

☐ **Nondisclosure Order:** The financial institution served with this warrant, including its employees and agents, shall not disclose any information regarding its content, existence, or execution pending further court order.

☐ **Blood draw:** (Not for HIV testing per Penal Code § 1524.1)**:** A blood sample shall be drawn from the person described in Exhibit 1A by trained medical personnel in accordance with accepted medical practices.

☐ **Anticipatory Warrant**: Having determined that probable cause for this search will exist upon the occurrence of the triggering event(s) described in Exhibit 3, and that there is probable cause said triggering event(s) will occur, this warrant shall be executed promptly after said triggering event(s) occur. Exhibit 3 is *attached* hereto and incorporated by reference.

☐ **Covert Warrant:** The property described in Exhibit 1B shall not be removed from the premises. An inventory shall be prepared showing the location of all such property discovered on the premises. Said property shall be photographed or videotaped to show its location when discovered. Compliance with the receipt requirements of Penal Code § 1535 is excused until _____ unless an extension is granted by this court. [Initial compliance date must not be more than 7 days following execution of the warrant.] Within two days after executing this warrant, the following shall be filed with this court: (1) the inventory, and (2) the original or copy of all photographs and/or videotape recordings made during the execution of this warrant.

☐ **Additional instructions:** Additional instructions pertaining to this search warrant are contained in Exhibit 4, *attached* hereto and incorporated by reference.

_____          _____
Date and time warrant issued          Judge of the Superior Court

*Source:* Reprinted with permission of the District Attorney's Office of Alameda County, California. Available online: http://le.alcoda.org/publications/files/sw_multi.pdf (accessed February 16, 2011).

**FIGURE 4.7 Example of a Special Instructions Warrant**

## Scope and Manner of the Search

Two additional restrictions with regard to the service of a search warrant concern the scope and manner of the search. *Scope* refers to where the police can look for evidence. *Manner* refers to the physical steps the police can take to find the evidence in question, including breaking down doors, forcibly opening locked cabinets, and other actions that could potentially damage property.

The scope of the search must be reasonable based on the object of the search. In other words, the police can only look where the item could reasonably be found. For example, assume the evidence in question is a stolen diamond ring. Such an item is relatively small, so the police will be authorized to look almost anywhere for the ring. However, if the evidence in question is large in size—for example, a big-screen television—then the police cannot look in small places, where such an item could not possibly be found. The Supreme Court's statement in *Harris v. United States*, 331 U.S. 145 (1947) provides further clarification: "[T]he same meticulous investigation which would be appropriate in a search for two small canceled checks could not be considered reasonable where agents are seeking a stolen automobile or an illegal still."

*Harris v. United States*
*(331 U.S. 145 [1947])*

The police may also detain people as needed while serving a search warrant. According to the Court in *Michigan v. Summers*, 452 U.S. 692 (1981), "[A] warrant to search for contraband founded on probable cause implicitly carries with it the limited authority to detain the occupants of the premises while a proper search is conducted." The law enforcement interests at stake in that decision were officer safety, assistance with completion of the search, and prevention of flight.

*Michigan v. Summers*
*(452 U.S. 692 [1981])*

This ruling was restricted by the 2013 decision in *Bailey v. United States* (No. 11-770). In that case, as officers were preparing to execute a warrant, two detectives surveilled the property searched. They noticed two men leave the property, get in a car, and drive away. The detectives followed the men, stopped the car, ordered the men out, patted them down, and found incriminating evidence. The Court held that *Summers* did not apply in this context: "The rule in *Summers* is limited to the immediate vicinity of the premises to be searched and does not apply here, where Bailey was detained at a point beyond any reasonable understanding of the immediate vicinity of the premises in question."

Although the police may detain people who are on the premises to be searched, they cannot search those people unless probable cause exists (*Ybarra v. Illinois*, 444 U.S. 85 [1979]). A frisk is permissible, though, as long as the police have a reasonable suspicion that there is a risk to officer safety. If a person does not live on the premises, does not house personal belongings there, and is not a threat, he or she will probably be allowed to leave.

As discussed in the section "Arrest with Warrants," federal law authorizes the police to break open doors and containers if they are refused admittance (18 U.S.C. § 3109). However, there are restrictions on such actions. The manner of the search must be limited to what is reasonably necessary to find the evidence in question. The Supreme Court has stated that "[e]xcessive or unnecessary destruction of property in the course of a search may violate the Fourth Amendment, even though the entry itself is lawful and the fruits of the search not subject to suppression" (*United States v. Ramirez*, 523 U.S. 65 [1998]). Additionally, the occupant of the place searched can be detained—even in handcuffs—for the duration of the search (*Muehler v. Mena*, 544 U.S. 93 [2005]).

### Procedure after Service of a Search Warrant

After a search warrant has been served, the police are required to inventory the items that were seized. Usually the inventory is taken by the searching officer in the presence of the

---

**DECISION-MAKING EXERCISE 4.8**

**DEFINING DAYTIME**

On August 26, at approximately 7:30 P.M., the Sunny County Sheriff's Department executed a search warrant on the premises of 5678 Cherry Lane. The defendants later argued that the search warrant and its execution were defective because the warrant directed that it be executed during the *daytime*. In fact, the warrant was executed at approximately 7:30 P.M., and sunset occurred at 6:43 P.M., according to the National Weather Service. Given this, was the warrant therefore defective?

### WHERE CAN POLICE REASONABLY LOOK?

Sheriff's deputies had a search warrant to look for a rare, stolen koala in the house of the local taxidermist. When serving the warrant, they looked through the kitchen cupboards, wherein they found small baggies of a white, powdery substance as well as a scale. They seized the items and arrested the taxidermist for drug possession. The koala was never found. May the seized items be admitted into evidence? What if the officers had been looking for a stolen circus elephant?

---

person whose property was searched. This procedure not only protects against claims of police theft, but also helps assure the person whose premises were searched that his or her property has been accounted for. A copy of the inventory is given to the person whose property was searched, and if no one was on the premises during the time of the search, the list must be left at the scene in a prominent place. In addition, the police typically have to complete some type of a search record form to be kept on file with the department. Interestingly, the police are not required to notify the property owner of the steps necessary for the return of the property or to remedy any perceived constitutional violation (see *City of West Covina v. Perkins*, 525 U.S. 234 [1999]).

*City of West Covina v. Perkins* *(525 U.S. 234 [1999])*

## Media Presence

In rare circumstances, the involvement of media in police activity results in constitutional issues. In *Wilson v. Layne*, 526 U.S. 603 (1999), the Supreme Court decided whether the police can bring members of the media along during the service of a arrest warrant. Early in the morning on April 16, 1992, deputy U.S. marshals and Montgomery County police officers entered the suspected home of Dominic Wilson. They were joined by a *Washington Post* reporter and a photographer as part of a marshals' service ride-along policy. Dominic's parents were asleep in bed when the officers arrived. They heard the officers enter the home and ran into the living room to investigate the disturbance. A verbal altercation ensued, and both the Wilsons were subdued. Dominic Wilson was never found. Even though the reporter observed what occurred and the photographer took pictures of what transpired, the story was never printed and the pictures were never published. The parents, Charles and Geraldine Wilson, nonetheless brought a *Bivens* action (the Section 1983 counterpart for lawsuits against *federal* officials) against the marshals, alleging the officers violated their Fourth Amendment rights by bringing the media into their home.

*Wilson v. Layne* *(526 U.S. 603 [1999])*

### DETENTION OF A THIRD PARTY DURING AN ARREST

As officers arrived at a house to serve a search warrant, they encountered Larry McVee descending the front steps. The officers asked McVee to help them gain entry into the house. McVee replied that he did not have keys to the house but would ring someone over the intercom. When he did so, another occupant answered the door but refused to allow the officers into the house. The officers then forced the door open and detained McVee as well as eight other people who were in the house. All nine people were frisked because the officers feared for their safety. One of the people had a gun on his person. The officers arrested that man, and in his later trial for weapons offenses, he moved to suppress the gun on the grounds that the officers did not have justification to detain him (or the other people in the house) during the execution of a search warrant. Will his motion be granted?

1. Time Constraints
    a. Search must be executed promptly after issuance
    b. Search must be conducted during daylight hours if possible
    c. Search must not last indefinitely
2. Scope and Manner
    a. Search must be based on object sought
    b. Search must avoid causing excessive and unnecessary property damage
    c. Cannot search guests or third parties if probable cause to do so is lacking

**FIGURE 4.8 Summary of Search Warrant Restrictions**

The case worked its way up through the courts and was ultimately heard by the Supreme Court, which decided that media presence during the service of arrest warrants violates the Fourth Amendment, as long as the presence serves no "legitimate law enforcement objectives." The Court declared that "it is a violation of the Fourth Amendment for police to bring members of the media or other third parties into a home during the execution of a warrant when the presence of the third parties in the home was not in aid of the execution of the warrant."

Chief Justice Rehnquist, writing for the majority, began by stating that the Fourth Amendment embodies the "centuries-old principle of respect for the privacy of the home." He went on to note that although the law enforcement officers were authorized to enter the Wilsons' home, "it does not necessarily follow that they were entitled to bring a newspaper reporter and photographer with them." The Court then considered whether the actions of both parties—the reporters and the police—were related to the objectives of the intrusion into the Wilsons' home. It ruled that they were not. Since the reporters were in the Wilsons' residence for their own purposes, they "were not present for any reason related to the justification for police entry into the home." However, if media presence *does* serve legitimate law enforcement objectives, then the Fourth Amendment will not be violated.

To many observers, the Court's decision in *Wilson v. Layne* seemed to decide the fate of the so-called reality-based police television shows—and to an extent, it did. The police cannot take a camera crew with them when an arrest warrant is served. Media accompaniment is still permissible outside people's homes, however.

Figure 4.8 provides a summary of the restrictions on the service of arrest warrants.

## ▶ Special Circumstances Involving Bodily Intrusions

The Supreme Court has been especially restrictive with regard to intrusions into the human body. A well-known example is *Rochin v. California*, 342 U.S. 165 (1952). In that case, the police had information that a man was selling narcotics. They entered his home and forced their way into his bedroom. When the police asked the man about two capsules that were lying on his bed, he put the capsules in his mouth. The officers could not successfully remove the drugs from the man's mouth, so they took him to the hospital, where his stomach was pumped. Drugs were found and the man was convicted in California state court for possession of morphine. *Rochin* was decided in 1952, prior to when the exclusionary rule was applied to the states. As a result, the Court ruled that the way the police handled the man shocked the conscience, thereby violating his Fourteenth Amendment right to due process.

In another case considering a search through a surgical procedure, *Winston v. Lee*, 470 U.S. 753 (1985), the Supreme Court decided whether the government could require a bullet to be surgically removed from a suspected robber. The Court required not only that a warrant be obtained before allowing such an intrusion but also that the suspect's safety and privacy interests should be weighed against society's interest in capturing lawbreakers. The Court noted,

> A compelled surgical intrusion into an individual's body for evidence . . . implicates expectations of privacy and security of such magnitude that the intrusion may be "unreasonable" even if likely to produce evidence of a crime. . . . The reasonableness of surgical intrusions beneath the skin depends on a case-by-case approach, in which the individual's interests in privacy and security are weighed against society's interests in conducting the procedure. In a given case, the question whether the community's need for evidence outweighs the substantial privacy interest at stake is a delicate one admitting of few categorical answers.

The Court did not expressly decide what the appropriate procedure would be before surgery would be permitted, but it did cite a lower court decision, *United States v. Crowder*, 543 F.2d 312 (1977), in which the D.C. Circuit Court of Appeals decided that before surgery would be permissible (even if a warrant were obtained), an adversarial hearing with appellate review must occur. Thus, under certain circumstances, it would appear that certain types of bodily intrusions require more than a warrant.

Given the extreme sensitivity of bodily intrusions, especially with regard to civil liberties, police departments should take special care when engaging in them. Accordingly, portions of the San Bernardino, California, Police Department's policy for strip and body cavity searches are reprinted in Figure 4.9. The body cavity discussion, in particular, deserves careful attention, as this type of search enjoys a high level of Fourth Amendment protection.

# ▶ Electronic Surveillance

The term *electronic surveillance* includes a variety of methods for spying on the activities of suspected criminals, including both conversations and suspected criminal actions. The methods used to spy on criminal suspects are quite diverse and include wiretapping, "bugging," hacking into computer transmissions, tracking movements of persons and equipment, video surveillance, and seeing through opaque surfaces using devices such as thermal imagers and "gun detectors."

Electronic surveillance law is exceedingly complex and rapidly changing, so a thorough introduction is beyond the scope of this text. However, by focusing some attention on legislative developments over time, sufficient familiarity can be gained with the general contours of the law in this important area of criminal procedure. The following subsections begin by looking at early legislative requirements in the area of electronic surveillance, then move into Title III of the Omnibus Crime Control and Safe Streets Act of 1968 (and its 1986 amendments), and finally consider the PATRIOT Act, which was passed following the September 11 terrorist attacks.

Most of the law in this area, especially Title III and the PATRIOT Act, restricts government interception of private communications. Thus, the bulk of the discussion that follows concerns the use of wiretaps and similar strategies to intercept communications. Other types of electronic surveillance—namely, the use of tracking devices, video recorders, and detection devices—are discussed in a separate subsection, as these types of activities are governed mostly by Supreme Court decisions.

Following *Katz v. United States*, 389 U.S. 347 (1967) (discussed in depth in the previous chapter), the Supreme Court decided *Berger v. New York*, 388 U.S. 41 (1967), in which it considered a statute that permitted eavesdropping orders to be issued by magistrates if the police showed reasonable grounds that evidence of a crime would be discovered. The Court declared the statute unconstitutional, holding that a warrant supported by probable cause is necessary to secure permission to intercept people's communications. Importantly, though, *Katz* and *Berger* do not apply to the interception of communications that can be considered consensual, such as when the government plants a listening device on an informant.

**PROCEDURES**

A. When an arrestee is taken into custody, that person may be subjected to a pat down search, metal detector search, and thorough clothing search in order to discover and retrieve concealed weapons and/or contraband prior to being transported to County Jail.

B. Before requesting authority for a strip search or body cavity search, an officer must determine there is a reasonable suspicion based on specific and articulable facts to believe an arrestee is concealing a weapon or contraband, and that a strip search or body cavity search will result in the discovery of the weapon or contraband.

No strip search or visual body cavity search may be conducted on a misdemeanor or infraction arrestee, without the prior written authorization of the supervisor on duty. A copy of the written authorization shall remain with the case file and shall be made available upon request. The time, date, and place of the search, the name and sex of the person conducting the search, and a statement of the results of the search, including a list of any items removed from the person searched shall be recorded in the case file and made available upon request of the person search or his/her authorized representative. The authorization shall include specific and articulable facts and circumstances upon which the reasonable determination was made by the supervisor.

C. No arrestee shall be subjected to a physical body cavity search except under the authority of a search warrant issued by a magistrate specifically authorizing the physical body cavity search.

A physical body cavity search shall be conducted under sanitary conditions, and only by a physician, nurse practitioner, registered nurse, licensed vocational nurse, or emergency medical technician licensed to practice in the State of California. Any physician engaged in providing health care to detainees or inmates of a facility may conduct the physical body cavity search. A copy of the warrant shall remain in the case file and shall be made available upon request of the person searched or his/her authorized representative. The time, date, and place of search, the name and sex of the person conducting the search, and a statement of the results of the search including a list of items removed from the person searched shall be recorded in the case file.

D. A person conducting a strip search or a visual body cavity search shall not touch the breasts, buttocks, or genitalia of the person being searched.

E. All persons conducting or present during a strip search or visual or physical body cavity search shall be of the same sex as the person being searched, except for physicians or licensed medical personnel.

F. All strip, visual, and physical body cavity searches shall be conducted in an area of privacy so that the search cannot be observed by persons not participating in the search. A person is considered to be participating in the search if his/her official duties relative to search procedure require him/her to be present at the time the search is conducted.

G. No strip or body cavity search shall be conducted on persons not under arrest, without their consent, or a valid search warrant for that person and the rules herein apply to infraction or misdemeanor arrestees. Officers will also adhere to all procedures when dealing with felony arrestees, except that no prior written authorization of the supervisor is required.

H. Employees are reminded that willful violations of Penal Code Section 4030 relating to strip searches and body cavity searches by persons authorizing or conducting such searches are punishable as misdemeanors and civil actions as well punitive damages are available to a person improperly searched.

*Source:* Chapter 29, Procedure 1, "Use of Force," from *Standard Operating Procedure*, San Bernardino, California, Police Department (rev. December 22, 2004). Reprinted with permission.

**FIGURE 4.9 Strip and Body Cavity Search Policy (San Bernardino, CA, Police Department)**

Electronic surveillance law is rapidly changing. There are several "hoops" authorities have to jump through in order to conduct electronic surveillance of the sort depicted in this picture.

## Title III and the Electronic Communications Privacy Act

In 1968, Congress passed **Title III of the Omnibus Crime Control and Safe Streets Act** (18 U.S.C. §§2510–20). Then, in 1986, Congress amended the act by passing the **Electronic Communications Privacy Act** (ECPA) (Pub. L. No. 99-508 [1986]). Both acts govern law enforcement electronic surveillance activities at both the federal and state levels. They are of particular importance because they preempt state laws addressing electronic surveillance. That is, for electronic surveillance to conform to constitutional requirements, it must not only abide by state law but also by the 1968 and 1986 acts.

Both acts protect virtually all wire, oral, and electronic communications among private parties. Title III restricts the *interception* of "wire, oral or electronic communications," unless such interception is authorized by statute (see the act for definitions of each). The 1986 amendments to the act added *electronic communications* to the list of protected activities. The amendments also covered the electronic storage and processing of information. In short, in order for the government to intercept almost any wire, oral, and electronic communications among private parties, it must obtain a valid search warrant.

Unlike communications between private parties, communications among government employees and communications between private parties and the general public are not protected. For example, if an individual posts a message to the World Wide Web, it will not be protected in any way. Also, as discussed earlier, communications that are consensual in nature—such as between a suspect and a government informant—do not come under the protection of Title III or its amendments.

The requirements for obtaining a Title III warrant go beyond the requirements for obtaining a typical warrant discussed earlier in this chapter. The application must contain:

- the identity of both the officer filing and the officer approving the application.
- "a full and complete statement of the facts and circumstances relied upon by the applicant to justify his belief that an order should be issued."
- "a particular description of the nature and location of the facilities from which or the place where the communication is to be intercepted."
- a "full and complete statement as to whether or not other investigative procedures have been tried and failed or why they reasonably appear to be unlikely to succeed if tried or to be too dangerous."
- "a statement of the period of time for which the interception is required to be maintained," including, if deemed necessary, "a particular description of facts establishing

probable cause to believe that additional communications of the same type will occur" after "the described type of communication has been first obtained."

- "a full and complete statement of the facts concerning all previous applications . . . involving any of the same persons, facilities, or places specified in the application, and the action taken by the judge on each such application."
- "a statement setting forth the results thus far obtained from the interception, or a reasonable explanation of the failure to obtain such results."

When preparing to serve a Title III warrant, authorities can covertly enter the place where the interception is to take place (see *Dalia v. United States*, 441 U.S. 238 [1979]). The entry must be reasonable and not result in excessive property damage. Indeed, too much, if any, property damage would alert that suspect that an investigation is taking place. Also, if the circumstances of the interception change during the course of the investigation, the Title III warrant will need to be amended. For example, if when listening to conversations, the police are alerted to additional criminal conduct that they would like to hear about, they must seek an amendment to the original warrant.

If all Title III requirements are not met, the remedy is suppression of the evidence. That is, the exclusionary rule will apply. In fact, Title III has its own set of exclusionary rules, but they are more or less the same as the rule described in Chapter 2. For example, if a Title III warrant fails to describe with particularity the communications to be intercepted, and assuming this is called to the attention of the court, any evidence resulting from the interception will be inadmissible in court. However, if authorities make a reasonable mistake, then the "good faith" exception announced in *United States v. Leon*, 468 U.S. 897 (1984) will apply. Also, in *United States v. Giordano*, 416 U.S. 505 (1974), the Court held that suppression of evidence is only required when the part of the act that has been violated "was intended to play a central role in the statutory scheme." In other words, trivial violations of the act will not likely result in suppression. For example, if fewer than all of the law enforcement officers involved in the investigation are identified in the warrant, then evidence will not be suppressed.

## The Foreign Intelligence Surveillance Act

The Foreign Intelligence Surveillance Act (FISA), passed in 1978, regulates electronic surveillance as it pertains to foreign intelligence gathering. In contrast, Title III and ECPA are mostly for domestic law enforcement purposes. FISA regulates a number of specific activities, including physical searches for intelligence-gathering purposes, the use of pen registers and so-called "trap-and-trace" devices, access to business records, and, of course, electronic surveillance. FISA also created the secretive Foreign Intelligence Surveillance Court, which hears requests for surveillance warrants. Before a warrant is issued, the court must find probable cause that:

- "the target of the surveillance is a foreign power or an agent of a foreign power . . . ; and
- each of the facilities or places at which the electronic surveillance is directed is being used, or is about to be used, by a foreign power or an agent of a foreign power." (50 U.S.C. Section 1805 (a)(2)(A)-(B))

Electronic surveillance law continues to change at a feverish pace. What's more, when changes are made, they often incorporate "sunset" clauses that essentially terminate the legislation at a specified date. One example of this is the Protect America Act, signed into law on August 5, 2007. Among other things, the act removed the warrant requirement for government surveillance of foreign intelligence targets. A sunset clause was included partly because of the controversy surrounding the legislation, but certain provisions have since been reauthorized more than once by federal legislation. Legislation in this area continues to face legal challenge, but with little success (for a recent example, see *Clapper v. Amnesty International USA*, No. 11-1025 [2013]).

# Summary

## 1. Outline the components of search and arrest warrants.

A warrant must meet three requirements in order to be valid: (1) approval by a neutral and detached magistrate; (2) a showing of probable cause; and (3) particularity. A prosecutor or law enforcement official cannot be considered neutral and detached. Neither can a judge who is paid for issuing warrants. *The showing of probable cause* differs depending on the type of warrant. An *arrest warrant* requires showing probable cause that the person to be arrested committed the crime. A *search warrant* requires showing probable cause that the evidence to be seized was connected with a crime *and* that it will be found in the place to be searched. Particularity in an arrest warrant is satisfied when the suspect's name or a detailed description of the person is given. Particularity in a search warrant is satisfied when the place to be searched and the item or items to be seized are described in detail.

## 2. Describe how search and arrest warrants are executed.

Arrest warrants are required in two situations: (1) arrests in the home and (2) arrests in third-party homes. Arrests in public do not require warrants. Similarly, exigent circumstances may allow an arrest without a warrant, regardless of location. The police are required to announce their presence during the execution of a search warrant unless exigent circumstances are present.

The police will generally not be liable for property damage during the service of a warrant; however, due process may be violated if the property damage is excessive. Deadly force can be used to effect an arrest, but only when the suspect seeks to escape and poses a significant threat to other officers or citizens. Finally, the courts will admit evidence resulting from a wrongful arrest, as long as the mistake was a reasonable one.

*Searches* with warrants are subject to many of the same restrictions as *arrests* with warrants. However, search warrants are also constrained in terms of time, insofar as the police cannot wait too long to serve the warrant or take too long to look for evidence. Also, the courts frequently require that search warrants be served during daylight hours. The scope of the search must be limited to the object of the search, the seized evidence must be inventoried and a list given to the homeowner, and the police cannot bring members of the media along when serving a search warrant if the media presence serves no legitimate law enforcement objectives.

## 3. Explain how bodily intrusions and electronic surveillance create "special circumstances" for Fourth Amendment purposes.

The traditional Fourth Amendment approach to determining constitutionality does not always work in the case of bodily intrusions or when electronic surveillance is used. Additionally, the interception of communications, in particular, is governed by a restrictive body of law (such as Title III of the Omnibus Crime Control and Safe Streets Act of 1968).

# Key Terms

arrests *103*
arrest warrant *98*
deadly force *111*

Electronic Communications Privacy Act *123*
Foreign Intelligence Surveillance Act *124*

Foreign Intelligence Surveillance Court *124*
neutral and detached magistrate *98*

## Key Cases

### Warrant Components

- *Coolidge v. New Hampshire*, 403 U.S. 443 (1971)
- *Lo-Ji Sales, Inc. v. New York*, 442 U.S. 319 (1979)
- *Maryland v. Garrison*, 480 U.S. 79 (1987)
- *Andresen v. Maryland*, 427 U.S. 463, 479 (1976)

### Arrests with Warrants

- *Davis v. Mississippi*, 394 U.S. 721 (1969)
- *Payton v. New York*, 445 U.S. 573 (1980)
- *Steagald v. United States*, 451 U.S. 204 (1981)

- *Hudson v. Michigan*, 547 U.S. 586 (2006)
- *Sabbath v. United States*, 391 U.S. 585 (1968)
- *Tennessee v. Garner*, 471 U.S. 1 (1985)
- *Graham v. Connor*, 490 U.S. 386 (1989)

### Searches with Warrants

- *Gooding v. United States*, 416 U.S. 430 (1974)
- *Harris v. United States*, 331 U.S. 145 (1947)
- *Michigan v. Summers*, 452 U.S. 692 (1981)
- *City of West Covina v. Perkins*, 525 U.S. 234 (1999)
- *Wilson v. Layne*, 526 U.S. 603 (1999)

## Further Exploration

1. Describe an encounter between a police officer and a citizen in which a reasonable person would believe that he or she is free to leave.

2. In *United States v. Montoya de Hernandez*, 473 U.S. 531 (1985), law enforcement officials detained a suspect drug "balloon swallower" for 16 hours while they waited for "nature to take its course," so to speak. The majority approved of the delay because the defendant's detention "resulted solely from the method by which she chose to smuggle illicit drugs into the country" (*Id.* at 559). Justices Brennan and Marshall strongly dissented, pointing out that the detention in this case—"indefinite confinement in a squalid back room cut off from the outside world, the absence of basic amenities that would have been provided to even the vilest of hardened criminals, repeated strip searches" was effectively an arrest, thus requiring probable cause (*Id.* at 556). Who was right?

3. Days before the statute of limitations was set to run out on five felony sex offense counts, a John Doe arrest warrant was issued based solely on a DNA profile from evidence that was gathered at the scene of one of the crimes. The defendant was arrested three weeks later once police secured an amended warrant that contained his name. Do you think the DNA profile satisfied the Fourth Amendment's particularity requirement? Does it matter that the statute of limitations was set to run out? Why or why not?

4. A search warrant listed the following items: "numerous customers' checks stolen from Cingular Wireless; checks and materials to make forged checks; computers, printers and scanners for forging checks; a big-screen television purchased with a counterfeit check; and a printer purchased with a counterfeit check" (*State v. Powell*, 306 S.W. 3d 761 [2010]). Not listed in the warrant was a safe that was also bought with a forged check. When serving the search warrant, the police seized, among other things, two safes. The safes were taken to the police station and the locks were "drilled out" by a locksmith. Methamphetamine was found in one of the safes. Was this seizure in compliance with the Fourth Amendment? A fully informed answer to this question may require an examination of the material presented in the next chapter.

5. A man used a pistol-gripped sawed-off shotgun to shoot a rival gang member—five times and in public. Police came to learn of the incident from the suspect's ex-girlfriend. A warrant was obtained to search for the gun, but the warrant listed, among other things, "all firearms." Does this language satisfy the Fourth Amendment's particularity requirement? Why or why not? Does it matter that the suspect was a known gang member and that the sawed-off shotgun was illegal? See *Messerschmidt v. Millender* (No. 10-704 [2012]) for further information and details.

6. Consider these facts from an actual case: "a California Superior Court judge issued a search warrant for a house in Merced County where Payton resided. Police believed that the occupants were selling drugs. The warrant directed officers to search for any item listed in 'Attachment A,' which included methamphetamine and materials used to cut and package it. Attachment A also included, among other things, '[s]ales ledgers showing narcotics transactions such as pay/owe sheets' and '[f]inancial records of the person(s) in control of the residence or premises, bank accounts, loan applications, [and] income and expense records.' The warrant did not explicitly authorize the search of computers. During the execution of the search, the officers found no evidence of drug sales. Officer Horn found a computer in Payton's bedroom with the screen saver activated. He moved the mouse, which removed the screen saver, and clicked open a file. It disclosed an image that he thought was child pornography. This and images like it eventually led to Payton's charge for possession of child pornography. Payton moved to suppress the evidence, challenging the search on the two grounds he raises on appeal . . . he argued that the search of the computer exceeded the scope of the warrant" (*United States v. Payton*, 573 F.3d 859 [9th Cir. 2010]). Was this a proper search? In other words, could the computer reasonably be considered a "place" in which the evidence sought could be found?

7. Assume police officers receive a tip from an informant that a particular house contains weapons and illegal drugs. If they obtain a warrant to search the residence, must they knock and announce their presence? Why or why not?

## Review Questions

1. Explain the three requirements of a valid warrant.

2. How does the showing of probable cause differ for an arrest warrant versus a search warrant?

3. How does particularity differ for an arrest warrant versus a search warrant?

4. Distinguish between a stop and an arrest.

5. Distinguish between a stop and a nonstop.

6. When is an arrest warrant required?

7. What reasons have been offered for the so-called "knock-and-announce" requirement with regard to arrest and search warrants?

8. When can the announcement requirement be dispensed with?

9. Briefly summarize the Supreme Court's view on property damage during the service of a warrant.

10. Summarize the Supreme Court's decisions in *Tennessee v. Garner* and *Graham v. Connor*. Why are these decisions important to criminal procedure?

11. What restrictions exist concerning the scope and manner of a search with a warrant?

12. What is the Supreme Court's view on the media's presence during the service of a search warrant? What is the leading case in this area?

13. Explain the two leading cases that address bodily intrusion during the course of a search.

14. What are the main statutes regulating electronic surveillance?

## Web Links and Exercises

1. Developing a policy manual: Read Chief W. Dwayne Orrick's article "Developing a Police Department Policy-Procedure Manual," published in the International Association of Chiefs of Police *Big Ideas for Smaller Police Departments* newsletter. What, according to him, is the best way to develop a policy-procedure manual? What role do court recommendations play in his recommendations? You can find the article on page 4 here: http://www.theiacp.org/LinkClick.aspx?fileticket=On 6JRot3kSc%3d&tabid=392 (accessed April 18, 2013).

2. Foreign Intelligence Surveillance Act: Read about recent developments in FISA. What activities has the FISA Court reported to Congress?

Suggested URL: http://www.fas.org/irp/agency/doj/fisa (accessed April 18, 2013).

3. Knock and announce: Read more about the knock-and-announce rule at the Federal Law Enforcement Training Center's website. Summarize the federal knock-and-announce rule. Is federal procedure different from state and local procedure?

Suggested URL: https://www.fletc.gov/training/programs/legal-division/downloads-articles-and-faqs/research-by-subject/4th-amendment/knockandannounce.pdf/view (accessed April 18, 2013).

# 5 Searches and Arrests without Warrants

### LEARNING OBJECTIVES

When you complete this chapter, you should be able to:

1. *Summarize the issues involved in warrantless searches and seizures.*

2. *Explain the search incident to arrest doctrine.*

3. *Explain the concept of hot pursuit.*

4. *Summarize the special issues involved in automobile searches.*

5. *Summarize the plain view doctrine.*

6. *Describe the situations in which warrantless arrests may be made.*

**OUTLINE**

---

# Introduction: Moving beyond the Warrant Requirement

If it was not for exceptions to the warrant requirement, the Fourth Amendment would take substantially less effort to understand. At the same time, the exceptions are what make the Fourth Amendment interesting. These exceptions also afford law enforcement an opportunity to arrest or search in situations when a warrant is neither practical nor possible to secure. However, a warrant is *always* preferable—whenever circumstances permit, one should be obtained.

The exceptions to the Fourth Amendment's warrant requirement considered in this chapter all require probable cause. Other exceptions to the warrant requirement that *do not* require probable cause are discussed in later chapters.

# ► Warrantless Searches

Broadly, there are four types of warrantless searches that require probable cause. They are called **exceptions to the warrant requirement** because the actions they cover do not need to be supported by a search warrant. The four types of warrantless searches are (1) searches incident to an arrest; (2) searches conducted under exigent circumstances; (3) searches involving automobiles; and (4) searches based on the "plain view" doctrine.

Other warrantless searches exist, such as consent searches, but they do not require probable cause. One may be inclined to put "frisks" in the warrantless search category, but they are not technically "searches." Consent, frisks, and other warrantless actions that require *less* than probable cause are taken up in later chapters.

## Searches Incident to Arrest

Imagine a situation in which a police officer has lawfully (with probable cause) arrested a suspect, is leading him away, and observes the suspect reach into his pocket. What would be going through the police officer's mind as he or she observed this behavior? Scenarios like this illustrate the reasoning behind the **search incident to arrest** exception to the warrant requirement. This exception recognizes that when arresting a suspect, police officers must be permitted to search the person and the immediate area in order to protect the officers from harm and to prevent the destruction of evidence. It would be dangerous to prohibit police from searching arrestees for weapons, and impractical to wait for a warrant before conducting such a search.

*Chimel v. California*
*(395 U.S. 752 [1969])*

The leading case in searches incident to arrest is *Chimel v. California*, 395 U.S. 752 (1969). Officers in that case arrested Chimel in his home and then searched both him *and* his house. The Supreme Court held that the full search of the house was unreasonable, but a search of the arrestee was permitted "to remove any weapons that the [arrestee] might seek to use in order to resist arrest or effect his escape" and to "seize any evidence on the arrestee's person in order to prevent its concealment or destruction."

### Restrictions on Searches Incident to Arrest

The most basic requirement concerning searches incident to arrest—and one that is often overlooked—is that the arrest itself must be lawful. When the arrest itself is not lawful, that is, when it is not based on probable cause, any search incident to that arrest is unlawful.

Another consideration with regard to searches incident to arrest is the nature or seriousness of the offense. Courts have grappled with the question as to whether a search should be permitted when the offense on which the arrest is based is not serious. Because one of the rationales of the exception is to protect officers from harm, then is officer safety likely to be compromised when the arrest is for a minor offense?

Two important Supreme Court cases have sought to answer this question. In *United States v. Robinson*, 414 U.S. 218 (1973), the Court held that a patdown of the suspect's outer clothing was permissible following an arrest for driving with a revoked license. And in a companion case to *Robinson*, *Gustafson v. Florida*, 414 U.S. 260 (1973), the Court upheld the search of a suspect after his arrest for failure to have his driver's license.

The Supreme Court offered two reasons for its opinions in *Robinson* and *Gustafson*. First, according to Chief Justice Rehnquist, "It is scarcely open to doubt that the danger to an officer is far greater in the case of the extended exposure which follows the taking of a suspect into custody and transporting him to the police station than in the case of the relatively fleeting contact resulting from the typical *Terry*-stop" (*Robinson*, 414 U.S. 218). Second, the Court believed a bright-line rule was necessary, given the need to protect police officers: "A police officer's determination as to how and where to search the person of a suspect whom he has arrested is necessarily a quick *ad hoc* judgment which the Fourth

▼

Amendment does not require to be broken down in each instance into an analysis of each step in the search."

Thus, *any* arrest justifies a warrantless search incident to that arrest. Another important requirement, however, is that the arrest must result in a person being *taken into custody*. This was emphasized in *Knowles v. Iowa*, 525 U.S. 113 (1998). In that case, a police officer stopped a person for speeding, and rather than arresting him (which the officer had justification to do), the officer issued him a citation. Then, the officer conducted a search of the car and found a marijuana pipe. The Court noted that traffic stops rarely pose the same threat to officer safety as arrests. This is not to suggest, however, that police officers cannot search people incident to lawful arrest for minor vehicle-related infractions. If the authority to arrest is present, a search incident to that arrest is permissible. The key factor is that the person must actually be arrested and taken into custody. Otherwise, the search will not conform with Fourth Amendment requirements.

*Knowles v. Iowa*
*(525 U.S. 113 [1998])*

## Timing of the Search

Timing of a search incident to arrest is also important. In particular, probable cause to arrest must *precede* the warrantless search (*Sibron v. New York*, 392 U.S. 40 [1968]). The reason for this is to restrict officers from engaging in "fishing expeditions," or searches based on less than probable cause that would presumably result in probable cause to make an arrest.

Note that if probable cause to arrest is in place, the officer is not required to formally arrest the suspect before engaging in the search (see *Rawlings v. Kentucky*, 448 U.S. 98 [1980]). In *Rawlings*, officers lawfully arrested a man in his home, but they first searched him after he claimed ownership of some narcotics. They found $4,500 cash in his pocket and a knife, *then* arrested him. The Supreme Court sanctioned this order of events.

If the search follows an arrest, as is typical, then it must take place *soon* after the arrest. In legal parlance, the search must be *contemporaneous* to the arrest. In *Preston v. United States*, 376 U.S. 364 (1964), Justice Black observed that the "justifications [for the search incident to arrest] are absent where a search is remote in time or place from the arrest." Police officers had arrested the occupants of a car and taken them to jail. After this, the officers searched the car, which had been towed to an impound lot. The Supreme Court noted that the possibilities of destruction of evidence and danger to the officers were no longer in place, as the suspects were no longer even present.

*Preston v. United States*
*(376 U.S. 364 [1964])*

Note that while a noncontemporaneous search is not justified under the search incident to arrest exception, it is authorized under the automobile exception, to be discussed later. Also, the Supreme Court authorizes inventory searches of automobiles that have been lawfully impounded. Inventory searches are discussed later, as well.

There is one significant exception to the requirement that a search incident to arrest be contemporaneous. In *United States v. Edwards*, 415 U.S. 800 (1974), the Supreme Court, in a 5 to 4 decision, upheld the warrantless search and seizure of an arrestee's clothing 10 hours after his arrest, during which time he was in jail. The Court noted that "searches and seizures that could be made on the spot at the time of arrest may legally be conducted later when the accused arrives at the place of detention." The Court did point out, however, that the taking of the individual's clothing at the time of the arrest would have been impractical because it "was late at night[,] no substitute clothing was then available for Edwards to wear, and it would certainly have been unreasonable for the police to have stripped respondent of his clothing and left him exposed in his cell throughout the night." Thus, this decision established the rule that a noncontemporaneous search incident to arrest is permissible when (1) an immediate search is nearly impossible and (2) the exigency still exists at the time of the later search.

## Scope of the Search

A search incident to arrest is also limited scope, or the area that may be searched. The case of *United States v. Rabinowitz*, 339 U.S. 56 (1950), was the first to set limits on the scope of a search incident to arrest. Officers armed with a valid arrest warrant arrested a man and then conducted a warrantless search of his one-room business, including the desk, safe, and file cabinets. The Supreme Court upheld the search because the room "was small and under the immediate and complete control of the respondent."

Nearly 20 years later, the Supreme Court heavily modified the *Rabinowitz* rule. In *Chimel*, discussed above, the Court argued that the *Rabinowitz* decision had been construed to mean that "a warrantless search 'incident to a lawful arrest' may generally extend to the area that is considered to be in the 'possession' or under the 'control' of the person arrested." Further, the Court noted that the *Rabinowitz* standard gave police "the opportunity to engage in searches not justified by probable cause, [but] by the simple expedient of arranging to arrest suspects at home rather than elsewhere." To get around this problem, Justice Stewart formulated the **armspan rule**. In the Court's words, a search incident to arrest would now be limited to the area "within [the] immediate control" of the person arrested—that is, "the area from within which he might have obtained either a weapon or something that could have been used as evidence against him."

An interesting twist was presented in *Washington v. Chrisman*, 455 U.S. 1 (1982). In that case, an officer stopped a student on suspicion of drinking under age, an action that the Court considered an arrest. The officer asked the student for his identification and followed him to his dorm room, where the student's identification was presumably located. While at the student's room, the officer observed in plain view marijuana and drug paraphernalia. The officer seized the evidence. The Supreme Court upheld the seizure of the evidence, stating that "[e]very arrest must be presumed to present a risk of danger to the arresting officer. . . . Moreover, the possibility that an arrested person will attempt to escape if not properly supervised is obvious." Thus, "it is not unreasonable, under the Fourth Amendment for an officer, as a matter of routine, to monitor the movements of an arrested person, as his judgment dictates, following the arrest."

The cases discussed thus far have focused narrowly on the scope of the incident search exception with reference only to the arrestee. What if another person *besides* the arrestee poses a threat to the police? This concern has led to several expansions and restrictions to the armspan rule.

**Expansions of the Armspan Rule.**   In *Maryland v. Buie*, 494 U.S. 325 (1990), the Supreme Court expanded the scope of the incident search in two ways. It held that the police may, as part of a search incident to arrest, look in areas immediately adjoining the place of arrest for other persons who might attack the officers. In such cases, no justification is required to search these persons. The key is that such a search must occur incident to an arrest. Next, the Court held that at any point up to the time the arrest is completed, the police may engage in a **protective sweep**, defined as "a cursory visual inspection of those places in which a person might be hiding." However, reasonable suspicion must exist for such a sweep to be justified. Thus, no justification is required *after* arrest, but reasonable suspicion is required to engage in a sweep up to the point of the arrest.

---

### DECISION-MAKING EXERCISE 5.1

#### TIMING OF A SEARCH INCIDENT TO ARREST

A locked suitcase was lawfully seized from the open trunk of a parked automobile during the arrest of two of the automobile's occupants. The suitcase was then transported by police officers to the police station. An hour later, the officers opened the suitcase without a search warrant and without the consent of the arrested persons. However, they did have probable cause to believe that the container held contraband. In fact, the suitcase contained large amounts of marijuana. Can this be considered a valid search incident to arrest?

▼

A warrantless search of a house following a lawful arrest has also been considered by the court, based on the need to secure the premises, usually pending the procural of a search warrant. Thus, if the police believe another person or persons are in the house and could potentially destroy evidence, the house may be secured but not searched until a warrant has been obtained. This was the decision reached in *Segura v. United States*, 468 U.S. 796 (1984). In that case, the Supreme Court, in another 5 to 4 decision, declared "that where officers, having probable cause, enter premises . . . , arrest the occupants . . . and take them into custody and, for no more than the period here involved [19 hours in this case], secure the premises from within to preserve the status quo while others, in good faith, are in the process of obtaining a warrant, they do not violate the Fourth Amendment's proscription against unreasonable seizures."

It is appropriate at this juncture to note that the Court has authorized the police to rely on the incident search exception to engage in searches well beyond the arrestee's armspan—and when no threat exists from people sympathetic to the arrestee. In particular, the Supreme Court has held that officers may engage in a warrantless, suspicionless search of a car and containers within it following the lawful arrest of the car's driver (*New York v. Belton*, 453 U.S. 454 [1981]), but "only if it is reasonable to believe that the arrestee might access the vehicle at the time of the search or that the vehicle contains evidence of the offense" (*Arizona v. Gant*, No. 07-542 [2009]). This issue is discussed at greater length later in this chapter in the section "Automobile Searches."

*New York v. Belton*
*(453 U.S. 454 [1981])*

*Arizona v. Gant*
*(No. 07-542 [2009])*

Aside from the possible danger to police officers from "confederates," there is the potential for such third parties to destroy evidence. Only one Supreme Court case appears to have addressed this specific issue: *Vale v. Louisiana*, 399 U.S. 30 (1970). Police officers had warrants authorizing the arrest of the defendant. While surveilling the house, the officers observed the defendant come out of the house and engage in what appeared to be a drug sale. They arrested the defendant outside the home, but then went back inside and searched it. According to the officers, two of the defendant's relatives had arrived at the house in the meantime and could have destroyed evidence. The Supreme Court decided that this action violated Fourth Amendment requirements.

## Summary: Requirements for Searches Incident to Arrest

A search incident to arrest may be conducted without a warrant, but it is subject to four restrictions. First, the arrest must be based on probable cause and result in custodial detention. Second, the search must be close in time to the arrest (it must be contemporaneous with the arrest). Third, the scope of the search must be limited. The police must limit their search to (1) the person arrested and any containers discovered from that search; (2) the arrestee's immediate grabbing area; (3) a protective sweep of the premises without justification following an arrest but with reasonable suspicion leading up to the arrest; or (4) securing the premises, if they have a reasonable belief that evidence may be destroyed by someone sympathetic to the arrestee (see Figure 5.1). Finally, the premises to be searched

| Level of Intrusion | Justification Required |
|---|---|
| Search of arrestee | None |
| Search of arrestee's grabbing area | None |
| Protective sweep | Reasonable suspicion that confederates are present |
| Secure residence | Reasonable suspicion to fear destruction of evidence |

**FIGURE 5.1 Permissible Scope of a Search Incident to Arrest (Assuming a Valid Arrest)**

**FIGURE 5.2 Search Incident to Arrest Policy (Gallatin, TN, Police Department)**

can be secured prior to procural of a warrant, but reasonable suspicion is required. Figure 5.2 presents the Gallatin, Tennessee, Police Department's policy for a search incident to arrest, which illustrates how police departments have attempted to grapple with the complexities of the law in this area. Figure 5.3 provides a timeline of key cases regarding searches incident to arrest.

## Searches Based on Exigent Circumstances

As discussed earlier, the exceptions to the search warrant requirement are premised, in part, on the impracticality of obtaining a warrant. Perhaps no exception illustrates this better than the **exigent circumstances** exception. When the exigencies, or emergency circumstances of the situation require the police to act immediately to avoid danger to

TIMELINE

**Scope of the Search Incident to Arrest over Time**

| 1950 | 1969 | 1981 | 1982 |
|---|---|---|---|
| *United States* v. *Rabinowitz,* 339 U.S. 561 1950 A full room search was sanctioned following an arrest. | *Chimel* v. *California,* 395 U.S. 752 The Court overruled Rabinowitz and the "armspan rule" was adopted. The arrestee can be searched, as can the arrestee's "grabbing area." | *New York* v. *Belton,* 453 U.S. 454 Officers may engage in a warrantless, suspicionless search of a car and containers within it following a lawful arrest of the car's driver. | *Washington* v. *Chrisman,* 455 U.S. 1 It is permissible to monitor the movements of an arrested person (in this case to his dorm to get his identification) and seize contraband found in plain view. |

**FIGURE 5.3**

**PROPER SCOPE FOR A SEARCH INCIDENT TO ARREST**

Two police officers arrived at Bobby Sheen's house with a valid warrant for his arrest. The officers were informed by a nosy neighbor that two of Sheen's accomplices were in the house with him. The officers knocked, announced their presence, and entered the house. They encountered Sheen as he was descending the stairs, and he was placed under arrest. Immediately after the arrest, one of the officers went upstairs and found drug paraphernalia on a nightstand. May this evidence be lawfully seized? What if the drug paraphernalia had been found in a drawer instead?

themselves, danger to others, the destruction of evidence, or the escape of the suspect, it would be unreasonable to require the police to take time to obtain a warrant.

Generally, three types of exigencies are recognized by the courts as authorizing the police to act without a warrant: (1) hot pursuit; (2) likelihood of escape or danger to others absent hot pursuit; and (3) evanescent evidence. Although these exceptions allow the police to act without a warrant, probable cause is still required. For example, police must have probable cause that the person being pursued is a suspect before they can enter a home or building without a warrant to arrest him or her.

## Hot Pursuit

Police officers must often enter a home or building without a warrant while in "hot pursuit" of a suspect who the police believed had just committed a serious crime. Under some circumstances, they are permitted to arrest the suspect, and evidence they encounter within the building may be admissible, under the **hot pursuit** exception. The Supreme Court first recognized this exception in the case of *Warden v. Hayden*, 387 U.S. 294 (1967), in which the police were called by taxicab drivers who reported that their taxi company had been robbed. The police followed the suspect to a house, where they were granted entry by the suspect's wife. The suspect was upstairs in the house, pretending to be asleep. While searching the house for the suspect, the police found and seized clothing, a shotgun, and a pistol, all of which were used against the suspect at trial. The Court found the warrantless entry reasonable because the "exigencies of the situation made that course imperative."

*Warden v. Hayden*
*(387 U.S. 294 [1967])*

Several reasons were offered for the decision. First, Justice Brennan stated that "[t]he Fourth Amendment does not require police officers to delay in the course of an investigation if to do so would gravely danger their lives or the lives of others." Also, "[s]peed . . . was essential, and only a thorough search of the house for persons and weapons could

**Scope of the Search Incident to Arrest over Time,** *continued*

| 1984 | 1990 | 2009 |
|---|---|---|
| ***Segura* v. *United States*, 468 U.S. 796** Premises can be secured pending the procural of a search warrant. A **protective sweep** (cursory visual inspection of the places in which someone may be hiding) can be conducted if the police have reason to believe evidence may be destroyed by someone sympathetic to the arrestee. | ***Maryland* v. *Buie*, 494 U.S. 325** The police may, as part of a search incident to arrest, conduct a protective sweep of the premises. | ***Arizona* v. Gant, No. 07-542** The rule in *Belton* v. *New York* is modified as follows: A search of the arrestee's vehicle is permissible "only if it is reasonable to believe that the arrestee might access the vehicle at the time of the search or that the vehicle contains evidence of the offense" in question. |

**FIGURE 5.3** *continued*

have insured that Hayden was the only man present and that the police had control of all weapons which could be used against them or to effect an escape." Despite the sweeping language of the *Hayden* decision, the Supreme Court has imposed a number of restrictions on searches and seizures premised on hot pursuit.

Hot pursuit permits warrantless entry only when the police have probable cause to believe that the person they are chasing has committed a crime and is on the premises entered. The police must also have reason to believe the suspect will escape or that further harm, either to evidence or to other people, will occur if the suspect is not immediately apprehended. With regard to this restriction, one court has observed that "[a] hot pursuit, by itself, creates no necessity for dispensing with a warrant" (*State v. Wren*, 115 Idaho 618 [1989]). Similarly, the Ninth Circuit has stated that police officers must reasonably believe (1) "that the suspect either know[s] or will learn at any moment that they are in immediate danger of apprehension"; (2) that "evidence is being currently removed or destroyed and it is impractical to advert the situation without immediately arresting the suspects or seizing the evidence"; or (3) that "a suspect is currently endangering the lives of themselves or others" (*United States v. George*, 883 F.2d 1407 [9th Cir. 1989]).

The police must also begin the hot pursuit from a lawful starting point. If, for example, officers initially observe the suspect while they are unlawfully on someone's private property, they cannot claim hot pursuit to justify any further warrantless action. However, in *United States v. Santana*, 427 U.S. 38 (1976), the Supreme Court upheld the warrantless arrest of a woman in her house when the police merely *observed* a crime on private property from a public vantage point. In that case, police officers observed Santana standing in the open doorway of her house with a brown paper bag, which they had probable cause to believe contained narcotics. They pursued her into the house and arrested her. This decision suggests that the police can pursue from a public vantage point a suspect whom they observe on private property.

The hot pursuit doctrine applies only to serious offenses, including felonies and some misdemeanors. This restriction on the hot pursuit doctrine—and, indeed, on exigent circumstance searches in general—is perhaps the most important one. As such, it is treated in a section by itself later.

Generally, the scope of a search based on hot pursuit is broad. The Supreme Court has stated that "[t]he permissible scope of search must, at the least, be as broad as may reasonably be necessary to prevent the dangers that the suspect at large in the house may resist or escape" (*Warden*, 387 U.S. 294). However, the search must be "prior to or immediately contemporaneous with" the arrest of the suspect. Also, officers may only search where the suspect or weapons might reasonably be found. A simple rule of thumb, then, is that the nature of the exigency defines the scope of the search. Another general with regard to hot pursuit is that if the police have a reasonable amount of time to obtain a warrant, they should always do so. For example, in *Welsh v. Wisconsin*, 466 U.S. 740 (1984), Justice Brennan argued that the government's "claim of hot pursuit . . . [was] . . . unconvincing because there was no immediate or continuous pursuit of the petitioner from the scene of [the] crime."

## Escape and Endangerment to Others Absent Hot Pursuit

Hot pursuit is justified when the suspect may escape or inflict harm on police officers or others. There are other situations, however, in which police must enter and arrest a suspect without a warrant to prevent the suspect from escaping or inflicting harm, but their actions cannot be characterized as "hot pursuit." In *Minnesota v. Olson*, 495 U.S. 91 (1990), for example, the prosecution sought to justify a warrantless entry and arrest of a suspect in a duplex that the police had surrounded. There was probable cause to believe that Olson, the man in the duplex, had been the driver of a getaway car involved in a robbery and murder the day before. The Supreme Court ruled that the officers acted unconstitutionally under the circumstances because Olson was only the driver, not the murder suspect, and the

**ARE EXIGENT CIRCUMSTANCES PRESENT?**

An officer attempted to stop a man for driving 73 miles per hour in a 55-mile-per-hour zone. Instead of stopping, the man sped away and led the officer (and others officers who quickly joined) on a high-speed pursuit down two-lane roads at speeds of nearly 90 miles per hour. After several unsuccessful attempts to stop the fleeing car, one of the pursuing officers deliberately rammed the fleeing suspect's car, causing it to crash. The suspect was severely injured and rendered quadriplegic. Now he is suing under Section 1983 (see Chapter 2), alleging that the officer who rammed his car used excessive force to effect an unreasonable seizure under the Fourth Amendment. Should his lawsuit go forward?

weapon had been recovered, which diminished the urgency of the situation. In addition, it was unlikely Olson would escape because the building was surrounded. On its face, then, this case is not useful on this point. However, the Court seemed to suggest that had Olson *not* been the driver (he had been the suspected murderer), had the weapon *not* been recovered, and had the building *not* been fully surrounded, the warrantless action would have been lawful.

A more recent case, *Brigham City v. Stuart*, 547 U.S. 398 (2006), has helped to clarify the issue. Police were called to a house that received complaints about a loud party. On arriving at the scene, officers witnessed a fight involving four adults and one juvenile. One of the adults hit the juvenile. The officers announced their presence, but they couldn't be heard above the commotion inside, so they entered without a warrant. In a unanimous decision, the Supreme Court held that such warrantless entries are constitutionally permissible so long as the police have an objectively reasonable basis to believe the occupant is "seriously injured or threatened with such injury."

## Evanescent Evidence

In some situations, warrantless searches may be permitted securing evanescent evidence, or evidence that may rapidly vanish or disappear. This may include certain types of evidence inside a person, as well as a house, a paper, or an effect.

One of the most common examples of vanishing or disappearing evidence inside a person is alcohol in the blood. In *Breithaupt v. Abram*, 352 U.S. 432 (1957), the Court upheld the warrantless intrusion (via a needle) into a man's body for the purpose of drawing blood to see if he had been drinking. This decision was effectively overruled in a recent case. In *Missouri v. McNeely*, 569 U.S. ___ (2013), the Supreme Court ruled that the natural dissipation of alcohol in a person's bloodstream does not necessarily constitute an exigency justifying a warrantless search. The Court stopped short of deciding that *all* blood-draws must be supported by a warrant, but it certainly sent a message that a warrant should be obtained whenever practical. Part of the Court's reasoning for the decision was that it is much easier to obtain warrants these days than it was in the *Breithaupt* era.

*Breithaupt v. Abram*
*(352 U.S. 432 [1957])*

The *Breithaupt* decision remains relevant, however, because it also established that warrantless searches for evanescent evidence are permissible only when (1) there is no time to obtain a warrant; (2) there is a "clear indication" that the search will result in obtaining the evidence sought; and (3) the search is conducted in a "reasonable manner." This three-prong approach remains more or less intact today.

In a later decision, *Schmerber v. California*, 384 U.S. 757 (1966), the Court offered the following reasoning in support of the reasonable manner requirement:

The interests in human dignity and privacy which the Fourth Amendment protects forbid any such intrusions on the mere chance that desired evidence might be obtained. In the

▼

absence of a clear indication that in fact such evidence will be found, these fundamental human interest require law officers to suffer the risk that such evidence may disappear unless there is an immediate search.

In *Rochin v. California*, 342 U.S. 165 (1952), police tried to extract evidence from a man's stomach. They were unsuccessful, took the man to a hospital, and had a doctor force an emetic into his stomach against his will. Capsules containing morphine were extracted. The Supreme Court declared that the evidence should not have been admitted, stating:

> . . . we are compelled to conclude that the proceedings by which this conviction was obtained do more than offend some fastidious squeamishness or private sentimentalism about combatting crime too energetically. This is conduct that shocks the conscience. Illegally breaking into the privacy of the petitioner, the struggle to open his mouth and remove what was there, the forcible extraction of his stomach's contents—this course of proceeding by agents of government to obtain evidence is bound to offend even hardened sensibilities.

As for the "clear indication" requirement, the Court has been somewhat flexible. For example, in *United States v. Montoya de Hernandez*, 469 U.S. 1204 (1985), the Court treated the clear indication requirement as being identical to the reasonable suspicion standard set forth in *Terry v. Ohio*. This case involved the detention for several hours of a woman who was suspected of smuggling narcotics in her alimentary canal.

It is important to remember that, like the hot pursuit exception, the exigency used to justify a warrantless search for evanescent evidence must be immediate. In other words, there must be good reason to believe that an immediate search will result in the seizure of the evidence in question. *Cupp v. Murphy*, 412 U.S. 291 (1973), illustrates this point. A man who had been informed of his wife's strangulation volunteered to come to the police station for questioning. While he was at the station, officers observed what appeared to be dried blood on the man's fingernails. The officers asked if they could take a scraping from his fingernails, and the man refused. He then started rubbing his hands behind his back and placing them in his pockets. At that point, the officers forcibly removed some of the material from under the man's fingernails. The Court upheld this action on the grounds that the police had probable cause to believe that "highly evanescent evidence" was in the process of being destroyed.

*Kentucky v. King*, 563 U.S. ___ (2011), is also illustrative. The Supreme Court held that police can make a forcible warrantless entry into a private residence if they have reason to believe evidence is being destroyed. In that case, officers smelled marijuana outside an apartment, knocked loudly, and announced their presence. They then heard what they believed was the sound of evidence being destroyed. They announced their intent to enter, kicked in the door, and found drugs in plain view—and other evidence during the course of a protective sweep. The Supreme Court ruled that the evidence was admissible.

In certain rare situations, the police may have reason to suspect that evidence may be lost or destroyed, not because of the actions of a person (the suspect or the suspect's confederates), but because of other causes. In *United States v. Chadwick*, 433 U.S. 1 (1977), for example, the Supreme Court noted that a warrant would not be required to search a footlocker if the officers believed that it contained evidence that would lose its value unless the footlocker were opened at once or if the officers had reason to believe that the footlocker contained explosives or other inherently dangerous items.

### Exigent Circumstances and the Seriousness of the Offense

The Supreme Court has also noted that the *seriousness* of the offense may be relevant in determining whether exigent circumstances are present. For example, in *Welsh*, 466 U.S. 740, a witness one night reported that an automobile was being driven erratically. Eventually, the car swerved off the road and stopped in a field. The driver walked away

*Cupp v. Murphy*
*(412 U.S. 291 [1973])*

**IMMEDIACY AND EVANESCENT EVIDENCE**

Federal agents believed that a motor home parked in a secluded area near a river was being used to house a methamphetamine laboratory. The agents maintained visual surveillance throughout the afternoon. Around 4.00 P.M., one of the agents smelled chemicals "cooking." Shortly after that, the agents observed a man dash out of the motor home, gasping for air. In light of this incident, the agents decided to search the motor home. They ordered all of the occupants out of the motor home and placed them under arrest. The agents then entered the motor home to see if any other people were inside, turn off any cooking apparatus, and inventory the contents. They found a methamphetamine laboratory behind a drawn curtain at the back of the motor home. Were their actions justified?

before police could arrive at the scene. When they did arrive, the police checked the registration of the car and found out it belonged to Welsh. They went to Welsh's house, gained entry, and arrested Welsh without a warrant. The Supreme Court held that the warrantless nighttime entry of a suspect's home to make an arrest for a *nonjailable* offense is a violation of the Fourth Amendment:

> Before government agents may invade the sanctity of the home, it must demonstrate exigent circumstances that overcome the presumption of unreasonableness that attaches to all warrantless home entries. An important factor to be considered when determining whether any exigency exists is the gravity of the underlying offense for which the arrest is being made . . . [A]pplication of the exigent circumstances exception in the context of home entry should rarely be sanctioned when there is probable cause that only a minor offense has been committed.

*Welsh* is controversial for at least two reasons. First, it is not always clear what constitutes a minor offense. The Court declared that warrantless entry to make an arrest for drunk driving is in violation of the Fourth Amendment, even though drunk driving is considered a serious offense in every state of the union. Second, the Court has implied that warrants are *not* required for warrantless home arrests in serious cases. The D.C. Circuit's opinion in *Dorman v. United States*, 435 F.2d 385 (D.C. Cir. 1970), highlighted seven factors that may permit warrantless entry:

- The offense is serious.
- The suspect is believed to be armed.
- The police have a high degree of probable cause for arrest.
- There is an especially strong reason to believe the suspect is on the premises.
- Escape is likely.
- The entry can be made peaceably.
- The entry can be made during the day.

## Summary: Searches Based on Exigent Circumstances

The common types of exigent circumstances recognized by the courts include hot pursuit, threats to persons, and threats to evidence. Warrantless action based on a hot pursuit exigency is constitutional only if the police have probable cause to believe any of the following:

- The person they are pursuing has committed a serious offense.
- The person will be found on the premises the police seek to enter.

**EXIGENT CIRCUMSTANCES AND THE SEVERITY OF THE OFFENSE**

An apartment was burglarized while no one was home, and a checkbook and a television were stolen. Someone in the apartment complex witnessed Brian Corman leaving the victim's unit and called the police. Officers responded and confronted Corman at the door to his apartment, which was in the same building. Without a warrant, the officers entered Corman's apartment, searched it, found the items stolen in the burglary, and arrested him. Are these actions constitutionally valid?

- The suspect will escape or harm someone or evidence will be lost or destroyed.
- The pursuit originates from a lawful vantage point.
- The scope and timing of the search are reasonable.

In situations where the hot pursuit exception does not apply (and, presumably, the automobile and search incident to arrest exceptions do not apply), a warrantless search for evanescent evidence is permissible when (1) there is probable cause to believe that evidence will be destroyed, lost, or devalued; (2) the procedures employed are reasonable; and (3) the exigency was not police created. A broad interpretation of the latter condition suggests that the same applies in the case of hot pursuit, but the Supreme Court has not ruled on the problem of police-created exigencies. Also, a warrantless search is permissible absent hot pursuit or the potential for damage or destruction to evidence, if probable cause exists to believe a person on the premises is in imminent danger of death or serious bodily harm.

## Automobile Searches

*Carroll v. United States*
*(267 U.S. 132 [1925])*

In the landmark case of *Carroll v. United States*, 267 U.S. 132 (1925), the Supreme Court carved out an **automobile exception** to the Fourth Amendment's warrant requirement. The Court declared that the warrantless search of an automobile is permissible when (1) there is probable cause to believe the vehicle contains evidence of a crime and (2) securing a warrant is impractical. *Carroll* was decided in 1925, during Prohibition. The case involved the stop of a vehicle driven by a suspect who was known to have previously engaged in the sale of bootleg whiskey. A warrantless search of the car revealed 68 bottles of illegal liquor. The Supreme Court upheld the warrantless search on the grounds that the evidence would be lost if the police had been required to take the time to secure a warrant.

**POLICE-CREATED EXIGENCIES**

The police knocked on the door of Patrick Warner, whom they suspected was an armed and dangerous narcotics dealer. When Warner came to the door, the police ordered him to place his hands on the glass door and then to slowly reach down and unlock it. Warner said he did not have a key and would need to go to another room to obtain one. Believing he would use the opportunity to retrieve a gun from elsewhere in the house, the officers kicked down the door and entered as the suspect retreated to another room. Once inside, the officers conducted a protective sweep of the apartment. During the course of the sweep, they found bales of marijuana. Were the entrance and the sweep justified?

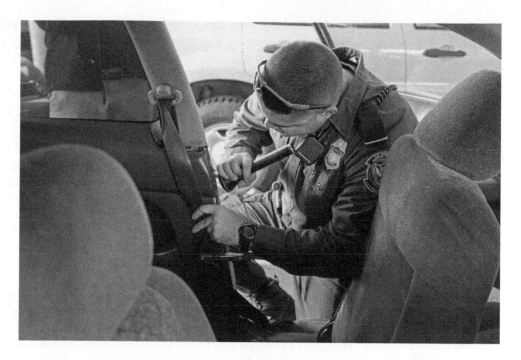

Vehicle searches must be based upon probable cause, but they do not require warrants. As long as probable cause is in place, a vehicle search can be quite extensive.

Note that *Carroll* deals with vehicle *searches*, not stops. A different standard is applied to vehicle stops, which are discussed in a separate section in Chapter 6.

## Rationale for the Automobile Exception

Three arguments can be offered in support of the automobile exception. First, because of the inherent mobility of vehicles, it is impractical to obtain warrants. According to the Court in *Carroll*:

> The guaranty [sic] of freedom from unreasonable searches and seizures by the Fourth Amendment has been construed, practically since the beginning of the Government, as recognizing a necessary difference between a search of a store, dwelling house or other structure in respect of which a proper official warrant readily may be obtained, and a search of a ship, motor boat, wagon or automobile, for contraband goods, where it is not practicable to secure a warrant because the vehicle can be quickly moved out of the locality in which the warrant must be sought.

Second, because vehicles are typically operated in public spaces, the Court has held that people have a lesser expectation of privacy. As the Court observed in *Cardwell v. Lewis*, 417 U.S. 583 (1974), an automobile serves a transportation function, not a privacy function—a car "seldom serves as one's residence or the repository of personal effects." Also, people have a lesser expectation of privacy in their automobiles because by their very nature, automobiles travel "public thoroughfares where [their] occupants and [their] contents are in plain view."

The third reason for the automobile exception hinges on the government regulations to which vehicles are subjected. The old adage that "driving is a privilege, not a right" applies in this context. The Court's opinion in *Chadwick* is illustrative. In that case, police opened and searched a locked footlocker being carried by the defendants. The government argued that the same exception should apply to the footlocker as an automobile, because the footlocker was mobile. The Court disagreed, citing five characteristics of automobiles: they (1) travel on public roads; (2) are subject to state regulations and licensing requirements;

(3) are subject to other strict regulations; (4) are subject to periodic inspections; and (5) may be impounded for public safety reasons (433 U.S. 1 [1977]). Thus, the Court declared that the automobile exception should not apply to the warrantless search of personal items, regardless of their mobility.

## Requirements for Warrantless Vehicle Searches

Three general requirements must be met for a valid warrantless vehicle search: (1) the exception must only apply to automobiles; (2) with one exception, such a search must be premised on probable cause; and (3) it must be impractical to obtain a warrant (i.e., the vehicle stop must be such that it is impractical, burdensome, or risky to take time to obtain a warrant). The third requirement is unresolved, as the courts have relied on lesser expectation of privacy analysis rather than an exigency argument to support warrantless searches of automobiles. Figure 5.4 shows the vehicle search requirements of the Pine Bluff, Arkansas, Police Department, illustrating the application of these requirements.

*Defining "Automobile."* With regard to the automobile exception for search warrants, the term *automobile* has a very specific meaning, which is very different from its meaning in everyday language. Some vehicles are covered by the automobile exception that do not meet the usual definition—cars, boats, and planes are all considered "automobiles."

*California v. Carney (471 U.S. 386 [1985])*

A more complex situation is presented by vehicles serving a dual purpose of both transportation and residence, such as a motor home, or a tractor trailer with a sleeper cab. The Court was confronted with this question in the case of *California v. Carney*, 471 U.S. 386 (1985). There, the Court applied the standard of objective reasonableness and refused to define explicitly the types of automobiles covered by the automobile exception. Instead, the Court held that whether a vehicle serves as transportation or as a residence requires looking at the *setting* in which the vehicle is located. If the setting "objectively indicates that the vehicle is being used for transportation," then the automobile exception applies.

Four additional factors are used in determining whether a vehicle serves a transportation function: (1) whether it is mobile or stationary; (2) whether it is licensed; (3) whether it is connected to utilities; and (4) whether it has convenient access to the road. If, for example, a trailer is on blocks, unlicensed, connected to utilities, and in a trailer park, it will almost certainly be treated as a residence for purposes of the Fourth Amendment.

**Probable Cause Requirement.** In *Carroll*, the Court noted that "where seizure is impossible except without warrant, the seizing officer acts unlawfully and at his peril unless he can show the court probable cause." In other words, although police may search a vehicle without a warrant, the search must still be based on probable cause. Note, however, that probable cause to *search* and probable cause to *arrest* are not one and the same. While probable cause to search may exist, it does not automatically give probable cause to arrest.

| | SUBJECT: | POLICY NUMBER 352 |
|---|---|---|
| | SEARCH: **MOTOR VEHICLE** | ISSUE DATE 02/19/2008 |
| | CHAPTER: **INVESTIGATIONS** | EFFECTIVE DATE 02/19/2008 |
| | ISSUED By: Chief of Police John E. Howell | TOTAL PAGES 5 |

**FIGURE 5.4 Vehicle Search Policy (Pine Bluff, AR, Police Department)**

In *Carroll*, for example, the police had probable cause to search the vehicle but not probable cause to arrest the occupants.

Probable cause to *arrest* does not authorize a full search of a vehicle, including the trunk, but it does authorize a search of the passenger compartment (*New York v. Belton*, 453 U.S. 454 [1981]). This rule was extended in *Thoraton v. United States*, 541 U.S. 615 (2004), to include searches where the initial contact between the officer and the suspect took place outside the vehicle, in a parking lot. However, in an even more recent decision, this rule was significantly limited. In *Arizona v. Gant*, 556 U.S. 332 (2009), a man was arrested for driving on a suspended license. After he was handcuffed and placed in a patrol car, officers searched his car and found cocaine in the pocket of a jacket. Based on this evidence, he was convicted of illegal drug possession. The Supreme Court held that a *Belton*-type search is permissible "only if it is reasonable to believe that the arrestee might access the vehicle at the time of the search or that the vehicle contains evidence of the offense of arrest." Whereas *Belton* was a bright-line decision, *Gant* now makes it somewhat difficult to determine whether a search is sanctioned. It forces officers to decide whether the vehicle contains evidence of the offense in question.

There is one important exception to the rule that probable cause must be in place before a vehicle search can be conducted. In *New York v. Class*, 475 U.S. 106 (1986), the Court held in a 5 to 4 decision that the warrantless, suspicionless search of a car for the purpose of ascertaining the vehicle identification number (VIN) is permissible. All that is required is a valid traffic stop. Importantly, though, this exception does not authorize the police to enter cars at will, without any basis for a search. In support of its opinion, the Court pointed to the lesser expectation of privacy argument. Also, it noted that the search was minimally intrusive.

**Impracticality of Obtaining a Warrant.** Given the circumstances surrounding most vehicle stops, it would seem foolish to require that the police obtain a warrant before searching an automobile. As the Court observed in *Carroll*, a warrant is required where it is reasonably practicable to obtain one. In most situations involving the stop of an automobile, securing a warrant is not reasonably practicable.

In *Husty v. United States*, 282 U.S. 694 (1931), for example, a police officer followed up on a tip from an informant and found contraband in Husty's unattended car. Given that the car was unattended, one could argue that a warrant should have been secured, but the Court argued that the officer "could not know when Husty would come to the car or how soon it would be removed." Contrast *Husty* with *Coolidge v. New Hampshire*, 403 U.S. 443 (1971), which involved the warrantless search of two cars located on defendant's property. In that case, the Court ruled that the automobile exception did not apply because the police had probable cause to act more than two weeks before the search.

*Coolidge v. New Hampshire (403 U.S. 443 [1971])*

*Husty* and *Coolidge* suggest that the warrantless search of an automobile will only be upheld if it was impractical to obtain a warrant. This third requirement is unresolved, however. For example, in *Chambers v. Maroney*, 399 U.S. 42 (1970), the Court held that as long as the vehicle is readily mobile, a warrantless search is permissible, even if it is conducted away from the scene at the stationhouse. The actual search of the automobile in *Chambers* was made at the police station many hours after the car had been stopped on the highway, when the car was no longer movable. Furthermore, at that point, exigent circumstances no longer existed and a magistrate could have required a warrant. Yet the Court sanctioned the search.

Another case, *United States v. Johns*, 469 U.S. 478 (1985), seems to suggest that the automobile exception requires some form of exigency. The Court held that the warrantless search of an automobile is impermissible if it "adversely affect[s] a privacy [or] possessory interest." This argument seems to suggest that a search under the automobile exception needs to be premised on the urgency of the situation; otherwise, a warrant should be secured. Nevertheless, the Court in *Johns* did state that a three-day delay between the initial stop and the arrest was permissible, partly because the car's owner did not claim that the delay caused hardship.

So, what is the role of exigency in the automobile exception? A safe rule of thumb is that the presence or absence of exigent circumstances is irrelevant. Instead, a showing that the automobile was readily mobile is enough to justify a warrantless search under the automobile exception (as long as probable cause is in place and the target of the search is, in fact, an automobile, as defined earlier).

## Scope of the Search

In *United States v. Ross*, 456 U.S. 798 (1982), the Supreme Court declared that as long as the police have justification to conduct a warrantless automobile search, it may be "as thorough as a magistrate could authorize in a warrant." The only limitation is "defined by the object of the search and the places in which there is probable cause to believe that it may be found." Accordingly, if the contraband sought is small (such as a single syringe), the scope of the vehicle search exception is almost limitless. Even passengers' personal belongings may be searched (*Wyoming v. Houghton*, 526 U.S. 295 [1999]).

Sometimes it is necessary to cause some damage (removing panels, headliners, etc.) in order to find the object sought. On the one hand, the suspect's due process may be violated if the damage inflicted is excessive. On the other hand, it would appear that a certain degree of physical damage to an automobile is permissible. The *Carroll* decision, for example, was based on a warrantless search in which the police sliced open the vehicle's upholstery to look for contraband.

Police often used search methods that do not involve physically entering a vehicle. The Supreme Court has considered whether allowing a drug dog to sniff a vehicle during a traffic stop violated the Fourth Amendment. In *Illinois v. Caballes*, 543 U.S. 405 (2005), an Illinois state trooper stopped a vehicle for speeding. During the 10-minute stop, while the trooper was going through all the usual motions associated with a traffic stop, another trooper arrived and allowed a drug dog to sniff the vehicle. The dog was alerted to the trunk. Marijuana was found, and the driver was arrested. The Supreme Court upheld the dog sniff, citing three factors: (1) the legality of the stop; (2) the short duration of the stop; and (3) the fact that no one can claim legal ownership to—and thereby assert a privacy interest in—contraband.

## Other Actions in a Traffic Stop

Under current case law, the police are permitted wide latitude in conducting traffic stops. The police may stop a car based on the belief that a crime has been committed, which includes any traffic violation (*Whren v. United States*, 517 U.S. 806 [1996]). In addition, once a person has been stopped, the officer may order him or her to stand outside the

---

**DECISION-MAKING EXERCISE 5.7**

### A TWIST ON *CARROLL*

Two police detectives have probable cause to believe that several illegal automatic weapons are in the trunk of Carmine Lord's car. However, Lord's car is broken down and has been left with the local auto mechanic. Furthermore, Lord has proven to be a difficult customer and has refused to pay for the full amount of the repair. Consequently, the mechanic has locked Lord's car in a bay at his service station and refused to release it until he receives payment. Assuming they have the mechanic's blessing, may the detectives search Lord's car for the weapons while it is at the station?

vehicle without any justification (*Maryland v. Wilson*, 519 U.S. 408 [1997]). The police may also engage in searches with consent (*Ohio v. Robinette*, 519 U.S. 33 [1996]), seize items that are in plain view (*Horton v. California*, 496 U.S. 128 [1990]), frisk the driver and/or search the passenger compartment of the vehicle out of concerns for safety (*Michigan v. Long*, 463 U.S. 1032 [1983]), and search the entire car if probable cause to arrest and/or search is developed (*Belton*, 453 U.S. 454). Finally, police are not required to provide the *Miranda* warnings when asking questions pursuant to a routine vehicle stop (*Miranda v. Arizona*, 384 U.S. 436 [1966]).

Some questions have been raised concerning the constitutional protections afforded to passengers who happen to be riding in a vehicle that is stopped. For example, in *Brendlin v. California* (551 U.S. 249 [2007]), the Supreme Court was presented with the question of whether a passenger is considered "seized" within the meaning of the Fourth Amendment when the vehicle is stopped. It held that passengers, like drivers, are seized in such situations. Why does this matter? Since the passenger was considered seized, he was able to challenge the constitutionality of the stop. He did so because police found contraband on his person.

What police *cannot* do during the course of a vehicle stop (or any other stop for that matter) is ascertain immigration status. In *Arizona v. United States*, 567 U.S. ___ (2012), the Supreme Court invalidated several parts of an Arizona law that required state officers to make a "reasonable attempt. . . . to determine the immigration status" of any person stopped provided that "reasonable suspicion exists that the person is an alien and is unlawfully present in the United States." The Court held that "[d]etaining individuals solely to verify their immigration status would raise constitutional concerns."

## When Other Doctrines Govern Searches of Automobiles

Note that the automobile exception cases are *not* the only cases governing warrantless searches of vehicles. Many warrantless searches of vehicles are better analyzed under other exceptions to the Fourth Amendment's warrant requirement. For example, the Supreme Court has rejected the use of the automobile exception in analyzing searches of automobiles crossing international borders. Such cases are better analyzed under the border checkpoints exception discussed in Chapter 7.

Still other warrantless searches of automobiles are permissible based on other decisions unrelated to the automobile exception initially set forth in *Carroll*. These include searches (1) incident to arrest (see earlier discussion); (2) during the course of a stop-and-frisk (see Chapter 6); (3) under the plain view doctrine (see later discussion); (4) based on the inventory search exception (see Chapter 7); and (5) with consent by the automobile's occupant (see Chapter 7). Therefore, searches of automobiles—like searches of other places as well as people—can simultaneously be governed by several different doctrines. Figure 5.5 summarizes the levels of justification required to conduct various types of vehicle searches. Figure 5.6 presents a timeline of key automobile search and seizure cases.

| Level of Intrusion | Justification Required |
|---|---|
| Search of entire car, including containers | Probable cause to search |
| Search of passenger compartment and containers | Probable cause to arrest occupant |
| Weapons search of passenger compartment | Reasonable suspicion/fear for safety |
| Order occupants out of car | Reasonable suspicion to stop |
| Inventory search | Administrative |

**FIGURE 5.5 Levels of Justification for Automobile Searches**

**Timeline of Key Automobile Search and Seizure Cases,** *continued*

| 1925 | 1970 | 1974 | 1975 |
|---|---|---|---|
| ***Carroll* v. *United States*** An automobile can be searched without a warrant if the police have probable cause.[0] | ***Chambers* v. *Maroney*** If it is necessary and/or reasonable to search a vehicle later at a police station, post arrest, the *Carroll* doctrine applies.[1] | ***Cardwell* v. *Lewis*** People enjoy a lesser expectation of privacy in their vehicles than in their homes and offices.[2] | ***Texas* v. *White*** The *Carroll* doctrine applies to all post-arrest vehicle searches conducted later at a police station, irrespective of need and/or reasonableness.[3] |

**FIGURE 5.6**

### Racial Profiling

Clearly, the police have numerous opportunities to detect contraband during the course of a vehicle stop. And since almost every driver violates a traffic law at some point or other, there is plenty of justification for stopping motorists to begin with. But whether every motorist is stopped for *legitimate* reasons is questionable. Further, even if the police have legal grounds to stop someone in his or her car, they may be motivated by some pretext. Should the police be able to use traffic laws to stop people when they really have other objectives in mind (such as, to gain consent to search)? The Supreme Court has yet to answer this question, which has led to the concern that the police may have *too* much discretion in terms of their authority to stop motorists. Closely tied to this concern are allegations of **racial profiling**, which have emerged in recent years. Racial profiling occurs when the police use race or ethnicity as a factor in determining whether to stop someone.

*Whren v. United States*
*(517 U.S. 806 [1996])*

A driver's race or ethnicity obviously does not provide the justification to stop him or her. But many argue that the police often use existing traffic laws, which are numerous and frequently violated, to single out certain drivers based on their race or ethnicity. The Supreme Court has yet to decide on the constitutionality of this type of conduct directly, but at least one of its decisions has come close. For example, in *Whren v. United States*, 517 U.S. 806 (1996), Washington, D.C., police made a traffic stop and observed two bags of crack cocaine in the hands of a passenger who was seated in the front of the car. The police testified that they stopped the driver because he had violated traffic laws. In contrast, the defendants claimed that the stop was made based on their race and that the police used alleged traffic violations as a reason to stop them.

The Supreme Court concluded that the "constitutional reasonableness of traffic stops" does not depend "on the actual motivations of the individual officers." The Court also concluded that the only relevant inquiry is whether the officer had cause to stop the car.

### DECISION-MAKING EXERCISE 5.8

#### PROPER SCOPE FOR AN AUTOMOBILE SEARCH

Joan Lee was pulled over on Interstate 10 after a highway patrol officer observed her aggressively weaving from one lane to another. The officer had probable cause to search the vehicle for drugs. Accordingly, Lee opened the trunk, at which point the officer's attention was drawn to the spare tire. To the officer, it looked as though the spare was the wrong size for the vehicle. In addition, there appeared to be a white, powdery substance on the rubber. Based on his knowledge that narcotics are smuggled in such a fashion, the officer pulled the spare out of the vehicle, slashed it open with a knife, and found drugs inside. The drugs were seized and Lee was arrested. In terms of scope, was this search justified?

| **1977** | **1970** | **1983** | **1985** |
|---|---|---|---|
| ***Pennsylvania v. Mimms*** During routine traffic stops, officers can order drivers out of their cars and frisk them.[4] | ***United States v. Ross*** With probable cause, police can search an automobile without a warrant, including any containers within.[5] | ***Michigan v. Long*** Police can frisk a driver and search the passenger compartment of a vehicle following a valid stop, provided they have reasonable suspicion that the driver poses a danger.[6] | ***California v. Carney*** If the setting "objectively indicates that the vehicle is being used for transportation," then the automobile exception applies.[7] |

**FIGURE 5.6** *(continued)*

It rejected the argument that the Fourth Amendment requires a court to consider whether "the officer's conduct deviated materially from usual police practices, so that a reasonable officer in the same circumstances would not have made the stop for the reasons given." Simply put, the Supreme Court has stated that individual officers' motivations—whether racial or of any other substance—are irrelevant. The only question worth asking and answering, according to the Court, is whether the officer had cause to stop. Needless to say, this decision did not satisfy critics of racial profiling.

**Equal Protection Claims.** The Court's opinion in *Whren* effectively closed the door on Fourth Amendment claims of racial discrimination. So what remedies are available for claims of racial profiling? One option is that motorists can sue, based on 42 U.S.C. 1983, for racial discrimination under the equal protection clause of the Fourteenth Amendment. At least two types of Fourteenth Amendment claims can be identified. The first is a challenge to a law or policy that intentionally classifies people based on race or some other classification. Second, plaintiffs can argue that a racially neutral policy or statute is being enforced in a discriminatory fashion.

For the first type of equal protection claim to succeed, it must be shown that (1) a practice or policy intentionally classifies persons based on race and (2) the practice or policy withstands "strict judicial scrutiny" (*Adarand Constructors, Inc. v. Pena*, 515 U.S. 200 [1995]a). These are known as *Pena's* first and second prongs.

Concerning *Pena's* first prong, one court has said that racial discrimination can be shown by a law that "expressly classifies persons on the basis of race" (*Hayden v. County of Nassau*, 180 F.3d 42 [2nd Cir. 1999]) or by a practice or policy that treats one differently from members of other racial groups. For example, if a police department's policy authorizes stops based on racial or ethnic characteristics, it would be discriminatory. According to another court, racial discrimination exists when law enforcement personnel "adopt a policy, employ a practice, or in a given situation take steps to initiate an investigation . . . based solely upon the citizen's race" (*United States v. Avery*, 128 F.3d 974 [6th Cir. 1997]).

There are no formal policies or practices that expressly authorize traffic stops based on race. It is therefore necessary to use statistical evidence to show that the police acted with intent to discriminate, even though discrimination is not a stated purpose of the policy. In *Hunter v. Underwood*, 471 U.S. 222 (1985), for instance, the Supreme Court sustained an equal protection claim by African Americans who claimed they were deprived of important rights for convictions under an Alabama law. The Court accepted statistical evidence to the effect that blacks were disenfranchised under the law at a rate 1.7 times more than whites.

However, the saying "you can prove anything with statistics" is at least partly true, and courts have had reservations about relying on statistical evidence of racial discrimination. In *McCleskey v. Kemp*, 481 U.S. 279 (1987), the Court rejected a statistical analysis related to the application of the death penalty in Georgia. The study presented in that case

| **1990** | **1996** | **1997** | **2000** |
|---|---|---|---|
| ***Michigan Dept. of State Police v. Sitz*** Suspicionless seizures of motorists are permissible for purposes of detecting drunk driving.[8] | ***Whren v. United States*** The constitutional reasonableness of a traffic stop does not depend on an officer's initial motivation. It depends only on whether there was justification to stop the vehicle.[9] | ***Maryland v. Wilson*** During a routine traffic stop, the officer can order a passenger out of the vehicle and frisk him or her.[10] | ***City of Indianapolis v. Edmund*** The police cannot operate roadblocks for the purpose of detecting illegal drugs.[11] |

**FIGURE 5.6** *(continued)*

claimed that the race of the victim was the factor most likely to influence jury members in their death penalty decisions. The Court claimed that the study showed only a correlation between the race of the victim and the decision to impose the death penalty. The Court took a similar approach in *United States v. Armstrong*, 517 U.S. 456 (1996), in which it rejected the defendants' argument that the federal government engaged in the racially selective prosecution of "crack" cocaine offenders. It held that the defendants "failed to satisfy the threshold showing . . . that the Government declined to prosecute similarly situated suspects of other races." These decisions suggest that it would be exceedingly difficult to show Fourteenth Amendment discrimination in the context of racial profiling.

As for *Pena's* second prong—that a policy or practice must withstand "strict judicial scrutiny"—the government must show the necessity of the classification scheme. Specifically, a Fourteenth Amendment equal protection claim will not succeed if the government can show that it has a compelling interest justifying the practice or policy. Or stated differently, if the government can show that unequal treatment is necessary to further some clear, legitimate government purpose, an equal protection claim will not succeed (see, for example, *Heller v. Doe*, 509 U.S. 312 [1993]). However, if the government cannot meet this strict scrutiny test, an equal protection claim will probably succeed, provided that *Pena's* first prong is also satisfied.

As for the second type of Fourteenth Amendment claim, courts sometimes hear lawsuits in which plaintiffs allege that a racially neutral policy or statute has been enforced in a racially discriminatory fashion. Indeed, as early as 1886, the Supreme Court recognized that laws and policies can be enforced in a discriminatory fashion. In *Yick Wo v. Hopkins*, 118 U.S. 356 (1886), the Supreme Court held that a racially neutral statute had been enforced "with a mind so unequal and oppressive as to amount to a practical denial by the state of that equal protection of the laws . . . which is secured . . . by the broad and benign provisions of the Fourteenth Amendment to the Constitution of the United States."

Some plaintiffs have argued that legal searches and seizures conducted with appropriate justification violate the Fourteenth Amendment if they are used to selectively target certain individuals over others. For example, a plaintiff may argue that even though he or she was detained lawfully, the police violated the Fourteenth Amendment's equal protection clause because they selectively targeted individuals for such actions based solely on race. These types of claims are fairly rare and not often successful, but one New Jersey court has stated that if a police department embarks "upon an officially sanctioned de facto policy of targeting minorities for investigation and arrest," then it may be held liable (*State v. Kennedy*, 588 A.2d 834 [N.J. Super. 1991]).

**Civil Rights Act of 1964.** It is exceedingly difficult, if not currently impossible, to succeed with a Fourteenth Amendment equal protection–based claim. Another available remedy is Title VII of the Civil Rights Act of 1964, which requires a showing of **disparate impact**. A policy or action has a disparate impact if it treats one group in a markedly different fashion than another.

| **2004** | **2007** | **2009** | **2011** |
|---|---|---|---|
| ***Illinois* v. *Lidster*** Police are constitutionally authorized to conduct suspicionless vehicle checkpoints for the purpose of gaining information about a crime recently committed in the area.[12] | ***Brendlin* v. *California*** Passengers, like drivers, are considered "seized" during traffic stops, meaning they enjoy Fourth Amendment protection from unreasonable searches and seizures.[13] | ***Arizona* v. *Gant*** If a motorist is arrested, police may search the vehicle only if it is reasonable to assume the arrestee could access the vehicle *or* the vehicle contains evidence of the offense of arrest.[14] | ***Davis* v. *United States*** The post-arrest seizure of evidence not connected with the offense of arrest is constitutionally permissible if based on objectively reasonable reliance on appropriate appellate precedent.[15] *Gant* would have invalidated the seizure in this case, but it had not been decided at the time the seizure took place. |

**FIGURE 5.6** *(continued)*

Title VII states, in relevant part, that recipients of federal funds

> may not . . . utilize criteria or methods of administration which have the effect of subjecting individuals to discrimination based on their race, color, national origin, or have the effect of defeating or substantially impairing accomplishment of the objectives of the program as respects individuals of a particular race, color, or national origin" (28 C.F.R. 42.104[b][2]).

On its face, this legislation looks like an attractive option for challenging racial profiling in traffic stops. But the statute is primarily used by the federal government to enforce certain rules against entities that receive federal funds—usually state and local units of government. The question of whether private parties (such as average citizens) can enforce Title VII is one that has been litigated extensively in the courts. Of particular interest has been the issue of *standing*. Specifically, a plaintiff must show that he or she was a direct participant in or intended beneficiary of a state or local program or activity that receives federal funds. The Civil Rights Act of 1987 defines "program or activity" as *all* operations of a governmental entity that receives federal funds. Thus, traffic stops would appear to fall within the meaning of the legislation, and in theory, people should be able to sue under Title VII for racially discriminatory traffic enforcement policies. The Supreme Court has not yet ruled on this issue, however.

## Plain View Searches

The everyday meaning of "plain view" would suggest that it applies to situations in which evidence can be seen without having to search for it. However, "plain view" has a very specific meaning in criminal procedure, and the doctrine applies only in certain situations.

The "plain view" doctrine first emerged in the Supreme Court's decision in *Coolidge* 403 U.S. 443. The issue in *Coolidge* was whether evidence seized during a search of cars belonging to Coolidge was admissible. The police had a warrant to search the cars, but it was later deemed invalid, so the state argued that the evidence should still be admissible because the cars were in plain view from a public street and from the house in which Coolidge was arrested. The Court did not accept this argument, pointing out that just because the police could *see* the cars from where they were was not enough to permit seizure of the evidence within. However, the Court did point out that if the police been *in* an area, such as a car or a house, if the evidence was "immediately apparent as such," and if the evidence was discovered "inadvertently," the evidence would have been admissible. In other words, part of the reason the evidence was not admissible in *Coolidge* was that the police officers were not lawfully in the cars when the evidence was seized.

To summarize, the Court decided in *Coolidge* that a plain view seizure is authorized when (1) the police are lawfully in the area where the evidence is located; (2) the items are immediately apparent as subject to seizure; and (3) the discovery of the evidence is inadvertent. The

## RACIAL PROFILING

While on patrol, Officer James observed a white van with an African American driver inside, idling in a fire lane adjacent to a shopping mall. Rather than issuing the driver a citation, James parked his cruiser and entered the van's license plate number into his Law Enforcement Information Network ("LEIN") computer, which revealed that the van was registered to a Curtis Ellison, who had an outstanding felony warrant. Following department policy, James called for backup and continued to observe the van. Before backup arrived, another African American male got into the van and drove it away. Officer James followed the van until his backup was close, at which point he activated his lights and stopped the van. James advised the driver that he was being stopped for parking in a fire lane and asked for his license, registration, and proof of insurance. When James learned that Ellison was the *passenger*, not the driver, he ordered Ellison out of the van, searched him, and found two firearms on his person. Ellison now alleges that he and his friend were victims of racial profiling and that the stop (and subsequent search) was invalid under the Fourth Amendment. Is this argument valid?

first prong of the *Coolidge* ruling—the lawful access prong—has remained relatively stable over time. The second and third prongs, however, have undergone significant interpretation in recent years. The remainder of this section more closely examines these three requirements.

### The Lawful Access Requirement

For the plain view doctrine to apply, the police must have **lawful access** to the object to be seized. As the Supreme Court stated in *Coolidge*:

> [P]lain view *alone* is never enough to justify the warrantless seizure of evidence. This is simply a corollary of the familiar principle . . . that no amount of probable cause can justify a warrantless search or seizure absent "exigent circumstances." Incontrovertible testimony of the senses that an incriminating object is on premises belonging to a criminal suspect may establish the fullest possible measure of probable cause. But even where the object is contraband, this Court has repeatedly stated and enforced the basic rule that the police may not enter and make a warrantless seizure.

The Court's opinion in *Coolidge* reinforces the point that just because the police may *see* contraband does not necessarily mean they can *seize* it. If, for example, evidence is seen lying in a vacant lot or other public place, it may be seized. In such a situation, a search has not occurred. However, evidence that may be viewed from a public place but is, in fact, on private property cannot be seized unless a warrant is obtained or exigent circumstances are present. So, if a police officer on foot patrol observes a marijuana plant in the window of a private residence, he or she may not enter the premises and seize the plant, even though such observation establishes, as the Court stated in *Coolidge*, "the fullest possible measure of probable cause."

What is meant by *lawful vantage point*? There are four specific situations in which police officers may be in a lawful vantage point for purposes of the plain view doctrine. The first is during a warranted search. For example, if an officer comes upon an article during the execution of a valid search warrant, the plain view doctrine may apply (subject to further restrictions described later). Second, officers are at a lawful vantage point during a valid arrest. This includes warrantless arrests in public, warrantless arrests based on exigent circumstances, and arrests with warrants. Third, when a warrantless search is conducted, the police officer is in a lawful vantage point—assuming, of course, that the warrantless search is based on probable cause. Finally, as illustrated in the previous paragraph, officers are always in a lawful vantage point during nonsearches.

## The "Immediately Apparent" Requirement

In addition to the requirement that the police have lawful access to an object, it must also be **immediately apparent** that the object is subject to seizure. *Immediately apparent* means that the officer has probable cause to seize the object.

This was the decision reached in *Arizona v. Hicks*, 480 U.S. 321 (1987). In that case, the police entered the defendant's apartment without a warrant because a bullet had been fired through his floor into the apartment below, injuring a person there. The warrantless entry was based on the exigency of looking for the shooter, for other potential victims, and for the weapon used in the incident. Once inside the apartment, the officer observed new stereo equipment that seemed out of place, given the surroundings. The officer suspected the stereo equipment was stolen but did not have probable cause to believe that it was, so he picked up a turntable in order to obtain its serial number. He then called in the information and confirmed that it was stolen. The Court held that this warrantless action did not satisfy the plain view doctrine. It was not immediately apparent to the officer that the stereo equipment was stolen.

Keep in mind that *immediately apparent* has virtually the same meaning as *probable cause to seize*. An officer does not need to be absolutely certain that the object is subject to seizure for the plain view doctrine to apply. That was the decision reached in *Texas v. Brown*, 460 U.S. 730 (1983). Brown was stopped late at night at a routine driver's license checkpoint. When he opened the glove box to look for his license, an opaque balloon, knotted at the opening, fell out onto the floor of the passenger side of the vehicle. The officer making the stop observed what he perceived to be drug paraphernalia in the glove compartment and ultimately seized the balloon and its contents. The balloon was later proven to contain heroin. Brown was convicted of narcotics offenses. The Texas Court of Criminal Appeals reversed Brown's conviction, pointing out that the plain view doctrine did not apply because the officer did not *know* incriminatory evidence was before him when he seized the balloon. A unanimous Supreme Court reversed the decision, stating, "The fact that [the officer] could not see through the opaque fabric of the balloon is all but irrelevant; the distinctive character of the balloon itself spoke volumes as to its contents—particularly to the trained eye of the officer."

*Arizona v. Hicks*
*(480 U.S. 321 [1987])*

## The Role of Inadvertency

The role of *inadvertency* in the plain view determination has received considerable attention. The original position of the Supreme Court in *Coolidge* was that an object seized under the plain view doctrine must not have been anticipated by the police. For example, assume that a police officer obtains a warrant to search a suspect's home for the proceeds from a robbery. Assume further that the officer *expects* to find guns in the house but does not state in the warrant that guns will be sought. If, during the search, the officer finds guns, under the Supreme Court's old ruling, the guns will not be admissible because the officers expected to find them. This limit on the plain view doctrine came to be known as the *inadvertency requirement*. The rationale was that an officer who anticipates discovering evidence of a crime should seek prior judicial authorization (a warrant). Further, the Fourth Amendment's particularity requirement would be compromised if general searches were permitted.

In *Horton v. California*, 496 U.S. 128 (1990), the Court abandoned the inadvertency requirement, declaring that inadvertency, although a "characteristic of most legitimate 'plain view' seizures, . . . is not a necessary condition" of the doctrine. The Court offered two reasons for abandoning the inadvertency requirement imposed in *Coolidge*. First, according to *Horton*, as long as a warrant particularly describes the places to be searched and the objects to be seized, the officer cannot expand the area of the search once the evidence has been found. In other words, it is unlikely that once officers have found the evidence listed in the warrant, they will go on a "fishing expedition," looking for evidence not

*Horton v. California*
*(496 U.S. 128 [1990])*

**CONSIDERING THE "IMMEDIATELY APPARENT" REQUIREMENT FOR PLAIN VIEW**

Police officers have a warrant for the arrest of Randy Whitbeck, who is the suspect in a rape. They lawfully execute the warrant and arrest Whitbeck in his home. While there, one of the officers observes a rifle leaning up against the wall in an adjacent bedroom. With probable cause to suspect that it is an illegal assault weapon, she enters the room and seizes the gun. May the gun be introduced into evidence? Assume further that the gun is not connected in any way to the rape. Does it matter that the seizure of the gun is not connected with the rape? Finally, if the officers knew the rifle was contraband *prior* to serving the warrant and if the rifle was not named in the search warrant accompanying the arrest warrant, could they still seize it lawfully?

listed in the warrant. According to the Court, the particularity requirement itself ensures that people's privacy is protected.

Second, the Court noted that "evenhanded law enforcement is best achieved by the application of objective standards of conduct, rather than standards that depend upon the subjective state of mind of the officer." An inadvertency requirement would force the courts to dwell on police officers' subjective motivations, which would be both time consuming and distracting. The Court went on to note that "[t]he fact that an officer is interested in an item of evidence and fully expects to find it in the course of a search should not invalidate its seizure if the search is confined in area and duration by the terms of the warrant or a valid exception to the warrant requirement."

### Plain Touch, Feel, and Smell

The term *plain view* seems to imply that the plain view doctrine is limited to items that the police can see with their eyes. However, in recent years, the Court has extended the plain view doctrine to incorporate items discovered using additional senses, especially smell (*United States v. Place*, 462 U.S. 696 [1983]) and feel (Cf., *Minnesota v. Dickerson*, 508 U.S. 366 [1993]). In *Dickerson*, for example, a police officer spotted Dickerson acting suspiciously near a notorious "crack house." The officer frisked Dickerson for a weapon, pursuant to *Terry v. Ohio*, but instead of finding a weapon, the officer found a small lump that he could not immediately identify. Instead of terminating the frisk, the officer carefully examined the object in Dickerson's pocket, which turned out to be cocaine. The Court ruled that this action was unlawful, arguing that the officer's actions fell outside the permissible scope of a seizure based on plain touch. Had it been immediately apparent to the officer that the object was contraband, the seizure would have been permissible. Additionally, the plain view doctrine can be extended to what police officers hear, as long as probable cause is in place and all the aforementioned requirements have been satisfied.

### Plain View as a Fallback Measure

It should be noted that the plain view doctrine is often thought of as something of a fallback measure. There are countless situations in which the plain view doctrine would seem to apply but in which the courts have based their decisions on other doctrines. An example of such a case is *Colorado v. Bannister*, 449 U.S. 1 (1980). A police officer approached a stopped vehicle and observed chrome lug nuts on the passenger seat that were of the same type that had reportedly been stolen in the vicinity. The occupants of the car also matched the description of those described by the victim. The officer engaged in a warrantless search of the vehicle and seized the lug nuts. The Supreme Court did not apply the plain view doctrine in this case but instead relied on the automobile exception to the warrant requirement set forth in *Carroll* (see earlier discussion). The Court argued that the warrantless search and seizure of the evidence was permissible, given the inherent mobility of the car, so the plain view doctrine did not apply.

However, if a warrantless search or seizure is not authorized by any other doctrine (such as a search incident to arrest, or search in the presence of exigent circumstances), then the plain view may apply to allow the evidence. Consider, for example, the discussion concerning search warrant requirements in Chapter 4. The particularity requirement states that the warrant must explicitly describe what is to be seized. But if during the course of a warranted search, the police stumble across evidence that they believe can be seized but is not set forth in the search warrant, the plain view doctrine may apply. In such a situation, the original authorization to engage in the search (the search warrant) does not clearly permit seizure of the evidence, yet plain view provides a fallback basis for seizing the evidence.

Similarly, evidence discovered during a hot pursuit (*Warden v. Hayden*), when accompanying an arrestee to his or her room (*Washington v. Chrisman*), when investigating a fire in a home (*Michigan v. Tyler*, 436 U.S. 499 [1978]), and in many other such situations can be seized but not always on the basis of the warrantless action itself. For example, assume police officers during the course of a hot pursuit find a cache of illegal weapons in a house. The hot pursuit exception to the warrant requirement does not authorize seizure of the weapons, but the plain view doctrine does. Again, the plain view doctrine serves as a fallback measure. Another such fallback measure is the inventory search exception, discussed in Chapter 7.

In summary, the plain view doctrine will apply only in situations in which the police have lawful access to the object in question. Provided that the appropriate level of justification is in place to engage in the warrantless action in question (such as probable cause, reasonable suspicion, administrative justification, or engaging in a nonsearch), the lawful access requirement will automatically be satisfied.

# ▶ Warrantless Arrests

Just as there are a number of types of searches that may be conducted without a warrant, the Supreme Court has also sanctioned certain types of arrests that may be made without a warrant. They include arrests in the presence of exigent circumstances and arrests in public places.

## Arrests Based on Exigent Circumstances

Exigent (emergency) circumstances may justify warrantless entry into a private home for the purpose of making an arrest. The five exigencies identified earlier in this chapter for justifying a search also justify warrantless entry for making an arrest. In other words, a warrantless arrest, with probable cause, is permissible if any of the following is present: (1) hot pursuit; (2) danger to officers; (3) danger to third parties; (4) escape; and (5) destruction of evidence. Figure 5.7 shows the San Bernardino, California, Police Department's policy for making warrantless arrests based on exigent circumstances.

## Arrests in Public Places

Unlike arrests made in a home (or in a third-party residence), arrests made in public do not require warrants. In *United States v. Watson*, 423 U.S. 411 (1976), the Supreme Court upheld the common-law rule that arrests made in public do not need to be predicated on a warrant. The Court expressed confidence in the ability of police officers to make probable cause determinations: "[W]e decline to transform [a] judicial preference [for arrest warrants] into a constitutional rule when the judgment of the Nation and Congress has for so long been to authorize warrantless public arrests on probable cause."

*United States v. Watson*
*(423 U.S. 411 [1976])*

The Court extended this decision to the curtilage of a home in *United States v. Santana*, 427 U.S. 38 (1976). In that case, the police who had probable cause to arrest Santana arrived

The "Ramey Decision" by the California Supreme Court commands that a police officer may not enter the residence of a suspect <u>for the purpose of effecting an arrest</u> without a warrant of arrest, unless "exigent (emergency) circumstances" justify such action, or lawful consent for entry is obtained.

The opinion defines exigent circumstances as "an emergency situation requiring swift action to prevent (1) <u>imminent</u> danger to life, (2) or <u>serious</u> damage to property, (3) or to forestall the <u>imminent</u> escape of a suspect, (4) or destruction of evidence."

The burden of proof of the existence of one or more of the exigent circumstances defined by the court will be upon the prosecution, and it appears that the courts will closely scrutinize any such claim of justification.

The prohibition includes arrests for felonies or misdemeanors whether by day or by night, and the prohibition encompasses arrest of adults and minors.

The Ramey rule will be applied to temporary residences such as hotels and motels. With the application of the "vicarious exclusionary rule", which acts to suppress evidence against any defendant when such evidence is obtained in the violation of any third party's rights, it appears that the prohibition will extend to residences of others where the suspect may be a guest regardless of the temporary nature of the suspect's tenancy.

The opinion of the court does not discuss the circumstances of "hot pursuit" or close pursuit from another place into a residence. It is believed that if probable cause for arrest exists during a pursuit but the arrest is not made due purely to the actions of the suspect in evading the officers and going into a residence, then the entry and arrest will be reasonable and justifiable in light of the imminent danger of escape.

Since the issue addressed by the court is the entry into a residence for the purpose of effecting the arrest and the necessity for judicial review of such process before the entry, it can be assumed that entry by means of a valid search warrant would satisfy the requirement for judicial review, and an arrest based on evidence uncovered during the search would be proper and not in violation of the rule in Ramey.

It appears also that if the officer enters the residence lawfully for any purpose other than the arrest of a suspect (in response to a call for service or in the legitimate course of an investigation) an ensuing arrest would be proper, although the courts would certainly scrutinize these circumstances.

In light of this opinion, the policy of the San Bernardino Police Department will be:

A warrant of arrest shall be obtained prior to any arrest of a suspect from a residence at any time for any offense except:

1. When one or more of the defined exigent circumstances are readily evident.
2. As a result of close pursuit wherein the arrest would have been lawful except for the suspect's evading the arrest and going into a residence.
3. When probable cause is developed during the execution of a valid search warrant for the residence and the suspect is present.
4. When entry has been lawfully made for another purpose (such as investigation of an offense or response to a call for service) and was not for the purpose of effecting an arrest.
5. When lawful consent for entry for the purpose of effecting an arrest is obtained. In the case of minors, proper consent may be obtained from the parent/s or responsible adult in charge, or, in the absence of a responsible adult, from the minor himself.

During normal business hours, an arrest warrant may be obtained by contacting the District Attorney's Office. Outside of normal business hours, it will be necessary to contact the "on call" deputy district attorney for review and assistance and then a magistrate for the issuance of a warrant. There is no statutory provision for a telephonic arrest warrant, consequently it will be necessary to contact the magistrate in person.

**FIGURE 5.7 Warrantless Arrest Policy (San Bernardino, CA, Police Department)**

**FIGURE 5.7** *(continued)*

at her house to find her standing in the opening of her front door. When she saw the officers approaching, she retreated into the house. The officers followed her into the house and made the arrest. The Supreme Court declared that the officers' actions were constitutional because when Santana was standing in the doorway, "[s]he was not in an area where she had any expectation of privacy." The entry into Santana's house was justified on exigent circumstances—namely, hot pursuit.

*Watson* and *Santana*, read together, permit another type of warrantless action authorized by the Fourth Amendment. As long as they have a probable cause, the police can make a warrantless arrest in a public place. A warrantless arrest in the curtilage of someone's home is also authorized. The key fact in *Santana*, though, was that the arrest was initiated by the police observing what they perceived to be criminal activity from a public place. This important qualification ensures that the police cannot just wander onto private property, looking for opportunities to make arrests. A crime must be observed from a lawful vantage point; otherwise, a warrant will be required.

What if the offense takes place out of view of the officer? The courts have stated that if probable cause exists, the police can arrest anyone for any offense, as long as the arrest is made in a public place. It is useful, though, to distinguish between (1) various types of offenses and (2) whether the offense in question was committed in the presence of the officer. Generally, any offense committed in an officer's presence permits an arrest. Also, there is no requirement that the offense for which a person is arrested be "closely related" to the conduct that led to the confrontation between officer and suspect (*Devenpeck v. Alford*, 543 U.S. 146 [2004]). Additionally, serious offenses (felonies) committed *out* of the officer's view permit a warrantless, public arrest—provided that probable cause exists. Less clear is the issue of a warrantless, public arrest for a minor offense committed out of the officer's presence.

## Arrests for Minor Offenses

The Supreme Court has declared that "the Fourth Amendment does not forbid a warrantless arrest for a minor criminal offense, such as a misdemeanor seatbelt violation punishable only by a fine" (*Atwater v. City of Lago Vista*, 532 U.S. 318 [2001]). Texas law makes it a misdemeanor for a front seat passenger in a car equipped with seatbelts to not wear the seatbelt. The law states that the police may arrest or issue a citation to the passenger. Atwater was arrested and later filed suit under Section 1983, arguing that the officer violated her Fourth Amendment rights. In the Court's words,

> Atwater has cited no particular evidence that those who framed and ratified the Fourth Amendment sought to limit peace officers' warrantless misdemeanor arrest authority to instances of actual breach of the peace, and the Court's review of framing-era documentary history has likewise failed to reveal any such design.

On its face, *Atwater* seems to be a controversial case. On closer examination, though, the decision is likely to have little impact on criminal procedure. The reason for this is, simply,

*Atwater v. City of Lago Vista*
*(532 U.S. 318 [2001])*

that it is unpractical (and usually undesirable) to arrest people for violations as trivial as failing to wear a seatbelt. Just because the Court has now said that such warrantless arrests do not violate the Fourth Amendment does not mean that the police will alter their behavior consistent with the *Atwater* decision.

*Virginia v. Moore*
*(553 U.S. 164 [2008])*

In a related case, *Virginia v. Moore*, 553 U.S. 164 (2008), police stopped a motorist for driving with a suspended license. Virginia state law required that the officers issue a citation and summons to appear in court. Instead, the officers arrested the driver. In a search incident to arrest, officers found cocaine. Moore's attorney sought suppression of the cocaine at trial. The trial court judge allowed the evidence, but the Virginia Supreme Court reversed. In a unanimous decision, the Supreme Court held that the officers did not violate Moore's constitutional rights. The *Moore* case is similar to *Atwater* in the sense that the offense that justified the arrest was relatively minor. And the Supreme Court sanctioned the officers' actions, even though they ran counter to Virginia law.

# Summary

## 1. Summarize the issues involved in warrantless searches and seizures.

The situations in which law enforcement officials *can* search without a warrant almost outnumber the number of situations in which they *cannot* search without a warrant. The Supreme Court has carved out several exceptions to the Fourth Amendment's warrant requirement. While the exceptions vary considerably, a common thread runs through them: The Court has decided that it is not always practical to obtain a warrant. Permissible warrantless searches can be categorized as searches incident to arrest, hot pursuit, automobile searches, and plain view searches.

## 2. Explain the search incident to arrest doctrine.

Searches incident to arrest are constitutionally permissible, but the arrest itself must, of course, be legal (based on probable cause). Also, the arrest must result in someone being taken into custody. In addition, the search must follow the arrest closely in time. The scope of the search is also limited. A search incident to arrest is limited to (1) the person arrested and any containers discovered from that search and (2) the arrestee's immediate grabbing area. Prior to an arrest, the police may engage in a protective sweep of the premises, if they have a reasonable belief that evidence may be destroyed by someone sympathetic to the arrestee. They may also engage in a protective sweep following arrest. No justification is required for such a postarrest sweep. Finally, the Supreme Court appears to agree that the premises can be searched for evidence that is likely to be destroyed, and in such cases, probable cause is not required.

## 3. Explain the concept of hot pursuit.

Hot pursuit, threats to persons, and threats to evidence are exigent circumstances that also permit dispensing with the Fourth Amendment's warrant requirement. Warrantless searches and arrests based on hot pursuit are constitutional only if the police have probable cause to believe (1) that the person they are pursuing has committed a serious offense; (2) that the person will be found on the premises the police seek to enter; and (3) that the suspect will escape or harm someone or that evidence will be lost or destroyed. Also, the pursuit must originate from a lawful vantage point and the scope and timing of the search must be reasonable. When hot pursuit does not apply, a warrantless search for evanescent evidence is permissible when (1) there is probable cause to believe that evidence will be destroyed, lost, or devalued; (2) the procedures employed are reasonable; and (3) the exigency was not police created. Finally, if neither hot pursuit nor the potential for damage or destruction to evidence exists, a warrantless search is permissible if the police have probable cause to believe a person on the premises is in imminent danger of death or serious bodily harm.

## 4. Summarize the special issues involved in automobile searches.

Warrantless automobile searches are constitutionally permissible because (1) automobiles are mobile, making it difficult to obtain warrants; (2) people enjoy a lesser expectation of privacy when in their cars; and (3) automobiles are subject to a host of government regulations. Even so, for an automobile search to be constitutional, it must be (1) directed at a vehicle that serves a transportation function; (2) premised on probable cause to believe the vehicle contains evidence of a crime; and (3) completed without unnecessary delay.

Racial profiling is of particular concern in the context of vehicle stops. It occurs when the police use race or ethnicity as a factor in determining whether they will stop someone. While a driver's race or ethnicity clearly does not provide justification to stop him or her, critics claim that the police can use existing traffic laws to single out certain individuals for improper reasons—say, for instance, pulling someone over for speeding regardless of whether any traffic laws were actually violated. The Supreme Court has yet to decide directly on the constitutionality of this type of conduct, but at least one decision has come close to the issue. In *Whren*, the Court stated that the "constitutional reasonableness of traffic stops" does not depend "on the actual motivations of the individual officers." Despite this controversial decision, claims may be made under the Fourteenth Amendment and under Title VI of the Civil Rights Act of 1964.

## 5. Summarize the plain view doctrine.

Items in plain view can be seized if the police have lawful access to the items and if it is immediately apparent that the items are contraband. The discovery of such items does not have to be inadvertent. The "plain view" doctrine has been extended to include plain smell and plain feel. The plain view doctrine should be viewed as something of a fallback measure, because the seizure of evidence can often be justified by other doctrines, such as hot pursuit, search incident to arrest, automobile searches, and so on.

## 6. Describe the situations in which warrantless arrests may be made.

Two types of warrantless arrests have been authorized by the Supreme Court. First, if exigent circumstances are present, the police may make a warrantless arrest. Probable cause is required, however. Second, an arrest in public can be made without a warrant. Even certain minor offenses can support arrest in public places.

# Key Terms

armspan rule *132*
automobile exception *140*
disparate impact *148*
evanescent evidence *137*
exceptions to the warrant
    requirement *130*

exigent circumstances *134*
hot pursuit *135*
immediately apparent *151*
lawful access *150*
"plain view" doctrine *149*
protective sweep *132*

racial profiling *146*
search incident to arrest *130*

# Key Cases

## Searches Incident to Arrest

- *Chimel v. California*, 395 U.S. 752 (1969)
- *Knowles v. Iowa*, 525 U.S. 113 (1998)
- *Preston v. United States*, 376 U.S. 364 (1964)

## Searches Based on Exigent Circumstances

- *Warden v. Hayden*, 387 U.S. 294 (1967)
- *Welsh v. Wisconsin*, 466 U.S. 740 (1984)
- *Minnesota v. Olson*, 495 U.S. 91 (1990)
- *Breithaupt v. Abram*, 352 U.S. 432 (1957)
- *Cupp v. Murphy*, 412 U.S. 291 (1973)

## Automobile Searches

- *Carroll v. United States*, 267 U.S. 132 (1925)
- *California v. Carney*, 471 U.S. 386 (1985)

- *New York v. Belton*, 453 U.S. 454 (1981)
- *Arizona v. Gant*, No. 07-542 (2009)
- *Whren v. United States*, 517 U.S. 806 (1996)

## Plain View Searches

- *Coolidge v. New Hampshire*, 403 U.S. 443 (1971)
- *Arizona v. Hicks*, 480 U.S. 321 (1987)
- *Horton v. California*, 496 U.S. 128 (1990)

## Warrantless Arrests

- *United States v. Watson*, 423 U.S. 411 (1976)
- *United States v. Santana*, 427 U.S. 38 (1976)
- *Atwater v. City of Lago Vista*, 532 U.S. 318 (2001)
- *Virginia v. Moore*, 553 U.S. 164 (2008)

# Further Exploration

1. A police officer is on foot patrol in a suburban neighborhood, and while walking by a residence, he views what is clearly a potted marijuana plant basking in the sun through a living room window. What can he do under these circumstances? Would a warrantless search exception apply? Why or why not? If not, then what can he do?

2. Officers have a search warrant for the home of an alleged child pornographer. Their warrant permits seizure of books, magazines, and documents. As they are conducting the search, they observe a computer. Although no images are displayed on the monitor, they seize the computer anyway. They justify the seizure under a plain view theory, claiming that the internet is frequently used to view and circulate images of child pornography. Will this seizure of the computer be upheld?

3. Review this chapter's discussion of the *Arizona v. Gant* decision. Assume that officers arrest a woman in her hotel room. She is handcuffed, moved into the hallway outside the room, and guarded by an officer. A remaining officer then searches the hotel room. Is this action justified? Would *Gant* come into play? If so, how would this decision apply? What other cases might apply to this case, and why?

4. A murder suspect was arrested pursuant to a vehicle stop. Officers found a cellular phone lying on the passenger seat. The vehicle was impounded, and the suspect was taken to the police station for questioning, along with his possessions (including the phone). As the suspect was being questioned, another officer scrolled through the phone numbers on the phone that had been taken from the car. Was the officer authorized to do this? If so, under what legal theory? Note that this scenario is based on an actual case: *State v. Boyd*, 992 A.2d 1071 (Conn. 2010).

5. Consider these facts from an actual case, *State v. Tibbles*, 236 P.3d 885 (Wa. 2010):

   Just before midnight on October 28, 2004, Trooper Larsen noticed that a vehicle driven by Tibbles had a defective taillight. He stopped the car and, upon making contact with Tibbles, detected a strong odor of marijuana. At the trooper's request, Tibbles provided his license but could not find his registration. Trooper Larsen asked Tibbles to step out of his vehicle, and Tibbles complied. The trooper informed Tibbles he could smell marijuana; Tibbles replied that he did not have any in his possession. Trooper Larsen then searched Tibbles but did not find either marijuana or drug paraphernalia. In response to the trooper's questioning, Tibbles denied smoking marijuana that day. Trooper Larsen then proceeded to search the interior of Tibbles's car. Under the front passenger seat inside a brown paper bag, he found a glass pipe, a glass container with what he believed was marijuana, a knife, and two lighters. Tibbles denied the marijuana was his. Trooper Larsen did not arrest Tibbles but cited and released him after confiscating the suspected marijuana and drug paraphernalia. Subsequent testing by the Washington State Patrol verified that the substance in the glass container was marijuana. The State charged Tibbles with misdemeanor possession of marijuana and drug paraphernalia. Before his trial in district court, Tibbles moved to suppress the evidence seized by Trooper Larsen as the poisonous fruits of an illegal search.

Should the evidence be suppressed? Why or why not? What doctrines and cases are relevant for deciding this case?

## Review Questions

1. Explain the term *exceptions* as applied to the Fourth Amendment.
2. Summarize the requirements for a valid search incident to arrest.
3. What type of law enforcement activities would be considered "exigent circumstances"?
4. Explain the Supreme Court's rationale for permitting warrantless searches of automobiles.
5. Summarize the requirements for a valid automobile search.
6. Explain the leading cases in the area of racial profiling.
7. What types of arrest are permissible without a warrant?
8. Explain how the term *plain view* means something different in criminal procedure than in everyday use.
9. Explain the lawful access prong of the plain view doctrine.
10. Explain the immediately apparent prong of the plain view doctrine.
11. To what extent is inadvertency relevant in the plain view context?
12. How has the plain view doctrine been extended by the Supreme Court?
13. What other Fourth Amendment doctrines may permit the seizure of evidence if the plain view doctrine does not apply?
14. Has the Supreme Court become too generous with exceptions to the Fourth Amendment's warrant requirement? Explain your position.

## Web Links and Exercises

1. Technology and search incident to arrest: Read about some recent lower court cases dealing with the intersection of technology and the search incident to arrest exception to the warrant requirement. One particularly relevant case is *United States v. Finley*, 477 F.3d 250 (5th Cir. 2007).
Suggested URL: http://cyb3rcrim3.blogspot.com/2007/05/search-incident-to-arrest.html (accessed May 3, 2013).
2. Read about policies and training in the area of police vehicle pursuits. What is the key dilemma underlying the decision of whether to pursue?
Suggested URL: http://www.ncjrs.gov/pdffiles/164831.pdf (accessed May 3, 2013).
3. Profiling and the war on terror: Read about racial profiling before and after 9/11. How has the worst terrorist attack on our nation altered profiling?
Suggested URL: http://www.scu.edu/ethics/publications/ethicalperspectives/profiling.html (accessed May 3, 2013).
4. Plain smell: Should the smell of burning marijuana justify a warrantless search? Read more in *United States v. Mowatt*, No. 06-4886 (4th Cir. 2008).
Suggested URL: http://pacer.ca4.uscourts.gov/opinion.pdf/064886.P.pdf (accessed May 3, 2013).

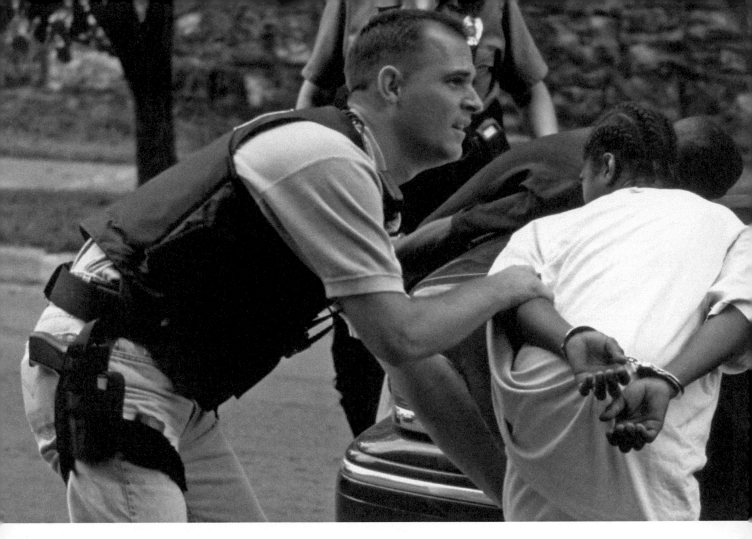

# 6 Actions Based on Reasonable Suspicion

**LEARNING OBJECTIVES**

When you complete this chapter, you should be able to:

1. *Distinguish between a stop and a nonstop.*

2. *Explain when a stop-and-frisk is permissible.*

3. *Summarize stop-and-frisk procedure.*

4. *Explain the relevance of drug courier profiling in the stop-and-frisk context.*

5. *Compare and contrast investigative detentions with stop-and-frisk.*

. . . . . . . . . . . . . . . . . . . . . . . . . . . . . . . . . . . . . . . . . . . . . . . . .

# Introduction: Loosening the Fourth Amendment's Restraints

Chapter 3 introduced "reasonable suspicion" as the justification required for a police officer to conduct a stop-and-frisk. Reasonable suspicion was defined as a lesser degree of certainty than probable cause, but a greater degree of certainty than a hunch or unsupported belief.

The term *reasonable suspicion* is found nowhere in the Constitution, but was created by the Supreme Court. The Court recognized that crime control could not be accomplished without a lower standard than probable cause. If probable cause was always required, police officers would not even be able to question people suspected of involvement in criminal activity without a high degree of justification.

Reasonable suspicion can be understood in terms of the due process and crime control viewpoints described in Chapter 1. The law governing stop-and-frisk attempts to achieve a balance between due process and crime control. On the one hand, controlling crime is in the public interest, and the police must be able to engage in certain activities to fulfill their duties. On the other hand, the public values their personal freedoms, and the Constitution is a highly prized guarantor of these freedoms. Many people, despite their desire to reduce crime, would object to aggressive search-and-seizure tactics by the police. Reasonable suspicion is something of a compromise between the conflicting goals of crime control and due process. It can be seen as achieving a balance between the needs of law enforcement and personal freedom.

Recall two critical points that were made in Chapter 3. First, when police activity does not constitute a search, the Fourth Amendment does not apply, and therefore probable cause is not required. Much the same logic applies to a stop and a frisk. If police conduct falls short of a stop or a frisk, the Fourth Amendment does not apply. Thus, when the Fourth Amendment does not apply, reasonable suspicion is not required. Second, if the police confront a person but such activity does not constitute a stop or a frisk, no justification is required. At the opposite extreme, though, if police conduct amounts to a more significant intrusion than a stop or a frisk, then a different standard of justification will be required—most likely, probable cause.

• • • • • • • • • • • • • • • • • • • • • • • • • • • • • • • • • • • • • • • • • • • • • • • • • • • •

# ▶ *Terry v. Ohio*: The facts

*Terry v. Ohio*
*(392 U.S. 1 [1968])*

*Terry v. Ohio*, 392 U.S. 1 (1968) forms the foundation for the law governing police actions that are based on reasonable suspicion. Because it is of critical importance, its facts are worth considering in some depth:

> . . . while he was patrolling in plain clothes in downtown Cleveland at approximately 2:30 in the afternoon of October 31, 1963, [Officer McFadden's] attention was attracted by two men, Chilton and Terry, standing on the corner of Huron Road and Euclid Avenue. He had never seen the two men before, and he was unable to say precisely what first drew his eye to them. However, he testified that he had been a policeman for 39 years and a detective for 35, and that he had been assigned to patrol this vicinity of downtown Cleveland for shoplifters and pickpockets for 30 years. He explained that he had developed routine habits of observation over the years, and that he would "stand and watch people or walk and watch people at many intervals of the day." He added: "Now, in this case, when I looked over, they didn't look right to me at the time."
>
> His interest aroused, Officer McFadden took up a post of observation in the entrance to a store 300 to 400 feet away from the two men. "I get more purpose to watch them when I seen their movements," he testified. He saw one of the men leave the other one and walk southwest on Huron Road, past some stores. The man paused for a moment and looked in a store window, then walked on a short distance, turned around and walked back toward the corner, pausing once again to look in the same store window. He rejoined his companion at the corner, and the two conferred briefly. Then the second man went through the same series of motions, strolling down Huron Road, looking in the same window, walking on a short distance, turning back, peering in the store window again, and returning to confer with the first man at the corner. The two men repeated this ritual alternately between five and six times apiece—in all, roughly a dozen trips. At one point, while the two were standing together on the corner, a third man approached them and engaged them briefly in conversation. This man then left the two others and walked west on Euclid Avenue. Chilton and Terry resumed their measured pacing, peering, and conferring. After this had gone on for 10 to 12 minutes, the two men walked off together, heading west on Euclid Avenue, following the path taken earlier by the third man.
>
> By this time, Officer McFadden had become thoroughly suspicious. He testified that after observing their elaborately casual and oft-repeated reconnaissance of the store window on Huron Road, he suspected the two men of "casing a job, a stick-up," and that he considered it his duty as a police officer to investigate further. He added that he feared "they may have a gun." Thus, Officer McFadden followed Chilton and Terry and saw them stop in front of Zucker's store to talk to the same man who had conferred with them earlier on the street corner. Deciding that the situation was ripe for direct action, Officer McFadden approached the three men, identified himself as a police officer and asked for their names. At this point, his knowledge was confined to what he had observed. He was not acquainted with any of the three men by name or by sight, and he had received no information concerning them from any other source. When the men "mumbled something" in response to his inquiries, Officer McFadden grabbed petitioner Terry, spun him around so that they were facing the other two, with Terry between McFadden and the others, and patted down the outside of his clothing. In the left breast pocket of Terry's overcoat, Officer McFadden felt a pistol. He reached inside the overcoat pocket, but was unable to remove the gun. At this point, keeping Terry between himself and the others, the officer ordered all three men to enter Zucker's

store. As they went in, he removed Terry's overcoat completely, removed a .38-caliber revolver from the pocket and ordered all three men to face the wall with their hands raised. Officer McFadden proceeded to pat down the outer clothing of Chilton and the third man, Katz. He discovered another revolver in the outer pocket of Chilton's overcoat, but no weapons were found on Katz. The officer testified that he only patted the men down to see whether they had weapons, and that he did not put his hands beneath the outer garments of either Terry or Chilton until he felt their guns. So far as appears from the record, he never placed his hands beneath Katz' outer garments. Officer McFadden seized Chilton's gun, asked the proprietor of the store to call a police wagon, and took all three men to the station, where Chilton and Terry were formally charged with carrying concealed weapons.

The Supreme Court sanctioned the stops, patdowns, and subsequent weapon seizures on the grounds that requiring a warrant could threaten officer safety or the safety of others.

# ▶ Stop and Frisk: Two Separate Acts

A *stop* is a separate act from a *frisk*. A stop always precedes a frisk, but a stop *does not* give a police officer permission to conduct a frisk. Rather, the officer must have separate justification for each act. Reasonable suspicion is required to stop a person, and it is also required to frisk a person.

In *Terry*, the Supreme Court ruled that in addition to the suspicion required to justify a stop, the officer must have reasonable suspicion that the person stopped is *armed* and *dangerous* in order to conduct a frisk. In support of this position, the Court used a balancing test: each intrusion by the government must be justified by a legitimate objective. In other words, no legitimate law enforcement objective is served when a police officer frisks a person whom the officer does not perceive as threatening.

For example, assume a police officer observes two men in an area with much drug traffic activity, whispering to each other and passing items back and forth. Arguably, the officer would have reasonable suspicion that criminal activity is afoot, thus permitting him or her to question the men. However, if the officer does not perceive that either suspect is armed and dangerous, then a frisk would be inappropriate.

# ▶ The Stop

In many situations, it is clear when a police officer has stopped someone. For instance, when a patrol officer legally pulls a motorist over, it is safe to say that such activity constitutes a stop. Similarly, if a police officer handcuffs a suspect, that person has clearly been stopped (and arrested). But what about a simple confrontation between a foot patrol officer and a pedestrian? If the officer directs general questions—such as "What is your name?"—at the pedestrian, can this be considered a stop? Given that there are many situations such as this, the definition of a *stop* must be given special attention.

## Definition of a Stop

Generally speaking, a stop is the detention of a person by a law enforcement officer for the purpose of investigation. The definition of a stop is important because if the police officer's activities amount to a stop, then the Fourth Amendment will apply. This is because a stop is the same thing as a seizure of a person. As the Court observed in *Terry*, "[W]henever a police officer accosts an individual and restrains his freedom to walk away, he has 'seized' that person."

In *Terry*, the Supreme Court stated that "obviously not all personal intercourse between policemen and citizens involves seizures of persons." Instead, the Fourth Amendment applies only "when the officer, by means of physical force or show of authority, has in some way restrained the liberty of [a] citizen." Thus, there is an important distinction to be drawn between (1) a forcible seizure or a stop and (2) a less intrusive type of confrontation in which, for example, the officer merely questions a person who is free to ignore the officer and leave. The seizure or stop requires reasonable suspicion (provided it is considered a *Terry* stop and not an arrest), but the simple questioning requires no justification.

There is no easy way to distinguish a *stop* from a *nonstop*, but the Supreme Court has attempted to clarify the differences with an objective test. In *United States v. Mendenhall*, 446 U.S. 544 (1980), the Court observed:

> [A] person has been "seized" within the meaning of the Fourth Amendment only if, in view of all the circumstances surrounding the incident, a *reasonable person would have believed that he was not free to leave.* Examples of circumstances that might indicate a seizure, even where the person did not actually attempt to leave, would be the threatening presence of several officers, the display of a weapon by an officer, some physical touching of the person of the citizen, or the use of language or tone of voice indicating that compliance with the officer's request might be compelled. (emphasis added)

The Court's decision in *Mendenhall* stemmed from a confrontation between plain-clothes Drug Enforcement Administration (DEA) agents and a 22-year-old African American woman in the Detroit airport. The agents had asked the woman for her ticket and identification, and she complied. When they realized the name on the ticket did not match her name, the agents asked the woman to accompany them into a nearby private room. The Court did not actually decide whether the woman had been stopped, but it did create the objective test described in the previous quote. Figure 6.1 lists several criteria used to distinguish between a stop and a consensual encounter.

*Florida v. Royer*, 460 U.S. 491 (1983) was the first case to apply the test set forth in *Mendenhall* in order to determine the conditions under which a seizure or stop may take place. The facts in *Royer* were virtually identical to the facts in *Mendenhall*, except that the officers did not return the detained individual's plane ticket or driver's license. The Supreme Court held, in a 5 to 4 decision, that given the circumstances, when the officers did not indicate that the individual was free to leave, a seizure had taken place. The Court wrote:

> The predicate permitting seizures on suspicion short of probable cause is that law enforcement interests warrant a limited intrusion on the personal security of the suspect. The

*United States v. Mendenhall* (446 U.S. 544 [1980])

1. Threatening behavior on the part of officers
2. The presence of several officers
3. Display of a weapon by an officer
4. Physical touching of the person by the officer
5. The issuing of orders as opposed to requests
6. The use of intimidating language or tone of voice
7. A lengthy time period
8. Intrusive actions, such as a full-body search
9. Use of lights or sirens
10. The officer blocking the person's path
11. Coercive police behavior
12. Taking place out of public view

**FIGURE 6.1 Factors Used to Distinguish between a Stop and a Consensual Encounter**

scope of the intrusion permitted will vary to some extent with the particular facts and circumstances of each case. This much, however, is clear: *an investigative detention must be temporary and last no longer than is necessary to effectuate the purpose of the stop. Similarly, the investigative methods employed should be the least intrusive means reasonably available to verify or dispel the officer's suspicion in a short period of time.* (emphasis added)

The detained individual was subjected to the functional equivalent of an arrest, and as a result, the agents needed probable cause to detain him for as long as they did (which, incidentally, was only about 15 minutes). Moving the subject from a public location to a private location was one of the key factors that helped turn the encounter from a stop into an arrest.

Contrast *Royer* with the Supreme Court's decision in *Florida v. Rodriguez*, 469 U.S. 1 (1984). In that case, the Court ruled that a seizure had *not* taken place when a plainclothes officer approached a man in an airport, displayed his badge, asked permission to talk with the man, and requested that he move approximately 15 feet to where the man's companions were standing with other police officers. The Court described this type of confrontation as "clearly the sort of consensual encounter that implicates no Fourth Amendment interest." It seems, therefore, at least in the airport context, that certain confrontations that take place in common areas do not amount to stops within the meaning of the Fourth Amendment.

Simply following a suspect, while such activity may be intimidating, is also insufficient to constitute a "stop." In *Michigan v. Chestnut*, 486 U.S. 567 (1988), police officers in their car followed a man who fled on foot when he spotted their patrol car. The officers did not activate their siren or lights, display weapons, ask the man to stop, or attempt to block the suspect's path. The Court acknowledged that this type of conduct can be "somewhat intimidating," but it ruled, nevertheless, that the act of police officers following the man did not amount to a stop. The situation would have been different, however, if the police officers had visibly chased the defendant. In the Court's words, "[W]hat constitutes a restraint on liberty prompting a person to conclude that he is not free to leave will vary, not only with the particular police conduct at issue, but also with the setting in which the conduct occurs."

Similarly, a person has not been "seized" unless the police have used force to apprehend the person or the person has yielded to police authority. The case of *California v. Hodari D.*, 449 U.S. 621 (1991), involved the apprehension of an individual who was chased by the police on foot. The Court ruled that the individual had not been seized at the time he threw away a rock of cocaine because the police had not yet caught up with him. The individual argued that he was "stopped" when he was being pursued by the police officers because the chase was sufficient to cause a reasonable person to believe he was not free to leave. In other words, he argued that he was subjected to a "show of authority" stop. Accordingly, the individual argued in court that the cocaine should not be admissible as evidence. Rejecting his argument, the Court ruled that the seizure of a person during a pursuit occurs only when there is an application of force by the police or the suspect submits to police authority (gives up).

*California v. Hodari D. (449 U.S. 621 [1991])*

The Court has also suggested that whether a reasonable person would feel they were free to leave depends on an analysis of all the circumstances surrounding the confrontation. In *Florida v. Bostick*, 501 U.S. 429 (1991), police officers approached a passenger on a bus and asked to inspect his ticket and identification and also his luggage. Both actions were conducted pursuant to a policy that permitted police officers to conduct suspicionless *Terry* stops for the purpose of detecting drug activity. The Supreme Court refused to adopt the Florida Supreme Court's analysis, which held that such drug sweeps were seizures, implicating the Fourth Amendment. Instead, the Court ruled that "in order to determine whether a particular encounter constitutes a seizure, a court must consider all the circumstances surrounding the encounter to determine whether the police conduct would have communicated to a reasonable person that the person was not free to decline

*Florida v. Bostick, 501 U.S. (429 [1991])*

## LOOKING FOR ILLEGAL ALIENS

Immigration and Customs Enforcement (ICE— formerly the INS) routinely conducts so-called factory surveys to determine whether illegal aliens are employed at certain worksites. In these surveys, uniformed and armed agents disperse themselves through the building and approach each employee in order to inquire about his or her citizenship. While this is going on, employees are free to continue with their work and move about the building. Does such activity amount to a stop, thereby implicating the Fourth Amendment?

the officer's requests or otherwise terminate the encounter." The Supreme Court remanded the case back to the Florida Supreme Court, instead of reversing it. Nevertheless, a portion of Justice O'Connor's opinion suggests that the majority was not satisfied with the Florida court's decision: the bus passenger's perception of not being free to leave was, according to O'Connor, "the natural result of his decision to take the bus."

In *United States v. Drayton*, 536 U.S. 194 (2002), the U.S. Supreme Court held that *Bostick*-like bus detentions are permissible and that passengers need not be advised of their right to deny consent to search. In that case, officers boarded a Greyhound bus as part of a drug interdiction effort. They spoke one-on-one with individual passengers and asked for consent to search. The officer asked one individual if he could search his person. The individual consented and drugs were found.

## Sources of Information

Just as there are many different sources of information that can give rise to probable cause to make an arrest, there are many different sources of information that can give rise to reasonable suspicion. The reasonable suspicion standard is of course lower than probable cause, so the "proof" that must be in place is somewhat less.

Permissible sources of information vary. First hand observations are preferable, but officers are not always able to witness suspicious activity while it occurs. This sometimes forces them to rely on more questionable sources, such as informants. For example, in *Adams v. Williams*, 407 U.S. 143 (1972), an officer, acting on a tip that a man in a nearby car had a gun at his waist, approached the car and asked the man to open the door. When the suspect rolled down his car window instead of opening the door, the officer reached into the car and removed a gun from the man's waistband. The officer did not identify himself, but the Supreme Court ruled that the seizure of the weapon was reasonable under the circumstances.

In a similar case, police acted on a very specific anonymous tip that a woman would leave a particular unit in an apartment complex, get into a specific car, and drive toward a named hotel. The informant further reported that the woman would be carrying an ounce of cocaine inside a brown attache case. Officers observed the woman leave the apartment, but without the case. They followed her, stopped her, obtained consent to search her vehicle, and found cocaine in a briefcase in the trunk. In a 6 to 3 decision, the Supreme Court sanctioned the stop and subsequent search/seizure: "the totality of the circumstances demonstrates that significant aspects of the informant's story were sufficiently corroborated by the police to furnish reasonable suspicion" (*Alabama v. White*, 496 U.S. 325 [1990]).

Still other sources of information may give rise to reasonable suspicion to stop or frisk. For example, drug courier profiling may be used, which is discussed more fully later in the chapter. Police may also rely on "wanted" flyers, radio bulletins, and other suspect descriptions, even from other jurisdictions (*United States v. Hensley*, 469 U.S. 221 [1985];

*Whitley v. Warden*, 401 U.S. 560 [1971]). The range of possible sources of reasonable suspicion is extensive and impossible to detail thoroughly in this limited space.

## Duration of a Stop

A stop must be limited in duration, and after a passage of time, the stop may evolve into a *de facto* arrest. However, there are no precise rules as to how long a stop may take. In *Royer*, discussed above, the Supreme Court held that a 15-minute detention exceeded the bounds of a proper stop—and became a *de facto* arrest. Yet, in certain exceptional circumstances, the Supreme Court has permitted detentions lasting much longer. For example, in *United States v. Sharpe*, 470 U.S. 675 (1985), officers followed two vehicles suspected of involvement in drug trafficking. One vehicle was stopped and the driver was detained for 40 minutes while the officers sought and stopped the second car and its driver. The Court did not establish a bright-line rule for what time period is considered permissible, but it did state that "in evaluating whether an investigative detention is unreasonable, common sense and ordinary human experience must govern over rigid criteria." Thus, the 40-minute detention of the driver of the first car was permissible.

In a controversial case, *Montoya De Hernandez*, 473 U.S. 531 (1985), even a detention of as long as 16 hours was allowed. In that case, a woman who was traveling from Colombia was detained for 16 hours in an airport because she was suspected of being a "balloon swallower" (a person who smuggles narcotics by hiding them in his or her alimentary canal). The woman was given two options: (1) to return on the next available flight to Colombia or (2) to remain in detention until she was able to produce a monitored bowel movement. She chose the first option, but officials were unable to place her on the next flight, and she refused to use toilet facilities. Officials then obtained a court order to conduct a pregnancy test (she claimed to be pregnant), an X-ray exam, and a rectal exam. The exams revealed 88 cocaine-filled balloons in her alimentary canal. She was convicted of numerous federal drug offenses, but the court of appeals reversed that decision, holding that her detention violated the Fourth Amendment. The Supreme Court, in turn, reversed the court of appeals decision and ruled that the 16-hour detention was permissible. According to the Court, "The detention of a traveler at the border, beyond the scope of a routine customs search and inspection, is justified at its inception if customs agents, considering all the facts surrounding the traveler and her trip, reasonably suspect that the traveler is smuggling contraband in her alimentary canal."

*Montoya De Hernandez*
*(473 U.S. 531 [1985])*

Unfortunately, there are few clear guidelines as to the appropriate duration of a stop. The Supreme Court has stated that the reasonableness of a stop turns on the facts and circumstances of each case. In particular, the Court has emphasized "(1) the public interest served by the seizure, (2) the nature and scope of the intrusion, and (3) the objective facts upon which the law enforcement officer relied in light of his knowledge and expertise" (*Mendenhall*, 446 U.S. 544). Moreover, the Court has ruled that "the use of a particular method to restrain a person's freedom of movement does not necessarily make police action tantamount to an arrest" and that "police may take reasonable action, based upon

---

**DECISION-MAKING EXERCISE 6.2**

**CREATING A "CONSTITUTIONALLY COGNIZABLE" POLICY**

The city mayor, frustrated with a wave of serious and violent crime in the area, instructs the police to stop and demand identification from each citizen they encounter. As the mayor's legal counsel, what would you advise regarding the constitutionality of these instructions to the police?

the circumstances, to protect themselves . . . or to maintain the status quo" (*United States v. Kapperman*, 764 F.2d 786 [11th Cir. 1985]).

## The Meaning of "Free to Leave"

If a person is confronted but not stopped, is he or she *really* free to leave? Many people tend to feel intimidated by police officers, even when asked nonincriminating, innocuous questions. Would it not appear strange to an officer for someone to simply walk away during a conversation with him or her? Would the officer just let the person walk away and go about his or her business? There are no easy answers to questions such as these, but they highlight the differences between theory and reality, as considered in Chapter 1.

Although in may interactions with a police officer, a reasonable person might believe he or she is technically free to leave, the act of actually leaving during the course of a conversation with a police officer could prove to be something of a risky endeavor. The same issue applies to situations in which a motorist is legally permitted to decline to give a police officer permission to search his or her surroundings, even though doing so may create suspicion.

In a similar vein, a person who is stopped has the right to refuse to answer questions—he or she cannot be *forced* to talk. However, refusing to answer questions could create enough fear on the part of the officer to justify a stop. The refusal, when combined with other factors, could also give rise to probable cause sufficient to justify an arrest. Despite all Supreme Court rulings to the contrary, then, it is risky to simply walk away from an inquisitive police officer or to refuse to provide answers to the officer's questions.

## Can Effects Be Seized?

*Terry* and subsequent cases have mostly focused on stops of *persons*, but a handful of cases have addressed the seizure of property based on less than probable cause. As indicated in Chapter 3, probable cause is required for the seizure of a person if that seizure amounts to an arrest. The same applies to *effects*, which are usually a person's personal items. If the detention or seizure of a person's effects amounts to an arrest, then probable cause is required.

The question, then, is, when does the seizure of a person's effects rise to the level of an arrest? The Supreme Court attempted to answer this question in *United States v. Place*, 462 U.S. 696 (1983). In that case, the Court ruled that a 90-minute detention of a person's

---

**DECISION-MAKING EXERCISE 6.3**

**STRETCHING THE TIME LIMITS OF A STOP**

Law enforcement officers kept a plane under surveillance because they had reasonable suspicion to believe that it was being used to transport narcotics. They approached the aircraft, which was ready for takeoff. Standing near the left wing of the plane, one of the officers raised his badge, identified himself, and, shouting over the noise of the speeding engine, ordered the pilot to shut off the engine and get down. The pilot looked from side to side and appeared hesitant about what to do. At that moment, the officer moved in front of the aircraft, drew his gun, pointed it at the pilot, and again yelled to him to shut off the engine and get out of the plane. The officer identified himself and said he wanted to speak to the pilot because he was suspected of narcotics smuggling. He then patted down the pilot in search of weapons; finding none, he placed his gun back in the holster. The officers then questioned the pilot about the plane's ownership. The pilot was evasive and ended up supplying inaccurate and contradictory information about who owned the plane. The officers then detained him for over an hour while *they* attempted to determine who owned the plane. Was this action justified?

▼

luggage in an airport to arrange for a drug dog "sniff" to detect drugs was unconstitutional because the detention was too long. Also, the Court stated that "the failure of the agents to accurately inform respondent of the place to which they were transporting his luggage, of the length of time he might be dispossessed, and of what arrangements would be made for return of the luggage if the investigation dispelled the suspicion" contributed to the unconstitutional nature of the detention. The Court went on to note that "some brief detentions of personal effects may be so minimally intrusive of Fourth Amendment interests that strong countervailing governmental interests will justify seizure based only on specific articulable facts that the property contains contraband or evidence of a crime."

There are some situations in which restraints on people's effects do not amount to a Fourth Amendment seizure. In *United States v. Leeuwen*, 397 U.S. 249 (1970), the police, who were contacted by a suspicious postal clerk, asked post office officials to hold two packages for 29 hours while they investigated the situation and obtained a search warrant. A unanimous Court ruled that the circumstances "certainly justified detention, without a warrant, while an investigation was made." Also, the Court ruled that "[n]o interest protected by the Fourth Amendment was invaded by forwarding the packages the following day rather than the day when they were deposited." In short, because the detention of the package did not invade any privacy interest in the package, a Fourth Amendment seizure did not take place.

## Stops and Seizures under *Terry*: A Summary

A *Terry* stop is characterized by two specific features: (1) the police question a person or communicate with him or her and (2) a reasonable person would believe that he or she is not free to leave. Reasonable suspicion is required in order to make a *Terry* stop conform to the Fourth Amendment. Conversely, if an officer detains a person in such a manner that a reasonable person would believe he or she *is* free to leave, the protections of the Fourth Amendment do not apply and reasonable suspicion is not required. If the officer wishes to conduct a frisk—a separate act from a stop—he or she must have reasonable suspicion that the suspect is armed and dangerous, not just reasonable suspicion that the person was involved in a crime, as required for a *Terry* stop.

There are no clear answers as to what is the appropriate duration for a stop. However, as the Supreme Court suggested in *Mendenhall*, a lengthy stop is constitutionally permissible when (1) the public interest is served by the seizure; (2) the nature and scope of the intrusion are not excessive; and (3) the officer possesses enough in the way of objective

---

**DECISION-MAKING EXERCISE 6.4**

### WHAT CONSTITUTES A PROPER STOP?

On a Wednesday afternoon at 3:00 P.M., Officer Weber was on patrol in a neighborhood that had recently experienced several daytime burglaries. Her attention was drawn to a car in the driveway of one residence, which had its trunk open. In the trunk were several plastic trash bags of the type reportedly used by the burglar to carry away the loot. Weber pulled her cruiser into the driveway behind the vehicle, blocking its path. At that point, the driver of the car was closing the trunk and preparing to leave. The driver approached Weber, appearing quite nervous, and asked her to move the cruiser. Instead of doing so, Weber asked the driver for identification, which he produced. The identification indicated an address on the other side of town. Weber then frisked the driver, found a gun in his left coat pocket, and arrested him. No evidence connected the driver to the burglaries, but he was prosecuted for unlawfully carrying a concealed weapon. He moved to exclude the gun on the grounds that the initial stop was illegal and that the gun was the fruit of that illegal stop. What should the court decide?

▼

facts to justify the stop. Thus, if a person is stopped and detained for a long time based on an officer's hunch, but poses no threat to public safety, then the stop is probably illegal. In such a situation, the stop would need to be justified by probable cause because it would amount to a *de facto* arrest.

# ▶ The Frisk

A **frisk** is a superficial examination by the officer of the person's body surface or clothing to discover weapons or items that could be used to cause harm. The additional step of frisking a suspect is a Fourth Amendment intrusion that requires justification apart from that required to stop the person. Specifically, in order to conduct a frisk, the officer needs reasonable suspicion that the suspect is armed and dangerous. This is in addition to the reasonable suspicion required to stop the person for questioning.

## Permissible Grounds for a Frisk

While *Terry* held that a frisk is permissible only when an officer reasonably fears for his or her safety, there is still considerable dispute over the situations in which a frisk is appropriate. What does it mean to *fear for one's safety*? A number of court decisions have wrestled with this question.

*Pennsylvania v. Mimms*
*(434 U.S. 106 [1977])*

For example, in *Pennsylvania v. Mimms*, 434 U.S. 106 (1977), police officers observed a man driving a vehicle with expired plates. The officers stopped the vehicle in order to issue the man a traffic summons. When the officers asked the man to step out of the car, the officers observed a large bulge in the pocket of his jacket. Fearing that the bulge might be a weapon, one of the officers frisked the man. It turned out that the bulge was a .38-caliber revolver. The man claimed at his trial that the gun was seized illegally, but the Supreme Court upheld the frisk. Even though a bulge in one's pocket does not necessarily indicate he or she has a weapon, the Court granted some latitude in its decision to law enforcement personnel.

*Ybarra v. Illinois*
*(444 U.S. 85 [1979])*

However, in *Ybarra v. Illinois*, 444 U.S. 85 (1979), the Court ruled that officers did not have grounds to frisk 12 bar patrons during a search of the bar itself. Justice Stewart stated in *Ybarra* that "[t]he 'narrow scope' of the *Terry* exception does not permit a frisk for weapons on less than reasonable belief or suspicion directed at the person to be frisked, even though that person happens to be on premises where an authorized narcotics search is taking place." Thus, just because someone happens to be in an area in which criminal activity is supposedly taking place does not make him or her eligible for a frisk.

*Minnesota v. Dickerson*
*(508 U.S. 366 [1993])*

Despite the limitations on frisks imposed by the *Ybarra* decision, the Court has since retreated somewhat from its decision in that case. In *Minnesota v. Dickerson*, 508 U.S. 366 (1993), police officers observed a man leaving a "crack" house. As he approached and saw the officers, he turned and began walking in the opposite direction. The officers stopped and frisked him and found drugs on him. The frisk was conducted without reasonable suspicion or any other level of justification. The Court ruled that the police exceeded the bounds of a valid frisk when they found drugs on the man's person, but the Court did *not* rule that the frisk was unconstitutional. It would seem, then, that under certain circumstances, a frisk is permissible on less than reasonable suspicion. Apparently, the act of leaving a "crack" house and acting evasively was sufficient justification to conduct a frisk, even though the police went too far in doing so.

In *Arizona v. Johnson*, 555 U.S. 323 (2009), the Court further expanded the frisk doctrine. In that case, gang task force officers were patrolling and stopped a vehicle for a traffic violation. The officers had no reason to suspect the vehicle's occupants of criminal activity, but they nevertheless ordered them out of the car. One of them was frisked and a weapon was found. The Court sanctioned this activity, noting that "a passenger's motivation to

1. When the person has a reputation for dangerousness
2. When the person is suspected of having committed a dangerous felony
3. When visual cues suggest the presence of a weapon or similar dangerous instrument
4. When the suspect makes suggestive or furtive gestures

**FIGURE 6.2 When a Frisk Is Permissible**

use violence during the stop to prevent apprehension for a crime more grave than a traffic violation is just as great as that of the driver."

There are no clear rules that establish when an officer can reasonably fear for his or her safety. Ultimately, the determination of a potential threat is a subjective one. Almost without exception, the courts will defer to the judgment of the officer, assuming that he or she is able to articulate some specific facts that contributed to reasonable suspicion that the suspect was armed and dangerous. Figure 6.2 summarizes the circumstances as to when a frisk is permissible.

## Scope of a Frisk

A number of cases have focused specifically on the permissible scope of a frisk. Two issues have been raised: (1) the definition of a *frisk*—that is, what the officer can physically do to a person that does not rise to the level of a search; and (2) the items that can be felt for during the course of a frisk.

With regard to the first issue, the Supreme Court in *Terry* described a *frisk* as "a carefully limited search of the outer clothing . . . in an attempt to discover weapons which might be used to assault [a police officer]." In *Sibron v. New York*, 392 U.S. 40 (1968), the Court offered additional clarification by declaring that the act of reaching into a suspect's pockets is impermissible when the officer makes "no attempt at an initial limited exploration for arms." Generally, then, a frisk is little more than an open-handed patdown of someone's outer clothing. Only if the officer feels something that resembles a weapon can he or she then reach into the suspect's pocket (or other area used to conceal it) to determine what the item is. And as the Sixth Circuit observed in *United States v. Richardson*, 949 F.2d 851 (6th Cir. 1991), "When actions by the police exceed the bounds permitted by reasonable suspicion, the seizure becomes an arrest and must be supported by probable cause."

*Sibron v. New York*
*(392 U.S. 40 [1968])*

With regard to the items that can be felt for during the course of a frisk, the Supreme Court in *Ybarra v. Illinois* emphasized that frisks must be directed at discovering weapons, not criminal evidence. In *Ybarra*, one of the police officers had removed what he described as a "cigarette pack with objects in it" from the suspect. The Court basically decided that the officer's actions were too intrusive; the package could not have been considered a threat to the safety of the officers conducting the search. Significantly, the Court did not declare the seizure illegal because the officer was not looking for weapons. Rather, the search was illegal because the officer did not have reasonable suspicion to frisk every patron in the bar. Nevertheless, a frisk should not be used as a "fishing expedition" to see if some kind of usable evidence can be found on the person.

Two additional points concerning the scope of a frisk need to be underscored at this juncture. First, a frisk must be *motivated* by the desire to remove weapons and other instruments of potential harm from a criminal suspect. Note, however, that although the purpose of a frisk is to preserve officer safety, the officer may, in some circumstances, seize contraband found during the course of a lawful frisk. This issue is discussed in the section on plain touch and feel later in this chapter.

| Proper | Improper |
|--------|----------|
| An officer observes a large "bulge" in the front waistband of a suspicious individual's pants and frisks him for a weapon. | A man is sitting in a car waiting to pick up a friend. An officer orders him out of the car and frisks him. |
| Two officers observe a man "casing" a convenience store. When they confront him, he becomes argumentative. They frisk him for a weapon. | An officer confronts a suspicious individual who is in an area that has been experiencing a number of daytime burglaries. He reaches into the man's pockets looking for weapons and/or contraband. |
| An officer stops a speeding vehicle. The driver gives the officer false identification, whereupon the officer orders him out and frisks him. | Several men are waiting in line for a nightclub. Officers approach them, block their path, and reach into each individual's jacket feeling for weapons and/or contraband. |

**FIGURE 6.3 Examples of Proper and Improper Frisks**

Second, a valid frisk can always evolve into a Fourth Amendment search, provided that probable cause develops along the way. For example, assume that a Chicago police officer frisks a suspect because she fears he may be carrying a gun. If it turns out that the suspect is carrying a pistol, which is illegal in the city of Chicago, she could arrest the suspect and conduct a full search incident to arrest. In this example, though, the object seized during the frisk (the gun) must be immediately apparent to the officer for the seizure to be legal. As the Supreme Court stated in *Dickerson* (508 U.S. 366):

> Although the officer was lawfully in a position to feel the lump in respondent's pocket, because *Terry* entitled him to place his hands upon respondent's jacket, the court below determined that the incriminating character of the object was not immediately apparent to him. Rather, the officer determined that the item was contraband only after conducting a further search, one not authorized by *Terry* or by any other exception to the warrant requirement.

In the example, then, had the object been seized after careful manipulation of the object by the officer, then the seizure based on the frisk would not conform to the Fourth Amendment. Figure 6.3 provides additional examples of proper and improper frisks.

## Frisks under *Terry*: A Summary

A frisk is permissible when an officer reasonably fears for his or her safety. However, there is no easy way to define exactly what facts would *cause* an officer to reasonably fear for his or her safety. If an officer can offer no facts or testimony to support the frisk, it will probably be declared unconstitutional. On the other hand, if the officer possesses some objective information that served as the basis for a frisk (such as observing a bulge in a suspect's pocket), the frisk is probably legal.

A number of cases have focused on the permissible scope of a frisk, and three important limits have been imposed. First, a frisk can be nothing more than a patdown of someone's outer clothing. Groping or squeezing is not permissible. Second, a frisk must be motivated by the desire to promote officer safety, not by the desire to seek out any form of contraband. That is, the sole purpose of a *Terry* patdown is to protect the officer from weapons that might be used by the suspect during the encounter. Finally, for an officer to legally seize an item during the course of a frisk, that item must be immediately apparent to the officer as contraband.

Figure 6.4 contains portions of the San Bernardino, California, Police Department's stop-and-frisk policy, which succinctly summarizes the discussion thus far.

**Cursory Patdown Search**

**A.** Detaining/Arresting

**1.** When an officer detains any subject suspected of committing a criminal offense and the officer has reasonable suspicion that subject may have a weapon, the officer shall conduct, or arrange for a cursory patdown search for weapons as soon as practical.

**2.** When an officer arrests any subject, the officer shall conduct or arrange for a cursory patdown or custody search prior to placing the suspect in a vehicle for transportation.

**3.** The cursory patdown search for weapons or contraband shall consist of patting the suspect's body and clothing. The squeezing of loosely fitting clothing, such as jacket seams and pockets or other unexplained masses is permitted. Detected potential weapons and contraband, or containers capable of concealing weapons or contraband shall be removed for inspection. Officers shall be cautious of the potential presence of sharp or pointed objects.

**B.** In the absence of consent or plain sight, other detected objects may not be removed or inspected unless the subject is under arrest or probable cause exists to arrest the subject. Officers are cautioned that probable cause to arrest must exist before non-weapon objects can be removed for inspection.

**C.** Absent exigent circumstances, an officer of the same sex <u>shall</u> conduct the cursory search. Exigent circumstances are defined as:

- An immediate articulable threat to the officer, public safety, or the potential destruction/disposal of physical evidence.

- Response of a same sex officer will result in an unreasonable period of detention.

Whenever possible, cursory patdown searches by an officer of the opposite sex of the detainee should be in direct sight of a second witnessing officer. Every reasonable effort shall be made to protect the dignity of the arrestee or detainee during the cursory patdown search.

*Source:* Chapter 29, Procedure 3, "Use of Force," from *Standard Operating Procedure*, San Bernardino, California, Police Department (rev. December 22, 2004). Reprinted with permission.

**FIGURE 6.4 Stop-and-Frisk Policy (San Bernardino, CA, Police Department)**

**DECISION-MAKING EXERCISE 6.5**

**THE PERMISSIBLE SCOPE OF A FRISK**

Two police officers were approached by a person (previously unknown to them) who stated that Jack Smith was in the Valley Grill on First Street and that he had several bags of cocaine for sale. The person provided detailed information concerning Smith and described the clothing he was wearing. The officers went to the Valley Grill and found no one of that description. After the officers left the bar, however, they observed a person walking on the sidewalk who matched the description they had been given. The officers approached him, blocked his path, and asked for his identification. The man's identification revealed that his name was Jack Smith. At that point, the officers ordered Smith to remove his shoes. As he did so, the officers continued to ask him questions. Was this action appropriate?

# ▶ The Evolution of Stop-and-Frisk Law

In *Terry*, the Supreme Court created an exception to the Fourth Amendment's requirement of probable cause for searches by holding that police officers can stop and frisk people based on reasonable suspicion. In the wake of *Terry*, a number of significant and controversial Supreme Court decisions have modified the scope of the stop-and-frisk exception to the Fourth Amendment's probable cause requirement. The cases fall into five categories:

- vehicle stops and weapons searches of automobiles,
- protective sweeps of residences,
- plain touch and feel,
- stops for loitering, and
- checks for identification.

## Vehicle Stops and Weapons Searches of Automobiles

*Delaware v. Prouse*
*(440 U.S. 648 [1979])*

As discussed in Chapter 5, automobile searches involve a specific set of rules as to what police officers can do with automobiles when they have reasonable suspicion. *Delaware v. Prouse*, 440 U.S. 648 (1979), sets forth the rule that police officers can stop and detain motorists in their vehicles so long as the officers have "at least articulable and reasonable suspicion" that the motorists are violating the law. For example, if a police officer observes a driver run a stop sign, the officer is justified in pulling the person over and detaining him or her because reasonable suspicion is present.

The decision in *Pennsylvania v. Mimms*, 434 U.S. 106 (1977), discussed earlier, also authorizes a police officer to order a driver out of a car. The logic is that doing so is a minimal intrusion that can be justified by safety concerns. Likewise, an officer is also permitted to frisk a motorist who has been pulled over if the officer reasonably fears for his or her safety.

Interestingly, if a police officer orders a driver (or a passenger, or both) out of the car, is reasonably suspicious that the driver is armed and dangerous, and frisks the driver, the officer may also search the area of the interior of the car within the suspect's immediate control. Such a search is permissible even when the driver has already been ordered to step out of the vehicle. The case that established this ruling was *Michigan v. Long*, 463 U.S. 1032 (1983). In *Long*, police officers saw a car swerve into a ditch. After stopping to investigate, they observed that the driver was intoxicated and that there was a large hunting knife on the floor of the vehicle. The Supreme Court ruled that the officers were justified in searching the passenger compartment and frisking the driver.

*Long* is an important decision because a search almost always requires probable cause. Note, however, that the scope of the search in this case was limited to the vehicle occupant's grabbing area, which included the whole of the interior of the car. Neither containers inside the car nor any in the trunk of the car (if any) can be searched during the course of a vehicle weapons search based on reasonable suspicion.

## Protective Sweeps of Residences

*Maryland v. Buie*
*(494 U.S. 325 [1990])*

Another decision that essentially expands *Terry* is *Maryland v. Buie*, 494 U.S. 325 (1990). If police lawfully make an arrest in a person's residence, a protective sweep of the home (defined in Chapter 5 as "a cursory visual inspection of those places in which a person might be hiding") is permitted based on the *Terry* rationale. A *sweep* is when one or more officers disperse throughout the home with the intent of looking for other people that could pose a threat to the officers making the arrest. In the Court's words, a *protective sweep* is a "quick and limited search of the premises, incident to arrest, and conducted to protect

▼

the safety of police officers or others." This protective sweep, which requires reasonable suspicion, should be distinguished from the automatic but more limited sweep that is permitted incident to a lawful arrest (see Chapter 5).

According to the Supreme Court, a sweep is permitted if the officer possesses "a reasonable belief based on specific and articulable facts that an area to be swept harbors an individual posing a danger to those at the arrest scene." In addition, a sweep "may extend only to a cursory inspection of those spaces where a person may be found" and may last only as long as is necessary to eliminate the suspicion of danger. *Buie* thus expands *Terry* in the sense that police officers can do more than just frisk a person who is arrested in a private residence. Note, however, that this case does not permit officers to *search* but only to *sweep* the area. A search would have to be supported by probable cause. However, items in plain view can be seized (see Chapter 5).

The Court's decision in *Buie* is not without its critics, however—the dissenters in the case being perhaps the most vocal. Consider Justice Brennan's observations in his dissent to *Buie*:

> *Terry* and its early progeny permitted only brief investigative stops and extremely limited searches based on reasonable suspicion . . . but this Court more recently has applied the rationale underlying *Terry* to a wide variety of more intrusive searches and seizures prompting my continued criticism of the emerging tendency on the part of the Court to convert the *Terry* decision from a narrow exception into one that swallows the general rule that [searches] are reasonable only if based on probable cause.

The exception Justice Brennan refers to is the exception made in *Terry* to the Fourth Amendment's requirement that reasonable searches be supported by probable cause. In a sense, *Terry* was intended to be only a minor exception to the Fourth Amendment. Brennan's concern in this case, then, is that the Fourth Amendment continues to be weakened in cases that continue to uphold police actions that would otherwise would have been considered searches, but for the Court's decision in *Terry*.

This is an important area of law that continues to evolve. No doubt, the Supreme Court will continue to consider cases that involve the relationship among probable cause, reasonable suspicion, and the police activities that each permits.

## Plain Touch and Feel

In *Dickerson*, when the police officer frisked the suspect, he exceeded the bounds of *Terry* because the officer "squeezed, slid, and otherwise manipulated the packet's content" before learning that it was cocaine. *Dickerson* is considered by many to be the case that officially recognized the doctrine known as *plain touch* (sometimes called *plain feel*). The Supreme Court has long recognized that the items in plain view fall outside Fourth Amendment protections. *Dickerson* is something of a hybrid between a *Terry*-based frisk and the "plain view" doctrine. According to one commentator, "[I]f the officer, while staying within the

---

**DECISION-MAKING EXERCISE 6.6**

**A VEHICLE SEARCH**

A police officer pulled a motorist over for exceeding the posted speed limit. The officer then ordered her out of the car. Without her consent and without probable cause, the officer searched the interior passenger compartment of the vehicle. He found marijuana and a "bong" under the seat, and arrested the woman. Was the search of the passenger compartment justified?

*Example 1*: An officer conducts a pat down of a man who seems intoxicated and smells like marijuana. When he feels a bulge in the man's jacket, the officer reaches into his pocket and finds a "bong."

*Example 2*: While serving an arrest warrant, an officer frisks a suspect and feels a bulge in his pocket. Upon reaching into the suspect's pocket, the officer feels two baggies full of rock-like objects. He seizes the items, which turn out to be crack cocaine.

*Example 3*: An officer responds to a complaint and notices a large bulge in the suspect's pocket. He reaches in the suspect's pocket and withdraws a bottle.

**FIGURE 6.5 Examples of Proper Seizures Based on Plain View, Feel, and Touch during the course of Stop-and-Frisks**

narrow limits of a frisk for weapons, feels what he has probable cause to believe is a weapon, contraband or evidence, the officer may expand the search or seize the object."[1]

The reason the Supreme Court frowned on the frisk conducted in *Dickerson* was that it was not immediately apparent to the officers that the suspect had contraband in his pocket. Thus, for the plain feel doctrine to apply, two conditions must be met: (1) Police must have reasonable suspicion to frisk, *and* (2) contraband must be immediately apparent for it to be lawfully seized. Stated more formally, "[T]he police may seize contraband detected solely through the officer's sense of touch, if, as with the plain-view doctrine, the officer had a right to touch the object in question (lawful vantage point and lawful access) and, upon tactile observation, the object's identity as contraband was immediately apparent."[2] Figure 6.5 presents examples of proper seizures based on plain view, touch, and feel during stop-and-frisk situations.

## Stops for Loitering

A somewhat lesser known but equally controversial expansion of *Terry* has been applied to stops for loitering. Generally, stopping a person requires reasonable suspicion. However, certain statutes, known collectively as *loitering statutes*, authorize the police to stop or arrest suspicious-looking individuals based on a lesser degree of certainty than even reasonable suspicion. Because these statutes often permit the police to stop people based on less than reasonable suspicion, many of them have been declared unconstitutional on the grounds that they are too vague.

*Papachristou v. City of Jacksonville (405 U.S. 156 [1972])*

In *Papachristou v. City of Jacksonville*, 405 U.S. 156 (1972), the Supreme Court declared unconstitutional a municipal ordinance that targeted "vagrants" and "rogues and vagabonds, or dissolute persons who go about begging . . . common drunkards, lewd, wanton and lascivious persons, . . . persons wandering or strolling around from place to place without any lawful purpose or object, habitual loafers, [and] disorderly persons." The Court concluded that the ordinance provided "no standards governing the exercise of . . . discretion" and thereby "permit[ted] and encourage[d] an arbitrary and discriminatory enforcement of the law" and resulted "in a regime in which the poor and the unpopular are permitted to 'stand on the sidewalk . . . only at the whim of any police officer.' "

*Kolender v. Lawson (461 U.S. 352 [1983])*

In a more recent case, *Kolender v. Lawson*, 461 U.S. 352 (1983), the Supreme Court struck down another statute that made a misdemeanant of any person "[w]ho loiters or wanders upon the streets or from place to place without apparent reason or business and who refuses to identify himself and to account for his presence when requested by any peace officer to do so, if the surrounding circumstances are such as to indicate to a

---

[1]S. L. Emanuel and S. Knowles, *Emanuel Law Outlines: Criminal Procedure* (Larchmont, NY: Emanuel, 1998), p. 129.

[2]J. Dressler, *Law Outlines: Criminal Procedure* (Santa Monica, CA: Casenotes, 1977), pp. 12–15.

**THE BOUNDS OF A PROPER FRISK**

An officer on foot patrol observed a known gang member leaving a notorious crack house. When the gang member spotted the officer, he turned and ran in the opposite direction. The officer gave chase, caught up with him, and ordered him to stop. The gang member did stop, at which point the officer administered a patdown frisk. No weapons were found, but the officer felt a lump in the gang member's pocket. Upon careful examination with her fingers, the lump was revealed to be a package of cellophane of the type commonly used to package "crack" cocaine. The officer seized the bag. May it be introduced as evidence at the gang member's trial for narcotics possession?

reasonable man that the public safety demands such identification." The Court ruled that the statute was too vague because it "vests virtually complete discretion in the hands of the police to determine whether the suspect has satisfied the statute and must be permitted to go on his way in the absence of probable cause to arrest."

After *Kolender*, a number of jurisdictions have attempted to devise sufficiently specific loitering statutes. For example, the City of Chicago passed a statute providing that "whenever a police officer observes a person whom he reasonably believes to be a criminal street gang member loitering in any public place with one or more other persons, he shall order all such persons to disperse and remove themselves from the area." *Loitering* was defined as "to remain in any one place with no apparent purpose." Despite the more specific language of this statute, though, the Supreme Court also struck it down. Specifically, in *Chicago v. Morales*, 527 U.S. 41 (1999), the Supreme Court ruled that the statute was unconstitutionally vague. The majority believed that the statute still gave police too much discretion to decide which people could be classified as gang members. However, the Court suggested that it may have upheld the statute if it had applied to gang members or to those with "an apparently harmful purpose or effect," but instead, that statute applied to "everyone in the city who may remain in one place with one suspected gang member as long as their purpose is not apparent to an officer observing them."

Generally, statutes allowing stops or arrests for loitering would seem to be constitutionally questionable. Nevertheless, loitering statutes can still be found on the books in some jurisdictions in the United States (some of which may not be as vague as those struck down by the Supreme Court). To be safe, the police should limit their stops to those that are based on reasonable suspicion that criminal activity is afoot. Any stop based on less than reasonable suspicion opens the police officer's actions to a great deal of constitutional scrutiny.

## Checks for Identification

In another line of cases, the Court has recognized the need for police to check for identification in the course of investigating an incident. In *Hiibel v. Sixth Judicial District Court of Nevada*, 542 U.S. 177 (2004), police received a call reporting an assault. The caller reported having seen a man assault a woman in a red and silver pickup truck on a particular road. As an officer arrived at the scene, he observed a truck matching the same description parked on the side of the road. A man was standing beside the truck and a young woman was sitting inside it. The officer approached the man and informed him that he was investigating a reported assault. The man appeared intoxicated. The officer asked for the man's identification. He refused and asked why the officer wanted to see his identification. The officer responded, once again saying that he was investigating a reported assault. The man became agitated, insisting he had done nothing wrong. During the confrontation, the officer asked the man 11 times for his identification and was refused every time. He arrested the man

*Hiibel v. Sixth Judicial District Court of Nevada (542 U.S. 177 [2004])*

and charged him with "willfully resist[ing], delay[ing], or obstruct[ing] a public officer in discharging or attempting to discharge any legal duty of his office," in violation of Nevada law. The question before the U.S. Supreme Court was whether officers can demand identification in situations such as this. The Court held that the officer was within his rights to do so.

This case followed somewhat on the heels of an earlier decision in which the Court authorized officers to stop (with reasonable suspicion) suspected criminals to ask questions and check identification (*United States v. Hensley*, 469 U.S. 221 [1985]). The twist in *Hiibel* was whether refusal to give an officer identification justified *arrest*. Clearly the Supreme Court feels it is important for officers to be permitted to ask for identification in stop encounters: ". . . the ability to briefly stop [a] person, ask questions, or check identification in the absence of probable cause promotes the strong government interest in solving crimes and bringing offenders to justice."

# ▶ Drug Courier Profiling

An especially controversial variety of *Terry*-like investigative stops is those based on so-called **drug courier profiling**. Almost without exception, drug courier profiling occurs during stop-and-frisk encounters—those in which a person is stopped and questioned because he or she appears suspicious in some way. Drug courier profiling is most common in airports but also occurs on U.S. highways and elsewhere.

Profiling of offenders is often used for other offenses, as well. Law enforcement officials have developed profiles for everything from car thieves and child abusers to sex offenders and terrorists. This type of profiling should be distinguished from racial profiling discussed in the last chapter. Here we are concerned primarily with whether certain characteristics permit authorities to conduct stops similar to the one permitted in *Terry*.

Controlled substances are often carried into the United States by airline passengers. Searching every person who passes through an airport would be costly, time consuming, unacceptable to passengers, and almost certainly unconstitutional. Warrantless searches that are based on no articulable justification are always considered unreasonable under the Fourth Amendment, unless one of a few "specifically established and well-delineated exceptions" applies (*Katz v. United States*, 389 U.S. 347 [1967]). In other words, such searches violate the Fourth Amendment because they are not based on probable cause.

Given that suspicionless searches are illegal, then, the police are left with two options when confronting people suspected of being drug couriers: "consensual encounters" and "investigative detentions." A consensual encounter, sometimes referred to as a "consent search," has been defined as an "encounter in which contact is initiated by a police officer without any articulable reason whatsoever and the citizen is briefly asked some questions."

---

**DECISION-MAKING EXERCISE 6.8**

**PUTTING IT ALL TOGETHER**

Deputy Smith was on patrol in his police cruiser when he heard a report over the radio that a bank had just been robbed and that four male perpetrators had fled in a blue 1976 Ford pickup without license plates. Several minutes later, Smith observed a vehicle matching the description given over the radio, except that it *had* license plates. He followed the truck and, after turning on his flashers, ordered the driver of the truck to pull over to the side of the road, which he did. Smith approached the truck and observed three men and a woman inside, each of whom appeared nervous and upset by the fact that they had been pulled over. After Smith ordered the occupants out of the car, he observed a bulge in the driver's pocket. He frisked the driver and found a weapon. Was Smith justified in stopping the vehicle and frisking the driver?

An investigative detention is "a temporary involuntary detention . . . which must be predicated on 'reasonable suspicion'" (*United States v. Bueno*, 21 F.3d [1978]). Both consent searches and investigative detentions are not considered searches, so they fall outside the Fourth Amendment's probable cause requirement.

Probable cause is not required for a consent search, because when a person gives consent to the police to conduct a search or ask questions, the Fourth Amendment does not apply. Assuming the citizen remains free to decline the officer's request to conduct a search, the officer can legally ask a person to look in his or her car, bag, house, or other area. The logic behind consent searches was touched on in *Terry*: "there is nothing in the Constitution which prevents a policeman from addressing questions to anyone on the streets." However, for a consent search to be truly consensual, the person must feel free to refuse. This is closely related to the definition of *stop* covered earlier in this chapter: "[T]he Fourth Amendment permits police officers to approach individuals at random in airport lobbies and other public places to ask them questions and to request consent to search their luggage, so long as a reasonable person would understand that he or she could refuse to cooperate" (*Bostick*, 501 U.S. 429). In other words, the constitutionality of a consent search is premised on the requirement that the person is truly free to decline when asked by a police officer to allow a search. (Consent searches are covered in greater detail in Chapter 7.)

Perhaps more common in the practice of drug courier profiling is the use of investigative detentions, or *Terry* stops. *Terry* permits police officers to stop people based on reasonable suspicion that criminal activity is afoot. *Terry* stops occur in airports and elsewhere when a person is involuntarily detained. For this type of stop to occur, however, the officer needs to show that there is, in fact, reasonable suspicion that the person is a drug courier. Drug courier profiling is a controversial topic, because it is open to debate as to what characteristics a person must display for reasonable suspicion to be established.

Clearly, not every person walking through an airport can be stopped. Thus, law enforcement officials must look for specific characteristics of drug couriers. As the Supreme Court observed in *Mendenhall*, "Much . . . drug traffic is highly organized and conducted by sophisticated criminal syndicates . . . And many drugs . . . may be easily concealed. As a result, the obstacles to detection . . . may be unmatched in any other area of law enforcement." Further, one of the most significant impediments in the war on drugs is the "extraordinary and well-documented difficulty of identifying drug couriers" (*Royer*, 460 U.S. 491).

The original "drug courier profile" is generally attributed to Paul Markonni, an agent of the DEA. He identified a number of suspicious characteristics of likely drug couriers

Drug courier profiling often takes place at airports. Some profiling is very visible, but much of it is conducted by officials who work undercover. Most profiling also takes place away from checkpoints, such as the one depicted here. If authorities have reasonable suspicion to stop an individual anywhere in an airport, they will do so.

when he was assigned to a drug interdiction unit at the Detroit airport. That profile has since been described as an "informally compiled abstract of characteristics thought typical of persons carrying illicit drugs" (*Mendenhall*, 446 U.S. 544). There is no single, nationally recognized drug courier profile or set of characteristics indicative of drug courier profiling. Instead, specific cases must be considered to ascertain which types of characteristics fit the drug courier profile.

The first drug courier profile case of note, *United States v. Van Lewis*, 409 F. Supp. 535 (E.D. Mich. 1976), listed several characteristics to be used in identifying drug couriers: (1) the use of small denominations of currency for ticket purchase; (2) travel to and from major drug import centers; (3) the absence of luggage or use of empty suitcases on trips that normally require extra clothing; and (4) travel under an alias. In a similar case, *Elmore v. United States*, 595 F.2d 1036 (5th Cir. 1979), the Fifth Circuit described these common characteristics of drug couriers:

> (1) arrival from or departure to an identified source city; (2) carrying little or no luggage; (3) unusual itinerary, such as rapid turnaround time for a very lengthy airplane trip; (4) use of an alias; (5) carrying unusually large amounts of currency in the many thousands of dollars, usually on their person, or in briefcases or bags; (6) purchasing airline tickets with a large amount of small denomination currency; and (7) unusual nervousness beyond that ordinarily exhibited by passengers.

Some secondary characteristics of drug couriers were also identified in *Elmore v. United States*, including "(1) the almost exclusive use of public transportation, particularly taxicabs, in departing from the airport; (2) immediately making a phone call after deplaning; (3) leaving a false or fictitious call-back telephone number with the airline being utilized; and (4) excessively frequent travel to source or distribution cities."

Still other characteristics of drug couriers include unusual dress, age between 25 and 35, and extreme paleness consistent with being extremely nervous.[3] Another study points to characteristics such as "not checking bags at the airport, not using identification tags on luggage, purchasing tickets on the day of a flight, exiting first or last from the plane, visually scanning the terminal for law enforcement, making no eye contact with airport personnel, walking quickly through the terminal while continuously checking over one's shoulder, and quickly leaving the airport on arrival."[4] See Figure 6.6 for a fairly comprehensive list of characteristics that have been identified as typical of drug couriers.

## Landmark Cases Regarding Drug Courier Profiling

*Reid v. Georgia*
*(448 U.S. 438 [1980])*

*Reid v. Georgia*, 448 U.S. 438 (1980) was one of the first Supreme Court cases to address drug courier profiling. The petitioner, Reid, arrived at the Atlanta airport on an early morning flight. A narcotics agent on duty at the time observed that Reid repeatedly looked over his shoulder at another man and that both were carrying shoulder bags. As the two men left the airport, the narcotics officer approached them and asked them for identification and to consent to a search. Reid tried to run away and, in doing so, left his bag behind, which turned out to contain cocaine. He was later apprehended and brought to trial on drug possession charges. He attempted to have the cocaine thrown out under the exclusionary rule, claiming that he had been unconstitutionally detained as he was leaving the airport with the other man.

---

[3]B. Wilson, "The War on Drugs: Evening the Odds through the Use of the Airport Drug Courier Profile," *Boston University Public Interest Journal* 6 (1994): 202–232.

[4]C. R. Williams and B. A. Arrigo, "Discerning the Margins of Constitutional Encroachment: The Drug Courier Profile in the Airport Milieu," *American Journal of Criminal Justice* 24 (1999): 31–46.

▼

1. Use small denominations of currency for ticket purchases
2. Travel to and from major drug import centers
3. Have no luggage or use empty suitcases on trips that normally require extra clothing
4. Travel under an alias
5. Have an unusual itinerary, such as a rapid turnaround time for a very lengthy airplane trip
6. Carry unusually large amounts of currency (i.e., many thousands of dollars)
7. Display unusual nervousness beyond that ordinarily exhibited by passengers
8. Use public transportation almost exclusively upon departing the airport
9. Immediately make a phone call after deplaning
10. Leave a false or fictitious call-back telephone number with the airline
11. Dress in an unusual manner
12. Are between 25 and 35 years old
13. Are extremely pale (consistent with being extremely nervous)
14. Do not use identification tags on luggage
15. Purchase tickets on the day of the flight
16. Exit first or last from the plane
17. Walk quickly through the terminal while continuously checking over his or her shoulder
18. Quickly leave the airport on arrival

**FIGURE 6.6 Typical Characteristics of Drug Couriers**

The trial court granted Reid's motion to suppress the cocaine. However, the Georgia Court of Appeals reversed the lower court's decision and ruled that the narcotics agent had performed a permissible stop based on the so-called drug courier profile. In its decision, the Georgia Court of Appeals noted that Reid (1) had arrived from Fort Lauderdale, Florida, a place of origin for drugs; (2) was traveling at an unusual hour; (3) was attempting to conceal the fact that he was traveling with another person; and (4) was not traveling with any luggage, other than the shoulder bag.

The U.S. Supreme Court granted *certiorari*, holding that "the judgment of the appellate court cannot be sustained insofar as it rests on the determination that the DEA agent lawfully seized the petitioner when he approached him." The Court went on to note that the agent "could not . . . have reasonably suspected the petitioner of criminal activity on the basis . . . that the petitioner preceded another person and occasionally looked backward at him." The other reasons for stopping Reid were also criticized by the Court because the unusual hour, lack of luggage, and place of origin "describe a very large category of presumably innocent travelers, who would be subject to virtually random seizures were the Court to conclude that as little foundation as there was in this case could justify the seizure." The Court declared that the DEA agent did not have reasonable suspicion to detain Reid.

*Mendenhall* was an essential decision in defining the *stop* in stop-and-frisk—it also had important implications for drug courier profiling in the United States. In that case, DEA agents, who were "present for the [purpose] of detecting unlawful traffic in narcotics," observed Mendenhall in the Detroit airport. They approached her in the airport and identified themselves. They then asked Mendenhall for her identification and airline ticket. When she complied, they noticed that the plane ticket was in another name. At that point, the agents asked Mendenhall if she would accompany them to a private room and consent

## DECISION-MAKING EXERCISE 6.9

### AN APPLICATION OF DRUG COURIER PROFILING

DEA agents at the Dallas/Fort Worth airport observed a woman exiting a plane that had just arrived from Miami. She was carrying a small bag on her shoulder and looking around as if she was expecting to meet another person. Still alone, she walked quickly into a restroom. When she came out, she went directly to a pay phone, where she made a phone call lasting 30 minutes. Finding her conduct suspicious, the DEA agents approached the woman, identified themselves, and asked if they could speak with her. The woman appeared very nervous, and her voice cracked when she conversed with them. The agents asked for the woman's identification and plane ticket. She furnished her plane ticket but stated that she had lost her identification. The agents asked how long she was going to stay in the Dallas/Fort Worth area. She replied that she would remain for one week, but one of the agents noticed that her ticket indicated that she would be leaving later that same day. Do the agents have justification to further detain the woman?

to a search of her bags. She was told that she had the right to decline, but she handed over her purse and agreed to the search. A female police officer then arrived to search Mendenhall's person. When she removed her clothing, they found a package that appeared to contain heroin. The Supreme Court sanctioned this action and declared that a certain degree of deference should be given to law enforcement agents to interpret the circumstances in each case, based on their experience and expertise. The Court reasoned that an experienced law enforcement officer may be "able to perceive and articulate meaning in given conduct which would be wholly innocent to the untrained observer" (*Mendenhall*, 446 U.S. 544).

Another significant drug courier profiling case decided by the Supreme Court is *Florida v. Royer*, 460 U.S. 491 (1983). In that case, two detectives at the Miami International Airport observed Royer, who had purchased a one-way ticket to New York under an assumed name. Believing that Royer displayed characteristics associated with the drug courier profile, the officers approached him. Royer produced his ticket and identification after being requested to do so. The officers did not return his ticket and identification and instead asked Royer to accompany them to a nearby room. One of the detectives retrieved the luggage that Royer had checked and brought it to the room. Royer produced a key for the suitcases, and marijuana was found in one of them. Royer was convicted for felony possession, but the Florida Court of Appeals reversed the trial court's decision, holding that the officers detained Royer without probable cause, which was required because of the intrusive nature of the stop.

The detectives argued that Royer fit the drug courier profile for a number of reasons. First, he was carrying luggage that appeared to be heavy. Second, he was young, dressed casually, and appeared nervous. Finally, he paid for his plane ticket in cash and did not complete the airline identification tag, opting instead to write only his name and destination on the tag. The court argued on appeal, however, that "any of these factors relied upon by Miami police may have been as consistent with innocence as with guilt" and that the drug courier profile alone was insufficient to establish reasonable suspicion, much less probable cause, to detain Royer. The case worked its way up to the U.S. Supreme Court, and the Court upheld the appeals court decision. According to the Court, Royer was detained illegally, in part because the detectives did not indicate at any point that he was free to leave. Further, the Court argued that "the detention . . . was a more serious intrusion on his personal liberty than is allowable on mere suspicion of criminal activity. What had begun as a consensual encounter . . . escalated into an investigatory procedure in an interrogation room, and [Royer] . . . was under arrest."

In contrast to *Royer*, in *United States v. Sokolow*, 490 U.S. 1 (1989), the Court upheld a stop that was premised on certain characteristics that the DEA had identified for drug couriers. In that case, DEA agents stopped Sokolow upon his arrival at Honolulu International Airport and found a large quantity of cocaine in his carry-on luggage. In support of the stop, the agents noted that Sokolow (1) had paid $2,100 for his airline ticket with a roll of $20 bills; (2) traveled under an assumed name; (3) had flown in from a major "source city," Miami; (4) had stayed in Miami for only 48 hours; (5) appeared nervous; and (6) did not check any luggage. The district court denied Sokolow's motion to suppress the drugs, finding that the agents had reasonable suspicion to stop him in the airport. However, the court of appeals declared that the stop was illegal, a violation of the Fourth Amendment. The court relied on a two-pronged test to assess the legality of the stop. It required a showing that (1) there was "ongoing criminal activity" and that there were (2) "personal characteristics" of drug courier profiles. While the second prong would seem to have been met in this case, the appeals court decided that the first prong had not been met because the government did not offer "empirical documentation that the combination of facts at issue did not describe the behavior of significant numbers of innocent persons." In other words, the court of appeals found no evidence of ongoing criminal activity and thus ruled that the stop was in violation of the Fourth Amendment.

*United States v. Sokolow*
*(490 U.S. 1 [1989])*

---

**DECISION-MAKING EXERCISE 6.10**

**TERRORIST PROFILING**

In 2004, two Arab gentlemen, Tarik Farag and Amro Elmasry, traveled from San Diego to New York's JFK airport on American Airlines Flight 236. As soon as they deplaned at JFK, they were met by no less than 10 armed agents in paramilitary gear with guns and police dogs. They were ordered to raise their hands and were frisked, handcuffed, and whisked off to an interrogation room. The investigation yielded no evidence of wrongdoing. The men sued, arguing that their arrests were unjustified, but the government cited the following as justification for the airport detention (note that these facts were reported to the captain by two counterterrorism agents who were on the flight):

- At the beginning of the flight, despite sitting on opposite sides of the aisle, plaintiffs spoke to each other over the heads of other passengers in a mixture of Arabic and English;

- Elmasry made an allegedly "unusual" initial seat change "from a window seat . . . to a middle seat . . . between two other male passengers";

- After Elmasry changed seats, he and Farag talked to each other "loudly" over the heads of other passengers in a mixture of Arabic and English;

- Elmasry looked at his watch when the plane took off, when the plane landed, and at other points during the flight;

- After the meal service, Elmasry "got out of his seat . . . , went into the aisle, leaned over to Farag, and spoke a 'very short sentence' to Farag in a mixture of Arabic and English";

- Immediately thereafter, plaintiffs moved together to the back of the plane, and did not take their carry-on luggage with them;

- Plaintiffs got up to return to the front of the cabin at the very end of the flight, after the "fasten seatbelt" indicator was lit;

- Upon returning to the front of the plane, Farag did not sit in his original seat (17E), but rather, in Elmasry's original seat (18A), which was located directly behind Smith; [and]

- After the plane landed, Elmasry took out his cellular phone and deleted five or six numbers (*Farag v. United States*, 2008 U.S. Dist. LEXIS 95331 [2008]).

Is there merit to the government's argument?

▼

The U.S. Supreme Court reversed the appeals court decision. It held that the agents *did* have reasonable suspicion that Sokolow was engaged in the transportation of narcotics. In criticizing the two-pronged test used by the appeals court, the Supreme Court noted that the test "created unnecessary difficulty in dealing with one of the relatively simple concepts embodied in the Fourth Amendment." In reference to the suspicious conduct observed by the agents, the Court went on to note that "although each of these factors [such as paying $2,100 for a plane ticket with small denomination bills] is not by itself proof of illegal conduct and is quite consistent with innocent travel, taken together they amount to reasonable suspicion that criminal activity was afoot."

## ► Investigative Detentions

The Supreme Court has held that certain police station detentions are justifiable on less than probable cause. One type of **investigative detention**, a stationhouse detention, is less intrusive than an arrest but more intrusive than a *Terry* stop. Stationhouse detentions are used in many locations for such purposes as obtaining fingerprints and photographs, ordering lineups, administering polygraph examinations, and securing other types of evidence.

In *Davis v. Mississippi*, 394 U.S. 721 (1969), involved a boy who was one of the 25 suspects in a rape investigation. Davis was 14 years old at the time of the case. Police conducted a dragnet-style investigation based on a victim's description that "negro youth" were responsible for her victimization. Davis, along with the other 24 suspects, were detained and fingerprinted without probable cause. The Court excluded fingerprint evidence obtained from all 25 rape suspects, but it did note that detention for fingerprinting would have been permissible if "narrowly circumscribed procedures" were in place. In other words, the Court suggested that to justify the detention, there had to be some objective basis for detaining a person, a clear investigation underway, and a court order stating that adequate evidence exists.

In another case, *Hayes v. Florida*, 470 U.S. 811 (1985), officers went to the home of a burglary-rape suspect (without a warrant) in the hopes of obtaining his fingerprints. The officers asked the man to accompany them to the stationhouse. The man expressed reluctance, so one officer said they would arrest him if he failed to comply. The man said he would rather accompany the officers to the police station than be arrested. He was taken to the police station and it was determined that his fingerprints matched those taken from the scene of the crime. The Supreme Court reversed his conviction, stating:

> Our view continues to be that the line is crossed when the police, without probable cause or a warrant, forcibly remove a person from his home or other place in which he is entitled to be and transport him to the police station, where he is detained, although briefly, for investigative purposes. We adhere to the view that such seizures, at least where not under judicial supervision, are sufficiently like arrests to invoke the traditional rule that arrests may constitutionally be made only on probable cause.

The key in *Hayes*, is that the detention was not consensual. In cases in which consent is obtained, probable cause is not necessary.

In summary, then, a stationhouse detention for the purpose of fingerprinting may be permissible when (1) there is reasonable suspicion to believe the suspect has committed a crime; (2) there is a reasonable belief that the fingerprints will inculpate or exculpate the suspect; and (3) the procedure is carried out promptly. The Supreme Court has not yet addressed the issue of stationhouse detentions for purposes other than fingerprinting.

# Summary

## 1. Distinguish between a stop and a nonstop.

A number of generalizations can be drawn from the stop-and-frisk discussion in this chapter and from the introduction to reasonable suspicion presented in Chapter 3. First, an encounter between a citizen and police is not governed by the Fourth Amendment unless it is considered a *stop*, which is one type of *seizure*. When the police activity in question rises to the level of a stop, then the Fourth Amendment applies, and the officer is required to have the appropriate level of justification for the stop to be legal.

Factors to consider in determining whether a "stop" has taken place include (1) whether the police action was threatening; (2) how long the detention lasted; (3) whether the person was physically detained or physically touched by the police; (4) whether the detention took place in public view or removed from public view, such as in a private room; and perhaps most importantly, (5) whether a reasonable person would, under the circumstances, have believed that he or she was free to leave. With regard to the last factor, it is not necessary that police communicate to the detainee that he or she is free to leave. A situation involving only brief questioning, then, is unlikely to be considered a stop that would implicate the Fourth Amendment.

## 2. Explain when a stop-and-frisk is permissible.

The Fourth Amendment generally requires that probable cause be in place before a Fourth Amendment seizure can occur. However, the Supreme Court in *Terry* ruled that a person can be seized on less than probable cause to arrest. The second conclusion, then, focuses on when this can occur. Generally, a seizure based on less than probable cause (reasonable suspicion) can occur under three circumstances: (1) when the officer observes a person engaging in unusual activity and can point to specific, articulable facts that contribute to reasonable suspicion that criminal activity is afoot; (2) when the officer receives information from an informant who is reliable; and (3) when the officer receives a communication from another police department that the person to be stopped is suspected of involvement in criminal activity.

## 3. Summarize stop-and-frisk procedure.

When reasonable suspicion is in place and a police officer is entitled to make a stop, he or she must make reasonable inquiries. These inquiries should be limited to testing the officer's suspicion. If the questioning becomes unreasonable, excessive, or too intrusive, probable cause may be required. Then, if the officer reasonably believes, during the course of questioning, that the person is armed and dangerous, he or she can frisk the person. Factors used in determining whether a frisk is reasonable include (1) whether the person has a reputation for dangerousness; (2) the type of criminal activity in which the person is presumably involved; (3) visual cues that suggest the presence of a weapon; and/or (4) suggestive or furtive gestures on the part of the suspect.

Frisks are also limited. A frisk is authorized if an officer reasonably fears for his or her safety, and it is limited to a patdown of the person's outer clothing. Recent decisions, however, permit a limited search of the area immediately surrounding the person, such as in automobiles and other situations in which several people may be found. Weapon-like objects and contraband can be removed during the course of the frisk, but both must be immediately apparent to the frisking officer. If a weapon or other item is not immediately apparent, then the officer risks exceeding the limits of a frisk, especially if he or she feels, gropes, or otherwise manipulates the object in an attempt to determine what it is. Such activity may arise to the level of a search, requiring probable cause.

## 4. Explain the relevance of drug courier profiling in the stop-and-frisk context.

Drug courier profiling is a controversial practice. While the courts have approved of practices that have characteristics of drug courier profiles, a number of cases concerning drug courier profiling have reached the Supreme Court. Even so, the Court has yet to rule definitively on the constitutionality of drug courier profiling. Racial discrimination is also at issue in drug courier profiling. There is no shortage of criticism concerning the role of race in profiling, but since the Supreme Court has not decided on the legality of profiling, it is unlikely that racially motivated investigative stops, to the extent they exist, will cease to occur.

## 5. Compare and contrast investigative detentions with stop-and-frisk.

Investigative detentions, also called a stationhouse detention, are less intrusive detentions than arrests, but more intrusive than a *Terry* stop. Stationhouse detentions are used in many locations for such purposes as obtaining fingerprints and photographs, ordering lineups, administering polygraph examinations, and securing other types of evidence.

# Key Terms

drug courier profiling *178*
frisk *170*

investigative detention *184*

stop *163*

# Key Cases

## Stop

- *Terry v. Ohio*, 392 U.S. 1 (1968)
- *United States v. Mendenhall*, 446 U.S. 544 (1980)
- *California v. Hodari D.*, 449 U.S. 621 (1991)
- *Florida v. Bostick*, 501 U.S. 429 (1991)
- *United States v. Montoya De Hernandez*, 473 U.S. 531 (1985)

## Frisk

- *Pennsylvania v. Mimms*, 434 U.S. 106 (1977)
- *Ybarra v. Illinois*, 444 U.S. 85 (1979)
- *Minnesota v. Dickerson*, 508 U.S. 366 (1993)
- *Sibron v. New York*, 392 U.S. 40 (1968)

## Evolving Nature of Stop-and-Frisk

- *Delaware v. Prouse*, 440 U.S. 648 (1979)
- *Maryland v. Buie*, 494 U.S. 325 (1990)
- *Papachristou v. City of Jacksonville*, 405 U.S. 156 (1972)
- *Kolender v. Lawson*, 461 U.S. 352 (1983)
- *Hiibel v. Sixth Judicial District Court of Nevada*, 542 U.S. 177 (2004)

## Drug Courier Profiling

- *Reid v. Georgia*, 448 U.S. 438 (1980)
- *United States v. Mendenhall*, 446 U.S. 544 (1980)
- *United States v. Sokolow*, 490 U.S. 1 (1989)

# Further Exploration

1. In *Florida v. J.L.*, 529 U.S. 266 (2000), police received an anonymous tip that a young black male wearing a plaid shirt was in possession of a gun at a bus stop. Officers went to the bus stop and found *three* young black males, only one of whom was wearing a plaid shirt. The officers frisked the male fitting the description and found a gun. Were they justified in conducting the frisk if all they had to go off of was an anonymous tip? Find and read the Court's opinion. What did the Court decide? Was the decision unanimous? If not, what argument did the dissent offer? The majority?

2. An officer conducts a routine stop for speeding. As she approaches the vehicle, she notices a bumper sticker that says "I Eat Cops for Breakfast." The officer has no other basis for concluding the motorist may be dangerous. Can she order the motorist out of the vehicle and conduct a frisk? What cases are relevant and why? Also consider reading the Fifth Circuit's opinion in *Estep v. Dallas County*, 310 F.3d 353 (5th Cir. 2002).

3. The day after a shooting in which a man was killed, police pulled over a vehicle for making an illegal U-turn. As he was approaching the driver's side of the vehicle, one of the officers noticed bullet holes in the door. The officer then asked for identification from both the driver and passenger. The passenger was identified as Nolan, who the officers knew was affiliated with a local gang. Following are other pertinent facts from this actual case:

   After running data checks on both the driver and the passenger, the officer saw that the Omaha police homicide unit had put out a "locate" for Nolan. A "locate" means that an officer wishes to speak with the individual, but it does not give the officers authority to arrest the individual.

   At that point, the officer asked Nolan to get out of his car and stand near the back fender area. Instead, Nolan went past that area and sat on the curb. The officer observed that Nolan moved "[v]ery quickly" and was grabbing his waistband. The officer also observed that Nolan's pants were falling down and that it appeared as if there was something heavy in his pants. Finally, when asked if he had any weapons or other dangerous objects on his person, Nolan did not respond. The officer conducted a patdown of Nolan, looking for weapons. The patdown revealed a .44-caliber gun, found

   in Nolan's waistband. A subsequent search of Nolan's person uncovered live ammunition, and Nolan was placed under arrest at that time. The gun and ammunition were admitted into evidence . . .

   Were the officer's actions justified? Why or why not? Read *State v. Nolan*, 807 N.W.2d 520 (Ne. 2012) for further information.

4. A 911 caller summoned police and asked that a man named Joshua Garcia be removed from the residence. As officer Stansell was getting close to the residence, he noticed a man walking across the street. The officer stopped his car near the man, shone his flashlight on him, exited his car, and told the man to "stop." The man kept walking and officer Stansell again ordered him to stop. The man had his hands in his pockets and was clearly fumbling with something. The officer then jumped in the man's path, pulled out his gun, and ordered the man to remove his hands from his pockets. The man kept on his way, still fumbling in his pockets. The officer then holstered his weapon and sprayed the man with a one-second burst of pepper spray. Before the man went down, he dropped something. After the officer arrested him, he determined that the item dropped was crack cocaine. Should the evidence be admissible at trial? What if you learned that the man in the scenario was the suspect in the domestic violence incident? See *State v. Garcia*, 217 P.3d 1032 (N.M. 2009).

5. Read these facts from *United States v. Foster*, 634 F3d 243 (4th Cir. 2011) and determine whether the evidence should have been admissible, citing applicable case law:

   On August 8, 2008, at approximately 1:00 P.M., Detective J. Ragland, a seventeen-year veteran of the Henderson Police Department, exited a restaurant after eating lunch with his wife. As Detective Ragland, in plain clothes, walked towards his unmarked police vehicle, he noticed a young black male sitting in the driver's seat of an SUV with his hands on the steering wheel. Detective Ragland saw the man's mouth move, but could not make out what he was saying. He then witnessed a second black male sit up in the passenger seat from a crouching position. The detective recognized the second individual as David Foster. . . . Detective Ragland knew Foster because he had previously dated Foster's cousin, and he had arrested Foster in the past for driving with a revoked license . . .

The moment the two saw one another, the detective observed Foster's arms "shifting" . . . However, Detective Ragland never saw Foster's actual hands, only his upper body and arms above the elbow. While continuing on his way towards the police vehicle, the detective walked past the SUV and asked its occupants "What are ya'll doing?" Foster replied that they were "just chilling." . . . Detective Ragland then responded . . . "Knowing you, you are up to something," Detective Ragland then entered his own vehicle and left the parking lot.

Detective Ragland drove across the street to a bank parking lot and continued to observe the SUV. He did not see anyone get into or approach the vehicle. He did not see anyone leave the vehicle. He called Sergeant Darnell, the drug unit supervisor, and was informed that Foster was under investigation. Detective Ragland understood this comment to mean that Foster was under investigation for a drug related offense. He also called Officer Macialek for assistance with a possible drug arrest. Approximately fifteen minutes after first encountering Foster, Detective Ragland returned to the still parked SUV with Officer Macialek.

The officers used their respective vehicles to block the SUV in, got out of their cars, and separately approached either side of the SUV. Officer Macialek approached the passenger side of the vehicle with his gun drawn. The officers asked Foster and the driver to show their hands, and they complied. Detective Ragland asked the driver for identification, and the driver informed him that his license was in his back pocket. While the driver and Foster remained in the car, Detective Ragland performed a pat-down search. He then allowed the driver to retrieve his license. Detective Ragland asked for the vehicle registration, and Foster opened the glove compartment to retrieve it. The moment the glove compartment opened, Detective Ragland saw a plastic bag containing a white powdery substance that he believed to be cocaine, these suspicions were ultimately confirmed. Detective Ragland immediately ordered the driver and Foster to put their hands up and placed them under arrest. A later search of the SUV revealed a set of digital scales in the glove compartment, and a small travel bag tucked under the passenger's seat containing both $6,570 in cash and more cocaine. The total amount of cocaine seized was 350.5 grams.

# Review Questions

1. Why is it important to treat a stop and a frisk as two separate acts?

2. Assuming a police officer has reasonable suspicion to stop a person, what must the officer do before stopping him or her?

3. Define a *stop.*

4. Why is the duration of a stop important?

5. Can *effects* be seized? Explain.

6. Summarize the permissible grounds for a frisk.

7. Summarize the Supreme Court's view on the proper scope of a frisk.

8. In what ways has the stop-and-frisk law been expanded? Summarize pertinent cases.

9. Why is it important to distinguish between theory and reality when discussing stop-and-frisk?

10. What is drug courier profiling?

11. Identify several characteristics of drug couriers.

12. Summarize the Supreme Court's view on drug courier profiling, citing relevant cases.

13. In what ways is race relevant to the drug courier profile?

14. What are investigative detentions? How do they differ from stops?

15. Reasonable suspicion is not mentioned in the Fourth Amendment. Has the Supreme Court overstepped its authority by essentially creating this level of justification? Why or why not?

# Web Links and Exercises

1. Stop-and-frisk: Read more about police actions that fall short of arrest.

URL (read the article called "Police Intervention Short of Arrest"): http://www.fbi.gov/stats-services/publications/law-enforcement-bulletin/2006-pdfs/nov06leb.pdf (accessed May 6, 2013).

2. Traffic stops: Read about traffic stops and the risks. What does it mean to "take AIM" in traffic stops?

Suggested URL: http://www.fbi.gov/stats-services/publications/law-enforcement-bulletin/2008-pdfs/may08leb.pdf (accessed May 6, 2013).

3. Read about the practice of criminal profiling. How does it differ from drug courier and other forms of profiling discussed in this chapter? How is it similar?

Suggested URL: http://www.forensicpsychology.net/resources/criminal-profiling/ (accessed May 6, 2013).

4. Terrorist profiling: Read about terrorist profiling.

Suggested URL (there is a section in the report at this URL): http://www.loc.gov/rr/frd/pdf-files/Soc_Psych_of_Terrorism.pdf (accessed May 6, 2013).

# 7 Actions Based on Administrative Justification and Consent

### LEARNING OBJECTIVES

When you complete this chapter, you should be able to:

**1** *Explain the justification for regulatory and administrative searches.*

**2** *Describe regulatory and administrative searches.*

**3** *Describe consent searches and the issues associated with them.*

# Introduction: Casting Off the Fourth Amendment's Restraints

This chapter briefly introduces several types of actions that the Supreme Court has authorized based on administrative justification. As discussed in Chapter 3, when an action is based on an administrative justification, its primary purpose is noncriminal. These actions resemble searches because they intrude on people's privacy—and can lead to the discovery of evidence. Technically, however, they are not searches. Instead of being based on probable cause or reasonable suspicion, administrative actions involve a balancing test, weighing citizens' privacy interests against the interest of ensuring public safety. When the latter outweighs the former, an administrative "search" is allowed, subject to certain limitations (such as department policy).

This chapter also introduces the topic of consent searches. When a person gives valid consent to search, neither a warrant nor probable cause is required. Closely tied to consent searches is the controversial police practice known as "knock and talk." The consent search section also delves into third-party consent or the extent to which one person can grant consent to have another person's property searched. Consent searches are similar to actions based on administrative justification because neither require probable cause—or any real measure of proof that a crime is being committed, or has been committed.

## ▶ Actions Based on Administrative Justification

The Supreme Court has authorized many types of actions under the administrative justification exception to the Fourth Amendment's probable cause and warrant requirements. Sometimes they are described as *special needs beyond law enforcement searches*; other times, they are called *regulatory searches*. To avoid confusion, this book groups all of them under the category of actions based on *administrative justification*. The actions that are considered include (1) inventories; (2) inspections; (3) checkpoints; (4) school discipline; (5) "searches" of government employees' offices; (6) drug and alcohol testing; and (7) parole and probation supervision. Note that when the term "search" appears in quotes, it is to indicate that although a particular action may look like a search on its face, it is not the same as a true Fourth Amendment search.

### Inventories

Like seizures based on plain view, inventories can be viewed as another type of fallback measure. An inventory can be of a vehicle or of a person's personal items. Usually, when a search occurs under the automobile exception, or as a search incident to arrest, an inventory is taken after the fact for the purpose of developing a record of what items have been taken into custody. Both types of inventories are "fallbacks" in the sense that they often occur *after* an earlier search.

#### Vehicle Inventories

*South Dakota v. Opperman*
*(428 U.S. 364 [1976])*

A **vehicle inventory** occurs in a number of situations, usually after a car has been impounded for traffic or parking violations. In *South Dakota v. Opperman*, 428 U.S. 364 (1976), the Supreme Court held that a warrantless inventory is permissible on administrative or regulatory grounds. However, it must (1) follow a *lawful* impoundment; (2) be of a routine nature, following standard operating procedures; and (3) not be a "pretext concealing an investigatory police motive." Thus, even though a vehicle inventory permits a search without probable cause for the limited purpose of creating a routine inventory of items, it cannot be used in lieu of a regular search requiring probable cause.

Why did the Court allow police to conduct an inventory without probable cause, despite the fact that it is still a "search" in the conventional sense of the term? The Court distinguished between administrative care-taking functions (such as inventories) and criminal investigations. It noted that the probable cause requirement of the Fourth Amendment is "unhelpful" in the context of care-taking functions, as opposed to criminal investigations. Probable cause is irrelevant in an inventory, "particularly when no claim is made that the protective procedures are a subterfuge for criminal investigations."

The Court offered three reasons in support of vehicle inventories. First, an inventory protects the owner's property while it is in police custody. Second, an inventory protects the police against claims of lost or stolen property. Finally, an inventory protects the police and public from dangerous items (such as weapons) that might be concealed in a car.

Note that permissible inventories include containers within the vehicle. That is, the police may examine *any* container discovered during the course of a vehicle inventory,

▼

provided that it is mandated by departmental procedures. This was the decision reached in *Colorado v. Bertine*, 479 U.S. 367 (1987), in which an officer opened a closed backpack during an inventory search and found drugs. *Bertine* is also significant in that the Court refused to alter the vehicle inventory exception to the Fourth Amendment when secure impound facilities are accessible. As the Court stated, "[T]he security of the storage facility does not completely eliminate the need for inventorying; the police may still wish to protect themselves or the owners of the lot against false claims of theft or dangerous instrumentalities."

*Colorado v. Bertine*
*(479 U.S. 367 [1987])*

In *Bertine*, the Court also rejected an argument that car owners should be able to make their own arrangements if their vehicles are impounded (such as having it towed by a private company, or having a friend drive it home). The Court stated, "The reasonableness of any particular governmental activity does not necessarily or invariably turn on the existence of alternative 'less intrusive' means."

Reading *Opperman* and *Bertine* together would suggest that inventories are relatively standard and intended mainly to take note of a car's contents. However, in *Michigan v. Thomas*, 458 U.S. 259 (1982), the Supreme Court concluded that the police could go even further. In that case, officers found a loaded .38 revolver in one of the impounded vehicle's air vents. The Court upheld the officers' actions because marijuana had been found in the vehicle shortly before the gun was detected.

In summary, then, two important issues must be understood with regard to vehicle inventories. First, if during the course of a valid inventory, the police discover evidence that gives rise to probable cause to search, then a more extensive search is permissible. But according to *Carroll v. United States*, 267 U.S. 132 (1925), discussed in Chapter 5, one of the requirements for such action to be constitutional is the impracticality of securing a warrant.

Second, despite the Supreme Court's apparent willingness to give police wide latitude with vehicle inventories, the police must set clear guidelines as to how the inventory should be conducted. In other words, the Court has authorized inventories without probable cause or a warrant only if, in addition to the other requirements discussed earlier, they are conducted in accordance with clear departmental policies and procedures. Requiring the police to follow appropriate policies minimizes the exercise of discretion and deters inventories from being used for criminal investigation purposes. An example of a typical inventory search policy, from the Pine Bluff, Arkansas, Police Department's *Policy and Procedure Manual*, is reprinted in Figure 7.1.

## Person Inventories

The inventory exception to the Fourth Amendment's warrant requirement also applies in the case of a **person inventory** often called an *arrest inventory*. The general rule is that the police may search an arrestee and his or her personal items, including containers found in his or her possession, as part of a routine inventory incident to the booking and jailing procedure. As decided in *Illinois v. Lafayette*, 462 U.S. 640 (1983), neither a search warrant nor probable cause is required. According to the Court:

*Illinois v. Lafayette*
*(462 U.S. 640 [1983])*

> Consistent with the Fourth Amendment, it is reasonable for police to search the personal effects of a person under lawful arrest as part of the routine administrative procedure at a police station incident to booking and jailing the suspect. The justification for such searches does not rest on probable cause, and hence the absence of a warrant is immaterial to the reasonableness of the search. Here, every consideration of orderly police administration—protection of a suspect's property, deterrence of false claims of theft against the police, security, and identification of the suspect—benefiting both the police and the public points toward the appropriateness of the examination of respondent's shoulder bag.

| | SUBJECT:<br><br>TOWING & STORAGE OF VEHICLES | POLICY NUMBER<br>260 |
|---|---|---|
| | | ISSUE DATE<br>02/19/2008 |
| | CHAPTER: PATROL | EFFECTIVE DATE<br>02/19/2008 |
| | ISSUED By:<br>Chief of Police John E. Howell | TOTAL PAGES<br>6 |

I. PROCEDURES

A. GENERAL

1. The Impoundment of motor vehicles shall be accomplished by the use of contract commercial towing services, towing vehicles, and impoundment lots as authorized by this law enforcement agency. All towing agencies must be a member of the Arkansas Towing and Recovery Board, certified for and display inspection documentation indicating they are authorized for nonconsent towing.

2. Vehicles impounded by or otherwise taken into the custody by this agency shall be inventoried in a manner consistent with this agencies policy on motor vehicle inventories as stated in Section F of this policy.

   a. Inventories should be performed at the scene or at a safe place nearby whenever this can be done safely and effectively.
   b. A Pine Bluff Police Department wrecker log will be completed on any impounded motor vehicles.
   c. Motor vehicles shall not be impounded for purposes other than those defined by statute or ordinance, (e.g., not as a form of punishment, or as a means of conducting vehicle searches when probable cause does not exist or consent to search cannot be obtained).

3. When impoundments are necessary, the operator and any passengers should not be stranded. Officers shall take those measures necessary to ensure that the operator and any passengers of the vehicle are offered transportation. To include but not limited to:

   a. Call a taxi cab for them.
   b. Call a friend or relative to pick them up.
   c. With supervisor approval, transport them to the nearest reasonably safe location.

4. If the driver/owner or passenger(s) decline assistance with transportation and the vehicle is towed at the direction of an officer for any reason, the officer shall document their refusal on an original Information /Incident Report, as Supplemental to and existing Information/Incident Report, or on an Accident Report, whichever is appropriate to the circumstances.

5. Vehicle operators may be permitted to remove unsecured valuables of a nonevidentiary nature from the vehicle prior to its removal for impoundment. The nature of these valuables shall be noted on the appropriate reporting document.

6. Impounded vehicles shall be released to owners with proof of ownership and personal identification, and following proof of payment of any impoundment, storage, or related fees and taxes.

*Source:* Reprinted courtesy of Pine Bluff, AR, Police Department.

**FIGURE 7.1 Vehicle Inventory Policy (Pine Bluff, AR, Police Department)**

It is important to understand that an inventory of person must follow a lawful arrest, so the probable cause to search requirement is essentially satisfied at the arrest stage.

The Supreme Court's decision in *Opperman*, which allowed searches of containers in vehicle inventories, has essentially been extended to person inventories. That is, as part of inventorying a person's possessions pursuant to a valid arrest, the police may also examine containers. The Court felt that it would be unduly burdensome to require the police to determine which containers may or may not contain evidence of criminal activity.

# Inspections

A variety of **inspections** is permissible without a warrant or probable cause. For all practical purposes, they are "searches." Even so, the courts have continually stressed the "invasion versus need" balancing act—that is, the benefits of some inspections outweigh the costs of inconveniencing certain segments of the population. Most of these exceptions to the warrant requirement are based on the Court's decision in *Camara v. Municipal Court*, 387 U.S. 523 (1967), where it was concluded that "there can be no ready test for determining reasonableness other than by balancing the need to search against the invasion which the search entails."

*Camara v. Municipal Court*
*(387 U.S. 523 [1967])*

## Home Inspections

Two types of home inspection have been considered by the Supreme Court. The first concerns health and safety inspections of residential buildings, such as public housing units. In *Frank v. Maryland*, 359 U.S. 360 (1959), the Court upheld the constitutionality of a statute designed to punish property holders for failing to cooperate with warrantless health and safety inspections. It noted that such inspections "touch at most upon the periphery of the important interests safeguarded by the Fourteenth Amendment's protection against official intrusion."

In 1967, the Supreme Court overruled the *Frank* decision in *Camara v. Municipal Court*, 387 U.S. 523 (1967). In *Camara*, the Court noted that nonconsensual administrative inspections of private residences amount to a significant intrusion upon the interests protected by the Fourth Amendment. Today, a warrant is required for authorities to engage in a home inspection. However, the meaning of *probable cause* in such a warrant differs from that applied to warrants typically used in criminal investigations. The Court has stated that if an area "as a whole" needs inspection, based on factors such as the time, age, and condition of the building, then the probable cause requirement will be satisfied. The key is that probable cause in the inspection context is not *individualized* as in the typical warrant. That is to say, inspections of this sort are geared toward buildings, not persons.

The Supreme Court *has* held that inspections of the homes of welfare recipients do not require a warrant, however. In *Wyman v. James*, 400 U.S. 309 (1971), the Supreme Court upheld the constitutionality of a statute that allowed welfare caseworkers to make warrantless visits to the homes of welfare recipients. The purpose of such inspections is to ensure that welfare recipients are conforming with applicable guidelines and rules. The Court declared that welfare inspections are not searches within the meaning of the Fourth Amendment, which means they can be conducted without a warrant *or* probable cause. Of course, such inspections should be based on neutral criteria and should not mask intentions to look for evidence of criminal activity.

## Business Inspections

Compared to home inspections, far more case law exists in the arena of business inspections. *See v. City of Seattle*, 387 U.S. 541 (1967), a companion case to *Camara*, was one of

---

## DECISION-MAKING EXERCISE 7.1

### INVENTORIED AND INVENTORIED AGAIN

At the time of a defendant's arrest, police officers inventoried his automobile and seized several items. Approximately eight hours after the car was impounded, an officer, without obtaining a warrant, searched the car a second time, seizing additional evidence. Note that both searches were inventory searches. Do these searches, as many courts have stated it, "pass Fourth Amendment muster"? What if only the second search was deemed unconstitutional?

---

the first to focus on the constitutionality of business inspections. *See* involved a citywide inspection of businesses for fire code violations. The Court noted that "[t]he businessman, like the occupant of a residence, has a constitutional right to go about his business free from unreasonable official entries upon his private commercial property" and therefore warrants were required for business inspections.

However, soon after *See*, the Court created what came to be known as the **closely regulated business** exception to the warrant requirement set forth in *Camara* and *See*. Specifically, in *Colonnade Catering Corp. v. United States*, 397 U.S. 72 (1970), the Court upheld a statute criminalizing the refusal to allow warrantless entries of liquor stores by government inspectors. According to the Court:

> We agree that Congress has broad power to design such powers of inspection under the liquor laws as it deems necessary to meet the evils at hand. The general rule laid down in *See v. City of Seattle* . . . —"that administrative entry, without consent, upon the portions of commercial premises which are not open to the public may only be compelled through prosecution or physical force within the framework of a warrant procedure"—is therefore not applicable here. In *See*, we reserved decision on the problems of "licensing programs" requiring inspections, saying they can be resolved "on a case-by-case basis under the general Fourth Amendment standard of reasonableness." . . . What we said in *See* reflects this Nation's traditions that are strongly opposed to using force without definite authority to break down doors. We deal here with the liquor industry long subject to close supervision and inspection. As respects that industry, and its various branches including retailers, Congress has broad authority to fashion standards of reasonableness for searches and seizures.

*United States v. Biswell*
*(406 U.S. 311 [1972])*

Similarly, in *United States v. Biswell*, 406 U.S. 311 (1972), the Court upheld the warrantless inspection of a firearms dealership. In *Biswell*, the Court observed that "[w]hen a dealer chooses to engage in this pervasively regulated business and to accept a federal license, he does so with the knowledge that his business records, firearms and ammunition

## DECISION-MAKING EXERCISE 7.2

### WELFARE-RELATED HOME INSPECTIONS

In *Calabretta v. Floyd*, 189 F.3d 808 (9th Cir. 1999), an anonymous party called the Department of Social Services at 1:30 A.M. and said that she was awakened by a child at the Calabretta home screaming, "no, Daddy, no." Four days after the call, a social worker went to the Calabretta home to investigate. Mrs. Calabretta, the mother, refused to let the social worker in. Then, 10 days after the first visit, the social worker returned to the Calabretta house with a police officer. The officer met the social worker at the Calabretta house, knowing nothing about the case except that he had been assigned to assist her. She told him that they had received a report of the children crying, and he understood her to mean that they might have been beaten. When the police officer knocked on the door of the home, Mrs. Calabretta responded but did not open the door. The police officer said they were checking on the children's welfare because someone had reported children crying. Mrs. Calabretta still did not open the door and said she was uncomfortable letting them in without her husband at home. The police officer had the opinion that any check on the welfare of children involved an exigent circumstance and thus that no search warrant was needed. Once the two gained entry, the social worker took the children into one room while the officer remained in another room with the mother. The social worker asked the 12-year-old to pull down the 3-year-old's pants to check for bruises on her buttocks. The 12-year-old refused and the 3-year-old began crying. At that point, the mother rushed in. The social worker then demanded that the mother pull down the 3-year-old's pants, which she did. There were no bruises. The Calabrettas sued the social worker, the police officer, and other defendants for, among other things, a violation of their Fourth Amendment rights. Was the entrance into the Calabretta home constitutional?

will be subject to effective inspection." A key limitation on this ruling, however, is that authorities cannot use unauthorized force for the purpose of gaining entrance.

In a later case, *Donovan v. Dewey*, 452 U.S. 494 (1981), the Court modified the closely regulated business exception. The Court decided that it is not enough that an industry is "pervasively regulated" for the business inspection exception to apply. Three additional criteria must be met: (1) the government must have a "substantial" interest in the activity at stake; (2) warrantless searches must be necessary to the effective enforcement of the law; and (3) the inspection protocol must provide "a constitutionally adequate substitute for a warrant."

The Court clarified the *Dewey* criteria in *New York v. Burger*, 482 U.S. 691 (1987). In that case, the Court upheld the warrantless inspection of a vehicle junkyard for the purpose of identifying "vehicle dismantlers." Justice Blackman noted that *Dewey's* first criterion was satisfied because vehicle theft was a serious problem in New York. The second criterion was satisfied because surprise inspections were necessary if stolen vehicles and parts were to be identified. The third criterion—adequate substitute—was satisfied because junkyard operators were notified that inspections would be unannounced and conducted during normal business hours. In the Court's words:

> The New York regulatory scheme satisfies the three criteria necessary to make reasonable warrantless inspections pursuant to [the statute in question]. First, the State has a substantial interest in regulating the vehicle-dismantling and automobile-junkyard industry because motor vehicle theft has increased in the State and because the problem of theft is associated with this industry . . . Second, regulation of the vehicle-dismantling industry reasonably serves the State's substantial interest in eradicating automobile theft . . . [and third, the statute] provides a "constitutionally adequate substitute for a warrant." . . . The statute informs the operator of a vehicle dismantling business that inspections will be made on a regular basis. . . . Thus, the vehicle dismantler knows that the inspections to which he is subject do not constitute discretionary acts by a government official but are conducted pursuant to the statute.

It is important to point out, though, that when business inspections become nonregulatory (such as for the purpose of criminal investigation or prosecution), then a warrant is required (see *G.M. Leasing Corp. v. United States*, 429 U.S. 338 [1977]). See Figure 7.2 for a timeline of business inspection cases.

## Fire Inspections

In *Michigan v. Tyler*, 436 U.S. 499 (1978), the Supreme Court authorized the warrantless inspection of a burned residence (a fire inspection) immediately after the fire had been put out. The key fact in the holding is that the inspection must be contemporaneous, not several days or weeks after the fire. The rationale offered by the Court was that it is necessary

*Michigan v. Tyler*
*(436 U.S. 499 [1978])*

---

### DECISION-MAKING EXERCISE 7.3

#### BUSINESS INSPECTIONS

Komfortable Kitty Drug Company manufactures and packages veterinary drugs. Several times during a one-year period, Food and Drug Administration (FDA) agents inspected the company's premises to ensure compliance with the Food, Drug, and Cosmetic Act. The agents cited Komfortable Kitty for several violations. Drugs that were allegedly in violation of the act were seized pursuant to an *in rem* arrest warrant (a warrant authorizing the seizure of property). Altogether, over $100,000 worth of drugs and equipment were seized. Komfortable Kitty has contested the constitutionality of the seizure. Does the company have a valid case?

| **1967** | **1970** |
|---|---|
| **See v. City of Seattle, 387 U.S. 541** A warrant is required for the unconsented administrative entry and inspection of a commercial business. | **Collonnade Catering Corp. v. United States, 397 U.S. 72** A statute criminalizing refusal to allow warrantless entry and inspection of liquor stores is upheld. The **closely regulated business** doctrine is created, meaning that certain businesses (liquor stores, firearms dealerships) can be subjected to warrantless inspections because they are closely regulated and there is a need to ensure compliance with applicable laws. |

**FIGURE 7.2**

to determine the cause of a fire as soon as possible after it has been extinguished. A warrant in such an instance, felt the Court, would be unduly burdensome.

In a related case, *Michigan v. Clifford*, 464 U.S. 287 (1984), the Court decided on the constitutionality of a warrantless arson-related inspection that was conducted five hours after the fire was extinguished. While the inspection began as an administrative inspection of the site, when evidence of arson was found, a more extensive search was conducted. The Court required a warrant because the officials engaging in the search admitted it was part of a criminal investigation. According to the Court:

> The warrantless intrusion into the upstairs regions of the Clifford house presents a telling illustration of the importance of prior judicial review of proposed administrative searches. If an administrative warrant had been obtained in this case, it presumably would have limited the scope of the proposed investigation and would have prevented the warrantless intrusion into the upper rooms of the Clifford home. An administrative search into the cause of a recent fire does not give fire officials license to roam freely through the fire victim's private residence.

Interestingly, in *Clifford*, the Court stated that "the home owner is entitled to reasonable advance notice that officers are going to enter his premises for the purposes of ascertaining the cause of the fire," which suggests that notice, but not a warrant, is required for the typical fire inspection. More extensive searches, however, still require warrants supported by probable cause.

## International Mail Inspections

*United States v. Ramsey*
*(431 U.S. 606 [1977])*

The Supreme Court has permitted government officials to open incoming international mail without a warrant to do so. For example, in *United States v. Ramsey*, 431 U.S. 606 (1977), customs agents opened mail that was coming into the United States from Thailand, a known source of drugs. Further, the agents felt that a specific envelope was heavier than what would have been considered usual. Considering these factors, the Supreme Court upheld the warrantless search:

> The border-search exception is grounded in the recognized right of the sovereign to control, subject to substantive limitations imposed by the Constitution, who and what may enter the country. It is clear that there is nothing in the rationale behind the bordersearch exception which suggests that the mode of entry will be critical. It was conceded at oral argument that customs officials could search, without probable cause and without a warrant, envelopes carried by an entering traveler, whether in his luggage or on his person. . . . Surely no different constitutional standard should apply simply because the envelopes were mailed, not carried. The critical fact is that the envelopes cross the border and enter this country, not that they are brought in by one mode of transportation rather than another. It is their entry into this country from without it that makes a resulting search "reasonable."

| **Supreme Court Business Inspection Cases,** continued | | |
|---|---|---|
| **1972** | **1981** | **1987** |
| **United States v. Biswell, 406 U.S. 311** The warrantless inspection of a firearms dealership during normal business hours does not violate the Fourth Amendment. | **Donovan v. Dewey, 452 U.S. 494** The closely regulated business doctrine is modified. In addition to demonstrating that the business is closely regulated, it is necessary that (1) the government have a "substantial" interest in the activity at stake, (2) warrantless inspections are *necessary* to ensure compliance with the law, and (3) the inspection protocol provides a "constitutionally adequate substitute for a warrant." | **New York v. Burger, 482 U.S. 691** Vehicle junkyard inspections are upheld under the *Dewey* criteria. |

**FIGURE 7.2** *Continued*

## Checkpoints

A **checkpoint** is a means of investigating a large number of people, and is distinguished from an inspection, which involves a single building or entity. Several types of checkpoints are constitutionally permissible without warrants. Whereas an *inspection* targets particular homes and/or businesses, a *checkpoint* possesses an element of randomness. Either *everyone* is stopped or every *n*th person (such as every tenth person) is stopped. A checkpoint is similar to an inspection insofar as its purpose is usually not criminal, as in a typical search by police. And to the extent that some checkpoints border on looking for evidence of crime (such as a checkpoint to look for illegal immigrants), they are often justified because they are not based on individualized suspicion.

### Border Checkpoints

In *Carroll v. United States*, 267 U.S. 132 (1925), the Supreme Court stated that brief border detentions are constitutionally permissible. Further, the Court stated that it is in the interest of "national self protection" to permit government officials to require "one entering the country to identify himself as entitled to come in . . ."

More recently, in *United States v. Montoya de Hernandez*, 473 U.S. 531 (1985), the Court reaffirmed the need for warrantless border inspections: "Routine searches of the persons and effects of entrants [at the border] are not subject to any requirement of reasonable suspicion, probable cause, or a warrant . . . [O]ne's expectation of privacy [is] less at the border." The Court wrote:

> [This case reflects] longstanding concern for the protection of the integrity of the border. This concern is, if anything, heightened by the veritable national crisis in law enforcement caused by smuggling of illicit narcotics . . . and in particular by the increasing utilization of alimentary canal smuggling. This desperate practice appears to be a relatively recent addition to the smugglers' repertoire of deceptive practices, and it also appears to be exceedingly difficult to detect.

Border checkpoints have also been upheld on U.S. waterways (*United States v. Villamonte-Marquez*, 462 U.S. 579 [1983]), at highway checkpoints well inside the international borders (*Almeida-Sanchez v. United States*, 413 U.S. 266 [1973]), and at international airports (*Illinois v. Andreas*, 463 U.S. 765 [1983]). According to another decision (*United States v. Flores-Montano*, 541 U.S. 149 [2004]), it also appears that officials may do more than just detain a vehicle at the border. In that case, the Supreme Court sanctioned the removal, disassembly, and reassembly of a vehicle's fuel tank.

### Illegal Immigrant Checkpoints

*United States v. Martinez-Fuerte (428 U.S. 543 [1976])*

In *United States v. Martinez-Fuerte*, 428 U.S. 543 (1976), the Court upheld the decision of the Immigration and Naturalization Service (INS) to establish roadblocks near the Mexican border for the purpose of discovering illegal aliens. The Court offered a number of reasons for its decision. First, "[t]he degree of intrusion upon privacy that may be occasioned by a search of a house hardly can be compared with the minor interference with privacy resulting from the mere stop for questioning as to residence." Second, motorists could avoid the checkpoint if they so desired. Third, the Court noted that the traffic flow near the border was heavy, so individualized suspicion was not possible. Fourth, the location of the roadblock was not decided by the officers in the field "but by officials responsible for making overall decisions." Finally, a requirement that such stops be based on probable cause "would largely eliminate any deterrent to the conduct of well-disguised smuggling operations, even though smugglers are known to use these highways regularly." Importantly, law enforcement officers must have justification to examine the bags and personal effects of individuals who are stopped at immigration checkpoints (or during any immigration check) (*Bond v. United States*, 529 U.S. 334 [2000]). Figure 7.3 summarizes these cases and the border checkpoint cases discussed in the previous subsection.

## Border and Immigration Checkpoint Cases

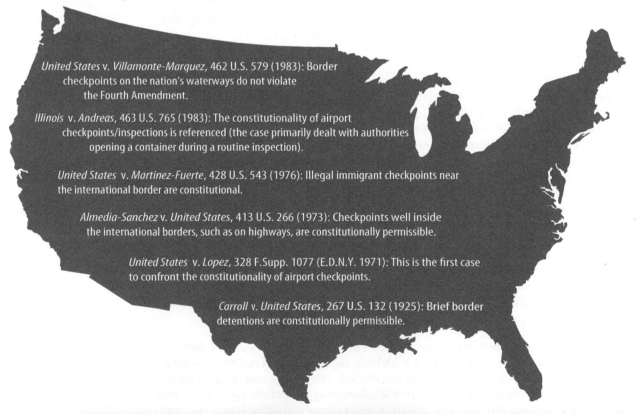

*United States* v. *Villamonte-Marquez*, 462 U.S. 579 (1983): Border checkpoints on the nation's waterways do not violate the Fourth Amendment.

*Illinois* v. *Andreas*, 463 U.S. 765 (1983): The constitutionality of airport checkpoints/inspections is referenced (the case primarily dealt with authorities opening a container during a routine inspection).

*United States* v. *Martinez-Fuerte*, 428 U.S. 543 (1976): Illegal immigrant checkpoints near the international border are constitutional.

*Almedia-Sanchez* v. *United States*, 413 U.S. 266 (1973): Checkpoints well inside the international borders, such as on highways, are constitutionally permissible.

*United States* v. *Lopez*, 328 F.Supp. 1077 (E.D.N.Y. 1971): This is the first case to confront the constitutionality of airport checkpoints.

*Carroll* v. *United States*, 267 U.S. 132 (1925): Brief border detentions are constitutionally permissible.

**FIGURE 7.3**

## DETECTING ILLEGAL ALIENS

The U.S. Border Patrol relies on checkpoints north of the Mexican border to look for illegal aliens. (In California, these can be found as far as 90 miles north of the border.) These checkpoints are often stationed in the middle of major freeways, where every car must slow down and, at a minimum, be waved through by one of several agents standing between the lanes. In addition, there is little, if any, opportunity to exit the freeway in order to avoid the checkpoints. Can these checkpoints be considered administrative? What if, instead of having the cars slow down, the border patrol required all vehicles to *stop*, at which point they would briefly search the trunk (or cargo compartment, in the case of a pickup truck, van, or tractor trailer), in an effort to find illegal aliens? Could they legally do this?

## Sobriety Checkpoints

In *Michigan Dept. of State Police v. Sitz*, 496 U.S. 444 (1990), the Court upheld a warrantless, suspicionless checkpoint designed to detect evidence of drunk-driving. In that case, police checkpoints were set up, at which all drivers were stopped and briefly (approximately 25 seconds) observed for signs of intoxication. If such signs were found, the driver was detained for sobriety testing, and if the indication was that the driver was intoxicated, an arrest was made. The Court weighed the magnitude of the governmental interest in eradicating the drunk-driving problem against the slight intrusion to motorists stopped briefly at such checkpoints. Two factors were key to the constitutionality of Michigan's checkpoint: (1) evenhandedness was ensured because the locations of the checkpoints were chosen pursuant to written guidelines and every driver was stopped; and (2) the officers themselves were not given discretion to decide whom to stop. Significantly, the checkpoint was deemed constitutional even though motorists were *not* notified of the upcoming checkpoint *or* given an opportunity to turn around and go the other way. According to the Court:

> No one can seriously dispute the magnitude of the drunken driving problem or the State's interest in eradicating it. Media reports of alcohol-related death and mutilation on the Nation's roads are legion. The anecdotal is confirmed by the statistical. . . . For decades, this Court has "repeatedly lamented the tragedy." . . . Conversely, the weight bearing on the other scale—the measure of the intrusion on motorists stopped briefly at sobriety checkpoints— is slight. . . . In sum, the balance of the State's interest in preventing drunken driving, the extent to which this system can reasonably be said to advance that interest, and the degree of intrusion upon individual motorists who are briefly stopped, weighs in favor of the state program. We therefore hold that it is consistent with the Fourth Amendment.

*Michigan Dept. of State Police v. Sitz (496 U.S. 444 [1990])*

## License and Safety Checkpoints

In *Delaware v. Prouse*, 440 U.S. 648 (1979), the Supreme Court held that law enforcement officials cannot randomly stop drivers for the single purpose of checking their drivers' licenses and registration. The Court's reasoning is interesting:

> An individual operating or traveling in an automobile does not lose all reasonable expectation of privacy simply because the automobile and its use are subject to government regulation. Automobile travel is a basic, pervasive, and often necessary mode of transportation to and from one's home, workplace, and leisure activities. Many people spend more hours each day traveling in cars than walking on the streets. Undoubtedly, many find a greater sense of security and privacy in traveling in an automobile than they do in exposing themselves by pedestrian or other modes of travel. Were the individual subject to unfettered

governmental intrusion every time he entered an automobile, the security guaranteed by the Fourth Amendment would be seriously circumscribed. . . . Accordingly, we hold that except in those situations in which there is at least articulable and reasonable suspicion that a motorist is unlicensed or that an automobile is not registered, or that either the vehicle or an occupant is otherwise subject to seizure for violation of the law, stopping an automobile and detaining the driver in order to check his driver's license and the registration of the automobile are unreasonable under the Fourth Amendment.

The Court did note, however, that "this holding does not preclude the State of Delaware or other States from developing methods for spot checks that involve less intrusion or that do not involve the unconstrained exercise of discretion." In particular, "Questioning of all oncoming traffic at roadblock-type stops is one possible alternative." If officers stopped every fifth, tenth, or twentieth vehicle, then the checkpoint would probably conform to the Court's requirement that roadblocks and checkpoints restrict individual officers' discretion to the fullest extent possible.

## Crime Investigation Checkpoints

*Illinois v. Lidster*
*(540 U.S. 419 [2004])*

In *Illinois v. Lidster*, 540 U.S. 419 (2004), the Supreme Court decided that checkpoints are also authorized for officers to ask questions related to crimes that had occurred earlier at the same area. In *Lidster*, police briefly detained motorists to ask them if they had any information about a hit-and-run accident between a vehicle and a bicycle that had taken place a week before at the same location. A driver entered the checkpoint, swerved, and nearly hit an officer. He was stopped and subjected to a field sobriety test. He was convicted of drunk-driving and later challenged the constitutionality of the checkpoint. The Supreme Court disagreed, thus permitting yet another type of checkpoint.

## Other Types of Checkpoints

Still other types of checkpoints have been considered by the Supreme Court. In *United States v. Villamonte-Marquez*, for example, the Court distinguished stops of boats on water from stops of vehicles on land. In that case, customs officers stopped and boarded a person's boat to inspect documents in accordance with 19 U.S.C. Section 1581(a), which permits officers to board any vessel, at any time, without justification, to examine the vessel's manifest or other documents. While onboard the defendant's boat, one of the customs officers smelled what he thought was marijuana. Looking through an open hatch, the officer spotted bales that turned out to contain marijuana. The Court noted that fixed checkpoints for boats are not possible, given the expansiveness of open water, so it relied on different reasoning. The Court noted that boardings such as that in *Villamonte-Marquez* are essential to ensure enforcement of the law in waters, "where the need to deter or apprehend drug smugglers is great." Key restrictions the Court *did* impose, though, were that such detentions be brief and limited to the inspection of documents. The reason the seizure of the marijuana was upheld in *Villamonte-Marquez* was that the contraband was in plain view.

Airport checkpoints are also authorized, with no need for probable cause or reasonable suspicion. According to the Ninth Circuit, "The need to prevent airline hijacking is unquestionably grave and urgent. . . . A pre-boarding screening of all passengers and carry-on articles sufficient in scope to detect the presence of weapons or explosives is reasonably necessary to meet the need" (*United States v. Davis*, 482 F.2d 893 [9th Cir. 1973]). Another court reached a similar conclusion (*United States v. Lopez*, 328 F. Supp. 1077 [E.D.N.Y. 1971]). And the Fifth Circuit's opinion in *United States v. Skipwith*, 482 F.2d 1272 (5th Cir. 1971) is particularly helpful:

[T]he intrusion which the airport search imposes on the public is not insubstantial. It is inconvenient and annoying, in some cases it may be embarrassing, and at times it can be incriminating. There are several factors, however, which make this search less offensive to the searched person than similar searches in other contexts. One such factor is the almost complete absence of any stigma attached to being subjected to search at a known, designated airport search point. . . . In addition, the offensiveness of the screening process is somewhat mitigated by the fact that the person to be searched must voluntarily come to and enter the search area. He has every opportunity to avoid the procedure by not entering the boarding area. Finally, the circumstances under which the airport search is conducted make it much less likely that abuses will occur. Unlike searches conducted on dark and lonely streets at night where often the officer and the subject are the only witnesses, these searches are made under supervision and not far from the scrutiny of the traveling public. Moreover, the airlines, which have their representatives present, have a definite and substantial interest in assuring that their passengers are not unnecessarily harassed. The officers conducting the search under these circumstances are much more likely to be solicitous of the Fourth Amendment rights of the traveling public than in more isolated, unsupervised surroundings.

Note that airport screenings are now conducted by *public* as opposed to *private* actors. Prior to the September 11, 2001, terrorist attacks, airport inspections were conducted by private security companies. Now, they are conducted by Transportation Safety Administration (TSA) officials, who are employed by the federal government. This change is of no consequence to the constitutionality of airport screenings, however, even though such inspections are today sometimes more intrusive than prior to September 11 (for example, "shoe searches" and searches at the boarding gate are now used in addition to the screening at the main security checkpoint).

## Unconstitutional Checkpoints

In conducting a checkpoint, the administrative rationale is *not* acceptable if it is relied upon in order to detect evidence of criminal activity. This was emphasized in *City of Indianapolis v. Edmond,* 531 U.S. 32 (2000), a case in which the Supreme Court decided whether a city's suspicionless checkpoints for detecting illegal drugs were constitutional. Here is how the Supreme Court described the checkpoints:

*City of Indianapolis v. Edmond (531 U.S. 32 [2000])*

> The city of Indianapolis operated a checkpoint program under which the police, acting without individualized suspicion, stopped a predetermined number of vehicles at roadblocks in various locations on city roads for the primary purpose of the discovery and interdiction of illegal narcotics. Under the program, at least one officer would (1) approach each vehicle, (2) advise the driver that he or she was being stopped briefly at a drug checkpoint, (3) ask the driver to produce a driver's license and the vehicle's registration, (4) look for signs of impairment, and (5) conduct an open-view examination of the vehicle from the outside. In addition, a narcotics-detection dog would walk around the outside of each stopped vehicle.

The Court held that stops such as those conducted during Indianapolis's checkpoint operations require individualized suspicion. In addition, "because the checkpoint program's primary purpose [was] indistinguishable from the general interest in crime control," it violated the Fourth Amendment.

## School Discipline

Public school administrators and teachers may "search" a student without a warrant if they have reasonable suspicion that the action will yield evidence that the student has violated the law or is violating the law or rules of the school. However, such **school discipline "searches"** must not be "excessively intrusive in light of the age and sex of the students and the nature of the infraction." This was the decision reached in *New Jersey v. T.L.O.,* 469 U.S. 325 (1985). In *T.L.O.,* a high school student was caught smoking in a school bathroom

*New Jersey v. T.L.O. (469 U.S. 325 [1985])*

▼

## A CONSTITUTIONALLY VALID CHECKPOINT?

Consider the facts from *Maxwell v. City of New York*, 102 F.3d 664 (2d Cir. 1996).

During the spring and summer of 1992, street crime, including four drive-by shootings, escalated in the Soundview neighborhood of the Bronx. In response, the 43rd precinct instituted the so-called Watson Avenue Special Operation. This involved a temporary vehicular checkpoint in an eight square-block narcotics-ridden area where most of the drive-by shootings had taken place. The checkpoint was to be active three days a week on a random basis and for approximately six hours a day, primarily in the evening hours. When the checkpoint was in operation, officers manning the barricade were to stop every vehicle seeking to enter the area in order to ascertain the driver's connection to the neighborhood. Drivers who approached the checkpoint were to be allowed to avoid questioning by driving around the area or by parking their cars and entering the area on foot. Area residents and commercial vehicles were to be allowed into the neighborhood. Officers manning the barricades were verbally instructed that they could also allow cars dropping off small children or visiting the local church to enter the area. Other than that, vehicles were not permitted beyond the barricades. The operation was in effect for six weeks, between August 26 and October 10, 1992.

Was this checkpoint constitutional? Why or why not?

(in violation of school policy) and was sent to the vice principal. When the vice principal searched the student's purse for cigarettes, he also found evidence implicating the student in the sale of marijuana. The Court held that the evidence was admissible because the administrator had sufficient justification to search the purse for evidence concerning the school's antismoking policy.

In support of its decision in *T.L.O.*, the Court noted that a warrant requirement "would unduly interfere with the maintenance of the swift and informal disciplinary procedures needed in the schools . . . [and] . . . the substantial need of teachers and administrators for freedom to maintain order in the schools." The majority further stated that the reasonableness test for school disciplinary "searches" involves a twofold inquiry: "First, one must consider 'whether the . . . action was justified at its inception . . .' second, one must determine whether the search as actually conducted 'was reasonably related in scope to the circumstances which justified the interference in the first place'."

Although *T.L.O.* gave school officials broad discretion to conduct disciplinary searches, that ability was significantly limited in *Safford Unified School District v. Redding*, 557 U.S. 364 (2009). In that case, Savana Redding, an eighth grader, was "strip searched" by school officials on a belief that she was in possession of certain nonprescription medications, in violation of school policy. Writing for the majority, Justice Souter found that the search violated the Fourth Amendment because there was no ". . . indication of danger to the students from the power of the drugs or their quantity and any reason to suppose that (Redding) was carrying pills in her underwear." More than just reasonable suspicion is necessary, then, to support particularly intrusive searches of this nature—not only in the context of school discipline, but also in the workplace.

Note that *T.L.O.* concerns students in kindergarten through grade 12. A different standard applies in the context of public and private universities. The courts have generally held that the Fourth Amendment is applicable at the university level. That is, for university personnel to conduct searches of students' dorm rooms, lockers, and so on, some level of justification is required.

### Locker Checks and Drug Dog "Sniffs"

A handful of lower court decisions concern inspections of public school students' lockers as well as drug dog "sniffs" for the purpose of detecting illicit drugs. First, random, suspicion-less locker inspections are generally permissible, assuming the students have been given some notification in advance that their lockers are subject to inspection at any time (see *Commonwealth v. Cass*, 709 A.2d 350 [Pa. 1998]). However, "searches" of *specific* lockers would still be subject to the reasonableness test set forth in *T.L.O.*

With regard to the use of drug dogs, the Fifth Circuit held that so-called "sniffs" of lockers and cars in public schools are constitutional (*Horton v. Goose Creek Independent School District*, 690 F.2d 470 [5th Cir. 1982]). The court reasoned that lockers and cars were inanimate objects located in a public place, and therefore there was a lower expectation of privacy in these locations.

The sniffing of *students*, as opposed to their property, is the subject of greater controversy. In *Doe v. Renfrow*, 631 F.2d 91 (7th Cir. 1980), the Seventh Circuit held that the exploratory sniffing of students was not a search. The Seventh Circuit agreed with the lower court's observation that "the presence of the canine team for several minutes was a minimal intrusion at best and not so serious as to invoke the protections of the Fourth Amendment" (*Doe v. Renfrow*, 475 F. Supp. 1012 [1979]). However, the Ninth Circuit has taken a contrary point of view, holding that dog sniffs of students' possession implicate the Fourth Amendment and require probable cause (*B.C. v. Plumas Unified School District*, 192 F.3d 1260 [9th Cir. 1999]). This is a disagreement between federal circuits that is ripe for some resolution by the Supreme Court.

## "Searches" of Government Employees' Offices

In a case very similar to *T.L.O.*, the Court held that neither a warrant nor probable cause was required to "search" a government employee's office, but the "search" must be "a non-investigatory work-related intrusion or an investigatory search for evidence of suspected work-related employee misfeasance" (*O'Connor v. Ortega*, 480 U.S. 709 [1987]). Justice O'Connor summarized the Court's reasoning: "[T]he delay in correcting the employee misconduct caused by the need for probable cause rather than reasonable suspicion will be translated into tangible and often irreparable damage to the agency's work, and ultimately to the public interest." It is important to note, however, that the Court limited its decision strictly to work-related matters: "[W]e do not address the appropriate standard when an employee is being investigated for criminal misconduct or breaches of other non-work-related statutory or regulatory standards." The Court further noted in *Ortega* that the appropriate standard by which to judge such "searches" is *reasonableness*:

> We hold, therefore, that public employer intrusions on the constitutionally protected privacy interests of government employees for noninvestigatory, work-related purposes, as well as for investigations of work-related misconduct, should be judged by the standard of reasonableness under all the circumstances. Under this reasonableness standard, both the inception and the scope of the intrusion must be reasonable.

Recently, the Supreme Court was confronted with the question of whether a police officer's employer could examine the content of messages sent via a pager. A police department issued its officers pagers, which were monitored by the department. When one officer's pager exceeded the number of allotted monthly messages, the department acquired transcripts of the officer's messages. Upon learning that some of them were sexually explicit, the department disciplined the officer accordingly. He sued under Section 1983, alleging his Fourth Amendment rights were violated. However, the Supreme Court disagreed, holding that the department's "search" of the pager message contents was reasonable (*City of Ontario v. Quon*, 560 U.S. ___ [2010]).

It should be pointed out that *reasonableness* in the context of public school student and government employee "searches" is not the same as *reasonable suspicion*. The latter refers to a certain level of suspicion, while the former focuses on the procedural aspects of the actions in question (such as, did authorities go too far in looking for evidence?). The distinction between *reasonableness* and *reasonable suspicion* is a subtle but important one—hence, the reason for discussing disciplinary and work-related "searches" in the section on administrative justification.

Perhaps more important, none of the foregoing cases apply to individuals employed in *private* companies. Recall that the Fourth Amendment applies only to *government action*, and private employers are not being bound by the strictures of the Fourth Amendment. Stated simply, private employers can search private employees' lockers, desks, and the like without infringing on any constitutional rights.

## Drug and Alcohol Testing

As **drug and alcohol testing** has become increasingly common at schools and in the workplace, the Supreme Court has turned its attention to the constitutionality of these practices. Three lines of cases can be discerned: (1) employee testing; (2) hospital patient testing; and (3) school student testing.

### Drug and Alcohol Testing of Employees

*Skinner v. Railway Labor Executives' Association (489 U.S. 602 [1989])*

With some limitation, the Supreme Court has permitted warrantless, suspicionless drug and alcohol testing of employees based on federal regulations. In *Skinner v. Railway Labor Executives' Association*, 489 U.S. 602 (1989) and *National Treasury Employees Union v. Von Raab*, 489 U.S. 656 (1989), the Court upheld the constitutionality of certain regulations that permit drug and alcohol testing. The Court cited two reasons for its decision. The first was deterrence—without suspicionless drug testing, there would be no deterrent to employees to stay off drugs. The second reason was that drug testing promotes businesses' interest in obtaining accurate information about accidents and who is responsible. In *Skinner*, Justice Stevens made this observation:

> Most people—and I would think most railroad employees as well—do not go to work with the expectation that they may be involved in a major accident, particularly one causing such catastrophic results as loss of life or the release of hazardous material requiring an evacuation. Moreover, even if they are conscious of the possibilities that such an accident might be a contributing factor, if the risk of serious personal injury does not deter their use of these substances, it seems highly unlikely that the additional threat of loss of employment would have any effect on their behavior.

Two interesting limitations should be noted about both these cases. The first is that the Court did not decide whether warrantless, suspicionless drug testing could be used for *law enforcement* purposes. Rather, such testing was held to be constitutional for *regulatory* reasons. Second, both cases focused on federal regulations: Federal Railroad Administration guidelines in *Skinner* and U.S. Customs Service Policy in *National Treasury Employees Union*. Left open was the question of private business policy. Nevertheless, the courts have since upheld drug and alcohol testing of teachers, police officers, and several other groups.[1]

This line of cases would seem to suggest that employee drug testing is becoming increasingly common across the United States. While it is certainly true that more employees are subject to drug testing now than in the past, the Supreme Court has clearly stated

---

[1]P. T. Bookspan, "Jar Wars: Employee Drug Testing, the Constitution, and the American Drug Problem," *American Criminal Law Review* 26 (1988): 359–400.

## SEARCHES OF GOVERNMENT EMPLOYEES

Federal law enforcement agents suspected that several employees in a government agency were engaged in criminal wrongdoing. Several of the agency's records were subpoenaed. To ensure that the records were being prepared in accordance with the subpoena, the agents visited the government agency. During the course of their visit, the director of the agency was asked to open an employee's office. Upon looking in the employee's office, the agents found incriminating documents and seized them. They also searched the employee's file cabinet and found more incriminating documents, which were also seized. Is this a valid search of a government employee's office, as authorized by *O'Connor v. Ortega*, 480 U.S. 709 (1987)?

that certain drug testing policies are unconstitutional. For example, in *Chandler v. Miller*, 520 U.S. 305 (1997), the Court struck down a Georgia statute that required every person seeking nomination or election to undergo a test for illegal drugs.

*O'Connor v. Ortega*
*(480 U.S. 709 [1987])*

## Drug and Alcohol Testing of Hospital Patients

In a recent case, *Ferguson v. Charleston*, 532 U.S. 67 (2001), the Supreme Court addressed the constitutionality of drug testing of hospital patients. In the fall of 1988, staff at the Charleston, South Carolina, public hospital became concerned over the apparent increase in the use of cocaine by patients who were receiving prenatal treatment. Staff at the hospital approached the city and agreed to cooperate in prosecuting pregnant mothers who tested positive for drugs. A task force was set up, consisting of hospital personnel, police, and other local officials. The task force formulated a policy for how to conduct the tests, preserve the evidence, and use it to prosecute those who tested positive. Several women tested positive for cocaine. The question before the Supreme Court was whether the Fourth Amendment is violated when hospital personnel, working with the police, test pregnant mothers for drug use without their consent. Not surprisingly, the Court held that:

*Ferguson v. Charleston*
*(532 U.S. 67 [2001])*

> Because the hospital seeks to justify its authority to conduct drug tests and to turn the results over to police without the patients' knowledge or consent, this case differs from the four previous cases in which the Court considered whether comparable drug tests fit within the closely guarded category of constitutionally permissible suspicionless searches. . . . Those cases employed a balancing test weighing the intrusion on the individual's privacy interest against the "special needs" that supported the program. The invasion of privacy here is far more substantial than in those cases. In previous cases, there was no misunderstanding about the purpose of the test or the potential use of the test results, and there were protections against the dissemination of the results to third parties. Moreover, those cases involved disqualification from eligibility for particular benefits, not the unauthorized dissemination of test results. The critical difference, however, lies in the nature of the "special needs" asserted. In each of the prior cases, the "special need" was one divorced from the State's general law enforcement interest. Here, the policy's central and indispensable feature from its inception was the use of law enforcement to coerce patients into substance abuse treatment.

## Drug and Alcohol Testing of Public School Students

The Supreme Court has recently extended its drug testing decisions to include public school students. Specifically, in *Vernonia School District 47J v. Acton*, 515 U.S. 646 (1995), the Court upheld a random drug testing program for school athletes. The program had been instituted because the district had been experiencing significant student drug use. Under the program, all students who wished to play sports were required to be tested at the

*Vernonia School District*
*47J v. Acton*
*(515 U.S. 646 [1995])*

beginning of the season and then retested randomly later in the season. The Court noted that athletes enjoy a lesser expectation of privacy, given the semi-public nature of locker rooms, which is where the testing took place. Also, athletes are often subject to other intrusions, including physical exams, so drug testing involved a "negligible" privacy intrusion, according to the Court.

*Board of Education v. Earls*
*(536 U.S. 822 [2002])*

Even more recently, the Supreme Court reaffirmed its holding in *Vernonia School District*, in the case of *Board of Education v. Earls*, 536 U.S. 822 (2002), which dealt with another student drug testing policy. The Student Activities Drug Testing Policy, implemented by the Board of Education of Independent School District no. 92 of Pottawatomie County, required students who participate in extracurricular activities to submit to random, suspicionless drug tests. Urine tests were intended to detect the use of illegal drugs. Together with their parents, two students, Lindsay Earls and Daniel James, brought a Section 1983 lawsuit against the school district, alleging that the drug testing policy violated the Fourth Amendment, as applied to the states through the due process clause of the Fourteenth Amendment. The district court found in favor of the school district, but the Tenth Circuit Court reversed the decision, holding that the policy violated the Fourth Amendment. It concluded that random, suspicionless drug tests would only be permissible if there were some identifiable drug abuse problem. However, the Supreme Court held that random, suspicionless drug testing of students who participate in extracurricular activities "is a reasonable means of furthering the School District's important interest in preventing and deterring drug use among its schoolchildren and does not violate the Fourth Amendment."

## Probation and Parole Supervision

*Griffin v. Wisconsin*
*(483 U.S. 868 [1987])*

A person on probation enjoys a lesser expectation of privacy than the typical citizen, and therefore enjoys a lesser degree of protection from government searches. In *Griffin v. Wisconsin*, 483 U.S. 868 (1987), the Supreme Court held that a state law or agency rule permitting probation officers to search a probationer's home without a warrant and based on reasonable suspicion was constitutional. The majority (of only five justices) concluded that probation supervision "is a 'special need' of the State permitting a degree of impingement upon privacy that would not be constitutional if applied to the public at large." The same principle almost certainly applies to parolees, but the Supreme Court has not addressed this issue.

The Court has also ruled that evidence seized by parole officers during an illegal search and seizure need not be excluded at a parole revocation hearing (see *Pennsylvania Board of Probation and Parole v. Scott*, 524 U.S. 357 [1998]). This latter decision can be interpreted to mean that the exclusionary rule does not apply in parole revocation

---

### DECISION-MAKING EXERCISE 7.7

#### DRUG TESTING OF STUDENTS

The school board approved a policy prohibiting a high school student from participating in any extracurricular activities or driving to and from school unless the student and his or her parent or guardian consented to and passed tests for drugs, alcohol, and tobacco in random, unannounced urinalysis examinations. (Extracurricular activities include not only athletic teams but also organizations such as the student council, foreign language clubs, and so on.) When consent for testing had been given and the individuals had taken and passed the tests, then participation in the extracurricular organizations or driving to and from school would be permitted. The testing was to be conducted by Acme Toxicology Services, which would collect the samples, and the local hospital's laboratory services division, which would perform the tests. Can this type of random, suspicionless drug testing be considered an administrative search?

▼

hearings. A warrant requirement, the Court noted, "would both hinder the function of state parole systems and alter the traditionally flexible, administrative nature of parole revocation proceedings."

More recently, in *United States v. Knights*, 534 U.S. 112 (2001), the Supreme Court held that warrantless searches of probationers are permissible not only for probation-related purposes (for example, to ensure that probation conditions are being conformed with) but also for investigative purposes. In that case, a probationer was suspected of vandalizing utility company facilities. A police detective searched the probationer's residence and found incriminating evidence. The Supreme Court held that "[t]he warrantless search of Knights, supported by reasonable suspicion and authorized by a probation condition, satisfied the Fourth Amendment."

Needless to say, all three of these decisions do not provide a great deal of guidance to probation officers on the streets. *Griffin*, for example, dealt with the constitutionality of one statute in one state. This means that probation officers are mostly forced to turn to state-level supreme court decisions for guidance. The California Supreme Court has offered some clarification with regard to searches-and-seizures by probation officers that the Supreme Court has not. However, those decisions are limited to California.

## Police-Probation Partnerships

A new challenge to Fourth Amendment rights has been presented by **police-probation partnerships**, a cutting-edge law enforcement strategy now being experimented with across the country. An example of this approach is Boston's Operation Night Light. The program began in 1992 as an informal collaboration between probation officers and Boston's Anti-Gang Violence Unit. Teams composed of one probation officer and two police officers serving as backup make surprise visits to the homes, schools, and worksites of high-risk youth probationers, mostly during the hours of 7 p.m. to midnight. The program grew to the extent that 50 police officers and 50 probation officers worked together in this program seven nights a week.

Another example of a police-probation partnership in action is the IMPACT project in San Bernardino, California. The program was virtually identical to Boston's, except that the teams consisted of one police officer and one probation officer. In addition, *all* new probationers were under scrutiny.

These and other police-probation partnerships are controversial from a Fourth Amendment standpoint in that they seem to have search-and-seizure implications. On one hand, these partnerships may be highly effective in reducing crime. On the other hand, critics of police-probation partnerships claim that they are little more than a way to circumvent the Fourth Amendment's probable cause and warrant requirements. In other words, critics claim that police officers use probation officers as "stalking horses" to skirt the Fourth Amendment. The California Supreme Court's *Bravo* decision (discussed earlier), for example, permits warrantless, suspicionless searches of probationers, even by police officers.

Here again, the interests of due process and crime control collide. Police-probation partnerships may effectively reduce crime, but they may also compromise due process. Eventually, the constitutionality of these partnerships will be decided in court. Most likely, the U.S. Supreme Court will decide on the matter in the near future, because the Fourth Amendment implications are simply too serious to ignore.

## Parole Supervision

In *Samson v. California*, 547 U.S. 843 (2006), the Supreme Court extended its earlier probation decision to parole supervision. It held that "[t]he Fourth Amendment does not prohibit a police officer from conducting a suspicionless search of a parolee." It's rationale for this decision was that "[p]arolees, who are on the 'continuum' of state-imposed punishments, have fewer expectations of privacy than probationers, because parole is more akin to imprisonment than probation is."

*Samson v. California*
*(547 U.S. 843 [2006])*

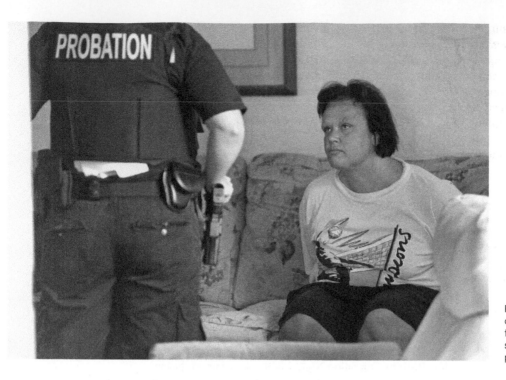

Probation officers are afforded more latitude than police officers for searches and seizures of probationers.

# ► Consent Searches

Technically, most administrative exceptions to having a warrant require no justification. Rather, the courts focus on balancing the interests of public safety against individual privacy. That said, there is one clear-cut situation in which absolutely no justification or balancing act is required in order to decide on the constitutionality of a search. When a person consents to a search, no justification is required. This is known as a **consent search**.

Cases involving consent searches can be placed into three categories, focusing on (1) whether consent is voluntary; (2) the *scope* of the search; and (3) whether a *third-party individual* can give consent to the search of another person.

## Voluntariness

*Schneckloth v. Bustamonte (412 U.S. 218 [1973])*

The general rule is that validly obtained consent justifies a warrantless search, with or without probable cause. However, for consent to be valid, it must be voluntary. Consent cannot be "the result of duress or coercion, express or implied" (*Schneckloth v. Bustamonte*, 412 U.S. 218 [1973]). However, there is no bright-line test as to whether there has been sufficient duress or coercion to render the consent involuntary. Instead, the Court has opted for a *totality of circumstances* test. This test requires looking at the *surrounding circumstances* of the consent, including whether a show of force was made; whether the person's age, mental condition, or intellectual capacities inhibited understanding; whether the person is or was in custody; and/or whether consent was granted "only after the official conducting the search [had] asserted that he possesses a warrant" (*Bumper v. North Carolina*, 391 U.S. 543 [1968]).

Importantly, consent to search may be valid even if the consenting party is unaware of the fact that he or she can refuse consent (*Schneckloth v. Bustamonte*). As the Court stated in *Ohio v. Robinette*, 519 U.S. 33 (1996), "[J]ust as it 'would be thoroughly impractical to impose on the normal consent search the detailed requirements of an effective warning,' so too would it be unrealistic to require police officers to always inform detainees that they are free to go before a consent to search may be deemed involuntary." This view was recently reaffirmed in *United States v. Drayton*, 536 U.S. 194 (2002), a case involving consent searches of bus passengers. Nevertheless, one's awareness of the right to refuse consent is still factored into the totality of circumstances analysis (as in *United States v. Mendenhall*, 446 U.S. 544 [1980]), although ignorance of the right to refuse is not enough, in and of itself, to render consent involuntary.

To ensure the constitutionality of consent searches, many police departments have suspects complete "consent to search" forms. An example of one such form, from the San Bernardino, California, Police Department, is shown in Figure 7.4.

## Scope Limitations

The person giving consent determines the limits of the consent search. For example, if a person tells the police that they may search his home for narcotics, it does not authorize the police to search his financial records for transactions related to drug sales (*United States v. Dichiarinte*, 445 F.2d 126 [7th Cir. 1971]). Likewise, if the person giving consent tells an officer she can search in a particular location, say the trunk of a car, then it does not mean the officer can search wherever she likes.

Another issue concerning the scope of a consent search is whether consent can be withdrawn once given. In *State v. Brochu*, 237 A.2d 418 (Me. 1967), the Maine Supreme

Crime Report No._____

**CONSENT TO SEARCH**

I, _____ give the San Bernardino Police Department my consent to search the below listed property.

Address: _____City _____

_____ Country _____

Address: _____City _____

_____ Country _____

Vehicle/s:      Make _____Year _____Veh. Lic. #

_____

            Make _____Year _____Veh. Lic. #

_____

Other:      _____

      _____

      _____

      _____

      _____

      _____

      _____

                              Signed: _____

Date: _____            Time: _____

Witness _____            Witness _____

*Source:* San Bernardino, California, Police Department. Reprinted with permission.

**FIGURE 7.4 Example of a Consent to Search Form**

Court held that a defendant's consent to search his house for evidence of his wife's murder did not extend to another search carried out the day after he was arrested as a suspect. Thus, although the man did not expressly request that the search be terminated, the Maine court still decided that consent had been effectively ended. The U.S. Supreme Court has not directly decided whether consent can be withdrawn, however.

## Third-Party Consent

A handful of Supreme Court cases have focused on whether a third party (someone other than the authority asking for consent to search and the individual whose property is the target of the search) can give consent to have another person's property searched. Examples of such third parties include a landlord consenting to have a tenant's apartment searched, or parents consenting to have their child's room searched. As far as the immediate family is concerned, there are several general rules: (1) Wives and husbands can give consent to have their partners' property searched and (2) parents can give consent to have their children's property searched, but (3) children cannot give consent to have their parents' property searched. Children cannot give consent because they are considered incompetent to give voluntary consent, given their age.

More confusing is the situation of a roommate, former girlfriend, friend, or extended family member. Two important Supreme Court cases are relevant here. First, third-party consent can be given if (1) the third-party individual possesses "common authority" over the area to be searched and (2) the nonconsenting party (such as the roommate) is not present (*United States v. Matlock*, 415 U.S. 164 [1974]). According to the Court, **common authority** rests on "mutual use of the property by persons generally having joint access or control for most purposes." Thus, a third party could give consent to have a shared bathroom searched but not to have his or her roommate's bedroom searched.

What happens, however, if the nonconsenting party is present and affirmatively objects to the search? The courts are divided on this issue. There are some clear-cut situations, in which two people possess common authority over a particular area. But it may not be clear to officers at the scene whether common authority exists. In response to this question, the Supreme Court has held that the warrantless entry of private premises by police officers is valid if based on the **apparent authority** doctrine. In other words, a warrantless entry of a residence is valid if it is based on the consent of a person whom the police reasonably believe has authority to grant consent, even if their beliefs are ultimately erroneous. In *Illinois v. Rodriguez*, 497 U.S. 177 (1990), consent was given by a former girlfriend

*United States v. Matlock*
*(415 U.S. 164 [1974])*

*Illinois v. Rodriguez*
*(497 U.S. 177 [1990])*

---

**DECISION-MAKING EXERCISE 7.8**

### WHAT CONSTITUTES VOLUNTARY CONSENT?

Several undercover police officers went to the apartment where it was believed a robbery suspect was hiding out. They did not have probable cause that the suspect was at that location, and indeed, they did not even know the suspect's name, so no warrant was obtained. Rather, the visit was to be merely investigative, and it was hoped that enough information would be gleaned from the visit so a valid warrant could be obtained. The officers knocked on the apartment door, and the man who answered the door fit the description of the suspect. The officers identified themselves, arrested the man, and conducted a protective sweep of the apartment, fearing that other dangerous individuals may be present. Once the premises had been secured, the officers asked the suspect, who was seated at a table in handcuffs, to sign a "consent to search" form. The suspect said, "You go ahead and search, but I ain't signing nothing." Setting aside the issue of the constitutionality of the arrest and protective sweep, was the suspect's consent voluntary?

▼

### SCOPE OF CONSENT

Hector Lopez is stopped by the highway patrol for speeding. The officer who approaches his car asks if he will consent to a search of his vehicle. As reinforcements arrive, the officer states that they are concerned about drug smuggling on this stretch of freeway. Lopez gives consent and says, "Yes, you can search my car," and so the officers subject the car to an intensive search. They remove every bag and every moveable item from the vehicle and scrutinize each one carefully. They further check the spare tire compartment, engine compartment, and glove box and even the panels providing access to lighting, electrical systems, and so on. Have the officers exceeded the scope of Lopez's consent? What if, instead, Lopez stated, "Yes you can search my car, but I'm late for a doctor's appointment, so I have to leave in less than five minutes"?

who possessed apparent authority to grant consent because she still had a key to her ex-boyfriend's apartment. The test for reasonableness in this situation, according to the Court, is as follows: "[W]ould the facts available to the officer at the moment [of the entry] . . . warrant a man of reasonable caution in the belief that the consenting party had authority over the premises?"

Despite the opinion in *Rodriguez*, in most cases, a third party cannot give consent to the search of another. For example, a landlord cannot give consent to search property rented to another person (*Stoner v. California*, 376 U.S. 483 [1964]), one lessor cannot give consent to search the premises of another lessor (*United States v. Impink*, 728 F.2d 1228 [9th Cir. 1985]), hotel clerks cannot give consent to search guests' rooms (*Stoner v. California*), and college officials cannot give consent to search students' dormitories (*Piazzola v. Watkins*, 442 F.2d 284 [5th Cir. 1971]). Note, however, that consent given by the driver of a vehicle to search any part of the vehicle is valid even if the driver is not the owner of the vehicle (*United States v. Morales*, 861 F.2d 396 [3rd Cir. 1988]).

What if both parties who have common authority are present when the police request consent, but one of them refuses consent and the other gives it? This issue arose in the case of *Georgia v. Randolph*, 547 U.S. 103 (2006), in which police were called to the scene of a domestic dispute. When the officers asked for consent to search, the husband unequivocally refused, but the wife readily consented. The officers followed through on her consent, searched the premises, and found cocaine. The husband sought to have the cocaine excluded from his subsequent trial, but a Georgia trial court denied his motion. The Georgia Supreme Court reversed and the U.S. Supreme Court affirmed, holding that "a physically present co-occupant's stated refusal to permit entry renders warrantless entry and search unreasonable and invalid."

## "Knock and Talk"

So-called "knock and talk" consent searches are popular with law enforcement officers because of the difficulty of securing warrants in particular instances. The typical "knock and talk" scenario occurs when police officers approach someone's house, knock on the front door, and request consent to search the home. In *State v. Smith*, 488 S.E.2d 210 (N.C. 1997), the North Carolina Supreme Court described the procedure as follows:

> The "knock and talk" procedure is a tactic used by law enforcement . . . when they get information that a certain person has drugs in a residence but the officers don't have probable cause for a search warrant. The officers then proceed to the residence, knock on the door, and ask to be admitted inside. Thereafter gaining entry, the officers inform the person

## THE BOUNDS OF "KNOCK AND TALK"

In response to a neighbor's complaint, two police officers arrive at a home where there is clearly a loud party taking place. They knock on the door and a person who is visibly intoxicated asks in a slurred manner, "What can I do for you, officers?" The officers respond, "We have received a complaint about the noise coming from your house. Would you please tone it down?" The drunk person at the door responds, "Yup, no problem." At that point, the officers ask, "Do you mind if we come in and take a look around?" The drunk responds, "Will you get a search warrant if I refuse?" The officers, in turn, respond, "Yes, we will." The drunk then gives the officers permission to enter. Is doing so acceptable? In particular, assuming the officers do not have probable cause to get a warrant but rather lied in an effort to gain entry, will any contraband that might turn up during the course of the search be considered admissible in a criminal trial?

that they're investigating information that drugs are in the house. The officers then ask for permission to search and apparently are successful in many cases in getting the occupant's "apparent consent."

"Knock and talk" searches are controversial because they are not predicated on warrants or probable cause. Such searches strike at the cardinal Fourth Amendment principle that "physical entrance into the home of another without a warrant is the chief evil the Fourth Amendment has sought to alleviate" (*Payton v. New York*, 445 U.S. 573 [1980]). What makes "knock and talk" *legal*, in the strictest sense, however, is that the subsequent search is based on consent. Of course, the extent to which ordinary people are aware of their right to *refuse* consent is not altogether clear. To date, the Supreme Court has not ruled on the constitutionality of "knock and talk" practices. More than likely, the tactic will continue as long as consent is validly obtained. See Figure 7.5 for a list of questions that are commonly raised during a "knock and talk" situation.

1. *How is it known what was said?* The wording used by the officer to gain consent is of paramount importance.
2. *To what extent was a show of authority relied on by the officer?* A show of authority may diminish voluntariness.
3. *What is the scope of the search?* The scope may be limited by the wording used by the officer or the consenting party.
4. *Can the party that gives consent also terminate consent?* Generally, yes, but who is to be trusted: the officer(s) or the consenting party?
5. *What if the officer threatens to obtain a warrant?* Doing so diminishes voluntariness, if not eliminates it.
6. *What if the officer makes false statements to gain entry?* There is no prohibition against using false statements, but doing so diminishes voluntariness.
7. *Should the consenting party be advised of his or her* Miranda *rights?* Giving the Miranda warnings is not necessary unless a custodial interrogation takes place.
8. *Can a third party give consent?* A third party can give consent only if he or she has authority (or apparent authority) to do so.
9. *What if the consenting party is intoxicated?* This factors into the voluntariness determination.
10. *What if, during the course of a "knock and talk" procedure, exigent circumstances develop?* A full search would be permissible under such circumstances.

**FIGURE 7.5 Questions Often Raised with Regard to "Knock and Talk" Searches**

# Summary

## 1. Explain the justification for regulatory and administrative searches.

Actions based on administrative justification and consent require neither reasonable suspicion nor probable cause. The term *administrative justification* is something of a euphemism. It is not really *justification* at all. Actions based on administrative justification require that the government's interest in protecting public safety outweighs individual privacy interests. Consent searches, in contrast, need to be predicated on little more than validly given consent.

Actions based on administrative justification are rich in variety. They have been labeled *special needs searches* and *regulatory searches*, but to promote clarity, this chapter has used the language *administrative justification* to refer to all such actions. The most common actions based on administrative justification are inventories, inspections, checkpoints, school discipline, "searches" of government employees' offices, drug and alcohol testing, and parole and probation supervision.

## 2. Describe regulatory and administrative searches.

Inventories fall into two categories: (1) vehicle inventories and (2) person inventories. A vehicle inventory must follow a lawful impoundment, be of a routine nature, follow department policy, and not be used as a pretext concealing an investigative police motive. A person inventory is justified on similar grounds, except that it must be preceded by a lawful arrest.

Four types of inspections have been recognized by the U.S. Supreme Court. First, a general home inspection, such as a building code inspection, requires a specific type of warrant, but a welfare inspection, conducted for the purpose of determining compliance with welfare conditions, requires no warrant. Second, an inspection of a closely regulated business is permissible without a warrant if (1) the government has a substantial interest in the activity at stake; (2) the search promotes effective enforcement of the law; and (3) the inspection protocol provides a constitutionally adequate substitute for a warrant. Third, a fire inspection, usually tied to an arson investigation, is permissible without a warrant but must be contemporaneous to the fire. Finally, authorities may open and inspect international mail without a warrant.

Several types of checkpoints have also been sanctioned by the Supreme Court. In general, for a checkpoint to conform to constitutional requirements, it must be minimally intrusive, brief, and not directly tied to a criminal investigation. More specifically, checkpoints at the nation's borders, well inside the borders, at airports, and on the nation's waterways are permissible but are limited to the purpose of identifying incoming individuals. Illegal alien checkpoints are permissible without a warrant or probable cause for the purpose of detecting illegal aliens entering the country but must conform to established policies and procedures. Checkpoints for determining sobriety, as well as license and safety checkpoints, are constitutionally permissible but must also conform to department policies. Other types of checkpoints, such as airport security checkpoints, have been acknowledged by the Supreme Court and deemed constitutional. Checkpoints intended for the sole purpose of detecting criminal activity are unconstitutional, however.

School disciplinary "searches" are constitutionally permissible, but they must be reasonable. Random, suspicionless locker inspections are permissible but only with ample notice to students. The foregoing applies only to schools for kindergarten through grade 12. A traditional Fourth Amendment approach has been adopted for searches of college students. Drug dog "sniffs" of public school students have not been ruled on by the Supreme Court. For now, it appears that the police have fairly wide latitude in this area.

"Searches" of government employees' offices are permissible with neither a warrant nor probable cause but must amount to noninvestigatory work-related intrusions or investigatory searches for evidence of suspected work-related employee misconduct. When the objective of the "search" is to find evidence of non-work-related criminal misconduct, a warrant is required. None of the foregoing applies to *private* employees. That is, private employees do not enjoy Fourth Amendment protection because their employers are not government actors.

As for drug and alcohol testing, employees and public school students can be screened for the use of controlled substances, but only by properly trained individuals following appropriate policies (such as nurses). Hospital patients, however, cannot be subjected to drug and alcohol testing. Probation supervision permits warrantless searches premised on reasonable grounds. Some state Supreme Court decisions have suggested that no justification is necessary—that such searches are consented to as a result of the probation agreement.

## 3. Describe consent searches and the issues associated with them.

Consent searches are constitutional, but consent must be voluntary, as determined by the totality of circumstances. The scope of a consent search is defined by the person giving consent. Third parties can give consent if they have actual or apparent authority over the premises or property to be searched. A controversial law enforcement practice tied to consent searches is "knock and talk," a strategy in which police seek to gain consent to enter a residence for the purpose of detecting evidence of criminal activity.

Figure 7.6 briefly summarizes, in question-and-answer format, the issues discussed in this and the last four chapters. It serves as a helpful guide for determining the constitutionality of searches, seizures, and similar types of law enforcement action.

---

**A.** Does the Fourth Amendment apply?

*Each of the questions 1–4 must be answered yes for the amendment to apply.*

1. Does the person have standing?
2. Is the evidence in question a person, house, paper, or effect?
3. Is the conduct governmental?
4. Has a reasonable expectation of privacy been infringed upon, or has a seizure occurred?

*If all of the questions were answered yes, then proceed to B.*

**B.** Was the conduct in question justified?

1. Identify the type of intrusion (e.g., search, stop, arrest, nonsearch).
2. For the type identified, identify the level of justification required (e.g., probable cause, reasonable suspicion, administrative justification).

*If there is a mismatch, between the type and level of justification, then the conduct in question was not justified. If there is not a mismatch, go to C.*

**C.** Was a warrant required?

*If yes, answer questions 1–3. If no, move to D.*

1. Was it issued by a neutral and detached magistrate?
2. Was it supported by probable cause?
3. Was the particularity requirement satisfied?

*All three questions must be answered yes for the warrant to be valid.*

**D.** If a warrant was not required, were the prerequisites met for a warrantless search or seizure?

*The answer to this question requires revisiting the material set forth in this and earlier chapters.*

**E.** Any no answers and/or inappropriate justification will result in exclusion of evidence.

**FIGURE 7.6 Guide to the Fourth Amendment**

# Key Terms

apparent authority *212*
checkpoints *199*
closely regulated business *196*
common authority *212*

consent search *210*
drug and alcohol testing *206*
"knock and talk" *213*
person inventory *193*

police–probation partnerships *209*
school disciplinary "searches" *204*
vehicle inventory *192*

# Key Cases

## Inventories

- *South Dakota v. Opperman*, 428 U.S. 364 (1976)
- *Colorado v. Bertine*, 479 U.S. 367 (1987)
- *Illinois v. Lafayette*, 462 U.S. 640 (1983)

## Inspections

- *Camara v. Municipal Court*, 387 U.S. 523 (1967)
- *Wyman v. James*, 400 U.S. 309 (1971)
- *Colonnade Catering Corp. v. United States*, 397 U.S. 72 (1970)
- *United States v. Biswell*, 406 U.S. 311 (1972)
- *Michigan v. Tyler*, 436 U.S. 499 (1978)
- *United States v. Ramsey*, 431 U.S. 606 (1977)

## Checkpoints

- *United States v. Martinez-Fuerte*, 428 U.S. 543 (1976)
- *Michigan Dept. of State Police v. Sitz*, 496 U.S. 444 (1990)

- *Illinois v. Lidster*, 540 U.S. 419 (2004)
- *City of Indianapolis v. Edmond*, 531 U.S. 32 (2000)

## Other Administrative Searches

- *New Jersey v. T.L.O.*, 469 U.S. 325 (1985)
- *O'Connor v. Ortega*, 480 U.S. 709 (1987)
- *Skinner v. Railway Labor Executives' Association*, 489 U.S. 602 (1989)
- *Ferguson v. Charleston*, 532 U.S. 67 (2001)
- *Vernonia School District 47J v. Acton*, 515 U.S. 646 (1995)
- *Board of Education v. Earls*, 536 U.S. 822 (2002)
- *Griffin v. Wisconsin*, 483 U.S. 868 (1987)
- *Samson v. California*, 547 U.S. 843 (2006)

## Consent

- *Schneckloth v. Bustamonte*, 412 U.S. 218 (1973)
- *United States v. Matlock*, 415 U.S. 164 (1974)
- *Illinois v. Rodriguez*, 497 U.S. 177 (1990)

# Further Exploration

1. Police officers are operating a sobriety checkpoint on New Year's Eve. After an hour of stopping vehicles, they notice a long line of traffic and decided to temporarily suspend the checkpoint to ease the flow of traffic. Once the line is diminished, the officers reinitiate the checkpoint. The first motorist they stop displays signs of intoxication and is asked to pull to the side for a field sobriety test. Officers determine the driver is drunk and arrest him. He challenges the arrest on the grounds that state law required *every* vehicle be stopped during a sobriety checkpoint. How should the court decide and why?

2. Read this brief excerpt from an actual case, *State v. Hedgcock*, 765 N.W.2d 469 (Ne. 2009):

On February 22, 2006, the Nebraska State Patrol strategically placed signs along Interstate 80, eastbound, indicating that there was a drug checkpoint farther down the road. The checkpoint signs were posted along the shoulder and the median of Interstate 80 near the Platte River rest area in Cass County. The checkpoint signs read "Nebraska State Patrol Check Point Ahead" and "Drug Dog in Use." The signs alternated prior to the exit for the rest area, and a couple of signs were placed after the rest area. However, there was no drug enforcement checkpoint on Interstate 80. The checkpoint signs were placed near the Platte River rest area exit to induce motorists engaged in drug-related activity to take the exit in order to avoid the drug checkpoint.

Five officers, including Officers Alan Eberle, Richard Lutter, and Jason Scott, waited in the rest area either on foot or in unmarked vehicles, with their weapons concealed, wearing plain street clothes. The officers at the rest area observed individuals' behaviors for any indicators or circumstances that would alert them to possible drug activity . . .

Another officer waited in an unmarked car, in the middle of Interstate 80, observing motorists' reactions to the checkpoint signs. The officer specifically watched for motorists who made a "rapid departure" into the rest area, as such activity was indicative of someone attempting to avoid the checkpoint. The officer was to alert the other officers waiting at the rest area of any motorists' reactions that were suspicious.

At approximately 10:30 A.M., an officer informed Eberle that the driver of a white Chevrolet Blazer, with Utah plates, rapidly applied the brakes and changed lanes to enter the rest area after seeing the checkpoint signs. Eberle testified that after he received that information, he, along with Lutter and Scott, observed the Blazer enter the rest area. Even though there were empty stalls in front of the building, the Blazer parked away from the rest area building.

Do the officers have reasonable suspicion to stop and confront the motorists? What if they waited a little longer and observed one person leave the vehicle for the restroom while another remained in the vehicle? Would that change the outcome? Why or why not?

3. The District of Columbia Metropolitan Police Department's Neighborhood Safety Zone (NSZ) program utilized checkpoints to limit motorist access to certain high-crime parts of the city. Motorists received advanced notice of the checkpoints, and signs clearly marked the access points. Any motorists who sought to enter an NSZ were asked if they had "legitimate reasons" to enter. Legitimate reasons for entry included being a resident; making a delivery; attending school or taking a child to school; visiting a relative; providing medical attention; or attending a verified civic, community, or religious event. Motorists who did fit into one of these six categories were denied access. Does the NSZ approach comply with the Fourth Amendment? Read *Mills v. District of Columbia*, 571 F.3d 1304 (D.C. Cir. 2009) and summarize the arguments for and against checkpoints of this nature.

4. Border checkpoints clearly comply with Fourth Amendment requirements, as do fixed checkpoints well inside the nation's borders. What about roving border patrols? What constitutional constraints, if any, should apply to the use of roving border patrols inside the nation's borders. What standards of justification should apply? Read *United States v. Brignoni-Ponce*, 422 U.S. 873 (1975) for more on this subject.

5. Read the following facts from an actual case, *State v. Best*, 987 A.2d 605 (2010):

On May 15, 2006, Peter Brandt, the assistant principal of Egg Harbor Township High School, received a report of a student suspected of being under the influence of drugs. Brandt met with the student, who admitted he ingested a green pill that eighteen-year-old defendant Thomas Best gave him during fifth period auto shop class. Brandt and another assistant principal interviewed Best, who denied any wrongdoing. Brandt searched Best and found three white capsules in his pants pocket, but no green pills. Best admitted that he sold a pill to a student, but claimed that the pill was merely a nutritional supplement. Brandt subsequently searched Best's locker, but discovered no pills . . . Brandt asked Best where his car was parked and indicated that he was going to search his car. Before searching the car, Brandt declined Best's request to call his father. A search of the car's passenger compartment revealed a liquid-filled syringe, a fake cigarette with a hole in it that could be used as a pipe, a wallet, a bottle of pills apparently belonging to Rose Foster, a bag of suspected marijuana, a bag containing a white powdery substance, and a vial.

Is the evidence admissible against Best? Why or why not? Cite specific cases in support of your decision.

# Review Questions

1. In what ways do actions based on administrative justification avoid the requirements of the Fourth Amendment?

2. What types of inventories have been permitted by the Supreme Court? Explain the restrictions on each.

3. What types of inspections have been permitted by the Supreme Court? Explain the restrictions on each.

4. Distinguish between border checkpoints and illegal immigrant checkpoints.

5. Are sobriety and license and safety checkpoints valid? If so, when?

6. At what point do checkpoints become unconstitutional?

7. What are school disciplinary searches? What, if any, justification is required to conduct such searches?

8. Under what circumstances are suspicionless searches of government employees' offices constitutional?

9. Summarize the Supreme Court case law involving drug testing.

10. Explain the Supreme Court's decision in *Griffin v. Wisconsin*. How influential is this case in terms of probation supervision?

11. Why are police–probation partnerships controversial?

12. Summarize the requirements for a valid consent search.

13. Under what circumstances can a third party give consent to have another person's property searched?

14. Explain the law enforcement practice known as "knock and talk."

# Web Links and Exercises

1. Border checkpoints: Read the Government Accountability Office's report concerning the performance of border checkpoints, particularly those located in interior areas.
URL: http://www.gao.gov/new.items/d05435.pdf (accessed May 7, 2013).

2. Vehicle checkpoints: Read about the opposition to vehicle checkpoints. Are the critics' argument meritorious?
Suggested URL: http://www.roadblock.org (accessed May 7, 2013).

3. Virtual strip searches: Read about how advanced imaging technology works.
Suggested URL: http://www.tsa.gov/approach/tech/ait/index.shtm (accessed May 7, 2013).

4. Police–probation partnerships: Read about varieties of police–probation partnerships. Which is likely to be most effective?
URL: http://www.ncjrs.gov/pdffiles1/175047.pdf (accessed May 7, 2013).

5. Consent searches: Read Carl Benoit's article about consent searches. Focus closely on the section about a "physically present objector." What rules should officers follow?
URL: http://www.fbi.gov/stats-services/publications/law-enforcement-bulletin/2008-pdfs/july08leb.pdf/at_download/file (accessed May 7, 2013).

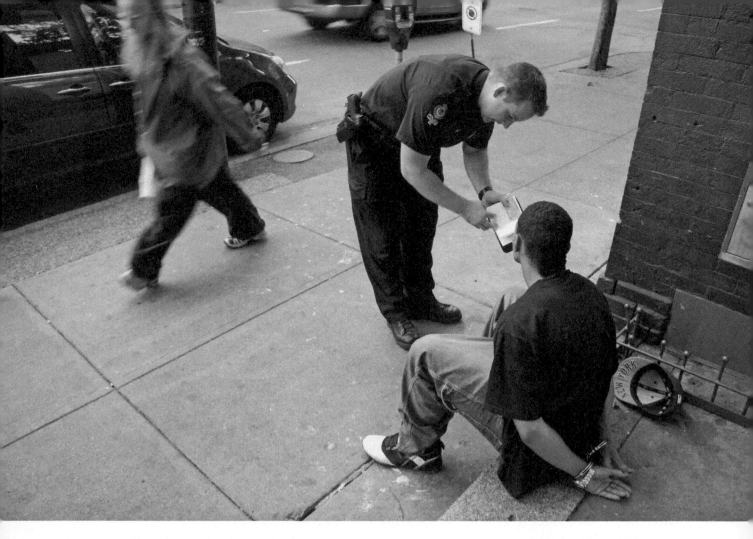

# 8 Interrogations and Confessions

## LEARNING OBJECTIVES

When you complete this chapter, you should be able to:

**1** *Summarize how due process and voluntariness impact interrogations and confessions.*

**2** *Summarize how the Sixth Amendment impacts interrogations and confessions.*

**3** *Explain the Fifth Amendment approach to interrogations and Miranda rights.*

**4** *Know when unconstitutionally obtained confessions are admissible in court to prove guilt.*

# OUTLINE

## Introduction: Getting Suspects to Talk

This chapter turns to the law of confessions and interrogations. The Fifth Amendment is what protects suspects from improper interrogation procedures and from being forced to supply illegally obtained confessions, but it is not the *only* protection offered to suspects in the confession context. Other amendments, namely the Sixth and the Fourteenth, also apply. The very fact that *three* amendments place restrictions on what the government can do in order to obtain confessions suggests that the U.S. Constitution places a high degree of value on people's rights to be free from certain forms of questioning.

## ▶ Interrogations and Confessions

A **confession** occurs when a person implicates himself or herself in criminal activity following police questioning and/or interrogation. An **admission**, by contrast, need not be preceded by police questioning; a person can simply admit to involvement in a crime without any police encouragement. Despite these differences, a confession and an admission will be treated as virtually synonymous throughout this chapter.

Most of the law concerning confessions and admissions has arisen in the context of police interrogation. The courts have imposed a litany of restrictions on what law enforcement officials can do in order to elicit incriminating statements from suspected criminals. Toward the end of the chapter, the discussion will turn to what steps law enforcement officials should take to secure a valid, documented confession.

### Various Approaches to Confession Law

Confessions and admissions are governed by the Fifth Amendment. The rights that must be read to suspects placed under custody, as required by the *Miranda* decision (such as the right to remain silent), stem, in part, from the Fifth Amendment. However, confessions and admissions are also protected by the Fourteenth Amendment's due process clause as well as the Sixth Amendment's right to counsel clause.

The primary focus in this chapter is on the Fifth Amendment, but for the sake of placing Fifth Amendment confession law into context, it is important to briefly consider the extent to which confessions are protected by other constitutional provisions. We begin with the Fourteenth Amendment due process voluntariness approach, then continue with the Sixth Amendment right to counsel approach. We conclude with an in-depth examination of the Fifth Amendment approach.

## ▶ The Due Process Voluntariness Approach

One approach to confessions and admissions can be termed the **due process voluntariness approach**. In general, when a suspect makes an involuntary statement, his or her statement will not be admissible in a criminal trial (or, as indicated earlier, in any other criminal proceeding) to prove his or her guilt.

At one time, the Fifth and Sixth Amendments did not apply to the states, and many defendants being prosecuted for state crimes did not receive the U.S. Constitution's guarantee of the right to counsel, or its protection against self-incrimination (see the previous discussion on "incorporation" in Chapter 1). In cases where it was alleged that a confession was extracted by violence or coercion, the Supreme Court instead applied the Fourteenth Amendment's due process clause. For example, in *Brown v. Mississippi*, 297 U.S. 278 (1936), police officers resorted to whippings and other brutal methods in order to obtain confessions from three African American defendants who were later convicted based on their confessions alone. The Supreme Court analyzed this case under the Fourteenth Amendment's due process clause, and found the convictions invalid because the interrogation techniques had been so offensive.

*Brown v. Mississippi*
*(297 U.S. 278 [1936])*

When analyzed under the due process clause of the Fourteenth Amendment, confessions are considered "involuntary" when, under the "totality of circumstances that preceded the confessions," the defendant is deprived of his or her "power of resistance" (*Fikes v. Alabama*, 352 U.S. 191 [1957]). Unfortunately there are no uniform criteria for determining voluntariness. Instead, the courts take a case-by-case approach to determining voluntariness. Usually, this requires focusing on two issues: (1) the police conduct in question and (2) the characteristics of the accused.

## Police Conduct

It has been made patently clear that physical brutality to coerce a confession violates the Fourteenth Amendment. As Justice Douglas stated in *Williams v. United States*, 341 U.S. 97 (1951), "Where police take matters into their own hands, seize victims, and beat them until they confess, they deprive the victims of rights under the Constitution."

*Williams v. United States (341 U.S. 97 [1951])*

In many other situations, however, the police conduct in question may not rise to the level of torture but may still be questionable. For example, in *Rogers v. Richmond*, 365 U.S. 534 (1963), a man confessed after the police told him they were going to take his wife into custody. And in *Lynumm v. Illinois*, 372 U.S. 528 (1963), a defendant confessed after being promised leniency. Both confessions were found to be coerced, and therefore involuntary. This is not to suggest that deception on the part of the police necessarily gives rise to an involuntary confession but only that it is one of several considerations in determining voluntariness.

It is safe to conclude that psychological pressures, promises of leniency, and deception are rarely *by themselves* enough to render a statement involuntary, but two or more such acts (especially if coupled with physical force) will more than likely result in an involuntary confession. Some illustrative cases are worth considering.

For example, in *Spano v. New York*, 360 U.S. 315 (1959), detectives relied on a police officer who was a friend of the accused to question him. The officer falsely stated that his job would be in jeopardy if he did not get a statement from the accused. The Supreme Court concluded that the false statement, including the sympathy thereby obtained, was sufficient to render the accused's statement involuntary.

Next, in *Leyra v. Denno*, 347 U.S. 556 (1954), police relied on a psychiatrist who posed as a doctor in order to give the accused relief from a sinus problem. The psychiatrist used subtle forms of questions and ultimately obtained a statement from the accused. The Court felt that the suspect was unable to resist the psychiatrist's subtle questioning.

Contrast *Spano* and *Denno* with *Frazier v. Cupp*, 394 U.S. 731 (1969), in which a police officer made a false statement that a co-defendant implicated the accused. The Supreme Court held that this was not sufficient to produce an involuntary statement. However, if the accused is questioned far from home and denied access to friends and family for several days, his or her resulting statements will probably be deemed involuntary (see *Fikes v. Alabama*). Similarly, an overly lengthy period of questioning or a denial of basic amenities, such as food, may result in a determination of involuntariness (see *Crooker v. California*, 357 U.S. 433 [1958]).

## Characteristics of the Accused

The personal characteristics of the accused, such as disabilities or age level, are also factors that have been considered in determining whether a confession is voluntary. For example, in *Haley v. Ohio*, 332 U.S. 596 (1948), the Supreme Court reversed a 15-year-old boy's confession because he was too young to have voluntarily confessed. In the Court's words, "Mature men possibly might stand the ordeal from midnight to 5 a.m. but we cannot believe that a lad of tender years is a match for the police in such a contest."[1]

---

[1] Note that *Haley* dealt with due process, not *Miranda*. The Court held in *Fare v. Michael C.*, 442 U.S. 707 (1979), that juveniles are not to be treated differently than adults in the *Miranda* context.

| Police Behavior | Characteristics of the Suspect |
|---|---|
| • Psychological pressure by the police | • Disability |
| • Promises of leniency | • Immaturity |
| • Deception | • Intoxication |
| • Length of detention | • Fatigue |
| • Duration of questioning | • Pain |
| • Intensity of questioning | • Age |
| • Deprivation of access to family, friends, nourishment, and counsel | • Level of education |
| • Whether the suspect was advised of his or her right | • Familiarity with the criminal process |

**FIGURE 8.1** Factors Considered in Determining Voluntariness

In some instances, fatigue and pain (such as from the result of an injury) can also render an accused's statement involuntary. However, such a result usually requires some questionable conduct on the part of the officials engaged in questioning of the accused.

As a general rule, a confession will be considered involuntary if (1) the police subject the suspect to coercive conduct and (2) the conduct is sufficient to overcome the will of the suspect. The court will also look at the totality of circumstances to determine if the suspect's vulnerabilities and condition, coupled with the police conduct, led to giving an involuntary confession (see *Colorado v. Connelly*, 479 U.S. 157 [1986]). See Figure 8.1 for a list of factors used to determine whether a confession is voluntary.

# ▶ The Sixth Amendment Approach

*Massiah v. United States* (377 U.S. 201 [1964])

The Sixth Amendment also limits what the police can do to obtain confessions and admissions from criminal suspects. In particular, the Supreme Court's decision in *Massiah v. United States*, 377 U.S. 201 (1964), established the rule that the Sixth Amendment's guarantee to counsel in all "formal criminal proceedings" is violated when the government "deliberately elicits" incriminating responses from a person. The two key elements to the Sixth Amendment approach are *deliberate elicitation* and *formal criminal proceedings*. The following subsections define each element.

## Deliberate Elicitation

**Deliberate elicitation** is a tactic in which officers create a situation likely to induce a suspect into making an incriminating statement. In *Massiah*, the defendant was released on bail pending a trial for violations of federal narcotics laws. He subsequently made an incriminating statement in the car of a friend who had allowed the government to install a

---

**DECISION-MAKING EXERCISE 8.1**

**POLICE CONDUCT AND VOLUNTARINESS**

A suspect was interrogated by five officers who, with their guns drawn, stood over him as he lay handcuffed on the ground, semiconscious from a gunshot he had received earlier (a wound that was not inflicted by the officers). The officers did not threaten to shoot the suspect if he failed to confess. Rather, they simply pointed their guns at him. Assuming the suspect confessed, would his confession be considered involuntary under the Fourteenth Amendment?

radio designed to eavesdrop on the conversation. Justice Stewart, writing for the majority, argued that if the Sixth Amendment's right to counsel is "to have any efficacy it must apply to indirect and surreptitious interrogations as well as those conducted in the jailhouse." Furthermore, "Massiah [the defendant] was more seriously imposed upon . . . because he did not even know that he was under interrogation by a government agent."

Another example of deliberate elicitation was presented in *Brewer v. Williams*, 430 U.S. 387 (1977). In that case, the defendant was suspected of killing a 10-year-old girl. Before he was to be taken by police officers to another city, his attorneys advised him not to make any statements during the trip. The attorneys were also promised by the police officers that they would not question the defendant during the trip. Nevertheless, during the trip, one of the officers suggested that the girl deserved a "Christian burial." The officer further mentioned that an incoming snowstorm would make it difficult to find the girl's body. The officer then stated, "I do not want you to answer me. I don't want to discuss it further. Just think about it as we're riding down the road." Shortly thereafter, the defendant admitted to killing the girl and directed the police to her body. The Court reversed the defendant's conviction, arguing that the officer had "deliberately and designedly set out to elicit information from Williams [the defendant] just as surely as—and perhaps more effectively than—if he had formally interrogated him."

*Brewer v. Williams*
*(430 U.S. 387 [1977])*

In a related case, *United States v. Henry*, 447 U.S. 264 (1980), the Supreme Court focused on whether the officers "intentionally creat[ed] a situation likely to induce Henry [the defendant] to make incriminating statements without the assistance of counsel." In that case, a man named Nichols, who was in jail with Henry, was enlisted by the police to be alert to any statements Henry made concerning a robbery. The police did not ask Nichols to start a *conversation* with Henry, only to be alert to what he said. The Supreme Court found that the officers created a situation likely to elicit an incriminating response, but only because Nichols was a paid informant.

*United States v. Henry*
*(447 U.S. 264 [1980])*

However, when law enforcement officers place an informant who is not paid, but is working closely with the police, in the same cell as the defendant, deliberate elicitation does not necessarily occur. This was the decision reached in *Kuhlmann v. Wilson*, 477 U.S. 436 (1986). Kuhlmann, the informant, did not ask the defendant any questions concerning the crime for which the defendant was charged but instead listened to (and later reported on) the defendant's "spontaneous" and "unsolicited" statements. Clearly, the line between these two cases is thin. The only distinction appears to be that Nichols, the informant in *Henry*, had worked with the police in the past and was being paid.

## Formal Criminal Proceedings

In *Massiah*, the Court held that the Sixth Amendment right to counsel applies once **formal criminal proceedings** have begun (a preliminary hearing, trial, or anything in between). Because Massiah was indicted, one might conclude that formal criminal proceedings once the indictment has been made. However, shortly after *Massiah*, the Court decided the case of *Escobedo v. Illinois*, 378 U.S. 478 (1964), which caused some confusion as to exactly when formal proceedings begin for the purposes of determining the right to counsel. Escobedo was arrested for murder, questioned, and released. Then, 10 days later, an accomplice implicated Escobedo and he was rearrested. He requested to consult with his attorney, but that request was denied. Escobedo was convicted of murder, based partly on the statement provided by his accomplice. The Supreme Court reversed the conviction, stating:

> We hold . . . that where, as here, the investigation is no longer a general inquiry into an unsolved crime but has begun to focus on a particular suspect, the suspect has been taken into police custody, the police carry out a process of interrogations that lends itself to eliciting incriminating statements, the suspect has requested and been denied an opportunity to

## SUSPECT CHARACTERISTICS AND VOLUNTARINESS

Ed Hornby approached a police officer on the street and said that he had killed someone and wanted to talk about it. He later confessed to an unsolved murder that had occurred several years earlier. Prior to trial, Hornby sought to have his confession excluded, arguing that it was involuntary. At trial, a psychiatrist testified for the defense that Hornby suffered from *command auditory* *hallucinations*, a condition that rendered him unable to resist what the "voices in his head" told him to do. How should the court decide? What if, instead, Hornby had become hesitant to talk and his confession had been preceded by a lengthy middle-of-the-night interrogation, during which he had been denied food and a desperately needed trip to the restroom?

consult with his lawyer, and the police have not effectively warned him of his absolute constitutional right to remain silent, the accused has been denied "the Assistance of Counsel" in violation of the Sixth Amendment . . . and that no statement elicited by the police during the interrogation may be used against him at a criminal trial.

In *Escobedo*, the Court seemed to broaden the scope of the Sixth Amendment by holding that it also applies once the accused becomes the focus of an investigation by the police. This left a significant question unanswered: When does a person become an accused? That is, when do formal criminal proceedings commence?

However, eight years after *Massiah*, the Supreme Court decided *Kirby v. Illinois*, 406 U.S. 682 (1972), holding that a defendant has a right to counsel whenever the "adverse positions of the government and defendant have solidified" so that "a defendant finds himself faced with the prosecutorial forces of organized society, and immersed in the intricacies of substantive and procedural criminal law." Fortunately, the Court clarified this statement by noting that the Sixth Amendment applies "whether by way of *formal charge, preliminary hearing, indictment, information, or arraignment*" (emphasis added). This was echoed in *Rothgery v. Gillespie County*, 554 U.S. 1 (2008), wherein the Court held that the Sixth Amendment right to counsel can attach at the initial appearance.

*Massiah* does not apply simply because a suspect or arrestee has retained the services of counsel. In *Moran v. Burbine*, 475 U.S. 412 (1986), the Supreme Court held that what is important in determining whether the Sixth Amendment right to counsel applies is whether "the government's role [has] shift[ed] from investigation to accusation." Similarly, in *Maine v. Moulton*, 474 U.S. 159 (1985), the Court held that "to exclude evidence pertaining to charges as to which the Sixth Amendment right to counsel had not attached at the time the evidence was obtained, simply because other charges were pending at that time, would unnecessarily frustrate the public's interest in the investigation of criminal activities."

It should be noted that the Sixth Amendment approach to interrogations and confessions is offense-specific. If formal proceedings have begun for one charge, but the defendant makes a confession regarding an offense he has not yet been charged with, the Sixth Amendment does not provide protection regarding the charge for which proceedings have not yet commenced. This was reiterated by the Supreme Court in *Texas v. Cobb*, 531 U.S. 162 (2001), where it held that a man's confession to a crime with which he had not been charged did not violate the Sixth Amendment. In that case, the defendant was indicted for burglary and given access to counsel, which obviously prohibits deliberate elicitation of incriminating information. However, he confessed to murdering the woman and child who lived in the home he allegedly burglarized. He later sought to have his confession excluded, but the Supreme Court disagreed, in essence, finding that the burglary charge did not trigger the Sixth Amendment protection for the murder charge.

## Waiver of the Sixth Amendment Right to Counsel (Confessions)

Once an accused individual has asserted his or her Sixth Amendment right to counsel, any statements obtained from subsequent questioning would be inadmissible at trial unless the accused initiated the communication (*Michigan v. Jackson*, 475 U.S. 625 [1986]). However, if a defendant adequately waives the right to counsel, postindictment questioning is not unconstitutional (*Patterson v. Illinois*, 487 U.S. 285 [1988]).

In *Montejo v. Louisiana*, 556 U.S. 778 (2009), the Court expanded the right of police to question defendants after a voluntary waiver of the right to counsel. Unbeknownst to police, Montejo had been appointed an attorney, but he was encouraged by a detective to write a letter of apology to the wife of the man he had killed. Before doing so, he was advised of his *Miranda* rights (detailed below), but again, he had been appointed counsel—although the police did not know this. The prosecution introduced the apology letter at trial. Montejo sought to have it excluded since his attorney was not present when it was written. The Supreme Court disagreed. It felt that other court decisions offered sufficient protection. Also, had Montejo asserted his right to counsel, the outcome would have likely been different.

What is the practical meaning of the *Montejo* decision? Law enforcement is now allowed, after reading a suspect the *Miranda* rights and receiving a voluntary waiver of the right to counsel, to interrogate a suspect who has been appointed counsel, provided that the suspect (1) has not previously asserted *Miranda* protection or (2) has previously asserted *Miranda* protection and subsequently waived it. The decision is beneficial to law enforcement because it offers more opportunities for them to secure incriminating statements from criminal suspects.

# ▶ The Fifth Amendment Approach

The Fifth Amendment lists a number of different rights in addition to the protection against self-incrimination that apply outside the scope of criminal procedure (for example, it also contains the so-called *eminent domain clause*, which prohibits the government from taking private property without just compensation). The provision that is relevant to criminal procedure is the *self-incrimination clause*, which states, in relevant part, that no person "shall be compelled in any criminal case to be a witness against himself."

## The Four Components of the Self-Incrimination Clause

The self-incrimination clause seems straightforward on its face, but it has been litigated extensively in the courts over the years. It can be broken into four specific components, each of which has been considered by the U.S. Supreme Court more than once. The four components are: (1) a person cannot be *compelled*; (2) in *any criminal case*; (3) *to be a witness*; and (4) *against oneself*.

### Compulsion

First, if a person is arrested and interrogated after asserting Fifth Amendment protection (and is not provided with counsel), then the Fifth Amendment will be violated. Second, a defendant in a criminal *trial* cannot be compelled to testify under *any* circumstances. The defendant enjoys absolute Fifth Amendment protection from self-incrimination during a criminal proceeding. However, once a defendant takes the stand, he or she can be compelled to answer questions. Indeed, the defendant can be held in contempt for failing to answer questions once he or she has taken the stand. The same rule applies to witnesses. The so-called **fair examination rule** ensures that witnesses at either a trial or a grand jury hearing can be compelled to answer questions once they waive their Fifth Amendment privilege and begin to testify.

## A Criminal Case

A murder trial is a classic case of a criminal proceeding, and would clearly fall within the definition of "a criminal case." However, determining whether a proceeding is "a criminal case" for Fifth Amendment purposes is not as easy as one might expect. Many types of civil proceedings (such as a lawsuit between private parties) have characteristics of criminal cases, but are not ordinarily thought of as criminal matters. For example, some civil cases have the potential to result in punitive sanctions (such as the forfeiture of one's property or punitive damages in a liability lawsuit). To deal with this complex issue, the courts usually focus on whether the case involves *punitive sanctions*, or consequences that are designed to punish someone, as opposed to compensating another for harm that was caused.

## To Be a Witness

In common speech, a *witness* is generally understood to be anyone who observes an event. But the term has a much more technical meaning in the context of the Fifth Amendment. The Supreme Court has defined the term *witness* as "one who supplies testimonial evidence," meaning that they might be called at trial to give testimony about what they observed. The Fifth Amendment protection against compelled self-incrimination also extends to things that people say which are communicative in nature—but not necessarily testimonial. An example is an incriminating statement given in a police interrogation room. *Testimony* thus comes in two forms: (1) that which is given at trial under oath and (2) that which is *communicative information* given by a person who is not under oath. However, the testimonial evidence requirement does not cover physical evidence (tangible property and the like). In other words, physical evidence is *not* protected by the Fifth Amendment.

## Against Oneself

*Couch v. United States*
*(409 U.S. 322 [1973])*

The only person who can assert Fifth Amendment protection is the person being compelled to answer a question. According to the Supreme Court, "The Constitution explicitly prohibits compelling an accused to bear witness 'against himself': it necessarily does not proscribe incriminating statements elicited from another. Compulsion upon the person asserting it is an important element of the privilege" (*Couch v. United States*, 409 U.S. 322 [1973]). Furthermore, the Court has noted that "[w]e cannot cut the Fifth Amendment completely loose from the moorings of its language and make it serve as a general protector of privacy—a word not mentioned in its text and a concept directly addressed in the Fourth Amendment" (*Fisher v. United States*, 425 U.S. 391 [1976]). For example, in *Couch*, the Fifth Amendment did not protect a business owner whose accountant turned over documents that incriminated the owner.

## *Miranda*

*Miranda v. Arizona*
*(384 U.S. 436 [1966])*

As discussed in Chapter 1, at one time the Bill of Rights did not apply to cases arising under state law, until one by one, the Court incorporated many of these rights. In *Malloy v. Hogan*, 378 U.S. 1 (1964), the Supreme Court held that the Fifth Amendment's self-incrimination clause applies to the states. In announcing that ruling some 40 years ago, the Court said that "today the admissibility of a confession in a state criminal prosecution is tested by the same standard applied in federal prosecution since 1897."

Not long after that decision, the Supreme Court moved beyond *Massiah*, *Escobedo*, and the due process voluntariness approaches to interrogation law, focusing instead on the Fifth Amendment. In *Miranda v. Arizona*, 384 U.S. 436 (1966), the Court announced the following important rule: "[T]he prosecution may not use statements, whether exculpatory or inculpatory, stemming from *custodial interrogation* of the defendant unless it demonstrates the use of procedural safeguards effective to secure the privilege against self-incrimination" (emphasis added). This wording clearly established that the Fifth Amendment should serve as the basis for determining the constitutionality of a confession. Pertinent facts from *Miranda* are as follows:

> On March 13, 1963, petitioner, Ernesto Miranda, was arrested at his home and taken in custody to a Phoenix police station. He was there identified by the complaining witness. The police then took him to "Interrogation Room No. 2" of the detective bureau. There he was questioned by two police officers. The officers admitted at trial that Miranda was not advised that he had a right to have an attorney present. Two hours later, the officers emerged from the interrogation room with a written confession signed by Miranda. At the top of the statement was a typed paragraph stating that the confession was made voluntarily, without threats or promises of immunity and "with full knowledge of my legal rights, understanding any statement I make may be used against me."

Importantly, the Sixth and Fourteenth Amendments still apply to interrogations and confessions in certain situations. For example, if the police conduct in question is not a custodial interrogation (as in *Miranda*) but formal charges have been filed, the Sixth Amendment will apply. Similarly, if custody and interrogation do not take place *and* formal charges are not filed, the due process voluntariness test can still be relevant for the purpose of determining the constitutionality of a confession or admission. In fact, think of the Fourteenth Amendment's due process clause, in particular, as being something of a fallback. If no other constitutional protections apply, the guarantee of procedural due process almost always does.

The *Miranda* warnings, which are most often read by police to an arrestee, often comprise a series of statements like this: "You have the right to remain silent. Anything you say can and will be used against you in a court of law. You also have the right to an attorney. If you cannot afford an attorney, one will be provided to you at no cost. Do you understand these rights as they have been read to you?"

*Miranda* is often interpreted as requiring a code of conduct for police interrogation. However, it is only a rule governing the admissibility of evidence. The judiciary is forbidden under the separation of powers doctrine from setting policy for the executive branch. As the Supreme Court observed in *United States v. Patane*, 542 U.S. 630 (2004), "the police do not violate a suspect's constitutional rights (or the *Miranda* rule) by negligent or even deliberate failures to provide full *Miranda* warnings. Potential violations occur, if at all, only upon the admission of unwarned statements into evidence." In other words, the failure to give *Miranda* warnings does not, by itself, constitute a violation of constitutional rights. It only impacts the admissibility of statements given by the defendant.

---

## DECISION-MAKING EXERCISE 8.3

### FORMAL CRIMINAL PROCEEDINGS

An arrest warrant was issued for Mark Eddie for the crime of burglary, following an indictment for his latest heist. A detective arrested Eddie, brought him to the stationhouse, and then interrogated him at length concerning the burglary without counsel present. The detective also interrogated Eddie about additional burglaries of which he was suspected of being involved in. While Eddie refused to talk about the most recent burglary (in which he made off with a substantial amount of money), he did admit to two prior burglaries. Was the questioning constitutional?

It should be underscored that a key component of *Miranda* is that the questioning (and detention) must be conducted by government actors. If the people engaged in questioning cannot be considered government actors, then Fifth Amendment protections do not apply. However, when a private individual conducts a custodial interrogation as an agent of (working for) the police, *Miranda* applies.

It is also critical to note that when neither custody nor interrogation (or both) occur, *Miranda* does not apply. So when a suspect who was not in custody or "interrogated" answered an officer's questions about a murder, but then fell silent when asked more detailed questions, and the prosecution used the suspect's silence as proof of guilt at his trial, the Supreme Court approved (*Salinas v. Texas*, 570 U.S. ___ [2013]). In support of its decision, the Court noted "...that petitioner's Fifth Amendment claim fails because he did not expressly invoke the privilege in response to the officer's question."

Since the Supreme Court limited its decision in *Miranda* to *custodial interrogations*, it is important to understand the definitions of these two important terms: *custody* and *interrogation*.

## Custody

Many people believe that *Miranda* rights apply whenever the police begin to question a person. However, if the person being questioned is not in *custody*, *Miranda* rights do not apply. Simple police questioning, or even a full-blown interrogation, is not enough to trigger the protections afforded by the Fifth Amendment. The Court ruled that *Miranda* applies when "a person has been taken into custody or otherwise deprived of his freedom of action in any significant way." A person is clearly in custody once they have been arrested, but what about a lesser intrusion? Unfortunately, there is no easy answer to this question. In determining whether a person is in "custody," the Supreme Court has held that "the only relevant inquiry is how a reasonable man in the suspect's position would have understood his situation" (*Berkemer v. McCarty*, 468 U.S. 420 [1984]).

*Berkemer v. McCarty*
*(468 U.S. 420 [1984])*

The question of whether a person is in custody for *Miranda* purposes has been considered in a number of contexts. Examples include: (1) traffic and field stops; (2) questioning in the home; (3) questioning at the police station or equivalent facility; (4) questioning of juveniles; (5) questioning between a probation officer and probationer; and (6) questioning for minor crimes.

### Traffic Stops

A person is not in custody in the typical traffic stop. This was the decision reached in *Berkemer*. There, a motorist was stopped for weaving in and out of traffic. After he admitted to drinking and smoking marijuana, the officer arrested him. The motorist argued that he should have been advised of his right to remain silent, but the Supreme Court disagreed, noting that vehicle stops are "presumptively temporary and brief" and sufficiently public to avoid the appearance of being coercive. The Court added, "From all that appears in the stipulation of facts, a single police officer asked [the defendant] a modest number of questions and requested him to perform a simple balancing test at a location visible to passing motorists" and thus did not violate the Fifth Amendment.

The same applies to stops not involving vehicles. *Miranda* permits law enforcement officers to engage in "[g]eneral on-the-scene questioning as to facts surrounding a crime or other general questioning of citizens in the factfinding process." With regard to *Terry* stops in particular, "[t]he comparatively nonthreatening character of [investigative] detentions explains the absence of any suggestion in our opinions that *Terry* stops are subject to the dictates of *Miranda*." However, if an investigative stop becomes more intrusive than a *Terry* stop, say, because it takes place over a long period of time or is in a private setting, then, the Fifth Amendment's self-incrimination clause, made known to suspects through the *Miranda* warnings, will usually apply.

## Questioning in the Home

It is possible for questioning in one's home to rise to the level of custody. In *Orozco v. Texas*, 394 U.S. 324 (1969), the Supreme Court declared that a man was in custody when four police officers woke him in his own home and began questioning him. However, *Orozco* can be contrasted with *Beckwith v. United States*, 425 U.S. 341 (1976). In *Beckwith*, Internal Revenue Service (IRS) agents interviewed a man in his home, an action that the Supreme Court declared noncustodial. The man argued that because he was the focus of a criminal investigation, he should have been advised of his right to remain silent. However, Chief Justice Burger noted that "*Miranda* specifically defined 'focus,' for its purposes, as 'questioning initiated by law enforcement officers *after* a person has been taken into custody or otherwise deprived of his freedom of action in any significant way.'"

## Questioning at a Police Station

Questioning at the police station or an equivalent facility can also rise to the level of custody. However, not all stationhouse questioning can be considered custodial. Consider *Oregon v. Mathiason*, 429 U.S. 492 (1977), a case involving a man who voluntarily agreed to meet officers at the police station for questioning. He admitted to involvement in a crime but later argued that his visit to the stationhouse was custodial because of its inherently coercive nature. The Court said:

> Any interview of one suspected of a crime by a police officer will have coercive aspects to it, simply by virtue of the fact that the police officer is part of a law enforcement system which may ultimately cause the suspect to be charged with a crime. But police officers are not required to administer *Miranda* warnings to everyone whom they question. Nor is the requirement of warnings to be imposed simply because the questioning takes place in the stationhouse, or because the questioned person is one whom the police suspect.

In a later case, *California v. Beheler*, 463 U.S. 1121 (1983), the Court offered some clarification concerning its decision in *Mathiason*. It pointed out that *Miranda* is not implicated "if the suspect is not placed under arrest, voluntarily comes to the police station, and is allowed to leave unhindered by the police after a brief interview."

*California v. Beheler*
*(463 U.S. 1121 [1983])*

## Questioning of Juveniles

If the person questioned is a juvenile, the police need to tread carefully. As the Court noted in *J.D.B. v. North Carolina*, 564 U.S. _____ (2011), "a reasonable child subjected to police questioning will sometimes feel pressured to submit when a reasonable adult would feel free to go." Police in that case had questioned a boy in a school conference room about his alleged involvement in the theft of a digital camera. He confessed, but the Supreme Court reversed his conviction.

## Questioning of Probationers

Custody questions have come up in the context of probation officer/probationer meetings. In *Minnesota v. Murphy*, 465 U.S. 420 (1984), a probationer was ordered to meet with his probation officer for questioning. During the meeting, the probationer confessed to a rape and a murder. He later argued that he should have been advised of his *Miranda* rights, but the Court disagreed, holding that Murphy's "freedom of movement [was] not restricted to the degree associated with formal arrest." Furthermore, while "[c]ustodial arrest is said to convey to the suspect a message that he has no choice but to submit to the officers' will and to confess . . . [I]t is unlikely that a probation interview, arranged by appointment at a mutually convenient time, would give rise to a similar impression." The Court commented further in *Murphy*:

> Many of the psychological ploys discussed in *Miranda* capitalize on the suspect's unfamiliarity with the officers and the environment. Murphy's regular meetings with his probation

**THE NATURE OF CUSTODY**

Carole Reynolds was being held in jail while awaiting trial on narcotics offenses. The police had been unable to get her to make an incriminating statement, so they decided to place an undercover agent in her cell. The two women eventually struck up a conversation, and the agent asked Reynolds, "What do you do for a living?" She responded, "I'm a drug kingpin." Could Reynolds's statement be used against her at her trial for narcotics offenses?

**CAN READING THE *MIRANDA* RIGHTS CREATE A CUSTODIAL SITUATION?**

Assume that with reasonable suspicion, police officers approach a man whom they suspect of recently robbing the First National Bank. They confront the man, and before initiating any questioning, they immediately read him his *Miranda* rights. Shortly after being read his rights, but before questioning, the suspect states, "I'm glad you guys found me. I can't go on like this. I robbed First National." Does the officers' reading of *Miranda* convert a noncustodial situation (the case here) into a custodial one?

officer should have served to familiarize him with her and her office and to insulate him from psychological intimidation that might overbear his desire to claim the privilege. Finally, the coercion inherent in custodial interrogation derives in large measure from an interrogator's insinuation that the interrogation will continue until a confession is obtained. . . . Since Murphy was not physically restrained and could have left the office, any compulsion he might have felt from the possibility that terminating the meeting would have led to revocation of probation was not comparable to the pressure on a suspect who is painfully aware that he literally cannot escape a persistent custodial interrogator.

### Minor Offenses

The fact that the offense being investigated is minor does not appear to affect the analysis. In *Berkemer*, the vehicle case discussed above, the offense was a misdemeanor. The Court declared that no distinction should be drawn between types of crimes as far as *Miranda* is concerned. Instead, the only relevant issue is whether a person is in custody (and, of course, interrogated). Even for a misdemeanor, the incentive for police to try to induce the defendant to incriminate himself or herself may well be significant.

Figure 8.2 provides a list of factors that are used to distinguish custodial from noncustodial encounters.

| Custodial Situation | Noncustodial Situation |
| --- | --- |
| Arrest | Typical traffic stop |
| Excessively lengthy confrontation | General on-the-scene questioning |
| Not free to leave | Free to leave |
| Involuntary encounter | Voluntary encounter |
| Private place, such as a police station | Public place, where movement is not restricted |

**FIGURE 8.2 Distinguishing between Custodial and Noncustodial Situations**

# Interrogation

The second major component of *Miranda* is interrogation. Custody by itself is not enough to require that the *Miranda* warnings be given. For a person to be afforded Fifth Amendment protection—and particularly, to be advised of his or her right to remain silent—he or she must be subjected to interrogation.

*Miranda* defined **interrogation** as "questioning initiated by law enforcement officers." Then, in *Rhode Island v. Innis*, 446 U.S. 291 (1980), the Court noted that interrogation "must reflect a measure of compulsion above and beyond that inherent in custody itself." Thus, any questions that tend to incriminate—that is, those that are directed toward an individual about his or her suspected involvement in a crime—are considered interrogation.

*Rhode Island v. Innis (446 U.S. 291 [1980])*

Unfortunately, many *questions* are not readily identifiable as such. In *Innis*, the Supreme Court noted that in addition to "express questioning," the "functional equivalent" of a question is also possible. As defined in *Innis*, the **functional equivalent of a question** includes "any words or actions on the part of the police (other than those normally attendant to arrest and custody) that the police should know are reasonably likely to elicit an incriminating response from the suspect."

In *Innis*, while police officers were driving the defendant to the police station after his arrest for armed robbery, they engaged in a conversation about the danger the missing robbery weapon posed to schoolchildren with disabilities. Apparently in response to the conversation, the defendant directed the officers to the location of the weapon. Interestingly, though, the Supreme Court held that the officers' conversation did not constitute interrogation: It was "nothing more than a dialogue between the two officers to which no response from the respondent was invited." The majority assumed implicitly that suspects will not respond to "indirect appeals to . . . humanitarian impulses," but Justice Stevens dissented and argued that such an assumption "is directly contrary to the teachings of police interrogation manuals, which recommend appealing to a suspect's sense of morality as a standard and often successful interrogation technique."

Even though *Innis* did not ultimately involve the functional equivalent of a question, the Court essentially expanded the definition of *questioning*. Namely, a mere conversation between police officers designed to elicit an incriminating response—even if the conversation is not directed toward the suspect—can require giving the *Miranda* warnings.

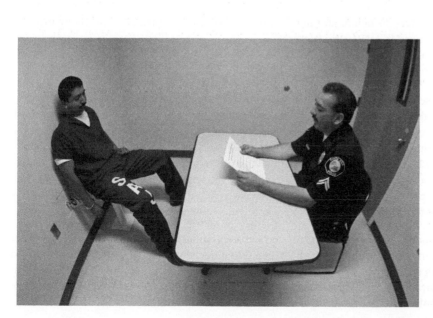

Suspects who are custodially interrogated must be advised of their *Miranda* rights. If the suspect is not in custody or is not interrogated, the *Miranda* rights do not need to be read.

| Interrogation | General Questioning |
|---|---|
| Guilt-seeking questions | Information-gathering questions |
| Conversation intended to elicit a response | Conversation not intended to elicit a response |

**FIGURE 8.3 Distinguishing between Interrogation and General Questioning**

Of course, the person must also be in custody for the *Miranda* warnings to apply. Figure 8.3 lists some of the factors considered when distinguishing between interrogation and general questioning.

## Other *Miranda* Issues

A number of important Supreme Court cases have hinged on other significant issues, including (1) the substance and adequacy of the *Miranda* warnings and (2) waivers of *Miranda*. If, for example, the *Miranda* warnings are not given adequately, then the police risk having a confession being thrown out of court. Also, like many rights, those provided by *Miranda* can be waived. That is, suspects can elect *not* to remain silent. Finally, suspects are not required to be advised of their *Miranda* rights when doing so could compromise public safety. These and other *Miranda* issues are considered in the four subsections that follow.

### Substance and Adequacy of the Warnings

In some cases, the police do not follow the exact wording of the warnings specified in *Miranda*. There is a long line of cases involving people who have sought to have their confessions excluded at trial because all or some of the *Miranda* warnings were not read adequately. For example, in *California v. Prysock*, 453 U.S. 355 (1981), a juvenile defendant was told, "You have the right to talk to a lawyer before you are questioned, have him present with you while you are being questioned, and all during the questioning." The defendant was then told that he had the right to a court-appointed lawyer but not that one would be provided for him if he was indigent.

*California v. Prysock (453 U.S. 355 [1981])*

The defendant challenged his conviction, but the Court concluded that the warnings given to him were sufficient and that "*Miranda* itself indicates that no talismanic incantation was required to satisfy its strictures."

In another interesting case, *Duckworth v. Eagan*, 492 U.S. 192 (1989), the following warnings were given:

> Before we ask you any questions, you must understand your rights. You have the right to remain silent. Anything you say can be used against you in court. You have the right to talk to a lawyer for advice before we ask you any questions, and to have him with you during questioning. You have this right to the advice and presence of a lawyer even if you cannot afford to hire one. We have no way of giving you a lawyer, but one will be appointed for you, if you wish, if and when you go to court. If you wish to answer questions now without a lawyer present, you have the right to stop answering questions at any time. You also have the right to stop answering at any time until you've talked to a lawyer.

Even though the warnings in this version suggested that counsel would only be provided at court, the Supreme Court held, in a 5 to 4 decision, that these warnings "touched all the bases required by *Miranda*." Thus, as long as all the essential *Miranda* information is communicated, simple departures from the exact words prescribed in *Miranda* will not render a confession inadmissible in a criminal trial.

**INCRIMINATING EVIDENCE AND INTERROGATION**

Police officers lawfully executed a search warrant on Don Cheney's house. Cheney was not at home, but the officers were let into the house by his wife. When Cheney arrived at home, he was immediately arrested. He was then seated on the living room couch, and one of the officers brought in a potted marijuana plant and placed it on the coffee table in front of him. When Cheney saw the plant, he began crying and said, "OK, you got me. The plant is mine. As you probably know, there are plenty more where that came from." At trial, Cheney sought to have his statement suppressed on the grounds that a custodial interrogation without the *Miranda* warnings took place in his living room on the night of the search. How should the court decide?

**ANOTHER INTERROGATION?**

The police permitted a man who was the suspect in a murder investigation to converse with his wife at the police station where he was being held. Their conversation occurred during the presence of a police officer and was recorded. The man made an incriminating response during the conversation, which was later introduced at his trial for the murder of his child. The man argued that he had been subjected to the functional equivalent of an interrogation when the police officer was present with a tape recorder. Is he correct?

Occasionally, police have added additional information not specified in *Miranda*. If more information than the original *Miranda* warnings is provided to a suspect, will any subsequent confession be inadmissible? For example, must the defendant be advised of the consequences of deciding to answer questions? The case of *Colorado v. Spring* (479 U.S. 564 [1987]) is a useful point of departure. There, the defendant was arrested and questioned on suspicion of transporting stolen firearms. He was also questioned about a homicide. He admitted that he had been given his *Miranda* warnings and that he understood them; however, he argued that the statements he made about the homicide were not admissible because he had not been informed that he was going to be questioned about the homicide (he was arrested on suspicion of transporting stolen firearms). Unfortunately for the defendant, the majority held that "a suspect's awareness of all the possible subjects of questioning in advance of interrogation is not relevant to determining whether the suspect voluntarily, knowingly, and intelligently waived his Fifth Amendment privilege." A similar issue came up in *Florida v. Powell*, 559 U.S. ___ (2010), a case in which the following was added to the *Miranda* warning: "You have the right to use any of these rights at any time you want during this interview." The Supreme Court held that advising a suspect that he or she has the right to talk with an attorney before answering any questions *and* that the suspect can invoke that right at any time during questions conformed to *Miranda*.

To ensure that the *Miranda* warnings are read properly, most police departments have a policy describing exactly what that should include. Figure 8.4 provides an example of one such policy, from the San Bernardino, California, Police Department.

### Waiver of *Miranda*

In *Miranda*, the Supreme Court stated that if a person talks after he or she has been read the warnings, "a heavy burden rests on the government to demonstrate that the defendant knowingly and intelligently waived his privilege against self-incrimination and his right to retained or appointed counsel." Furthermore, "a valid waiver will not be presumed simply

**FIGURE 8.4** *Miranda* **Advisement Policy (San Bernardino, CA, Police Department)**

from the silence of the accused after warnings are given or simply from the fact that a confession was in fact eventually obtained." According to the Supreme Court:

> Whatever the testimony of the authorities as to waiver of rights by an accused, the fact of lengthy interrogation or incommunicado incarceration before a statement is made is strong evidence that the accused did not validly waive his rights. In these circumstances the fact that the individual eventually made a statement is consistent with the conclusion that the compelling influence of the interrogation finally forced him to do so. It is inconsistent with any notion of a voluntary relinquishment of the privilege. Moreover, any evidence that the accused was threatened, tricked, or cajoled into a waiver will, of course, show that the defendant did not voluntarily waive his privilege.

*Colorado v. Connelly*
*(479 U.S. 157 [1986])*

In recent years, the courts have interpreted this language loosely. That is, whereas *Miranda* declared that a waiver should be viewed with considerable caution, later decisions have suggested that the burden of demonstrating a valid waiver is not difficult to meet. For example, in *Colorado v. Connelly*, 479 U.S. 157 (1986), the Court held that the government need only show the validity of a waiver by a "preponderance of evidence." And in *Fare v. Michael C.*, 442 U.S. 707 (1979), the Court held that the "totality of the circumstances approach is adequate to determine whether there has been a waiver." This latter test is not unlike the due process voluntariness test, discussed earlier in this chapter. It is used to assess juvenile waivers, as well.

### Express Waiver Required?

Must a person affirmatively state something to the effect that "I am willing to answer questions" for a waiver of *Miranda* to take place? In *North Carolina v. Butler*, 441 U.S. 369

**WERE THE *MIRANDA* RIGHTS READ PROPERLY?**

William Wentworth was interrogated while in police custody. He wore an expensive suit, sported lavish jewelry, and otherwise exhibited an aura of financial success. Before being interrogated, he was read the following rights: "You have the right to remain silent. Anything you say can and will be used against you in court. You have the right to talk with an attorney, either retained by you or appointed by the court, before giving a statement, and to have your attorney present when answering any questions." Wentworth made an incriminating statement during the interrogation and later moved to suppress it on the grounds that he was not informed that counsel would be provided if he was indigent. How should the court decide?

(1979), the Court held, "The question [of a waiver] is not one of form, but rather whether the defendant in fact knowingly and voluntarily waived his rights delineated in the *Miranda* case." Further, a "course of conduct indicating waiver" (such as the suspect deciding to converse with the police) is also sufficient for a valid waiver to take place. Based on this decision, the current rule is that the government must show a valid waiver based on "the particular facts and circumstances surrounding [the] case, including the background, experience, and conduct of the accused." In other words, the courts now take a case-by-case approach in determining whether *Miranda* waivers are obtained legally.

## Duration of a *Miranda* Waiver

In *Wyrick v. Fields*, 459 U.S. 42 (1982), a question arose concerning the duration of a *Miranda* waiver. The defendant was advised of his *Miranda* rights and agreed to take a polygraph examination without counsel present. The polygrapher determined there was some deceit and asked the defendant if he could explain his answers, which he did. He later argued that his post-examination explanation was inappropriate, and that his *Miranda* waiver did not carry forward to cover it. The Supreme Court held that ". . . he validly waived his right to have counsel present at 'post-test' questioning unless the circumstances changed so seriously that his answers no longer were voluntary, or unless he no longer was waiving his rights knowingly and voluntarily."

## Defining a "Knowing and Intelligent" Waiver

As was made clear in *Butler*, a valid *Miranda* waiver requires a showing that the waiver was "knowing and intelligent." What, then, is a *knowing and intelligent waiver*? There is no clear answer to this question, but the Court has noted that a full and complete understanding of the *Miranda* warnings is not necessary for a valid waiver to take place. This was the decision reached in *Connecticut v. Barrett*, 479 U.S. 523 (1987), a case in which the defendant refused to give the police any written statements before he talked to an attorney. He did state, however, that he had no problem *talking* to the police. As it turned out, the defendant thought that only written statements could be used against him in court. The Court called his actions "illogical" but nonetheless held that his oral statements were admissible.

A similar conclusion was reached in *Berghuis v. Thompkins*, 560 U.S. ___ (2010). The Court held that "where the prosecution shows that a *Miranda* warning was given and that it was understood by the accused, an accused's uncoerced statement establishes an implied waiver of the right to remain silent."

## Police Trickery and Waiver

A waiver of *Miranda* rights maybe valid in some cases even if a defendant has been deceived, or "tricked" into waiving his or her rights. Two additional Supreme Court decisions focused on whether the police can use certain forms of deception to obtain a *Miranda* waiver or statement. In *Colorado v. Spring*, 479 U.S. 564 (1987), the Court held that trickery *had not* taken place when the police failed to advise the defendant that he would be questioned about a different crime than the one for which he was arrested. It did point out, however, that "any evidence that the accused was . . . tricked . . . into a waiver will, of course, show that the defendant did not voluntarily waive his privilege."

In another interesting case, *Moran v. Burbine*, 475 U.S. 412 (1986), the Supreme Court held that a confession was validly obtained even though the police questioned the defendant after assuring his attorney that he would not be questioned until the following day. In a 6 to 3 decision, the Court held that this action did not result in a coerced confession. As Justice O'Connor noted, "[T]he same defendant, armed with the same information and confronted with precisely the same police conduct, would have knowingly waived his *Miranda* rights had a lawyer not telephoned the police station to inquire about his status."

In light of these two cases, it seems somewhat difficult to determine what constitutes "trickery." As a general rule, if officials lead a defendant to believe that he or she has no right to remain silent, then the waiver is not a knowing and intelligent waiver. However, if the police merely lead a defendant to believe there is no point in remaining silent (as in *Butler, Barrett, Fields, Spring*, and *Burbine*), then any subsequent incriminating statements that are made will probably be viewed as knowing and intelligent.

### Interruptions of the Reading of *Miranda* Rights and Waiver

In a recent twist regarding *Miranda* waivers, the Supreme Court considered whether police officers' failure to complete the *Miranda* warnings—after the suspect interrupted midway through by saying, "I understand my rights"—violated the Fifth Amendment. In *United States v. Patane*, 542 U.S. 630 (2004), after the suspect had interrupted the reading of *Miranda* rights and said he understood his rights, he informed police of the location of a pistol. He was indicted for possession of a firearm by a convicted felon and sought suppression of the pistol, claiming his Fifth Amendment privilege was violated. The Supreme Court disagreed and held that the evidence was admissible.

### Voluntariness

In addition to the requirement that a valid *Miranda* waiver must be knowing and intelligent, it must also be voluntary. The test for voluntariness is similar to the due process voluntariness test discussed earlier in this chapter. Threats, physical force, and the like can lead to defendants issuing involuntary confessions. However, in *Fare v. Michael C.*, 442 U.S. 707 (1979), the Court held that the confession obtained from a 16-year-old was not involuntary. In a strongly worded dissent, Justice Powell argued that the juvenile in this case "was immature, emotional, and uneducated, and therefore was likely to be vulnerable to the skillful, two-on-one, repetitive style of interrogation to which he was subjected." This case indicates that for the waiver to be considered involuntary, the conduct of the police must be seriously questionable.

Again, to be safe, many police departments require that each suspect completes a *Miranda* waiver before interrogation commences. Doing so helps ensure that the waiver is documented. An example of a *Miranda* waiver form, from the San Bernardino, California, Police Department, is reprinted in Figure 8.5.

### Continuation of Questioning after Asserting One's Right to Remain Silent

As a general rule, questioning must cease once the accused asserts his or her right to remain silent. As the Supreme Court emphasized in *Miranda*:

> If the individual indicates in any manner, at any time prior to or during questioning, that he wishes to remain silent, the interrogation must cease. . . . Without the right to cut off questioning, the setting of in-custody interrogation operates on the individual to overcome free

## WAIVER

I have been advised that:

1.  I have the absolute right to remain silent.

2.  Anything I say can and will be used as evidence against me in court.

3.  I have the right to be represented by an attorney and to consult with him before making any statement or answering any questions and I have the right to have an attorney present during any questioning.

4.  If I cannot afford an attorney, one will be appointed by the court, free of charge, to represent me before any questioning, if I desire.

I understand these rights. These rights have been explained to me. With these rights in mind, I am willing to talk to officers about the charges against me.


Date_____     Signed_____

Witness_____    Witness_____

*Source:* San Bernardino, California, Police Department. Reprinted with permission.

**FIGURE 8.5** *Miranda* Waiver Form (San Bernardino, CA, Police Department)

choice in producing a statement after the privilege has been once invoked. If the individual states that he wants an attorney, the interrogation must cease until an attorney is present. . . . If the individual cannot obtain an attorney and he indicates that he wants one before speaking to police, they must respect his decision to remain silent. . . . If authorities conclude that they will not provide counsel during a reasonable period of time in which investigation in the field is carried out, they may refrain from doing so without violating the person's Fifth Amendment privilege so long as they do not question him during that time.

This issue arose in *Edwards v. Arizona,* 451 U.S. 477 (1981). After being arrested, Edwards was questioned on January 19. He stopped answering questions and asked for his attorney. Questioning ceased, but the next day officers came back to the jail and resumed questioning, after informing Edwards of his *Miranda* rights. He confessed. The Supreme Court reversed his conviction, holding that "[h]aving exercised his right on January 19 to have counsel present during interrogation, petitioner did not validly waive that right on the 20th."

However, the Court has indicated that in some circumstances, the police can question a suspect after he or she has asserted the *Miranda* rights. In *Michigan v. Mosley,* 423 U.S. 96 (1975), two hours after the defendant had stated that he did not want to talk, a

*Michigan v. Mosley*
*(423 U.S. 96 [1975])*

## DECISION-MAKING EXERCISE 8.9

### THE CIRCUMSTANCES FOR A VOLUNTARY WAIVER

Fred Nicholas was arrested for murder, taken to the police station, and advised of his *Miranda* rights. He stated that he wished his attorney could be present but that he was away on business. Given that, Nicholas said that he "might as well talk." Unknown to Nicholas, his attorney was in town after all, had heard about Nicholas's arrest, and had tried unsuccessfully to contact him. In fact, the police had explicitly refused to let Nicholas meet with his attorney. Nicholas made an incriminating statement. Should it be admissible at trial?

different police officer confronted him in a different room about another crime and read him the *Miranda* rights for a second time. After this, the defendant made incriminating statements. In a 7 to 2 decision, the Court held that the suspect's *Miranda* rights had been "scrupulously honored." The Court said that the second officer's actions were acceptable because "the police here immediately ceased the interrogation, resumed questioning only after the passage of a significant period of time and the provision of a fresh set of warnings, and restricted the second interrogation to a crime that had not been a subject of the earlier interrogation."

In *Bobby v. Dixon*, 565 U.S. ___ (2011), police did not warn Dixon of his *Miranda* rights before questioning him about his suspected involvement in a forgery case. In a subsequent interrogation during which he *was* informed of his *Miranda* rights, Dixon confessed to a murder. Both crimes arose out of the same act (Dixon and an acquaintance were accused of burying a man alive and stealing his identity), but Dixon was questioned separately about his involvement in each. Dixon's conviction was upheld. The Court stated: "Dixon received *Miranda* warnings before confessing to Hammer's murder; the effectiveness of those warnings was not impaired by the sort of 'two-step interrogation technique' . . ." used in the investigation.

The common thread running throughout these last two cases is that the second set of questions either involved a separate crime or led to a confession to a second crime. However, it is not entirely clear if police may continue to ask questions about the *same* crime. In *Maryland v. Shatzer*, 559 U.S. ___ (2010), a different officer resumed questioning about the same crime more than *two weeks* after the suspect was released following initial questioning. The suspect was reread his *Miranda* rights, which he then waived. In this second session of questioning, he confessed to various crimes of sexual abuse. The Supreme Court decided that his confession was admissible, in part because "[h]is change of heart [was] . . . likely attributable to the fact that further deliberation in familiar surroundings [had] caused him to believe (rightly or wrongly) that cooperating with the investigation [was] in his interest."

## The Public Safety Exception to *Miranda*

In some circumstances when public safety is in jeopardy, interrogation is permissible without the *Miranda* warnings when a suspect is in custody. This issue came to light during the 2013 questioning of Boston Marathon bombing suspect, Dzhokhar Tsarnaev, who was questioned for a time without having first being advised of his *Miranda* rights.

*New York v. Quarles*
*(467 U.S. 649 [1984])*

The public safety exception to *Miranda* was first established in *New York v. Quarles*, 467 U.S. 649 (1984). The facts from *Quarles* are as follows: after receiving information that a man with a gun had just entered a supermarket, Officer Kraft, along with three other officers, entered the store. Kraft spotted the defendant, drew his gun, and ordered the man to stop and put his hands over his head. When the officers frisked the man, they found an empty shoulder holster on him. When they asked where the man had put the gun, he replied, "The gun is over there." Officer Kraft retrieved the revolver, placed the man under arrest, and read him the *Miranda* warnings. The trial court and the lower appellate courts excluded the gun on the grounds that the man had not been advised of his right to remain silent at the time the gun was found.

The Supreme Court disagreed. Justice Rehnquist wrote the majority opinion, arguing that rigid application of *Miranda* is not always warranted, particularly when public safety is a concern:

> [T]he need for answers to questions in a situation posing a threat to public safety outweighs the need for the prophylactic rule protecting the Fifth Amendment's privilege against self-incrimination. We decline to place officers such as Officer Kraft in the untenable position of having to consider, often in a matter of seconds, whether it best serves

society for them to ask the necessary questions without the *Miranda* warnings and render whatever probative evidence they uncover inadmissible, or for them to give the warnings in order to preserve the admissibility of evidence they might uncover but possibly damage or destroy their ability to obtain that evidence and neutralize the volatile situation confronting them.

The Court also made it clear that the appropriate test for determining whether a threat to public safety exists is an objective one—it is based on what a reasonable person in the same circumstances would believe. As the Court explained, "[W]here spontaneity rather than adherence to a police manual is necessarily the order of the day, the application of the [public safety] exception . . . should not be made to depend on *post hoc* findings at a suppression hearing concerning the subjective motivation of the arresting officer." The majority in *Quarles* apparently believed that an objective threat to public safety existed. Insofar as the officers did not know where the gun was located, not knowing that information "obviously posed more than one danger to the public safety: an accomplice might make use of it [or] a customer or employee might later come upon it."

The *Quarles* decision is a controversial one. As Justice O'Connor noted:

> *Miranda* has never been read to prohibit the police from asking questions to secure the public safety. Rather, the critical question *Miranda* addresses is who shall bear the cost of securing the public safety when such questions are asked and answered: the defendant or the state. *Miranda*, for better or worse, found the resolution of that question implicit in the prohibition against compulsory self-incrimination and placed the burden on the State.

*Quarles* appears to place the burden on the defendant to show that the failure to give *Miranda* warnings was not justified. As Justice O'Connor pointed out, shifting that burden does not ensure that public safety is preserved, but creates a *Miranda* loophole that allows otherwise inadmissible evidence to be used against the defendant.

## Challenging *Miranda*

The *Miranda* decision was very controversial after it was handed down. In 1968, shortly after the decision was announced, Congress passed the Omnibus Crime Control and Safe Streets Act, which contained various provisions intended to tighten gun control laws and expand the ability of police to use wiretaps. A portion of the statute, **18 U.S.C. Section 3501**, attempted to overrule the *Miranda* decision. It states that in any federal prosecution, a confession "shall be admissible in evidence if it is voluntarily given." Under the law, suspects are not required to be advised of their right to counsel, their right not to incriminate themselves, and so on.

For several years, Section 3501 remained dormant. The U.S. attorneys general knew that to utilize the statute would be to challenge the authority of the U.S. Supreme Court. But critics of *Miranda* were looking for an opportunity to bring Section 3501 before the Court. That opportunity arose in 2000 in a case involving a bank robbery. The defendant, Charles Dickerson, moved to suppress a statement he made to Federal Bureau of Investigation (FBI) agents on the ground that he had not received his *Miranda* warnings. The district court granted Dickerson's motion to suppress but also noted that the confession was voluntary, despite the apparent *Miranda* violation.

Then, the Court of Appeals for the Fourth Circuit held (in a 2 to 1 decision) that "Congress, pursuant to its power to establish the rules of evidence and procedure in the federal courts, acted well within its authority in enacting Section 3501, [and] Section 3501, rather than *Miranda*, governs the admissibility of confession in federal court" (*United States v. Dickerson*, 166 F.3d 667 [4th Cir. 1999]). The case, *Dickerson v. United States*, 530 U.S. 428

*Dickerson v. United States*
*(530 U.S. 428 [2000])*

(2000), then went before the Supreme Court. In a 7 to 2 opinion, Chief Justice Rehnquist wrote for the Court:

> We hold that *Miranda*, being a constitutional decision of this Court, may not be in effect overruled by an Act of Congress, and we decline to overrule *Miranda* ourselves. We therefore hold that *Miranda* and its progeny in this Court govern the admissibility of statements made during custodial interrogation in both state and federal courts.

The Court further noted:

> Whether or not we would agree with *Miranda's* reasoning and its resulting rule, were we addressing the issue in the first instance, the principles of *stare decisis* weigh heavily against overruling it now. . . . While *stare decisis* is not an inexorable command, particularly when we are interpreting the Constitution, even in constitutional cases, the doctrine carries such persuasive force that we have always required a departure from precedent to be supported by some special justification.
>
> We do not think there is such justification for overruling *Miranda*. *Miranda* has become embedded in routine police practice to the point where the warnings have become part of our national culture.

## *Miranda* and Section 1983

In *Chavez v. Martinez*, 538 U.S. 760 (2003), the Supreme Court seems to have shifted its view on *Miranda*. In that case, a police officer interrogated a man while he was receiving treatment for a gunshot wound. The man was *not* advised of his *Miranda* rights. He was never charged with a crime, but later sued under 42 U.S.C. Section 1983 (see Chapter 2), arguing that his constitutional rights were violated. The Supreme Court disagreed because the man was not compelled to be a "witness" against himself in a "criminal case." This decision would seem to suggest *Miranda* warnings are never required, unless statements obtained without the warnings are actually used against the accused in a criminal case.

# ▶ The Exclusionary Rule and Confession Analysis

It is often said that the exclusionary rule applies only to the Fourth Amendment. Part of the reason for this is that the Fifth Amendment essentially contains its own exclusionary rule by prohibiting compulsion of testimony. Whatever view one takes, the debate is largely semantic. In the end, evidence obtained in violation of *any* constitutional amendment will not be admissible in a criminal trial.

Generally speaking, a confession obtained in violation of *Miranda* or some constitutional provision will be excluded. However, just because a confession is obtained illegally does not mean that any subsequently obtained evidence will automatically be excluded. In fact, illegally obtained statements are themselves considered admissible in certain instances.

There are essentially three lines of cases involving confessions and the exclusionary rule: (1) cases involving the standing of a party to challenge a confession, (2) cases where the prosecution seek to use a confession for impeachment, and (3) cases where a defendant seeks to exclude evidence that is "fruit of the poisonous tree."

## Confessions and Standing

For a confession (or evidence thereby obtained) to be excluded, the person arguing for exclusion must have *standing*; that is, one person cannot seek to exclude the confession of another, even if that confession was obtained in violation of *Miranda*. As noted in *Couch v.*

*United States*, 409 U.S. 322 (1973), being advised of *Miranda* is considered a personal right. Thus, a person arguing for exclusion of an (unconstitutionally obtained) incriminating statement must have standing to challenge its use; otherwise, the statement and subsequent evidence will be deemed admissible.

## Confessions and Impeachment

In some cases, the prosecution may use a confession, not for the purposes of proving the defendant's guilt, but to impeach the defendant's testimony. In other words, the prosecution attempts to undermine the witness's credibility by showing that something the defendant said in the confession is inconsistent with the defendant's testimony at trial. A key limitation on this rule is that the statement must be obtained voluntarily in the due process sense.

For an example of a *Miranda* case, consider *Harris v. New York*, 401 U.S. 222 (1971). The prosecution sought to introduce an out-of-court statement that was inconsistent with the defendant's in-court testimony, even though the out-of-court statement was obtained in violation of *Miranda*. The Supreme Court held that the out-of-court-statement was admissible—to use only for impeachment purposes, and not to be used as evidence against Harris. The Court noted further that such a statement must be obtained voluntarily, which it was in Harris's case (see also *Oregon v. Hass*, 420 U.S. 714 [1975]; *New Jersey v. Portash*, 437 U.S. 385 [1978]).

*Harris v. New York*
*(401 U.S. 222 [1971])*

Note that for a statement obtained in violation of *Miranda* to be admissible for impeachment purposes, the statement must be an oral communication. The prosecution cannot introduce evidence of an accused's out-of-court *silence* for impeachment purposes. This issue arose in the case of *Doyle v. Ohio*, 426 U.S. 610 (1976), in which after the defendant's in-court exculpatory story, the prosecution sought to introduce evidence that the defendant did not offer the same explanation to the police. The Supreme Court held that the defendant's silence was not admissible for purposes of impeachment (see also *Wainwright v. Greenfield*, 474 U.S. 284 [1986]).

The Sixth Amendment approach was considered in *Michigan v. Harvey*, 494 U.S. 344 (1990). In that case, police questioned the defendant after he invoked his right to counsel and later waived it. The Supreme Court held that a statement obtained in violation of the right to counsel could be admitted for impeachment purposes. Recently, in *Kansas v. Ventris*, 556 U.S. ___ (2009), the Supreme Court reached a similar conclusion. In that case, police relied on an informant to obtain a statement from Ventris—after Ventris had been formally charged with a crime. It admitted the statement for impeachment purposes only, and not as part of the government's case in chief, even though the incriminating statement was obtained in violation of the Sixth Amendment.

## Confessions and "Fruit of the Poisonous Tree"

As discussed in Chapter 2, if evidence is obtained in violation of the constitution, any evidence derived from it is also not admissible under the so-called "fruit of the poisonous tree" doctrine. However, the Supreme Court has not been so quick to apply the same rule in the case of illegally obtained confessions. It has held that physical evidence derived from a confession obtained in violation of *Miranda* is admissible, as long as the information supplied by the accused is voluntary in the due process sense.

The first case of note concerning the fruit of the poisonous tree in the confession context was *United States v. Bayer*, 331 U.S. 532 (1947), a case decided well before the *Miranda* decision was handed down. There, the Court held that the Fourth Amendment "fruit of the poisonous tree" doctrine did not control the admissibility of improperly obtained confessions.

*United States v. Bayer*
*(331 U.S. 532 [1947])*

Then, in *Michigan v. Tucker*, 417 U.S. 433 (1974), a case decided after *Miranda*, but involving an interrogation that took place before *Miranda*, the Court suggested that it had not changed its position. In *Tucker*, a suspect was questioned about a rape without being advised of his right to counsel. Tucker claimed he was with a friend at the time of the crime.

**SHOULD THE EXCLUSIONARY RULE APPLY?**

Assume the police have Jack Richter in custody and are interrogating him about his suspected involvement in a gruesome murder. They do not advise him of his *Miranda* rights. Further, one of the officers, who is notorious for his aggressive interrogation techniques, holds a .357-caliber revolver (loaded with one round) to Richter's head and plays "Russian roulette" in order to obtain a confession. Richter succumbs to the pressure and admits to the murder. He also points the police to the location of the murder weapon. Obviously, his statement will not be admissible. What about the murder weapon?

The police then obtained incriminating evidence against Tucker from the friend. Although this information was clearly fruit of the initial interrogation, the Court stated that "[t]he police conduct at issue here did not abridge respondent's constitutional privilege against compulsory self-incrimination, but departed only from the prophylactic standards later laid down by this Court in *Miranda* to safeguard this privilege." In other words, the Court saw no reason to exclude the friend's statement.

In *Oregon v. Elstad*, 470 U.S. 298 (1985), the Court reaffirmed its *Tucker* decision, making clear that it would continue to treat *Miranda* as a "prophylactic" rule, at least insofar as it governs the admissibility of derivative evidence. Moreover, derivative evidence obtained from a violation of *Miranda* is admissible, but only if voluntarily obtained. In sum, these decisions govern derivative evidence, not the initial incriminating statements (such as Tucker's claim that he was with a friend). The latter are inadmissible when obtained in violation of the Fifth Amendment.

## ▶ The Importance of Documenting a Confession

So far, the case law presented in this chapter should have illustrated that the police must take great care in methods they use to extract incriminating information from a criminal suspect. It is also vital that police appropriately document a resulting confession. Assuming the police are successful in terms of eliciting an incriminating response, it is not enough for the suspect to say, "I did it" or to otherwise offer some form of verbal confession. In fact, if the police hand the suspect a pencil and paper and say, "Write down your confession," this will not be enough, either. Instead, the police need to follow specific procedures for documenting and reporting a confession.

According to one authority,[2] the police should document every interrogation and even keep an *interview log*: a document containing information about the individuals involved in the interrogations and the actions taken by both sides. A list of topics to be cited in an interview log is shown in Figure 8.6.

Also, a signed statement from the accused should be obtained, if possible. First, the signed statement should identify the suspect, the investigators, and the crime involved. Second, the statement should describe, in language the suspect can understand, the details of the crime, what the suspect did, and how he or she did it. The statement should then be carefully reviewed with the suspect, even read aloud, so its content is clear. Finally, the statement should be signed by the suspect, the officer who conducted the interrogation, and at least one witness—preferably another officer. Figure 8.7 shows a model statement form for securing a written confession from a criminal suspect.

---

[2]T. T. Burke, "Documenting and Reporting a Confession with a Signed Statement: A Guide for Law Enforcement," *FBI Law Enforcement Bulletin* 70 (2001): 17–22.

**Interview Log**

1. Identity of person interviewed
2. Identity of officers conducting interview
3. Location of interview
4. Date of interview
5. Time of arrest, if applicable
6. Location of arrest
7. Identity of officers making arrest
8. Time interview began
9. Time officers informed subject or suspect of his or her rights, and if more than one officer, name of officer advising subject or suspect
10. Time subject or suspect waived his or her rights
11. Time interview concluded
12. Time preparation of statement commenced
13. Identity of person preparing statement
14. Time statement completed
15. Time subject or suspect reviewed statement
16. Time subject or suspect signed written statement
17. A record of request and complaints of subject and the action taken thereon, such as the time a subject requests permission to call an attorney, the time he or she made a call to his attorney, the time subject complained of illness, the time and action taken on this complaint, the time subject requested food, the time and action taking on this request, and the details as to how this request was handled.

*Source:* T.T. Bruke, "Documenting and Reporting a Confession with a Signed Statement: A Guide for Law Enforcement," *FBI Law Enforcement Bulletin* (February 2001): 21.

**FIGURE 8.6  Content of Typical Interview Log**

---

**Signed Statement Format White-Collar Crime Sample**

I, (*subject's name and address*) hereby make the following free and voluntary statement to (*officer's official name and title*) who has identified himself/herself as a (*title of officer and name of department or agency*). I have been advised that I have been interviewed concerning my involvement in (*phrase describing scheme or nature of crime and victim, such as "the misappropriation and theft of $100,000 from the First National Bank while I was employed there during 1999"*).

I was born on (*subject's date of birth*) at (*subject's place of birth*). I attended (*last school attended*) and completed (*last grade or graduation date*). I read and write the English language.

> Officers should use the next few paragraphs to summarize what the subject did and how the subject did it, in his own words. Because this statement occurs after the subject's confession, officers can assist the subject in formulating the statement, using information previously provided. Officers should include any information the subject provides regarding what happened to the stolen money, how it was spent, items purchased, and other related details.

I knew that what I was doing was wrong, and I regret my actions. I wish to cooperate with the (*name of agency*) investigation and get this matter resolved. (*Optional paragraph, depending on circumstances and subject's remorse*)

I have read this (*number of pages*) page statement, have initialed all corrections, and I am signing it because it is true and correct. (*The subject writes this after reading the statement aloud and accepting its contents.*)

**FIGURE 8.7  Sample Form for Securing a Written Confession: White-Collar Crime**

**FIGURE 8.7** *Continued*

# Summary

## 1. Summarize how due process and voluntariness impact interrogations and confessions.

An involuntarily obtained confession violates due process clause of the Fourteenth Amendment. Figure 8.8 illustrates the relationships among the various constitutional provisions governing police interrogation procedures. The due process voluntariness approach acts as a fallback and is always applicable. The Sixth and Fifth Amendments, by contrast, apply in specific circumstances, as described. It is possible (albeit rare) for all three provisions to come into play.

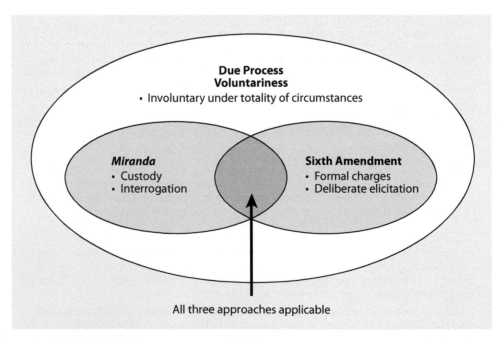

*Source:* Adapted from R. M. Bloom and M. S. Brodin, *Criminal Procedure: Examples and Explanations,* 2nd ed. (New York: Little, Brown, 1996)

**FIGURE 8.8 Relationship among the Various Approaches to Confession Law**

## 2. Summarize how the Sixth Amendment impacts interrogations and confessions.

Confessions are also governed by the Sixth Amendment's right to counsel clause, but only when formal charges have been filed. If the police deliberately elicit information from a person who has already been charged with a crime, the charged individual has the right to have counsel present during questioning.

## 3. Explain the Fifth Amendment approach to interrogations and *Miranda* rights.

The Fifth Amendment's self-incrimination clause is frequently relied on in challenges to the constitutionality of confessions. However, for the Fifth Amendment to be successfully invoked, several requirements must be met. First, the police must compel a statement that is incriminating as well as testimonial. And, of course, the accused individual is the only one who can assert his or her Fifth Amendment protection against an unconstitutionally obtained confession.

A confession will be thrown out, as was the decision in *Miranda v. Arizona*, if a suspect's incriminating statement is a result of custodial interrogation in which the suspect was not advised of his or her constitutional right to have counsel present. Before custodial interrogation can commence, suspects must be advised of their so-called *Miranda* rights.

## 4. Know when unconstitutionally obtained confessions are admissible in court to prove guilt.

For a confession (or evidence thereby obtained) to be excluded, the person arguing for exclusion must have *standing*; that is, one person cannot seek to exclude the confession of another, even if that confession was obtained in violation of *Miranda*. Another situation in which improperly obtained incriminating statements may be admissible is when such statements are used for purposes of impeachment. A key restriction on this rule, however, is that the statement must be obtained voluntarily in the due process sense. Finally, the Supreme Court has held that physical evidence obtained in violation of *Miranda* is admissible, as long as the information supplied by the accused is voluntary in the due process sense.

---

# Key Terms

18 U.S.C. Section 3501 *241*
admission *222*
confession *222*
custody *230*
deliberate elicitation *224*

due process voluntariness
approach *222*
fair examination rule *227*
formal criminal proceeding *225*
functional equivalent of a question *233*

interrogation *233*
*Miranda* warnings *229*
physical evidence *228*
testimonial evidence *228*

---

# Key Cases

## Due Process Voluntariness Approach

- *Brown v. Mississippi*, 297 U.S. 278 (1936)
- *Williams v. United States*, 341 U.S. 97 (1951)
- *Colorado v. Connelly*, 479 U.S. 157 (1986)

## Sixth Amendment Approach

- *Massiah v. United States*, 377 U.S. 201 (1964)
- *Brewer v. Williams*, 430 U.S. 387 (1977)
- *United States v. Henry*, 447 U.S. 264 (1980)

## Miranda

- *Miranda v. Arizona*, 384 U.S. 436 (1966)
- *Berkemer v. McCarty*, 468 U.S. 420 (1984)
- *California v. Beheler*, 463 U.S. 1121 (1983)
- *Rhode Island v. Innis*, 446 U.S. 291 (1980)
- *California v. Prysock*, 453 U.S. 355 (1981)
- *Michigan v. Mosley*, 423 U.S. 96 (1975)
- *Maryland v. Shatzer*, 08-680 (2010)
- *New York v. Quarles*, 467 U.S. 649 (1984)
- *Dickerson v. United States*, 530 U.S. 428 (2000)

## Exclusionary Rule and Confessions

- *Couch v. United States*, 409 U.S. 322 (1973)
- *Harris v. New York*, 401 U.S. 222 (1971)
- *United States v. Bayer*, 331 U.S. 532 (1947)

# Further Exploration

1. Dzokhar Tsarnaev was 19 when he was caught and charged in the Boston marathon bombing. While he was in the hospital undergoing treatment for a bullet wound, authorities began questioning him (as soon as he was able to respond) *without* advising him of his *Miranda* rights. The "public safety" exception was invoked. He was questioned for 16 hours without being read his *Miranda* rights. As Tsarnaev was en route to the hospital for treatment, the U.S. Justice Department made this announcement:

   The suspect is en route to the hospital for immediate treatment [. . .] But we plan to invoke the public safety exception to Miranda in order to question the suspect extensively about other potential explosive devices or accomplices and to gain critical intelligence

   Why was the announcement made? Was it good practice to do so? Why or why not? What would have been the consequence if the government did not make this announcement?

2. Iowa Code section 804.20 provides in part that "[a]ny peace officer or other person having custody of any person arrested or restrained of the person's liberty for any reason whatever, shall permit that person, without unnecessary delay after arrival at the place of detention, to call, consult, and see a member of the person's family or an attorney of the person's choice, or both . . ." An arrestee asks to "phone a friend," but the custody officer does not make the call or give him the phone. The arrestee subsequently makes incriminating statements. He seeks to have the statements thrown out on the grounds that he was denied his phone call. Should he succeed? Would it matter if the person he sought to call was not an attorney? What if the person he was trying to call was another police officer, with whom the arrestee was hoping to "make a deal?" See *State v. Garrity*, 765 N.W.2d 592 (Iowa 2009). Note that in this hypothetical there is an actual statute providing a right

   to a phone call. Not all states have such laws, so the "one phone call" rights claimed by arrestees on television and in the movies may not exist in some jurisdictions.

3. Police officers surrounded a property in which a barricaded suspect was threatening to kill two hostages. A hostage negotiator calls the man on the phone and, without administering *Miranda* warnings, converses with him multiple times over the course of several hours. The man makes incriminating statements on several occasions. At trial, his attorney seeks to exclude the statements he made during the phone conversation with the hostage negotiator. Should the statements be excluded? Was the man in custody for *Miranda* purposes? A similar set of facts were at issue in *United States v. Mesa*, 638 F.2d 582 (3rd Cir. 1980).

4. Evaluate this actual recorded exchange (*Wedgeworth v. State*, 288 S.W.3d 234 [Ark. 2008]) between detective Jaime Morrow and capital murder suspect James Wedgeworth. Did a *Miranda* violation occur?

   MORROW: "O.k., James when . . . ah . . . when I read you your rights . . . ah . . . you said you wanted your attorney present . . . I give you an opportunity to . . . to . . . to tell me who your attorney was so we could get him up here . . . Is that correct?"

   WEDGEWORTH: "Yes sir."

   MORROW: "At that time you told me you didn't have one but you wanted to go ahead and speak to me, is that correct?"

   WEDGEWORTH: "Yes sir."

   Morrow: "O.k., you wasn't forced to give me . . . to talk to me or anything like that was you?"

   WEDGEWORTH: "No sir."

   Wedgeworth then confessed to shooting the victim with a twenty gauge shotgun.

   MORROW: "And you . . . you . . . you understand you had the right to talk to a lawyer before any questions were asked . . . you may have had one present . . . you understood that?"

WEDGEWORTH: "Yes sir."

MORROW: "O.k. if you couldn't afford one . . . one would be appointed to represent you free of cost . . . you understood that . . . that correct?"

WEDGEWORTH: "Yes sir."

MORROW: "O.k., as I said earlier . . . when I started talking to you . . . you said you wanted your attorney . . . but you didn't have . . . you . . . you didn't you didn't have an attorney and you . . . you choose to go ahead and speak to me of your own free will . . . is that correct?"

WEDGEWORTH: "Yes . . . I did not know of a name of an attorney right off hand."

MORROW: "So . . . did I threaten you for your statement?"

WEDGEWORTH: "No sir."

MORROW: "Did I make you any promises for statement?"

WEDGEWORTH: "No sir."

MORROW: "O.k., your statement made of your own free will?"

WEDGEWORTH: "Yes sir."

5. Assume two burglary suspects insist on being interviewed together. Police grant their request. *Miranda* warnings are read. One waiver form is provided and one suspect signs it. Subsequently, both suspects made incriminating statements. Whose statements should be admissible? Which statements should not? This question came up in an actual case. Read *United States v. Lafferty*, 503 F.2d 293 (3rd Cir. 2007) for more details.

# Review Questions

1. Explain the means by which compulsion can occur, in Fifth Amendment terms.

2. How might the self-incrimination clause come into play in a noncriminal proceeding?

3. What does it mean to be a witness, in Fifth Amendment terms?

4. What does it mean, in Fifth Amendment terms, to be a witness against oneself?

5. Summarize the due process voluntariness approach to interrogations and confessions.

6. What factors affect voluntariness?

7. Summarize the Sixth Amendment approach to interrogations and confessions.

8. Explain the concept of deliberate elicitation.

9. What are formal criminal proceedings, for purposes of the Sixth Amendment approach to interrogations and confessions?

10. What are the *Miranda* warnings?

11. Describe the types of cases in which *Miranda* may apply.

12. Citing relevant cases, distinguish between custody and interrogation, for *Miranda* purposes.

13. Summarize the requirements for a valid *Miranda* waiver.

14. Explain the public safety exception to *Miranda*.

15. How does the exclusionary rule operate in the context of confessions and interrogations?

# Web Links and Exercises

1. Interviewing: Read Simon and Boetig's article about how to conduct a structured investigative interview.
URL (read the article, "The Structured Investigative Interview"): http://www.fbi.gov/stats-services/publications/law-enforcement-bulletin/2007-pdfs/june07leb.pdf (accessed May 9, 2013).

2. More on *Miranda*: Learn more about the Supreme Court's important decision in *Miranda v. Arizona*.
URL: http://www.mirandawarning.org (accessed May 9, 2013).

3. Vague invocations of the right to counsel: What if a suspect makes an ambiguous reference to his or her right to counsel in the interrogation context?

Suggested URL: http://www.aele.org/interrogations.html (accessed May 9, 2013).

4. The *FBI Law Enforcement Bulletin* contains an in-depth examination of the "public safety" exception to the *Miranda*. Read the article and answer this question: Do you agree with the author? Why or why not?

Suggested URL: http://www.fbi.gov/stats-services/publications/law-enforcement-bulletin/february2011/legal_digest (accessed May 9, 2013).

5. How interrogation works: Read more about how interrogation actually plays out.

Suggested URL: http://people.howstuffworks.com/police-interrogation4.htm (accessed May 9, 2013).

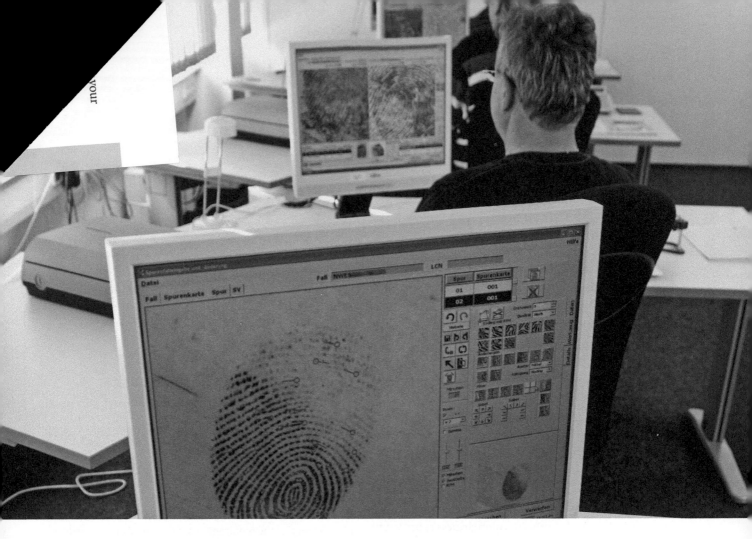

# 9 Identification Procedures and the Role of Witnesses

## LEARNING OBJECTIVES

When you complete this chapter, you should be able to:

**1** *Outline pretrial suspect identification techniques.*

**2** *Explain the problem of witness misidentification.*

**3** *Summarize identification techniques during the trial and issues involving witness credibility.*

**4** *Explain how the exclusionary rule operates in the identification context.*

# Introduction: Dealing with Witnesses to Crimes

*Identification procedures* are systems and activities that allow witnesses of crimes to identify suspected perpetrators. The three most common types of identification procedures are lineups, showups, and photographic arrays. In a **lineup**, the suspect is placed alongside several other people who resemble him or her (sometimes called "fillers," "foils," or "distractors"), and the witness (or victim) picks the suspect out of the lineup. The fillers may be jail inmates, actors, or volunteers. In a **showup**, the suspect is brought before the witness alone, so the witness can be asked whether that person is the perpetrator. Finally, in a **photographic array** (or photographic display), several photographs, including one of the suspect, are shown to a witness or victim, and he or she is asked to pick out the perpetrator.

Identification procedures fall into two broad categories: (1) out of court and (2) in court. The three identification procedures just described—lineups, showups, and photographic arrays—occur *out of court* and prior to trial. There are, however, many occasions in which the prosecution may wish to have a witness identify the suspect *in court* and during trial. Of course, not all witnesses recollect a suspect accurately or can be trusted with regard to the identification of a suspect. A *witness examination process* can help determine whether witnesses are reliable and trustworthy.

Naturally, a prosecutor will want to introduce evidence that a witness or victim picked the perpetrator out of a lineup. However, the prosecutor must do more than simply demonstrate that a witness identified the perpetrator. The identification procedure must be fair, and it must conform to constitutional requirements. Those constitutional requirements place restrictions on what officials can do in terms of arranging lineups, showups, and photographic arrays. These restrictions are critical because witnesses to crimes are frequently inaccurate in their descriptions.

Accordingly, this chapter begins with a discussion of the constitutional restrictions that govern the identification process. Next, out-of-court identification procedures are considered followed by in-court identification procedures and the witness examination process. The chapter concludes with a look at the role of the exclusionary rule as it applies to in-court and out-of-court identification procedures.

. . . . . . . . . . . . . . . . . . . . . . . . . . . . . . . . . . . . . . . . . . . . . . . . .

# ▶ Constitutional Challenges to Identification Procedures

Identification procedures have been challenged on four primary grounds, stemming from the Fourteenth Amendment's due process clause, the Fifth Amendment's self-incrimination clause, and the Sixth Amendment's right to counsel clause. The constitutionality of identification procedures has also been challenged on Fourth Amendment grounds.

## Right to Counsel

*United States v. Wade*
*(388 U.S. 218 [1967])*

After an indictment has been filed, the Sixth Amendment right to counsel applies to the witness identification process. In *United States v. Wade*, 388 U.S. 218 (1967), a defendant was placed in a police lineup, without his attorney present, *after* he had been indicted for a crime. The Supreme Court held that this violated the Sixth Amendment because a postindictment lineup is a "critical stage" in the criminal process. Further, "the presence of counsel [at postindictment lineups] is necessary to preserve the defendant's basic right to a fair trial." Indeed, the right to counsel extends well beyond the identification stage, as will be discussed in Chapter 11.

The key in *Wade* was that the lineup was postindictment—that is, conducted after charges had been filed. Had charges *not* been filed, a different decision would have probably resulted. Another important aspect of the *Wade* decision was that it distinguished lineups from "various other preparatory steps, such as systematized or scientific analyzing of the accused's fingerprints, blood sample, clothing, hair and the like." Counsel is not required for these types of activities because

> [k]nowledge of the techniques of science and technology is sufficiently available, and the variables in techniques few enough, that the accused has the opportunity for a meaningful confrontation of the Government's case at trial through the ordinary processes of cross-examination of the Government's expert witnesses and the presentation of the evidence of his own experts.

Recently, the Supreme Court has extended the Sixth Amendment right to counsel to include other hearings, such as preliminary hearings and arraignments (see *Kirby v. Illinois*, 406 U.S. 682 [1972]).

---

**DECISION-MAKING EXERCISE 9.1**

### COUNSEL DURING A LINEUP

Sam Linde has been arrested and charged with burglarizing Paul's Appliance Store. Authorities also suspect that Linde has burglarized several other appliance stores in the area, including John's Appliance Store. Suppose the police want to place Linde in a lineup for a witness who saw him leave John's Appliance Store in the middle of the night. Must counsel be present? (You may recall a similar exercise from the previous chapter, which dealt with confessions, but here the issue is a lineup.)

▼

# Due Process

The Supreme Court has also clearly stated that the Fourteenth Amendment's due process clause also applies to identification procedures. In *Stovall v. Denno*, 388 U.S. 293 (1967), the Court held that the accused is entitled to protection against procedures "so unnecessarily suggestive and conducive to irreparable mistaken identification" as to amount to a due process violation. In general, for an identification procedure to satisfy the due process clause, it must be (1) reliable and (2) minimally suggestive.

*Stovall v. Denno (388 U.S. 293 [1967])*

Whether an identification procedure is *reliable* is determined in light of the facts and circumstances surrounding the case. The following factors are used in determining whether an identification procedure is reliable:

> The opportunity of the witness to view the criminal at the time of the crime, the witness's degree of attention, the accuracy of the witness's prior description of the criminal, the level of certainty demonstrated by the witness at the confrontation, and the length of time between the crime and the confrontation. (*Neil v. Biggers*, 409 U.S. 188 [1972])

*Suggestiveness* has also been important in determining whether an identification procedure violates the due process clause. If the procedure is set up such that the witness or victim is almost guaranteed to pick the perpetrator, it is unnecessarily suggestive. If, for example, an offender is 6 feet tall and placed in a lineup with several others who are considerably shorter, then the procedure will be considered suggestive.

Although suggestiveness is a key factor, the Court stated in *Biggers* that reliability is more important than suggestiveness. In the Court's words, it is "the likelihood of misidentification which violates a defendant's right to due process." This position was reaffirmed in the case of *Manson v. Braithwaite*, 432 U.S. 98 (1977), where the Court held that the totality of circumstances determines whether an identification procedure is unreliable.

*Manson v. Braithwaite (432 U.S. 98 [1977])*

The Supreme Court has been fairly judicious in terms of due process violations during witness identification, and has set the bar very high for challenging identifications on this basis. In *Perry v. New Hampshire*, 565 U.S. ___ (2012), police were interviewing a woman in her apartment who had reported that a man was breaking into cars in the parking lot. When the woman was asked to describe the man, she pointed out the window and said the culprit was standing right next to one of the police officers outside. Barian Perry, the man she pointed to, was arrested. He sought exclusion of the woman's identification, but the Supreme Court, in an 8 to 1 decision, concluded that happenstance was responsible for the identification procedure. It was not by design: "The Due Process Clause does not require a preliminary judicial inquiry into the reliability of an eyewitness identification when the identification was not procured under unnecessarily suggestive circumstances *arranged* by law enforcement" (emphasis added).

# Self-Incrimination

The Fifth Amendment's self-incrimination clause has also been invoked with regard to identification procedures. In particular, some defendants have argued that being forced to participate in a lineup or photographic array is itself incriminating and, as such, violates the Fifth Amendment. However, in *United States v. Wade*, 388 U.S. 218 (1967), the Court held that the privilege against self-incrimination does not limit the use of identification procedures.[1] The Court's rationale was that even though incriminating information can result from identification procedures, such evidence is physical or real as opposed to testimonial. In *Wade*, the Court decided on the constitutionality of an identification procedure,

---

[1]Note that the Fifth Amendment would apply if a defendant in a lineup was forced to answer questions from the police or witnesses.

in which the accused was required to utter words that were presumably uttered by the perpetrator. The Court concluded that this type of identification procedure was valid because the defendant's voice was used as an identifying characteristic, not as a means for him to express his guilt. Thus, the Fifth Amendment does not apply to identification procedures.

## The Fourth Amendment

Lastly, identification procedures have been challenged on Fourth Amendment grounds. Like the Fifth Amendment, the Fourth Amendment has yet to be used to successfully challenge identification procedures. According to the Supreme Court, no one enjoys a reasonable expectation of privacy in characteristics that are exposed to the public. For example, if an offender is viewed by a witness, the witness's identification of the offender will be admissible in court, even though the identification is incriminating. The defendant may argue that the act of being viewed by the witness is incriminating, but the courts consider this sort of knowing exposure as beyond constitutional protection.

Although the Fourth Amendment does not apply directly to witness identification procedures, the police must still comply with its probable cause requirement when seizing a suspect for the purposes of identifying him or her. Obviously, if the police want to seize a person so as to obtain fingerprints, a voice exemplar, or some other form of evidence, they are bound by Fourth Amendment restrictions. As noted elsewhere in this book, probable cause is required before the police can seize a person. Assuming a seizure is justified, however, then any real or physical evidence obtained by the arrestee will be admissible.

There may be at least one exception to the Fourth Amendment's probable cause requirement as it pertains to identification. In *Hayes v. Florida*, 470 U.S. 811 (1985), the Court stated:

*Hayes v. Florida*
*(470 U.S. 811 [1985])*

> There is . . . support in our cases for the view that the Fourth Amendment would permit seizures for the purpose of fingerprinting, if there is reasonable suspicion that the suspect has committed a criminal act, if there is a reasonable basis for believing that fingerprinting will establish or negate the suspect's connection with that crime, and if the procedure is carried out with dispatch.

> However, if conducted in the home, such a seizure must be preceded by judicial authorization.

# ▶ Summary: Constitutional Challenges to Witness Identification Procedures

Only two constitutional provisions actually place restrictions on identification procedures: the Fourteenth Amendment's due process clause and the Sixth Amendment's right to counsel clause. The Fifth Amendment, while important to confession law, does not come into play when identification procedures are at issue. Similarly, the Fourth Amendment does not apply to identification procedures directly, but it does apply indirectly insofar as probable cause is required if law enforcement officials plan to seize somebody for the purpose of identifying him or her. See Figure 9.1 for a summary of these issues.

# ▶ Pretrial Identification Techniques

As described earlier, there are three types of pretrial identification techniques: lineups, showups, and photographic arrays. Each of these identification procedures is described in the following section, with particular focus on how the constitutional restrictions already discussed apply to it.

- **Fourth Amendment:** The Fourth Amendment protects from an unlawful search or seizure conducted for the purpose of securing an identification. There is an exception, however: A witness can identify a suspect who is wrongfully seized if the identification is sufficiently independent of the illegal seizure.
- **Fifth Amendment:** Technically, the Fifth Amendment does not apply to identification procedures. This is true even if a suspect is asked to supply a voice exemplar, if this is done for the purpose of identification (and not a confession or admission).
- **Sixth Amendment:** The Sixth Amendment right to counsel exists in the context of making an identification but only in limited circumstances. First, the right to counsel only applies if formal adversarial charges have commenced. Second, a suspect in a photographic array does not enjoy Sixth Amendment protection, regardless of whether charges have been filed.
- **Fourteenth Amendment:** The Fourteenth Amendment's due process clause always applies to identification procedures. In particular, if an identification procedure is too suggestive, it will violate the Fourteenth Amendment.

**FIGURE 9.1 Summary of Constitutional Issues in Identification Procedures**

## Lineups

Suspects may be forced to participate in lineups because lineups exhibit physical characteristics, not testimonial evidence. Suspects placed in lineups may also be required to supply voice exemplars, but solely for identification purposes, not as a confession. If a suspect refuses to participate in a lineup, he or she can be cited with contempt and the prosecutor may comment at trial about the suspect's refusal to cooperate.

### Steps to Minimize Suggestiveness

As noted earlier, the due process clause limits identification procedures. In particular, an overly **suggestive lineup** violates due process. In *United States v. Wade*, 388 U.S. 218 (1967), the Supreme Court noted that a lineup becomes suggestive when, for instance,

> all in the lineup but the suspect were known to the identifying witness, . . . the other participants in a lineup were grossly dissimilar in appearance to the suspect, . . . only the suspect was required to wear distinctive clothing which the culprit allegedly wore, . . . the suspect is pointed out before or during a lineup, and ... the participants in the lineup are asked to try on an article of clothing which fits only the suspect.

The Project on Law Enforcement Policy and Rulemaking proposes several guidelines for minimizing suggestiveness in a police lineup:

- The lineup should consist of at least five people, including the suspect.
- The persons in the lineup should have similar physical characteristics.
- The suspect should be permitted to choose his or her place in line.
- Each person in the lineup should be required to take whatever specialized action is required (to utter certain words).
- The persons in the lineup should be warned to conduct themselves such that the suspect does not stand out.
- A lineup should be photographed or videotaped.[2]

---

[2]From Project on Law Enforcement Policy and Rulemaking, "Eyewitness Identification," *Model Rules for Law Enforcement* (Tempe, AZ: Arizona State University, 1974).

The International Association of Chiefs of Police (IACP) Legal Center has recommended similar guidelines:

- A lineup should consist of five to six people.
- Each participant in the lineup must sign the appropriate waiver form, unless his or her counsel is present.
- Everyone in the lineup should be of the same sex and race, approximately the same age, and approximately the same height, weight, coloring, build, and so on.
- Everyone in the lineup should wear approximately the same clothing.
- The accused should be placed in the lineup at random, so as not to stand out.
- Persons known to the witness should not be placed in the lineup.
- Private citizens participating in the lineup (if insufficient numbers of prisoners are available) should sign a written consent form indicating they are aware that no charges have been filed against them, that they are free to leave at any time, and so on.
- Each witness should view the lineup separately so one witness does not unduly influence another in his or her identification of the perpetrator.
- Each participant in the lineup should be given the same instructions and should perform the same acts (supply a voice exemplar).
- Participants in the lineup should be instructed not to make any statements or comments unless ordered to do so.
- Frontal and side-profile photographs of the lineup should be taken.
- A single officer should oversee the lineup procedure.
- A written waiver of counsel should be obtained if the suspect waives his or her Sixth Amendment right to have counsel present at a *postindictment lineup*.[3]

An important restriction concerning lineups is that people cannot be indiscriminately picked off the street for participation. If a person is *not* already in custody, the police must have reasonable suspicion that he or she has committed the crime in question (see *Hayes v. Florida*). However, if the person *is* in custody prior to the lineup, then he or she can be forced to stand in a lineup without any judicial authorization (see *United States v. Anderson*, 490 F.2d 785 [D.C. Cir. 1974]).

## Showups

A *showup* is a one-on-one confrontation between the victim and the offender, usually conducted outside the courtroom setting. Specifically, a showup is usually held when the suspect has been apprehended shortly after having committed the crime and the witness is still at or near the scene of the crime. A lineup is always preferable to a showup because a lineup includes several potential suspects, and a showup is usually unnecessarily suggestive. However, a showup is necessary under certain circumstances.

For example, when a witness is immobile and cannot be present at a lineup, a showup is an effective alternative. In *Stovall v. Denno*, 388 U.S. 293 (1967), the Supreme Court noted, "Faced with the responsibility for identifying the attacker, with the need for immediate action and with the knowledge that [the victim] could not visit the jail, the police followed the only feasible procedure and took [the accused] to the hospital room." In a similar vein, a showup is preferable when the *suspect* is immobile.

---

[3]International Association of Chiefs of Police, "Eyewitness Identification," in *Legal Points* (Gaithersburg, MD: IACP Legal Center, 1975).

▼

A showup is sometimes desirable to facilitate prompt identification when time is of the essence. If the witness is required to wait for a lineup, for instance, misidentification is more likely to result as the witness's memory fades. A showup conducted more than 60 minutes after the crime, however, will usually not be upheld (see *United States v. Perry*, 449 F.2d 1026 [D.C. Cir. 1971]). But in at least one case, the Supreme Court upheld a stationhouse showup in which no emergency existed. In *Neil v. Biggers*, 409 U.S. 188 (1972), the Court sanctioned an arranged one-on-one showup, even though it took place well after the point at which the crime in question was committed. The Court noted that there was "no substantial likelihood of misidentification" because the witness had an opportunity to view the suspect for almost 30 minutes, under good lighting, prior to the showup.

*Neil v. Biggers*
*(409 U.S. 188 [1972])*

The same constitutional provisions that govern lineups also govern showups. Specifically, the Sixth Amendment right to counsel applies, but only after adversarial proceedings have commenced (see *Moore v. Illinois*, 434 U.S. 220 [1977]). Due process protections also exist—if the showup is unnecessarily suggestive under a totality of circumstances analysis, then any identification that comes from it will not be admissible in court.

## In-Court Showups

Occasionally, a witness will identify the accused for the first time in *court*, which is referred to as an **in-court showup**. The key feature of an in-court showup is that the witness has *not* identified the suspect, either in a lineup or related procedure, prior to trial. Such identifications are highly suggestive because the suspect has already been identified by virtue of having been named as a defendant in the case.

The leading case dealing with in-court showups is *Moore v. Illinois*, 434 U.S. 220 (1977). Although the focus of the case was on the preliminary hearing, not the trial, the Court's

*Moore v. Illinois*
*(434 U.S. 220 [1977])*

---

### DECISION-MAKING EXERCISE 9.2

#### ALTERING THE SUSPECT'S APPEARANCE

On December 24, the Toy Emporium was robbed. The suspect escaped before security guards and police could capture him, but store security cameras and several witnesses indicated that the crime was committed by a white male who was 6 feet, 3 inches tall, approximately 270 pounds, between 25 and 30 years of age, wearing a green trench coat, and having long hair. Two hours after the robbery, a man was arrested in a nearby town because he fit the general description of the robber. However, he was bald and wearing a brown trench coat. A lineup was conducted, in which the suspect was required to wear a wig resembling the long hair of the perpetrator. He was positively identified by several witnesses. Does the act of requiring the suspect to alter his appearance conform to constitutional requirements?

---

### DECISION-MAKING EXERCISE 9.3

#### WHAT CONSTITUTES A VALID SHOWUP?

The police believe that Anna Delgado was involved in a hit-and-run car accident in which a man was killed. They do not have the reasonable suspicion required to seize Delgado for appearance in a lineup, but they do have a witness to the accident. The police decide to take the witness to Delgado's place of work to make an identification. Delgado is identified at her place of employment. Is this type of showup valid?

---

decision would be expected to apply to criminal trials, as well as other adversarial proceedings. Here are the facts from that case, as described by the Supreme Court:

> After petitioner had been arrested for rape and related offenses, he was identified by the complaining witness as her assailant at the ensuing preliminary hearing, during which petitioner was not represented by counsel nor offered appointed counsel. The victim had been asked to make an identification after being told that she was going to view a suspect, after being told his name and having heard it called as he was led before the bench, and after having heard the prosecutor recite the evidence believed to implicate petitioner. Subsequently, petitioner was indicted, and counsel was appointed, who moved to suppress the victim's identification of petitioner. The Illinois trial court denied the motion on the ground that the prosecution had shown an independent basis for the victim's identification. At trial, the victim testified on direct examination by the prosecution that she had identified petitioner as her assailant at the preliminary hearing, and there was certain other evidence linking petitioner to the crimes. He was convicted and the Illinois Supreme Court affirmed.

Notwithstanding the clear violation of the Sixth Amendment in this case (which the Supreme Court also pointed out), the Court pointed to the suggestiveness that occurs when a witness identifies a suspect for the first time at a formal hearing:

> It is difficult to imagine a more suggestive manner in which to present a suspect to a witness for their critical first confrontation than was employed in this case. The victim who had seen her assailant for only 10 to 15 seconds, was asked to make her identification after she was told that she was going to view a suspect, after she was told his name and heard it called as he was led before the bench, and after she heard the prosecutor recite the evidence believed to implicate petitioner. Had petitioner been represented by counsel, some or all of this suggestiveness could have been avoided.

What message is to be gleaned from *Moore*? In general, law enforcement officials should have witnesses identify suspects via lineups, showups, or photographic arrays *prior* to the point at which adversarial proceedings commence. Any of these identification procedures would result in a less suggestive identification than would be likely at trial. Clearly, though, lineups, showups, and photographic arrays can also be suggestive.

## Photographic Identifications

The last type of identification procedure to be considered in this text is the photographic identification array. It involves displaying a picture of the suspect along with those of several other people to a victim or witness for the purpose of identification.

Photographic identification procedures approximate real-life lineups by including several people, but they are not subjected to the same constitutional restrictions that lineups are. In particular, there is no Sixth Amendment right to counsel during a photographic identification. However, due process protections *do* apply.

---

**DECISION-MAKING EXERCISE 9.4**

**MAKING A VALID IDENTIFICATION**

Wilma Hobbes was unable to identify the man suspected of raping her, even after the police presented her with a photographic array *and* a lineup. Some weeks later, in a chance encounter while walking through the local courthouse, Wilma passed a person whom she believed was her rapist. He was subsequently arrested, and she identified him at the trial. Should this identification be considered valid?

To minimize due process problems, several photographs of like individuals should be shown to the witness or victim so as to minimize unnecessary suggestiveness. In *Simmons v. United States*, 390 U.S. 377 (1968), the Supreme Court shed some light on the importance of a carefully constructed photographic array:

*Simmons v. United States*
*(390 U.S. 377 [1968])*

> Despite the hazards of initial identification by photograph, this procedure has been used widely and effectively in criminal law enforcement, from the standpoint both of apprehending offenders and of sparing innocent suspects the ignominy of arrest by allowing eyewitnesses to exonerate them through scrutiny of photographs. The danger that use of the technique may result in convictions based on misidentification may be substantially lessened by a course of cross-examination at trial which exposes to the jury the method's potential for error. We are unwilling to prohibit its employment, either in the exercise of our supervisory power or, still less, as a matter of constitutional requirement. Instead, we hold that each case must be considered on its own facts, and that convictions based on eyewitness identification at trial following a pretrial identification by photograph will be set aside on that ground only if the photographic identification procedure was so impermissibly suggestive as to give rise to a very substantial likelihood of irreparable misidentification.

To conform to due process requirements, multiple photographs of like individuals are ideal. However, in one case, the Supreme Court sanctioned an identification based on only one picture. In *Manson v. Braithwaite*, 432 U.S. 98 (1977), the Court permitted an in-court identification based on an earlier identification from a single photograph because it was reliable based on the totality of circumstances. In particular, the Court described how Glover, the witness, who was also a police officer, arrived at his conclusion that the suspect (the "vendor" of illegal drugs) in the photograph was, in fact, the perpetrator. Here are the criteria on which the Court focused:

1. *The opportunity to view.* Glover testified that for two to three minutes he stood at the apartment door, within two feet of the respondent. The door opened twice, and each time the man stood at the door. The moments passed, the conversation took place, and payment was made. Glover looked directly at his vendor. It was near sunset, to be sure, but the sun had not yet set, so it was not dark or even dusk or twilight. Natural light from outside entered the hallway through a window. There was natural light, as well, from inside the apartment.

2. *The degree of attention.* Glover was not a casual or passing observer, as is so often the case with eyewitness identification. Trooper Glover was a trained police officer on duty—and specialized and dangerous duty—when he called at the third floor of 201 Westland in Hartford on May 5, 1970. . . . It is true that Glover's duty was that of ferreting out narcotics offenders and that he would be expected in his work to produce results. But it is also true that, as a specially trained, assigned, and experienced officer, he could be expected to pay scrupulous attention to detail, for he knew that subsequently he would have to find and arrest his vendor. In addition, he knew that his claimed observations would be subject later to close scrutiny and examination at any trial.

3. *The accuracy of the description.* Glover's description was given to D'Onofrio [a backup officer] within minutes after the transaction. It included the vendor's race, his height, his build, the color and style of his hair, and the high cheekbone facial feature. It also included clothing the vendor wore. No claim has been made that respondent did not possess the physical characteristics so described. D'Onofrio reacted positively at once. Two days later, when Glover was alone, he viewed the photograph D'Onofrio produced and identified its subject as the narcotics seller.

4. *The witness's level of certainty.* There is no dispute that the photograph in question was that of respondent.

5. *The time between the crime and the identification.* Glover's description of his vendor was given to D'Onofrio within minutes of the crime. The photographic identification took place only two days later. We do not have here the passage of weeks or months between the crime and the viewing of the photograph.

Taken together, these five considerations led the Court to this conclusion:

These indicators of Glover's ability to make an accurate identification are hardly outweighed by the corrupting effect of the challenged identification itself. Although identifications arising from single-photograph displays may be viewed in general with suspicion, see *Simmons v. United States*, 390 U.S., at 383, we find in the instant case little pressure on the witness to acquiesce in the suggestion that such a display entails. D'Onofrio had left the photograph at Glover's office and was not present when Glover first viewed it two days after the event. There thus was little urgency and Glover could view the photograph at his leisure. And since Glover examined the photograph alone, there was no coercive pressure to make an identification arising from the presence of another. The identification was made in circumstances allowing care and reflection.

The *Manson* decision suggests that single-photograph identifications are constitutionally permissible, but it must be emphasized that the witness in this case was a police officer and that the facts were somewhat unusual. It is doubtful that the Supreme Court would uphold a similar identification today, and it is always preferable to place multiple pictures of like individuals in a photographic array.

Figure 9.2 shows the Gallatin, Tennessee, Police Department's policy for the use of showups, lineups, and photographic arrays, which summarizes many of the points made so far.

---

**9.29 Showup, Lineup, and Photographic Identification**

*9.29.1 Showup*

A showup is the presentation of a suspect to an eyewitness a short time after the commission of a crime. Many courts have suppressed evidence from a showup due to the inherent suggestiveness of the event. Because of this, a lineup is preferred over a showup when possible. However, when exigent circumstances require the use of a showup, the following guidelines will be used:

1. A showup will not be conducted when the suspect is in a cell, restrained, or dressed in jail clothing;
2. A showup will not be conducted with more than one witness present at a time. Witnesses will not be allowed to communicate with each other regarding the identification of the suspect;
3. The same suspect will not be presented to the same witness more than once;
4. The suspect will not be required to put on clothing worn by the perpetrator, speak words uttered by the perpetrator, or perform other actions of the perpetrator; and
5. Officers will not say or do anything that might suggest to the witness that the suspect is or may be the perpetrator.

*9.29.2 Photographic Identification*

In conducting a photographic identification, an officer must use multiple photographs shown individually to a witness or simultaneously in a book or array. Additionally,

**FIGURE 9.2 Lineup, Showup, and Photographic Array Policy (Gallatin, TN, Police Department)**

▼

an officer will adhere to the following guidelines when conducting a photographic identification:

1. Use at least six photographs of individuals who are reasonably similar in age, height, weight, and general appearance and of the same sex and race;
2. Whenever possible, avoid mixing color and black and white photos, use photos of the same size and basic composition, and never mix mug shots with other snapshots or include more than one photo of the same suspect;
3. Cover any portions of mug shots or other photographs that provide identifying information on the subject, and similarly cover those used in the array;
4. Show the photo array to only one witness at a time;
5. Never make suggestive statements that may influence the judgement or perception of the witness; and
6. Preserve the photo array, together with full information about the identification process, for future reference.

### 9.29.3 Lineup

A lineup is the live presentation of at least five individuals to a victim. In conducting a lineup, an officer will schedule the lineup on a date and at a time that is convenient for all concerned parties. Additionally, the officer must fulfill necessary legal requirements for the transfer of a subject to the lineup location should he/she be incarcerated at a detention center; make timely notice to the detention center concerning the pickup; and make arrangements for picking up the prisoner. Finally, the officer must make arrangements to have at least four other persons act as "fill ins" at the lineup who are of the same race, sex, and approximate height, weight, age, and physical appearance and who are similarly clothed.

The officer in charge of conducting the lineup will ensure that the following requirements are adhered to:

1. Ensure that the prisoner has been informed of his/her right to counsel if formal charges have been made against him/her, and also ensure that he/she has the opportunity to retain counsel or request that one be provided;
2. Obtain a written waiver on the prescribed departmental form should the prisoner waive his/her right to counsel;
3. Allow counsel representing the accused an opportunity to observe the manner in which the lineup is conducted;
4. Advise the accused that he/she may take any position in the lineup which he/she prefers and may change positions prior to summoning a new witness;
5. Ensure that all persons in the lineup are numbered consecutively and are referred to only by number;
6. Ensure that a complete written, audio, and video record of the lineup proceedings are made and retained when possible;
7. Ensure that witnesses are not permitted to see nor are they to be shown any photographs of the accused immediately prior to the lineup;
8. Ensure that not more than one witness views the lineup at a time and that they are not permitted to speak with one another during lineup proceedings; and
9. Scrupulously avoid using statements, clues, casual comments, or providing unnecessary or irrelevant information that in any manner may influence the witnesses' decision-making process or perception.

*Source:* From *General Directives Manual*, Gallatin, Tennessee, Police Department (December 28, 1999). Used courtesy of the Gallatin Police Department.

**FIGURE 9.2** *Continued*

# ▶ Identification Procedures: Flaws and Fixes

Nearly every suspect identification procedure can be flawed in some fashion, some more than others. Consider showups. No matter what steps police take to ensure fairness, showups are prone to mistaken identification. And the consequences of mistaken identification can be serious:

> Billy Wayne Miller was asleep in a back bedroom of his father's modest Oak Cliff home when three Dallas police officers burst through the front door around 3 A.M., guns in hand, yelling another man's name. Still groggy and clad only in his underwear, Mr. Miller was taken to the front porch. There he spotted a woman in a squad car glance at him and nod to an officer seated beside her before the car drove away. That split-second, one-man lineup cost Mr. Miller 22 years of his life on a rape conviction that DNA evidence later invalidated.[4]

Stories like Billy Wayne Miller's could be less common if authorities relied exclusively on lineups and photographic identification procedures. However, even lineups can be flawed. And so can photographic arrays. The Innocence Project, an organization that works to exonerate wrongfully convicted inmates, claims that "eyewitness misidentification is the single greatest cause of wrongful convictions nationwide."[5] The organization highlights some situations in which lineups and photographic procedures led to wrongful convictions:

- A witness in a rape case was shown a photo array where only one photo—of the person police suspected was the perpetrator—was marked with an "R."
- Witnesses substantially changed their description of a perpetrator (including key information such as height, weight, and presence of facial hair) after they learned more about a particular suspect.
- Witnesses only made an identification after multiple photo arrays or lineups—and then made hesitant identifications (saying they "thought" the person "might be" the perpetrator, for example), but at trial the jury was told the witnesses did not waver in identifying the suspect.[6]

---

### DECISION-MAKING EXERCISE 9.5

#### CREATING A VALID PHOTOGRAPHIC ARRAY

A rapist tells each of his victims that he has already been imprisoned for rape. His latest victim, Sandy, tells the police what he said. The police then show Sandy a single photograph of a rape suspect who was previously imprisoned. Sandy identifies the man in the photo as her rapist. Is this photographic array constitutional? Next, assume that the rapist does not tell his victims he has previously been imprisoned and that the police place his photo in a photographic array with the photos of two other individuals. Is this procedure appropriate? What if five photos are shown: three of the rapist (each from different points in time, with different clothes and hair styles) and one each of the other two individuals?

---

### DECISION-MAKING EXERCISE 9.6

#### THE PHOTO ARRAY REVISITED

Consider again the scenario in Exercise 9.5. What if the police tell the second witness who the first witness identified, then tell the third witness who the first and second witnesses identified, and so on? What if, instead, the police show five different photographic arrays to a single witness, but the suspected rapist appears once in each array?

---

4S. McGonigle and J. Emily, "DNA Exoneree Fell Victim to 'Drive-by' Identification," *Dallas Morning News*, October 13, 2008: http://www.public.iastate.edu/~nscentral/mr/08/1017/exoneration.html (accessed May 10, 2013).
5http://www.innocenceproject.org/understand/Eyewitness-Misidentification.php (accessed May 10, 2013).
6Ibid.

CHAPTER 9   Identification Procedures and the Role of Witnesses   262
▼

Some might take issue with the Innocence Project's arguments, but many researchers have also found that identification procedures can be problematic—so much so that in May of 1998, then U.S. attorney general Janet Reno organized a working group of prosecutors, defense attorneys, police officers, and other experts who were tasked with creating a set of "best practices" for identification procedures. The working group's findings were echoed in an article published by a group of psychologists at around the same time. They identified "four simple rules of procedure that follow from the scientific literature that we argue could largely relieve the criminal justice system of its role in contributing to eyewitness identification problems."[7] The rules were:

- The person who conducts the lineup or photospread should not be aware of which member of the lineup or photospread is the suspect.

- Eyewitnesses should be told explicitly that the person in question might not be in the lineup or photospread and therefore should not feel that they must make an identification. They should also be told that the person administering the lineup does not know which person is the suspect in the case.

- The suspect should not stand out in the lineup or photospread as being different from the distractors based on the eyewitness's previous description of the culprit or based on other factors that would draw extra attention to the suspect.

- A clear statement should be taken from the eyewitness at the time of the identification and prior to any feedback as to his or her confidence that the identified person is the actual culprit.[8]

## Double-Blind Lineups

When the investigator conducting a lineup knows who the suspect is, he or she can unintentionally (and even intentionally) influence the witness and thereby taint the identification procedure. For example, the investigator may say to the witness, "Why don't you take another look at number three" (the suspect is in the number three position in a lineup). Clearly this comment could sway the witness in the direction the investigator prefers.

A **double-blind lineup** is one in which the investigator conducting the lineup (or assembling a photo array) does not know who the suspect is. This helps ensure that the investigator will not lead the witness in a particular direction. Studies have shown that double-blind procedures reduce the risks of mistaken identifications.[9] Here is a summary of the findings from one of the most recent studies in this area:

> Administrator knowledge had the greatest effect on identifications of the suspect for simultaneous photospreads paired with biased instructions, with single-blind administrations increasing identifications of the suspect. When biased instructions were given, single-blind administrations produced fewer foil identifications than double-blind administrations. Administrators exhibited a greater proportion of biasing behaviors during single-blind administrations than during double-blind administrations.[10]

---

[7]G. L. Wells, M. Small, S. Penrod, R. S. Malpass, S. M. Fulero, and C. A. E. Brimacombe, "Eyewitness Identification Procedures: Recommendations for Lineups and Photospreads," *Law and Human Behavior* 22 (1998): 603–647.

[8]Ibid., pp. 627–635.

[9]See, S. M. Greathouse and M. B. Kovera, "Instruction Bias and Lineup Presentation Moderate the Effects of Administrator Knowledge on Eyewitness Identification," *Law and Human Behavior* 33 (2009): 70–82; R. M. Haw and R. P. Fisher, "Effects of Administrator-Witness Contact on Eyewitness Identification Accuracy," *Journal of Applied Psychology* 89 (2004): 1106–1112; M. B. Russano, J. J. Dickinson, S. M. Greathouse, and M. B. Kovera, "Why Don't You Take Another Look at Number Three: Investigator Knowledge and Its Effects on Eyewitness Confidence and Identification Decisions," *Cardozo Public Law, Policy, and Ethics Journal* 4 (2006): 355–379.

[10]Greathouse and Kovera, p. 70.

**MISTAKEN IDENTIFICATION?**

Janice Bolan, a rape victim, was examined at a hospital and a rape kit was used to collect DNA evidence. No sperm cells were identified in the first examination of the swabs. Bolan then gave police a description of her attacker, saying he was an African American male between 25 and 30 years of age, approximately 6 feet tall, and had a beard. She then helped officers create a sketch of the perpetrator, which was circulated throughout the community. A week later, police received a call that a man fitting the description was working in a nearby grocery store. Police took Bolan to the store and asked if the man, Dean Cage, was her attacker. She answered yes. Police then conducted a lineup at the police station. Once again, Bolan identified Cage as her attacker. Cage was arrested and convicted in a bench trial, after she testified in court that she was "100 percent sure" Cage was the rapist—and pointed to him in court. Is there anything wrong with these events?

## Virtual Officer Lineups

Despite their increased reliability, double-blind lineups are often not used because they demand greater resources to implement. A double-blind lineup requires at least two investigators instead of the usual one—one to know the identity of the suspect and another to administer the lineup without knowing the suspect's real identity. One solution to this problem is to use a "virtual officer" to conduct the procedure.[11] One team of researchers has gone so far as to develop software in which a virtual officer (called "Officer Garcia") conducts a photographic array. Because the virtual officer does not know the identity of the suspect or his or her placement in the array, the procedure is not susceptible to investigator influence. A "YouTube" demonstration of this procedure is available online.[12]

## ▶ Identification During Trial

Often, a witness will be called on to identify the perpetrator of a crime (usually, the defendant) *during* the trial. Sometimes, this process is straightforward and subject to little dispute by either party to the case. Other times, an in-court identification can be tainted by a previous out-of-court identification. (This problem is discussed in the exclusionary rule section toward the end of this chapter.) To better understand this issue, it is useful to examine the process of questioning witnesses at trial.

A criminal trial is a carefully choreographed event, in which each party—the defense and the prosecution—has the right to ask questions as well as attack the credibility or believability of a witness's testimony. The state has the burden of persuasion, so that party presents its case first. During the state's case-in-chief, the prosecutor calls all his or her witnesses and presents the evidence required to build the case. When the state rests, then the defense has its turn.

Although this description seems simple, the process of examining witnesses is much more complex. The following discussion will shed light on this often confusing aspect of criminal procedure.

---

[11]O. H. MacLin, L. A. Zimmerman, and R. S. Malpass, "PC-Eyewitness and the Sequential Superiority Effect: Computer-Based Lineup Administration," *Law and Human Behavior* 29 (2005): 303–321.

[12]http://www.youtube.com/watch?v=SEhcLQmwtjQ (accessed November 4, 2008).

A witness is often called on to identify a suspect at trial.

## Refreshing a Witness's Memory

Witnesses frequently forget the facts to which they are supposed to testify, particularly if a great deal of time has passed between the event and the date of the in-court testimony. To remedy this problem, the *Federal Rules of Evidence* state that a witness's memory of a prior experience may be *refreshed* by referring the witness to his or her prior statements.[13] Of course, if a witness has no memory whatsoever of the event, then he or she is not competent to testify to that event. However, if a refresher is all that is needed, then the examining party should be able to remind the witness of what he or she said in the past.

Under the rules of evidence, refreshing a witness's memory may be accomplished through one of two methods: (1) present memory revived and (2) past memory recorded. With regard to *present memory revived*, the in-court testimony of the witness is the evidence. By contrast, in *past memory recorded*, a written account is the evidence, not the witness's in-court testimony.

In the first method, *present memory revived*, a witness's present memory is revived when, for example, he or she is asked to refer to records or other written documents. After the witness views the documents and has his or her memory refreshed, his or her statement to this effect is admitted as evidence. The documents shown to the witness are not read or shown to the jury because the *documents themselves* are not evidence, only the witness's testimony. Assume, for example, that a witness to a car accident is asked whether she remembers the license plate number of the car that sped away from the scene. She replies that she is uncertain but may be able to recall the number if she can consult some notes she wrote on the day she witnessed the car leaving the scene. If the witness is permitted to rely on her notes and she then remembers the license plate number, then she will be permitted to testify to this effect under a theory of present memory revived.

---

[13]Ibid., Rule 612.

**IDENTIFY THE LEADING QUESTIONS**

What follows are several hypothetical questions that a prosecutor would ask a witness. Decide whether each is a leading question: (1) "Is the man who assaulted you in the courtroom today?" (2) "Could you point to the man who assaulted you?" (3) "Isn't the man who assaulted you sitting in this courtroom today?" (4) "Isn't that the man who assaulted you?" (5) "Isn't it true that the man who assaulted you is sitting right there?"

In the second method, *past recollection recorded*, it is the recording itself that is admitted into evidence. That is, the jury is allowed to consider the document as opposed to the witness's testimony. The written document essentially becomes a substitute for the witness's memory.

Certain requirements must be met before documents offered through the past recollection recorded method will be admitted into evidence. First, the witness must testify that he or she had personal knowledge of the facts at one time. Second, the witness must testify that the recording was accurate. Third, the witness must testify that he or she does not have adequate recollection of the facts such that he or she could testify to them in court. In addition, the trial judge must be satisfied with the document in order for it to be admissible into evidence. Finally, once a past recollection recorded has been admitted into evidence, the opposing side should have the opportunity to view the document (see *United States v. Kelly*, 349 F.2d 720 [2nd Cir. 1965]; *People v. Banks*, 50 Mich. App. 622 [1974]).

## Witness Credibility

**Credibility** pertains to whether the witness's testimony should be believed. In other words, can the witness's statements be judged as truthful? If the witness is able to remember events, communicate clearly to the jury, and come across as convincing, he or she will probably be regarded as credible. *Credibility* should be distinguished from **competence**, which pertains to a witness's ability to remember events, communicate effectively, and understand the importance of telling the truth, as well as the consequences of not doing so.

When discussing competence, courts often refer to the processes of **accrediting** and **discrediting**. A witness can be *discredited* when the prosecution or defense challenges his or her credibility. The process of *accrediting* is the opposite, or when the prosecution or defense attempts to support, bolster, or improve a witness's credibility.

It is important to note that specific rules govern the processes of accrediting and discrediting. First, it is universally agreed that unless a witness's credibility has been attacked, no evidence may be introduced to support or bolster his or her credibility. According to the court in *United States v. Price*, 722 F.2d 88 (5th Cir. 1983), "[T]here is no reason why time should be spent in proving that which may be assumed to exist. Every witness must be assumed to be of normal moral character for veracity, just as he is assumed to be of normal sanity." Simply put, a witness generally cannot be *accredited* until someone, whether the prosecution or the defense, attempts to *discredit* him or her.

Although a witness may not be accredited without a prior attempt to discredit, a witness may be asked introductory questions, such as asking the witness to introduce himself or herself and describe his or her background. The prosecution or defense may also ask direct questions about the witness's familiarity with the case or, in the case of an expert witness, questions about the witness's occupation, background, and professional accomplishments. This type of questioning would appear to be accrediting, but a certain amount of background information can be supplied by introductory questions without it being considered accreditation. However, there is a point where accrediting must stop, absent an attack on the witness's credibility. Unfortunately, there are few clear rules as to what amount of accrediting background information is permissible. According to the court in *Government of Virgin Islands v. Grant*, 938 F.2d 401 (1985):

> The jurisprudence of "background" evidence is essentially undeveloped. "Background" or "preliminary" evidence is not mentioned in the evidence codes, nor has it received attention in the treatises. One justification for its admission, at least in terms of the background of a witness qua witness, is that it may establish absence of bias or motive by showing the witness's relationship (or non-relationship) to the parties or to the case.

It is safe to conclude, though, that when the introduction process turns to aggrandizing—that is, into more than an introduction—the accrediting of a witness must stop.

In one interesting case, *Pointer v. State*, 74 So.2d 615 (Ala. Ct. App. 1954), the prosecutor, during his closing statement, said that if the prosecution witness had been of bad character, the issue would have been raised by the defense. The court reversed the ensuing conviction, holding that because there was no attack on the witness's credibility during trial, the prosecutor was not permitted to bolster the witness's credibility.

A controversial issue with regard to accrediting concerns what can be done to bolster a witness's credibility when he or she cannot remember important events. If, for example, a witness testifies to a series of events but states that she is unable to remember everything, may another witness be called to offer reasons for the woman's memory lapse? A question similar to this was raised in *United States v. Awkward*, 597 F.2d 667 (9th Cir.), *cert. denied*, 444 U.S. 885 (1979). In that case, the Ninth Circuit Court of Appeals ruled that the prosecution could not have a witness testify that he had been hypnotized, and could not call an expert who had hypnotized the witness to testify about the effects of hypnosis on him or her. As the court observed:

> [U]nless an adverse party attacks the witness's ability to recall by bringing out or exploring the fact of hypnosis, the use of expert testimony to support the efficacy of hypnosis is improper. The party calling a witness should not be permitted to inquire in any way into the witness's ability to recall, or methods of pretrial memory refreshment, until such questions have been raised by the adversary.

In sum, witness accrediting is permissible, but usually "only after the character of the witness for truthfulness has been attacked by opinion or reputation evidence or otherwise" (*Blake v. Cich*, 79 F.R.D. 398 [D. Minn. 1978]). In legal parlance, accrediting of this sort is also known as *witness rehabilitation* (which is addressed following the discussion of impeachment, below). Note, however, that this limit on accrediting is not recognized in most modern evidence statutes, except with regard to character evidence. That is, most modern statutes do not allow accrediting of a witness's character but remain silent as to other types of accrediting.[14]

## Impeachment

Attacking a witness's credibility is referred to as **impeachment**. When faced with a witness whose credibility may be questionable, the prosecution or defense may decide to challenge the witness's credibility before the jury. The jury will then draw its own conclusions as to the witness's truthfulness and believability.

---

[14]Ibid., Rule 608(a)(2).

1. Establish bias or prejudice.
2. Point to prior convictions.
3. Allege uncharged crimes and immoral acts.
4. Identify contradictions and prior inconsistent statements.
5. Suggest inability to observe events.
6. Challenge reputation.

**FIGURE 9.3 Methods of Witness Impeachment**

Impeachment is most often used during cross-examination, when the adverse party has the opportunity to ask questions of a witness who has just testified. The prosecution or the defense can attack a witness's credibility for a number of different, well-established reasons (see Figure 9.3). However, there is little value in attempting to impeach a witness if his or her testimony does not carry much weight or is unpersuasive to the jury. Alternatively, if there is no basis for an attack on a witness's credibility but the opposing side attempts to do so anyway, the impeachment effort could backfire.

## Rehabilitation

When the credibility of a witness is attacked, the side that produced the witness can take steps to bolster his or her credibility, either by calling other witnesses or introducing other evidence. This process is known as rehabilitation. Rehabilitation occurs during redirect examination, which follows cross-examination. For example, assume the defense calls a witness. The defense attorney will question the witness in an effort to absolve the defendant of guilt. If the prosecution sees fit to impeach the defense witness and succeeds in doing so, the defense attorney will work to rehabilitate its witness during the redirect examination stage.

In discussing the importance of rehabilitation, one court observed that "it is well recognized that once a witness's credibility has been attacked, whether it be by the introduction of evidence of bad reputation, conviction of crime, inconsistent statements, evidence of misconduct, or by incisive cross-examination, the party calling the witness has a right to present evidence designed to rehabilitate the witness's credibility" (*State v. Bowden*, 439 A.2d 263 [R.I. 1982]).

Three common approaches are used to rehabilitate witnesses. The first is to argue that the witness was untruthful in the past but is telling the truth now. Perhaps the witness was once a deceptive miscreant but has been reformed to the extent that he or she can now be trusted. Second, the party seeking to rehabilitate its own witness may argue that a contradictory or inconsistent statement alluded to by the other side was taken out of context. For example, suppose that part of a police report is used to impeach an officer who is giving testimony. The party seeking to rehabilitate the officer may then introduce other portions of the police report that shed light on the part used to impeach the officer (see *Short v. United States*, 271 F.2d 73 [9th Cir. 1959]).

A third way to rehabilitate a witness is to introduce other evidence to bolster his or her credibility. For example, suppose that a witness makes a statement *prior* to trial that contradicts his or her statement *at* trial. The other side may then elect to introduce additional pretrial statements supportive of his or her statements at trial. Recall the infamous O. J. Simpson case when Detective Mark Fuhrman was impeached by the defense because he had made racially discriminatory statements in the past. Had the prosecution called other police witnesses to testify as to Fuhrman's objectivity with regard to race, their testimony may have rehabilitated Fuhrman as a witness.

Given the importance of witness identification, it is useful to know how to be a good witness to criminal activity as well as a good in-court witness. This information is provided in Figures 9.4 and 9.5, respectively.

1. Try to remember the basics:
   a. *Who* was the person?
   b. *What* did he or she do?
   c. *When* and *where* did he or she do this?
2. Was the offender an acquaintance or a stranger? Would you recognize the offender if you saw him or her again?
3. Pay attention to details: Was the offender male or female? What race or ethnicity was he or she? What was his or her approximate age? Height? Weight? Body build? Hair color and length? Any distinguishing features? What clothes was he or she wearing? Was he or she wearing a coat? Hat? Glasses? Did he or she have any weapons? What car was he or she driving, if any? What was the license plate number? What were the make, model, and color of the car? Features of the vehicle?
4. What did the offender say? What did he or she do? How did he or she act? Was anyone injured?
5. Where is the offender, or where did he or she go? How did he or she leave? How long ago did this happen?

**FIGURE 9.4 Tips for Being a Good Witness to Criminal Activity**

1. Jurors and other witnesses may be present in the same public areas as you. For that reason, you should not discuss the case with anyone. In addition, jurors may have the opportunity to observe how you act outside of the courtroom. If you see a juror, you are not allowed to speak to the juror, even to say hello.
2. When you are called to testify, you will first be sworn in. You will be asked to raise your right hand and place your left hand on the Bible. When you take the oath, pay attention to the clerk, and say "I do" clearly.
3. When a witness gives testimony, he/she is first asked some questions by the lawyer calling him or her to the stand; in your case, this is an Assistant U.S. Attorney. This is called "direct examination." Then, the witness is questioned by the opposing lawyer (the defense counsel) in "cross examination." (Sometimes the process is repeated two or three times to help clear up any confusion.) The basic purpose of direct examination is for you to tell the judge and jury what you know about the case. The basic purpose of cross-examination is to explore the accuracy of your testimony. Don't get mad if you feel you are being doubted in cross examination. DO NOT LOSE YOUR TEMPER. An angry or impolite witness will probably not be believed. Always be polite and courteous. In Grand Jury, there is NOT any cross-examination because the defense is not present.
4. Objection is a legal term that means one of the attorneys feels you are being asked an improper question. When you hear a lawyer say "objection", simply stop speaking and wait for the judge to rule on the objection. If the judge decides the question is proper, he/she will overrule the objection. If the judge decides the question is not proper, he/she will sustain the objection. You may not answer the question if it has been sustained. You will be told by the judge or the attorney whether to answer the question if you get confused. In Grand Jury, there are NOT any objections because the defense is not present.
5. Before you testify, try to picture the scene, the objects there, the distances, and exactly what happened so that you can recall the facts more accurately when you are asked. If the question is about distances or time, and if your answer is only an estimate, be sure to say it is only an estimate. Beware of suggestions by attorneys as to distances or times when you do not recall the actual time or distance. Do not agree with their estimate unless you independently arrive at the same estimate.
6. Speak in your own words. Don't try to memorize what you are going to say. Doing so will make your testimony sound rehearsed and unconvincing. Instead, be yourself, and prior to trial go over in your own mind those matters about which you will be questioned.

**FIGURE 9.5 Tips for Testifying in Federal Court**

7. Most important of all, you are sworn to TELL THE TRUTH. Tell it. Every true fact should be readily admitted. Do not stop to figure out whether your answer will help or hurt either side. You are expected to be impartial.

8. The judge and jury are interested in facts that you have observed or personally know about. Do not give your opinion unless asked. Give positive, definite answers when at all possible. Avoid saying, "I think," or "I believe", if you can be positive. If you do not know, say so. Do not make up an answer. Be positive about things you can remember. If you can not remember details, simply say you don't remember.

9. You should only answer the question asked and not volunteer information.

10. The court reporter must be able to hear all your answers, so do not nod your head for a "yes' or 'no' answer. Speak loudly and clearly. Also, you will sound best if you do not use words like "yah", "nope", and "uh-huh".

11. Explain your answer if necessary. Give answers in your own words and if the question cannot be answered with a yes or no answer, say so and explain.

12. Do not exaggerate. Don't make overly broad statements that you may have to correct. Be particularly careful in responding to a question that begins, "Wouldn't you agree that . . .?" The explanation should be in your own words. Do not allow an attorney to put words in your mouth.

13. Listen carefully to the whole question you are asked. If you do not understand the question or did not hear it, ask to have it rephrased or repeated.

14. If your answer was not correctly stated, correct it immediately. If your answer was not clear, clarify it immediately. It is better to correct a mistake yourself than to have the attorney discover an error in your testimony. If you realize you have answered incorrectly, say "May I correct something I said earlier?"

15. Sometimes witnesses give inconsistent testimony-something they said before doesn't agree with something they said later. If this happens to you, don't get flustered. Just explain honestly why you were mistaken. The jury, like the rest of us, understands that people make honest mistakes.

16. Sometimes an attorney may ask if you have talked to anybody about the case. It is perfectly proper for you to have talked to people, including the Assistant U.S. Attorney and the case agent before you testified, and you should, of course, respond truthfully to this question.

17. After you have completed testifying, you should not tell other witnesses what was said during your testimony. Thus, do not ask other witnesses about their testimony and do not volunteer information about your own. Once you have been formally excused as a witness, you are free to go.

*Source:* United States Attorney's Office, Western District of Louisiana, *Coming to Court: General Resource Guide* (Shreveport, LA: United States Attorney's Office, ND), http:// www.justice.gov/usao/law/vicwit/vns_comingtocourt.pdf (accessed May 10, 2013).

**FIGURE 9.5** *Continued*

# ▶ The Exclusionary Rule and Identifications

When identification procedures violate constitutional protections, the identifications made during such procedures will not be admissible in a criminal trial. Generally, there are two means by which identifications will be excluded: (1) when an in-court identification is tainted by an out-of-court identification and (2) when a suspect is searched or seized improperly and then identified by a witness.

## Tainted Identifications

In-court identifications are viewed cautiously by courts. In most such situations, the defendant is sitting in the court room, not surrounded by anyone else matching his or her description (as in a lineup), and sometimes having features that give the appearance of being guilty (such as wearing prison coveralls). Furthermore, given the fact that the defendant has been identified—at least, for trial purposes—as the one suspected of having committed a crime, witnesses often jump to the conclusion that the defendant is the one who should be held responsible. Nevertheless, courts routinely permit in-court identifications.

However, if an in-court identification is tainted by an illegal out-of-court identification, it may be excluded. In this situation, a witness has previously identified the witness during an identification that was obtained illegally (such as where a postindictment lineup was conducted in violation of the defendant's Sixth Amendment right to counsel). When identifying the defendant again at trial, the witness might be influenced by the prior identification. This is known as a **tainted identification**. Unfortunately, it is not always easy to decide whether an in-court identification is "fruit of the poisonous tree." In *United States v. Wade*, the Supreme Court held that an illegally conducted lineup does not invalidate later identifications resulting from an "independent source." The independent source in this context does not have to be another person. Instead, if the witness had plenty of time to view the perpetrator prior to the police lineup, showup, or photographic array, then his or her in-court identification may be admissible. According to the opinion in *Wade*, some factors that may be considered include

> the prior opportunity to observe the alleged criminal act, the existence of any discrepancy between any pre-lineup description and the defendant's actual description, any identification prior to lineup of another person, the identification by picture of the defendant prior to the lineup, failure to identify the defendant on a prior occasion, and the lapse of time between the alleged act and the lineup identification.

Also, if the witness did not experience intense anxiety or pressure during the criminal act (and thus had plenty of opportunity to absorb what was occurring), it is likely that his or her in-court identification will not be tainted by questionable police conduct during a lineup (see *United States v. Johnson*, 412 F.2d 753 [1st Cir. 1969], *cert. denied*, 397 U.S. 944 [1970]).

## Identifications Resulting from Illegal Searches and Seizures

What happens if a person is wrongfully arrested—say, based on less than probable cause—and then placed in a lineup and identified by a witness? Can the witness's identification be considered admissible in a criminal trial? What if, further, the lineup is nonsuggestive and otherwise abides by constitutional requirements? The Supreme Court has not offered clear guidance in these situations.

In *Davis v. Mississippi*, 394 U.S. 721 (1969), the fingerprint identification of a rape suspect was deemed inadmissible because it was the product of an illegal arrest. However, in a similar case, *United States v. Crews*, 445 U.S. 463 (1980), the Supreme Court decided otherwise. Crews was illegally arrested and photographed and then his photograph was shown to a witness, who identified him as the perpetrator. He was tried and convicted based, in part, on the witness's identification. The Supreme Court agreed with the trial court that the arrest was illegal but still upheld Crews's conviction. Three members of the majority justified this decision by arguing that the "fruit" was gathered at the point of the illegal arrest, as opposed to later, so the derivative evidence doctrine should not apply. The Court further noted that the identification had not "'been come at by exploitation' of the violation of the defendant's Fourth Amendment rights."

*United States v. Crews*
*(445 U.S. 463 [1980])*

Inasmuch as *Crews* was decided well after *Davis v. Mississippi*, it would seem that an identification resulting from an illegal search or seizure would be admissible. Recall, as well, how the exclusionary rule applies in the *Miranda* context. The Supreme Court held in *United States v. Bayer*, 331 U.S. 532 (1947), that the "fruit of the poisonous tree" doctrine does not control the admissibility of physical evidence obtained from illegal confessions. These decisions, taken together, chip away at the exclusionary rule and reinforce the notion that the "fruit of the poisonous tree" doctrine applies only in limited circumstances—primarily, when an illegal search or seizure (as opposed to an improper confession or identification) results in the subsequent seizure of tangible evidence.

▼

## WHEN IS AN IN-COURT IDENTIFICATION TAINTED?

Joan Vines heard noises emanating from Sarah Locklear's apartment and minutes later saw two men, one with black gloves and a brown paper bag, exit from the basement of the building and leave in a green 1956 Plymouth. Vines left her apartment immediately to check on things. She found the door to the Locklear apartment open, and she located a piece of stereo equipment just outside the building. Suddenly, the Plymouth returned, so Vines retreated to her apartment. Through her window, she watched the same two men put the piece of stereo equipment into the car. The men left again in the car, but not before Vines jotted down the license plate number. She later gave it to the police, together with physical descriptions of the two men. Vines was then brought to the station for the purpose of identifying one of the suspects. She was taken to a room in which the suspect was seated. The suspect was requested to stand and turn around, which he did. Vines identified him as one of the two participants in the burglary of Locklear's apartment. Vines later identified the man at his trial for burglary. Will the in-court identification be tainted by the station-house identification?

## WHEN IS AN IN-COURT IDENTIFICATION VALID?

Valerie DeLuca's house has been burglarized so many times that she has given up all hope that the police will be able to find the perpetrator. She has told them the burglar's *modus operandi* several times and even that he has worn dark clothes and a black ski cap, but the police have still been unable to catch the burglar. Then, one night, the police apprehend a suspicious man, wearing dark clothing and a black ski cap, walking the streets of DeLuca's neighborhood. They don't have probable cause but arrest him anyway. They call DeLuca in to the stationhouse, hoping she can identify the burglar in a lineup. In fact, she is not sure precisely who the burglar is, but she doesn't tell the police she is uncertain. Instead, she is so desperate to put an end to the burglaries that she plays the odds and identifies one of the men in the lineup. That man is then charged with burglary. Later, at trial, DeLuca identifies the man as the one who burglarized her house on several occasions. Will her in-court identification be valid? In other words, even though her testimony would not be truthful, would her in-court identification of the suspect conform to constitutional requirements?

# Summary

## 1. Outline pretrial suspect identification techniques.

Identification procedures are of three types: (1) lineups, (2) showups, and (3) photographic identifications or arrays. All are bound by the Fourteenth Amendment's due process clause. That is, if they are too suggestive, they will be declared unconstitutional. Lineups and showups are also restricted by the Sixth Amendment's right to counsel clause, but this clause does not apply to photographic identifications. Identification procedures are not protected by the Fifth and Fourth Amendments because an identification itself is not considered testimony or a seizure.

## 2. Explain the problem of witness misidentification.

Witnesses are prone to mistaken identification, especially in showup situations. Even lineups and photo arrays can result in mistaken identification. As such, various procedures have been developed to improve identification procedures. Two recent examples include double-blind lineups and virtual officer lineups.

### 3. Summarize identification techniques during the trial and issues involving witness credibility.

Identification during trial is critical at determining the outcome of a case. As such, it is subject to a number of important restrictions. A criminal trial is a carefully choreographed event, so the order of the questioning proceeds in specific stages. Witnesses sometimes require assistance recollecting events. Also, since some witnesses tend to be untrustworthy, steps can be taken to cast doubt on their credibility. This process is known as impeachment.

### 4. Explain how the exclusionary rule operates in the identification context.

An identification, whether occurring during trial or prior to trial, can be excluded as evidence. First, if an in-court identification is tainted by an improper out-of-court identification, it will be inadmissible. Similarly, if an identification takes place following the illegal arrest and/or search of a suspect, it can be excluded, as well. There are exceptions to these rules, however. Usually, if the identification is sufficiently divorced from any prior illegality, it will be admissible at trial.

## Key Terms

accrediting *266*
competence *266*
credibility *266*
discrediting *266*
double-blind lineup *263*

impeachment *267*
in-court showup *257*
lineup *251*
photographic array *251*
rehabilitation *268*

showup *251*
suggestive lineup *255*
tainted identification *271*

## Key Cases

### Constitutional Restrictions on Identifications

- *United States v. Wade*, 388 U.S. 218 (1967)
- *Stovall v. Denno*, 388 U.S. 293 (1967)
- *Manson v. Braithwaite*, 432 U.S. 98 (1977)
- *Hayes v. Florida*, 470 U.S. 811 (1985)

### Pretrial Identification

- *Neil v. Biggers*, 409 U.S. 188 (1972)
- *Moore v. Illinois*, 434 U.S. 220 (1977)

- *Simmons v. United States*, 390 U.S. 377 (1968)
- *Manson v. Braithwaite*, 432 U.S. 98 (1977)

### Exclusionary Rule and Identifications

- *United States v. Crews*, 445 U.S. 463 (1980)

## Further Exploration

1. This exchange took place at trial (*Neil v. Biggers*, 409 U.S. 188 [1972]) as the victim was recounting events one evening when a youth with a butcher knife grabbed her in the doorway of her kitchen:

"A. [H]e grabbed me from behind, and grappled—twisted me on the floor. Threw me down on the floor."
"Q. And there was no light in that kitchen?"

"A. Not in the kitchen."

"Q. So you couldn't have seen him then?"

"A. Yes, I could see him, when I looked up in his face."

"Q. In the dark?"

"A. He was right in the doorway—it was enough light from the bedroom shining through. Yes, I could see who he was."

"Q. You could see? No light? And you could see him and know him then?"

"A. Yes."

Is the identification trustworthy? If not, what additional information would be needed?

2. Justice Sotomayor was the sole dissenter in *Perry v. New Hampshire*, 565 U.S. ___ (2012), a case we examined in the due process section at the early part of this chapter. She argued in part:

This Court has long recognized that eyewitness identifications' unique confluence of features—their unreliability, susceptibility to suggestion, powerful impact on the jury, and resistance to the ordinary tests of the adversarial process—can undermine the fairness of a trial. Our cases thus establish a clear rule: The admission at trial of out-of-court eyewitness identifications derived from impermissibly suggestive circumstances that pose a very substantial likelihood of misidentification violates due process. The Court today announces that that rule does not even "com[e] into play" unless the suggestive circumstances are improperly "police-arranged." . . . Our due process concern, however, arises not from the act of suggestion, but rather from the corrosive effects of suggestion on the reliability of the resulting identification. By rendering protection contingent on improper police arrangement of the suggestive circumstances, the Court effectively grafts a *mens rea* inquiry onto our rule. The Court's holding enshrines a murky distinction—between suggestive confrontations intentionally orchestrated by the police and, as here, those inadvertently caused by police actions—that will sow confusion. It ignores our precedents' acute sensitivity to the hazards of intentional and unintentional suggestion alike and unmoors our rule from the very interest it protects, inviting arbitrary results.

Evaluate Justice Sotomayor's argument. Do you agree with her? Why or why not?

3. Read the following facts from an actual case (*State v. Chen*, 27 A.3d 930 [N.J. 2011]) and determine whether the April 17 identification should be excluded:

Late in the evening on January 23, 2005, Johann Christian Kim (JC) received a phone call from his ex-girlfriend, defendant Cecilia X. Chen. The two had not spoken since June 2000, around the time their relationship ended. During the call, defendant told JC that she was not doing well and had recently broken up with her boyfriend. She apologized for having taken JC for granted and wondered aloud how things might have turned out had they remained together. JC stated that he was happily married and expecting a child. Defendant cried at times before the conversation ended.

Three days after that phone call, JC's wife, Helen, was home alone recovering from surgery. At 4:00 in the afternoon, she received a phone call from an unknown woman who asked for Mr. Kim. The woman explained that she was calling about a second mortgage with Bank of America, but the Kims had no such mortgage. The caller ID listed a liquor store located in Neptune City. The Kims lived nearby in Ocean Township. A short time later Helen was disturbed by loud knocking on the front door. A young woman who Helen did not know, but who Helen later identified as defendant, was at the door. The woman explained that her car had broken down and asked to use a phone and the bathroom. Helen let the woman into the house, but called JC to tell him about the strange phone call and woman. While they were speaking, the woman returned from the bathroom, grabbed Helen, and stabbed her with a kitchen knife in the back of the shoulder. Helen fought back. A neighbor who lived across the street, Lori Schoch, heard Helen's screams and saw part of the struggle on the front porch. Schoch called the police. Helen was able to disarm her attacker, and the woman ran off.

Helen described her assailant to police as an Asian or Filipino woman who was about 5'4", twenty to twenty-five years old, and wearing black frame glasses. Schoch provided a similar description to the police within about two hours of the attack. Helen drew a picture of her assailant that night. She showed it to JC who thought it looked familiar. Between the drawing and the unusual phone call, JC thought that perhaps it might be defendant. JC had access to defendant's personal website and showed Helen five to ten pictures of defendant on the computer. When she saw one picture, Helen "just jumped" and was "ninety percent positive" that defendant was her attacker . . .

On April 17, 2006, defendant was indicted on charges of aggravated assault, armed robbery, and weapons offenses. Nearly twenty-two months after the attack, on November 14, 2006, the police presented a photo array to Helen and Schoch for the first time. A detective testified that one of the reasons the police waited to show the photo array was out of concern that the website pictures might have prejudiced Helen. Helen and Schoch separately selected defendant's picture.

# Review Questions

1. Explain how the Sixth Amendment's right to counsel applies in the identification context.

2. Explain how due process applies in the identification context.

3. Why are the Fourth and Fifth Amendments not applicable in the identification context?

4. Explain the three types of pretrial identification procedures. How do they differ from one another?

5. What are some methods of reducing the suggestiveness of a lineup?

6. What is an in-court showup?

7. What does a constitutionally valid photographic array look like?

8. Distinguish between credibility and competence.

9. Distinguish between impeachment and rehabilitation.

10. What is a tainted identification? Why is it important in criminal procedure?

11. Explain the Supreme Court's view on identifications that result from illegal searches or seizures.

12. Summarize the tips for being a good witness to criminal activity.

13. Summarize the tips for being a good witness during court.

# Web Links and Exercises

1. Improving identification procedure: what steps can be taken to improve identification procedures?
Suggested URL: http://www.ncjrs.gov/pdffiles1/nij/178240.pdf (accessed May 10, 2013).

2. Wrongful convictions: read about the causes of wrongful convictions, according to the Innocence Project.
URL: http://innocenceproject.org (accessed May 10, 2013).

3. Double-blind lineups: read more about making eyewitness identification more reliable. Do they improve on traditional lineup procedures?
Suggested URL: http://www.ojp.usdoj.gov/nij/journals/258/police-lineups.html (accessed May 10, 2013).

4. Virtual identification procedures: see a video demonstration with "Officer Garcia," the virtual officer.
URL: http://www.youtube.com/watch?v=SEhcLQmwtjQ (accessed May 10, 2013).

# 10   The Pretrial Process

**LEARNING OBJECTIVES**

When you complete this chapter, you should be able to:

1. *Explain the purpose and process of the initial appearance.*

2. *Explain the purpose and the process of the probable cause hearing.*

3. *Summarize bail and other types of pretrial release.*

4. *Explain the purpose and process of the preliminary hearing.*

5. *Summarize the arraignment process.*

6. *Summarize the discovery process.*

. . . . . . . . . . . . . . . . . . . . . . . . . . . . . . . . . . . . . . . . . . . . .

# Introduction: The Road to Trial

The criminal process begins with one of two events: a warrantless arrest or a criminal complaint. If a person is arrested without a warrant—say, for committing a crime in the presence of a police officer—then the arresting officer will file a criminal complaint against the individual and the formal criminal process will commence. On the other hand, if a warrant is obtained before making an arrest, the warrant must be preceded by a criminal complaint. Before an arrest warrant will be issued, the officer needs to convince a judge that a crime has been committed. The complaint serves as a basis for issuing an arrest warrant. The same logic applies if a private party complains as to someone's presumed involvement in criminal activity. In such a situation, an officer will probably investigate the private party's complaint and, if it is meritorious, the officer will apply for a warrant.

Once a person has been arrested, with or without a warrant, he or she will be booked at the arresting officer's police station or the sheriff's station (sheriffs usually run jails). **Booking** involves documenting who was arrested, the time of the arrest, and the offense involved. Next, the arrestee's personal items will be inventoried. The arrestee may be photographed and fingerprinted, depending on the offense and the jurisdiction involved. The police are also authorized to take and analyze a cheek swab of the arrestee's DNA (*Maryland v. King*, 569 U.S. ___ [2013]). Finally, the arrestee will be placed in a holding cell, jail cell, or similar confinement facility and allowed to contact counsel, family, friends, and other individuals, as needed.

This chapter focuses on the pretrial process. The procedures described are common to many jurisdictions, but may vary depending on the jurisdiction and the nature of the offense. This is a critically important point to keep in mind as you work through this chapter.

## ▶ The Initial Appearance

Once arrested and booked, the suspect is then brought before a magistrate or judge in what is known as the **initial appearance**. Not all jurisdictions require an initial appearance (also referred to as *presentment*), but for those that do, the suspect must be brought before a judge in a relatively short period of time. Delays of more than 6 hours are usually unacceptable, but they may be necessary on occasion, however, if the time of arrest precludes appearance before a judge (such as 1 A.M. on Monday).

The initial appearance is designed to serve a number of purposes. In a misdemeanor case, such as minor in possession, the trial may take place at this stage. In a more serious case, however, the accused will be advised of:

- the reason he or she is being detained (notification of formal charges often comes later at arraignment),
- his or her protection against self-incrimination, and
- his or her right to appointed counsel, if necessary. The judge may also set bail at the initial appearance, but the bail determination often requires a separate hearing. (For ease of understanding, this chapter treats the bail determination as its own hearing, independent of the initial appearance.)

The initial appearance is usually swift and subject to few procedural constraints. In fact, only one Supreme Court decision has dealt explicitly with the initial appearance. In *Rothgery v. Gillespie County*, 554 U.S. 191 (2008), the Court held that the Sixth Amendment right to counsel applies at the initial appearance. In contrast, the probable cause, bail, and preliminary hearings have received much more of the Court's attention.

## ▶ The Probable Cause Hearing

*Gerstein v. Pugh*
*(420 U.S. 103 [1975])*

In *Gerstein v. Pugh*, 420 U.S. 103 (1975), the Supreme Court held that the Fourth Amendment requires a **probable cause hearing** either before or promptly after arrest.[1] A probable cause hearing *before* an arrest usually results in an arrest warrant being issued. Recall that an arrest warrant is issued based on a judge's determination as to whether probable cause existed. No hearing to determine probable cause after such an arrest is necessary because it would be redundant. However, when an arrest is made *without* a warrant, then a probable cause determination must often be made. The purpose of the probable cause hearing is, in essence, to determine whether there is probable cause to keep a person detained.

The *Gerstein* decision challenged the preliminary hearing system in Florida. Probable cause was determined at preliminary hearings in that state, but those hearings were not required until 30 days after arrest. Basically, a person could be held following a warrantless

---

[1]Probable cause hearings are not required in certain jurisdictions.

arrest for 30 days, sometimes longer. The Court held that such a lengthy detention required a judicial determination of probable cause *early on*:

> [W]hile the State's reasons for taking summary action subside, the suspect's need for a neutral determination of probable cause increases significantly. The consequences of prolonged detention may be more serious than the interference occasioned by arrest. Pretrial confinement may imperil the suspect's job, interrupt his source of income, and impair his family's relationship. . . . When the stakes are this high, the detached judgment of a neutral magistrate is essential if the Fourth Amendment is to furnish meaningful protection from unfounded interference with liberty.

The Court decided, in essence, that the prosecutor's decision to charge is not in itself enough to satisfy the probable cause requirement. However, the Court also noted that a probable cause hearing is *not* required after every arrest. An arrest with a warrant need not be followed by a probable cause hearing. Likewise, when an arrest is based on a grand jury indictment, a probable cause hearing is not required, either. The rationale for this is that the grand jury performs an investigative function, makes its probable cause determination, and then issues its indictment. In the course of this process, the probable cause requirement is satisfied. Finally, if the detention is relatively short, such as when a preliminary hearing follows shortly after arrest, a probable cause hearing will not be required.

## Procedural Issues Surrounding the Hearing

The lower court's decisions leading up to the Supreme Court's opinion in *Gerstein* required that a probable cause hearing resemble an adversarial trial, complete with counsel, compulsory process, and other procedures. The Supreme Court reversed the lower court's decisions as to these issues, declaring that the probable cause hearing is a not a "critical stage" of the criminal process. In support of its decision, the Court observed:

> Criminal justice is already overburdened by the volume of cases and the complexities of our system. The processing of misdemeanors, in particular, and the early stages of prosecution generally are marked by delays that can seriously affect the quality of justice. A constitutional doctrine requiring adversary hearings for all persons detained pending trial could exacerbate the problem of pretrial delay.

## Timing of the Hearing

In *Gerstein*, the Court stated that if a probable cause hearing must be held, it must take place "promptly after arrest." It did not define what was meant by *promptly*, but in *Riverside County v. McLaughlin*, 500 U.S. 44 (1991), the Court provided some clarification. In a 5 to 4 decision, the Court held that for a hearing to comply with the Fourth Amendment, it must take place within 48 hours of arrest:

*Riverside County v. McLaughlin (500 U.S. 44 [1991])*

> In order to satisfy *Gerstein*'s promptness requirement, a jurisdiction that chooses to combine probable cause determinations with other pretrial proceedings must do so as soon as is reasonably feasible, but in no event later than 48 hours after arrest. Providing a probable cause determination within that time frame will, as a general matter, immunize such a jurisdiction from systemic challenges. Although a hearing within 48 hours may nonetheless violate *Gerstein* if the arrested individual can prove that his or her probable cause determination was delayed unreasonably, courts evaluating the reasonableness of a delay must allow a substantial degree of flexibility, taking into account the practical realities of pretrial procedures. Where an arrested individual does not receive a probable cause determination within 48 hours, the burden of proof shifts to the government to demonstrate the existence

## THE PROBABLE CAUSE HEARING

Conner Case was arrested for robbery. He was taken to the police station, booked, and placed in detention. The police department maintains a policy that arrestees may be detained in the city detention facility at the request of an investigatory officer without having formal charges filed against them. Persons who are so detained are said to be "on hold." The main reason for doing so is to stage a lineup, in which a witness or a complainant can view and identify the suspect. If the arrestee is suspected of committing multiple offenses, the police department will hold several lineups,

extending the period of detention longer than usual. The average time for investigative hold is 26 hours if no charges are filed and 35 hours if charges are filed. Case was held for 35 hours. He is now suing pursuant to 42 U.S.C. Section 1983, claiming that the police violated his Fourth Amendment rights and denied him a prompt probable cause hearing. In particular, he claims that the only valid reasons for delaying a probable cause hearing are those associated with transporting arrestees to the police station, booking them into the jail, and filing charges. How should the court rule?

## TIMING OF THE PROBABLE CAUSE HEARING

With probable cause, Officer Jones arrested three men for impersonating police officers. The men were brought to the police station at 4:30 A.M. and subsequently fingerprinted, photographed, and given breathalyzer tests. The test results showed that all three men were legally intoxicated, with blood-alcohol levels well above the legal limit. The police department maintains a policy that arrestees with blood-alcohol

levels of over 0.05 cannot be interviewed until they are sober, so the three men were placed into custody. Eighteen hours later, after sobering up, they were interviewed. All charges against them were dropped following the interviews. The three men sued Officer Jones under Section 1983, arguing that they were denied a prompt probable cause hearing. How should the court rule?

of a bona fide emergency or other extraordinary circumstance, which cannot include intervening weekends or the fact that in a particular case it may take longer to consolidate pretrial proceedings.

Acceptable excuses for delay include "unavoidable delays in transporting arrested persons from one facility to another, handling late-night bookings where no magistrate is readily available, [and] obtaining the presence of an arresting officer who may be busy processing other suspects or securing the premises of an arrest." Unacceptable reasons for delay, by contrast, include the need to gather additional evidence to support the arrest in hindsight and issues of bad faith, such as inconveniencing the individual or making him or her wait for no legitimate reason.

## ▶ Pretrial Release

Once a person has been arrested, the question as to whether he or she should be temporarily released invariably arises. If the arrestee does not pose a significant risk of flight and has been arrested for a relatively minor offense, pretrial release is often a sensible decision. However, if it is likely that the arrestee will fail to appear in later proceedings, he or she should probably be jailed, pending additional court proceedings.

Bail is a deposit taken by the court from the defendant upon release to ensure that they will appear for later proceedings. The Eighth Amendment states, "Excessive bail shall not be required." This simply means that bail cannot be set at a level that is out of line with the offense. Not everyone enjoys a constitutional right to bail, however. In capital cases, for example, bail has always been denied. Consider the Supreme Court's statement in *Carlson v. Landon*, 342 U.S. 524 (1952): "In England, [the Bail] clause has never been thought to accord a right to bail in all cases, but merely to provide that bail shall not be excessive in those cases where it is proper to grant bail. When this clause was carried over into our Bill of Rights, nothing was said that indicated any different concept."

Critics of some courts' decisions to deny bail have argued that because the U.S. criminal justice system presumes innocence, everyone should be released. After all, a defendant cannot be considered guilty until the state proves his or her guilt beyond a reasonable doubt. However, in *Bell v. Wolfish*, 441 U.S. 520 (1979), the Supreme Court stated that the presumption of innocence is merely "a doctrine that allocates the burden of proof in criminal trials."[2]

*Bell v. Wolfish*
*(441 U.S. 520 [1979])*

It is also important to point out that the Eighth Amendment prohibition against excessive bail *has not* been incorporated so as to apply to the states. For example, in *Murphy v. Hunt*, 455 U.S. 478 (1982), a detainee sued under Section 1983, claiming that his Eighth Amendment right was violated. The Supreme Court held that his suit was moot because he was convicted in Nebraska state court. This important decision, coupled with the realization that the Eighth Amendment's excessive bail provision has not been incorporated, explains some of the discrepancies in bail decisions.

## The Pretrial Release Hearing

The Constitution does not specify whether bail should be set in a separate hearing, but numerous Court decisions seem to suggest a separate hearing is warranted. For example, in *Stack v. Boyle*, 342 U.S. 1 (1951), the Court stated that as part of the bail determination, the judge should consider "the nature and circumstances of the offense charged, the weight of the evidence against [the accused], [and] the financial ability of the defendant to give bail and the character of the defendant." The Court also stated:

*Stack v. Boyle*
*(342 U.S. 1 [1951])*

> Since the function of bail is limited, the fixing of bail for any individual defendant must be based upon standards relevant to the purpose of assuring the presence of that defendant. The traditional standards as expressed in the Federal Rules of Criminal Procedure . . . are to be applied in each case to each defendant. . . . It is not denied that bail for each petitioner has been fixed in a sum much higher than that usually imposed for offenses with like penalties and yet there has been no factual showing to justify such action in this case. The Government asks the courts to depart from the norm by assuming, without the introduction of evidence, that each petitioner is a pawn in a conspiracy and will, in obedience to a superior, flee the jurisdiction. To infer from the fact of indictment alone a need for bail in an unusually high amount is an arbitrary act. Such conduct would inject into our own system of government the very principles of totalitarianism which Congress was seeking to guard against in passing the statute under which petitioners have been indicted.

Assuming a bail hearing is required, it is also not clear whether a simple probable cause–type hearing is all that is needed or if a more adversarial proceeding is necessary. Since bail is set once charges have already been filed, it would seem that, at a minimum, counsel should be provided. In *United States v. Salerno*, 481 U.S. 739 (1987), the Court concluded that a federal preventive detention statute that provided for counsel, evidence presentation, and cross-examination was acceptable, but it did not state whether such

---

[2]Note that some states have preset bail schedules for low-level offenses. For these states, some of the following discussion is not applicable.

rights should be afforded to the accused in every bail hearing. Thus, the question of what type of bail hearing is required, if any, remains unanswered. In some situations (and in certain jurisdictions), the bail decision is made during another hearing, such as the initial appearance.

## The Pretrial Release Decision

The pretrial release decision has traditionally taken one of three forms. The first, and most common, results in release on bail. Second, some arrestees are released on their own recognizance, which means they simply promise to show up when required. Finally, in recent years, the courts have adopted a policy of preventive detention for certain individuals, which involves a calculation as to the arrestee's level of dangerousness and flight risk. Release is denied to those individuals likely to pose a threat to others or not likely to appear at their scheduled hearings.

### Release on Bail

18 U.S.C. Section 3142 provides that "upon all arrests in criminal cases, bail shall be admitted, except where the punishment may be death." Most states have adopted similar language in their constitutions. California's constitution, for example, provides that "all persons shall be bailable by sufficient sureties, unless for capital offenses when the proof is evidence or the presumption great" (Cal. Const. Art. I, Section 6). There is variability from state to state, however, because, once again, the Eighth Amendment's excessive bail provision has not been incorporated to the states through the due process clause of the Fourteenth Amendment.

The bail decision is sometimes problematic. More often than not, a judge sets bail according to the nature of the offense in question, not according to the accused's ability to pay.[3] The frequent result of this is that indigent defendants—no matter what they are accused of—languish in jail cells until their court dates because they cannot afford to post bail.

In response to the inability of many defendants to post bail, the professional **bail bond agent** has stepped in.[4] These individuals collect a fee from the accused, usually a percentage of bail, and then post a bond so the accused can be released. If the accused shows up at trial, the agent collects his or her fee and gets his or her money back from the court. If the accused fails to show up, then the agent loses the amount posted. In order to avoid this loss, bail bonds agents employ *bounty hunters* to catch the accused and bring him or her before the court. There is a misperception, however, that bail bonds agents can with impunity do whatever it takes to apprehend those who "skip" bail. Indeed, in response to concerns that such agents have been given too much authority, some states have adopted legislation to restrict their activities. Texas is perhaps most restrictive. Figure 10.1 reprints a Texas statute that sets forth the procedures bail bonds agents must follow to rearrest those who skip bail.

The bail bonds agent system is flawed in that the agents, rather than the courts, are given a certain degree of power. Regardless of what amount the court sets as bail, bonds agents can then decide who gets released or who stays in jail based on the accused's ability to pay. Those who can pay the fee effectively buy their freedom, if only temporarily. Those who cannot pay stay in jail. The courts sit on the sidelines, essentially, while the whole bail bonds process plays out. As described in the decision for *Pannell v. United States*, 320 F.2d 698 (D.C.Cir. 1963):

> Certainly the professional bondsman system as used in this District is odious at best. The effect of such a system is that the professional bondsmen hold the keys to the jail in their pockets. They determine for whom they will act as surety—who in their judgment is a

---

[3]See, for example, M. Paulsen, "Pre-Trial Release in the United States," *Columbia Law Review* 66 (1966): 109–125, 113.
[4]Not all states have bail bonds agents.

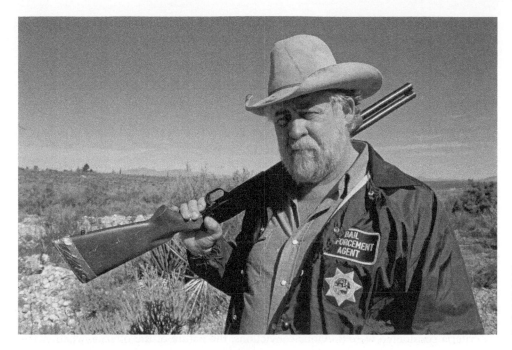

Bail bond agents employ bounty hunters who are given broad authority to track down defendants who fail to appear for their court dates.

**(a)** Any [bail bond agent], desiring to [apprehend] his [bond recipient] and after notifying the [bond recipient's] attorney, if the [bond recipient] is represented by an attorney, in a manner provided by Rule 21a, Texas Rules of Civil Procedure, of the [bail bond agent's] intention to surrender the [bond recipient], may file an affidavit of such intention before the court or magistrate before which the prosecution is pending. The affidavit must state:

    **(1)** the court and cause number of the case;
    **(2)** the name of the defendant;
    **(3)** the offense with which the defendant is charged;
    **(4)** the date of the bond;
    **(5)** the cause for the [apprehension]; and
    **(6)** that notice of the [bail bond agent's] intention to surrender the [bond recipient] has been given as required by this subsection.

**(b)** If the court or magistrate finds that there is cause for the [bail bond agent] to [apprehend] his [bond recipient], the court shall issue a warrant of arrest for the [bond recipient]. It is an affirmative defense to any liability on the bond that:

    **(1)** the court or magistrate refused to issue a warrant of arrest for the principal; and
    **(2)** after the refusal to issue the warrant the [bond recipient] failed to appear.

**(c)** If the court or magistrate before whom the prosecution is pending is not available, the [bail bond agent] may deliver the affidavit to any other magistrate in the county and that magistrate, on a finding of cause for the [bail bond agent] to [apprehend] his [bond recipient], shall issue a warrant of arrest for the [bond recipient].

**(d)** An arrest warrant issued under this article shall be issued to the sheriff of the county in which the case is pending, and a copy of the warrant shall be issued to the [bail bond agent] or his agent.

**(e)** An arrest warrant issued under this article may be executed by a peace officer, a security officer, or a private investigator licensed in this state.

*Source:* Adapted from *Texas Code of Criminal Procedures*, Chapter 17, Article 17.19 (2002).

**FIGURE 10.1 Example of Bail Bonds Agent Rearrest Procedures**

good risk. The bad risks, in the bondsmen's judgment, and the ones who are unable to pay the bondsmen's fees, remain in jail. The court and the commissioner are relegated to the relatively unimportant chore of fixing the amount of bail. The result of this system in the District of Columbia is that most defendants, for months on end, languish in jail unable to make bond awaiting disposition of their cases. Instead of being allowed the opportunity of obtaining worthwhile employment to support their families, and perhaps to pay at least in part for their defense, almost 90 percent of the defendants proceed in forma pauperis, thus casting an unfair burden on the members of the bar of this community who are required to represent these defendants without pay.

## Release on Recognizance

Even though release on bail is the most common form of pretrial release, the courts have experimented with releasing people on their own recognizance. **Release on recognizance (ROR)** means that the accused is released with the assumption that he or she will show up for scheduled court hearings. Naturally, this method of pretrial release is reserved for those individuals who pose a minimal risk of flight.

New York City's Manhattan Bail Project was the first significant effort to explore the possibilities of ROR. This program, administered by the Vera Institute, focused on indigent defendants who, according to carefully set criteria, posed a minimal flight risk. Among the criteria considered were previous convictions, the nature of the offense, whether the accused was employed, and whether the accused had roots in the community (such as a family to go back to). The program was a resounding success: Only 1.6 percent of those individuals recommended for ROR intentionally failed to appear at court.

The results of the Manhattan Bail Project prompted other cities around the United States to adopt similar programs. And in 1984, Congress passed the federal Bail Reform Act, which provided that any person charged with a noncapital offense "be ordered released pending trial on his personal recognizance or upon the execution of an unsecured appearance bond in an amount specified by the judicial officer, unless the officer determines . . . that such a release will not reasonably assure the appearance of the person as required" (18 U.S.C. Sections 3146–3152).

An important feature of this new legislation was that bail was to be considered only as one of many options to ensure the accused's appearance at trial. Among the other options were restrictions on travel and association, along with other conditions that would ensure the appearance of the accused (see 18 U.S.C. Section 3146[a]). The Bail Reform Act also provided that when bail was to be used, the money should be deposited with the court, not with a bail bonds agent. The Bail Reform Act further provided that

the judge shall . . . take into account the available information concerning: the nature and the circumstances of the offense charged, the weight of evidence against the accused, the accused's family ties, employment, financial resources, character and mental condition,

---

**DECISION-MAKING EXERCISE 10.3**

### AMOUNT OF BAIL

Mike Rhodes has been arrested for the crime of robbery, which carries a possible life sentence. The judge sets bail in the amount of $100,000. Rhodes has $12 to his name and no assets. (He rides the bus and lives with his parents.) As such, he cannot even afford the 10 percent deposit typically required to secure a bail bond. His only recourse is to sue under 42 U.S.C. Section 1983, claiming that his Fourteenth Amendment right to equal protection was violated when the judge set bail well beyond his means. Should his lawsuit succeed?

the length of his residence in the community, his record of convictions, and his record of appearances at court proceedings or of flight to avoid prosecution or failure to appear at court proceedings. (Section 3146[b])

This is in stark contrast to the notion that judges simply consider the nature of the offense in setting bail.

While the federal government and many states still release people on their own recognizance, this practice is not usually relied on for serious offenses. In fact, when the offense in question is serious and the accused presents a significant risk of flight, bail may be altogether denied.

### Preventive Detention: Denying Pretrial Release

Growing concern over crimes committed by defendants out on pretrial release prompted some reforms. In 1970, for example, the District of Columbia passed the first **preventive detention** statute, which authorized denial of bail to dangerous persons charged with certain offenses for up to 60 days (D.C. Code 1970 Section 23-1322). Then, Congress passed the federal Bail Reform Act, which authorized judges to revoke pretrial release for firearms possession, failure to comply with curfew, and failure to comply with other conditions of release. The act also permitted detention for up to 10 days of an individual who "may flee or pose a danger to any other person or the community" (Section 3142[d]).

Somewhat controversially, the Bail Reform Act of 1984 permitted pretrial detention for *more than* 10 days of certain individuals. Thus, under the act, if it is deemed that no pretrial release condition "will reasonably assure the appearance of the person as required and the safety of any other person and the community," then indefinite detention is acceptable. For a detention of this nature to conform to Fourth and Eighth Amendment restrictions, a hearing must be held to determine whether the case "involves a serious risk that the person will flee; [or] a serious risk that the person will obstruct or attempt to obstruct justice, or threaten, injure, or intimidate, a prospective witness or jury" (Section 3142[f]).

## Criteria for Release

As noted above, the Constitution does not guarantee the right to bail. Some people are denied bail, and others are granted bail. Three factors are typically considered by the judge: (1) the accused's flight risk; (2) the level of dangerousness of the accused; and (3) the accused's financial status.

### Flight Risk

In *Stack v. Boyle*, the Supreme Court declared that the purpose of bail is to ensure the accused's appearance at trial:

> Like the ancient practice of securing the oaths of responsible persons to stand as sureties for the accused, the modern practice of requiring a bail bond or the deposit of a sum of money subject to forfeiture serves as additional assurance of the presence of an accused. . . . Since the function of bail is limited, the fixing of bail for any individual defendant must be based upon standards relevant to the purpose of assuring the presence of that defendant.

This does not mean, though, that a judge can set an amount that is unrealistic, in light of the Eighth Amendment's prohibition of excessive bail:

> Admission to bail always involves a risk that the accused will take flight. That is a calculated risk which the law takes as the price of our system of justice. . . . In allowance of bail, the duty of the judge is to reduce the risk by fixing an amount reasonably calculated to hold the accused available for trial and its consequence. But the judge is not free to make the sky the limit, because the Eighth Amendment to the Constitution says: "Excessive bail shall not be required."

### PREVENTIVE DETENTION

The Bail Reform Act of 1984 provided that judges can deny bail to certain individuals charged with specific crimes and after finding that "no condition or combination of conditions [attaching to release] will reasonably assure the appearance of the person as required and the safety of any other person and the community" (18 U.S.C. Section 3142[e]). Marty Corelli is a drug kingpin charged with serious narcotics offenses and is presumed to be a significant flight risk. Accordingly, the judge denies bail to Corelli, thereby requiring him to remain in jail until his trial. Is this action constitutional?

In short, a delicate balance needs to be struck to ensure the accused's appearance at trial. Bail should be set at an amount designed to minimize the risk of flight, yet the amount set should not be so much that the accused cannot reasonably afford to pay it, either by cash or by bond.

### Dangerousness

Aside from the obvious risk of flight, some defendants are particularly dangerous individuals that pose a threat to society. In these cases, the courts sometimes see fit either to deny bail or to set the amount relatively high because of such perceived dangerousness. In *Salerno*, the Supreme Court dealt with a challenge to the provision in the Bail Reform Act of 1984 that dangerousness could be considered in a bail determination. In the Court's words:

> Nothing in the text of the Bail Clause [of the Eighth Amendment] limits permissible government considerations solely to questions of flight. The only arguable substantive limitation of the Bail Clause is that the Government's proposed conditions of release or detention not be "excessive" in light of the perceived evil. . . . [W]hen the government has admitted that its only interest is in preventing flight, bail must be set by a court at a sum designed to ensure that goal, and no more. . . . We believe that when Congress has mandated detention on the basis of a compelling interest other than prevention of flight, as it has here, the Eighth Amendment does not require release on bail.

*Schall v. Martin*
*(467 U.S. 253 [1984])*

The issue of dangerousness, as it pertains to the bail decision, also came up in the case of *Schall v. Martin*, 467 U.S. 253 (1984). There, the Supreme Court upheld a statute that provided for detention of a juvenile who posed a serious risk of committing a crime while on release. The statute was criticized as essentially amounting to punishment without trial, but the Court decided that *punishment* only exists when the government's *intent* is to punish. And since the purpose of the state's detention policy was not to punish but rather to protect the community from a dangerous individual, it was deemed constitutional. Of course, given the problems inherent in predicting criminal behavior, the Court's argument is somewhat specious.

### Financial Status

The courts usually take into account the accused's financial status in making a bail decision. Failure to do so can lead to irrational bail determinations. For example, if bail is set at a fixed amount, a poor individual will have a considerably more difficult time coming up with the required funds than a wealthy individual. Perhaps more important, if the wealthy individual views the amount as a "drop in the bucket," then he or she may not be motivated to show up for trial.

Surprisingly, bail can be denied simply because the accused is unable to pay it. In *Schilb v. Kuebel*, 404 U.S. 357 (1971), the Supreme Court took it upon itself to decide on the constitutionality of a state statute that provided that a criminal defendant who was not released on his or her own recognizance could (1) deposit 10 percent of the amount of set bail with the court, 10 percent of which would be forfeited to the court as *bail bonds costs*, or (2) pay the full amount of bail, all of which would be refunded if the accused showed up at court. The defendant argued that the statute unfairly targeted indigent individuals because they were forced to choose the first option. However, the Supreme Court upheld the statute because "[i]t should be obvious that the poor man's real hope and avenue for relief is the personal recognizance provision." Furthermore, in the words of the Court, "[I]t is by no means clear that [the second option, paying the full amount,] is more attractive to the affluent defendant."

*Schilb v. Kuebel*
*(404 U.S. 357 [1971])*

## Treatment of Pretrial Detainees

If bail is denied, or a defendant is unable to make bail, the defendant is relegated to a pretrial detention facility pending trial. These facilities must only serve the purposes of ensuring appearance at trial and maintaining the security of the facility. Treatment of detainees is unconstitutional if the purpose of that treatment is "punishment." The Supreme Court has dealt with several cases alleging unconstitutional conditions at pretrial detention facilities. For example, in *Bell v. Wolfish*, 441 U.S. 520 (1979), the Court upheld several of the rules promulgated by New York City's Metropolitan Correctional Center (MCC), including rules prohibiting inmates from receiving books from entities other than publishers, bookstores, and book clubs, as well as outside packages. The Court also upheld unannounced searches of living quarters but was careful to state that when such prohibitions are intended to punish (instead of to serve some legitimate governmental purpose, such as to ensure the safety and security of inmates), they can violate due process. Quoting the Court:

> [If] a particular condition or restriction of pretrial detention is reasonably related to a legitimate governmental objective, it does not, without more, amount to "punishment." Conversely, if a restriction or condition is not reasonably related to a legitimate goal—if it is arbitrary or purposeless—a court permissibly may infer that the purpose of the governmental action is punishment that may not constitutionally be inflicted upon detainees *qua* detainees.

In one case, a pretrial detainee argued that unannounced searches of his cell violated the Fourth Amendment. The Court concluded, however, in *Hudson v. Palmer*, 468 U.S. 517 (1984), that prisoners do not enjoy a reasonable expectation of privacy in their cells:

> A prisoner has no reasonable expectation of privacy in his prison cell entitling him to the protection of the Fourth Amendment against unreasonable searches. While prisoners enjoy many protections of the Constitution that are not fundamentally inconsistent with imprisonment itself or incompatible with the objectives of incarceration, imprisonment carries with it the circumscription or loss of many rights as being necessary to accommodate the institutional needs and objectives of prison facilities, particularly internal security and safety. It would be impossible to accomplish the prison objectives of preventing the introduction of weapons, drugs, and other contraband into the premises if inmates retained a right of privacy in their cells. The unpredictability that attends random searches of cells renders such searches perhaps the most effective weapon of the prison administrator in the fight against the proliferation of weapons, drugs, and other contraband. A requirement that random searches be conducted pursuant to an established plan would seriously undermine the effectiveness of this weapon.

**FINANCIAL STATUS AND BAIL DETERMINATION**

A prosecution for mail fraud against a postal worker resulted in her conviction. During the trial, the defendant was 30 minutes late in returning after a recess, which the judge had granted so the defendant could go to her office to gather evidence for the defense. Because she was late, the judge ordered her to be held in jail for the balance of the trial. She had not been held in jail prior to the judge's decision. Is this action constitutional?

**TREATMENT OF PRETRIAL DETAINEES**

Several pretrial detainees at the county jail brought a class action in federal district court against the county sheriff and other officials, claiming that the jail's policy of denying pretrial detainees contact visits with their spouses, relatives, children, and friends violates due process. Should pretrial detainees be constitutionally entitled to contact visits of this nature? If so, why?

Furthermore, "society would insist that the prisoner's expectation of privacy always yield to what must be considered the paramount interest in institutional security." Prison guards, then, can seize "any articles which, in their view, disserve legitimate institutional interests."

The Supreme Court has also sanctioned strip searches of all arrestees during the pretrial phase (*Florence v. County of Burlington*, 566 U.S. ___ [2012]). In that case, Florence was arrested for failure to appear. Once he was in jail, he was required to remove his clothes, open his mouth, lift his tongue, lift his genitals, and squat and cough. He argued that the strip search procedure was unnecessary because he was not accused of smuggling drugs. The Supreme Court disagreed. Justice Kennedy noted that the offense of record "is a poor predictor of who has contraband."

## ▶ The Preliminary Hearing

The **preliminary hearing** should be distinguished from the initial appearance, the probable cause hearing, and the pretrial release hearing. It almost always takes place after one of these hearings as well as after the charging decision. As one court stated, the purpose of the preliminary hearing is intended to prevent "hasty, malicious, improvident, and oppressive prosecutions" and to ensure that "there are substantial grounds upon which a prosecution may be based" (*Thies v. State*, 178 Wis. 98 [1922]). The preliminary hearing resembles a criminal trial in that it is usually adversarial.

*Lem Woon v. Oregon*
*(229 U.S. 586 [1913])*

A preliminary hearing is not required by the Constitution (*Lem Woon v. Oregon*, 229 U.S. 586 [1913]). It is up to each state to determine under what circumstances it is required. Fortunately, most states, as well as the federal government, require preliminary hearings, at least to a certain extent. Whether a preliminary hearing is required typically depends on a jurisdiction's method of filing criminal charges. In jurisdictions that *require* that charges be filed in the form of a grand jury indictment, no preliminary hearing is required if the prosecutor secures an indictment within a specified time period. However, in states where a prosecutor proceeds by information, the defendant will usually be entitled to a preliminary hearing before the charges are filed.

Whether a jurisdiction proceeds by indictment or information has important implications concerning the defendant's rights. As discussed further in Chapter 11, the defendant does *not* enjoy the right to counsel during a grand jury proceeding. The defendant does not even enjoy the right to challenge the state's case. In a preliminary hearing, however, both rights exist. Thus, a zealous prosecutor in a jurisdiction that proceeds by either indictment or information may opt for an indictment because the accused will enjoy fewer rights. Of course, this issue may be moot because accused individuals can and often do waive their right to a preliminary hearing.

## The Probable Cause Requirement

Assuming a preliminary hearing is required, the prosecutor has the burden of proving that the case should be *bound over* (handed over) to a grand jury or go to trial. The standard of proof at a preliminary hearing is *probable cause*. Invariably, this step is confused with the probable cause hearing. The two hearings can be distinguished as follows: A probable cause hearing considers the justification to arrest, whereas a preliminary hearing considers whether probable cause exists to proceed with a trial. This is a critical distinction and is often the reason why there are separate probable cause and preliminary hearings in some states.

Preliminary hearings only require a showing of probable cause, since setting a *higher* standard would essentially make trial pointless. To require proof beyond a reasonable doubt, for example, would make holding a later criminal trial redundant. On the other hand, some people favor requiring more proof than probable cause because once a probable cause hearing has taken place, the preliminary hearing seems somewhat redundant. To minimize some of the confusion, one court observed that "probable cause to arrest does not automatically mean that the Commonwealth has sufficient competent legal evidence to justify the costs both to the defendant and to the Commonwealth of a full trial" (*Myers v. Commonwealth*, 363 Mass. 843 [1973]).

Basically, at a preliminary hearing, the prosecutor needs to convince the judge that there is enough evidence to proceed with a trial. More specifically, there must be enough evidence to make a judge or jury contemplate which case is more convincing: that of the prosecution or the defense. If it is clear that the state has no case but perhaps had probable cause for arrest, the court will order that the would-be defendant be released.

## Procedural Issues at Preliminary Hearings

Since a preliminary hearing is adversarial in nature, it seems sensible that the right to counsel should apply. According to the Supreme Court, in *Coleman v. Alabama*, 399 U.S. 1 (1970), it does, and the state must provide counsel if the accused is indigent. The Court declared that the preliminary hearing is a critical stage of the criminal process: "Plainly the guiding hand of counsel at the preliminary hearing is essential to protect the indigent accused against an erroneous and improper prosecution."

*Coleman v. Alabama* *(399 U.S. 1 [1970])*

Evidence procedures in a preliminary hearing are markedly different than those in a criminal trial. First, the *Federal Rules of Criminal Procedure* allow hearsay evidence in preliminary hearings, though not explicitly.[5] By contrast, *hearsay evidence* (i.e., what one person previously heard and then repeats while testifying in court) is restricted in a criminal trial. Also, the exclusionary rule does not technically apply in preliminary hearings. Actually, it is not so much that the rule does not apply but rather that the preliminary

[5]The hearsay language was removed from the *Federal Rules* in 2002, but the Advisory Committee notes make it clear that hearsay can still be admitted. See http://www.law.cornell.edu/rules/frcrmp/NRule5_1.htm (accessed November 5, 2008).

**PRELIMINARY HEARINGS**

Assume that a jurisdiction maintains a policy that people charged with misdemeanors will not be given preliminary hearings. Is such a restriction constitutional?

hearing is an inappropriate stage of the criminal process in which to object to evidence. As the *Federal Rules of Criminal Procedure* also state, the defendant "may not object to evidence on the ground that it was unlawfully acquired."[6] (Note that the *Federal Rules of Criminal Procedure* apply to federal courts, not state courts. So some states may maintain different procedures.)

Cross-examination of witnesses is sometimes permitted, as is the use of compulsory process (subpoenas) to require their appearance. While these rights exist at criminal trials, preliminary hearings restrict them somewhat. In fact, the Supreme Court stated that there is no constitutional right to cross-examine at the preliminary hearing (*Goldsby v. United States*, 160 U.S. 70 [1895]). The court has discretion over the extent of cross-examination, but the bulk of it is reserved for trial.

Some commentators have expressed concern that too much cross-examination at a preliminary hearing may turn it into a full-blown criminal trial. But one court has stated that "past experience indicates that trial strategy usually prevents such a result as both the prosecution and the defense wish to withhold as much of their case as possible" (*Myers v. Commonwealth*). Furthermore, "defense tactics usually mitigate against putting the defendant on the stand or presenting exculpatory testimony at the preliminary hearing unless defense counsel believes this evidence is compelling enough to overcome the prosecution's case."

## ▶ The Arraignment

Once a person has been formally charged, he or she will be arraigned. The purpose of the **arraignment** is to formally notify the defendant of the charge lodged against him or her. Also at the arraignment, the defendant enters one of three pleas: (1) **guilty**; (2) **not guilty**; or (3) **nolo contendere**. A plea of guilty is an admission by the defendant of every allegation in the indictment or information. Such a plea may be entered for a number of reasons. For example, the defendant may simply elect to admit responsibility. The defendant may also plead guilty after having made a plea agreement with the prosecution.

In making a plea of not guilty, the defendant formally contends that he or she did not commit the crime in question. A plea of not guilty will result in a criminal trial, especially for a serious crime. Finally, a plea of *nolo contendere* means, "I do not desire to contest the action." It resembles a guilty plea but is different in the sense that it is not a formal admission of responsibility for the crime. A plea of *nolo contendere* may not be used against the defendant in any later civil litigation that arises from the acts that led to the criminal charge. Also, in some jurisdictions, if the defendant enters a plea of *nolo contendere*, the court may not ask the defendant whether he or she committed the crime in question. But with a guilty plea, the defendant is required to make an **allocution**, in which the defendant explains to the judge exactly what he or she did and why. The allocution is documented in court records and can be used against the defendant in related civil proceedings.

---

[6]*Federal Rules of Criminal Procedure*, Rule 5.1(e). Available online at http://www.law.cornell.edu/rules/frcrmp/ (accessed September 19, 2013).

## ▶ Summary of Pretrial Proceedings

So far, the discussion has distinguished among five potential pretrial proceedings: (1) the initial appearance; (2) the probable cause hearing; (3) the pretrial release hearing; (4) the preliminary hearing; and (5) the arraignment. The initial appearance usually always takes place, regardless of the method of arrest or even of the charges in question, but it is not constitutionally required. Indeed, for a misdemeanor, the trial may take place at this stage.

The probable cause hearing is also not *required* by the Constitution. Nevertheless, a probable cause determination needs to be made at some stage of the criminal process. If the arrest is by warrant, the hearing is not necessary. If the arrest is warrantless, then a probable cause hearing is necessary but only if a preliminary hearing is not set to take place immediately. Also, if the arrest is premised on a grand jury indictment, a probable cause hearing will not be necessary. In short, the purpose of the probable cause hearing is to avoid an unnecessarily lengthy detention that is unsupported by probable cause.

A few court decisions seem to suggest that a separate pretrial release hearing is required, but the Supreme Court has offered no clarification on this matter. As a practical matter, it is sometimes worthwhile to make the bail decision in another hearing, such as the initial appearance. Today, whether a bail hearing is required hinges on the jurisdiction in question and the nature of the offense.

Finally, the preliminary hearing is required but only in limited circumstances and for certain offenses—usually felonies. If a prosecutor obtains a grand jury indictment within a short period of time, a preliminary hearing may not be necessary. On the other hand, if the prosecutor proceeds by information, then a preliminary hearing may be required. Once a person has been charged with a crime, he or she will be arraigned. At the arraignment, the defendant will be notified of the charges against him or her and be allowed to enter a formal plea of guilty, not guilty, or *nolo contendere*.

## ▶ Discovery

If one learned of the criminal process only by watching courtroom dramas on prime-time television, his or her understanding of the process would be sorely limited. It is rarely the case that prosecutors and defense attorneys are bitter enemies or that one side springs surprise evidence on the other side. Instead, criminal (as well as civil) trials in the United States are carefully choreographed events with few unpredictable twists and turns. In fact, as many a litigator will attest, criminal trials are relatively boring and predictable. Even the most celebrated criminal trial of the 1990s, the O. J. Simpson trial, put the most attentive of observers to sleep at times.

Trials in this country are rarely exciting for several reasons. First, most prosecutors and defense attorneys are not great orators. And second, through the process of *discovery*, each side *knows* what evidence the other side will present, with few exceptions.

**Discovery** is the process by which each party to a case learns of the evidence that the opposition will present. The *Federal Rules of Criminal Procedure* provide that the defendant may, upon request, *discover* from the prosecution (1) any written statements or transcriptions of oral statements made by the defendant that are in the prosecution's possession; (2) the defendant's prior criminal record; and (3) documents, photographs, tangible items, results from physical and mental evaluations, and other forms of real evidence considered *material* to the prosecution's case.[7] Evidence is considered *material* if it is consequential to the case or, more simply, capable of influencing the outcome of the case. If the defense requests items in the second or third categories, then the prosecution will be granted *reciprocal discovery*, where it learns of the defense's evidence. Relevant portions of Rule 16 are reprinted in Figure 10.2.

---

[7]*Federal Rules of Criminal Procedure*, Rule 16. Available online at http://www.law.cornell.edu/rules/frcrmp/ (accessed September 19, 2013).

▼

### (a) GOVERNMENT'S DISCLOSURE.

**(1)** *Information Subject to Disclosure.*

- Defendant's Oral Statement.
- Defendant's Written or Recorded Statement.
- Defendant's Prior Record.
- Documents and Objects.
- Reports of Examinations and Tests.
- Expert Witnesses.

*Information Not Subject to Disclosure.* . . . this rule does not authorize the discovery or inspection of reports, memoranda, or other internal government documents made by an attorney for the government or other government agent in connection with investigating or prosecuting the case. Nor does this rule authorize the discovery or inspection of statements made by prospective government witnesses . . .

### (b) DEFENDANT'S DISCLOSURE.

**(1)** *Information Subject to Disclosure.*

- Documents and Objects.
- Reports of Examinations and Tests.
- Expert Witnesses.

*Information Not Subject to Disclosure.* Except for scientific or medical reports, . . . discovery or inspection of reports, memoranda, or other documents made by the defendant, or the defendant's attorney or agent, during the case's investigation or defense; or a statement made to the defendant, or the defendant's attorney or agent, by (i) the defendant; a government or defense witness; or a prospective government or defense witness.

### (c) CONTINUING DUTY TO DISCLOSE.

A party who discovers additional evidence or material before or during trial must promptly disclose its existence to the other party or the court if:

**(1)** the evidence or material is subject to discovery or inspection under this rule; and

**(2)** the other party previously requested, or the court ordered, its production.

*Source: Federal Rules of Criminal Procedure, Rule 16*

**FIGURE 10.2 Discovery under the Federal Rules of Criminal Procedure.**

Rule 16 of the *Federal Rules of Criminal Procedure* seems to permit a great deal of information to be exchanged in discovery, but it is actually quite restrictive. Several states permit even more discovery, such as the names and addresses of all persons known to have any information concerning the case. This means that each side must provide their opponent with a list of *all* individuals likely to give testimony at trial.

It should be noted that parties to a case are also protected by *attorney–client* privilege. This is a rule of evidence that allows a party to refuse to disclose any confidential communication between the client and his or her attorney (such as discussions between the attorney and the client about the case, or information provided by the client to his or her attorney). Attorney–client privilege protects this information from disclosure at all times, including during discovery.

Similar to the confidential communications protected by attorney–client privilege, trial strategy is also protected from disclosure. For example, the method of argument that the prosecution wishes to use in order to convince the jury of a particular fact is not subject to discovery. Similarly, the order in which the defense seeks to call witnesses need not be communicated to the prosecution. Strategy is also referred to as *work product*. Work product is not shared during the discovery process.

The sections that follow focus on discovery by the prosecution, discovery by the defense, and constitutional issues raised in the discovery process. It is essential to keep in mind that discovery is part of the *pretrial process*. It takes place in the hours and days leading up to the criminal trial. But if, for example, a new witness becomes available during the course of a trial, then discovery can take place later in the criminal process, as well.

## Discovery by the Prosecution

Discovery by the prosecution is relatively limited because of the constitutional rights enjoyed by criminal defendants. For example, the defense cannot be compelled to provide the prosecution with incriminating information, particularly in the form of statements and admissions. The scope of prosecutorial discovery has been addressed repeatedly in the courts via the Fifth and Sixth Amendments.

### Fifth Amendment Restrictions

Although the Fifth Amendment protects the defendant from disclosing certain incriminating information, he or she may be required to disclose information regarding the defenses he or she intends to use at trial, such as alibis. In *Williams v. Florida*, 399 U.S. 78 (1970), the Court considered Florida's *notice of alibi statute*, which required the defendant, at the prosecution's request, to disclose alibi defenses coupled with a list of witnesses who would support them. The Court found that this type of discovery does not violate the Fifth Amendment because it is not self-incriminating. In fact, the purpose of an alibi defense is to exculpate (clear) the defendant. According to the Court, "Nothing in the Fifth Amendment privilege entitles a defendant as a matter of constitutional right to await the end of the State's case before announcing the nature of his defense, any more than it entitles him to await the jury's verdict on the State's case-in-chief before deciding whether or not to take the stand himself."

*Williams v. Florida (399 U.S. 78 [1970])*

The *Williams* decision extends to other defenses, as well. For example, if the defense intends to argue that the defendant is not guilty by reason of insanity, then the prosecutor must be notified in advance of this intention. Alternatively, if the defense intends to argue that the defendant acted in self-defense, then the prosecution should also be notified. The reason for requiring this notification is that it provides the prosecutor with an opportunity to plan its argument to the contrary.

The defense often must also supply the prosecution with a witness list containing the names of all the witnesses that may be called to testify. Often, the defense also must provide the prosecution with information about the testimony the witness is expected to give. Some critics believe that compelling the defense to supply a witness list to the prosecution is incriminatory, but in fact, the prosecution would eventually discover the names and identities of the witnesses, as well as their testimony, at trial anyway.

Although some states require the disclosure of witnesses, the defense *cannot* be required to tell the prosecutor whether the defendant will testify. In *Brooks v. Tennessee*, 406 U.S. 605 (1972), the Supreme Court declared unconstitutional a state statute that required the defendant, if he or she wished to testify, to do so immediately after the prosecution rested its case, and before any other defense witnesses are called. The Court held that the statute violated the Fifth Amendment's privilege against self-incrimination and diminished the defense counsel's ability to make such determinations as to when certain witnesses will testify. In reaching its decision, the Court cited *United States v. Shipp*, 359 F.2d 185 (1966):

> If the man charged with a crime takes the witness stand in his own behalf, any and every arrest and conviction, even for lesser felonies, can be brought before the jury by the prosecutor, and such evidence may have devastating and deadly effect, although unrelated to the offense charged. The decision as to whether the defendant in a criminal case shall take the stand is, therefore, often of utmost importance, and counsel must, in many cases,

meticulously balance the advantages and disadvantages of the prisoner's becoming a witness in his own behalf. Why, then, should a court insist that the accused must testify before any other evidence is introduced in his behalf, or be completely foreclosed from testifying thereafter? . . . This savors of judicial whim, even though sanctioned by some authorities; and the cause of justice and a fair trial cannot be subjected to such a whimsicality of criminal procedure.

It may prove useful, for example, to let the defendant take the stand at the *end* of the defense case if it is believed (1) that the defense's case was not particularly persuasive and (2) the defendant can offer testimony likely to sway the jury to support his or her version of events. The Fifth Amendment prohibits a court from denying defendants the ability to make this strategic decision.

In addition to witnesses, discovery extends to other forms of proof, including real evidence (such as a murder weapon) and documentary evidence (such as a falsified tax return). In general, the Fifth Amendment is not violated when the defense is compelled to disclose real and documentary evidence that will be introduced at trial. This is because the Fifth Amendment's protection against self-incrimination is considered a *personal* right—that is, it applies to *people*, not to real or documentary evidence. However, the defense *cannot* be compelled to disclose evidence that will *not* be used at trial because of attorney–client privilege.

In summary, the Fifth Amendment is *not* violated when the defense is forced to provide the prosecution, in advance of trial, any of the following: (1) an alibi or other affirmative defense that will be raised at trial; (2) notice of witnesses who are to testify, including their statements; or (3) real or documentary evidence concerning the crime in question. The Fifth Amendment *is* violated when the defense is compelled to (1) notify the prosecution as to whether the defendant intends to testify; (2) identify witnesses who will not testify at trial; or (3) disclose evidence that will not be introduced at trial.

### Sixth Amendment Restrictions

The Sixth Amendment provides, in relevant part, that the accused enjoys the right "to have compulsory process for obtaining witnesses in his favor." Compulsory process means compelling a witness to testify in court, and typically involves the use of a court-ordered subpoena. Some constitutional challenges to the discovery process have been raised on the grounds that the defendant was denied the right to call a witness to testify.

*United States v. Nobles*
*(422 U.S. 225 [1975])*

In *United States v. Nobles*, 422 U.S. 225 (1975), the defense attempted to call a private investigator to the stand whose testimony would have cast doubt on the prosecution's case. The trial judge ruled that the investigator could not testify until the prosecution received portions of the investigator's pretrial investigative report. The Supreme Court upheld this decision. The defense argued that this decision infringed on the accused's right to compulsory process—namely, to call the investigator to the stand. But according to the Court, "The Sixth Amendment does not confer the right to present testimony free from the legitimate demands of the adversarial system; one cannot invoke the Sixth Amendment as a justification for presenting what might have been a half-truth." The defense further argued that being forced to supply information from the investigator's report violated attorney–client privilege, but the Court countered by concluding that attorney–client privilege was basically waived when the defense decided to have the investigator testify about the contents of his report.

A second Sixth Amendment issue that has been raised with regard to discovery is whether the testimony of a witness can be excluded if the defense does not inform the prosecution that the witness will testify. In *Taylor v. Illinois*, 484 U.S. 400 (1988), the defense called a witness who had not been on a witness list supplied to the prosecution before trial. The trial court excluded the witness's testimony, citing a violation of discovery procedure. The defendant appealed, arguing that exclusion of the witness's testimony violated the

**PROSECUTORIAL DISCOVERY**

Anne Tator, the local prosecutor, learns from defendant Fred Lyons that he has a list of potential witnesses who will testify on his behalf. Tator learns further that Lyons will not call at least half of the potential witnesses. Nevertheless, Tator demands that Lyons supply her with the full names of everyone on the list, even the names of those who will not testify. Is Tator constitutionally entitled to discover the identities of witnesses whom the defense will not call to testify?

compulsory process clause of the Sixth Amendment. However, the Supreme Court ruled that exclusion of the testimony was appropriate and did not violate the Sixth Amendment. The purpose of discovery, the Court noted, is to "minimize the risk that fabricated testimony will be believed." (See also *Michigan v. Lucas*, 500 U.S. 145 [1991], for further discussion of the relationship between certain Sixth Amendment rights and the discovery process.)

In summary, *Nobles* and *Taylor* suggest that it is relatively difficult to infringe on a defendant's Sixth Amendment rights, as far as discovery is concerned. If the defense attempts to gain a tactical advantage either by failing to supply a complete list of witnesses, or failing to disclose documents the witnesses will rely on, then the trial court will be able to exclude the testimony without violating the Sixth Amendment right to compulsory process. Compulsory process must be preceded by making the appropriate disclosures in discovery.

## Discovery by the Defense

Naturally, discovery should benefit the *defense* more than the *prosecution*. After all, the prosecution presents the state's case against the defendant; it is only sensible that the defense should learn the nature of the prosecution's case. Usually, the prosecution will have more information than the defense because it must prove *beyond* a reasonable doubt that the defendant committed the crime. The defense, by contrast, only needs to raise reasonable doubt in the minds of the jurors that the defendant did *not* commit the crime.

### Cases Dealing with Discovery by the Defense

In *Williams v. Florida*, discussed previously, the Supreme Court required the defense to notify the prosecution as to any defenses, alibi or otherwise, it would assert as well as a list of witnesses who would testify in support of those defenses. In *Wardius v. Oregon*, 412 U.S. 470 (1973), the Court declared that this type of discovery must be *reciprocal*. That is, the Court held that the prosecution must provide the defense with a list of witnesses who will testify in rebuttal to the defendant's alibi or defense:

*Wardius v. Oregon*
*(412 U.S. 470 [1973])*

> [I]n the absence of a strong showing of state interests to the contrary, discovery must be a two-way street. The State may not insist that trial be run as a "search for truth" so far as defense witnesses are concerned, while maintaining "poker game" secrecy for its own witnesses. It is fundamentally unfair to require a defendant to divulge the details of his own case while at the same time subjecting him to the hazard of surprise concerning refutation of the very pieces of evidence which he disclosed to the State.

A key feature of the *Wardius* decision is that it applies only to evidence that is truly "reciprocal." More specifically, if the defense supplies the prosecution with a list of

## DEFENSE DISCOVERY

The so-called Jencks Act, 18 U.S.C. § 3500 (1976), provides, in part, that "[i]n any criminal prosecution brought by the United States, no statement or report in the possession of the United States which was made by a Government witness or prospective Government witness (other than the defendant) shall be the subject of subpoena, discovery, or inspection until said witness has testified on direct examination in the trial of the case." Assume that a defendant wishes to obtain a written statement made by one of the prosecution's witnesses *prior* to the witness's testimony. Clearly, the Jencks Act prohibits this. Thus, the defendant claims that the act seriously restricts his ability to conduct an effective defense. If you represented the appellate court charged with deciding on the constitutionality of this section of the Jencks Act, how would you decide?

witnesses who will testify, the prosecution is not necessarily required to supply the defense with something wholly disconnected from a witness list. This was the decision reached in *United States v. Armstrong*, 517 U.S. 456 (1996), in which the Supreme Court held that the prosecution need only supply the defense with evidence that is "material to the preparation of the defendant's case."

Basically, if the evidence the defense wants to discover is a "shield," or used to refute the state's case, access will be granted. If, by contrast, the evidence is a "sword," or intended to challenge prosecutorial conduct, access will not be granted.

In *State v. Eads*, 166 N.W.2d 766 (Iowa 1969), one court summarized the restrictions on defense discovery even for "shield" purposes. If a *state interest* is likely to be compromised, then the prosecution is not required to disclose evidence to the defense, even if such evidence is intended to be used by the defense to challenge or refute the state's case. State interests preclude discovery by the defense under these circumstances:

(1) It would afford the defendant increased opportunity to produce perjured testimony and to fabricate evidence to meet the State's case; (2) witnesses would be subject to bribe, threat and intimidation; (3) since the State cannot compel the defendant to disclose . . . evidence [protected by the Fifth Amendment], disclosure by the State would afford the defendant an unreasonable advantage at trial; and (4) disclosure is unnecessary in any event because of the other sources of information which defendant has under existing law.

In the wake of *Eads*, several states have imposed restrictions on defense discovery when certain state interests have been called into question. For example, many states prohibit discovery of the identities of prosecution witnesses until after they have testified so as to prevent defense from tampering with (or threatening) prosecution witnesses.

## Nonreciprocal Discovery

With few exceptions, discovery is a two-way street: The defense must supply the prosecution with certain information and vice versa. For example, as mentioned above, when the defense wants to assert an alibi, it must supply the prosecution with that alibi; the prosecution must, in turn, supply the defense with a list of witnesses who will testify in rebuttal to the alibi.

The restrictions on the discovery that may be sought by the defense, although controversial, do not leave the defense at a disadvantage. In fact, in some circumstances, the prosecution is required to supply information, but without a reciprocal obligation by the defense. Specifically, the prosecution has a constitutional duty to disclose exculpatory evidence. This duty is significant because typically, such evidence may be critical to the outcome of the case. A requirement to disclose exculpatory evidence—evidence that would otherwise not be offered by the prosecution at trial—would seem to disadvantage the prosecution. Meanwhile, the defense is not required to disclose evidence that *it* will not use at trial.

The prosecution also has a constitutional duty to preserve evidence, but the defense does not. These two methods of so-called **nonreciprocal discovery** are discussed in the two subsections that follow.

## The Prosecution's Duty to Disclose Exculpatory Evidence

As a matter of due process, the prosecution has a constitutional duty to reveal exculpatory evidence to the defense. If the prosecution obtains evidence suggesting that the defendant is not guilty, it needs to inform the defense of this fact. This requirement is an ongoing duty, both before and during trial. However, if the evidence clearly establishes factual innocence, it should be disclosed before the trial (*United States v. Ruiz*, 536 U.S. 622 [2002]). Numerous Supreme Court cases have emphasized this important requirement.

In *Mooney v. Holohan*, 294 U.S. 103 (1935), the prosecution knowingly used perjured testimony to convict the defendant. The Court held that due process is violated when the prosecution "has contrived a conviction through the pretense of a trial which in truth is but used as a means of depriving a defendant of liberty through a deliberate deception of court and jury by the presentation of testimony known to be perjured." In *Mooney*, the prosecution *arranged* to have a witness give false testimony. Later, the Court applied the rule in *Mooney* to cases where perjured testimony is *not* arranged by the prosecution but, rather, given by a witness on his or her own volition. If the prosecution later learns that the testimony is false, it is bound to notify the defense (*Alcorta v. Texas*, 355 U.S. 28 [1957]).

In *Napue v. Illinois*, 360 U.S. 264 (1959), the Supreme Court held that the prosecution is also bound to disclose its knowledge of false testimony that affects the credibility of a witness. In that case, a witness testified falsely that the prosecution had not promised him leniency for his willingness to cooperate. Since the prosecutor knew the witness's testimony was false and did nothing to correct it, the defendant's conviction was reversed, since "[t]he jury's estimate of the truthfulness and reliability of a given witness may well be determinative of guilt or innocence, and it is upon such subtle factors as the possible interest of the witness in testifying falsely that a defendant's life or liberty may depend."

In *Brady v. Maryland*, 373 U.S. 83 (1963), perhaps the most important case in this area of law, the Supreme Court drastically altered its previous decisions concerning the prosecution's duty to disclose exculpatory evidence. The Court held that "the suppression by the prosecution of evidence favorable to an accused upon request violates due process where the evidence is *material either to guilt or to punishment*, irrespective of the good faith or bad faith of the prosecution" (emphasis added). The Court also eloquently stated:

*Brady v. Maryland*
*(373 U.S. 83 [1963])*

> Society wins not only when the guilty are convicted but when criminal trials are fair; our system of the administration of justice suffers when any accused is treated unfairly. An inscription on the walls of the Department of Justice states the proposition candidly for the federal domain: "The United States wins its point whenever justice is done its citizens in the courts." . . . A prosecution that withholds evidence on demand of an accused which, if made available, would tend to exculpate him or reduce the penalty helps shape a trial that bears heavily on the defendant. That casts the prosecutor in the role of an architect of a proceeding that does not comport with standards of justice, even though, as in the present case, his action is not "the result of guile."

▼

Whether evidence is *material* is not entirely clear, but in *United States v. Agurs*, 427 U.S. 97 (1976), the Supreme Court offered some clarification. The defendant stabbed and killed a man with the victim's knife. She claimed self-defense but was nevertheless found guilty. The defense argued that because the prosecution had not disclosed that the victim had a prior criminal record, the conviction should be reversed. The Court disagreed, stating that the victim's prior criminal record was not material enough to the question of guilt or innocence. Important to this decision is the fact that the defense did not request information about the victim's prior criminal record at trial, only on appeal. Had the defense explicitly requested such information at trial, a different decision probably would have resulted.

An obvious problem is posed by the *Agurs* decision: If the defense does not know what exculpatory evidence the prosecution has, it cannot request that evidence. Does this mean that the defense should be denied access to exculpatory evidence if it does not request it? In *United States v. Bagley*, 473 U.S. 667 (1985), the Court sought to answer this question but, unfortunately, offered little clarification. The defense had posed a broad request to the prosecution for discovery of "any deals, promises or inducements made to [prosecution] witnesses in exchange for their testimony." The prosecution failed to disclose some of the requested information, but on appeal, the Supreme Court held that this action did not constitute a due process violation. According to the Court, there was no "reasonable probability" that the exculpatory evidence would have influenced the outcome of the case.

What amounts to a "reasonable probability" that the outcome of the case may be altered by failure to disclose exculpatory evidence? In *Kyles v. Whitley*, 514 U.S. 419 (1995), the Court identified four elements that should be considered. First, reasonable probability does not mean a preponderance of evidence but something less. Second, when exculpatory evidence is included, the reasonable probability standard does not require the defense to show that the other evidence presented by the prosecution is insufficient to prove guilt. Third, once the defense demonstrates a reasonable probability of a different outcome, its job is done; the appellate court cannot decide that the prosecution's failure to disclose evidence amounted to a harmless error. Finally, while the prosecution is not required to present every shred of evidence that may prove helpful to the defense, it "must be assigned the consequent responsibility to gauge the likely net effect of all such evidence and make disclosure when the point of 'reasonable probability' is reached."

In summary, the prosecution's constitutional duty to disclose exculpatory evidence hinges on whether such evidence would have a reasonable probability of changing the outcome of the case. Who makes the decision as to what constitutes a reasonable probability that the outcome of a case will be changed if exculpatory evidence is not disclosed? Depending on the case, it is usually the judge or the prosecutor who makes the decision.

If the defense can show that the prosecution possesses exculpatory evidence, then a hearing to determine the reasonable probability issue may be required. However, if the defense has no knowledge of specific evidence possessed by the prosecution that may prove exculpatory, the prosecution can make the decision. Indeed, in *Pennsylvania v. Ritchie*, 480 U.S. 39 (1987), the Supreme Court held that the "defendant's right to discover exculpatory evidence does not include the unsupervised authority to search through the Commonwealth's files."

In *District Attorney v. Osborne*, 557 U.S. 52 (2009), the Court was confronted with the question of whether the due process clause requires the state to turn over DNA evidence to those found guilty of criminal activity. It decided that there is no such duty and that legislatures are the proper forum to set appropriate rules governing the release of DNA evidence. This decision makes clear, then, that there is no constitutional duty to disclose

*Kyles v. Whitley*
*(514 U.S. 419 [1995])*

**A Timeline of Cases Involving the Prosecution's Duty to Disclose Exculpatory Evidence**

| 1935 | 1957 | 1959 | 1963 |
|---|---|---|---|
| **Mooney v. Holohan, 294 U.S. 103** "A criminal conviction procured by the state prosecuting authorities solely by the use of perjured testimony known to them to be perjured and knowingly used by them in order to procure the conviction, is without due process of law and in violation of the Fourteenth Amendment." | **Alcorta v. Texas, 355 U.S. 28** If the prosecution knows a witness gives or gave perjured testimony, it must notify the defense. | **Napue v. Illinois, 360 U.S. 264** Prosecutorial fabrication concerning the credibility of a witness constitutes a due process violation. | **Brady v. Maryland, 373 U.S. 83** "[S]uppression by the prosecution of evidence favorable to an accused upon request violates due process where the evidence is *material either to guilt or to punishment*, irrespective of the good faith or bad faith of the prosecution" (emphasis added). |

**FIGURE 10.3**

possibly exculpatory evidence *after* trial. "After trial" means post sentencing. If a prosecutor withholds evidence that could affect the defendant's sentence, then a due process violation occurs (see, *Cone v. Bell*, 556 U.S. ___ [2009]).

In 2011, the Supreme Court decided another DNA-related case (*Skinner v. Switzer*, 562 U.S. ___ [2011]). Convicted inmates who seek access to DNA evidence to prove their innocence may file Section 1983 lawsuits, but not proceed via petitioning for habeas corpus relief. So while the Court seemed to close the door on DNA access in *Osborne*, it cracked it open again in *Skinner*. Federal courts may hear inmates claims that their state DNA testing procedures are flawed, but the mechanism for doing so is via filing a Section 1983 civil rights lawsuit.

Most recently, *Smith v. Cain*, 565 U.S. ___ (2012), the Supreme Court decided whether disclosure to the defense of police files containing eyewitness statements was material, where such statements are the only evidence linking the defendant to the crime in question. It held in part: ". . . the eyewitness's testimony was the *only* evidence linking Smith to the crime, and the eyewitness's undisclosed statements contradicted his testimony. The eyewitness's statements were plainly material, and the State's failure to disclose those statements to the defense thus violated *Brady*."

See Figure 10.3 for a summary of cases governing the prosecution's duty to disclose exculpatory evidence.

## The Prosecution's Duty to Preserve Evidence

The prosecution is also constitutionally bound to *preserve* evidence. This means that the prosecution cannot destroy exculpatory evidence in an effort to gain a conviction. To do so would be a violation of due process. For the defense to convince the court that the prosecution has failed to meet its duty to preserve evidence, it must demonstrate three facts: (1) that the evidence was expected to "play a significant role in the suspect's defense"; (2) that the evidence was of "such a nature that the defendant would be unable to obtain comparable evidence by other reasonably available means"; and (3) that the destruction of the evidence was a result of "official animus toward [the defendant] or . . . a conscious effort to suppress exculpatory evidence" (*California v. Trombetta*, 467 U.S. 479 [1984]). Note that the third requirement departs from the *Brady* decision discussed in the previous section. *Brady* did not consider the prosecution's state of mind relevant.

In *Arizona v. Youngblood*, 488 U.S. 51 (1988), the Supreme Court clarified the third factor—the motivation of the prosecution. The Court stated that "unless a criminal

*Arizona v. Youngblood* (488 U.S. 51 [1988])

| **1976** | **1985** | **1995** |
|---|---|---|
| ***United States* v. *Agurs,* 427 U.S. 97** Some clarification is brought to the *Brady* notion of "material" information. The prosecution's failure to disclose the victim's prior criminal record was not material enough to the question of guilt or innocence. | ***United States* v. *Bagley,* 473 U.S. 667** The prosecution's failure to disclose information about "any deals, promises or inducements made to [government] witnesses in exchange for their testimony" was deemed not to have a "reasonable probability" of changing the outcome of the case. | ***Kyles* v. *Whitley*, 514 U.S. 419** Clarification is brought to the *Bagley* notion of "reasonable probability." First, reasonable probability does not mean a preponderance of evidence but something less. Second, when exculpatory evidence is included, the reasonable probability standard does not require the defense to show that the other evidence presented by the prosecution is insufficient to prove guilt. Third, once the defense demonstrates a reasonable probability of a different outcome, its job is done. Finally, while the prosecution is not required to present every shred of evidence that may prove helpful to the defense, it "must be assigned the consequent responsibility to gauge the likely net effect of all such evidence and make disclosure when the point of 'reasonable probability' is reached." |

**FIGURE 10.3** *Continued*

defendant can show bad faith on the part of the police [or prosecution], failure to preserve potentially useful evidence does not constitute due process of law."

Not only must prosecutors preserve evidence but so, too, must police. A careful record must be maintained documenting everyone who possessed each item since the time it was acquired by the police, and exactly what was done with the item at each step in the process. One of the purposes of a **chain of custody** is to avoid claims by the defense that evidence has been tainted or tampered with. Figure 10.4 presents portions of the Gallatin, Tennessee, Police Department's policy for processing and preserving evidence.

---

**9.30.2 Statutory Authority and Departmental Authorization**

Any property used in commission or furtherance of certain crimes or used for the transportation of stolen property may be confiscated and forfeited as per TCA 40-33-101 through TCA 40-33-204.

Any time an officer wishes to seize or confiscate property under these circumstances (i.e. seizure of vehicle driven by an individual whose license is revoked), the officer will contact his or her shift supervisor for authorization. The shift supervisor will in turn notify the Field Operations Commander and/or the Chief of Police, or his or her designee, for authorization prior to the vehicle being seized by the requesting officer.

**9.30.3 Processing Evidence**

An officer that has evidence to be placed in the evidence room will make an inventory of the evidence at the location it was found or recovered. The seizing officer will properly handle, mark, and package all evidence, and place the evidence in the collection box in the processing room, if practical, or directly to the evidence room as soon as practical. The seizing officer must turn in evidence no later than the end of his or her tour of duty.

Evidence that cannot be marked directly for identification will be placed in a sealed container or package and the package will be marked for identification. Items will be placed in separate packages when the possibility of contamination exists. Items requiring lab analysis or processing must be placed in separate packages. Money and controlled substances will be counted or weighed by two officers, placed in envelopes separate from other evidence, and then sealed. Both officers will sign the envelopes.

**FIGURE 10.4 Example of a Chain of Custody Policy**

**A Timeline of Cases Involving the Prosecution's Duty to Disclose Exculpatory Evidence,** *continued*

| 2004 | 2009 | 2009 | 2011 | 2012 |
|------|------|------|------|------|
| ***Banks* v. *Dretke*, 540 U.S. 668** The prosecution's failure to disclose that a key witness was a paid government informant was considered "material" to whether Banks was "dangerous," an aggravating factor under the state's death penalty statute (the information should have been shared with the jury). | ***District Attorney* v. *Osborne*, 557 U.S. 52** There is no constitutional duty to disclose possibly exculpatory evidence (in this case, DNA evidence) *after* trial. | ***Cone* v. *Bell*, 556 U.S. \_\_\_** If a prosecutor with holds evidence that could affect the defendant's sentence, then a due process violation occurs. | ***Skinner* v. *Switzer*, 562 U.S. \_\_\_** Federal courts may hear inmates' claims that their state DNA testing procedures are flawed, but the mechanism for doing so is via filing a Section 1983 civil rights lawsuit. | ***Smith* v. *Cain*, 565 U.S. \_\_\_** Failure to disclosur to the defense police files containing eyewitness statements was material, particularly because the eyewitness statements were the only evidence linking the defendant to the crime. |

**FIGURE 10.3** *Continued*

---

Evidence of a hazardous nature will be appropriately packaged and stored in accordance with necessary safety precautions. Such substances include, but are not limited to, items that may have been exposed to or contaminated by communicable diseases, hazardous chemicals or waste products, or explosive or highly combustible products. When appropriate, the Property Officer will make arrangements and assume responsibility for storage and control of such items outside the evidence room.

An evidence envelope will be filled out and sealed for all evidence. If the items or evidence is too large to be placed into an envelope, only the evidence control form will be placed with the item. The chain of custody form will be forwarded with all required reports.

The reporting officer will document all evidence on the evidence control form. The reporting officer will fill out a chain of custody form. The departmental case number will be placed on all evidence forms.

If an officer needs a particular piece of property processed, the officer may request Investigations to make arrangements or assist in making arrangements, or may process the property himself or herself. Vehicles are to be processed at the scene, the impound lot, or other appropriate location.

### 9.30.4 Impounding Evidence

The Property Officer will be responsible for receiving, storing, maintaining, releasing, and accounting for all evidence in compliance with this policy. When evidence is deposited with the Property Officer or in an approved holding facility, an evidence receipt will be completed by the seizing officer. The evidence receipt will include all information necessary to both document and ensure the integrity or the chain of custody. All drugs will be weighed and monies counted by the Property Officer and recorded on the evidence receipt. The Property Officer will be responsible for developing and maintaining a master file of all evidence invoices and evidence tags completed. This file will be cross-indexed with the chain of custody file.

### 9.30.5 Storage of Evidence

The Property Officer will assign a storage location for each item of evidence and record this information on the evidence receipt and evidence tag. Evidence requiring added security, including money, precious metals, jewelry, gemstones, weapons,

**FIGURE 10.4** *Continued*

narcotics, and dangerous drugs, will be stored in a separate secured area. Perishable items will be stored in a refrigerator or other suitable container.

### 9.30.6 Access to the Evidence Room

Only employees authorized by the Chief may enter the evidence room. A log will be kept by the Property Officer to identify each authorized employee entering the evidence room.

### 9.30.7 Inspections of the Evidence Room

On a monthly basis, the Staff Services Commander will make an inspection of the evidence room to ensure adherence to appropriate policies and procedures. Unannounced inspections of the evidence room will be conducted semiannually as directed by the Chief. An annual inventory of evidence held by the Department will be conducted by a commanding officer, appointed by the Chief, not routinely or directly connected with evidence control.

### 9.30.8 Recording Transfers of Custody

The Property Officer will be responsible for developing and maintaining a file that documents all changes in custody of physical evidence. The file will be capable of readily identifying the individual or organization currently maintaining custody of all evidence. A written record of all transfers of physical evidence will be made. Officers who assume custody of evidence from the evidence room bear full responsibility for ensuring its security, proper storage, and maintenance, and for the ready retrieval of such evidence upon demand.

### 9.30.16 Removing Evidence from Storage

When evidence is needed for court, it may be obtained from the Property Room. This will be done during the Property Room hours. The officer will sign the Chain of Custody Form and assume full responsibility for the evidence. The Property Room Officer will note the officer's name and reason for removing the evidence on the appropriate log. All evidence will be returned at the end of the day's proceedings. If the Property Room Officer is not on-duty at the time the evidence is returned, the officer will have his or her supervisor place the evidence in the Evidence Locker. This will be noted on the Chain of Custody Form. If the evidence is in a sealed container or envelope, it will not be opened unless directed by the court or is needed for processing.

*Source*: From *General Directives Manual*, Gallatin, Tennessee, Police Department (December 28, 1999). Used courtesy of the Gallatin Police Department.

**FIGURE 10.4** *Continued*

## DECISION-MAKING EXERCISE 10.10

### DISCLOSURE OF EXCULPATORY EVIDENCE

Leonard Baum was convicted of first-degree murder and sentenced to death. In preparing an appeal, Baum's attorney learned that the state never disclosed certain evidence favorable to Baum. That evidence included eyewitness statements taken by the police following the murder; statements made to the police by an informant, who was never called to testify; and a list of the license numbers of cars parked at the crime scene on the night of the murder, which did not include Baum's car. Baum argues that had this evidence been disclosed at his trial, there would have been a reasonable probability that he would not have been found guilty. Should Baum be granted a new trial?

# Summary

## 1. Explain the purpose and process of the initial appearance.

It is important to underscore the fact that the pretrial process differs substantially across the United States. Some jurisdictions follow the procedures outlined in this chapter, in the order presented (see Figure 10.5). Others follow the same basic procedures but in a different order. Still others combine various hearings into a single hearing or do not require them at all. Readers are advised to familiarize themselves with the procedures followed in the jurisdiction where they reside.

That said, the pretrial process always begins with an initial appearance. This is where, at a minimum, the accused is advised of the charges against him or her. In a misdemeanor case, the trial may take place at this stage. Also, the accused may be advised of his or her privilege against self-incrimination as well as the right to appointed counsel, if he or she is indigent.

## 2. Explain the purpose and the process of the probable cause hearing.

After the initial appearance, a probable cause hearing may be required. If the defendant is arrested without a warrant, a separate court hearing may be held to determine whether there was probable cause to arrest. This determination can be made independently of any other hearing. The probable cause hearing, if required, needs to be held promptly after arrest, usually within 48 hours.

## 3. Summarize bail and other types of pretrial release.

Following the probable cause hearing is the pretrial release determination. The accused may be released on bail, in which case he or she deposits a certain amount of money with the court (possibly through a bail bonds agent) as an incentive to show up for later hearings. Failure to show up will result in, among other things, forfeiture of the bail money. A defendant can also be released on his or her own recognizance (ROR). At the other extreme, a defendant who is presumed to pose a significant risk of flight may be held without bail. This tactic is known as preventive detention. Three different criteria are considered in making the pretrial release determination: the accused's (1) flight risk, (2) level of dangerousness, and (3) financial status.

## 4. Explain the purpose and process of the preliminary hearing.

The preliminary hearing is the next stage in the pretrial process. The preliminary hearing differs from the other hearings already discussed in that it is intended to be a check on the prosecution's charging decision. A preliminary hearing is generally not required, however, if (1) the defendant waives it or (2) the prosecutor proceeds by indictment. In the latter instance, the grand jury essentially serves as an appropriate check on the charging decision.

## 5. Summarize the arraignment process.

After the preliminary hearing (or grand jury indictment), the arraignment is held. At this stage, the defendant is formally notified of the charges against him or her. In addition, he or she enters a plea of guilty, not guilty, or *nolo contendere*.

**Initial Appearance**

a. Not required in all jurisdictions
b. Trial may take place at this stage for a misdemeanor
c. Accused informed of complaint against him or her, of protection against self-incrimination, of right to appointed counsel if need be

**Probable Cause Hearing**

a. Only required if arrest is warrantless
b. Must be held within 48 hours, but clear time limit has not been set

**Pretrial Release/Bail Determination**

a. Methods of ensuring defendant's return are bail, release on recognizance, preventive detention
b. Bail cannot be excessive

**Preliminary Hearing**

a. Serves as a check on charging decision and is not same as probable cause hearing
b. May not be held if defendant waives it or prosecution proceeds by indictment

**Arraignment**

a. Suspect advised of formal charges filed against him or her
b. Suspect enters plea of guilty, not guilty, or *nolo contendere*

**Discovery**

a. Prosecution advises defense of evidence to be used in securing conviction
b. Defense advises prosecution of evidence to be used in securing acquittal
c. Prosecution must disclose exculpatory evidence and preserve it

*Note:* There are several variations to this order of events throughout the United States.

**FIGURE 10.5 Summary of the Pretrial Process**

# 6. Summarize the discovery process.

The last stage of the pretrial process discussed in this chapter is discovery. In actuality, however, discovery can take place early on, perhaps prior to a preliminary hearing, or well into a trial. Discovery is the process whereby the prosecution advises the defense of the evidence it will use to secure a conviction. The defense must also disclose the evidence it intends to use to exonerate the defendant. The prosecution has a duty to disclose the defendant's statements in its possession, tangible evidence that will be introduced at trial, test results that are material to the case, and a list of witnesses who will testify for the prosecution as well as the substance of their testimony. The defense, by contrast, must supply the prosecution with its intended alibi or other defense as well as a list of witnesses (and their statements) who will testify in support of the defense. Finally, the due process clause of the Fourteenth Amendment requires the prosecution to disclose exculpatory evidence to the defense *and* to preserve evidence while in its custody.

## Key Terms

allocution *290*

arraignment *290*

bail *280*

bail bond agent *282*

booking *277*

chain of custody *300*

discovery *291*

guilty *290*

initial appearance *278*

*nolo contendere 290*

nonreciprocal discovery *297*

not guilty *290*

preliminary hearing *288*

pretrial release *280*

preventive detention *285*

probable cause hearing *278*

release on recognizance (ROR) *284*

## Key Cases

### Probable Cause Hearing

- *Gerstein v. Pugh*, 420 U.S. 103 (1975)
- *Riverside County v. McLaughlin*, 500 U.S. 44 (1991)

### Pretrial Release

- *Stack v. Boyle*, 342 U.S. 1 (1951)
- *Schall v. Martin*, 467 U.S. 253 (1984)
- *Schilb v. Kuebel*, 404 U.S. 357 (1971)
- *Bell v. Wolfish*, 441 U.S. 520 (1979)

### Preliminary Hearing

- *Lem Woon v. Oregon*, 229 U.S. 586 (1913)
- *Coleman v. Alabama*, 399 U.S. 1 (1970)

### Discovery

- *Williams v. Florida*, 399 U.S. 78 (1970)
- *United States v. Nobles*, 422 U.S. 225 (1975)
- *Wardius v. Oregon*, 412 U.S. 470 (1973)
- *Brady v. Maryland*, 373 U.S. 83 (1963)
- *Kyles v. Whitley*, 514 U.S. 419 (1995)
- *Arizona v. Youngblood*, 488 U.S. 51 (1988)

## Further Exploration

1. Shawn Drumgold was convicted and imprisoned for the murder of a 12-year-old girl. The key witness against him, Ricky Evans, a homeless man, was given cash, meals, and housing at a Howard Johnson Hotel for several months, all paid for by the police department. Drumgold is now challenging his conviction on the grounds that the prosecution failed to disclose this information. How should the court rule? See *Drumgold v. Callahan*, 806 F.Supp.2d 405 (D. Mass. 2011).

2. Read the following facts from a real case (*United States v. Rodriguez*, 489 Fed.Appx. 528 [3d Cir. 2012]) and decide whether the *Brady* claim has merit:

   In September 2007, Philadelphia plainclothes police officers on patrol in an unmarked car observed Stanley Rodriguez conversing with the driver of a car stopped in the middle of the street. In plain view, Rodriguez passed a rolled-up bookbag to the driver, who placed two rectangular objects wrapped in green tape into the bag and returned it to Rodriguez. One of the officers identified the objects as kilogram packages of cocaine from their shape and wrapping, and the officers followed Rodriguez. Alerted by a bystander to the presence of the police, Rodriguez fled on foot, throwing the bookbag onto the roof of a nearby garage. The officers apprehended Rodriguez, and then retrieved the bookbag containing the two green-wrapped objects. Laboratory analysis subsequently determined the packages contained two kilograms of cocaine.

Rodriguez was subsequently indicted [for drug offenses]. Prior to trial, the government informed Rodriguez that several officers involved in his arrest had been subject to complaints unrelated to his case investigated by the Philadelphia Police Internal Affairs Division (IAD). The government subsequently informed Rodriguez that most of the investigations involved Officer Norman, whose credibility had been undermined in the course of an investigation and against whom one investigation remained open, but that allegations of improper search had resulted in a finding of departmental violation against Officers

Reynolds and Walker and remained open against Officers Betts, O'Malley, and McGrory. Rodriguez filed a motion for . . . review of the internal affairs files concerning the open investigations, which the government opposed, noting in its brief that it did not intend to call Officer Norman. The District Court denied the motion, holding the IAD investigation into an alleged improper search was neither material nor exculpatory as required under *Brady*.

3. Should a prosecutor be required to inform members of the jury that a witness was told he would not be charged with a crime in exchange for his testimony against the defendant? Read the Supreme Court's decision in *Giglio v. United States*, 405 U.S. 150 (1972). Also read the article at the following URL: http://www.fbi.gov/stats-services/publications/law-enforcement-bulletin/october-2011/disclosure-in-the-modern-age (accessed May 13, 2013). How did *Giglio* create its own category of discovery material? How is the case relevant to police officers who give testimony?

# Review Questions

1. What is booking?
2. What is the initial appearance? What is its purpose?
3. What is the probable cause hearing? What is its purpose? When is it required?
4. How soon after arrest must the probable cause hearing be held?
5. What methods of pretrial release are available? Define each.
6. What are the criteria for pretrial release? How have they been used in court decisions?
7. Summarize the key cases dealing with the treatment of pretrial detainees.
8. What is the preliminary hearing? What is its purpose? When is it required?
9. What rights does the defendant enjoy during the preliminary hearing?
10. What is discovery?
11. Citing cases, what are the restrictions on discovery by the prosecution?
12. Citing cases, what are the restrictions on discovery by the defense?
13. What is nonreciprocal discovery?
14. Explain what it means to require the prosecution to disclose exculpatory evidence. What are the consequences if the prosecution fails to do so?
15. Is the prosecution bound to preserve evidence? The police? If so, how?

# Web Links and Exercises

1. The pretrial process: read more about the pretrial process and browse back issues of *The Pretrial Reporter*.
URL (click on the "Resources" tab): http://www.pretrial.org (accessed May 13, 2013).

2. Bail: read more about how bail works:
Suggested URL: http://www.aboutbail.com/pages/how-bail-bonds-work (accessed May 13, 2013).

3. Bail bonds agents: read more about bail bonds agents at the Web site for the Professional Bail Agents of the United States. Click on the "Bail Information" tab and then on the "History of Bail" tab to read about the history of bail in the United States.
URL: http://pbus.com (accessed May 13, 2013).

4. *Federal Rules of Criminal Procedure*: read about the rules of criminal procedure (including discovery rules) in federal court.
Suggested URL: http://www.law.cornell.edu/rules/frcrmp (accessed May 13, 2013).

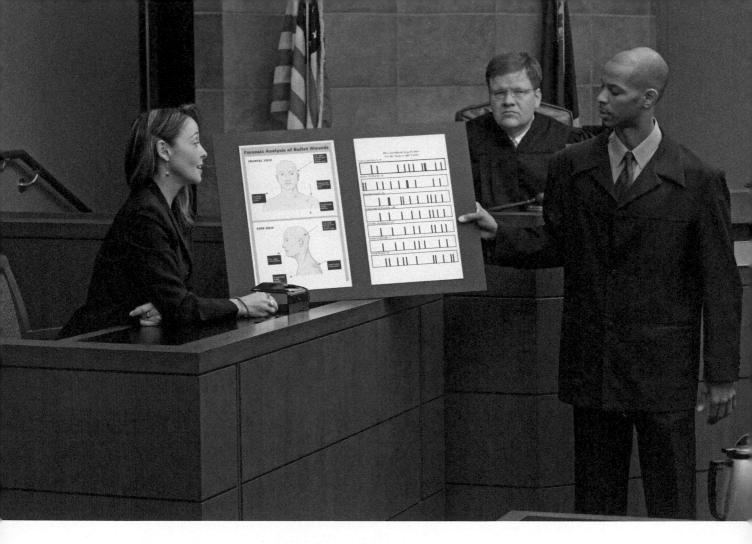

# 11 Prosecutors, Grand Juries, and Defense Attorneys

## LEARNING OBJECTIVES

When you complete this chapter, you should be able to:

**1** *Describe the prosecutor's role, prosecutor's discretion, and the issues surrounding prosecutorial misconduct.*

**2** *Explain the concept of joinder and reasons for it.*

**3** *Explain the purpose, functions, and powers of a grand jury.*

**4** *Outline the development of the right to counsel.*

**OUTLINE**

## Introduction: Bringing Charges and Mounting a Defense

This chapter will focus on the roles of the prosecutor, grand jury, and defense attorney. It must be emphasized that all of these entities have an important role to play in the case *even before the pretrial process begins*. For example, the right to counsel attaches to varying degrees well before the pretrial process is set into motion. Similarly, when the services of the grand jury are required, it can perform an investigative function well before the arrest stage of the criminal process. Prosecutors, too, perform a great deal of work before the pretrial process.

# ▶ The Prosecutor

The prosecutor is the official given the task of charging criminal suspects in the name of the government and obtaining convictions of those responsible for violating the law. There are several types of prosecutors in the United States. U.S. attorneys are prosecutors in the federal criminal justice system. District attorneys, or state's attorneys, are the elected chief prosecutors in state criminal justice systems. Most often, they are elected to head county offices. Below the district attorney are deputy district attorneys or assistant state's attorneys who actually litigate most criminal cases in court. Attorneys general, whether state or federal, are the main legal advisor to the government in their jurisdictions. Their role is primarily one of legal advising, rather than prosecution. City attorneys are, with some exceptions, the chief legal advisors to city government officials. Most criminal prosecutions are handled at the county level, so this chapter's discussion is focused primarily on district attorneys and state's attorneys and their deputies.

Article II, Section 3, of the U.S. Constitution states that the executive branch of the federal government "shall take Care that the Laws be faithfully executed." This constitutionally mandated duty to execute the law falls on prosecutors. Of course, police officers also execute the law, but prosecutors possess the authority to decide whether to bring formal charges against suspected criminals. As the Supreme Court noted in *Bordenkircher v. Hayes*, 434 U.S. 357 (1978), "[S]o long as the prosecutor has probable cause to believe that the accused committed an offense defined by statute, the decision whether or not to prosecute, and what charge to file or bring before a grand jury, generally rests entirely on his discretion." Prosecutors do not have *unlimited* discretion, however. There are important restrictions on their decision to charge. Some of these limitations stem from the Constitution, while others stem from statutes and other sources.

## The Charging Decision

The prosecutor generally has the authority to decide whether to proceed with charges. This is known as **prosecutorial discretion**. He or she can elect not to charge for a number of reasons, even over strenuous objection by the victim or the person reporting the alleged crime. The prosecutor's discretion also comes into play in the process of *plea bargaining* (discussed in Chapter 12) in which the defendant can accept a guilty plea for a lesser offense than the one charged. Finally, prosecutors sometimes must answer to authorities that mandate, or at least strongly encourage, prosecution of particular types of offenses. Figure 11.1 presents portions of a federal prosecutor's charging document (also referred to in some jurisdictions as "information").

## Deciding Not to Prosecute

The most obvious reason for deciding not to prosecute is lack of evidence. The prosecutor may determine that, based on the evidence presented by the police, the suspect is innocent.

UNITED STATES OF AMERICA  )
                          )
v.                        )        No.____
                          )
ANTHONY MATTHEWS          )        Violations: Title 18, United States Code,
                          )        Section 1343

<u>COUNT ONE</u>

The UNITED STATES ATTORNEY charges:

**1.** At times material to this information:
   **a.** Defendant ANTHONY MATTHEWS owned and controlled Express Mortgage, a licensed Illinois mortgage brokerage located on Wabash Street and on Western Boulevard in Chicago, Illinois.
   **b.** Bank One was a financial institution, the deposits of which were insured by the Federal Deposit Insurance Corporation ("FDIC"). Wells Fargo Home Mortgage was a subsidiary of Wells Fargo Bank.
   **c.** MIT Lending and St. Francis Mortgage were mortgage companies engaged in the business of issuing mortgage loans for the purchase of residential property.
**2.** Beginning no later than 2003 and continuing through at least 2006, at Chicago, in the Northern District of Illinois, Eastern Division, and elsewhere,

ANTHONY MATTHEWS,

defendant herein, together with other co-schemers known to the United States Attorney, devised, intended to devise, and participated in a scheme to defraud and to obtain money by means of materially false and fraudulent pretenses, representations, and promises, which scheme affected financial institutions. More specifically, defendant schemed to fraudulently obtain over $1 million in mortgage loan proceeds from various banks and mortgage lending institutions, including Bank One, Wells Fargo Bank. MIT Lending. St. Francis Mortgage and Wells Fargo Home Mortgage, among others (hereinafter referred to collectively as "lenders"), as described below.

*Source*: http://www.usdoj.gov/usao/iln/pr/chicago/2008/pr0619_01i.pdf (accessed November 7, 2008).

**FIGURE 11.1 Portions of a Federal Prosecutor's Charging Document (Information)**

In this event, there would be no point in proceeding to trial because there would be only a slight chance that a conviction would be obtained. If there is not enough *evidence* to obtain a conviction, then the prosecutor will likely decide not to prosecute, even if he or she *believes* the suspect is guilty.

There are other reasons not to prosecute, other than lack of evidence. For example, even if the state's case is strong, there may be an incentive not to prosecute. If it appears the defense's case is *stronger*, then it may behoove the prosecutor to proceed with charges against a different individual.

Nonetheless, prosecutors are human and, as such, can be influenced by the facts of a particular case. Say, for instance, that a law mandates life in prison for growing in excess of 1,000 marijuana plants. Assume further that a suspect apprehended for violating such a

**REASONS FOR NONPROSECUTION**

Another controversial reason for nonprosecution is a by-product of the U.S. so-called war on drugs. Civil asset forfeiture statutes permit the forfeiture of money and property tied to criminal activity—most frequently, the illicit drug trade. Many asset forfeiture statutes permit forfeited proceeds to go to the executive branch, which usually means the police, but sometimes prosecutors. Some have argued that when there is not enough evidence to proceed with a criminal case, prosecutors can opt to pursue civil

forfeiture, for which the burden of proof is generally lower. And as an added bonus, if a forfeiture action succeeds and a person's property is forfeited to the state, then the prosecutor may reap a financial reward for selecting a civil proceeding instead of a criminal one. Is the possibility of civil asset forfeiture a legitimate reason not to prosecute? That is, if a prosecutor chooses not to press criminal charges against someone, instead opting for forfeiture, should the decision be considered constitutional?

law has a spotless record, is married, and has four children. Would life in prison be the best punishment for such an individual? Or would a fine, community service, or some other sanction be more appropriate? This decision is often up to the prosecutor, and depending on the nature of the case, he or she may elect not to proceed with charges.

Another reason for not charging is related to economic factors. It is not possible, given the limited resources that exist in most public agencies (including prosecutors' offices), to proceed with charges against every suspect. Not having the time to build a case because of a high caseload may effectively force a prosecutor to be lenient with certain individuals.

## Challenging the Decision Not to Prosecute

A prosecutor's decision to not press charges is rarely challenged, but on occasion, higher authorities may get involved when they disagree with a prosecutor's decision. Failure to press charges can sometimes be questioned by a court, which can provide relief to individuals who wish to proceed with the case. Other times, a prosecutor's supervisor or other high-ranking official may step in. According to one source, "Many states by statute confer upon the attorney general the power to initiate prosecution in cases where the local prosecutor has failed to act. In practice, however, attorneys general have seldom exercised much control over local prosecuting attorneys."[1]

Another way of preventing prosecutors from failing to act or otherwise abusing their discretion is to require them to abide by standards of conduct. These standards provide rules for deciding which cases are worthy of prosecution, while ensuring that prosecutors act in accordance with the law. Figure 11.2 presents portions of the *Code of Conduct for Judicial Employees*, published by the Administrative Office of the U.S. Courts.

Some U.S. jurisdictions require court approval of a prosecutor's decision not to pursue charges. The prosecutor is typically required to explain to the court in writing his or her reasons for failing to prosecute. While this approach may seem sensible on its face, the Supreme Court has been somewhat critical of judicial review of prosecutorial decisions. In *Wayte v. United States*, 470 U.S. 598 (1985), the Court stated that it refused to question a prosecutor's discretion because "[s]uch factors as the strength of the case, the prosecution's general deterrence value, the Government's overall enforcement plan are not readily susceptible to the kind of analysis the courts are competent to make."

In general, if the prosecutor's decision not to press charges stems from legitimate factors, such as lack of evidence or case backlog, then the decision should be honored. This

---

[1]Y. Kamisar, W. LaFave, and J. Israel, *Modern Criminal Procedure*, 9th ed. (St. Paul, MN: West, 1999), p. 894.

**A. Code of Conduct for Judicial Employees.**

**CANON 1: A JUDICIAL EMPLOYEE SHOULD UPHOLD THE INTEGRITY AND INDEPENDENCE OF THE JUDICIARY AND OF THE JUDICIAL EMPLOYEE'S OFFICE**

An independent and honorable Judiciary is indispensable to justice in our society. A judicial employee should personally observe high standards of conduct so that the integrity and independence of the Judiciary are preserved and the judicial employee's office reflects a devotion to serving the public. Judicial employees should require adherence to such standards by personnel subject to their direction and control. The provisions of this code should be construed and applied to further these objectives. The standards of this code shall not affect or preclude other more stringent standards required by law, by court order, or by the appointing authority.

**CANON 2: A JUDICIAL EMPLOYEE SHOULD AVOID IMPROPRIETY AND THE APPEARANCE OF IMPROPRIETY IN ALL ACTIVITIES**

A judicial employee should not engage in any activities that would put into question the propriety of the judicial employee's conduct in carrying out the duties of the office. A judicial employee should not allow family, social, or other relationships to influence official conduct or judgment. A judicial employee should not lend the prestige of the office to advance or to appear to advance the private interests of others. A judicial employee should not use public office for private gain.

**CANON 3: A JUDICIAL EMPLOYEE SHOULD ADHERE TO APPROPRIATE STANDARDS IN PERFORMING THE DUTIES OF THE OFFICE**

In performing the duties prescribed by law, by resolution of the Judicial Conference of the United States, by court order, or by the judicial employee's appointing authority, the following standards apply:

**A.** A judicial employee should respect and comply with the law and these canons. A judicial employee should report to the appropriate supervising authority any attempt to induce the judicial employee to violate these canons.

*Note:* A number of criminal statutes of general applicability govern federal employees' performance of official duties. These include:

> 18 U.S.C. § 201 (bribery of public officials and witnesses);
>
> 18 U.S.C. § 211 (acceptance or solicitation to obtain appointive public office);
>
> 18 U.S.C. § 285 (taking or using papers relating to government claims);
>
> 18 U.S.C. § 287 (false, fictitious, or fraudulent claims against the government);
>
> 18 U.S.C. § 508 (counterfeiting or forging transportation requests);
>
> 18 U.S.C. § 641 (embezzlement or conversion of government money, property, or records);
>
> 18 U.S.C. § 643 (failing to account for public money);
>
> 18 U.S.C. § 798 and 50 U.S.C. § 783 (disclosure of classified information);
>
> 18 U.S.C. § 1001 (fraud or false statements in a government matter);
>
> 18 U.S.C. § 1719 (misuse of franking privilege);
>
> 18 U.S.C. § 2071 (concealing, removing, or mutilating a public record);
>
> 31 U.S.C. § 1344 (misuse of government vehicle);
>
> 31 U.S.C. § 3729 (false claims against the government).

In addition, provisions of specific applicability to court officers include:

> 18 U.S.C. § § 153,154 (court officers embezzling or purchasing property from bankruptcy estate);
>
> 18 U.S.C. § 645 (embezzlement and theft by court officers);

**FIGURE 11.2 Code of Conduct for Judicial Employees**

▼

18 U.S.C. § 646 (court officers failing to deposit registry moneys);

18 U.S.C. § 647 (receiving loans from registry moneys from court officer).

This is not a comprehensive listing but sets forth some of the more significant provisions with which judicial employees should be familiar.

**B.** A judicial employee should be faithful to professional standards and maintain competence in the judicial employee's profession.

**C.** A judicial employee should be patient, dignified, respectful, and courteous to all persons with whom the judicial employee deals in an official capacity, including the general public, and should require similar conduct of personnel subject to the judicial employee's direction and control. A judicial employee should diligently discharge the responsibilities of the office in a prompt, efficient, nondiscriminatory, fair, and professional manner. A judicial employee should never influence or attempt to influence the assignment of cases, or perform any discretionary or ministerial function of the court in a manner that improperly favors any litigant or attorney, nor should a judicial employee imply that he or she is in a position to do so.

**D.** A judicial employee should avoid making public comment on the merits of a pending or impending action and should require similar restraint by personnel subject to the judicial employee's direction and control. This proscription does not extend to public statements made in the course of official duties or to the explanation of court procedures. A judicial employee should never disclose any confidential information received in the course of official duties except as required in the performance of such duties, nor should a judicial employee employ such information for personal gain. A former judicial employee should observe the same restrictions on disclosure of confidential information that apply to a current judicial employee, except as modified by the appointing authority.

**E.** A judicial employee should not engage in nepotism prohibited by law.

*Note*: See also 5 U.S.C. § 3110 (employment of relatives); 28 U.S.C. § 458 (employment of judges' relatives).

**F.** Conflicts of Interest.

(1) A judicial employee should avoid conflicts of interest in the performance of official duties. A conflict of interest arises when a judicial employee knows that he or she (or the spouse, minor child residing in the judicial employee's household, or other close relative of the judicial employee) might be so personally or financially affected by a matter that a reasonable person with knowledge of the relevant facts would question the judicial employee's ability properly to perform official duties in an impartial manner. . . .

**CANON 4: IN ENGAGING IN OUTSIDE ACTIVITIES, A JUDICIAL EMPLOYEE SHOULD AVOID THE RISK OF CONFLICT WITH OFFICIAL DUTIES, SHOULD AVOID THE APPEARANCE OF IMPROPRIETY, AND SHOULD COMPLY WITH DISCLOSURE REQUIREMENTS**

**A.** *Outside Activities.* A judicial employee's activities outside of official duties should not detract from the dignity of the court, interfere with the performance of official duties, or adversely reflect on the operation and dignity of the court or office the judicial employee serves. Subject to the foregoing standards and the other provisions of this code, a judicial employee may engage in such activities as civic, charitable, religious, professional, educational, cultural, avocational, social, fraternal, and recreational activities, and may speak, write, lecture, and teach. If such outside activities concern the law, the legal system, or the administration of justice, the judicial employee should first consult with the appointing authority to determine whether the proposed activities are consistent with the foregoing standards and the other provisions of this code. . . .

**FIGURE 11.2** *Continued*

decision should be honored even if he or she agrees to dismiss criminal charges if the defendant agrees not to file a civil suit.

# Restrictions on Bringing Charges

Although the prosecutor has broad discretion in deciding whether to bring charges, there are limitations on that discretion. Often, charges may be dropped or a conviction may be reversed if the charges were brought for inappropriate reasons. The prosecution may not be selective in its decision to charge, and prosecution may not be pursued for vindictive reasons.

If a prosecutor acts unfairly, selectively, or vindictively, the prosecuting decision may be overruled. That is, the charges against the accused will be dropped, or in the event that the person is charged and convicted, his or her conviction will be overturned. However, if a prosecutor brings charges for inappropriate reasons and this decision is uncontested, then the charges will most likely stand.

## Selective Prosecution

If an individual is targeted for prosecution merely because he or she is a member of a certain group, such as being a minority, then his or her constitutional rights may be violated. This is known as **selective prosecution**. If a prosecutor's decision to press charges is selective in nature, the Fourteenth Amendment's equal protection clause may be violated. For example, in *Yick Wo v. Hopkins*, 118 U.S. 356 (1886), the Supreme Court stated:

Though the law itself be fair on its face and impartial in appearance, yet, if it is applied and administered by public authority with an evil eye and an unequal hand, so as practically to

## THE DECISION NOT TO CHARGE

Following are the facts reported by the U.S. District Court for the District of Columbia in *NAACP v. Levi*:

> On May 31, 1971, Carnell Russ, a 24-year-old black, while operating his motor vehicle on an Arkansas highway, was arrested for an alleged speeding violation by Jerry Mac Green, a white state trooper. Russ was accompanied by his wife, their minor children, and an adult cousin. The trooper directed him to the county courthouse. Russ complied and upon arrival, parked his vehicle and was escorted into the courthouse by the arresting trooper and two other white law enforcement officers, Charles Ratliff and Norman Draper. Minutes later, Russ returned to the vehicle where his family awaited. He requested and received from his wife sufficient money to post the necessary collateral. He then joined the three officers who were close by

observing his actions. The four retraced their steps with Russ again in custody. A short time thereafter, Mrs. Russ first observed two of the officers leave and minutes later an ambulance depart from the rear of the courthouse area where her husband had just entered in the officers' custody. She later learned that Mr. Russ, while under detention, had been shot in the center of his forehead by Ratliff and then transported to a hospital. Green and Draper were the sole witnesses to the shooting. Her husband died from the gunshot wound within hours.

Ratliff was indicted and found not guilty of voluntary manslaughter pursuant to an investigation by the state police. Criminal charges were not brought against the other two officers, and the case was closed. Does the prosecutor's decision not to pursue charges against the other officers seem reasonable?

## ANOTHER DECISION NOT TO CHARGE

Chief Lord, of the Springfield Police Department, arrested Nancy Simpson for tampering with a witness, Terri Flanders, the alleged victim of an assault by a friend of Simpson's. Simpson hired an attorney, and discussions with the local prosecutor ensued. Simpson agreed to sign a written release—in which she promised not to sue the city, its officials, or the alleged victim of the assault—if the prosecutor dismissed the criminal charges. The criminal charges were dropped. Is fear of being sued a valid reason not to prosecute?

make unjust and illegal discriminations between persons in similar circumstances, material to their rights, the denial of equal justice is still within the prohibition of the Constitution.

*Oyler v. Boles, 368 U.S.*
*(448 [1968])*

Since *Yick Wo*, the Supreme Court has become more specific as to what constitutes selective prosecution. In *Oyler v. Boles*, 368 U.S. 448 (1968), the Court held that the prosecution's selection of cases violates the equal protection clause only when it is intentional and is intended to target "a certain class of cases . . . or specific persons." In that case, the defendant presented evidence that he was the only individual of six sentenced under a particular statute. The Court held that this was not discriminatory because the defendant was unable to demonstrate intent by the prosecutor or provide evidence that he fit the group targeted for prosecution. The Court noted:

> The conscious exercise of some selectivity in enforcement is not in itself a federal constitutional violation. Even though the statistics in this case might imply a policy of selective enforcement, it was not stated that the selection was deliberately based upon an unjustifiable standard such as race, religion, or other arbitrary classification.

Since the *Oyler* decision, the courts have applied a three-pronged test for determining whether prosecution is selective. It must be shown that (1) similarly situated individuals were not prosecuted, (2) the prosecutor intended for this to happen, and (3) the decision resulted from an arbitrary, rather than rational, classification scheme. An *arbitrary* classification scheme would be based on, for example, race or sex. A *rational* classification scheme would be one that considers the evidence against each individual without regard to the color of his or her skin, country of origin, religious preference, sex, or other such criteria.

Selective prosecution is not always prohibited, and may be permissible in some instances. Sometimes, prosecutors aggressively pursue *conspicuous individuals*, such as celebrities. The courts have allowed prosecution of certain individuals for the sole purpose of discouraging other people from committing the same offense. As one court noted, "Selective enforcement may . . . be justified when a striking example or a few examples are sought in order to deter other violators" (*People v. Utica Daw's Drug Co.*, 16 A.D.2d 12 [1962]).

Prosecutors can also get into trouble for targeting the most *significant offender* in a group of offenders. Sometimes, the prosecution may choose to charge one offender instead of another, even though both were suspected of having committed the same offense. When a group of individuals is suspected of having committed various degrees of the same offense, then it is problematic for a prosecutor to charge just one of them. An example of this practice was considered in *State v. McCollum*, 159 Wis.2d 184 (App. 1990), a case in which a court dismissed prostitution charges against nude female dancers because the dancers' male patrons were not charged, even though Wisconsin law criminalized their behavior, as well.

Prosecutors may also open themselves up to allegations of selective prosecution by engaging in pretextual prosecution. This occurs when the prosecutor lacks the evidence to charge someone with a particular crime and so charges him or her with a lesser crime. However, prosecutors are rarely chastised for this type of conduct. For example, in *United States v. Sacco*, 428 F.2d 164 (9th Cir. 1970), a court noted that allowing a prosecutor to pursue lesser charges when the evidence to mount a more serious charge does not exist is perfectly acceptable.

The most recent Supreme Court case addressing selective prosecution was *United States v. Bass*, 536 U.S. 862 (2002). At issue was a defendant's request for discovery of the Department of Justice's charging practices in capital cases. He alleged that blacks were disproportionately charged in such cases and that he was charged because of his race. His argument did not succeed, however. The Court noted that he was required to show ". . . evidence of both discriminatory effect and discriminatory intent" and that ". . . raw statistics regarding overall charges say nothing about charges brought against similarly situated defendants."

## Vindictive Prosecution

If a prosecutor's charging decision is motivated by revenge, then the resulting charge violates the due process clause of the Fourteenth Amendment. Specifically, if a prosecutor charges an individual simply because he or she is exercising his or her constitutional rights, such vindictive prosecution will not be allowed.

In *Blackledge v. Perry*, 417 U.S. 21 (1974), the defendant was convicted in a lower court for misdemeanor assault with a deadly weapon. The defendant filed an appeal with the county superior court for a trial *de novo* (a new trial), which is sometimes permitted in misdemeanor cases. The prosecutor then obtained an indictment charging the offender with *felony* assault for the same conduct. The defendant pleaded guilty to this offense and was sentenced to five to seven years. The Supreme Court concluded that "vindictiveness against a defendant for having successfully attacked his first conviction must play no part in the sentence he receives after a new trial." The Court concluded further that

*Blackledge v. Perry*
*(417 U.S. 21 [1974])*

## WHAT IS SELECTIVE PROSECUTION?

In July 1980, a presidential proclamation was issued requiring certain young males to register with the Selective Service System. This information is used for drafting potential soldiers if the need arises. David Elders refused to register and even went so far as writing letters to government officials, including the President, in which he declared no intention to register. Elders' case, along with cases involving other men who refused to register, was placed in a "Selective Service" file. Only cases in the Selective Service file were selected for prosecution. Elders was prosecuted for failure to register. He claims the prosecution was selective. Is he right?

## WHAT IS PRETEXTUAL PROSECUTION?

The district attorney (D.A.) suspects that Corinne Dwyer is running a call-girl service out of her suburban home. The D.A. does not have enough evidence to prosecute Dwyer for her prostitution activities, but he does have sufficient evidence to prosecute Dwyer for abandoning an appliance. Dwyer had put a refrigerator at the end of her driveway with a "Free" sign on it, in violation of a statute that provides that "any person who discards or abandons or leaves in any place accessible to children, any refrigerator, icebox, deep freeze locker, . . . which is no longer in use, and which has not had the door removed or the hinges and such portion of the latch mechanism removed to prevent latching or locking of the door, is guilty of a misdemeanor" (California Penal Code, Section 402b). Dwyer is thus charged and argues that she has been unfairly targeted for pretextual prosecution, in violation of her Fourteenth Amendment right to equal protection. What should the court decide?

such punishment after the fact must be overturned, unless the prosecutor can explain the increase in charges.

In *United States v. Goodwin*, 457 U.S. 368 (1982), a misdemeanor defendant decided not to plea bargain and requested a trial by jury. Before trial, the government obtained a felony indictment against the defendant arising out of the same incident. The defendant was convicted in federal district court on the felony charge. The Court held that "a presumption of prosecutorial vindictiveness was not warranted in this case, and absent such

## WHAT IS VINDICTIVE PROSECUTION?

Cesar Fresco was arrested for uttering (giving, offering, cashing, or passing or attempting to pass) a forged document, which is a felony punishable by a prison term of 2 to 10 years. He has an extensive criminal history and has committed forgery in the past. The prosecutor offers a plea bargain to Fresco, giving him two choices: (1) He can plead guilty to the crime and the prosecutor will recommend a five-year sentence; or (2) he can reject the plea, be prosecuted under the habitual offender statute, and face a potential life term. The prosecutor tells Fresco, "If you do not accept this agreement, I will prosecute you as a habitual offender and you will go to prison for the rest of your life." Fresco rejects the plea and is convicted. Later, he sues, claiming that the prosecution was vindictive. Will he succeed?

a presumption, no due process violation was established." The Court went on to note that ". . . only in rare cases [will] a defendant be able to overcome the presumptive validity of the prosecutor's actions through such a demonstration." In other words, if the more serious charging decision is made *prior* to trial, as it was in this case, it is presumed that the prosecutor is not acting vindictively.

## Dealing with Overzealous Prosecutors

By charging offenders, prosecutors serve as advocates for the government. In this capacity, they are immune from suit for charging suspects with crimes.[2] This is reasonable because imagine what would happen to the criminal process if prosecutors could be sued at every turn for charging offenders!

Prosecutors also act as advocates when they argue the government's case. They can do almost anything in this capacity to secure a conviction without fear of being held liable. Prosecutors have been shielded from being sued for a variety of actions, including:

- using false statements at pretrial hearings (*Burns v. Reed*, 500 U.S. 478 [1991]),
- using false testimony at trial (*Imbler v. Pachtman*, 424 U.S. 409 [1976]),
- failing to disclose exculpatory evidence (*Kalina v. Fletcher*, 522 U.S. 118 [1997]),
- fabricating evidence, influencing witnesses, and
- breaching plea agreements.

In a recent case, *Connick v. Thompson*, 563 U.S. ___ (2011), the Supreme Court held that a district attorney's office may not be held liable for failing to train its prosecutors in the event of a single failure by one prosecutor to disclose exculpatory evidence to the defense. This and decisions before it have set the bar to prove prosecutorial misconduct quite high.

Not everyone agrees prosecutors should enjoy absolute immunity, especially in light of recent DNA exonerations and high-profile scandals. According to one critic, prosecutors should only enjoy qualified immunity.

> Absolute immunity frustrates the purpose of civil rights legislation by failing to deter frequent and egregious misconduct. It also hinders the development of constitutional standards and the implementation of structural solutions for systemic problems. Prosecutorial liability—with the safeguard of qualified immunity to prevent vexatious litigation—is necessary to ensure the integrity of the criminal justice system.[3]

Prosecutors are immune from liability (1) when they act as administrators or investigators and (2) when they make reasonable mistakes. However, if the plaintiff in a lawsuit can show a prosecutor acted as an administrator or investigator and violated clearly established constitutional law, the prosecutor can be held liable.

### Recourse

Despite the immunity they enjoy, there is recourse for dealing with overzealous prosecutors. Such consequences may include:

- Private admonition or reprimand
- Public reprimand

---

[2]M. Z. Johns, "Reconsidering Absolute Prosecutorial Immunity," *Brigham Young University Law Review* 2005 (2005): 53–154.
[3]Ibid., p. 56.

- Suspension from law practice
- Permanent disbarment
- In the case of an elected district attorney, being thrown out of office

Despite the availability of these potential consequences, prosecutors are seldom punished for their wrongdoing. According to the Center for Public Integrity, out of more than 11,000 cases of prosecutorial misconduct, only two prosecutors were disbarred.[4] Reprimand was the most common sanction.

The story of Mike Nifong sheds some light on the problem of prosecutorial misconduct. Nifong was the prosecutor in the infamous Duke lacrosse case, where three white Duke University lacrosse players were accused of rape by a black stripper. He was the prototypical overzealous prosecutor. For example, he repeatedly made statements to the press that were unsupported and controversial. He also continued to pursue criminal charges, even as new evidence came to light that would have made securing a conviction difficult.

The state bar association filed complaints against Nifong, and he was ultimately disbarred and held in contempt of court. Since some of Nifong's actions may not have been consistent with the role of an "advocate," his immunity may have been "qualified" rather than absolute. He was sued by the wrongfully accused lacrosse players and their families and claimed bankruptcy.

# Joinder

**Joinder** is the combining of separate parties or separate charges into a single legal action. A prosecutor may either (1) bring multiple charges against the same individual in the same trial or (2) bring charges against multiple individuals in the same trial. In determining whether either is appropriate, two questions must be asked: First, based on the jurisdiction in question, is joinder appropriate? Second, if joinder is appropriate, will it be unfairly prejudicial? If joinder is determined to be inappropriate and unfairly prejudicial, the court may allow **severance**, in which the defendants or charges are separated into separate trials.

*United States v. Lane*
*(474 U.S. 438 [1986])*

The question of whether joinder is appropriate is best resolved prior to trial, but sometimes joinder is not addressed until *after* trial. Assume, for example, that a single defendant is charged in the same trial for assault and robbery. Assume further that he is convicted on both counts. If joinder is shown to have been inappropriate, the two charges may be severed and decided in separate trials. According to the Supreme Court in *United States v. Lane*, 474 U.S. 438 (1986), if this joinder has "a substantial and injurious effect or influence in determining the jury's verdict," then new and separate trials must be held.

## Multiple Charges against the Same Individual

According to the *Federal Rules of Criminal Procedure*, multiple charges may be brought against the same individual under the following circumstances:

When the charges arise out of

1. the same criminal event (such as robbery of a convenience store and assault when fleeing the scene of that robbery);
2. two separate criminal acts that are tied together in some fashion (such as a convenience store robbery to obtain cash to buy and sell illegal drugs); or
3. two criminal acts that are the same or similar in character.[5]

---

[4]Center for Public Integrity, *Harmful Error: Investigating America's Local Prosecutors*, http://projects.publicintegrity.org/pm (accessed November 7, 2008).
[5]*Federal Rules of Criminal Procedure*, Rule 8. Available online at http://www.law.cornell.edu/rules/frcrmp/

The third situation can be better understood with an example: If a serial killer uses the same *modus operandi* against his victims, he may be tried for several homicides in the same criminal trial.

There are a number of strategic reasons for the defense to argue against joinder. First, there is the concern that the jury will not consider the criminal acts for which the accused is charged separately. Another concern is that the jury will view all the evidence against the accused in a cumulative, rather than separate, fashion. Say, for example, that the prosecution presents eyewitness testimony against a defendant accused of robbery. Also assume that the prosecution presents a murder weapon allegedly used by the defendant against the victim of the robbery. The jury may consider together the eyewitness testimony and the murder weapon and arrive at the conclusion that the accused is guilty. But if the robbery and homicide were tried separately, the jury may not arrive at this conclusion so easily. Finally, another defense argument against joinder is that by trying an individual on several charges in the same trial, he or she will have difficulty asserting separate defenses to the criminal acts at issue.

When trying a person for several related crimes in the same trial, the prosecutor must proceed carefully. If the criminal acts are identical, there is the risk that the convictions may be overturned on the basis of the double jeopardy clause in the Fifth Amendment. For example, if the prosecutor charges an individual for both first-degree and second-degree murder of the same victim in the same trial and the individual is convicted of both offenses, then it will be deemed unconstitutional.

### Charges against Multiple Defendants

Joinder may also involve charging multiple defendants in the same criminal trial. The *Federal Rules of Criminal Procedure* state, "Two or more defendants may be charged in the same indictment or information if they are alleged to have participated in the same act or transaction or in the same series of acts or transactions constituting an offense or offenses."[6] In other words, joinder of defendants is reserved in most instances for crimes of conspiracy (crimes where two or more individuals plan or cooperate in a criminal act).

As with joinder of *charges*, joinder of *defendants* raises a number of concerns. For instance, the jury may get confused as to who, if anyone, is guilty and simply convict all of the defendants. Or the jury may convict a defendant simply because he or she is associated with another defendant who bore a greater responsibility for the crime. Also, it is conceivable that one defendant may testify against another but then refuse to answer questions on cross-examination, citing self-incrimination concerns.

Although there are strong arguments against joinder, it serves the important goal of promoting efficiency in the court system. Allowing prosecutors to join charges and defendants reduces court backlog and speeds up the administration of justice.

# ▶ The Grand Jury

According to the Fifth Amendment, "No person shall be held to answer for a capital, or otherwise infamous crime, unless on a presentment or indictment of a grand jury." This part of the Fifth Amendment cannot be fully understood without considering the time in which it was written. The framers of the Bill of Rights fear that in certain situations, the prosecutor, as a representative of government, could become too powerful in making charging decisions. The framers believed that the **grand jury** would be a method of keeping the power of government in check.

Despite that intent, the grand jury is no longer quite as independent as the framers had hoped. Instead, it is now highly dependent on the actions of the prosecutor. Grand juries

---

[6]Ibid.

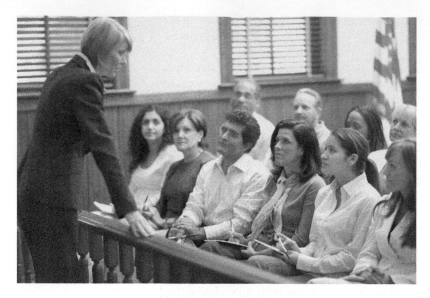

The pool from which a grand jury is selected must be a fair cross-section of the community.

still perform important investigative functions, and they are quite powerful in terms of, for instance, being able to subpoena witnesses and records. But their role today is tied closely to the goals of the prosecutor. In fact, almost every state makes the prosecutor the main legal adviser of the grand jury and requires him or her to be present during all grand jury sessions.

Even though the Fifth Amendment suggests that indictment by grand jury is guaranteed for certain offenses, this right has not been incorporated so as to apply to the states. In the 1884 decision of *Hurtado v. California*, 110 U.S. 516 (1884), the Supreme Court stated that indictment by a grand jury is not a right guaranteed by the due process clause of the Fourteenth Amendment. The Court stated:

> [W]e are unable to say that the substitution for a presentment or indictment by a grand jury of [a] proceeding by information after examination and commitment by a magistrate, certifying to the probable guilt of the defendant, with the right on his part to the aid of counsel, and to the cross-examination of the witnesses produced for the prosecution, is not due process of law.

It should be emphasized that although the right to grand jury indictment has not been incorporated to the states, many states do, in fact, require this method of prosecution. Several states do require that, for the most part, felonies are to be prosecuted only by grand jury indictment. The same is true for the federal system. Most states, however, permit prosecution by either indictment or information. See Figure 11.3 for an overview of the mechanisms for filing serious charges in each state.

In states that permit either indictment or information, the choice of one or the other depends on the circumstances of each case. Typically, grand jury indictment will be chosen when (1) the case is of great public or political significance; (2) the investigative power of the grand jury is useful; (3) the grand jury may be able to issue an indictment more quickly compared to holding a preliminary hearing and then issuing an information indictment; or (4) one or more witnesses is hesitant to speak in open court, preferring the secrecy of grand jury proceedings.

## How a Grand Jury Is Constructed

A grand jury can be impaneled by either the court or the prosecutor. Usually, the court has this responsibility, but prosecutors are increasingly given the ability to decide whether a grand jury is necessary.

*Hurtado v. California*
*(110 U.S. 516 [1884])*

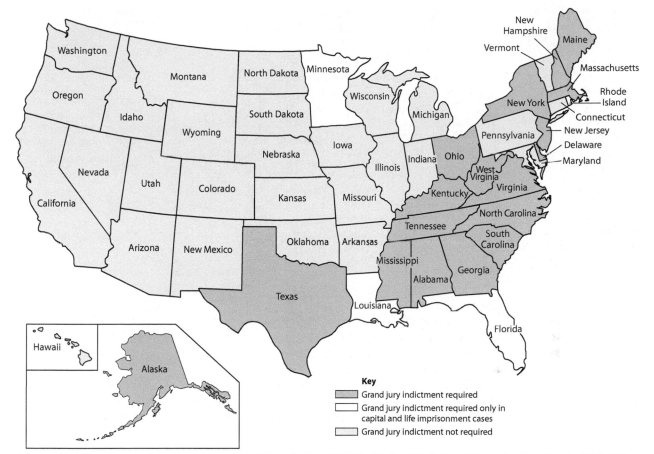

*Source*: D. B. Rottman and S. M. Strickland, *State Court Organization, 2004* (Washington, DC: National Center for State Courts, 2004). Note that some states requiring grand jury indictment do so only for certain offenses. For example, Texas requires grand jury indictments for felonies, not misdemeanors.

**FIGURE 11.3 Charging Methods for Serious Crimes by State**

In larger jurisdictions, a grand jury may not be a single body—several grand juries may be acting at the same time. One or more could be performing investigative functions, and others could be working on specific cases.

### Duration

Once a grand jury has been convened, its members serve for a specified period of time. A term can last from one to three months, but sometimes less, if the court or prosecutor believes that further deliberation is unnecessary. Under the *Federal Rules of Criminal Procedure*, a regular grand jury cannot serve for a period longer than 18 months, unless the court extends the service "upon a determination that such extension is in the public interest."[7] Fortunately, people selected for grand juries do not have to meet every day; usually, a grand jury meets several days a month.

### Size

Grand juries are larger than ordinary trial juries. In the past, grand juries consisting of 24 or so people were not uncommon. Today, grand juries are usually smaller, ranging from 16 to 20 people. One state, Tennessee, permits a grand jury of 13 individuals, but the voting

---
[7]Ibid., Rule 6.

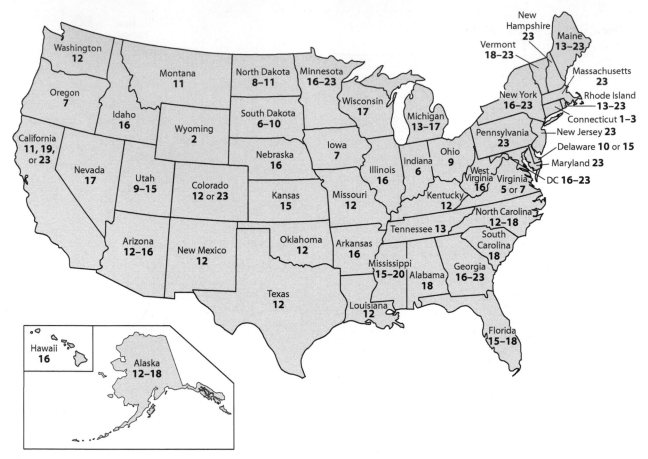

Source: Based on data from University of Dayton, http://campus.udayton.edu/~grandjur/stategj/sizegj.htm (accessed May 14, 2013).

**FIGURE 11.4 Grand Jury Size Requirements by State**

requirements in that state are fairly restrictive. See Figure 11.4 for an illustration of grand jury size requirements by state.

## Voting Requirements

Grand jury voting requirements also vary by state. The most common voting requirement is that 12 grand jury members must agree on an indictment. However, one state, Virginia, requires only four votes for issuance of a **true bill**, which is the endorsement made by a grand jury when it finds sufficient evidence to warrant a criminal charge. By contrast, Texas requires a vote of 9 out of 12.

As with a *petit jury* (trial jury), a grand jury is headed by a foreperson, who is charged with, among other duties, signing the indictment and keeping track of the votes of each member. Figure 11.5 shows portions of the indictment against Ahmed Abassi, a Tunisian man who was accused of radicalizing a Canadian resident who was charged with plotting to derail a train in the United States. Abassi was indicted for trying to stay in the United States illegally, presumably to build a terror cell that could operate inside U.S. borders.

## Selection of Members

In some states, prospective grand jury members are randomly selected from a list of eligible voters. In others, they are randomly selected from a list of licensed drivers. Still other states pull prospective grand jury members from a list of tax returns, telephone directories, and

UNITED STATES DISTRICT COURT
SOUTHERN DISTRICT OF NEW YORK

UNITED STATES OF AMERICA

    – v. –                            **INDICTMENT**

AHMED ABASSI,                      **13 cr.**

                Defendant.

## COUNT ONE

### FRAUD AND MISUSE OF VISAS

The Grand Jury charges:

1. On or about April 15, 2013, in the Southern District of New York and elsewhere, AHMED ABASSI, the defendant, as permitted under penalty of perjury under Title 28, United States Code, Section 1746, did knowingly subscribe as true a false statement with respect to a material fact in an application, affidavit, and other document required by the immigration laws and regulations prescribed thereunder, and did knowingly present such application, affidavit, and other document which contained such false statement and which failed to contain a reasonable basis in law and fact, in order to facilitate an act of international terrorism as defined in Title 18, United States Code, Section 2331, to wit, ABASSI completed a form I-765, Application for Employment Authorization, falsely Stating that he intended to remain in the United States for employment, When in fact he sought to remain in the United States to facilitate an act of international terrorism.

(Title 18, United States Code, Sections 1546(a) and 2.)

## COUNT TWO

### FRAUD AND MISUSE OF VISAS

The Grand Jury further charges:

2. On or about April 15, 2013, in the Southern District of New York and elsewhere, AHMED ABASSI, the defendant, as permitted under penalty of perjury under Title 28, United States Code, Section 1746, did knowingly subscribe as true, a false statement with respect to a material fact in an application, affidavit, and other document required by the immigration laws and regulations prescribed thereunder, and did Knowingly present such application, affidavit, and other document which contained such false statement and which failed to contain a reasonable basis in law and fact, in order to facilitate an act of international terrorism as defined at Title 18, United States Code, Section 2331, to wit, ABASSI completed a Form I-485, Application to Register Permanent Residence or Adjust Status, falsely stating that he intended to remain in the United States for employment, when in fact he sought to remain in the United States to facilitate an act of international terrorism.

(Title 18, United States Code, Sections 1546(a) and 2.)

### FORFEITURE ALLEGATIONS

3. As a result of committing the visa fraud offenses alleged in Counts One and Two of this Indictment, AHMED ABASSI, the defendant, shall forfeit to the United States, pursuant to Title 18, United States Code, Section 982(a)(6), all conveyances used in the commission of the offenses; all property, real and personal, that constitutes and is derived from and is traceable to proceeds obtained directly and indirectly from the commission of the offenses; and all property, real and personal, that was used to facilitate, and was intended to be used to facilitate, the commission of the offenses.

**FIGURE 11.5 Portions of Ahmed Abassi Indictment**

<u>Substitute Assets Provision</u>

4. If any of the above-described forfeitable property, as a result of any or omission of AHMED ABASSI, the defendant:

**a.** cannot be located upon the exercise of due diligence;

**b.** has been transferred or sold to, or deposited with, a third person;

**c.** has been placed beyond the jurisdiction of the court;

**d.** has been substantially diminished in value;

or

**e.** has been commingled with other property

which cannot be subdivided without difficulty, it is the intent of the United States, pursuant to Title 21, United States Code, Section 853(p), to seek forfeiture of any other property of ABASSI up to the value of the above forfeitable property described above.

(Title 18, United States Code, Section 982(a) (6) (A), and Title 21, United States Code, Section 854.)

FOREPERSON

_____

PREET BHARARA

United States Attorney

FORM NO. USA-33s-274    (Ed. 9-25-58)

UNITED STATES DISTRICT COURT
SOUTHERN DISTRICT OF NEW YORK

UNITED STATES OF AMERICA

– v. –

AHMED ABASSI,

Defendant.

<u>INDICTMENT</u>

13 Cr.

(18 U.S.C.  § §   1546 & 2)

PREET BHARARA

United States Attorney

**A TRUE BILL**

_____

FOREPERSON

*Source:* http://www.justice.gov/usao/nys/pressreleases/May13/AbassiUnsealing/U.S.%20v.%20 Ahmed%20Abassi%20Indictment.pdf (accessed May 14, 2013).

**FIGURE 11.5** *Continued*

so on. Most people will not have the opportunity to serve on a grand jury because they are not convened that frequently.

The grand jury selection process usually involves two stages. First, a list of potential grand jury members is compiled by any of the methods (or others) just described. This pool of prospective grand jury members is known as the *venire*. Next, grand jury members are selected from this pool. At both stages, constitutional complications can arise.

First, special steps need to be taken to ensure that the pool of potential grand jurors, like that for a typical petit jury, is fair and impartial. In particular, the defendant can raise constitutional challenges to the grand jury selection process if it is *not* fair and impartial. One such challenge is based on the *equal protection clause*. This requires showing that there is a significant disparity between a group's representation in the community and its representation on the grand jury (see *Casteneda v. Partida*, 430 U.S. 482 [1977]).

Another constitutional challenge against the composition of the grand jury pool stems from the *fair cross-section requirement* announced in *Taylor v. Louisiana*, 419 U.S. 522 (1975). The Court in that case held that "systematic exclusion" of a "large distinct group" from the pool from which the (petit) jury is chosen violates the Sixth Amendment. The same logic carries over to the grand jury. If, for example, a grand jury consists of all white members and 40 percent of the community is black, the fair cross-section requirement will have been violated. By contrast, if the grand jury does not contain a snake handler, a militant feminist, a rabbi, or some such specific type of individual, the fair cross-section requirement will not have been violated because these and other individuals do not constitute large, distinct groups.

*Taylor v. Louisiana
(419 U.S. 522 [1975])*

When grand jury members are selected from the initial pool, similar constitutional concerns can be raised. If, for instance, the grand jury pool is representative of a fair cross-section of the community, it is still possible that people could be excluded from the jury on a systematic basis. In *Rose v. Mitchell*, 443 U.S. 545 (1979), the Court held that the "right to equal protection of the laws [is] denied when [the defendant] is indicted from a grand jury from which members of a racial group purposefully have been excluded."

*Rose v. Mitchell
(443 U.S. 545 [1979])*

## Secrecy of Grand Jury Proceedings

Grand jury proceedings are kept intensely secret. In *United States v. Rose*, 215 F.2d 617 (3rd Cir. 1954), the Third Circuit Court of Appeals provided several reasons for this:

(1) to prevent the escape of those whose indictment may be contemplated; (2) to insure the utmost freedom to the grand jury in its deliberations, and to prevent persons subject to indictment or their friends from importuning the grand jurors; (3) to prevent subornation of perjury or tampering with the witnesses who may testify before the grand jury and later appear at the trial of those indicted by it; (4) to encourage free and untrammeled disclosures by persons who have information with respect to the commission of crimes; [and] (5) to protect the innocent accused who is exonerated from disclosure of the fact that he has been under investigation, and from the expense of standing trial where there was no probability of guilt.

Notwithstanding these concerns, there are two categories of case law challenging grand jury secrecy: (1) cases addressing whether grand jury witness testimony should be supplied to the defense and (2) cases addressing the extent to which grand jury witnesses can share their testimony with other parties, such as other government officials.

### Disclosure of Witness Testimony to the Defense

According to the *Federal Rules of Criminal Procedure*, grand jury proceedings can be shared with the defense when the defendant makes "a showing that grounds may exist for a motion to dismiss the indictment because of matters occurring before the grand jury."[8] This type of

---

[8]Ibid.

disclosure is exceedingly rare and generally limited to situations in which there is evidence that prosecutorial misconduct occurred before the grand jury proceedings commenced.

### Disclosure of Witness Testimony to Other Parties

*Butterworth v. Smith*
*(494 U.S. 624 [1990])*

In *Butterworth v. Smith*, 494 U.S. 624 (1990), the Supreme Court declared that the First Amendment may provide an exception to the grand jury secrecy requirement. In that case, the Court held that a Florida statute that prohibited grand jury witnesses from recounting their own testimony violated freedom of speech.

*Butterworth* involved a defendant who wanted to share his grand jury testimony with third parties. However, many more cases deal with the issue of whether other third parties besides the defense should be able to access the records of grand jury proceedings. One such case is *Douglas Oil Co. of California v. Petrol Stops Northwest*, 441 U.S. 211 (1979), in which the Supreme Court held that parties seeking access to grand jury records "must show that the material they seek is needed to avoid a possible injustice to another judicial proceeding, that the need for disclosure is greater than the need for continued secrecy, and that their request is structured to cover only material so needed."

The government has traditionally been given greater latitude than other third parties in terms of access to grand jury proceedings. In fact, the *Federal Rules of Criminal Procedure* provide that no showing of "particularized need" is necessary in order to disclose information to other government attorneys who are assisting in prosecution.[9] However, when disclosure is sought by government officials who are *not* assisting in the prosecution, the Supreme Court has held that a showing of need *does* have to be made (see *United States v. Sells Engineering, Inc.*, 463 U.S. 418 [1983]).

## Rights of Witnesses Testifying before Grand Juries

Grand juries rely heavily on witness testimony. However, the rights afforded to grand jury witnesses differ significantly from those afforded to witnesses in other settings (such as at trial). Also, the rights afforded to the individuals targeted by grand jury investigations differ from those afforded to criminal defendants.

The cases in this area revolve around three issues: (1) the right of the individual targeted by a grand jury investigation to testify, (2) whether grand jury witnesses are required to be advised of their right not to testify, and (3) the right to counsel as applied in grand jury proceedings.

### Right to Testify

It is well known that the defendant in a criminal trial has a constitutional right to decide whether or not to testify in his or her own defense. In contrast, someone who is the target of a grand jury investigation usually *does not* enjoy the right to testify. Indeed, several states do not even grant the target of a grand jury investigation the right to be present. This restriction is justified on the same secrecy grounds discussed earlier. Also, since many grand jury proceedings have an investigative purpose, there may not be a specific target until the proceedings have concluded. In such a situation, it would be cumbersome to allow all potential targets to be present in order to give testimony in their defense.

### Being Advised of the Right Not to Testify

When witnesses appear before grand juries, they are protected by the Fifth Amendment's privilege against self-incrimination. This is no different than in a criminal trial. However, a question has arisen in the courts over whether grand jury witnesses must be *told* that they can remain silent. In other words, the courts have grappled with whether the *Miranda* warnings should apply in the grand jury context.

---

[9]Ibid.

As noted previously, the *Miranda* warnings are only required during custodial interrogation. Therefore, the following question has been asked: Are grand jury proceedings akin to custodial interrogations? At least one decision suggests that *Miranda* does not apply in the grand jury context because the proceedings are not as "inherently coercive" as traditional custodial interrogations (see *Gollaher v. United States*, 419 F.2d 520 [9th Cir. 1969]). However, some states require by law that the targets of grand jury investigations, as well as grand jury witnesses, be advised of their right not to testify. The Supreme Court has yet to rule on this issue.

### Right to Counsel

Grand jury witnesses and the targets of grand jury investigations generally are not guaranteed a right to counsel under the Sixth Amendment. The Supreme Court has maintained this position in at least two cases: *In re Groban's Petition*, 352 U.S. 330 (1957), and *United States v. Mandujano*, 425 U.S. 564 (1976). However, a person who has already been charged may have a right to counsel before a grand jury proceeding, but such an individual is rarely the target of such a proceeding (see *Kirby v. Illinois*, 406 U.S. 682 [1972]). The typical grand jury witness is someone called upon to shed light on a particular case. Such witnesses do not enjoy the right to counsel in grand jury proceedings, but they can of course assert Fifth Amendment protection and refuse to incriminate themselves. As we will see shortly, though, the grand jury may offer a grant of immunity in exchange for a witness's testimony.

*United States v. Mandujano*
*(425 U.S. 564 [1976])*

The Supreme Court has stated that grand jury proceedings take place before the initiation of adversarial criminal proceedings and, as such, are outside the scope of the Sixth Amendment's right to counsel. There are also several additional reasons for not allowing counsel to be present during grand jury proceedings: (1) the investigation could be delayed if the witness repeatedly confers with his or her attorney; (2) the investigation could be disrupted if the witness raises objections and arguments; and, of course, (3) secrecy could be compromised.

## Investigative Powers of the Grand Jury

One of the main duties of a grand jury is to investigate alleged wrongdoing in order to determine whether an indictment should be issued. Because of the importance of this function, a grand jury has a great deal of power in conducting their investigation. For example, as decided in *United States v. Calandra*, 414 U.S. 338 (1974), a grand jury "may compel the production of evidence or the testimony of witnesses as it considers appropriate, and its operation generally is unrestrained by the technical procedural and evidentiary rules governing the conduct of criminal trials." In this vein, a grand jury can subpoena witnesses and evidence. However, it can also extend grants of immunity to certain individuals in exchange for their testimony, and it can find people in contempt for failing to cooperate with an investigation.

*United States v. Calandra*
*(414 U.S. 338 [1974])*

### Subpoenas

Two types of subpoenas are available to grand juries: (1) a subpoena *ad testificandum* and (2) a subpoena *duces tecum*. The former compels a witness to appear before the grand jury, and the latter compels the production of tangible evidence (such as a suspected murder weapon). The power of the grand jury to utilize both of these mechanisms is virtually unrestricted. However, there have been a few constitutional objections to their use.

First, some have argued that a subpoena to appear before the grand jury amounts to a seizure within the meaning of the Fourth Amendment. The Supreme Court acknowledged in *United States v. Dioniso*, 410 U.S. 1 (1973) that being forced to appear before a grand jury may be inconvenient but not in comparison to the "historically grounded obligation of every person to appear and give his evidence before the grand jury." Furthermore, Fourth Amendment restrictions on the grand jury's subpoena power "would assuredly impede its investigation and frustrate the public's interest in the fair and expeditious administration of the laws."

Regarding tangible evidence, the Supreme Court has likewise held that a subpoena *duces tecum* does not amount to a Fourth Amendment seizure. However, according to the

*Hale v. Henkel*
*(201 U.S. 43 [1906])*

Court in *Hale v. Henkel*, 201 U.S. 43 (1906), such a subpoena must comport with the Fourth Amendment's particularity requirement. And in *United States v. Gurule*, 437 F.2d 239 (10th Cir. 1970), the Tenth Circuit announced a three-prong test for ensuring that a grand jury subpoena satisfies the Fourth Amendment's reasonableness requirement: "(1) the subpoena may command only the production of things relevant to the investigation being pursued; (2) specification of things to be produced must be made with reasonable particularity; and (3) production of records covering only a reasonable period of time may be required."

It has been noted above that grand jury witnesses enjoy the Fifth Amendment privilege against self-incrimination, but could the fact of being forced to appear before a grand jury, by itself, be incriminating? Not surprisingly, people have objected to grand jury subpoenas for this reason. Few, if any, have succeeded, however, because someone who is appearing before a grand jury does not know in advance what questions will be asked and, as such, cannot assert the Fifth Amendment privilege prior to his or her appearance.

### Grants of Immunity

Although witnesses appearing before a grand jury enjoy the Fifth Amendment privilege against self-incrimination, the grand jury can avoid this limitation by extending *grants of immunity* to witnesses in exchange for their testimony. A grant of transactional immunity prohibits future prosecution on the acts for which the witness testifies. In contrast, so-called "use and derivative use immunity" only bars the use of the witness's testimony against him or her in the future. If evidence is obtained after the fact, independent of the witness's testimony before the grand jury, then he or she can be charged (see *Kastigar v. United States*, 406 U.S. 441 [1972]).

### Findings of Contempt

When someone is subpoenaed to appear before the grand jury but does not show up, the jury's **contempt power** can be utilized to compel their appearance. That is, the grand jury can impose civil and criminal sanctions on the individual for failing to appear. For example, an individual may be jailed until he or she agrees to appear. Note that the grand jury's contempt power is limited to compelling the presence of the witness, not his or her testimony. The witness who *does* appear can still invoke the Fifth Amendment privilege and refuse to make a statement.

## Challenging a Grand Jury Indictment

Just as restrictions are placed on a prosecutor's decision to charge, the power of the grand jury to hand down indictments is also not unlimited. It is possible to challenge a grand jury indictment on constitutional and similar grounds, including (1) lack of evidence; (2) misconduct by the prosecutor as the adviser of the grand jury; (3) unfair selection of grand jury members; and (4) use of different evidence at trial from that presented to the grand jury. When any of these circumstances exist, a grand jury indictment will be *quashed* or declared invalid.

### DECISION-MAKING EXERCISE 11.7

#### GRAND JURY INVESTIGATIONS

Assume that the grand jury is investigating a major case of corporate fraud. Assume further that the grand jury issues a subpoena *duces tecum*, calling for "all understandings, contracts or correspondence between the Fabulous Widgets Company and all of its business partners, as well as all reports made and accounts rendered by such companies from the date of the organization of the Fabulous Widgets Company, as well as all letters received by that company since its organization from all of its business partners." Is this subpoena sufficiently particular?

**DECIDING ON VARIANCE**

A grand jury returned an indictment against two women, charging them both with conspiracy to commit murder. Typically, a criminal *conspiracy* exists when two or more persons agree to commit a crime and then commit some sort of overt act in furtherance of that agreement (see *People v. Cockrell*, 63 Cal. 2d 779 [1965]). The grand jury was presented with a recorded telephone call between the two women, in which they agreed to murder their husbands. The grand jury was *not* presented with evidence that the women bought handguns for themselves. That evidence was introduced by the prosecutor at trial, however. The women were convicted and are now appealing their convictions, claiming that there was a variance between their indictment and the prosecutor's case. Will they succeed?

There is considerable variation among the states as to what amount of evidence is necessary to secure a valid indictment. In some states, probable cause is required. In others, the grand jury can only issue an indictment when all the evidence before it would, if unexplained, warrant a conviction at trial. In Utah, an indictment can only be issued on clear and convincing evidence that a crime was committed and that the person charged committed it. In either case, a grand jury indictment can be quashed if the evidence relied on to obtain the indictment is insufficient. Also, if the evidence used to obtain an indictment is obtained through unconstitutional means, the indictment can be quashed by essentially invoking the exclusionary rule.

Flagrant prosecutorial misconduct can also lead to an indictment being quashed. If, for instance, the prosecutor fails to supply the grand jury with exculpatory evidence, a subsequent indictment *may* be quashed but only if such misconduct violates existing law. There is, surprisingly, very little existing case law in this area. Indeed, the Supreme Court held in *United States v. Williams*, 504 U.S. 36 (1992), that federal courts cannot easily dismiss an indictment because of prosecutorial misconduct. "Because the grand jury is an institution separate from the courts, over whose functioning the courts do not preside, we think it clear that, as a general matter at least, no such 'supervisory' judicial authority exists."

While the courts have been hesitant to quash indictments based on insufficient evidence and prosecutorial misconduct, discrimination in the selection of grand jury members is taken very seriously. As indicated earlier in this chapter, the composition of the grand jury must comply with the due process and equal protection requirements. When it does not, subsequent indictments can be quashed. The Court noted in *United States v. Mechanik*, 475 U.S. 66 (1986), that "racial discrimination in the selection of grand jurors is so pernicious and other remedies so impractical, that the remedy of automatic reversal [may be] necessary as a prophylactic means of deterring grand jury discrimination in the future."

Finally, if the prosecutor presents evidence at trial that departs significantly from the one relied on by the grand jury for the purpose of issuing an indictment, sanctions will be imposed. If this **variance** between the trial evidence and the grand jury evidence is minimal, the indictment will probably not be quashed. Interpreted differently, if the evidence presented by the prosecutor to secure an indictment is "in no way essential to the offense on which the jury convicted," the indictment will probably not be quashed (see *United States v. Miller*, 471 U.S. 130 [1985]).

# ▶ The Defense Attorney

The defense attorney is a lawyer who advises, represents, and acts for the defendant. All defense attorneys perform essentially the same task—helping criminal defendants navigate the sometimes rough waters of the justice process. They perform a number of specific functions:

- provide a knowledgeable, objective perspective on what the defendant's situation is and what is likely to happen should his or her case go to trial.

- zealously defend the accused at all stages of the criminal process.
- understand the law and legal rules, including court interpretations of federal and state constitutions.
- are familiar with local court customs and procedures.
- understand the possible hidden costs of various outcomes, particularly those associated with a plea of guilty.
- immerse themselves in and spend time on the case.
- gather information from various sources, including the prosecution's witnesses.
- hire and manage investigators, who assist in building the defense case.[10]

There are many types of defense attorneys: Some adopt a narrow specialty, such as defending suspected drunk drivers. Some represent indigent defendants, whereas others represent only the most affluent clients. Some are skilled litigators who have convinced numerous juries that the wrong person has been charged, whereas others have mastered plea bargaining and rarely see the inside of a courtroom. Some work in small firms, while others work in large firms with hundreds of attorneys. Some work for the government as public defenders, and some even work for free, perhaps by representing indigent death-row inmates.

## The Right to Counsel in a Criminal Prosecution

The right to counsel in a criminal prosecution stems primarily from the Sixth Amendment to the U.S. Constitution, which provides that "in all criminal prosecutions, the accused shall enjoy the right . . . to have the Assistance of Counsel for his defense." The right to counsel also has due process origins. Indeed, even in the *Miranda* rule, there is even a Fifth Amendment component because individuals who are custodially interrogated must be advised of their right to counsel.

### Due Process Origins

*Powell v. Alabama*
*(287 U.S. 45 [1932])*

At one time, the right to counsel did not exist for many individuals. Usually, counsel was only available for defendants who could afford an attorney. Eventually, the Supreme Court began to recognize the need to provide counsel to criminal defendants who could *not* afford it. The constitutional right of an indigent defendant to be represented by counsel was first announced in *Powell v. Alabama*, 287 U.S. 45 (1932). In that case, the Supreme Court reversed the convictions of several indigent defendants who were not represented by counsel at trial. Significantly, though, the Court based its decision on due process, not the Sixth Amendment. In the Court's words:

> The right to be heard would be, in many cases, of little avail if it did not comprehend the right to be heard by counsel. Even the intelligent and educated layman has small and sometimes no skill in the science of law. If charged with crimes, he is incapable, generally, of determining for himself whether the indictment is good or bad. He is unfamiliar with the rules of evidence. Left without aid of counsel he may be put on trial without a proper charge, and convicted upon incompetent evidence, or evidence irrelevant to the issue or otherwise inadmissible. He lacks both the skill and knowledge adequately to prepare his defense, even though he may have a perfect one. He requires the guiding hand of counsel at every step in the proceedings against him. Without it, though he be not guilty, he faces the danger of conviction because he does not know how to establish his innocence.

---

[10]Larry J. Siegel, Frank Schmalleger, and John L. Worrall, *Courts and Criminal Justice in America* (Columbus, OH: Pearson, 2011), p. 233.

▼

The right to counsel announced in *Powell* was not without limitations. It applied only to "capital case[s], where the defendant is unable to employ counsel, and is incapable adequately of making his own defense because of ignorance, feeble-mindedness, illiteracy, or the like."

## The Contemporary Sixth Amendment Approach

In *Johnson v. Zerbst*, 304 U.S. 458 (1938), the Court recognized the Sixth Amendment right to counsel in all federal prosecutions, stating that the Sixth Amendment "embodies a realistic recognition of the obvious truth that the average defendant does not have the professional legal skill to protect himself."

*Johnson v. Zerbst*
*(304 U.S. 458 [1938])*

But in *Johnson*, the Sixth Amendment's right to counsel was applied only to federal prosecutions, and was not extended to the states. This position was reaffirmed a few years later in the case of *Betts v. Brady*, 316 U.S. 455 (1942), where the Court held that "[t]he Due Process Clause of the Fourteenth Amendment does not incorporate, as such, the specific guarantees found in the Sixth Amendment." It was not until the 1963 decision in *Gideon v. Wainwright*, 372 U.S. 335 (1963), that the Sixth Amendment right to counsel became incorporated. In that case, the Court recognized that "lawyers in criminal courts are necessities, not luxuries."

*Gideon v. Wainwright*
*(372 U.S. 335 [1963])*

*Gideon* involved a prosecution for a felony, which meant for a time that the Sixth Amendment right to counsel applied only in felony proceedings, but in *Argersinger v. Hamlin*, 407 U.S. 25 (1972), the Supreme Court extended the right to counsel to misdemeanor cases, as well. According to the Court, "The requirement of counsel may well be necessary for a fair trial even in petty-offense prosecution. We are by no means convinced that legal and constitutional questions involved in a case that actually leads to imprisonment even for a brief period are any less complex than when a person can be sent off for six months or more."

However, the right to counsel was subsequently limited in *Scott v. Illinois*, 440 U.S. 367 (1979). In that case, a defendant was not provided with court-appointed counsel and was convicted of shoplifting and fined $50. The Court upheld his conviction and decided that the right to counsel does not apply when imprisonment is not part of the punishment. In other words, when there is no possibility of confinement, the Sixth Amendment right to counsel does not apply.

A modification of the *Scott* decision was handed down in *Alabama v. Shelton*, 535 U.S. 654 (2002), in which the Court held that "[a] suspended sentence that may 'end up in the actual deprivation of a person's liberty' may not be imposed unless the defendant was accorded 'the guiding hand of counsel' in the prosecution for the crime charged." *Shelton* was distinguished from *Scott* because Shelton was placed on probation and could have faced imprisonment if his probation was revoked. Scott, by contrast, was only fined and not placed on probation.

# The Right to Counsel at Other Stages of the Criminal Process

Until the Supreme Court's 1963 decision in *Gideon*, its cases on the right to counsel had addressed this right primarily in the context of trials. After *Gideon*, however, the Court began to turn its attention to the right to counsel at other stages of the criminal process. This right is tied primarily to the Sixth Amendment, but the Court found support for the right to counsel on the grounds of self-incrimination, due process, and equal protection.

## The Sixth Amendment Approach

In order to determine whether the Sixth Amendment right to counsel applies outside the trial context, the Court once applied what was sometimes referred to as the "critical stage analysis." In *United States v. Wade*, 388 U.S. 218 (1967), the Supreme Court announced a two-prong test for determining when counsel is required under the Sixth Amendment: (1) "whether potential substantial prejudice to the defendant's rights inheres in the particular confrontation;" and (2) whether counsel can "help avoid that prejudice." In support of its decision, the Court stated, "The trial which might determine the accused's fate may well not be that in the courtroom but that at the pretrial confrontation, with the State aligned against the accused, the witness the sole jury, and the accused unprotected against the overreaching, intentional or unintentional, [influence of the government]."

What, then, was considered a *critical stage*? The Court stated that the period from arraignment to trial was arguably the most critical period of the proceedings. Preliminary hearings and sentencing hearings were also considered critical stages in the criminal process (see *Mempa v. Rhay*, 389 U.S. 128 [1967]; *Coleman v. Alabama*, 399 U.S. 1 [1970]). Even so, it was not completely clear what constituted a "critical stage."

*Kirby v. Illinois*
*(406 U.S. 682 [1972])*

In *Kirby v. Illinois*, 406 U.S. 682 (1972), the Court became even more specific and held that the right to counsel applies not only in criminal prosecutions but also at the "initiation of adversary proceedings." This means that the Sixth Amendment right to counsel applies not only after indictment, formal charging, and on through sentencing, but also as early on at the initial appearance (*Rothgery v. Gillespie County*, 554 U.S. 191 [2008]).

### The Fifth Amendment Approach

The right to counsel has also been applied through the Fifth Amendment. The familiar *Miranda* case held that the Fifth Amendment's privilege against self-incrimination grants suspects the right to counsel during custodial interrogations because of the "inherent coerciveness" of such activities. Furthermore, the right to counsel during custodial interrogations applies before or after commencement of formal adversary proceedings.

### The Due Process Approach

The right to counsel also stems from the due process clause of the Fourteenth Amendment, but only in certain circumstances. The Fourteenth Amendment has been used to justify the right to counsel primarily in criminal appeals and probation or parole revocation hearings. For example, in *Douglas v. California*, 372 U.S. 353 (1963), the Court held that the right to counsel extends to convicted indigents for appeals of right (appeals to which the individual is legally entitled). And in *Gagnon v. Scarpelli*, 411 U.S. 778 (1973), the Court held that as a matter of due process, indigents are entitled to counsel at probation and parole revocation hearings, but only on a case-by-case basis (such as whether the complexity of the issues at stake is significant).

In contrast, the right to counsel does not necessarily exist to provide indigent convicts with assistance in preparing petitions for *discretionary* appeals (those in which the reviewing court decides whether to hear them) (see *Ross v. Moffitt*, 417 U.S. 600 [1974]). The Court noted that the government "does not automatically . . . act . . . unfairly by refusing to provide counsel to indigent defendants at every stage of the [appellate process]." Similarly, in *Pennsylvania v. Finley*, 481 U.S. 551 (1987), the Court announced that the state is not required to provide convicted criminals with counsel for the purpose of preparing *habeas corpus* petitions. The reason offered by the Court is that "[post-]conviction relief is even further removed from the criminal trial than is discretionary direct review."

## Waiver of the Right to Counsel

Though the Sixth Amendment provides for the right to counsel, accused individuals sometimes prefer to mount a **pro se defense**—to represent themselves in court. Indeed, according to the Supreme Court, criminal defendants have a constitutional right to represent themselves at trial (*Faretta v. California*, 422 U.S. 806 [1975]). In reaching this decision, the Court noted that the Sixth Amendment only guarantees the *assistance* of counsel, not necessarily *representation* by counsel:

The language and spirit of the Sixth Amendment contemplate that counsel, like the other defense tools guaranteed by the Amendment, shall be an aid to a willing defendant—not an organ of State interposed between an unwilling defendant and his right to defend himself personally. . . . An unwanted counsel "represents" the defendant only through a tenuous and unacceptable legal fiction. Unless the accused has acquiesced in such representation, the defense presented is not the defense guaranteed him by the Constitution, for in a very real sense, it is not his defense.

The Court also emphasized in *Faretta* that the framers viewed the "inestimable worth of free choice" as more important than the right to counsel. Also, "[t]o force a lawyer on a defendant can only lead [the defendant] to believe that the law contrives against him."

Not every defendant who wishes to proceed without counsel is allowed to do so, however. In *Johnson v. Zerbst*, 304 U.S. 458 (1938), the Supreme Court stated that a defendant may only waive counsel if the waiver is "competent and intelligent." This language was clarified in *Carnley v. Cochran*, 369 U.S. 506 (1962), when the Court noted that "the record must show, or there must be an allegation and evidence must show, that an accused was offered counsel but intelligently and understandingly rejected the offer. Anything less is not a waiver." The Court elaborated further in *Von Moltke v. Gillies*, 332 U.S. 708 (1948):

To be valid such waiver must be made with an apprehension of the nature of the charges, the statutory offenses included within them, the range of allowable punishments thereunder, possible defenses to the charges and circumstances in mitigation thereof, and all other facts essential to a broad understanding of the whole matter. A judge can make certain that an accused's professed waiver of counsel is understandingly and wisely made only from a penetrating and comprehensive examination of all the circumstances.

A number of subsequent cases have grappled with what constitutes a proper waiver. For example, in *Massey v. Moore*, 348 U.S. 105 (1954), the Court held that "[o]ne might not be insane in the sense of being incapable of standing trial and yet lack the capacity to stand trial without benefit of counsel." But in *Godinez v. Moran*, 509 U.S. 389 (1993), the Court held that a person who is competent to stand trial is also competent to waive counsel at trial and for pleading purposes.

In certain circumstances, while permitting waiver of counsel, the court can also require that *standby counsel* be available to the defendant—that is, an attorney who is standing by in order to assist the accused, if necessary. This was the decision reached in *McKaskle v. Wiggins*, 465 U.S. 168 (1984). The Court held that a judge can appoint standby counsel "to relieve the judge of the need to explain and enforce basic rules of courtroom protocol or to assist the defendant in overcoming routine obstacles that stand in the way of the defendant's achievement of his own clearly indicated goals." When waiver of counsel is knowing and intelligent, a judge's decision to appoint standby counsel will not be unconstitutional as long as (1) the defendant retains control over the case and (2) the jury understands that the defendant represents himself or herself.

## DECISION-MAKING EXERCISE 11.9

### RIGHT TO COUNSEL IN THE PRETRIAL PHASE

A man was arrested without a warrant when a police officer caught him robbing the First Street branch of American Bank. Four hours later, the man was brought before a judge for a probable cause hearing. The judge decided that the officer had probable cause to arrest. The man was convicted of the crime and sentenced to prison. He is now appealing his conviction, claiming that he should have been given access to counsel at the probable cause hearing. Is he right?

In 2004, the Supreme Court considered the obligation of a court to warn a defendant of the consequences of waiving the right to counsel. Essentially, the court decided that waiver of the right to counsel is one that the defendant takes, potentially, at his or her own peril. In *Iowa v. Tovar*, 541 U.S. 77 (2004), the Court held that a trial court was not required to warn the accused that waiving the right to counsel at a plea hearing involves two risks: (1) the possibility that valid defenses will be overlooked and (2) the accused will be deprived of advice as to whether a guilty plea is warranted. At the same time, though, the Constitution does not prohibit a court from insisting on representation of counsel for criminal defendants who are competent to stand trial but who also suffer from serious mental illness that would compromise their ability to put on an effective defense (*Indiana v. Edwards*, 554 U.S. 164 [2008]).

## Indigent versus Nonindigent Defendants' Right to Counsel of Their Choice

Many defendants who have the financial means are able to hire counsel of their choosing. Unfortunately, the indigent defendant does not have such a choice. The Sixth Amendment does not guarantee the indigent defendant the right to *choose* counsel; rather, it states that counsel will be *provided*. Usually, counsel will be a public defender. If, however, an indigent can show good cause that the attorney appointed to represent him or her is not doing so adequately, another attorney can be appointed. What constitutes *inadequate representation* is discussed in the next section.

Surprisingly, there are situations in which defendants, if they can afford representation, cannot hire counsel of their choice. If, for example, the defendant's choice of an attorney poses serious conflict-of-interest problems, the defendant may be forced to hire another attorney (see *Wheat v. United States*, 486 U.S. 153 [1988]). Or if the defendant's attorney is not qualified to practice law, then another attorney may be required (e.g., cf. *Leis v. Flynt*, 439 U.S. 438 [1979]). And somewhat controversially, if a defendant's assets are frozen pursuant to a civil forfeiture statute and he or she cannot afford counsel of his or her choosing, then a less expensive attorney may be required or a public defender may be appointed (see *Caplin v. Drysdale v. United States*, 491 U.S. 617 [1989]).

On the other hand, if a defendant with means has his or her eye on a particular attorney who is qualified to practice law and does not have any conflicts of interest, the defendant must be able to hire the attorney. If a judge wrongfully prohibits the defendant from hiring the attorney of his or her choice, the defendant's ensuing conviction must be overturned (*United States v. Gonzalez-Lopez*, 548 U.S. 140 [2006]).

An issue related to counsel of one's choice is whether indigent defendants can retain expert witnesses of their own choosing. In *Ake v. Oklahoma*, 470 U.S. 68 (1985), the Supreme Court held that an indigent defendant enjoys a constitutional right to an expert witness when his or her sanity is at issue. However, the Court limited its holding to provide for only one expert, and one who is state employed. States vary in their rules concerning expert witnesses for indigent defendants. Often there are price caps that limit how much an indigent defendant's expert can be paid. At some point, it becomes necessary to assume that the *state*'s experts (such as ballistics experts) present objective and accurate testimony that is not prejudicial to the accused.

## Effective Assistance of Counsel

Unfortunately, some defendants who are innocent are convicted because their attorneys are overworked, unprepared, or incompetent. All attorneys are not the same. Some, while authorized to practice law, prove to be totally ineffective in their duties. The Supreme Court has held that the Sixth Amendment requires that defendants be provided with **effective assistance of counsel**, but numerous cases have grappled with exactly what "effective assistance" means.

## When the Right Applies

The right to *effective assistance* applies when the *right to counsel* applies. For example, the Supreme Court has held that a defense attorney's failure to file a timely discretionary appeal is not ineffective because the right to counsel does not extend to such appeals (*Wainwright v. Torna*, 455 U.S. 586 [1982]). Only when counsel is required can an ineffective assistance claim be made.

It is important to understand that claims of ineffective assistance can be filed against both retained and appointed counsel. For a time, the Supreme Court held that a non-indigent defendant who retained his or her own attorney was bound by that attorney's representation, for better or worse, because there was no state action responsible for the ineffective representation. However, in *Cuyler v. Sullivan*, 446 U.S. 335 (1980), the Court held that privately retained counsel can be ineffective in the same way a public defender can:

> The vital guarantee of the Sixth Amendment would stand for little if the often uninformed decision to retain a particular lawyer could reduce or forfeit the defendant's entitlement to constitutional protection. Since the State's conduct of a criminal trial itself implicates the State in the defendant's conviction, we see no basis for drawing a distinction between retained and appointed counsel that would deny equal justice to defendants who must choose their own lawyers.

## The Meaning of "Effective Assistance"

A number of Supreme Court cases have sought to define "effective assistance." In, *McMann v. Richardson*, 397 U.S. 759 (1970), the Court held that counsel is effective when his or her legal advice is "within the range of competence demanded of attorneys in criminal cases." This was a somewhat vague standard, so the Court created a new test in *Strickland v. Washington*, 466 U.S. 668 (1984). It held that a two-prong test must be applied in order to determine whether counsel is ineffective:

*Strickland v. Washington* *(466 U.S. 668 [1984])*

> First, the defendant must show that counsel's performance was deficient. This requires showing that counsel made errors so serious that counsel was not functioning as the "counsel" guaranteed the defendant by the Sixth Amendment. Second, the defendant must show that the deficient performance prejudiced the defense. This requires showing that counsel's errors were so serious as to deprive the defendant of a fair trial, a trial whose result is unreliable.

*Performance.* The two prongs announced in this case are now known as the *performance* prong and the *prejudice* prong. Most cases have focused on the performance prong. The Court noted in *Strickland* that "[t]he proper measure of attorney performance remains simply reasonableness under prevailing professional norms." Defense counsel's performance will be considered adequate if he or she avoids conflicts of interest, serves as an advocate for the defendant's case, and brings to bear "such skill and knowledge as will render the trial a reliable adversarial testing process." Furthermore, defense counsel "has a duty to make reasonable investigations or to make a reasonable decision that makes particular investigations unnecessary."

A defense attorney's conflict of interest is certain to raise claims of poor performance. Ineffective assistance is likely if the attorney:

1. tries to represent more than one defendant in the same trial;
2. has represented one of the prosecution's witnesses in a previous trial;
3. is being paid by a third party; or
4. is contracted with a publishing company to write the defendant's story.

## Examples of Effective and Ineffective Assistance of Counsel

| 2002 | 2004 | 2005 |
|---|---|---|
| *Bell* v. *Cone,* 535 U.S. 685 Defense counsel's failure to present any mitigating evidence or to make a closing statement at the defendant's capital sentencing hearing was not ineffective. Among the reasons for the Court's decision was that the mitigating evidence that was not presented during the sentencing hearing *was* presented at trial, so the jury did have an opportunity to review it. | *Florida* v. *Nixon,* 543 U.S. 175 Defense counsel was permitted to acknowledge—in open court—his client's guilt and instead focus the defense on reasons why the defendant's life should be spared. The evidence was so clearly indicative of the defendant's guilt, that the Supreme Court did not feel the defense attorney's strategy was ineffective. | *Rompilla* v. *Beard,* 545 U.S. 374 Defense counsel is bound to make reasonable efforts to obtain and review material that it knows the prosecution will probably rely on as part of its case. |

**FIGURE 11.6**

Numerous other conflict-of-interest scenarios are possible, as well. In *Mickens v. Taylor*, 535 U.S. 162 (2002), the Supreme Court considered the question of whether a defense attorney's conflict of interest violates the defendant's Sixth Amendment rights. The defendant claimed his conviction should have been overturned because the judge should have inquired about the conflict of interest at trial but did not. However, the Supreme Court held that the judge's failure to do so did not entitle the defendant to an automatic reversal. Instead, the Court held that the defendant had to establish that the potential conflict of interest adversely affected the trial attorney's performance.

A number of other Supreme Court cases in recent years have sought to bring more clarification to what constitutes effective and ineffective assistance. A list of cases and their holdings appears in Figure 11.6.

Attorneys make errors in a variety of ways, even beyond those presented in Figure 11.6. Generally, though, the defendant must point to a specific error or set of errors, not the overall performance of his or her counsel. If defense counsel makes a specific error and can offer no explanation for the error, then the defendant will have a good chance in succeeding with a claim of ineffective assistance of counsel.

*Proving Prejudice.* With regard to the prejudice prong, the Court stated in *Strickland* that "[a]ctual or constructive denial of the assistance of counsel" and "various kinds of state interference with counsel's assistance" are "legally presumed to result in prejudice." State interference of this sort can occur when the defendant is either denied counsel or provided with counsel too late. Also, if the state blocks counsel's performance to some degree or otherwise interferes with the attorney–client relationship, an ineffective assistance of counsel claim is likely to succeed. In other words, such action is prejudicial.

Proving defense counsel's ineffective assistance is not enough to ensure a conviction will be overturned. In addition, as stated in *Strickland*, the defendant must prove that "there

## DECISION-MAKING EXERCISE 11.10

### EFFECTIVE ASSISTANCE OF COUNSEL

A woman has been convicted of check fraud. On appeal, she claims that she was denied access to effective counsel. She argues that her attorney, a young public defender, had never tried a jury case and did not have enough time to prepare an adequate defense. Will her appeal succeed?

**Examples of Effective and Ineffective Assistance of Counsel,** *continued*

| 2007 | 2008 | 2011 |
|---|---|---|
| ***Schriro* v. *Landrigan,* 550 U.S.\_\_\_**<br>A defense attorney was not ineffective when his client instructed him not to present mitigating evidence during the death penalty sentencing phase. | ***Wright* v. *Van Patten,* 552 U.S.\_\_\_**<br>If the defense attorney participates in a plea hearing by speakerphone, rather than in person, it does not mean he or she provides ineffective assistance. | ***Harrington* v. *Richter,* 562 U.S.\_\_\_**<br>Defense counsel was not ineffective when it failed to utilize the testimony of its own blood evidence expert who could have testified to the defendant's account of the events. Blood evidence was not central to the case, and it was apparent that even the defense attorney questioned the defendant's account of the crime for which he was on trial. |

**FIGURE 11.6** *Continued*

is a reasonable probability that, but for counsel's unprofessional errors, the result of the proceeding would have been different." In other words, the burden falls on the defendant to show that the outcome of the case was a result of the ineffective assistance provided by his or her defense attorney. If the defense counsel acted ineffectively but such actions did not influence the outcome of the case, then a *Strickland* claim cannot succeed. The Supreme Court has not elaborated extensively on these issues, but they have been touched upon extensively in the lower courts.

# Summary

## 1. Describe the prosecutor's role, prosecutor's discretion, and the issues surrounding prosecutorial misconduct.

A prosecutor's decision whether to charge is rarely challenged. Reasons for nonprosecution include a lack of evidence and court backlog. However, a prosecutor's decision not to press charges *can* be challenged. On rare occasions, a court can effectively overrule a prosecutor's decision not to charge someone. Also, a prosecutor's superior can demand that charges be brought.

Prosecutors' charging decisions are subject to certain constitutional restrictions. Unfair and selective prosecutions are inappropriate and violate the equal protection clause of the Fourteenth Amendment. Vindictive prosecutions violate due process. Prosecutors generally enjoy absolute immunity for their charging decisions. Methods of dealing with overzealous prosecutors range from reprimand to disbarment.

## 2. Explain the concept of joinder and reasons for it.

Joinder refers either to (1) bringing several charges against the same individual in the same trial or to (2) bringing charges against multiple defendants in the same trial. Both methods of joinder are generally considered appropriate, but if the crimes (or defendants) in question are only tied together because they are similar, separate trials may be warranted. Assuming the court permits joinder, then for separate trials to be held, the defendant must prove that his or her interests will be prejudiced in some fashion by a joint trial.

**Examples of Effective and Ineffective Assistance of Counsel,** *continued*

| 2011 | 2012 | 2012 | 2012 |
|---|---|---|---|
| ***Premo* v. *Moore*, 562 U.S.\_\_\_** Defense counsel was not ineffective for failing to seek suppression of the defendant's unconstitutionally-obtained confession. | ***Missouri* v. *Frye*, 566 U.S.\_\_\_** Defense counsel must inform the defendant of formal plea offers that contain favorable terms and conditions. Defense counsel in this case failed to notify the defendant of a prosecutor's favorable plea agreement and the agreement subsequently expired. | ***Lafler* v. *Cooper*, 566 U.S.\_\_\_** Flawed advice leading to the rejection of a plea offer can form the basis of an ineffective assistance claim. Defense counsel in this advised his client to reject a plea agreement on the mistaken belief that the defendant could not be convicted of assault with intent to murder. | ***Maples* v. *Thomas*, 565 U.S.\_\_\_** If defense counsel "abandons" the defendant, causing him or her to miss a key appellate deadline, a second chance to appeal the conviction must be given. |

**FIGURE 11.6** *Continued*

## 3. Explain the purpose, functions, and powers of a grand jury.

Approximately one-third of all states and the federal system require that prosecution in felony cases proceed by grand jury indictment. In the remaining states, prosecution can proceed by indictment or information. Grand juries are closely related to prosecutors in terms of their charging decisions. Frequently, the grand jury serves as a means of formalizing the prosecutor's decision to charge. A grand jury is useful when the case in question is of great public or political significance, when its extensive investigative powers are helpful, when time is of the essence, and when one or more witnesses is hesitant to speak in open court, preferring the secrecy that surrounds grand jury proceedings.

The size of a grand jury varies, depending on location. Typically, the smaller the grand jury, the higher the voting requirement. Grand jury selection pools must be representative in terms of race and gender. That is, a grand jury selection procedure that purposefully discriminates on the basis of race or gender will be unconstitutional. Indeed, if the selection procedure systematically excludes an identifiable segment of society, then it is inappropriate. The final grand jury itself does not need to be representative of the community.

Grand jury proceedings are typically held in secret. Thus, there are significant restrictions on what information from grand jury proceedings can be shared with the defense as well as other parties. There are several reasons for secrecy: (1) to prevent the escape of possible indictees, (2) to ensure freedom to the grand jury in its deliberations, (3) to prevent tampering with the witnesses who may testify, (4) to encourage persons who have information with respect to the commission of crimes to come forward, and (5) to protect the innocence of those who are ultimately exonerated by grand jury investigations.

An individual who is the target of a grand jury investigation does not have the right (1) to appear in front of the grand jury, (2) to have the assistance of counsel during the grand jury's investigation, (3) to be told he or she is the target of the investigation, or (4) to be reminded that he or she has the right to remain silent. In short, many of the constitutional rights that apply in the context of a criminal trial do not apply during the course of a grand jury investigation.

Grand juries possess extensive investigative powers. They can issue subpoenas *ad testificandum*, which require witnesses to appear and testify, and subpoenas *duces tecum*, which compel the production of evidence. Unlike subpoenas to elicit testimony, subpoenas to compel the production of tangible evidence must be sufficiently particular, relevant to the investigation, and not overly burdensome. As part of their investigative powers, grand juries can also grant immunity and hold people in contempt.

Just as there are constraints on prosecutors' charging decisions, there are restrictions on grand juries' indictment decisions. However, a grand jury indictment is rarely quashed. Only when there is evidence of serious prosecutorial tampering, discrimination in the composition of the grand jury pool, or variance between the evidence presented during the grand jury investigation and that presented at trial will a grand jury indictment possibly be quashed.

## 4. Outline the development of the right to counsel.

Criminal defendants enjoy the Sixth Amendment right to counsel once adversarial criminal proceedings have commenced. This usually means the right attaches once charges have been filed. Also, when the offense is such that there is possibility of confinement, the right to counsel does not apply. Like many constitutional rights, the right to counsel can be waived, but the court can appoint standby counsel in certain circumstances. Finally, the Supreme Court has interpreted the right to counsel to mean the right to *effective* counsel. Counsel is ineffective when specific errors are made that are prejudicial to the defendant's case.

## Key Terms

contempt power *330*
effective assistance of counsel *336*
grand jury *321*
joinder *320*
pretextual prosecution *317*

prosecutorial discretion *310*
*pro se* defense *334*
selective prosecution *315*
severance *320*
subpoena *ad testificandum* *329*

subpoena *duces tecum* *329*
true bill *324*
variance *331*
vindictive prosecution *317*

## Key Cases

### Prosecutor
- *Oyler v. Boles*, 368 U.S. 448 (1968)
- *Blackledge v. Perry*, 417 U.S. 21 (1974)
- *United States v. Lane*, 474 U.S. 438 (1986)

### Grand Jury
- *Hurtado v. California*, 110 U.S. 516 (1884)
- *Taylor v. Louisiana*, 419 U.S. 522 (1975)
- *Rose v. Mitchell*, 443 U.S. 545 (1979)
- *Butterworth v. Smith*, 494 U.S. 624 (1990)

- *United States v. Mandujano*, 425 U.S. 564 (1976)
- *United States v. Calandra*, 414 U.S. 338 (1974)
- *Hale v. Henkel*, 201 U.S. 43 (1906)

### Defense Attorney
- *Gideon v. Wainwright*, 372 U.S. 335 (1963)
- *Powell v. Alabama*, 287 U.S. 45 (1932)
- *Kirby v. Illinois*, 406 U.S. 682 (1972)
- *Johnson v. Zerbst*, 304 U.S. 458 (1938)
- *Strickland v. Washington*, 466 U.S. 668 (1984)

# Further Exploration

1. To what extent does *Connick v. Thompson*, 563 U.S. ___ (2011), affect the potential for prosecutorial misconduct? First read the case, then examine the article here for a different perspective: http://www.yalelawjournal. org/images/pdfs/1018.pdf (accessed May 13, 2013).

2. The National Association of Criminal Defense Lawyers (NACDL) has remarked that " . . . today's grand jury is a rubber stamp . . . " and that " . . . a good prosecutor could get a grand jury to indict a ham sandwich" (http://www.nacdl.org/grandjury/). Consequently, the NACDL has called upon Congress to reform the grand jury process, going so far as calling for a federal grand jury "bill of rights." You can read the proposed bill of rights here: http://www.nacdl. org/criminaldefense.aspx?id=10372&libID=10345 (accessed May 13, 2013). Do you agree with the proposed rights? What other reforms have been called for? What are the arguments against proposed reform? Is grand jury reform really necessary?

3. Public defender offices around the country are feeling a financial squeeze. What problems can flow from this? Listen to the NPR interview with Columbus, Ohio, public defender, Steven Nolder: http://www .npr.org/2013/04/10/176682852/some-public-defenders-warn-we-have-nothing-left-to-cut (accessed May 13, 2013).

4. Read these facts from *State v. Holmes*, 302 S.W.3d 831 (Tenn. 2010):

   The appellant, Tommy Holmes ("Defendant"), was indicted for attempted murder, aggravated rape, intimidation of a witness, and aggravated assault, and an assistant public defender ("Counsel") was appointed to represent him . . . [S]hortly before one of Defendant's trials, an "impromptu hearing" was held with Defendant present. During this "hearing," Counsel sought permission to withdraw from representing Defendant on the basis of Defendant's behavior toward him. Counsel told the trial court,

   On two occasions, Your Honor, including this morning—the reason I had [the defendant] brought up was so I could visit with him up here. He has threatened physical violence in the past at our last meeting. Today he put hands on me and I had to leave. He punched me in the face with his finger, knocked my glasses off. And I don't believe that I can represent [the defendant]; so I'm asking the Court to relieve me.

   If you were the judge, how would you react to the defense attorney's request? Should alternate counsel be appointed or should the defendant be forced to proceed *pro se*?

5. Assume it is learned at trial that the defense attorney was involved in an intimate relationship with an assistant district attorney in the appellate division of the local prosecutor's office. Assume further that the defense attorney was at one point involved in an intimate relationship with the prosecutor in the same case. Could the defendant make a conflict of interest claim, thus rendering counsel's assistance ineffective? Does it matter how long ago the relationship ended? What if it ended 17 years ago? Read *Commonwealth v. State*, 922 N.E.2d 768 (Mass. 2010).

# Review Questions

1. What is the role of the prosecutor?

2. What are some reasons for nonprosecution? What can be done to challenge a prosecutor's decision not to pursue charges?

3. What types of restrictions exist on the ability of the prosecutor to bring charges? Cite relevant cases.

4. How does qualified immunity and absolute immunity operate in the prosecution context?

5. What can be done with overzealous prosecutors?

6. What is joinder? Explain the differences between joinder of charges and joinder of defendants.

7. Referring to Figure 11.4, what is the size of the grand jury in your state? Investigate the voting requirements and selection methods of grand juries in your state.

8. Explain some significant Supreme Court decisions with regard to the secrecy of grand jury proceedings.

9. Explain the rights of witnesses testifying before grand juries.

10. Distinguish among three types of investigative powers that grand juries possess.

11. Can a grand jury indictment be challenged? If so, how? If not, why not?

12. What two constitutional provisions does the right to counsel in a criminal prosecution come from?

13. Explain how the right to counsel applies at other stages of the criminal process.

14. Can the Sixth Amendment right to counsel be waived? If so, what are the requirements for a valid waiver? Also, can a judge overrule a defendant's decision to waive counsel?

15. When might a defendant not be able to hire counsel of his or her choice?

16. Explain the meaning of *effective assistance of counsel*.

17. What must a defendant show in order to succeed with an ineffective assistance of counsel claim?

## Web Links and Exercises

1. Prosecutors: read more about prosecutors at the Web site of the National District Attorneys Association.
URL: http://www.ndaa.org (accessed May 14, 2013).

2. Grand juries: read more about grand juries. How do federal grand juries differ from state grand juries?
URL: http://campus.udayton.edu/~grandjur (accessed May 14, 2013).

3. Defense attorneys: read more about defense attorneys.
URL: http://www.nacdl.org (accessed May 14, 2013).

4. Public defenders: read more about public defenders.
URL: http://www.nlada.org (accessed May 14, 2013).

# 12 Plea Bargaining and Guilty Pleas

## LEARNING OBJECTIVES

When you complete this chapter, you should be able to:

**❶** *Explain the concept of plea bargaining.*

**❷** *Outline the history of plea bargaining and arguments for and against its use.*

**❸** *Summarize the procedures in the plea-bargaining process and the effects of plea bargaining.*

**❹** *Outline the elements of a valid guilty plea.*

**❺** *Summarize how a guilty plea may be contested.*

**OUTLINE**

# Introduction: Methods of Avoiding Trial

Obtaining a guilty plea through plea bargaining is the most common method of securing a conviction. The overwhelming majority of criminal convictions in the United States—90 percent, by some estimates—result from guilty pleas, rather than trials. These pleas usually derive from some bargaining between the defense attorney and the prosecutor. Both parties stand to gain something from a plea bargaining rather than going to trial: the prosecutor obtains a conviction, and the defense attorney usually succeeds in getting lenient treatment for his or her client.

Plea bargaining is essential to the administration of justice. If every defendant demanded his or her right to a jury trial, the criminal justice system would literally collapse. For this reason, arguments against plea bargaining are somewhat academic—plea bargaining is necessary because there are simply too many criminals and not enough prosecutors, courts, and prisons.

At the same time, though, criticism of plea bargaining should not be entirely dismissed. Americans are taught that judges and juries should determine guilt. However, plea bargaining essentially permits attorneys to decide the outcome of a case without ever going to trial. And it is well known that when two defendants face the same charge, the one who plea bargains invariably receives a lesser sentence than the one who does not.

Importantly, plea bargaining is not the only way to arrive at a guilty plea. Many defendants plead guilty to the charges against them even when no bargaining takes place. Although the bulk of this chapter focuses on plea bargaining, the section "Elements of a Valid Guilty Plea" is especially important for both types of guilty pleas: those that engage in bargaining and those that do not. A sample of the plea form that is submitted to the court is presented in Figure 12.1.

• • • • • • • • • • • • • • • • • • • • • • • • • • • • • • • • • • • • • • • • • • • • • • • • • • • • • • • • • • •

---

| | **PLEA FORM** | **CAUSE NUMBER:** |
|---|---|---|
| **STATE OF TEXAS** | § | **IN THE MUNICIPAL COURT** |
| **VS.** | § | **CITY OF** _____ |
| _____ | § | _____**COUNTY, TEXAS** |

### *PLEA OF NOLO CONTENDERE*

I, the undersigned, do hereby enter my appearance on the complaint of the offense, to wit: _____
_____
charged in Municipal Court Cause Number _____. I have been informed of my right to a jury trial and that my signature on this plea of *nolo contendere* (meaning "no contest") will have the same force and effect as a plea of guilty on the judgment of the Court. I do hereby plead *nolo contendere* to said offense as charged, waive my right to a jury trial or hearing by the Court, and agree to pay the fine and costs the judge assesses. I understand that my plea may result in a conviction appearing on either a criminal record or a driver's license record.

_____          _____
Date                                                                  Defendant's Signature

                                                                      _____
                                                                      Address

### PLEA OF GUILTY

I, the undersigned, do hereby enter my appearance on the complaint of the offense, to wit: _____
_____
charged in Municipal Court Cause Number . I have been informed of my right to a jury trial and that my signature to this plea of guilty will have the same force and effect as a judgment of the Court. I do hereby plead guilty to the offense as charged, waive my right to a jury trial or hearing by the Court, and agree to pay the fine and costs the judge assesses. I understand that my plea may result in a conviction appearing on either a criminal record or a driver's license record.

_____          _____
Date                                                                  Defendant's Signature

                                                                      _____
                                                                      Address

### PLEA OF NOT GUILTY

I, the undersigned, do hereby enter my appearance on the complaint of the offense, to wit:_____
_____
charged in Municipal Court Cause Number _____. I plead not guilty.

**FIGURE 12.1 Sample Plea Form**

---

**FIGURE 12.1** *Continued*

# ▶ Plea Bargaining

The practice of **plea bargaining** is often thought of simply as a process that results in a defendant accepting a guilty plea to lesser charge in exchange for a lighter sentence. However, the process is much more complex, and may take many forms depending on the case or situation. There are also a variety of concessions that may be offered to a defendant in exchange for a guilty plea.

*Charge bargaining* refers to the prosecutor's ability to negotiate with the defendant in terms of the charges that could be filed. *Sentence bargaining*, by contrast, is when the defendant agrees to plead guilty in exchange for a less serious sentence. Charge bargaining is largely carried out between the prosecution and the defense. Sentence bargaining requires getting the judge involved because he or she usually hands down the sentence. In fact, there is even such a thing as *count bargaining*, in which the defense negotiates to have the defendant charged with fewer counts of a certain offense.

Although, as will be noted later, a plea bargain must be intelligent and voluntary, it does not usually result in the most favorable outcome desired by the parties. For example, the prosecutor may simply be *forced* to present a favorable offer to the defendant because of procedural errors that would make it difficult to prove the state's case. Or the prosecutor may present the defendant with equally unfavorable choices. As one researcher observed, "[T]he right to reject the proposed plea bargain is largely chimerical. Fear of heavier sentence after trial and deference to advice of defense counsel might lead defendants to accept virtually all plea agreements."[1]

Usually, a plea agreement reached by the parties is subject to court approval. However, the plea-bargaining process is mostly carried on between the defense and the prosecution with little judicial oversight. For example, prosecutors can do a great deal to drop or alter charges against an individual prior to bringing any subsequent agreement to the attention of the trial judge.

Although in a typical plea agreement, the defendant accepts a plea to a lesser offense in exchange for a lighter sentence, there are many other concessions that can be offered to the defendant in exchange for a guilty plea. For example, sentence-bargaining concessions may include, but are not limited to, (1) the judge agreeing to impose certain probation conditions; (2) the prosecutor recommending a certain sentence to the judge; (3) the prosecutor agreeing not to invoke certain sentencing provisions, say, for multiple offenders; and (4) an agreement that the defendant will serve his or her sentence in a certain institution.[2]

---

[1]Anonymous Author, "Plea Bargaining and the Transformation of the Criminal Process," *Harvard Law Review* 90 (1977): 564–595, 579.

[2]See, for example, H. S. Miller, W. F. McDonald, and J. A. Cramer, *Plea Bargaining in the United States* (Ann Arbor, MI: Inter University Consortium for Political and Social Research, 1978), p. 17.

# The History and Rise of Plea Bargaining

The right to trial by jury has been a central part of the American legal system since the time of its founding. Plea bargaining, in effect, supplants trial by jury, and early in the nation's history, courts were reluctant to approve the practice. However, despite criticism, plea bargaining has gradually gained acceptance, and is now generally approved by the Supreme Court.

## Historical Origins

One of the earliest reported cases addressing plea bargaining was decided in the early 1800s. In that case, *Commonwealth v. Battis*, 1 Mass. 95 (1804), a court was hesitant to permit a guilty plea by a defendant charged with a capital crime. The court gave the defendant time to contemplate his plea and even "examined, under oath, the sheriff, the jailer and justice (before whom the examination of the prisoner was had [sic] previous to commitment), as to the sanity of the prisoner; and whether there had been tampering with him, either by promises, persuasions, or hopes of pardon if he would plead guilty."

Following *Battis*, other cases involving some degree of plea bargaining were reported. One court's opinion focused on a Michigan statute that set forth specific requirements necessary for a valid guilty plea. The court expressed concern that some of what could be called *plea bargaining* was taking place without the approval of the courts (*Edwards v. People*, 39 Mich. 760 [1878]). The court observed that Michigan passed the statute "for the protection of prisoners and of the public" in response "to serious abuses caused by [prosecutors] procuring prisoners to plead guilty when a fair trial might show they were not guilty, or might show other facts important to be known." The court also found it "easy to see that the Legislature thought there was danger that prosecuting attorneys . . . would procure prisoners to plead guilty by assurances [that] they have no power to make[,] of influence in lowering the sentence, or by bringing some other unjust influence to bear on them." These statements suggest that plea bargaining was a somewhat common practice by the second half of the nineteenth century.

Plea bargaining became even more common in the early to mid-1900s. Many states had, by then, impaneled commissions to study the workings of their criminal justice systems. An example of one such commission was the New York State Crime Commission, which was impaneled in 1927. The studies published by these commissions reported an increase in the practice of plea bargaining. For example, the Georgia Department of Public Welfare reported that the rate of pleading guilty increased 70 percent from 1916 to 1921.[3] Similarly, statistics in New York revealed that between 1839 and 1920, the guilty plea rate rose to some 90 percent of all cases.[4]

## Reasons for the Rise in Plea Bargaining

In the early days of the English criminal justice system, defendants were rarely represented by counsel, and trials were concluded very rapidly. Historical accounts show that a jury would hear 12–20 felony cases in a single day.[5] Trials played out in a similar fashion in U.S. courts during the 1800s. One historian points out that many early trials in the United States were carried out without defense attorneys, and in some cases, without prosecuting attorneys.[6] As the U.S. legal system began to mature and lawyers became regular participants, trials slowed down and guilty plea rates increased out of necessity. According to one source,

---

[3]Georgia Department of Public Welfare, "Crime and the Georgia Courts," *Journal of the American Institute of Criminal Law and Criminology* 16 (1924): 16.

[4]R. Moley, "The Vanishing Jury," *Southern California Law Review* 2 (1928): 97–127, 107.

[5]J. H. Langbein, "The Criminal Trial before Lawyers," *University of Chicago Law Review* 45 (1978): 263–316, 277.

[6]L. M. Friedman, *Crime and Punishment in American History* (New York: Basic Books, 1993), p. 235.

▼

"[P]lea bargaining should be viewed as a natural outgrowth of a progressively adversarial criminal justice system."[7]

Despite its apparent necessity, plea bargaining was criticized extensively by early commentators. Some called it an "incompetent, inefficient, and lazy method of administering justice."[8] Others suggested that plea bargaining was just a means of avoiding trials for individuals charged with committing criminal acts.

## Arguments in Support of Plea Bargaining

Plea bargaining is a widely accepted practice in the U.S. justice system, largely because of the costs associated with trials, and the benefits it provides for the court system. Plea bargaining benefits all members of the courtroom work group:

- the prosecutor
- the defense attorney
- the defendant
- the court (the judge)

Thus, the arguments in support of plea bargaining are really arguments concerning the *benefits* of reaching plea agreements. Each of these arguments needs to be viewed in context, however. In some situations, as played out in a few highly celebrated cases, the costs of plea bargaining may outweigh the benefits.

Plea bargaining benefits the prosecutor because it provides him or her with a greater ability to dispose of a busy case load. District attorneys are often faced with limited resources and, as such, cannot prosecute every case that comes before them. Specifically, a district attorney may opt to pursue charges on cases that have a highly public element or are likely to result in guilty convictions. Cases that do not look promising may be prime candidates for plea bargaining. And according to one observer, plea bargaining may be favored by the prosecution simply because it allows the courtroom work group to further its "mutual interest in avoiding conflict, reducing uncertainty, and maintaining group cohesion."[9]

Defense attorneys also benefit from plea bargaining. Public defenders, who are the most common type of counsel in criminal trials, face resource constraints similar to those of prosecutors. Thus, plea bargaining benefits public defenders by allowing quick disposition of cases. It also allows them to focus on cases that they perceive as being worthy of trial. Bargaining also benefits privately retained counsel because it speeds up the process, which translates into "more money for less work." This is not to suggest, however, that this is the prime motivation of defense attorneys. Many zealously guard the interests of their clients.

Plea bargaining benefits the defendant perhaps more than the prosecutor or the defense attorney. The obvious reason for this is that the defendant generally receives a lesser sentence (or charge) as a result of plea bargaining. On another level, as will be discussed later, the defendant loses his or her chance at an acquittal and, sometimes, important rights, including the right to a trial by jury. But the Supreme Court has said that these costs may be outweighed by the benefits of "avoiding the anxieties and uncertainties of trial" (*Blackledge v. Allison*, 431 U.S. 63 [1977]).

---

[7]Guidorizzi, "Should We Really 'Ban' Plea Bargaining?" pp. 753, 760.
[8]A. W. Alschuler, "Plea Bargaining and Its History," *Law and Society Review* 13 (1979): 211–245, 211 (quoting the *Chicago Tribune*, April 27, 1928, p. 1).
[9]R. A. Weninger, "The Abolition of Plea Bargaining: A Case Study of El Paso County, Texas," *UCLA Law Review* 35 (1987): 265–313, 267, n. 5.

| Arguments For | Arguments Against |
|---|---|
| Contributes to cohesion in the courtroom work group | Behooves the prosecutor to choose the most serious charge from which to begin bargaining |
| Helps the prosecutor dispose of a busy case load | Contributes to inefficiency |
| Helps the public defender dispose of a busy case load | Wastes time; most defendants plead guilty anyway |
| Benefits the defendant by providing a reduction in charges and/or a favorable sentencing recommendation | Undermines the integrity of the justice system |
| Saves on judicial resources by avoiding the costs of going to trial | Decides the defendant's guilt without having a trial |
| May give the victim the satisfaction of having a prompt resolution of the case | Allows the criminal to get away with his or her crime |
| May benefit the victim who does not wish to testify at trial | An innocent individual may be coerced to plead guilty (i.e., legal versus factual guilt) |

**FIGURE 12.2 Arguments For and Against Plea Bargaining**

The court also benefits from plea bargaining. The prompt disposition of cases saves judicial resources, as reviewing a plea agreement takes less time than holding a full-blown trial. The victims of crime may also benefit from resolving a case sooner. A quickly reached plea bargain may give the victim the satisfaction of having the case closed quickly. Moreover, the victim may also not want to testify or risk the possibility that the prosecution will not succeed in obtaining a conviction.[10] Figure 12.2 summarizes the arguments for and against plea bargaining.

## Criticisms of Plea Bargaining

Apart from the misgivings over having the prosecutor and defense attorney effectively deciding a defendant's guilt, there are other problems posed by plea bargaining.

In an effort to secure a conviction, the prosecutor will start with the most serious charge and work down. That is, the prosecutor may *overcharge* as a first step in the bargaining process. This negotiation process is much like that of buying a used car at a dealership, in which the dealer usually starts with a ridiculously high price but is willing to negotiate. In the end, however, some buyers end up purchasing a car for more than its fair market value. The concern with plea bargaining, then, is that the defendant will be encouraged to plead guilty to an offense that is more serious than that for which he or she would be convicted at trial.

Plea bargaining may also contribute to *inefficiency*. As one researcher observed, "[D]efense attorneys commonly devise strategies whose only utility lies in the threat they pose to the court's and prosecutor's time."[11] Critics further contend that not only is plea bargaining inefficient, but also wastes time. They claim that plea bargaining is not necessary to obtain guilty pleas and that most defendants plead guilty anyway, if they think it is highly likely that going to trial will result in a verdict of guilty.[12]

Plea bargaining is also viewed as undermining the integrity of the criminal justice system. Throughout this book, discussion has examined the complex rules of criminal procedure set forth by the U.S. Constitution and interpreted by the Supreme Court. Critics

[10]C. E. Demarest, "Plea Bargaining Can Often Protect the Victim," *New York Times*, April 15, 1994, p. A30.
[11]A. W. Alschuler, "The Prosecutor's Role in Plea Bargaining," *University of Chicago Law Review* 36 (1968), 50–112, 54.
[12]P. Arenella, "Rethinking the Functions of Criminal Procedure: The Warren and Burger Courts' Competing Ideologies," *Georgetown Law Journal* 72 (1983): 185–248, 216–219.

▼

of plea bargaining claim that plea bargaining circumvents these "rigorous standards of due process and proof imposed during trials."[13]

Another reason that plea bargaining may undermine the criminal process is that it effectively decides the defendant's guilt without having a trial, an exhaustive investigation, or the presentation of evidence and witness testimony. As mentioned earlier in this section, the defendant's guilt is effectively decided by the prosecutor. One critic has argued that plea-bargaining decisions result from improper considerations:

> One mark of a just legal system is that it minimizes the effect of tactical choices upon the outcome of its processes. In criminal cases, the extent of an offender's punishment ought to turn primarily upon what he did and, perhaps, upon his personal characteristics rather than upon a postcrime, postarrest decision to exercise or not to exercise some procedural option.[14]

Plea bargaining may also allow criminals to get away with their crimes—or at least to receive lenient sentences. Further, critics claim that providing reduced sentences may reduce the deterrent effect of harsh punishment. In both cases, plea bargaining may give the impression that defendants can negotiate their way out of being adequately punished for their crimes.

Perhaps the most serious consequence of plea bargaining is that innocent individuals may be coerced into pleading guilty. In such a situation, a plea bargain amounts to an admission of legal guilt, when, in fact, the defendant may not be guilty. An example of the pressure on innocent defendants to plead guilty occurred in *North Carolina v. Alford*, 400 U.S. 25 (1970). In that case, the defendant, facing the death penalty if he was convicted, pleaded guilty to the crime, but did not admit to all elements of it. His plea (and other similar pleas) was promptly dubbed the **Alford plea**. Certain jurisdictions permit *Alford* pleas (also called "best-interests pleas"). A defendant who makes an *Alford* plea does not allocute, which means he or she does not—and indeed is not required to—explain the details of the offense to the judge.

## Attempts to Restrict Plea Bargaining

Concerns over plea bargaining have led some jurisdictions to abandon the practice. In fact, at one point, the Attorney General of Alaska banned plea bargaining throughout the state's criminal justice system, which led researchers to conclude that "the efficient operation of Alaska's criminal justice system did not depend upon plea bargaining."[15] Several other jurisdictions have also experimented with restricting the practice of plea bargaining, ranging from outright bans to bans on bargaining in certain types of crimes.

One method by which some jurisdictions have limited plea bargaining is to impose a cutoff date, which prohibits plea bargaining after a case has been in process for a certain amount of time. For example, the Brooklyn (New York) District Attorney has adopted a cutoff date of 74 days after indictment.[16] And if a case goes all the way to trial within the cutoff period, plea bargaining could conceivably take place all the way through jury deliberations.

Another method of restricting plea bargaining has been to ban some or all types of plea agreements. Alaska is, of course, the most notable example of a total ban. In 1975,

---

[13]A. P. Worden, "Policymaking by Prosecutors: The Uses of Discretion in Regulating Plea Bargaining," *Judicature* 73 (1990): 335–340, 336.

[14]A. W. Alschuler, "The Changing Plea Bargaining Debate," *California Law Review* 69 (1981): 652–730, 652.

[15]M. L. Rubenstein and T. J. White, "Alaska's Ban on Plea Bargaining," *Law and Society Review* 13 (1979): 367–383, 367.

[16]C. Mirsky, "Plea Reform Is No Bargain," *New York Newsday*, March 4, 1994, p. 70.

the Alaska attorney general banned all forms of plea bargaining in an effort to increase convictions and restore public confidence in the justice system.[17] In a study on the ban, the Alaska Judicial Council concluded the following:

> Plea bargaining as an institution was clearly curtailed. The routine expectation of a negotiated settlement was removed; for most practitioners justifiable reliance on negotiation to settle criminal cases greatly diminished in importance. There is less face-to-face discussion between adversaries, and when meetings do occur, they are not usually as productive as they used to be.[18]

It is important to understand that Alaska banned plea bargaining but not the entering of guilty pleas. Defendants could still plead guilty to the crimes for which they were charged. In fact, the Judicial Council also found that the rate of guilty pleas remained essentially the same after the ban, suggesting that perhaps some degree of behind-the-scenes plea bargaining was still taking place. Also, in Alaska, the attorney general can hire and fire the district attorneys, which gives him or her substantial leverage to ban plea bargaining. (In most jurisdictions around the United States, district attorneys are elected officials and do not serve at the desire of the state attorney general.)

Some jurisdictions have also experimented with banning plea bargaining for certain offenses. For example, the Bronx County (New York) district attorney banned plea bargaining whenever a grand jury returned a felony indictment. This move was seriously criticized, as are most attempts to restrict plea bargaining, but the district attorney stated that the ban "means that society has ceded control to those it has accused of violating its laws; and it means that our system is running us, instead of the other way around."[19] Critics challenged the Bronx County district attorney's ban on postfelony indictment plea bargaining for at least two reasons: (1) It did not eliminate plea bargaining, and (2) it encouraged plea bargaining prior to indictment.[20]

Another approach tried in Philadelphia was the *jury waiver*, which gives the defendant the opportunity to engage in plea negotiations in exchange for giving up his or her right to a jury trial. Actually, this approach is not plea bargaining in the traditional sense. Instead, the defendant gets his or her day in court, but to receive concessions from the state, he or she must not demand a jury trial. This process has come to be known as the *slow plea of guilty*, insofar as it does not result in the disposition of a case prior to trial. One researcher described the process in more detail:

> Slow pleas are informal and abbreviated, and consist largely of the defense's presentation of statements concerning the defendant's allegedly favorable personal characteristics. . . . The defense presentation is not concerned with guilt or innocence since it usually is implicitly assumed by all parties involved in the process that the defendant is guilty of at least some wrongdoing.[21]

California attempted to abandon plea bargaining by popular referendum in 1982. The resulting statute (Cal. Penal Code 1192.7) imposed the following restrictions: no plea bargaining is permitted in any case involving (1) a serious felony, (2) a felony in which a firearm was used, or (3) the offense of driving under the influence. Plea bargaining is permissible, however, if the prosecution's evidence is weak, witnesses are unavailable, or a

---

[17]T. W. Carns and J. A. Kruse, "Alaska's Ban on Plea Bargaining Reevaluated," *Judicature* 75 (1992): 310–317, 317.
[18]Guidorizzi, "Should We Really 'Ban' Plea Bargaining?" pp. 753, 775.
[19]Press release, statement from R. T. Johnson, District Attorney, Office of the District Attorney of Bronx County, New York, November 24, 1992.
[20]Guidorizzi, "Should We Really 'Ban' Plea Bargaining?" pp. 753, 778.
[21]M. A. Levin, *Urban Politics and the Criminal Courts* (Chicago, IL: University of Chicago Press, 1977), p. 80.

plea agreement does not result in a significantly reduced sentence. Despite the statute, plea bargaining continues almost unabated in the state of California (*People v. Brown*, 223 Cal. Rptr. 66 [Ct. App. 1986]).

Judges have also experimented with plea-bargaining restrictions within their jurisdictions. In El Paso County, Texas, in 1987, two state district judges adopted a policy of prohibiting all plea negotiations in their courts as a method of ensuring equal treatment for similarly situated defendants.[22] Maricopa County, Arizona, adopted a similar approach in 1995. Five Maricopa County Superior Court judges adopted a policy that prohibited plea agreements based on stipulated (agreed upon) sentences. In other words, the judges refused to accept any plea agreement that included a negotiated sentence, believing that sentencing should be a decision left to the trial courts (*Espinoza v. Martin*, 894 P.2d. 688 [Ariz. 1995]).

## The Supreme Court's View on Plea Bargaining

Notwithstanding the criticism of plea bargaining, the Supreme Court has essentially laid the debate to rest by generally upholding the validity of the practice. In *Brady v. United States*, 397 U.S. 742 (1970), for example, the Court stated, "Of course, that the prevalence of guilty pleas is explainable does not necessarily validate those pleas or the system which produces them. But we cannot hold that it is unconstitutional for the State to extend a benefit to a defendant who in turn extends a substantial benefit to the State." Next, in the case of *Santobello v. New York*, 404 U.S. 257 (1971), the Court offered the following rationale in support of plea bargaining: "The disposition of criminal charges by agreement between the prosecutor and the accused, sometimes loosely called 'plea bargaining,' is an essential component of the administration of justice. Properly administered, it is to be encouraged." Although plea bargaining is permitted in most jurisdictions, the process is subject to some constitutional limitations.

*Brady v. United States*
*(397 U.S. 742 [1970])*

*Santobello v. New York*
*(404 U.S. 257 [1971])*

# ▶ The Plea-Bargaining Process

The prosecutor can make several different types of offer in order to obtain a guilty plea. The most straightforward and common method is to reduce the charge or charges against the defendant. Other alternatives include dismissing other pending charges and promising to recommend a particular sentence.

Assuming that what is offered by the prosecution is acceptable to the defendant, then he or she can make one of two pleas: a simple plea of guilty or a plea of *nolo contendere*. The former is akin to saying, "I am guilty," and the latter is akin to saying, "I do not contest this." Both pleas have essentially the same effect—the only difference is that the *nolo* plea cannot be used as an admission of guilt in a subsequent civil case.

## Constitutional Rights during Plea Bargaining

Plea bargaining is a method of circumventing criminal trial, and the rights available to the defendant during bargaining are not the same as those available during trial. Even so, there are important rights that the defendant still enjoys during the plea-bargaining process, including the rights to effective assistance of counsel and to be informed of exculpatory evidence. The defendant does not have the right to be present at important stages of the bargaining process, however.

The Sixth Amendment right to counsel applies during plea bargaining because charges have already been filed before bargaining commences. According to the Supreme Court in

---

[22]Weninger, "The Abolition of Plea Bargaining," p. 275.

*Kirby v. Illinois*, 406 U.S. 682 (1972), the right to counsel attaches when, after charges have been filed, the "defendant finds himself faced with the prosecutorial forces of organized society, and immersed in the intricacies of substantive and procedural criminal law." This means that the prosecutor cannot bargain directly with the defendant unless counsel has been waived.

The Sixth Amendment also requires that defense counsel be effective during the plea-negotiation process. This means that the defense attorney must, at a minimum, investigate the case so as to make an informed decision with regard to what sentences and charges are offered by the prosecution. To be effective, counsel must also ensure that his or her client understands the consequences of the plea-bargaining process. In addition, defense counsel must share with his or her client any and all plea offers presented by the prosecution (*Missouri v. Frye*, 566 U.S. ___ [2012]).

It is not easy for a defendant to make out a claim of ineffective assistance of counsel during negotiation. According to the Court in *Hill v. Lockhart*, 474 U.S. 52 (1985), the defendant must show "a reasonable probability that, but for counsel's errors, he would not have pleaded guilty and would have insisted on going to trial."

Next, the defendant enjoys the right to be informed of exculpatory evidence in possession of the prosecution. That is, if the prosecutor has evidence that casts doubt on the accused's guilt, he or she must inform the defense of that evidence. For evidence to be considered *exculpatory*, it must have a reasonable probability of affecting the outcome of the case. Evidence that is inconsequential to the question of guilt, which is rare, need not be provided to the defense (*United States v. Bagley*, 473 U.S. 667 [1985]).

No court has required that a criminal defendant be provided a constitutional right to be present during plea bargaining. This could change, but for now, all that is required is that the defense attorney effectively communicates to his or her client the nature of the sentence or charges offered by the prosecution.

Finally, in *United States v. Ruiz*, 536 U.S. 622 (2002), the Supreme Court decided that the defendant *does not* have the right to impeachment information relating to informants and other witnesses nor does he or she have the right to information supporting any affirmative defense that he or she might raise if the case went to trial. Thus, there are limitations to the information a defendant may have available when making a decision as to whether to accept an offer from the prosecution.

## Acceptable Inducements by the Prosecution

The Constitution places few restrictions on offers the prosecution may make during the bargaining process, which are known as **prosecutorial inducements**. In *Brady*, the first Supreme Court case to condone plea bargaining, the Court considered extent pressure may be applied to induce a defendant into entering a guilty plea. The defendant in *Brady* was charged with kidnapping under a statute that permitted (1) a jury to recommend the death penalty if it saw fit *or* (2) a judge to sentence the defendant to life in prison, if guilt was determined via a bench trial. The defendant opted for a jury trial but then changed his plea to guilty and was sentenced to 30 years. He then argued that the statute effectively compelled him to plead guilty because of fear of the death penalty. The Supreme Court rejected this claim.

The reasoning the Court offered for its decision is somewhat complicated but important. Justice White emphasized that the statute in *Brady caused* the guilty plea but did not *coerce* it. He then emphasized that coercion is possible only when physical force or mental pressure is applied. This means that if "Brady was so gripped by fear of the death penalty or hope of leniency that he did not or could not, with the help of counsel, rationally weigh the advantages of going to trial against the advantages of pleading guilty," then his argument would have succeeded. However, Justice White found that the statute at most *influenced*

▼

Brady and that the coercion argument was exaggerated. In further support of his opinion, Justice White quoted an appellate court decision dealing with plea bargaining, *Shelton v. United States*, 246 F.2d 571 (5th Cir. 1957):

> [A] plea of guilty entered by one fully aware of the direct consequences, including the actual value of any commitments made to him by the court, prosecutor, or his own counsel, must stand unless induced by threats (or promises to discontinue improper harassment), misrepresentation (including unfulfilled or unfulfillable promises), or perhaps by promises that are by their nature improper as having no proper relationship to the prosecutor's business (e.g., bribes).

In short, a guilty plea resulting from an inducement from the prosecution, like a confession obtained in a police interrogation room, should not be involuntary. A guilty plea will be considered involuntary when it results from prosecutorial coercion, such as physical force or strong psychological pressuring. If, by contrast, the prosecutor causes a guilty plea simply because the accused thinks that pleading as such is his or her best way of avoiding a long prison term, then the defendant cannot succeed by claiming such a plea is involuntary.

There are also very limited constitutional restrictions on the kinds of offers or inducements the prosecution can properly make. In *Bordenkircher v. Hayes*, 434 U.S. 357 (1978), the defendant was indicted by a grand jury for forging a check for $88.30. The range of punishment was 2–10 years in prison. The prosecutor offered to recommend a five-year sentence but threatened to seek an indictment under a habitual criminal statute if the defendant did not accept the offer. Since the defendant had two prior felony convictions, a conviction under the habitual criminal statute could have resulted in life in prison.

*Bordenkircher v. Hayes*
*(434 U.S. 357 [1978])*

Somewhat controversially, in a 5 to 4 decision, the Supreme Court upheld the defendant's conviction under the habitual criminal statute on the theory that it resulted from a choice among known alternatives. Basically, the Court said that the defendant had the choice to accept five years in prison and neglected to take the opportunity. The defendant argued that his second conviction was vindictive, but the Court countered by stating that "the imposition of these difficult choices [is] an inevitable—'and permissible'—attribute of any legitimate system which tolerates and encourages the negotiation of pleas" (*Bordenkircher v. Hayes*).

Reduced to its most fundamental elements, the Court's opinion in *Bordenkircher* implies that the prosecution has great latitude in terms of being able to persuade the defendant to accept a plea, as long as the higher charges are authorized by law and are openly presented to the defense. This suggests, as well, that the prosecution may offer a charge or sentencing concession in exchange for the defendant agreeing not to appeal or claim that some constitutional right has been violated. The Court stated further:

> There is no doubt that the breadth of discretion that our country's legal system vests in prosecuting attorneys carries with it the potential for both individual and institutional abuse. And broad though that discretion may be, there are undoubtedly constitutional limits upon its exercise. We hold only that the course of conduct engaged in by the prosecutor in this case, which no more than openly presented the defendant with the unpleasant alternatives of forgoing trial or facing charges on which he was plainly subject to prosecution, did not violate the Due Process Clause of the Fourteenth Amendment.

In a related case, *United States v. Goodwin*, 457 U.S. 368 (1982), the Court reached a similar decision. In that case, the defendant was indicted on additional charges after plea negotiations broke down. The Court held that the prosecutor could file additional charges if an initial expectation that the defendant would plead guilty to a lesser charge proved unfounded. The Court refused to accept the defendant's argument that the prosecution was vindictive and, once again, gave broad authority to prosecutors in the plea-bargaining process.

*United States v. Goodwin*
*(457 U.S. 368 [1982])*

Nonetheless, certain prosecutorial inducements are *not* permissible. For example, the Supreme Court has stated that "a prosecutor's offer during plea bargaining of adverse or lenient treatment for some person *other* than the accused . . . might pose a greater danger of inducing a false guilty plea by skewing the assessment of the risks a defendant must consider" (*Bordenkircher v. Hayes*). Also, if the prosecutor flagrantly deceives the accused or fabricates evidence and/or starts rumors concerning the accused's level of involvement in the offense, a resulting guilty plea will be deemed unconstitutional.

## Questionable Inducements

Occasionally, plea bargaining results in strange concessions by defendants as part of a plea agreement. One commentator, Judge Joseph Colquitt, has used the term **ad hoc plea bargaining** to refer to some of these agreements. He has stated:

> Ad hoc bargains exist in at least five forms: (1) the court may impose an extraordinary condition of probation following a guilty plea, (2) the defendant may offer or be required to perform some act as a quid pro quo for a dismissal or more lenient sentence, (3) the court may impose an unauthorized form of punishment as a substitute for a statutorily established method of punishment, (4) the State may offer some unauthorized benefit in return for a plea of guilty, or (5) the defendant may be permitted to plead guilty to an unauthorized offense, such as a 'hypothetical' or nonexistent charge, a nonapplicable lesser-included offense, or a nonrelated charge.[23]

Colquitt also states that ad hoc plea bargaining "may involve neither a plea nor a sentence. For example, if a defendant charged with public intoxication seeks to avoid a statutorily mandated minimum sentence of 10 days in the county jail, the prosecutor might agree to dismiss the charges if the defendant agrees to make a monetary contribution to a local driver's education program."

### DECISION-MAKING EXERCISE 12.1

**WHAT CONSTITUTES COERCION?**

The prosecutor approaches the defendant and his attorney and says, "I am prepared to charge you with petty larceny in lieu of grand larceny. If you plead guilty to the petty larceny charge, you will avoid being prosecuted under the state's 'three strikes' statute. If you don't plead guilty, I will charge you under the 'three strikes' law and I will make sure that you will go to prison for the rest of your natural life." The defendant accepts the plea agreement but later appeals it, claiming that it was coerced by the prosecution. How should the court rule?

### DECISION-MAKING EXERCISE 12.2

**PROSECUTORIAL DECEPTION**

Assume that a prosecutor and a defendant are negotiating a plea agreement. In the negotiation, the prosecutor lies to the defendant, saying, "We have a videotape recording of you engaged in the crime. If you do not plead guilty, this evidence will be used against you at trial. No jury in its right mind would acquit you based on the recording. However, if you plead guilty to petty larceny, then you will be out of jail in no time flat." The defendant pleads guilty but later appeals his conviction, claiming that his plea was the result of prosecutorial deception. What should the court decide?

---

[23]J. A. Colquitt, "Ad Hoc Plea Bargaining," *Tulane Law Review* 75 (2001): 695–776, 695.

Judges can even get involved in ad hoc plea bargaining. Colquitt points to one shocking example of this method of bargaining run amok. The case, *Ryan v. Commission on Judicial Performance*, 754 P.2d 724 (Cal. 1988), involved a woman who was required to participate in a drug treatment program as a result of several narcotics convictions. The probation officer asked to have the woman removed from the program because she supposedly failed to follow program guidelines. At a hearing to decide on the matter, the woman, "who was wearing a low-cut sweater, bent over several times to remove documents from her purse. Thereafter the judge dismissed all criminal charges against her. When his clerk asked why the charges had been dropped, [the judge] replied, 'she showed me her boobs.'" The judge was subsequently removed from the bench. Some less extreme examples of ad hoc plea concessions, as well as some relevant cases, are described in Figure 12.3.

# Statutory and Judicial Inducements

So far, the discussion has considered only what the prosecution can and cannot do as far as inducing the defendant to plead guilty. Defendants may also be motivated to enter pleas as a result of statutory and judicial inducements. **Statutory inducements** refer to laws that provide lenient sentences in exchange for guilty pleas. **Judicial inducements** are actions by judges that influence the bargaining process.

## Statutory Inducements

In *Corbitt v. New Jersey*, 439 U.S. 212 (1978), the defendant was charged with first-degree murder. The statute provided that if he decided to plead guilty to the crime, he could be

*Corbitt v. New Jersey*
*(439 U.S. 212 [1978])*

---

1. Charitable contributions in lieu of fines or jail terms: *State v. Stellato* (523 A.2d 1345 [Conn. App. Ct. 1987]); *Ratliff v. State* (596 N.E.2d 241 [Ind. Ct. App. 1992])

2. Relinquished property ownership: *United States v. Thao Dinh Lee* (173 F.3d 1258 [10th Cir. 1999])

3. Agreement to surrender a professional license or not work in a particular profession: *United States v. Hoffer* (129 F.3d 1196 [11th Cir. 1997])

4. Voluntary agreement to undergo sterilization: *State v. Pasicznyk* (1997 WL 79501 [Wash. Ct. App. Feb. 25, 1997])

5. Voluntary agreement to undergo surgical castration: *ACLU v. State* (5 S.W.2d 418 [Ark. 1999])

6. Agreement to enter the army on a four-year enlistment: *State v. Hamrick* (595 N.W.2d 492 [Iowa 1999])

7. Agreement not to appeal: *People v. Collier* (641 N.Y.S.2d 181 [App. Div. 1996])

8. Shaming punishments, such as bumper stickers for convicted DUI offenders: *Ballenger v. State* (436 S.E.2d 793 [Ga. Ct. App. 1993])

9. Agreement to seal the records of a case: *State v. Campbell* (21 Media L. Rep. 1895 [Wash. Super. Ct. 1993])

10. Ordering offenders to surrender profits, such as from books written about their crimes: *Rolling v. State ex rel. Butterworth* (741 So. 2d 627 [Fla. Dist. Ct. App. 1999])

11. Banishment to another location: *State v. Culp* (226 S.E.2d 841 [N.C. Ct. App. 1976]); *Phillips v. State* (512 S.E.2d 32 [Ga. Ct. App. 1999])

12. Pleading guilty to nonexistent crimes (i.e., crimes that are not prohibited by law): *Bassin v. Israel* (335 N.E.2d 53 [Ill. App. Ct. 1975])

*Source: Adapted from J. A. Colquitt, "Ad Hoc Plea Bargaining," Tulane Law Review 75 (2001): 69. See Colquitt's article for a thorough discussion of various, sometimes stranger concessions made as a result of ad hoc plea bargaining (i.e., note 26).*

**FIGURE 12.3 Examples of Ad Hoc Plea-Bargaining Concessions**

sentenced either to life imprisonment or to a term of 30 years. The defendant opted to take his chances and go to trial. He was convicted and sentenced to life in prison. The defendant claimed that the statute violated due process, but the Supreme Court upheld it in the interests of consistency. That is, the Court stated that it could not permit prosecutorial bargaining as in *Bordenkircher* "and yet hold that the legislature may not openly provide for the possibility of leniency in return for a plea." Further, the Court stated:

> It cannot be said that defendants found guilty by a jury are "penalized" for exercising the right to a jury trial any more than defendants who plead guilty are penalized because they give up the chance of acquittal at trial. In each instance, the defendant faces a multitude of possible outcomes and freely makes his choice. Equal protection does not free those who made a bad assessment of risks or a bad choice from the consequences of their decision.

The Court also noted, though, that plea bargaining should be an *executive*, as opposed to *legislative*, function. That is, legislatures should not be permitted to decide "that the penalty for every criminal offense to which a defendant pleads guilty is to be one-half the penalty to be imposed upon a defendant convicted of the same offense after a not guilty plea."

### Judicial Inducements

Traditionally, plea bargaining results from the prosecution and the defense reaching an agreement independently of the court—the judge is usually not part of the negotiation process. Today, however, certain jurisdictions permit a degree of judicial involvement in the plea-bargaining process. For example, the American Bar Association standards regarding guilty pleas permit judicial participation when it is requested but only for the purpose of clarifying acceptable charges and sentences. The judge cannot at any point, "either directly

---

**DECISION-MAKING EXERCISE 12.3**

**AN INDUCEMENT OF BANISHMENT**

Carl Moore was arrested for sodomy and other crimes. With the assistance of his counsel, Moore negotiated a guilty plea to three counts of sodomy, one count of violating the Controlled Substances Act, and one count of sexual exploitation of children. The trial judge accepted the guilty plea and followed the state's recommendation to impose (1) a 20-year sentence (3 years to serve and 17 years on probation), (2) banishment from the state, and (3) a $10,000 fine. Is banishment an acceptable inducement by the prosecution?

---

**DECISION-MAKING EXERCISE 12.4**

**JUDICIAL INDUCEMENTS**

The prosecutor, defense attorney, and defendant appear before Judge Dubois in one of the cases slated to be heard in her court. The defense attorney and prosecutor tell the judge that they have reached a plea agreement and that Charles Down, the defendant, has agreed to plead guilty to manslaughter instead of first-degree murder. Judge Dubois then questions Down to ensure that the plea is voluntary, intelligent, and based in fact. During the questioning, Down begins to express reservations about the plea agreement and says, "On second thought, I don't want to plead guilty." Judge Dubois then looks at Down and says, "You should really plead guilty, because from the looks of things, you're going to get the chair if you don't." Down agrees to plead guilty but later appeals, arguing that his plea was not voluntary. How should the court rule?

or indirectly, [communicate] to the defendant or defense counsel that a plea agreement should be accepted or that a guilty plea should be entered."[24]

In order to summarize the plea-bargaining process, Figure 12.4 presents relevant portions of Rule 11 of the *Federal Rules of Criminal Procedure*. The procedures outlined are those by which the federal courts must abide.

---

**(c) Plea Agreement Procedure.**

**(1)** *In General.*
An attorney for the government and the defendant's attorney, or the defendant when proceeding pro se, may discuss and reach a plea agreement. The court must not participate in these discussions. If the defendant pleads guilty or nolo contendere to either a charged offense or a lesser or related offense, the plea agreement may specify that an attorney for the government will:

  **(A)** not bring, or will move to dismiss, other charges;

  **(B)** recommend, or agree not to oppose the defendant's request, that a particular sentence or sentencing range is appropriate or that a particular provision of the Sentencing Guidelines, or policy statement, or sentencing factor does or does not apply (such a recommendation or request does not bind the court); or

  **(C)** agree that a specific sentence or sentencing range is the appropriate disposition of the case, or that a particular provision of the Sentencing Guidelines, or policy statement, or sentencing factor does or does not apply (such a recommendation or request binds the court once the court accepts the plea agreement).

**(2)** *Disclosing a Plea Agreement.*
The parties must disclose the plea agreement in open court when the plea is offered, unless the court for good cause allows the parties to disclose the plea agreement in camera.

**(3)** *Judicial Consideration of a Plea Agreement.*

  **(A)** To the extent the plea agreement is of the type specified in Rule 11(c)(1)(A) or (C), the court may accept the agreement, reject it, or defer a decision until the court has reviewed the presentence report.

  **(B)** To the extent the plea agreement is of the type specified in Rule 11(c)(1)(B), the court must advise the defendant that the defendant has no right to withdraw the plea if the court does not follow the recommendation or request.

**(4)** *Accepting a Plea Agreement.*
If the court accepts the plea agreement, it must inform the defendant that to the extent the plea agreement is of the type specified in Rule 11(c)(1)(A) or (C), the agreed disposition will be included in the judgment.

**(5)** *Rejecting a Plea Agreement.*
If the court rejects a plea agreement containing provisions of the type specified in Rule 11(c)(1)(A) or (C), the court must do the following on the record and in open court (or, for good cause, in camera):

  **(A)** inform the parties that the court rejects the plea agreement;

  **(B)** advise the defendant personally that the court is not required to follow the plea agreement and give the defendant an opportunity to withdraw the plea; and

**FIGURE 12.4 Plea-Bargaining Procedure**

---

[24]American Bar Association, Standard 14-3.3[d], from *Standards for Criminal Justice*, 2nd ed., supp., vol. 3 (Washington, DC: American Bar Association, 1986).

# ▶ Effects of Plea Bargaining

A plea bargain ultimately affects four separate parties: (1) the court, (2) the prosecutor, (3) the defendant, and (4) the victim.

## Effects on the Court

The court is not bound to accept a plea agreement. In deciding whether to accept the bargain, the court weighs the sometimes competing interests of the agreement and the public interest. Thus, if accepting a plea agreement poses a significant risk to the public—say, because a dangerous criminal will be spared prison and placed on probation (an unlikely event)—then the court has the discretion to deny it.

An illustrative case is *United States v. Bean*, 564 F.2d 700 (5th Cir. 1977). The facts were as follows: Bean was charged on October 22, 1976, with theft of a car and burglary of a habitation, in violation of state law. At the initial arraignment, Bean pleaded not guilty to both counts. On November 30, another arraignment was held on Bean's request. At that time, the court was informed that a plea bargain had been reached between the government prosecutor and Bean and his counsel. Under the agreement, Bean would plead guilty to the theft count and cooperate with the prosecutor in investigating others involved in the burglary. In return, the prosecutor would move for a dismissal of the burglary charge. Judge Spears rejected the plea because the offense of entering a home at night where people were sleeping was a much more serious offense than the theft of an automobile. The Fifth Circuit Court of Appeals upheld Judge Spears's decision, stating:

> Without deciding what unusual circumstances may result in the refusal of a plea bargain being an abuse of discretion, we find that Judge Spears' action in this case was well within the scope of his discretion. A decision that a plea bargain will result in the defendant's receiving too light a sentence under the circumstances of the case is a sound reason for a judge's refusing to accept the agreement. . . . In this case, Judge Spears was faced with a man who was charged with burglarizing at night a home on Fort Sam Houston in Texas, while Lieutenant

Colonel Robert W. Oppenlander, his wife, two daughters and one son were asleep inside. In addition, the presentence report indicated that Bean had previously been committed to four years in the Texas Department of Corrections for state charges of burglary and theft of a business at nighttime. Bean had also served twenty days for unlawfully carrying a weapon in San Antonio. Given this information Judge Spears was reluctant to accept a plea bargain that would allow Bean to plead guilty to only the theft of an automobile.

## Effects on the Prosecutor

The consequences of plea bargaining are of far greater magnitude for the prosecutor than for the court. Assuming the court accepts a plea bargain, whether it is a charge or sentence reduction, then the prosecutor must fulfill his or her part of the agreement. Importantly, though, the prosecutor is not bound by the plea bargain prior to the point at which it is accepted by the court.

### Prosecutorial Obligations Before the Court Accepts the Bargain

The prosecutor has a considerable amount of latitude with regard to fulfilling a plea bargain before it is accepted by the court. However, when the court accepts the bargain, it becomes formalized, at which point the prosecutor must fulfill his or her promises.

In *Mabry v. Johnson*, 467 U.S. 504 (1984), the Supreme Court considered the extent to which a prosecutor must uphold his or her end of the bargain prior to the point at which the court accepts it. In that case, the defense attorney called the prosecutor to accept a plea offer, but the prosecutor told him that the offer was a mistake and withdrew it. The prosecutor then offered a harsher offer in its place, one that would have resulted in a longer prison term. The Supreme Court upheld this practice, arguing that the plea agreement was reached with full awareness on the part of the defendant and "was thus in no sense the product of governmental deception; it rested on no 'unfulfilled promise' and fully satisfied the test for voluntariness and intelligence."

*Mabry v. Johnson (467 U.S. 504 [1984])*

In an analogous decision, the prosecution agreed to a plea agreement, but then reneged when it became clear the defendant had aided a fellow inmate in another crime while awaiting sentencing. The Supreme Court sided with the prosecution (*Puckett v. United States*, 556 U.S. ___ [2009]).

### Prosecutorial Obligations After the Court Accepts the Bargain

In general, the prosecution is bound to its plea-bargaining promises after the court accepts the bargain. An illustrative case is *Santobello v. New York*, 404 U.S. 257 (1971). The defendant was indicted for two felonies. He first entered a plea of not guilty on each count. After subsequent negotiations, however, the prosecutor agreed to allow the defendant to plead guilty to a lesser offense. The defendant then withdrew his pleas of not guilty and agreed to plead guilty to the lesser offense. The court accepted the plea. At sentencing, a new prosecutor, who was unaware of what had transpired earlier, requested the maximum sentence. The defense objected on the grounds that the previous prosecutor promised not to make any particular sentencing recommendation. The judge then stated that he was not influenced by the second prosecutor's sentencing recommendation and imposed the maximum sentence.

The Supreme Court declared that the sentence should be declared unconstitutional as a matter of due process. The Court stated that "when a plea rests in any significant degree on a promise or agreement of the prosecutor, so that it can be said to be part of the inducement or consideration, such promise must be fulfilled."

Unfortunately, the Court was not altogether clear as to what remedy is appropriate when the prosecutor breaches his or her agreement. In *Santobello*, the Court voided the defendant's conviction, but the Justices seemed mixed on the appropriate remedy for future

**JUDICIAL REJECTIONS**

Roger Moss has been arrested and charged with intentionally, and with premeditation, killing his wife. He reaches an agreement with Terry Stand, the local district attorney, to plead guilty to negligent manslaughter. Stand has a poor track record in the district attorney's office and has lost countless cases to shrewd defense attorneys. He figures entering into this plea agreement is his best shot at finally obtaining a guilty verdict. When Stand and Moss's defense attorney present the plea agreement to the judge, she rejects it on the ground that it is unduly lenient. Can the judge reject the plea for this reason?

cases. Some agreed that if the prosecution breaches its promise after the court has accepted the bargain, then it must be forced to uphold the bargain or the defendant should be able to withdraw the guilty plea. Others felt that the trial court should decide what remedy is necessary. This issue remains unresolved.

*United States v. Benchimol*
*(471 U.S. 453 [1985])*

Some years after *Santobello*, in the case of *United States v. Benchimol*, 471 U.S. 453 (1985), the Supreme Court seemed to change its opinion with regard to a prosecutor's breach of a plea agreement after it has been accepted by the court. The prosecutor agreed to recommend a sentence of probation with restitution, but the presentence report mentioned nothing of the agreement. The defense attorney pointed out the error, and the prosecution admitted that an agreement had been reached. Even so, the trial court sentenced the defendant to six years. The defendant then sought to have his sentence vacated, and the court of appeals agreed. However, the Supreme Court reversed, holding that unless the prosecution supports a recommendation "enthusiastically" or sets forth its reasons for a lenient recommendation, the court is under no obligation to honor the agreement. According to the Supreme Court:

> It may well be that the Government in a particular case might commit itself to "enthusiastically" make a particular recommendation to the court, and it may be that the Government in a particular case might agree to explain to the court the reasons for the Government's making a particular recommendation. But respondent does not contend, nor did the Court of Appeals find, that the Government had in fact undertaken to do either of these things here. The Court of Appeals simply held that as a matter of law such an undertaking was to be implied from the Government's agreement to recommend a particular sentence. But our view of Rule 11(e) [of the *Federal Rules of Evidence*, which sets forth procedures for plea bargaining] is that it speaks in terms of what the parties in fact agree to, and does not suggest that such implied-in-law terms as were read into this agreement by the Court of Appeals have any place under the Rule.

## Effects on the Defendant

The defendant who accepts an offer to plead guilty often faces consequences besides a reduced sentence or charge. Important rights are often waived, such as the right to appeal, the right to a jury trial, and the privilege against self-incrimination. Also, if the defendant supplies inaccurate information during the course of plea negotiations, he or she may not benefit from lenient treatment. Furthermore, in exchange for pleading guilty, the prosecution may require that the defendant testify against a codefendant.

*Ricketts v. Adamson*
*(483 U.S. 1 [1987])*

A significant Supreme Court case dealing with the latter consequence—possible testimony against a codefendant—is *Ricketts v. Adamson*, 483 U.S. 1 (1987). The defendant in that case testified against both of his codefendants in exchange for a reduction in the charge he was facing. He was then sentenced on the reduced charge. After that, the codefendants' convictions were overturned on appeal. The prosecution then retried the codefendants, but the original defendant refused to testify at the second trial, claiming that his duty had been fulfilled. The prosecution then filed an information charging him with first-degree murder. The Supreme Court did not bar the first-degree murder prosecution because the original agreement contained a clause to the effect that the agreement would be void if the defendant refused to testify against his codefendants. Justice Brennan did acknowledge, however, that the defendant could have construed the plea agreement only to require his testimony at the first trial. The Court noted that the proper procedure, if such a situation were to arise in the future, would be to submit a disagreement over the plea to the court that accepted the plea. That way, the expense of a further trial and appeals could be avoided.

At the other extreme, the defendant can sometimes *preserve* certain rights following a plea agreement. These types of arrangements are known as *conditional guilty pleas*. For example, New York law provides that an order denying a motion to suppress evidence

---

### DECISION-MAKING EXERCISE 12.6

#### THE PROSECUTOR'S DUTY TO FULFILL THE BARGAIN

Connor Leaves was charged with armed robbery and possession of a firearm during the commission of a felony. A plea agreement was reached wherein Leaves would plead guilty to attempted armed robbery and to the possession charge. In exchange for this reduction in charges, Leaves would assist the police and prosecution in investigating an unrelated crime. Leaves proceeded to fulfill his end of the agreement and told authorities that his friend, Bill Wright, was the man they were looking for. The prosecutor then withdrew the plea offer, stating that it was contrary to his office's policy. Leaves moved to reinstate the negotiated plea agreement, and the motion was granted. The prosecution has now appealed this decision. How should the appellate court rule?

---

### DECISION-MAKING EXERCISE 12.7

#### TWO PROSECUTORS, ONE BARGAIN

A plea bargain was reached between Prosecutor 1 and the defendant, in which the defendant agreed to plead guilty to less serious charges. Three months later, at the defendant's sentencing hearing, a different prosecutor, Prosecutor 2, represented the state. The following exchange took place between the judge and Prosecutor 2:

**Prosecutor 2:** At this time, Your Honor, the government calls for sentencing the case of the *United States of America v. Defendant.*

**Judge:** Anything you wish to say, Mr. Prosecutor 2?

**Prosecutor 2:** Well, Your Honor, in light of the plea-bargaining agreement, the government, at this time, is recommending three years' incarceration. We also recommend that, if possible, the defendant be incarcerated at a minimum security prison.

**Judge:** Why?

**Prosecutor 2:** Well, Your Honor, that was part of the plea bargain.

**Judge:** Not because you believe in it?

**Prosecutor 2:** Well, Your Honor, I do have some problems with that, but this is the way I understand it.

**Judge:** Anything else?

**Prosecutor 2:** Nothing further.

The defendant was then sentenced to four years in prison at a different institution. He has appealed his sentence. How should the appellate court rule?

**WAIVING RIGHTS AS A CONSEQUENCE OF PLEA BARGAINING**

Here are the facts from *United States v. Black*, 201 F.3d 1296 (10th Cir. 2000):

On November 20, 1997, a grand jury charged Mr. Black with five federal firearms offenses. . . . On April 15, 1998, Mr. Black entered into a plea agreement with the government. . . . Under the agreement, Mr. Black agreed to plead guilty to count three of the indictment. . . . He also agreed to waive his right to appeal his sentence. . . . The agreement stated that "the defendant agrees to waive his right to appeal the sentence he receives as a result of this Plea Agreement." . . . The government agreed to dismiss the remaining counts of the indictment and to recommend that Mr. Black receive a three-level downward adjustment in his offense level for acceptance of responsibility. It also agreed that if it appealed the district court's sentencing decision, Mr. Black would be released from the waiver of his right to appeal.

Should a defendant be required to give up his or her right to appeal pursuant to a plea agreement?

alleged to have been obtained as a result of unlawful search-and-seizure "may be reviewed on appeal from a judgment of conviction notwithstanding the fact that such judgment of conviction is predicated upon a plea of guilty" (N.Y. Crim. Proc. Law §§ 710.20 [1], 710.70 [2]). These types of agreements are rare, however. Indeed, the Supreme Court in *Tollett v. Henderson*, 411 U.S. 258 (1973), stated that "[w]hen a criminal defendant has solemnly admitted in open court that he is in fact guilty of the offense with which he is charged, he may not thereafter raise independent claims relating to the deprivation of constitutional rights that occurred prior to the entry of the guilty plea."

## Effects on the Victim

While plea bargaining mainly occurs between the prosecution and defense, it is also important to consider the impact on the victim. Victims are affected by plea bargaining in at least two respects. First, a plea agreement may give the victim a measure of closure relatively quickly. On the other hand, a plea agreement may be viewed by the victim as too lenient. That is, he or she may feel the offender was not adequately "punished" for the offense in question. To address this problem, several states have laws that require victim involvement or input during the bargaining process.[25]

## ▶ Elements of a Valid Guilty Plea

Assuming the prosecutor offers an acceptable inducement to the defendant, and assuming the defendant agrees to plead guilty in exchange for leniency, the judge must determine that the plea conforms to statutory and other requirements, as discussed earlier. The judge must then confirm that the defendant understands the plea and has agreed to it voluntarily.

*Boykin v. Alabama*
*(395 U.S. 238 [1969])*

*McCarthy v. United States*
*(394 U.S. 459 [1969])*

In *Boykin v. Alabama*, 395 U.S. 238 (1969), the Supreme Court held that it would be unconstitutional "for the trial judge to accept [a] guilty plea without an affirmative showing that it is intelligent and voluntary." In order to determine that the plea is voluntary, the judge usually questions the defendant. As the Court noted in *McCarthy v. United States*, 394 U.S. 459 (1969):

---

[25]U.S. Department of Justice, *Victim Input into Plea Agreements* (Washington, DC: U.S. Department of Justice, 2002). Available online: http://www.ojp.usdoj.gov/ovc/publications/bulletins/legalseries/bulletin7/ncj189188.pdf (accessed November 7, 2008).

A guilty plea must be intelligent, voluntary, and based in fact.

By personally interrogating the defendant, not only will the judge be better able to ascertain the plea's voluntariness, but he also will develop a more complete record to support his determination in a subsequent post-conviction attack. . . . Both of these goals are undermined in proportion to the degree the district court judge resorts to "assumptions" not based upon recorded responses to his inquiries.

For a guilty plea to be valid, it must conform to three requirements: (1) it must be intelligent; (2) it must be voluntary, not coerced; and (3) it must be based in fact. That is, if the defendant pleads guilty to a crime he or she did not commit, then technically, the plea will be invalid. The following subsections consider the case law regarding these three important requirements.

## Intelligence

In general, for a plea to be *intelligent* (understood), it must conform to specific requirements. The defendant must understand (1) the nature of the charge or charges of which he or she is accused, (2) the possible sentence or sentences associated with the charges, and (3) the rights he or she may waive if a guilty plea is entered. A person whose mental capacity is called into question may be declared incompetent at a pretrial hearing and treated in order to restore his or her competency.

### Understanding the Charge

In *Henderson v. Morgan*, 426 U.S. 637 (1976), the defendant was charged with first-degree murder. He pleaded guilty to second-degree murder following an offer by the prosecution. Several years later, he sought to have his conviction voided on the grounds that at the time he entered his plea, he did not understand that one of the elements of second-degree murder was intent to cause death. The Supreme Court held that "since respondent did not receive adequate notice of the offense to which he pleaded guilty, his plea was involuntary and the judgment of conviction was entered without due process of law." The element of intent (the *mens rea*) in second-degree murder was viewed as critical, which meant it should have been explained to the defendant.

*Henderson v. Morgan*
*(426 U.S. 637 [1976])*

## A VALID GUILTY PLEA?

Bill Dover, a federal prisoner, filed a *habeas corpus* petition (a method of challenging his confinement; see Chapter 15), claiming that his guilty plea was not knowing and intelligent because of ineffective assistance of counsel. Specifically, Dover claimed that his attorney mistakenly advised him that if he pleaded guilty, he would become eligible for parole after serving one-third of his prison sentence. In actuality, because Dover was a second-time offender, he was required under state law to serve one-half of his sentence before being eligible for parole. In other words, Dover claimed that he was not advised of the actual sentence that would result from his plea bargaining. Should he succeed with his petition?

It is not clear based on *Henderson* whether the *judge* must explain the elements of the offense to the defendant or whether this is the job of *counsel*. The Court intimated that if defense counsel explains the offense to the accused, then little else is needed: "[I]t may be appropriate to presume that in most cases defense counsel routinely explain the nature of the offense in sufficient detail to give the accused notice of what he is being asked to admit." Nevertheless, the judge should at least inquire as to whether the defendant understands the charge.

### Understanding the Possible Sentences

The *Federal Rules of Criminal Procedure* expressly require that the defendant understand the consequences of the plea.[26] This includes an understanding of the minimum and maximum sentences as well as applicable sentencing guidelines that the judge might be required to abide by.

Whether other consequences attendant to plea bargaining and sentencing have to be explained depends on the situation. On the one hand, at least one lower court has held that the defendant does not need to be informed of the loss of the right to vote (*People v. Thomas*, 41 Ill.2d 122 [1968]). On the other hand, failure to tell the defendant that deportation is a possible consequence of a guilty plea may result in a decision that such a plea is invalid (see *Padilla v. Kentucky*, 559 U.S. ___ [2010]).

### Understanding of Rights Waived as a Result of Pleading Guilty

The rights *waived* as a result of plea bargaining are different than the rights *denied* as a result of plea bargaining. For example, loss of the right to vote is not a loss due to voluntary waiver; it is a consequence tied to being convicted (even if by guilty plea) of a serious crime. The rights *waived* are those the defendant would otherwise be granted by the Constitution but are essentially given up voluntarily in exchange for lenient treatment.

The constitutional rights typically waived through plea bargaining are the right to trial by jury, the privilege against self-incrimination, and the right to confront adverse witnesses. By pleading guilty, the defendant forgoes having a trial, which is when these rights are frequently applicable. The privilege against self-incrimination, however, still applies outside the trial context, such as in pretrial custodial interrogations. Regardless, the defendant must be clearly informed of the constitutional rights that are waived as a result of plea bargaining. According to the Supreme Court in *Boykin v. Alabama*, 395 U.S. 238 (1969), there can be no presumption of "a waiver of these three important federal rights from a silent record."

---

[26] *Federal Rules of Criminal Procedure*, Rule 11, Available online at http://www.law.cornell.edu/rules/frcrmp/.

## Voluntariness

In addition to the requirement that a plea be understood, it also must be voluntary. Even though a plea may be understood, it may have resulted from coercion, threats, physical abuse, or the like. Thus, the *Federal Rules of Criminal Procedure* require that a plea be "voluntary and did not result from force, threats, or promises (other than promises in the agreement)."[27]

## Factual Basis

For a plea bargain to be valid, the plea must result from conduct that has a basis in fact. In other words, a defendant cannot (in the view of the court, anyway!) plead guilty to a crime he or she did not commit. This means that the court should inquire about the crime in question by, perhaps, having the accused describe the conduct giving rise to his or her guilty plea. This does not always occur, but according to the Supreme Court in *McCarthy v. United States*, 394 U.S. 459 (1969):

> Requiring this examination of the relation between the law and the acts the defendant admits having committed is designed to "protect a defendant who is in the position of pleading voluntarily with an understanding of the nature of the charge but without realizing that his conduct does not actually fall within the charge."

Importantly, the Court in *McCarthy* did not state that a factual basis for the plea bargain is a *constitutional* requirement, only that there should be one.

The Supreme Court elaborated on this issue in a similar case, in which the defendant pleaded guilty but insisted on his innocence. The Court stated that "an express admission of guilt . . . is not a constitutional requisite to the imposition of a prison sentence even if he is unwilling or unable to admit his participation in the acts constituting the crime" (*North Carolina v. Alford*, 400 U.S. 25 [1970]). The Court upheld the man's plea but also pointed out the following:

> Because of the importance of protecting the innocent and of insuring that guilty pleas are a product of free and intelligent choice, various state and federal court decisions properly caution that pleas coupled with claims of innocence should not be accepted unless there is a factual basis for the plea . . . and until the judge taking the plea has inquired into and sought to resolve the conflict between the waiver of trial and the claim of innocence.

---

### DECISION-MAKING EXERCISE 12.10

#### ANOTHER VALID GUILTY PLEA?

Caroline Wynn pleaded guilty to federal drug charges and was sentenced to 247 months in prison by the U.S. District Court. At sentencing, the court neglected to inform Wynn of her right to appeal her sentence. Several months later, while Wynn was in prison, she filed a *habeas corpus* petition, alleging that the district court's failure to advise her of her right to appeal her sentence violated the express terms of Rule 32(a)(2) of the *Federal Rules of Criminal Procedure*, which provides that "[t]here shall be no duty on the court to advise the defendant of any right of appeal after sentence is imposed following a plea of guilty or *nolo contendere*, except that the court shall advise the defendant of any right to appeal the sentence." Wynn knew of her right to appeal at the time of sentencing but did not file an appeal. Now, she seeks postconviction relief. How should the court decide?

---

[27]*Federal Rules of Criminal Procedure*, Rule 11, Available online at http://www.law.cornell.edu/rules/frcrmp/.

Thus, while there appears to be no constitutional basis for requiring that a guilty plea be tied to specific criminal acts, the courts—including the Supreme Court—prefer to avoid guilty pleas entered by otherwise innocent defendants. Unfortunately, it would be purely conjecture to estimate how many innocent criminal defendants plead guilty in order to "play the odds" and avoid potentially lengthy prison terms.

In summary, a valid guilty plea must consist of several elements: knowledge, intelligence, voluntariness, and factual basis. Figure 12.5 presents relevant portions of Rule 11 of the *Federal Rules of Criminal Procedure*, which succinctly summarizes the elements of a valid guilty plea from a perspective other than that of the Supreme Court.

**(a) Entering a Plea.**

    **(1)** *In General.*
    A defendant may plead not guilty, guilty, or (with the court's consent) nolo contendere.

    **(2)** *Conditional Plea.*
    With the consent of the court and the government, a defendant may enter a conditional plea of guilty or nolo contendere, reserving in writing the right to have an appellate court review an adverse determination of a specified pretrial motion. A defendant who prevails on appeal may then withdraw the plea.

    **(3)** *Nolo Contendere Plea.*
    Before accepting a plea of nolo contendere, the court must consider the parties' views and the public interest in the effective administration of justice.

    **(4)** *Failure to Enter a Plea.*
    If a defendant refuses to enter a plea or if a defendant organization fails to appear, the court must enter a plea of not guilty.

**(b) Considering and Accepting a Guilty or Nolo Contendere Plea.**

    **(1)** *Advising and Questioning the Defendant.*
    Before the court accepts a plea of guilty or nolo contendere, the defendant may be placed under oath, and the court must address the defendant personally in open court. During this address, the court must inform the defendant of, and determine that the defendant understands, the following:

        **(A)** the government's right, in a prosecution for perjury or false statement, to use against the defendant any statement that the defendant gives under oath;
        **(B)** the right to plead not guilty, or having already so pleaded, to persist in that plea;
        **(C)** the right to a jury trial;
        **(D)** the right to be represented by counsel—and if necessary have the court appoint counsel—at trial and at every other stage of the proceeding;
        **(E)** the right at trial to confront and cross-examine adverse witnesses, to be protected from compelled self-incrimination, to testify and present evidence, and to compel the attendance of witnesses;
        **(F)** the defendant's waiver of these trial rights if the court accepts a plea of guilty or nolo contendere;
        **(G)** the nature of each charge to which the defendant is pleading;
        **(H)** any maximum possible penalty, including imprisonment, fine, and term of supervised release;
        **(I)** any mandatory minimum penalty;
        **(J)** any applicable forfeiture;
        **(K)** the court's authority to order restitution;
        **(L)** the court's obligation to impose a special assessment;

**FIGURE 12.5 Elements of a Valid Guilty Plea**

**FIGURE 12.5** *Continued*

# ► Contesting a Guilty Plea

The defendant may wish to contest the guilty plea he or she enters for at least three reasons:

1. if the plea was the product of coercion by the prosecution;
2. if the prosecution has failed to fulfill its end of the bargain; and
3. if other problems emerge, such as unconstitutional conduct on the part of law enforcement officials.

A defendant who challenges his or her guilty plea does so in several ways, which include withdrawal of the plea and appeal.[28]

## Withdrawing a Guilty Plea

Any time the court refuses to accept a plea agreement reached by the prosecution and the defense, the defendant can usually withdraw the plea. Similarly, if the defendant pleads guilty even when there has been no plea bargaining, he or she can seek to withdraw his or her plea. However, if the prosecution disagrees with the court's decision to refuse the plea, then the defendant might *not* be able to withdraw his or her plea.

Once a plea has been accepted by the court, then it can only be withdrawn in limited circumstances. The *Federal Rules of Criminal Procedure* provide that a plea can be withdrawn prior to sentencing if the defendant shows a "fair and just" reason for overturning the plea.[29] Fair and just reasons are the same as those mentioned at the outset of this section: involuntary pleas, prosecutorial breaches, and lack of evidence or similar deficiency. Once a sentence has been entered, however, the only methods to challenge a plea are to appeal and, to a lesser extent, to have a *habeas corpus* review (see Chapter 15). Also, many jurisdictions place a time limit on plea withdrawals; usually, withdrawal is not permitted once a sentence has been imposed.

Readers may recall the case of Idaho Senator Larry Craig, who was arrested in the Minneapolis-St. Paul International Airport on suspicion of lewd conduct in a public rest room. Craig quickly pled guilty to criminal charges but later attempted to withdraw his

---

[28]*Habeas corpus* review is also possible. This is discussed further in Chapter 15.
[29]Federal Rules of Criminal Procedure, Rule 11.

guilty plea, claiming that it was not knowing and intelligent. A judge denied his motion. Craig served out his term as senator and did not run for re-election.

## Appealing a Guilty Plea

If the defendant moves to withdraw his or her plea and is denied this request, then an appeal is appropriate. If the withdrawal period has *passed*, then the only other method of appealing a guilty plea is through direct appeal. This creates something of a difficult situation for the defense. Since an appeal is mostly considered based on the trial court record, then the defendant has limited resources with which to prepare an argument (there is no transcript of a trial because by entering a guilty plea—the defendant elected to forgo trial). The only record left may be that from the arraignment or a similar pretrial proceeding, making it is *very difficult* to succeed with a direct appeal of a guilty plea.

Fortunately, some states, as well as the federal courts, permit appeals based on specific pretrial motions, such as a motion to exclude evidence on constitutional grounds. This is the case in New York and in other jurisdictions that maintain conditional plea mechanisms, as mentioned earlier. These issues aside, there are few Supreme Court precedents addressing appeals of guilty pleas. In *McCarthy v. United States*, 394 U.S. 459 (1969), the Supreme Court held that the trial court's failure to abide by proper arraignment procedure required reversal of a guilty plea on appeal. This is because the arraignment procedure—especially when there is no trial—"is designed to assist the district judge in making the constitutionally required determination that a defendant's guilty plea is truly voluntary."

Note that the decision to appeal a court's denial of a motion to withdraw a guilty plea is not necessarily the same as an appeal of one's conviction. The former may go to the voluntariness of the plea. The latter may concern some other procedural matter, such as an improper search or seizure, and may be appealable, provided the defendant has not waived his or her right to appeal as a result of plea bargaining.

Finally, note that *plea bargaining* and *pleading guilty* are not the same. Plea bargaining often results in a guilty plea, but a defendant does not have to engage in bargaining to plead guilty. Regardless of how the guilty plea is arrived at, the defendant can still seek to withdraw the plea. By contrast, a guilty plea that is entered *without* plea bargaining is more appealable than one reached as a result of bargaining. In the latter instance, the accused often gives up important rights, such as the right to appeal.

---

# Summary

## 1. Explain the concept of plea bargaining.

Plea bargaining occurs when the prosecution offers some concession to the defendant in exchange for a guilty plea. Two common forms of plea bargaining can be discerned. The first, charge bargaining, occurs when the prosecutor offers to charge the accused with a less serious offense in exchange for a guilty plea. The second, sentence bargaining, occurs when the prosecutor promises the defendant a favorable sentencing recommendation.

## 2. Outline the history of plea bargaining and arguments for and against its use.

Plea bargaining is how most cases in the U.S. criminal justice system are disposed of. By some estimates, 90 percent of all criminal cases are resolved through plea bargaining. Supporters of the practice claim that bargaining is necessary to ensure the orderly and prompt flow of criminal cases. Critics claim, among other things, that defendants are forced to give up important constitutional rights as a result of the plea bargaining process.

▼

In response to criticism, some jurisdictions have experimented with banning or restricting plea bargaining. Despite these attempts at reform, plea bargaining flourishes today. One of the reasons for this is that the Supreme Court condones the practice.

## 3. Summarize the procedures in the plea-bargaining process and the effects of plea bargaining.

Despite the Supreme Court's support for plea bargaining, it still requires that certain procedures be followed. First, the defendant must be represented by counsel and that counsel must be effective. Second, the defendant has the right to be informed by the prosecution of exculpatory evidence in the state's possession. Third, the prosecution can offer a wide range of inducements to the defense in order to secure a guilty plea, but those inducements cannot be coercive in nature. Further, there is some question about the propriety of so-called "ad hoc" plea bargaining: the practice of offering inducements to the defendant other than charge reductions and sentencing recommendations. Finally, statutory and judicial inducements for the defendant to plead guilty should be kept to a minimum.

Plea bargaining affects four parties: (1) the court, (2) the prosecutor, (3) the defendant (most often through the defense attorney), and (4) the victim. It affects the court only insofar as the court has to decide whether to accept the plea. A plea agreement that is excessively lenient is likely to be rejected by the court. The prosecutor is affected by plea bargaining only after the agreement has been accepted by the court. That is, the prosecutor must honor the agreement after the judge has accepted it but is under no obligation to do so beforehand. The defendant is perhaps the party most affected by plea bargaining. He or she often gives up certain rights by pleading guilty but can preserve certain rights pursuant to conditional plea agreement statutes. Victims get closure but may also be put off by agreements that are perceived as "soft."

## 4. Outline the elements of a valid guilty plea.

A court will not accept just any plea agreement put before it. All plea agreements must be valid—that is, they must be knowing and intelligent, voluntary, and based in fact. A knowing and intelligent waiver is one in which the defendant understands the charge, the possible sentences, and the rights waived as a result of bargaining. A voluntary plea is one that is not coerced by the state. Finally, a plea agreement should be based in fact—that is, premised on conduct that actually took place. In other words, the defendant should not plead guilty to a crime he or she did not commit, although this clearly happens from time to time.

## 5. Summarize how a guilty plea may be contested.

A guilty plea can be contested in at least two ways. First, the defendant can seek to withdraw his or her guilty plea. Doing so is fairly difficult once the court has accepted the plea. The defendant must show, for example, that the plea was involuntary to have it withdrawn after the court accepts it. Next, if the defendant is denied a request to withdraw his or her guilty plea, he or she can appeal that decision. Also, the defendant can sometimes appeal his or her conviction (as opposed to a court's decision to reject a motion to withdraw a guilty plea). The latter is increasingly rare because the defendant often agrees to waive his or her right to appeal as a result of plea bargaining.

---

# Key Terms

ad hoc plea bargaining *356*
*Alford* plea *351*

judicial inducements *357*
plea bargaining *347*

prosecutorial inducements *354*
statutory inducements *357*

# Key Cases

## Supreme Court's View on Plea Bargaining

- *Brady v. United States*, 397 U.S. 742 (1970)

## Plea-Bargaining Process

- *Bordenkircher v. Hayes*, 434 U.S. 357 (1978)
- *United States v. Goodwin*, 457 U.S. 368 (1982)
- *Corbitt v. New Jersey*, 439 U.S. 212 (1978)

## Effects of Plea Bargaining

- *Mabry v. Johnson*, 467 U.S. 504 (1984)
- *Santobello v. New York*, 404 U.S. 257 (1971)
- *United States v. Benchimol*, 471 U.S. 453 (1985)
- *Ricketts v. Adamson*, 483 U.S. 1 (1987)

## Valid Guilty Pleas

- *Henderson v. Morgan*, 426 U.S. 637 (1976)
- *Boykin v. Alabama*, 395 U.S. 238 (1969)
- *McCarthy v. United States*, 394 U.S. 459 (1969)

# Further Exploration

1. Courts are strapped for cash and trials are expensive. This has led to plea bargaining becoming more prevalent than ever. Some 97 percent of federal cases are disposed of by plea agreements. This turn of events raises an interesting question: has the fiscal crunch increased the risk that innocent defendants plead guilty? Before answering, read the article on plea bargaining and the innocent defendant at this link: http://gritsforbreakfast.blogspot.com/2012/09/plea-bargaining-and-innocent-defendant.html (accessed May 13, 2013).

2. Read Rule 12 of the *Federal Rules of Criminal Procedure* available here: http://www.law.cornell.edu/rules/frcrmp/rule_12 (accessed May 13, 2013). What pretrial motions can be made in a federal criminal trial? How might these motions affect plea negotiations? More specifically, if a defense attorney seeks to have government evidence excluded and succeeds, what could such an outcome do to the plea-bargaining process?

3. In what ways might a jurisdiction's plea-bargaining rate affect the re-election of a district attorney?

4. The Innocence Project has featured the cases of 28 individuals who pleaded guilty to crimes they did not commit. They collectively served over 150 years in prison before they were exonerated. Read about the cases here: http://www.innocenceproject.org/Content/When_the_Innocent_Plead_Guilty.php (accessed May 13, 2013). What do the cases have in common?

5. Ray Bitar turned Full Tilt Poker into one of the world's largest online gambling companies. He was indicted in 2012 as part of the federal government's crackdown on the online gaming industry. He was also accused of defrauding clients. In April 2013, Bitar reached a plea agreement. Following his guilty plea, he was sentenced to time served and ordered to forfeit his assets, including various homes and an estimated $40 million in cash. Does an agreement like this allow a high-profile defendant to "buy" his or her way out of a prison term? Should asset forfeiture be permitted in the plea-bargaining process? Does it matter that Title 9 (Section 9-113.100) of the U.S. Attorney's Manual says "Settlements to forfeit property are encouraged to conserve the resources of both the United States and claimants in situations where justice will be served?" See the following site for more details on the federal government's perspective on forfeiture in plea agreements: http://www.justice.gov/usao/eousa/foia_reading_room/usam/title9/113mcrm.htm#9-113.100 (accessed May 13, 2013).

# Review Questions

1. What is plea bargaining? Can a defendant plead guilty without plea bargaining?
2. Explain the historical origins of plea bargaining.
3. What are the reasons for the prevalence of plea bargaining?
4. Summarize the arguments against plea bargaining.
5. What has been done in response to criticisms of plea bargaining?
6. Summarize the arguments in support of plea bargaining.
7. Explain the accused's constitutional rights during plea bargaining.
8. What are some examples of acceptable inducements by the prosecution?
9. Describe ad hoc plea bargaining. Cite some examples.
10. Explain how judges and statutes can induce guilty pleas.
11. Summarize the effects of plea bargaining on the court.
12. What are the prosecutor's duties before and after the court accepts a plea bargain?
13. In what ways does plea bargaining affect the defendant?
14. Explain the elements of a valid guilty plea.
15. How can a plea of guilty be contested, if at all?

# Web Links and Exercises

1. Plea bargaining frequency: how common is plea bargaining?
Suggested URL: http://www.uscourts.gov/uscourts/Statistics/StatisticalTablesForTheFederalJudiciary/2012/june/D04Jun12.pdf (accessed May 15, 2013).

2. The case against plea bargaining: read more about arguments against plea bargaining.

Suggested URL: http://www.cato.org/pubs/regulation/regv26n3/v26n3-7.pdf (accessed May 13, 2013).

3. Victim input in plea bargaining: read about the state of law as it concerns victim input into plea bargaining.
URL: http://www.ncjrs.gov/ovc_archives/bulletins/legalseries/bulletin7/2.html (accessed May 13, 2013).

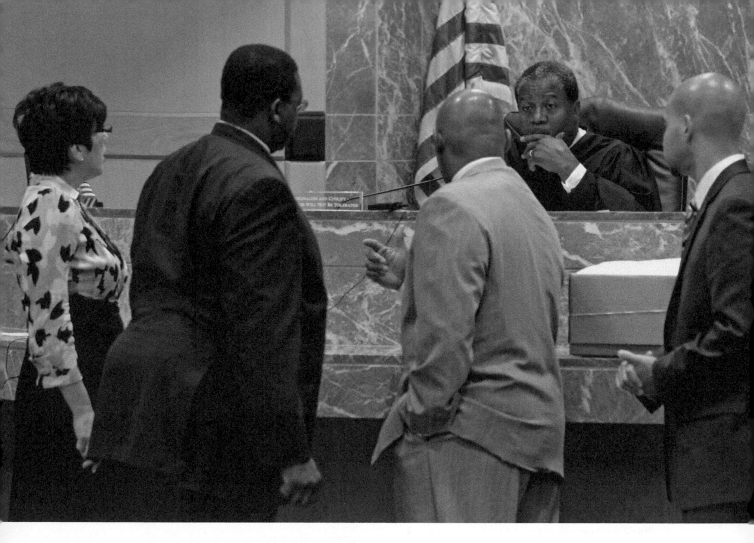

# 13 Rights at Trial

**LEARNING OBJECTIVES**

When you complete this chapter, you should be able to:

**1** *Summarize the right to a speedy trial.*

**2** *Explain the right to an impartial judge.*

**3** *Summarize the right to a jury trial.*

**4** *Outline the jury selection process.*

................................................

# Introduction: Ensuring an Expeditious and Fair Trial

Assuming a defendant does not plea-bargain, a trial will probably result. In the trial phase, the defendant is afforded a number of important constitutional rights. Three rights considered in this chapter are: (1) the right to a speedy trial, (2) the right to an impartial judge, and (3) the right to an impartial jury. Additional rights afforded to the defendant at trial are covered in Chapter 14.

................................................

# ▶ The Right to a Speedy Trial

The Sixth Amendment provides, in part, "In all criminal prosecutions, the accused shall enjoy the right to a **speedy trial**." When the framers of the Bill of Rights wrote this clause, they hoped to avoid the long delays in the criminal process that often resulted in great injustices to criminal defendants. If it took too long for a case to go to trial, the amount of time spent in jail could be oppressive, and might exceed the actual punishment following conviction. And a long delay in trying a case may make a trial less fair, as the memories of witnesses faded and evidence disappeared. These issues are no less important today than when the Sixth Amendment was written. The federal "Speedy Trial Act" (18 U.S.C. Sections 3161–3174), in addition to statutes in every state, are designed to ensure that defendants receive a "speedy trial." But exactly what constitutes a "speedy" trial, as well as the types of proceedings that are subject to this right, have not been clearly defined by the courts.

Despite the apparent importance of this significant right, the Supreme Court did not address the Sixth Amendment's speedy trial provision until 1966. In *United States v. Ewell*, 383 U.S. 116 (1966), the Court identified three purposes in having a speedy trial: (1) It prevents excessive incarceration; (2) it minimizes anxiety experienced by the accused as a result of a publicized accusation; and (3) it prevents damage to the defendant's case resulting from too much delay.

*Barker v. Wingo*
*(407 U.S. 514 [1972])*

In *Barker v. Wingo*, 407 U.S. 514 (1972), the Court elaborated on these purposes:

> If an accused cannot make bail, he is generally confined, as was Barker [the defendant] for 10 months, in a local jail. This contributes to the overcrowding and generally deplorable state of those institutions. Lengthy exposure to these conditions "has a destructive effect on human character and makes the rehabilitation of the individual offender much more difficult." At times the result may even be violent rioting. Finally, lengthy pretrial detention is costly. The cost of maintaining a prisoner in jail varies from $3 to $9 per day, and this amounts to millions across the Nation. In addition, society loses wages which might have been earned, and it must often support families of incarcerated breadwinners.

A speedy trial not only benefits the defense, but also the government and the society at large. First, having a speedy trial provides the opportunity for a guilty verdict to be secured quickly (assuming, of course, that the defendant is guilty). It also minimizes the opportunity for an individual out on bail to commit additional crimes while awaiting trial. However, if the accused is kept in detention prior to trial, too much delay can take a financial toll on the government.

Despite the advantages, pressure for a speedy trial can be a double-edged sword. Having a speedy trial may promote efficiency, but too much efficiency may prevent a defendant from receiving a fair trial. For example, if the defense is not given adequate time to prepare, then an erroneous guilty verdict could result. In *Ewell*, the Court stated that "[t]he essential ingredient is orderly expedition and not mere speed." Likewise, the defense may wish to delay trial for as long as possible on the hopes that the memories of prosecution witness will fade.

## When the Right to a Speedy Trial Applies

A fair amount of case law addresses the threshold issue of *when* the right to a speedy trial applies. In general, the right applies once a person has been *accused* of a crime. This is known as the **accusation rule**. Although this rule seems simple on its face, the timing of the accusation and the number of accusations can complicate the determination.

### The Accusation Rule

*United States v. Marion*
*(404 U.S. 307 [1971])*

In *United States v. Marion*, 404 U.S. 307 (1971), the defendants sought to dismiss the indictment against them by arguing that the government had known of their identities for three years prior to the indictment. More specifically, they argued that their Sixth Amendment right to a speedy trial had been violated because the government had known of them prior to the point at which they had been indicted. Their argument failed; the Court held that the Sixth Amendment's guarantee to a speedy trial attaches only *after* the person (or persons) has been accused of a crime. The Court further stated that being accused of a crime did not necessarily mean that formal charges had to be filed. Namely, "[T]he actual restraints imposed by arrest and holding to answer on a criminal charge" can be sufficient to amount to an accusation.

## Charged and Charged Again

Matters are further complicated when a person is charged, has the charges against him or her dropped, and is then charged again at some point in the future. This issue arose in *United States v. MacDonald*, 456 U.S. 1 (1982), in which there was a delay of four years between the dismissal of charges against the accused and a re-indictment on the same charges. According to the Court, "Following dismissal of charges, any restraint on liberty, disruption of employment, strain on financial resources, and exposure to public obloquy, stress, and anxiety is no greater than it is upon anyone openly subject to a criminal investigation." The Court also observed that MacDonald had been "free to go about his affairs, to practice his profession, and to continue his life" in the period between the two sets of charges. The Court thus held that the right to a speedy trial does not apply until the second set of charges is filed.

An interesting twist on *MacDonald* was presented in *United States v. Loud Hawk*, 474 U.S. 302 (1986). Charges against the defendant were dismissed, but the prosecution appealed the dismissal. The defendant was granted unconditional release while the prosecution continued to mount its case. Nevertheless, the Court still held that the defendant's right to a speedy trial was not implicated. Thus, if an individual is accused but then released to go about his or her business *with no charges pending*, any attempt to claim a violation of the Sixth Amendment's speedy trial provision will likely fail. However, if a person is released *while* charges are pending, a speedy trial argument could be successfully raised.

*United States v. Loud Hawk*
*(474 U.S. 302 [1986])*

## Ignorance of Charges

In *Doggett v. United States*, 505 U.S. 647 (1992), the defendant was charged with a crime, but did not know that he had been charged and was not restrained in any way. Doggett left the United States just prior to the government's attempt to arrest him and, still unaware of the charges against him, returned over two years later. Doggett was eventually found (although he never *evaded* authorities) and arrested over eight years after he was indicted.

*Doggett v. United States*
*(505 U.S. 647 [1992])*

The Supreme Court held in *Doggett* that the speedy trial clause of the Sixth Amendment was implicated. This was a surprising decision because Doggett was never detained nor could he claim any anxiety associated with the charges being filed against him (since he failed to learn of them until some eight years later). Also, Doggett carried on a law-abiding life, so he was not a threat to society. The Court's rationale for finding a violation of the speedy trial clause was that the ability of the defendant to mount an effective defense was undermined by the delay. Despite the Court's somewhat controversial decision in this case, *Doggett* has probably had little influence on subsequent defendants' speedy trial claims. The simple reason is that in most cases, defendants *know* when they are charged.

## Due Process and Speedy Trials

In many cases, a defendant is not charged for a long period of time after the crime is committed. Usually, most jurisdictions do not have statutes of limitations for serious offenses (laws that place time limits on bringing charges for particular types of offense). For less serious offenses, however, failure to bring charges in a timely manner can amount to a due

*United States v. Lovasco*
*(431 U.S. 783 [1977])*

process violation. Indeed, even if the time period for bringing charges has not expired, failure to bring charges quickly can rise to the level of a constitutional violation.

*United States v. Lovasco*, 431 U.S. 783 (1977), illustrates how a delay can result in a due process violation. There, the Supreme Court held that even when the statute of limitations period has not expired, the due process clause is violated if the delay exceeds "the community's sense of fair play and decency." In that case, two witnesses died during an 18-month delay between the crime and the indictment. The Court developed an *either/or* rule for determining whether this type of delay is unconstitutional: The delay must be for the purpose of gaining "a tactical advantage over the accused" or "in reckless disregard of circumstances . . . suggesting that there existed an appreciable risk that delay would impair the ability to mount an effective defense."

### Summary: The Application of the Right to a Speedy Trial

In general, the right to a speedy trial applies when a person is accused of a crime. In most cases, the right to a speedy trial attaches when charges are filed. However, if a person is charged, let go, and later recharged, the right to a speedy trial does not apply until the latter charge is filed. Due process can also be violated if charges are not brought in a timely fashion. This is sometimes true even if charges are not brought against a person before an applicable statute of limitations expires.

## When the Right to a Speedy Trial Is Violated

The Supreme Court has not created any bright-line test when the government violates the Sixth Amendment right to a speedy trial. In *Barker v. Wingo*, 407 U.S. 514 (1972), the Court established that this issue should be determined on a case-by-case basis. In *Barker*, the defendant did not assert his Sixth Amendment right until after the prosecution had sought 16 continuances, which lasted over five years. The Supreme Court announced a four-element test to determine when the right to a speedy trial is violated: "(1) length of delay; (2) the reason for the delay; (3) the defendant's assertion of his right; and (4) prejudice to the defendant." According to the Court, none of these four criteria is, by itself, determinative. Instead, the courts must balance one against the others in deciding whether a Sixth Amendment violation has taken place.

### When Too Much Time Has Elapsed

In *Doggett v. United States*, introduced earlier, the Supreme Court suggested that a delay of one year could be "presumptively prejudicial"—that is, in violation of the Sixth Amendment. It also held that the lengthy period between the point at which charges

---

**DECISION-MAKING EXERCISE 13.1**

**PUTTING CHARGES ON HOLD**

A prosecutor can sometimes use what is known as a *nolle prosequi* device, which involves charging a person with a crime but deciding, for the time being, not to prosecute the matter any further. The charges are not dismissed; rather, they are put on hold. The suspect can essentially be prosecuted any time thereafter at the whim of the prosecutor. Assume that a prosecutorial *nolle prosequi* is issued in Rick

O'Shea's case. O'Shea has been charged with aggravated assault, but the primary witness against him is in a coma. Assume further that the witness does not come out of the coma for an entire year. O'Shea is then convicted and later appeals, claiming his Sixth Amendment right to a speedy trial was implicated once the *nolle prosequi* commenced. What should the court decide?

were first filed and Doggett's trial violated the Sixth Amendment right to a speedy trial. However, in *Loud Hawk*, also discussed earlier, the delay was longer than seven years and the Court found no violation of the right to a speedy trial. In another case, *United States v. Eight Thousand Eight Hundred & Fifty Dollars*, 461 U.S. 555 (1983), the Court held that 18 months of delay prior to an asset forfeiture proceeding was "quite significant" but still not of constitutional magnitude.

These decisions seem controversial, but in light of the other three criteria announced in *Barker*, the delay itself was deemed insufficient to cause any prejudice to the defendant. That is, a violation of one of the four criteria is not, in itself, determinative.

## When the Delay Is Intentional

*Barker* also suggested that the reason or reasons for the delay can also be important:

> A deliberate attempt to delay the trial in order to hamper the defense should be weighted heavily against the government. A more neutral reason such as negligence or overcrowded courts should be weighted less heavily but nevertheless should be considered since the ultimate responsibility for such circumstances must rest with government rather than the defendant. [Finally,] a valid reason, such as a missing witness . . . should serve to justify appropriate delay.

A key element of this analysis is that the delay should be *deliberate*. An accidental delay, or one that is beyond the control of the prosecution, would probably be constitutional. For example, if defense counsel is responsible for the delay, the speedy trial right will not be violated (see, e.g., *Vermont v. Brillon*, 556 U.S. ___ [2009]). But even if the prosecution deliberately seeks to delay the case, it must be shown that the delay is prejudicial to the defense's case. If it does not actually prejudice the defendant, it is unlikely to violate the Sixth Amendment.

To further clarify, consider the Supreme Court's rationale in *Loud Hawk*, mentioned earlier. Part of the reason for the delay in that case was that the prosecution sought numerous appeals with regard to the trial court's decision. The Supreme Court then stated that courts should focus on "the strength of the Government's position on the appealed issue, the importance of the issue in the posture of the case, and—in some cases—the seriousness of the crime." As to the seriousness of the crime, the Court also stated, "[T]he charged offense usually must be sufficiently serious to justify restraints that may be imposed on the defendant pending the outcome of the appeal." In other words, if the government delays a trial by appealing, for instance, a decision on a motion to suppress, its position must be persuasive and the case serious. Legitimate motions that cause delay are not by themselves problematic (see *United States v. Tinklenberg*, 563 U.S. ___ [2011]), but frivolous delays for the purpose of weakening the defense should be avoided.

When delay is a result of prosecutorial negligence (as opposed to problems beyond the prosecution's control, such as unavailable witnesses or court backlog), the Supreme Court has been considerably more strict. Recall that in *Doggett*, six years elapsed between the defendant's return to the United States and his arrest. The Supreme Court pointed out that

---

### DECISION-MAKING EXERCISE 13.2

#### WHEN THE DEFENDANT IS RESPONSIBLE FOR THE DELAY

Charles Pitt escaped from jail while awaiting his trial on narcotics offenses. He was apprehended by the police nine months later. He was then tried, convicted, and sentenced to prison for 10 years. He has appealed his conviction, claiming that his Sixth Amendment right to a speedy trial was denied because of the nine-month delay. How should the appellate court rule?

this delay occurred because the government failed to continue tracking Doggett once he left the country. In their words:

> Although negligence is obviously to be weighted more lightly than a deliberate intent to harm the accused's defense, it still falls on the wrong side of the divide between acceptable and unacceptable reasons for delaying a criminal prosecution once it has begun. And such is the nature of the prejudice presumed that the weight we assign to official negligence compounds over time as the presumption of evidentiary prejudice grows. Thus, our toleration of such negligence varies inversely with its protractedness, and its consequent threat to the fairness of the accused's trial.

### When the Defendant Asserts the Right

Obviously, if the defendant does not assert his or her right to a speedy trial, then the courts should view any subsequent appeals with skepticism. However, if the defendant does not *formally* assert his or her right, can the courts then infer a waiver of the right? That is, if a defendant does not expressly state that his or her right to a speedy trial has been violated, should the defendant be able to make this claim in a subsequent appeal?

In *Barker*, the Supreme Court stated that "failure to assert the [speedy trial] right will make it difficult for a defendant to prove that he was denied a speedy trial." The Court also stated that the "frequency and force of the [defense] objections [to delay]" need to be taken into account. This means that formally asserting the right to a speedy trial may not be enough—the defendant should be sincere in his or her claims that the right was violated.

Recall from the *Miranda* discussion in Chapter 8 that silence cannot be construed as a waiver of the right to remain silent. The same does not hold true, then, with regard to the right to a speedy trial; total silence by the defense concerning the Sixth Amendment right to counsel means that, for all practical purposes, the defendant has waived the right.

### When the Delay Is Prejudicial to the Defendant

The fourth and final requirement for a defendant to succeed in raising a speedy trial claim is that the delay actually caused prejudice to him or her. In other words, the delay impaired the ability of the defendant to mount an adequate defense. If this and the three other requirements in *Barker* have been met, the Sixth Amendment right to a speedy trial may have been violated.

What exactly constitutes *prejudice* to the defendant? The Supreme Court provided some guidance in *Dickey v. Florida*, 398 U.S. 30 (1970), where it held that a seven-year delay, during which time two defense witnesses died and another became unavailable, warranted dismissal of charges. Thus, it would seem that an excessively lengthy delay, if it results in the unavailability of witnesses, may constitute prejudice to the defense.

---

**DECISION-MAKING EXERCISE 13.3**

**COURT BACKLOG**

Lorna Bath robbed the First Street branch of State Bank because she believed the bank did not care about its customers and needed to be "hit where it hurts." Unfortunately, she was caught and indicted for first-degree robbery. However, because the court had a significant case backlog, Bath was not tried until 15 months after the robbery. During that time, she never asserted her right to a speedy trial. She was tried, convicted, and later appealed. The appeal, which is before the court now, claims that Bath's Sixth Amendment right to a speedy trial was violated because of the 15-month delay. How should the court decide?

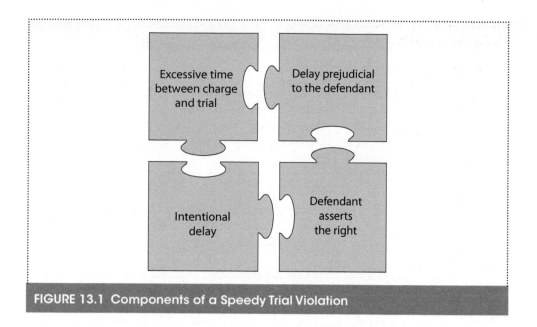

**FIGURE 13.1** Components of a Speedy Trial Violation

Note that the opinion in *Barker* seems to suggest that a lengthy delay by itself (in that case, over five years) is not always prejudicial. The question of prejudice hinged on the ability of a witness to remember certain events. The Court said that it would be difficult to show a memory lapse and, consequently, that such a memory lapse hurt the defense. More concrete reasons for prejudice—such as deceased defense witnesses, as in *Dickey*—are needed to show prejudice.

It is clear, then, that succeeding in a claim that one's constitutional right to a speedy trial has been violated is exceedingly difficult. The defense must show clear and substantial damage to its case for a prejudice claim to succeed. The mere possibility that prejudice occurred is not enough. Coupled with the three other requirements announced in *Barker*, there are significant barriers to raising a constitutional challenge based on the speedy trial clause. These requirements are summarized in Figure 13.1.

## Consequences of Violating the Right to a Speedy Trial

Assuming prosecution is delayed to an unconstitutional degree, we next have to determine the appropriate remedy. This question was answered in *Strunk v. United States*, 412 U.S. 434 (1973). The defendant was found guilty of a crime in a federal district court after a 10-month delay between indictment and arraignment. The Seventh Circuit Court of Appeals held that the defendant was denied a speedy trial, but only remanded the case for a reduction in the defendant's sentence. The U.S. Supreme Court reversed, holding that dismissal is the *only* remedy. Thus, any time a defendant's right to a speedy trial is denied, the charges against him or her will be dismissed altogether. This is in contrast to the plea-bargaining discussion in Chapter 12; in that context, if the prosecution fails to fulfill its end of a plea bargain, the accused does not necessarily go free.

*Strunk v. United States*
*(412 U.S. 434 [1973])*

## ▶ The Right to an Impartial Judge

In describing a person's right to a fair trial, the Sixth Amendment speaks only of juries (in addition to other important provisions), not judges. But the Supreme Court has held that the due process clause of the Fourteenth Amendment guarantees a criminal defendant the

**DECEASED WITNESSES**

Recall the facts of the case in Decision-Making Exercise 13.3. Suppose, now, that Lorna Bath is prepared to file another appeal. This time, she argues that during the 15-month time lapse, the lead defense witness—who was prepared to testify that Bath was nowhere near the scene of the crime on the day of the robbery—died of a massive heart attack. Bath argues this time that the delay was prejudicial to her case and that her conviction should be overturned. Will she succeed with this appeal?

right to trial by an **impartial judge**. This right applies in two situations: (1) a *bench trial*, in which the judge decides the defendant's fate instead of a jury; and (2) a *jury trial*, in which the judge acts solely as a trier of law (one who makes decisions about the law, not the facts of the case).

Recall from Chapter 4 that judges are not considered impartial when issuing warrants if they seek to gain financially from doing so. Likewise, judges presiding over criminal trial cannot have a financial stake in the outcome. For example, in *Tumey v. Ohio*, 273 U.S. 510 (1927), the judge of court that heard the defendant's case was also the city mayor. In addition, he received the fines and fees that he levied against those convicted in his courtroom. The Supreme Court concluded that due process is violated when the judge "has a direct, personal, substantial pecuniary interest in reaching a conclusion against him in his case."

*Tumey v. Ohio, 273 U.S. (510 [1927])*

A similar decision was reached in *Ward v. Monroeville*, 409 U.S. 57 (1972). However, in that case, the fees or fines collected by the judge did not go directly to the judge, but instead were paid into the town's budget. The amount of money collected was apparently substantial. The Court concluded, again, that due process was violated, this time stating that "the mayor's executive responsibilities for village finances may make him partisan to maintain the high level of contribution from the mayor's court." Contrast this decision with that of *Dugan v. Ohio*, 277 U.S. 61 (1928), in which the Supreme Court held that due process was *not* violated because the judge was one of several members of a city commission and, as such, did not have substantial control over the city's funding sources.

*Ward v. Monroeville (409 U.S. 57 [1972])*

## Methods of Removing a Judge Who Is Not Impartial

In most jurisdictions, either the defense or the prosecution can seek to have a judge removed *for cause*. That is, the individual seeking the judge's removal will argue that the judge is biased for or against a particular party to the case, usually by filing a motion for a new judge. Strangely, though, the only person who can remove such a judge is usually the judge himself!

Some jurisdictions allow either party to a case to *peremptorily* remove a judge. This is akin to the jury selection process (covered in the latter part of this chapter). Basically, the judge can be removed without any reason whatsoever. The number of peremptory removals, if permitted, is very small—usually one per case. Once the first judge has been removed, the parties can only seek to remove the second judge for cause.

In many situations, the judge does not need to be removed at the request of one of the parties. Responsible judges may remove themselves when conflicts of interest exist. Indeed, most judicial codes of ethics require that a judge *recuse* (disqualify) himself or herself if, among other things, he or she has a personal bias or prejudice concerning a party, personal knowledge of disputed evidentiary facts concerning the proceeding, or some conflict of interest in the case (see American Bar Association, Code of Judicial Conduct, Canon 3-C). Figure 13.2 presents relevant ethical canons from the Code of Judicial Conduct for United States Judges.

**Canon 1**

A judge should uphold the integrity and independence of the judiciary

**Canon 2**

A judge should avoid impropriety and the appearance of impropriety in all activities

**Canon 3**

A judge should perform the duties of the office impartially and diligently

**Canon 4**

A judge may engage in extra-judicial activities to improve the law, the legal system, and the administration of justice

**Canon 5**

A judge should regulate extra-judicial activities to minimize the risk of conflict with judicial duties

**Canon 6**

A judge should regularly file reports of compensation received for law-related and extra-judicial activities

**Canon 7**

A judge should refrain from political activity

*Source:* Administrative Office of the U.S. Courts. Available online: http://www.uscourts.gov/rulesandpolicies/CodesOfConduct.aspx (accessed February 16, 2011).

**FIGURE 13.2 Code of Conduct for United States Judges**

---

**DECISION-MAKING EXERCISE 13.5**

**AN IMPARTIAL JUDGE?**

During Beau Archer's criminal trial for assault, Archer, who represented himself, engaged in disruptive conduct and made insulting and slanderous remarks against the judge, calling him a "dirty, tyrannical old dog," "stumbling dog," and "fool" and further charged him with running a "Spanish Inquisition" and telling him to "keep your mouth shut." Archer was found guilty of assault by a jury. At a subsequent sentencing hearing, the trial judge also pronounced Archer guilty of criminal contempt arising from his conduct during the trial. The judge further sentenced Archer to an extra 11–22 years in prison on the contempt accounts. Archer appealed, claiming that he was denied an impartial judge. What should the court decide?

---

# ▶ The Right to an Impartial Jury

It is often fairly easy to determine whether a judge is impartial. However, deciding on what constitutes an **impartial jury** is far more difficult and complex. For this reason, the remainder of this chapter focuses on the right to trial by an impartial jury.

While the right to an impartial judge applies in *all* proceedings, whether petty or serious, pretrial or otherwise, the right to a trial by jury is *qualified*. That is, it does not *always* apply, even though the Sixth Amendment seems to suggest otherwise. For example, the process of plea bargaining can eliminate the need to have a trial altogether, but even if the defendant opts not to plea-bargain, the right to a jury trial may not exist.

# When the Right to a Jury Trial Applies

The right to a jury trial has always been recognized in the federal courts, but this right was not extended to the states until 1968 in the case of *Duncan v. Louisiana*, 391 U.S. 145 (1968). In that case, the Court noted that the right to a jury trial is "an inestimable safeguard against the corrupt or overzealous prosecutor and against the compliant, biased, or eccentric judge." The right to a jury trial has therefore been incorporated so as to apply to the states, but subsequent decisions have limited this right.

## The Noncriminal Proceeding Rule

The Sixth Amendment states, "In all *criminal prosecutions*, the accused shall enjoy the right to a . . . trial, by an impartial jury" (emphasis added). There is no Sixth Amendment constitutional right to a jury trial in *noncriminal* proceedings. (In civil lawsuits, trial by jury is guaranteed by the Seventh Amendment). More specifically, the Sixth Amendment does not provide a right to a jury trial in noncriminal proceedings that are nevertheless part of the "criminal" process. This has come to be known as the **noncriminal proceeding rule.**

*McKeiver v. Pennsylvania*
(403 U.S. 528 [1971])

Unfortunately, it is not always clear what constitutes a "noncriminal" proceeding. An example is a juvenile delinquency hearing. In *McKeiver v. Pennsylvania*, 403 U.S. 528 (1971), the Court held that juveniles charged with delinquent acts do not enjoy a right to a jury trial. Also, civil commitment hearings do not need to be conducted before a jury (see *Lynch v. Baxley*, 386 F. Supp. 378 [M.D. Ala. 1974]). In other words, both juvenile delinquency hearings and civil commitment hearings are noncriminal for Sixth Amendment purposes, even though they are still a part of the "criminal" process.

## The Petty Crime Exception

*Baldwin v. New York*
(399 U.S. 66 [1970])

Although the Sixth Amendment states that the right to a jury trial applies to *all* criminal prosecutions, the Supreme Court has carved out a *petty crime exception* to this right. In *Duncan*, mentioned earlier, the Court expressly stated that there is no right to a jury trial for *petty offenses*. In *Baldwin v. New York*, 399 U.S. 66 (1970), the Court explained its rationale for this exception, stating that the "disadvantages, onerous though they may be," of denying a jury trial for a petty crime are "outweighed by the benefits that result from speedy and inexpensive nonjury adjudication."

*Duncan* failed to define exactly what constitutes a *petty* offense, but in *Baldwin*, the Court concluded that any crime that can bring punishment of more than six months is no longer considered "petty." This has come to be known as the **six-month imprisonment rule;** thus, defendants do not enjoy a right to jury trial when the punishment they face is less than six months in jail or prison.

In some cases, a defendant may be charged with several crimes for which the combined term of imprisonment exceeds six months. It would seem that in such a case, the defendant arguable should have a right to a jury. However, in *Lewis v. United States*, 518 U.S. 322 (1996), the Court announced that a defendant charged in a single proceeding with several petty crimes does not have a right to jury trial even if the maximum penalty for *all* offenses could exceed six months in prison.

It is also possible that a person may be charged with a crime that has a possible six-month imprisonment term, but is sanctioned in some other manner. Such a case was considered in *Blanton v. City of North Las Vegas*, 489 U.S. 538 (1989). The Court announced in that case that the right to a jury trial in such a situation applies "only if [the defendant] can demonstrate that any additional statutory penalties, viewed in conjunction with the maximum authorized period of incarceration, are so severe that they clearly reflect a legislative determination that the offense in question is a 'serious' one." The defendant was charged with drunk-driving, a crime that carried a penalty of, at most, six months as well as a 90-day suspension of his driver's license. The Court stated, "[W]e cannot say that a

DECISION-MAKING EXERCISE 13.6

**A TWIST ON THE SIX-MONTH RULE**

During their criminal trial for auto theft, defendants Ray Katz and Jacob Apple committed various disrespectful and disruptive acts. After a verdict of guilty was returned on the theft charge, the judge sentenced Katz and Apple on contempt charges, as well. The combined sentence for Katz was three years and that for Apple was two years and eight months. Both have appealed their contempt convictions, claiming that they were denied a jury trial because their individual sentences exceeded six months. Is it conceivable that they could succeed in light of *Lewis v. United States*, 518 U.S. 322 (1996)?

90-day suspension is that significant as a Sixth Amendment matter, particularly when a restricted license may be obtained after only 45 days." In another case, *Muniz v. Hoffman*, 422 U.S. 454 (1975), the Court stated that a potential sentence of six months coupled with a *fine* does not require a jury trial.

In summary, the right to a jury trial applies in a criminal proceeding when the penalty for a single offense exceeds six months. In no other situation does the Sixth Amendment right to a jury trial apply, even if multiple charges for petty offenses could result in a lengthy prison term.

## Jury Size and Voting Requirements

Although many juries traditionally consist of 12 members, the Supreme Court has stated that a 12-member jury is not a constitutional requirement. In *Williams v. Florida*, 399 U.S. 78 (1970), the Court pointed out that the 12-member jury was a "historical accident" and "unnecessary to effect the purposes of the jury system." The Court noted that a six-member jury would even provide "a fair possibility for obtaining a representative cross-section of the community, . . . [a]s long as arbitrary exclusions of a particular class from the jury rolls are forbidden."

However, in *Ballew v. Georgia*, 435 U.S. 223 (1978), the Court concluded that a five-member jury was unconstitutional and found it unlikely that such a small group could engage "in meaningful deliberation, . . . remember all the facts and arguments, and truly represent the common sense of the entire community." Thus, to comply with the Sixth Amendment, the jury must be at least six members.

Jury size varies by state. See Figure 13.3 for a map of jury sizes in each state, specifically for courts of general jurisdiction (those with jurisdiction to try several types of cases, including more serious criminal cases). There is more variability in the sizes of juries for misdemeanors than felonies—the vast majority of states require 12-member juries in felony cases.

When a jury decides a case, a unanimous decision is not always required. In two companion cases, *Johnson v. Louisiana*, 406 U.S. 356 (1972) and *Apodaca v. Oregon*, 406 U.S. 404 (1972), the Court upheld a Louisiana statute that permitted 9 to 3 jury verdicts as well as an Oregon statute permitting 10 to 2 decisions. According to the Court:

*Johnson v. Louisiana*
*(406 U.S. 356 [1972])*

> In our view, disagreement of three jurors does not alone establish reasonable doubt, particularly when such a heavy majority of the jury, after having considered the dissenters' views, remained convinced of guilt. . . . That want of jury unanimity is not to be equated with the existence of reasonable doubt emerges even more clearly from the fact that when a jury in a federal court, which operates under the unanimity rule and is instructed to acquit a defendant if it has a reasonable doubt, . . . cannot agree unanimously upon a verdict, the defendant is not acquitted, but is merely given a new trial.

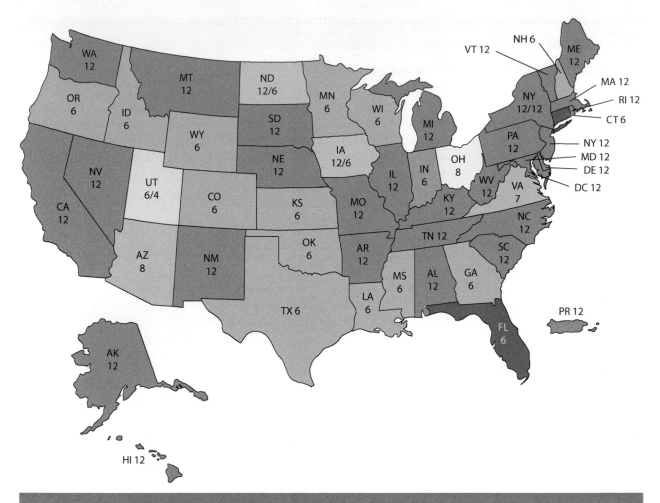

Map labels:
WA 12, OR 6, ID 6, MT 12, ND 12/6, MN 6, WI 6, VT 12, NH 6, ME 12, MA 12, RI 12, CT 6, NY 12/12, NY 12, MD 12, DE 12, DC 12, WY 6, SD 12, IA 12/6, MI 12, PA 12, NV 12, UT 6/4, NE 12, IL 12, IN 6, OH 8, WV 12, VA 7, CA 12, CO 6, KS 6, MO 12, KY 12, NC 12, AZ 8, NM 12, OK 6, AR 12, TN 12, SC 12, MS 6, AL 12, GA 6, TX 6, LA 6, FL 6, PR 12, AK 12, HI 12

**FIGURE 13.3 Jury Sizes by State for Misdemeanor Cases in Courts of General Jurisdiction**

In short, guilt can be determined by less than a unanimous jury in certain jurisdictions. This is somewhat controversial, however, because according to the dissent in *Johnson* and *Apodaca*, permitting a less than a unanimous decision diminishes reliability. This is because jurors may not debate as fully as they would if a unanimous decision were required, and some jurors may be more likely to succumb to group pressure. See Figure 13.4 for a list of jury voting requirements by state, again for courts of general jurisdiction.

## Waiving the Right to a Jury Trial

Although, as the Supreme Court pointed out in *Duncan*, a jury can be an important safe-guard against the potential abuses of judges and prosecutors, there are occasions on which the defendant wishes to waive his or her right to a jury trial. If the case is one that might inflame the emotions of a jury, or prior media exposure might cause a jury to be biased, then obtaining a fair and impartial jury may be difficult. In such a situation, the defendant may opt for a *bench trial*, in which the judge decides the question of guilt.

The leading case dealing with waiver of the right to a jury trial is *Patton v. United States*, 281 U.S. 276 (1930). In that case, the defendants argued that their decision to waive the right to a jury trial was invalid because they lacked the authority to do so. The Supreme Court disagreed and stated that the right to a jury trial can be waived at the

| State | Felony | Trial Type Misdemeanor | Civil |
|---|---|---|---|
| Alabama | U | U | U |
| Alaska | U | U | 5/6 |
| Arizona | U | U | 3/4 |
| Arkansas | U | U | 3/4 |
| California | U | U | 3/4 |
| Colorado | U | U | U |
| Connecticut | U | U | U |
| Delaware | U | U | U |
| Florida | U | U | U |
| Georgia | U | U | U |
| Hawaii | U | U | 5/6 |
| Idaho | U | U | 3/4 |
| Illinois | U | U | U |
| Indiana | U | U | U |
| Iowa | U | U | 7/8 or U |
| Kansas | U | U | 5/6 or U |
| Kentucky | U | U | 3/4 |
| Louisiana | 10/12* | U | 5/6 |
| Maine | U | U | 3/4 |
| Maryland | U | U | U |
| Massachusetts | U | U | 5/6 |
| Michigan | U | U | 5/6 |
| Minnesota | U | U | 5/6 or U |
| Mississippi | U | U | 3/4 |
| Missouri | U | U | 3/4 |
| Montana | U | U | 2/3 |
| Nebraska | U | U | 5/6 or U |
| Nevada | U | U | 3/4 |
| New Hampshire | U | U | U |
| New Jersey | U | U | 5/6 |
| New Mexico | U | U | 5/6 |
| New York | U | U | 5/6 |
| North Carolina | U | U | U |
| North Dakota | U | U | U |
| Ohio | U | U | 3/4 |
| Oklahoma | U | U | U |
| Oregon | 5/6** | 5/6 | 3/4 |
| Pennsylvania | U | U | 5/6 |
| Rhode Island | U | U | U |
| South Carolina | U | U | U |
| South Dakota | U | U | 5/6 |
| Tennessee | U | U | U |
| Texas | U | U | 5/6 |
| Utah | U | U | 3/4 or majority |
| Vermont | U | U | U |
| Virginia | U | U | U |
| Washington | U | U | 5/6 |
| West Virginia | U | U | U |
| Wisconsin | U | U | 5/6 |
| Wyoming | U | U | U |

Key: U = Unanimous; 5/6 = 5 out of 6 jurors must agree (3/4, 7/8, etc., interpreted similarly)

*Some sentences.

**Not capital cases.

Note: There are exceptions to these size requirements in each state. Also, where two voting requirements are listed, the voting requirement differs depending on the crime or the nature of the case.

Source: D. B. Rottman and S. M. Strickland, State Court Organization, 2004 (Washington, DC: Bureau of Justice Statistics, 2006).

**FIGURE 13.4 Jury Voting Requirements by State for Courts of General Jurisdiction**

**SMALL-JURY VOTING REQUIREMENTS**

A man was charged with the offense of obscenity and convicted in a state trial court before a six-person jury. A poll of the jury after the verdict indicated that the jury had voted 5 to 1 to convict. The man appealed his conviction, claiming that his right to trial by jury under the Sixth Amendment was violated when the state permitted a less than unanimous verdict by a six-member jury. How should the appellate court decide?

request of the defendant. The waiver must, however, be "express and intelligent." It must also be voluntary, not a product of government coercion (see *United States v. Jackson*, 390 U.S. 570 [1968]).

It is important to note that waiver of the right to a jury trial can be vetoed. That is, the judge can *require* a jury trial, even if the defendant desires otherwise. Often, such a veto is requested by the prosecutor. In *Singer v. United States*, 380 U.S. 24 (1965), the Court upheld a federal statute permitting vetoes of a jury waiver. According to the Court, refusal to grant the defendant a waiver merely subjects the defendant to "the very thing that the Constitution guarantees him"—namely, a jury trial. As the Court reasoned, "The Constitution recognizes an adversary system as the proper method of determining guilt, and the Government, as a litigant, has a legitimate interest in seeing that cases in which it believes a conviction is warranted are tried before the tribunal which the Constitution regards as most likely to produce a fair result." Thus, if the government feels that a jury trial will produce a fairer result than a bench trial, then a veto of the defendant's waiver of a jury trial is constitutionally permissible.

## Selection of Potential Jurors

Selection of impartial jurors is a multistep process. To begin, a list of potential, or prospective, jurors must be compiled. The creation of this list is critical, and must reflect a fair cross-section of the community. Once a list has been put together, then a panel of jurors is selected from this pool for *jury duty*. Jury selection can be thought of as a three-stage process: (1) a list of potential jurors is compiled; (2) potential jurors are selected from that list; and then (3) the jury itself is chosen. This section addresses the first and second stages; the third stage, *voir dire*, is addressed later.

The list of potential jury members can be called the *jury pool, master jury wheel,* or *jury list*. For simplicity, the term jury list will be used here. The jury list can be compiled from a number of sources. One of the most common methods is to draw from voter registration lists. The federal courts, the state of Washington, and several other states rely on this method. Another source, used in California, is the driver's license registration list. Some states even use telephone directory lists. Still other states rely on jury commissioners: individuals appointed by a judge who are responsible for compiling jury lists.

To be on the jury list, potential jurors usually must meet certain minimum requirements. For example, they must be of a certain age—usually, over 18. They must also be U.S. citizens and free of felony convictions. The requirements to serve on a jury vary considerably from one state to the next.

Once the jury list has been compiled, potential jurors are selected from the list for service. Individuals selected from the jury list are called a *panel* or *venire*. The term jury panel will be used here.

Anyone who has been called on for jury duty has, at one time, been part of a jury panel. And as most people know, there are several means by which one can be excused from a jury panel. Examples of people typically exempted from jury service are aliens, individuals unable to speak English, those under 18, those charged with a felony or who are serving a sentence, and those for whom jury service could cause severe hardship. People in law enforcement positions or who work in so-called critical occupations, such as the military and government, are typically exempted, as well.

Many defendants have appealed their convictions on the grounds that the jury list or panel was unconstitutional because of some form of bias. These challenges generally fall into two categories: (1) equal protection challenges and (2) fair cross-section challenges.

Both types of challenges can be made when the defendant examines the jury list for evidence of constitutional issues. Indeed, *Test v. United States*, 420 U.S. 28 (1975), grants federal defendants the right to inspect and copy jury lists in order to mount equal protection or fair cross-section challenges. Some jurisdictions publish the list automatically. Others make the list available to the attorneys on request. The information revealed in the lists also varies. For example, in Virginia, the list is required to contain names, addresses, ages, occupations, and employers (Virginia Code, Section 8.01-353). Other jurisdictions require prospective jurors to complete "eligibility questionnaires" prior to their service. The results of these questionnaires are then made available on request. The intent is to assist defendants with challenging the jury list if it so desires. Unfortunately, jury lists often provide little more than individuals' names—sex and race must be inferred.

Note that an unbiased jury list or panel may not necessarily result in an unbiased jury. Although the jury list or panel may be unbiased and highly representative of the community at large, the final jury may not be. Clearly, it is difficult to represent the entire community with 12 or fewer people. It is much easier to do so via the jury panel, however. Thus, the constitutional challenges discussed in the following sections apply to the selection of jury *lists* and *panels*, not to juries themselves. Jury selection is considered in the *voir dire* section.

## Equal Protection Challenges

Before the Sixth Amendment was incorporated to the states, the only method of challenging the fairness of a jury pool or panel was based on the equal protection clause of the Fourteenth Amendment. In one case, *Strauder v. Virginia*, 100 U.S. 303 (1879), the Supreme Court declared unconstitutional a statute that explicitly excluded African Americans from jury service. The statute was a violation of equal protection, according to the Court.

*Strauder* was a fairly easy and predictable decision, given that the statute was discriminatory on its face. But what about exclusion of a particular group for other than statutory reasons? In *Whitus v. Georgia*, 385 U.S. 545 (1967), the Court held that an equal protection challenge will succeed when there is a significant disparity between, in that case, the proportion of African Americans on the jury panel and the proportion in the community. In another case, *Castaneda v. Partida*, 430 U.S. 482 (1977), the Supreme Court used the equal protection argument again. There, it held that systematic exclusion of people with Spanish surnames violated equal protection. In both cases, a *significant disparity* was deemed one that cannot be attributed to chance.

In summary, an equal protection challenge against the composition of a jury list or panel succeeded when (1) there was purposeful discrimination against certain individuals and (2) the discrimination was significant. The past tense is used here because the equal protection approach was abandoned in the 1975 case of *Taylor v. Louisiana*, 419 U.S. 522 (1975). That and similar cases are considered next.

## Fair Cross-Section Challenges

In *Glasser v. United States*, 315 U.S. 60 (1942), the Supreme Court required that jury selection procedures be based on "the concept of the jury as a cross-section of the community."

That decision, however, only applied to the federal courts. It was not until 1975 and the case of *Taylor v. Louisiana* that the Supreme Court stated, "We accept the fair cross-section requirements as fundamental to the jury trial guaranteed by the Sixth Amendment." *Taylor* was therefore significant because (1) it abandoned the equal protection approach and (2) it applied the Sixth Amendment's fair cross-section requirement to the state courts through the due process clause of the Fourteenth Amendment.

*Taylor* was also significant because it abandoned the requirement of *significant exclusion*, replacing it with the lower standard of **systematic exclusion**. That is, in order to succeed with a fair cross-section challenge, the defendant need only show systematic exclusion of a distinctive group, not necessarily exclusion that was significant. *Taylor* also permitted fair cross-section challenges with regard to *any* distinctive group, not just racial and ethnic minorities, which were the only groups discussed in the equal protection cases from the previous section.

*Duren v. Missouri* (439 U.S. 357 [1979])

In a later case, *Duren v. Missouri*, 439 U.S. 357 (1979), the Court clarified *Taylor* by requiring that the defendant prove three elements in a fair cross-section challenge:

> (1) that the group alleged to be excluded is a *"distinctive"* group in the community; (2) that the representation of this group in venires from which juries are selected is not fair and reasonable in relation to the number of such persons in the community; and (3) that this *underrepresentation* is due to *systematic exclusion* of the group in the jury-selection process. (emphasis added)

The following paragraphs focus on these three elements: the distinctive group requirement, underrepresentation, and systematic exclusion.

First, a **distinctive group** must be large and identifiable. The group must also comply with the spirit of the Sixth Amendment, which is to guarantee a fair cross-section of the community. In *Lockhart v. McCree*, 476 U.S. 162 (1986), the Court noted that the distinctive group requirement

> (1) "guards against the exercise of arbitrary power" and [ensures] that the "commonsense judgment of the community" will act as a "hedge against the overzealous or mistaken prosecutor;" (2) [preserves] "public confidence in the fairness of the criminal justice system;" and (3) [implements] our belief that "sharing in the administration of justice is a phase of civic responsibility."

Examples of distinctive groups are racial and ethnic minorities, including African Americans, Hispanic Americans, Native Americans, Jews, and others. Women are also considered a distinctive group. *Nondistinctive* groups include, for example, blue-collar workers (see *Anaya v. Hansen*, 781 F.2d 1 [1st Cir. 1986]) and young adults (see *Ford v. Seabold*, 841 F.2d 677 [6th Cir. 1988]). Basically, any group that has received protection via legislation and the equal protection clause (most notably, women and minorities) is considered "distinctive" for jury purposes.

Next, underrepresentation refers to a proportion of distinctive groups within the pool that is too small compared to the population of that group in the community at large. For example, in *Taylor*, the Court concluded that women were underrepresented in the jury panel because while they made 53 percent of the population of people eligible for jury service, only 10 percent of the people in the jury panel were women. Similarly, in *Duren*, 54 percent of the adults in the county were women, but only 15 percent of the people on the jury panel were women.

It was easy for the Court to determine underrepresentation based on these startling percentages. When the discrepancies are not as readily apparent, however, determining underrepresentation can be quite difficult. It appears that a discrepancy of 10 percent or more between the jury panel and the distribution of a particular group in the community is unacceptable (*United States v. Rodriguez*, 776 F.2d 1509 [11th Cir. 1985]).

The last requirement for a fair cross-section challenge is whether the exclusion in question is a systematic exclusion or an accidental one. The only guidance the Supreme Court has offered with regard to this matter was announced in *Duren v. Missouri*: "[I]n Sixth Amendment fair-cross-section cases, systematic disproportion itself demonstrates an infringement of the defendant's interest in a jury chosen from a fair cross-section." Proving systematic exclusion can be quite difficult, as was made clear in a recent case, *Berghuis v. Smith*, 559 U.S. ___ (2010).

## The *Voir Dire* Process

Thus far, the focus has been on the composition of jury lists (lists that consist of all possible jurors) and jury panels (those actually called for jury duty). If either of these excludes a particular group of people to the extent that the defendant's equal protection rights are violated or the Sixth Amendment's fair cross-section requirement is violated, then any resulting conviction could be reversed. Once the jury panel has been chosen, then **voir dire** commences, which is the process of selecting a jury from a jury panel.

It is important to understand that once *voir dire* commences, the concern is not to ensure that the jury represents a fair cross-section of the community. Instead, *voir dire* is concerned with the selection of jury members who can be *impartial*, as the Sixth Amendment requires. The term *voir dire* means "to see what is said." At this stage, the judge, prosecutor, and defense have an opportunity to review potential jurors for evidence of bias.

*Voir dire* can be simple or complicated. In some jurisdictions, the judge decides who will serve on the jury. The prosecution and defense merely suggest questions to the judge in these jurisdictions. Doing so speeds up the process and also helps ensure that jurors do not develop preconceived ideas about the case in question.

Usually, however, it is the attorneys who do the questioning. This process can take anything from a few hours to a few weeks, depending on the nature of the case. *Voir dire* can also take time because nothing precludes the attorneys from investigating jurors' backgrounds, interviewing their acquaintances, and even hiring social scientists who are experts in anticipating probable decisions of prospective jurors.

During the *voir dire* process, each side—the defense and prosecution—has an unlimited number of *challenges for cause* in which the attorney argues that a particular person should be excluded from service on the jury because of bias or a similar reason. Each side is also given a certain number of *peremptory challenges*, which permit the attorney

---

**DECISION-MAKING EXERCISE 13.8**

**WHAT COMPOSES A DISTINCTIVE GROUP?**

Tanya Oki, a resident of an elite suburban neighborhood, was charged with burglary. She was tried and convicted by a 12-member jury and later sentenced to five years in prison. While in prison, she acquired a copy of the jury list (which, incidentally, is now permitted following the Supreme Court's decision in *Test v. United States*, 420 U.S. 28 [1975]). She concluded, based on the addresses in the list, that none of the jurors who convicted her were "yuppies." As such, she had her privately retained attorney draft an appeal, claiming that her Sixth Amendment right to an impartial jury was violated. In particular, she claimed that "yuppies" are a distinctive group and should be more adequately represented in the jury list. How should the appellate court decide?

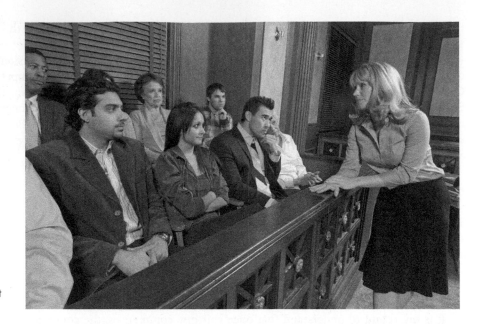

A jury need not be a representative cross section of the community, but it must be fair and impartial.

to exclude members of the jury panel without giving any reason. Before either challenge is used, however, the judge usually opens by asking questions of the jurors. Each of these three methods is considered in a following subsection. See Figure 13.5 for a summary of the *voir dire* process by state, including who conducts *voir dire* and the number of peremptory challenges allocated by specific type of crime.

| State | Number of peremptory challenges | | | | | |
|---|---|---|---|---|---|---|
| | Criminal | | | | | |
| | Capital | | Felony | | Misdemeanor | |
| | State | Defense | State | Defense | State | Defense |
| Alabama | 12 | 12 | 6 | 6 | 3 | 3 |
| Alaska | N/A | N/A | 10 | 10 | 3 | 3 |
| Arizona | 10 | 10 | 6 | 6 | 6 | 6 |
| Arkansas | 10 | 12 | 6 | 8 | 3 | 3 |
| California | 20 | 20 | 20/10 | 20/10 | 10/6 | 10/6 |
| Colorado | 10 | 10 | 5 | 5 | 3 | 3 |
| Connecticut | 25 | 25 | 15/6 | 15/6 | 3 | 3 |
| Delaware | 12 | 20 | 6 | 6 | 6 | 6 |
| District of Columbia | N/A | N/A | 10 | 10 | 3 | 3 |
| Florida | 10 | 10 | 10/6 | 10/6 | 3 | 3 |
| Georgia | 10 | 20 | 6 | 12 | 2 | 4 |
| Hawaii | N/A | N/A | 12/3 | 12/3 | 3 | 3 |
| Idaho | 10 | 10 | 10/6 | 10/6 | 4 | 4 |
| Illinois | 14 | 14 | 7 | 7 | 5 | 5 |
| Indiana | 20 | 20 | 10 | 10 | 5 | 5 |
| Iowa | N/A | N/A | 10/6 | 10/6 | 4 | 4 |

**FIGURE 13.5** *Voir Dire* Processes by State for Courts of General Jurisdiction

| State | Number of peremptory challenges | | | | | |
|---|---|---|---|---|---|---|
| | Criminal | | | | | |
| | Capital | | Felony | | Misdemeanor | |
| | State | Defense | State | Defense | State | Defense |
| Kansas | 12 | 12 | 12/8/6 | 12/8/6 | 3 | 3 |
| Kentucky | 8 | 8 | 8 | 8 | 3 | 3 |
| Louisiana | 12 | 12 | 12/6 | 12/6 | 6 | 6 |
| Maine | N/A | N/A | 10/8 | 10/8 | 4 | 4 |
| Maryland | 10 | 20 | 5 | 10 | 4 | 4 |
| Massachusetts | N/A | N/A | 12/4 | 12/4 | 4 | 4 |
| Michigan | N/A | N/A | 12/5 | 12/5 | 5 | 5 |
| Minnesota | N/A | N/A | 9/3 | 15/5 | 3 | 5 |
| Mississippi | 12 | 12 | 6 | 6 | 6 | 6 |
| Missouri | 9 | 9 | 6 | 6 | 2 | 2 |
| Montana | 8 | 8 | 6/3 | 6/3 | 6/3 | 6/3 |
| Nebraska | 12 | 12 | 6 | 6 | 3 | 3 |
| Nevada | 8 | 8 | 4 | 4 | 4 | 4 |
| New Hampshire | 10 | 20 | 15/3 | 15/3 | 3 | 3 |
| New Jersey | N/A | N/A | 12 | 20 | 10 | 10 |
| New Mexico | N/A | N/A | 3 | 5 | 3 | 5 |
| New York | N/A | N/A | 20/15 | 20/15/10 | 10 | 10 |
| North Carolina | 14 | 14 | 6 | 6 | 6 | 6 |
| North Dakota | N/A | N/A | 6/4 | 6/4 | 6/4 | 6/4 |
| Ohio | 6 | 6 | 4 | 4 | 3 | 3 |
| Oklahoma | 9 | 9 | 5 | 5 | 3 | 3 |
| Oregon | 12 | 12 | 6 | 6 | 6/3 | 6/3 |
| Pennsylvania | 20 | 20 | 7 | 7 | 5 | 5 |
| Puerto Rico | N/A | N/A | 10/5 | 10/5 | 5 | 5 |
| Rhode Island | N/A | N/A | 6 | 6 | 3 | 3 |
| South Carolina | 5 | 10 | 5 | 10 | 5 | 5 |
| South Dakota | 20 | 20 | 20/10 | 20/10 | 3 | 3 |
| Tennessee | 15 | 15 | 8 | 8 | 3 | 3 |
| Texas | 15 | 15 | 10 | 10 | 5 | 5 |
| Utah | 10 | 10 | 4 | 4 | 3 | 3 |
| Vermont | N/A | N/A | 6 | 6 | 6 | 6 |
| Virginia | 4 | 4 | 4 | 4 | 3 | 3 |
| Washington | 12 | 12 | 6 | 6 | 3 | 3 |
| West Virginia | N/A | N/A | 2 | 6 | 4 | 4 |
| Wisconsin | N/A | N/A | 6/4 | 6/4 | 4 | 4 |
| Wyoming | 12 | 12 | 8 | 8 | 4 | 4 |

*Note:* The following states/territories do not have a death penalty statute or have abolished the death penalty: Alaska, District of Columbia, Hawaii, Iowa, Maine, Massachusetts, Michigan, Minnesota, New Jersey, New Mexico, New York, North Dakota, Puerto Rico, Rhode Island, Vermont, West Virginia, and Wisconsin.

*Sources:* D. B. Rottman and S. M. Strickland, *State Court Organization, 2004* (Washington, DC: Bureau of Justice Statistics, 2006); http://www.deathpenaltyinfo.org/states-and-without-death-penalty (accessed February 24, 2011).

**FIGURE 13.5** *Continued*

## Questioning by the Judge

*Voir dire* usually begins with the judge asking questions—for instance, dealing with potential jurors' familiarity with the case, attitudes toward one or the other party to the case, demographic information, and so on. In high-profile cases, prospective jurors are often asked to complete a questionnaire intended to divulge information that might lead to their disqualification or excusal. This is often done to guide the attorneys in their *voir dire* questioning. The Supreme Court has upheld this type of questioning, noting that it is perfectly acceptable for the judge to question jurors about their knowledge and opinions concerning the case (*Mu'Min v. Virginia*, 500 U.S. 415 [1991]).

Generally, the judge is not required to ask any questions, but the Supreme Court has held that in certain types of cases—notably, those dealing with racial prejudice and capital punishment—judges must ask specific questions. In *Ham v. South Carolina*, 409 U.S. 524 (1973), the Court noted that questions about racial prejudice must be asked if racial issues are closely tied to the criminal conduct at issue. *Ham* was a case in which an African American defendant was tried for marijuana possession. The defendant claimed that because he was a well-known civil rights activist, the police had framed him on the narcotics charge. The Supreme Court stated that the general introductory questions asked by the judge were insufficient and that special attention should have been given to the race issue.

In another case, *Ristaino v. Ross*, 424 U.S. 589 (1976), a black defendant was convicted of a violent crime committed against a white security guard. The trial judge denied the defendant's request that specific questions about racial prejudice be asked of potential jurors. Instead, the judge just asked basic questions about *general* prejudice, not any directed at the facts of the case in question. Surprisingly, the Supreme Court upheld the trial judge's decision. This decision seems contradictory to *Ham*, but the Court noted in *Ristaino* that racial issues did not permeate the case. Instead, the fact that the defendant was black and the victim was white was secondary to the question of guilt.

The Supreme Court has also considered whether judges should ask detailed questions of potential jurors who serve on *death-qualified juries*—that is, juries that may recommend a death sentence.[1] The Court has actually been more emphatic with regard to death penalty cases than with those involving racial issues. It has stated that the judge *must*, at the request of either party, and only in cases in which capital punishment is a possible outcome, ask specific questions of jurors so as to assess their attitudes toward capital punishment. This rule was announced in *Morgan v. Illinois*, 504 U.S. 719 (1992). There, the Court held that defendants in capital cases may require potential jurors to state whether they would automatically impose the death penalty on conviction.

More recently, the Court held that appellate courts "owe deference to the trial court, which is in a superior position to determine the demeanor and qualifications of a potential juror" (*Uttecht v. Brown*, 551 U.S. 1 [2007]). This means that trial judges are in the best position to determine whether certain potential jurors should be excused because of reservations concerning capital punishment.

In summary, there are few constitutional restrictions on judges' questioning of potential jurors. With the exceptions of capital cases and those in which racial and ethnic matters permeate the trial, judges are under no obligation to ask questions of potential jurors. By the same token, judges are given considerable latitude in terms of asking almost any questions they desire. Detailed questions, however, are mostly asked by the attorneys in the case.

---

[1]A *death-qualified jury* is one in which each juror is at least open to the idea of sentencing someone to death. Death-qualified jurors are selected after being asked questions about whether they support the death penalty and would hand down a sentence of death, if the need arose.

## Challenges for Cause

The prosecution and defense are given unlimited opportunities to make **challenges for cause**. Potential jurors may be excluded for a number of reasons, some of which even have statutory origins. For example, if a member of the jury panel is related to the defendant, a challenge for cause will almost certainly succeed. Also, if the potential juror served on a past jury in a case dealing with a similar crime, a challenge for cause will probably succeed. If a potential juror stands to benefit financially from the outcome of the case, he or she will probably be excused based on a challenge for cause. While the list goes on, only two challenges have been considered by the Supreme Court: (1) those based on bias and (2) those based on attitudes toward capital punishment.

### Challenges Based on Bias.

Generally, if a juror is unable or unwilling to hear the case fairly and impartially, he or she may be excluded in a challenge for cause. However, as Supreme Court precedent seems to indicate, challenges for cause based on alleged bias rarely succeed. That is, in situations in which a person *appears* biased but does not state anything to this effect, it is difficult to succeed with a challenge for cause.

In fact, there is only one case in which the Supreme Court sanctioned exclusion of a potential juror because of alleged bias. In *Leonard v. United States*, 378 U.S. 544 (1964), the Court held that jury panel members who had heard the guilty verdict at the defendant's previous trial should have been excluded from serving on the jury in the present trial. The Court believed that the previous verdict may have influenced jurors in the second trial.

*Leonard* stands alone, however, in upholding a challenge based on bias. In *Dennis v. United States*, 339 U.S. 162 (1950), the Court required a showing of *actual* bias, not *alleged* bias. In that case, the defendant claimed that his conviction on contempt charges for failure to appear before the Committee on Un-American Activities was tainted because the jury consisted mostly of federal employees, who were all subject to discharge if they were not loyal to the government. The Court disagreed with Dennis's argument, stating that "[p] reservation of the opportunity to prove actual bias is a guarantee of a defendant's right to an impartial jury."

In a more recent case, *Smith v. Phillips*, 455 U.S. 209 (1982), the Court held once again that *actual* bias must be shown for a challenge for cause to succeed. In that case, the Court did not infer bias from the fact that a potential juror had been seeking employment from the prosecutor's office. However, this decision and *Leonard* should not be construed to suggest that actual bias must *always* be shown rather than alleged bias. Alleged, or implied, bias may be sufficient in certain limited circumstances for exclusion of a potential juror based on a challenge for cause.

*Smith v. Phillips*
*(455 U.S. 209 [1982])*

### Challenges in Death Penalty Cases.

Defendants in capital trials have the right to exclude jurors who have certain preconceived ideas about the death penalty. In *Witherspoon v. Illinois*, 391 U.S. 510 (1968), the Court considered the constitutionality of a statute that provided for exclusion of all potential jurors who "expressed scruples" against the death penalty. The Court held that a death sentence returned from such a jury would be unconstitutional because the jury resulting from the statute would be "organized to return a verdict of death." Importantly, in Witherspoon, it was only the defendant's death sentence that was invalidated, not his conviction. Also, note that nothing prohibits a prosecutor from excluding a juror who would *never* return a verdict of death.

*Witherspoon v. Illinois*
*(391 U.S. 510 [1968])*

In short, successful challenges for cause in death penalty cases usually fall into two categories. If the defendant can show that a potential juror is predisposed to return a verdict of death, such a juror will probably be excluded. Similarly, if the prosecution can show that a potential juror is almost certain to oppose capital punishment, that juror will probably be excluded, as well.

## Peremptory Challenges

**Peremptory challenges** call for removal of potential jurors *without* any reason. A peremptory challenge may be thought of as a fallback measure. If, say, the defense fails with a challenge for cause to exclude a potential juror who it believes will be biased against the defendant, a peremptory challenge can be used without making any kind of argument. As the Supreme Court stated in *Swain v. Alabama*, 380 U.S. 202 (1965), the peremptory challenge "is often exercised upon the 'sudden impressions and unaccountable prejudices we are apt to conceive upon the bare looks and gestures of another,' upon a juror's 'habits and associations,' or upon the feeling that the 'bare questioning [of a juror's] indifference may sometimes provoke a resentment'."

Because peremptory challenges need not be predicated on any type of argument, there are not many Supreme Court cases dealing with them. Of those that do, most have involved attempted exclusion based on race or ethnicity.

### Challenges by the Prosecution.

Generally, if the prosecution exercises a *challenge for cause* arguing that a person's race or ethnicity will cause him or her to be biased, that challenge will never succeed. But what if a *peremptory challenge* is used to exclude a juror based on race or ethnicity? This question was addressed in *Swain v. Alabama*, cited earlier. In that case, the defendant argued that the prosecutor excluded all minority jurors through peremptory challenges and, as such, violated the equal protection clause of the Fourteenth Amendment. The Court rejected this argument, as follows:

> [The peremptory challenge] is often exercised upon the "sudden impressions and unaccountable prejudices we are apt to conceive upon the bare looks and gestures of another," . . . upon a juror's "habits and associations," . . . or upon the feeling that "the bare questioning [a juror's] indifference may sometimes provoke a resentment." . . . It is no less frequently exercised on grounds normally thought irrelevant to legal proceedings or official action, namely, the race, religion, nationality, occupation or affiliations of people summoned for jury duty. For the question a prosecutor or defense counsel must decide is not whether a juror of a particular race or nationality is in fact partial, but whether one from a different group is less likely to be.

---

**DECISION-MAKING EXERCISE 13.9**

### STRONG OPINIONS ON THE DEATH PENALTY

Assume that during *voir dire*, the following exchange takes place between a defense attorney and a potential juror:

**Defense Attorney:** Do you have any reservations against the death penalty?

**Potential Juror:** No, of course not. I firmly support capital punishment. I think we should execute all criminals.

**Defense Attorney:** Do you think you can set aside your personal convictions for the purposes of this trial and make an objective decision based on the evidence?

**Potential Juror:** I suppose so. I think I could probably keep an open mind.

Now, assume that the defense attorney seeks to exercise one of her challenges for cause and asks the judge to exclude this juror. The judge denies the request. Assuming that the remaining jurors are not as opinionated, do you think the resulting jury will conform to the Sixth Amendment requirements discussed thus far?

The Court continued:

Hence veniremen are not always judged solely as individuals for the purpose of exercising peremptory challenges. Rather they are challenged in light of the limited knowledge counsel has of them, which may include their group affiliations, in the context of the case to be tried.

Had the prosecutor in this case sought to exclude minorities from all juries and had this come to light, a successful equal protection challenge probably could have been mounted.

Several years after *Swain*, the Supreme Court revisited the issue of using peremptory challenges for excluding racial and ethnic minorities. In *Batson v. Kentucky*, 476 U.S. 79 (1986), the Court decided that prosecutors can be called on to explain their use of peremptory challenges to exclude minorities, but only if the defense shows that the challenges were used for this purpose. This showing requires that the people excluded through the peremptory challenges constitute a distinct group, that these people were excluded by the prosecution through the use of peremptory challenges, and that "these facts and any other relevant circumstances raise an inference that the prosecutor used [peremptories] to exclude the veniremen from the petit jury on account of their race" (see also *Johnson v. California*, 125 S.Ct. 2410 [2005], *Miller El v. Dretke*, 125 S.Ct. 2317 [2005], and *Snyder v. Louisiana*, 554 U.S. 472 [2008]).

*Batson v. Kentucky* (476 U.S. 79 [1986])

If the defense makes the showing, then the prosecutor will be required to explain his or her reasons for excluding jurors based on race and ethnicity. However, this explanation does not need to be as convincing as one that would accompany a challenge for cause. It simply needs to be what the Court calls *race neutral*.

What is a race-neutral explanation? In *Hernandez v. New York*, 500 U.S. 352 (1991), the prosecutor sought to use peremptory challenges to exclude four potential jurors of Hispanic descent. They were the only three people on the panel with apparent Hispanic origins. The prosecutor argued that the jurors were excluded for two reasons: (1) that two of the panel members were involved in criminal activity and (2) that the other two "looked away" from him during questioning. The Court declared that this explanation was race neutral. Had the prosecution argued that the excluded jurors would likely decide a case in a certain way, given their Hispanic descent, the Court would have decided differently. Thus, a race-neutral argument is one that really has nothing to do with race or ethnicity.

To summarize, peremptory challenges used to exclude racial and ethnic minorities are constitutionally valid only when (1) the prosecutor offers a race-neutral explanation for doing so and (2) the judge believes the reason is genuine. These two requirements only matter, however, if the defendant raises the argument that race or ethnicity was a

## DECISION-MAKING EXERCISE 13.10

### APPROPRIATE USE OF THE PEREMPTORY CHALLENGE

An African American defendant, who was charged in a state trial court with robbery, objected to the prosecutor's use of peremptory challenges to excuse two black men from the jury panel. The prosecutor explained that he excused the first juror because the juror had long unkempt hair, a mustache, and a beard. The prosecutor then said that he excluded the second juror because the juror had a mustache and a beard. The trial court overruled the defendant's objection, impaneled the jury, and convicted the defendant of robbery. How should the appellate court decide?

motivating factor behind the prosecutor's use of peremptory challenges. In other words, the defense has the initial burden of showing racial or ethnic bias in the peremptory challenge stage. These guidelines apply not only to peremptory exclusion of racial and ethnic minorities (see *Powers v. Ohio*, 499 U.S. 400 [1991]; *Holland v. Illinois*, 493 U.S. 474 [1990]; *J.E.B. v. Alabama*, 511 U.S. 127 [1994]).

**Challenges by the Defense.** The defense also cannot exclude potential jurors through peremptory challenges based on race and ethnicity. For example, in *Georgia v. McCollum*, 502 U.S. 1056 (1992), the Court refused to sanction the exclusion of black panel members in the trial of white defendants charged with assaulting black individuals. At the same time, though, the defense cannot be forced to use a peremptory challenge to excuse a juror he or she argues should have been excused for cause.

*Gray v. Mississippi*
*(481 U.S. 648 [1987])*

Many Supreme Court cases concerning peremptory challenges by the defense have revolved around the question of how many, if any, peremptory challenges should be constitutionally permissible. The Court stated in *Gray v. Mississippi*, 481 U.S. 648 (1987), that peremptory challenges are not constitutionally guaranteed. And in *Stilson v. United States*, 250 U.S. 583 (1919), the Court held that in trials of codefendants, the number of peremptories should be reduced to the number each defendant would have if tried separately. Other cases suggest that the defense can be required to exercise its peremptory challenges before the government does (*Pointer v. United States*, 151 U.S. 396 [1894]) and that the defense can be required to exclude, through use of its peremptory challenges, jurors that the judge should have excused for cause (*Ross v. Oklahoma*, 487 U.S. 81 [1988]).

What if the court mistakenly denies a defense counsel request to exercise a peremptory challenge? This issue arose in *Rivera v. Illinois*, 556 U.S. ___ (2009). In that case, the Court held that the due process clause does not require automatic reversal of a conviction because the trial court erred in denying the defendant's right to exercise a peremptory challenge.

## When Impartial Jurors Cannot Be Found

It is sometimes exceedingly difficult to find impartial jurors. This is especially true in cases involving high-profile defendants that receive substantial media coverage. In this era of readily accessible news and information, the details of any particular case can quickly sweep across the whole country and be read by anyone with a television or internet connection.

If prospective jurors are influenced by media coverage, the defense may file a motion for change of venue, which permits the trial to be carried out elsewhere. Not many Supreme Court cases have dealt with change of venue questions, but in *Skilling v. United States*, 561 U.S. ___ (2010), the Court considered this issue. The defendant, Jeffrey Skilling, was a high-level executive of the now-defunct Enron energy corporation. He was charged with fraudulent financial manipulations that destroyed the company. He argued that an impartial jury could not be found in Houston, the location of the company, because thousands of Enron's employees and family members lived in the area. More than two-thirds of prospective jurors either knew victims of the company's failure or were victims themselves. The Supreme Court did not directly address the question of whether a change of venue should have been granted (Skilling was convicted in a federal district court in Houston and his conviction was upheld by the U.S. Court of Appeals for the Fifth Circuit), but it did infer that the defendant's argument was without merit because he was acquitted on nine counts in the indictment, suggesting impartiality on the jury's part. Also, 11 of the jurors in the trial had no connection to Enron.

## When Judges Preempt Juries

Recently, the Supreme Court gave some attention to what the jury must consider during its deliberations—and to what extent judges can preempt juries. In *Blakely v. Washington*, 542 U.S. 296 (2004), a man was convicted of kidnapping his estranged wife. After the jury returned its verdict, the judge decided that the man acted with "deliberate cruelty" and he handed down a harsher sentence than would have otherwise been authorized had he not identified such aggravating factors. The Supreme Court declared that the defendant's right to a jury trial was violated because the facts supporting the judge's finding of "deliberate cruelty" were not admitted by the accused *or* found by a jury. In other words, the judge could not preempt the jury's fact-finding role (see also *United States v. Booker*, 543 U.S. 220 [2005]).

---

# Summary

## 1. Summarize the right to a speedy trial.

The defendant has three important rights at trial: (1) the right to a speedy trial, (2) the right to an impartial judge, and (3) the right to an impartial jury. The first and third rights have origins in the Sixth Amendment. However, the right to an impartial judge does not—it is a right created by the Supreme Court, in much the same way the exclusionary rule is a judicial creation.

The right to a speedy trial applies once a person has been accused of a crime. If the defendant is charged, let go, and then charged again, the right does not apply until the second set of charges has been filed. Even if the defendant does not know he or she has been accused of or charged with a crime, the right to speedy trial can apply. This right sometimes extends beyond the Sixth Amendment and, according to the Supreme Court, can have a due process component.

Four criteria are used to determine when the right to a speedy trial has been *violated*: (1) too much delay between accusation and trial, (2) intentional delay, (3) whether the defendant asserts the right to a speedy trial, and (4) whether the delay is prejudicial. No criterion by itself is necessarily enough for the right to be violated, however. If, for instance, the delay is too long, intentional, prejudicial, and accompanied by the defendant's demand for a speedy trial, the right will almost certainly be violated. The consequence of violating the right to a speedy trial is dismissal of charges.

## 2. Explain the right to an impartial judge.

The defendant also enjoys the right to trial by an impartial judge. A judge cannot be considered impartial if he or she has a pecuniary interest in the outcome of a case. Usually, judges will remove themselves if they believe they cannot be impartial, but some jurisdictions permit the peremptory removal of judges. This allows counsel to remove one judge and request a second one. This method is extreme, however.

## 3. Summarize the right to a jury trial.

Finally, the defendant enjoys the right to trial by an impartial jury. However, the Supreme Court has held that this right applies only to criminal proceedings in which the possible punishment exceeds six months' detention. Jury size and voting requirements vary by jurisdiction, but as a general rule, the smaller the jury, the more unanimous the verdict must be.

Like many constitutional rights, the right to a jury trial can be waived, in which case the defendant opts for a bench trial.

## 4. Outline the jury selection process.

Jury selection occurs in three stages. First, a list of potential jurors, known as the jury list, is compiled. From that list, potential jurors are selected for jury service. Those selected for jury service are part of a jury panel. From the jury panel, some people are selected and required to go to a courtroom, where *voir dire* commences. *Voir dire* begins with the judge asking questions, some of which he or she is required to ask. Next, the attorneys on both sides will exercise their peremptory challenges and challenges for cause. The former are almost unrestricted but limited in number. The latter must be argued before the judge and are not limited in number.

It is important to understand that the jury list and panel must be representative of the community at large, but not the final jury. The only way for a defendant to succeed in arguing that the jury itself is not representative of the community is if he or she can show that the prosecution used its peremptory challenges to exclude individuals from distinctive groups and engages in this practice during the *voir dire* process for *all* juries. If the prosecution uses its peremptory challenges to occasionally excuse a juror based on race or ethnicity, the Sixth Amendment will not be violated. Finally, judges cannot preempt the jury's role.

## Key Terms

accusation rule *376*
challenges for cause *395*
distinctive group *390*
impartial judge *382*
impartial jury *383*

jury list *388*
jury panel *388*
noncriminal proceeding rule *384*
peremptory challenges *396*
six-month imprisonment rule *384*

speedy trial *376*
systematic exclusion *390*
*voir dire 391*

## Key Cases

### Speedy Trial

- *United States v. Marion*, 404 U.S. 307 (1971)
- *United States v. Loud Hawk*, 474 U.S. 302 (1986)
- *Doggett v. United States*, 505 U.S. 647 (1992)
- *United States v. Lovasco*, 431 U.S. 783 (1977)
- *Barker v. Wingo*, 407 U.S. 514 (1972)
- *Strunk v. United States*, 412 U.S. 434 (1973)

### Impartial Judge

- *Tumey v. Ohio*, 273 U.S. 510 (1927)
- *Ward v. Monroeville*, 409 U.S. 57 (1972)

### Impartial Jury

- *McKeiver v. Pennsylvania*, 403 U.S. 528 (1971)
- *Baldwin v. New York*, 399 U.S. 66 (1970)
- *Johnson v. Louisiana*, 406 U.S. 356 (1972)
- *Duren v. Missouri*, 439 U.S. 357 (1979)
- *Smith v. Phillips*, 455 U.S. 209 (1982)
- *Witherspoon v. Illinois*, 391 U.S. 510 (1968)
- *Batson v. Kentucky*, 476 U.S. 79 (1986)
- *Gray v. Mississippi*, 481 U.S. 648 (1987)

# Further Exploration

1. After years of studying jury decision making, researchers have concluded that "decisions are based on past experience in the form of scripts, schemas, stereotypes, and other cognitive mechanisms as well as personal beliefs and values about what is right, wrong, and fair."[2] What are your reactions to this conclusion? Read the cited article for more details.

2. In the event a jury becomes hopelessly deadlocked during its deliberations, a court may give the jury a so-called "*Allen* charge," after the Supreme Court's decision in *Allen v. United States*, 164 U.S. 492 (1896). The text of the "*Allen* charge" may read like this:

   You have informed the Court of your inability to reach a verdict in this case.

   At the outset, the Court wishes you to know that although you have a duty to reach a verdict, if that is not possible, the Court has neither the power nor the desire to compel agreement upon a verdict.

   The purpose of these remarks is to point out to you the importance and the desirability of reaching a verdict in this case, provided, however, that you as individual jurors can do so without surrendering or sacrificing your conscientious scruples or personal convictions.

   You will recall that upon assuming your duties in this case each of you took an oath. The oath places upon each of you as individuals the responsibility of arriving at a true verdict upon the basis of your opinion and not merely upon acquiescence in the conclusions of your fellow jurors.

   However, it by no means follows that opinions may not be changed by conference in the jury room. The very object of the jury system is to reach a verdict by a comparison of views and by consideration of the proofs with your fellow jurors.

   During your deliberations you should be open-minded and consider the issues with proper deference to and respect for the opinions of each other and you should not hesitate to re-examine your own views in the light of such discussions.

   You should consider also that this case must at some time be terminated; that you are selected in the same manner and from the same source from which any future jury must be selected; that there is no reason to suppose that the case will ever be submitted to twelve persons more intelligent, more impartial or more competent to decide it, or that more or clearer evidence will ever be produced on one side or the other.

   You may retire now, taking as much time as is necessary for further deliberations upon the issues submitted to you for determination. (http://www.courtswv.gov/supreme-court/docs/fall2005/32693.htm, accessed May 16, 2013).

   Could a set of judge's instructions like this be construed as coercive, especially insofar as they may be interpreted as pressure from a judge to reach a unanimous verdict? Consider the Eighth Circuit Court of Appeals' decision in *United States v. Ybarra*, No. 08-3137 (Eighth Cir. 2009).

3. What factors affect how long a jury takes to deliberate? Read the article "Factors Affecting the Length of Time a Jury Deliberates: Case Characteristics and Jury Composition" in the *Review of Law and Economics* (Volume 5, Issue 1, Pages 555–78). What factor is most important and why?

4. Mark Twain once lamented that the jury system "puts a ban upon intelligence and honesty, and a premium upon ignorance, stupidity, and perjury."[3] He said, "I desire to tamper with jury law. I wish to so alter it as to put a premium on intelligence and character, and close the jury box against idiots, blacklegs, and people who do not read newspapers."[4] Do you agree or disagree with his statements? Why or why not? Interestingly, one study concluded that "jurors that are able to serve on lengthier trials are more likely to be unemployed or retired, female, or unmarried and are less likely to have a college education."[5] How does this affect the quality of the jury system in the United States? Could it be time for paid professional jurors?

---

[2]D. J. Devine, L. D. Clayton, B. B. Dunford, R. Seying, and J. Pryce, "Jury Decision Making: 45 Years of Empirical Research on Deliberating Groups," *Psychology, Public Policy, and the Law* 7(2001): 622–725, p. 700.

[3]Cited in R. N. Jonakait, *The American Jury System* (New Haven, CT: Yale University Press, 2003), pp. 57–58.

[4]Ibid.

[5]D. G. Smith, "Structural and Functional Aspects of the Jury: Comparative Analysis and Proposals for Reform," *Alabama Law Review* 48(1997): 491.

5. Could jurors become victims in their own right while performing their civic duty? Read the article here before answering the question: http://tinyurl.com/ahw9fqz (accessed May 16, 2013).

6. Read these facts from *State v. Gonzales*, 808 P.2d 40 (1991):

Defendant and a codefendant, Victor Cordova, were tried jointly. Jury selection in this case took two days. On the first day, thirty-seven potential jurors were called. The trial court allowed each defendant four peremptory challenges and the state five. On this first day of jury selection, each defendant exercised all of his peremptory challenges, and the state exercised three of its five available challenges. All three of those challenges were used to remove Hispanic men from the jury. Ten of the necessary twelve jurors were selected from this venire.

The next day an additional twenty-four jurors were called. The trial court again allowed each defendant four peremptory challenges and the state five. The peremptory challenges allowed on the second day could only be used on the group of jurors that had been called for that day. On this second day, the state and each of the defendants exercised all of their peremptory challenges. All five of the state's peremptory challenges were used to remove Hispanic men from the jury.

The composition of the jury that was selected by this process was as follows. Ethnically, the jury consisted of four Hispanics, one Native American, and seven Anglos. In terms of gender, the jury was composed of eleven women and one man.

Should the defendants prevail on a claim challenging the composition of this jury?

# Review Questions

1. Explain when the right to a speedy trial applies.

2. What criteria are used to determine when the right to a speedy trial has been violated?

3. Summarize the consequences of violating the accused's right to a speedy trial.

4. Briefly outline important provisions of the federal Speedy Trial Act, including the consequences of violating it.

5. Under what circumstances could a judge be considered *not* impartial (biased)? Cite relevant cases.

6. What methods are available for removing a judge who cannot be considered impartial?

7. When does the right to a jury trial apply?

8. Explain the jury size and voting requirements in your state.

9. Can the right to a jury trial be waived? If so, what are the requirements for doing so?

10. Identify the methods used for creating a jury list.

11. What are the three stages of jury selection?

12. What are the requirements for a successful fair cross-section challenge of a jury panel?

13. Summarize the *voir dire* process.

14. What questions has the Supreme Court required judges to ask during *voir dire*?

15. Under what circumstances has the Supreme Court imposed restrictions on the use of peremptory challenges?

# Web Links and Exercises

1. Speedy Trial Act of 1974: What do the federal courts require with respect to the Sixth Amendment's speedy trial provision?

Suggested URL: http://www4.law.cornell.edu/uscode/uscode18/usc_sup_01_18_10_II_20_208.html (accessed May 16, 2013).

2. Code of Conduct for United States Judges: read more about the canons introduced in Figure 13.2.

URL: http://www.uscourts.gov/rulesandpolicies/CodesOfConduct.aspx (accessed May 16, 2013).

3. Origins of the American Jury: Why do we rely on trial by jury in this country, apart from what the Constitution requires?

Suggested URL: http://www.crfc.org/americanjury/origins.html (accessed May 16, 2013).

4. Is there a "CSI Effect?" There is concern that jurors expect the same evidence presented in popular television programs like *CSI: Crime Scene Investigation*. Are such concerns merited?

URL: http://www.ncjrs.gov/pdffiles1/nij/221501.pdf (accessed May 16, 2013).

5. Jury Nullification: read about the controversial practice of jury nullification.

Suggested URL: http://www.law.umkc.edu/faculty/projects/ftrials/zenger/nullification.html (accessed May 16, 2013).

# 14 More Rights at Trial

## LEARNING OBJECTIVES

When you complete this chapter, you should be able to:

**1** *Summarize the right to a public trial.*

**2** *Summarize the right to confrontation.*

**3** *Summarize the right to compulsory process.*

**4** *Explain the concept of double jeopardy.*

**5** *Outline the classifications and origins of the entrapment defense.*

## OUTLINE

# Introduction: More Protections for the Accused

In addition to guaranteeing the right to counsel, the Sixth Amendment provides that "[i]n all criminal prosecutions, the accused shall enjoy the right to . . . [a] public trial[,] to be confronted with the witnesses against him [and] to have compulsory process for obtaining witnesses in his favor." These rights are intended to assist the accused in mounting an effective defense. Without them, a criminal prosecution would be largely one-sided; that is, it would favor the prosecution.

In addition to the rights to a public trial, confrontation, and compulsory process, criminal defendants in the United States also enjoy other important rights at trial. One such right, known as protection from *double jeopardy*, is found in the Fifth Amendment: "[N]or shall any person be subject for the same offence to be twice put in jeopardy of life or limb." This means that an accused person cannot be convicted of or punished for the same offense twice. Finally, a defendant can assert the well-known *entrapment defense*. Protection from entrapment is not a constitutional right, but is worthy of discussion because of its close connection with criminal procedure—namely, police conduct.

# ► The Right to a Public Trial

*In re Oliver*
*(333 U.S. 257 [1948])*

In *In re Oliver*, 333 U.S. 257 (1948), the Supreme Court elaborated on the purpose of a **public trial**—one that is open to the public. The Court stated, "The knowledge that every criminal trial is subject to contemporaneous review in the forum of public opinion is an effective restraint on possible abuse of power. . . . Without publicity, all other checks are insufficient; in comparison of publicity, all other checks are of small account." Furthermore, "the presence of interested spectators may keep [the defendant's] triers keenly alive to a sense of their responsibility and to the importance of their functions."

*Oliver* dealt expressly with criminal trials, but the Supreme Court has held that openness also applies to other hearings. For example, suppression hearings should be open to the public (*Waller v. Georgia*, 467 U.S. 39 [1984]), as should *voir dire* (*Presley v. Georgia*, No. 09-5270 [2010]). By extension, most other hearings (with the exception of grand jury proceedings, which are traditionally carried out in secret) should be considered public, as well.

## When the Right May Not Apply

Most trials are open to the public, but occasionally they are not. Indeed, the defendant, whose interests are frequently served by openness, may want the trial closed to the public. This could be in an effort to minimize negative publicity, especially when the trial is for a heinous crime. In this way, the defendant's Sixth Amendment rights can be waived, just like many other constitutional rights can. The government can also seek to close a trial to the public. At present, the threat of terrorism is being used as justification by the government for the closure of certain judicial hearings.

### Government-Sought Closure

*Waller v. Georgia*
*(467 U.S. 39 [1984])*

In *Waller v. Georgia*, 467 U.S. 39 (1984), the Supreme Court limited the ability of the government to close proceedings to the public, and created a test for determining when closing proceedings is warranted. The government must show (1) that there is an overriding interest, such as protection of certain witnesses; (2) that the closure is no broader than absolutely necessary; and (3) that reasonable alternatives have been considered.

*Waller* dealt with the closure of a suppression hearing in which a video of people not yet indicted was played. The Court held that closure of the hearing was unconstitutional because the government did not identify "whose privacy interests might be infringed, how they would be infringed, what portions of the tape might infringe on them, and what portion of the evidence consisted of the tapes."

### Defense-Sought Closure

*Sheppard v. Maxwell*
*(384 U.S. 333 [1966])*

*Sheppard v. Maxwell*, 384 U.S. 333 (1966), illustrates the negative effects that publicity may have at trial. In that case, the courtroom was packed with members of the public and media for all nine weeks of the trial. This made it difficult for people to hear one another. The press also handled and took pictures of evidentiary exhibits. The Supreme Court reversed the defendant's conviction, citing the "carnival atmosphere" of the trial.[1]

In another case, *Estes v. Texas*, 381 U.S. 532 (1965), the Court also reversed the defendant's conviction, noting that the presence of television cameras distracted parties to the case in addition to the witnesses who gave testimony. This ruling does not provide a blanket prohibition of television cameras in courtrooms, however. In *Chandler v. Florida*, 449 U.S. 560 (1981), the Supreme Court upheld Florida's rule permitting the use of still photography

---

[1]While the defense in *Sheppard* did not directly seek closure of the trial, it did make requests for a continuance, a change of venue, and a mistrial.

and television cameras in court. Cameras are impermissible only if the defendant can show that "the media's coverage of his case—be it printed or broadcast—[compromises] the ability of the . . . jury . . . to adjudicate fairly."

# The First Amendment and Public Trials

The First Amendment guarantees freedom of speech and of the press. Thus, any effort to close a trial or pretrial hearing to the public—be it by the government or the defense—may cause the press to rally in opposition. The Supreme Court precedent suggests that unless the government or the defense can demonstrate that significant prejudice is likely to result from a public trial, closure of a trial is unlikely.

In *Gannett Co., Inc. v. DePasquale*, 443 U.S. 368 (1979), the Supreme Court held that the trial judge may, at the defendant's request, close a pretrial suppression hearing in an effort to avoid the "reasonable probability of prejudice." The Supreme Court sanctioned closure of this nature because it was at the defendant's request and because the media did not oppose closure.

In *Richmond Newspapers, Inc. v. Virginia*, 448 U.S. 555 (1980), however, the Court indicated that closure will seldom be allowed if the media asserts an interest in having access to the hearing. The defendant in *Richmond Newspapers* sought closure of his trial because he had been through four previous mistrials, one of which stemmed from a juror telling other jurors about press reports of the case. The Court rejected the defendant's argument, noting that "the right to attend criminal trials is implicit in the guarantees of the First Amendment; without the freedom to attend such trials, which people have exercised for centuries, important aspects of freedom of speech and of the press could be eviscerated."

In another case, *Globe Newspaper Co. v. Superior Court*, 457 U.S. 596 (1982), the Court noted that the First Amendment serves "to ensure that the individual citizen can effectively participate in and contribute to our republican system of self-government" and "fosters an appearance of fairness, thereby heightening public respect for the judicial process." Trial closures will therefore be rare.

## Dealing with Media Influence

The media can seemingly influence the fairness of a criminal trial in two ways: (1) by its pretrial coverage and/or (2) by being present in the courtroom, as just discussed. Several alternatives to closure are available and generally preferable. Each is aimed at ensuring a fair trial for the accused while maintaining as much openness as possible. The alternatives are:

- *voir dire* with special attention to pretrial publicity,
- a change of venue,
- jury sequestration,
- a gag order on the media, and
- a gag order on other parties.

**Voir Dire.**   As explained in Chapter 13, *voir dire* is the process by which jury members are selected from a panel of potential jurors. The judge can ask several questions, and the attorneys can exclude jurors for cause and by use of peremptory challenges. When media coverage of a crime is extensive and presumed to have influenced members of the jury panel, *voir dire* can be used to detect that bias.

In *Marshall v. United States*, 360 U.S. 310 (1959), the Supreme Court held that potential jurors who have learned from news coverage of a defendant's prior record are presumed to be prejudiced. Similarly, in *Irvin v. Dowd*, 366 U.S. 717 (1961), media coverage was so influential that the Court discounted jurors' statements about being willing to make impartial decisions. But in two later cases, *Murphy v. Florida*, 421 U.S. 794 (1975), and *Patton v. Yount*, 467 U.S. 1025 (1984), the Court indicated that unless a juror candidly admits bias due to pretrial publicity, a defendant's constitutional challenge to jury impartiality is unlikely to succeed. This point was echoed recently in *Skilling v. United States*, No. 08-1394 (2010), a case involving a former Enron executive who claimed that most prospective jurors were biased because of press coverage of Enron's actions. In that case, the Court held that a change of venue was not constitutionally required.

### Change of Venue.

Another method to address bias induced by press coverage is a **change of venue**. This involves moving the trial to a different jurisdiction where the jury pool is less likely to be influenced by the media coverage.

*Rideau v. Louisiana*
*(373 U.S. 723 [1963])*

In *Rideau v. Louisiana*, 373 U.S. 723 (1963), the Court overturned a defendant's death sentence because the trial court refused to grant the defendant's motion for a change of venue. In that case, Rideau's confession had been broadcast all over local television. The Court stated that "due process of law in this case required a trial before a jury drawn from a community of people who had not seen and heard Rideau's interview."

Of course, a change of venue is not a realistic option when pretrial publicity has influenced potential jurors in multiple jurisdictions. A change of venue rarely succeeds, then, in the trial of someone whose crime is well known over a wide geographical area.

### Jury Sequestration.

A third method of dealing with the influence of the press is **jury sequestration**. This method is mostly used to minimize the influence of press coverage *during* the trial. Sequestration is basically jury isolation—members are usually put up in a hotel and denied access to television and print media coverage of the trial. Sequestration is an extreme method, but necessary in certain cases. After all, judges' warnings to jury members to avoid media accounts while at home are probably naïve. The Supreme Court has recognized that jury sequestration is a valid option in certain extreme circumstances (see *Sheppard*, 384 U.S. 333).

### Media Gag Orders.

A **gag order** is a court order to keep the media quiet concerning a particular matter. In *Nebraska Press Ass'n v. Stuart*, 427 U.S. 539 (1976), the trial judge prohibited the media from reporting information regarding the defendant. While the Supreme Court disagreed in that case, it did indicate that a gag order would be permissible given "(a) the nature and extent of pretrial coverage; (b) whether other measures [such as changes of venue, continuances, *voir dire*, sequestration, or instructions to jury to ignore press coverage] would be likely to mitigate the effects of unrestrained pretrial publicity; and (c) how effectively a restraining order would operate to prevent the threatened danger."

*Nebraska Press Ass'n v. Stuart*
*(427 U.S. 539 [1976])*

### Other Gag Orders.

The courts have also experimented with gag orders on one or the other party in a criminal trial. This is an indirect method of reducing media coverage of a trial because it seeks to quiet the media's sources of information. This practice appears to have met with greater approval by the Supreme Court. In *Sheppard v. Maxwell*, for instance, the Court suggested that under certain circumstances, the judge has a constitutional obligation "to control the release of leads, information, and gossip to the press by police officers, witnesses and the counsel for both sides." For a gag order of this nature to succeed, it should be clear that the absence of a gag order presents a "clear and present danger" to the impartiality of the trial.

It is worth mentioning that professional codes of ethics prohibit attorneys from making certain types of statements to the public. For example, the *Annotated Model Rules of Professional Conduct* of the American Bar Association (ABA) prohibit lawyers from making "extrajudicial statements" that "will have a substantial likelihood of materially prejudicing an adjudicative proceeding." This includes statements as to "the character, credibility, reputation or criminal record of a party, suspect, . . . or witness, . . . the expected testimony of a party or witness, . . . [or the] . . . possibility of a plea of guilty, . . . the performance or results of any examination or test, [and] . . . any opinion as to . . . guilt or innocence."[2] The Supreme Court has even held that state bars can reprimand attorneys for making statements that cause "a substantial likelihood of material prejudice" to the case, apparently expanding on the relevant provisions of the ABA's *Annotated Model Rules of Professional Conduct* (see *Gentile v. Nevada State Bar*, 501 U.S. 1030 [1991]).

# ▶ The Right to Confrontation

The Sixth Amendment's provision that an accused person enjoys the right to be "confronted with the witnesses against him" is manifested in three ways. The first type of **confrontation** is to allow the defendant to appear at his or her own trial. In *Illinois v. Allen*, 397 U.S. 337 (1970), the Supreme Court expressly stated that "[o]ne of the most basic of rights guaranteed by the Confrontation Clause is the accused's right to be present in the courtroom at every state of his trial." The other two types of confrontation extended to the defendant are to require the live testimony of witnesses before the defendant and to permit him or her to challenge witnesses' statements in open court. See Figure 14.1 for a summary.

*Illinois v. Allen*
*(397 U.S. 337 [1970])*

---

[2]American Bar Association, *Annotated Model Rules of Professional Conduct* (Washington, DC: Center for Professional Responsibility, 2002), Rule 3.6[a][b].

## The Defendant's Right to Be Present

The defendant would be seriously hampered in his or her ability to confront adverse witnesses if he or she was not allowed to attend the trial. But allowing the defendant to be physically present in the courtroom may not be enough to satisfy the Sixth Amendment's strictures. For example, if the accused is not competent and is unable to understand what is taking place so as to be able to challenge the opposition, the Sixth Amendment may be violated. Some Supreme Court cases have addressed the requirement of physical confrontation, and some have addressed the defendants' mental competence as it pertains to confrontation. Before considering these types of cases, however, it might be helpful to refer to Figure 14.2, which presents Rule 43 of the *Federal Rules of Criminal Procedure*. It succinctly summarizes the discussion that follows.

### Physical Presence

The Supreme Court's opinion in *Illinois v. Allen* seems to suggest that the accused enjoys an unqualified right to **physical presence** in the proceedings, but nothing could be further from the truth. In the cases decided after *Allen*, the Court placed significant restrictions on when the defendant is permitted to be physically present. There are three key restrictions:

- physical presence is not required in noncritical proceedings,
- the right to physical presence may be waived, and
- physical presence may be impermissible due to the defendant's inappropriate conduct.

First, even though *Allen* spoke of the right to be present "at every stage of [the] trial," the Supreme Court changed course in *United States v. Gagnon*, 470 U.S. 522 (1985), and *Kentucky v. Stincer*, 479 U.S. 1028 (1987). In *Gagnon*, the defendant was denied physical presence at a meeting between a judge and juror, while in the latter, the defendant was not allowed to attend a pretrial determination of a child witness's competence. The Court sanctioned the trial court's actions in both cases. Part of the rationale was that both were noncritical stages of the trial process.

**Rule 43. Defendant's Presence**

**(a) When Required.**
Unless this rule, Rule 5, or Rule 10 provides otherwise, the defendant must be present at:

**1.** the initial appearance, the initial arraignment, and the plea;
**2.** every trial stage, including jury impanelment and the return of the verdict; and
**3.** sentencing.

**(b) When Not Required. A defendant need not be present under any of the following circumstances:**

**1.** *Organizational Defendant.*
The defendant is an organization represented by counsel who is present.

**2.** *Misdemeanor Offense.*
The offense is punishable by fine or by imprisonment for not more than one year, or both, and with the defendant's written consent, the court permits arraignment, plea, trial, and sentencing to occur in the defendant's absence.

**3.** *Conference or Hearing on a Legal Question.*
The proceeding involves only a conference or hearing on a question of law.

**4.** *Sentence Correction.*
The proceeding involves the correction or reduction of sentence under Rule 35 or 18 U.S.C. § 3582(c).

**(c) Waiving Continued Presence.**

**1.** *In General.*
A defendant who was initially present at trial, or who had pleaded guilty or nolo contendere, waives the right to be present under the following circumstances:

**A.** when the defendant is voluntarily absent after the trial has begun, regardless of whether the court informed the defendant of an obligation to remain during trial;
**B.** in a noncapital case, when the defendant is voluntarily absent during sentencing; or
**C.** when the court warns the defendant that it will remove the defendant from the courtroom for disruptive behavior, but the defendant persists in conduct that justifies removal from the courtroom.

**2.** *Waiver's Effect.*
If the defendant waives the right to be present, the trial may proceed to completion, including the verdict's return and sentencing, during the defendant's absence.

*Source: Federal Rules of Criminal Procedure, Rule 43.*

**FIGURE 14.2 Policy on Defendant's Presence**

Second, the defendant can waive his or her Sixth Amendment right to confrontation. Only the defendant can make this determination though. In *Taylor v. Illinois*, 484 U.S. 400 (1988), the Court held that the defense attorney cannot waive the defendant's right to be physically present without his or her consent.

*Taylor v. Illinois*
*(484 U.S. 400 [1988])*

The defendant can waive his or her right to be present through an express request (*Diaz v. United States*, 223 U.S. 442 [1912]) or by implying waiver. As an example of an implied waiver, in *Taylor v. United States*, 414 U.S. 17 (1973), the Court decided that the defendant's refusal to return to the courtroom after a lunch recess, even though it was not an intentional waiver, could have amounted to a violation of his Sixth Amendment right:

It is wholly incredible to suggest that [Taylor, the defendant,] . . . entertained any doubts about his right to be present at every stage of the trial. It seems equally incredible to us, as it did to the Court of appeals, "that a defendant who flees from a courtroom in the midst of a trial—where judge, jury, witnesses and lawyers are present and ready to continue—would not know that as a consequence the trial could continue in his absence."

Finally, the defendant may be prohibited from being physically present at his or her own trial for reasons related to the defendant's conduct. In *Illinois v. Allen*, for instance, the defendant was removed from his trial following repeated warnings by the judge to cease his disruptive behavior. The Supreme Court sanctioned the trial court judge's decision to exclude the defendant, holding that the right to be physically present can be waived if, after several warnings, the defendant acts "in a manner so disorderly, disruptive, and disrespectful of the court that his trial cannot be carried on with him in the courtroom." The Court also noted, however, that the defendant can reappear in the courtroom when he is "willing to conduct himself consistently with the decorum and respect inherent in the concept of courts and judicial proceedings."

## Mental Competence

Due process—and by implication, the right to confrontation—is violated when the defendant cannot understand what is happening to him or her in a criminal trial. In other words, the defendant must demonstrate **mental competence** in order to stand trial.

*Dusky v. United States*
*(362 U.S. 402 [1960])*

In *Dusky v. United States*, 362 U.S. 402 (1960), the Court set forth a test for determining whether a defendant is mentally competent to stand trial. The test assesses whether the defendant "has sufficient present ability to consult with his lawyer with a reasonable degree of rational understanding—and whether he has a rational as well as factual understanding of the proceedings against him." The burden of proving *incompetence* falls on the defendant (*Medina v. California*, 505 U.S. 437 [1992]).

It is important to understand that this test for competency is different from the insanity defense often discussed in criminal law texts. *Competency to stand trial*—the type of competency considered here—deals with the defendant's ability to understand what is happening at trial (as well as at pretrial hearings and other important proceedings). The

The right to confrontation provides that an accused person can appear at his or her own trial, face the live testimony of witnesses, and challenge witness testimony.

*insanity defense* concerns the defendant's competence at the time he or she committed the crime. The issue of the defendant's competency to stand trial is narrowly concerned with the defendant's ability to understand what is happening and communicate with counsel.

The defendant's competency is usually considered in a separate pretrial hearing. This was the rule announced in *Pate v. Robinson*, 383 U.S. 375 (1966), a case dealing with an Illinois trial judge's decision not to hold a hearing on the question of the defendant's mental condition, even though he had a long history of mental problems. The Supreme Court held that a hearing was necessary, noting that "[the Illinois court's] reasoning offers no justification for ignoring the uncontradicted testimony of Robinson's [the defendant's] history of pronounced irrational behavior. While Robinson's demeanor at trial might be relevant to the ultimate decision as to his [present] sanity, it cannot be relied upon to dispense with a hearing on that very issue."

If the defendant is declared incompetent to stand trial, he or she will be hospitalized until his or her competency is restored, if ever. However, in *Jackson v. Indiana*, 406 U.S. 715 (1972), the Supreme Court held that there are constitutional limitations on how long a defendant can be hospitalized for the purpose of restoring competency. That case dealt with a 27-year-old deaf-mute individual with the intellectual level of a preschooler, who was being hospitalized until the staff declared him sane. The Court concluded that it was likely the defendant's condition would *never* improve:

> We hold . . . that a person charged by a State with a criminal offense who is committed [to an institution] solely on account of his incapacity to proceed to trial cannot be held more than the reasonable period of time necessary to determine whether there is a substantial probability that he will attain that capacity in the foreseeable future. If it is determined that this is not the case, then the State must either institute the customary civil commitment proceeding that would be required to commit indefinitely any other citizen, or release the defendant.

## Drawbacks of Being Present

Although the Sixth Amendment, subject to some limitations, guarantees the right to be present at trial, the defendant's presence could in some cases be prejudicial or harmful to his or her case. First, if the defendant is present but exercises his or her Fifth Amendment rights by refusing to take the stand, the jury may conclude that he or she has something to hide. The Supreme Court has been so concerned with this possibility that it has prohibited the prosecution from calling attention to the defendant's refusal to testify (*Griffin v. California*, 380 U.S. 609 [1965]) and even required judges to advise jury members that no adverse inferences can be drawn from a defendant's refusal to testify (*Carter v. Kentucky*, 450 U.S. 288 [1981]).

---

### DECISION-MAKING EXERCISE 14.3

#### INDIGENCE AND THE RIGHT TO BE PRESENT

Adam Fish was a soldier in the U.S. Army and stationed in Arizona. He was arrested and charged with the sale of marijuana, in violation of state law. Prior to his trial on this charge, Fish was discharged from the army and voluntarily left Arizona for New York. When the trial date was set, Fish's court-appointed attorney requested that he return to Arizona. However, because Fish lacked the funds necessary to travel from New York to Arizona, he did not appear in Arizona on the date set for the trial. The trial proceeded without Fish's presence, and the jury returned a guilty verdict. After the verdict was rendered, Fish obtained the necessary travel funds and returned to Arizona in time for his sentencing. He was sentenced to not less than five or more than five-and-one-half years in prison. He is now appealing his conviction, claiming that his Sixth Amendment right to confrontation was violated. What should the court decide?

The defendant's appearance in the courtroom may also prejudice his or her case by reminding jurors about the crime. In *Estelle v. Williams*, 425 U.S. 501 (1976), the Supreme Court held that a state may not compel the defendant to wear jail attire in the courtroom. The Court concluded that a "constant reminder of the accused's condition implicit in such distinctive, identifiable attire may affect a juror's judgment." This decision was extended to the sentencing phase in *Deck v. Missouri* (544 U.S. 622 [2005]) when the Court held that defendants cannot be forced to wear leg irons during their capital sentencing hearings.

## The Defendant's Right to Live Testimony

*Mattox v. United States (156 U.S. 237 [1895])*

Confrontation also includes the defendant's right to **live testimony**. In general, this means the defendant enjoys the right to have witnesses *physically appear* in the courtroom to give their testimony, but this right has become qualified over the years. Over a century ago, the Supreme Court stated in *Mattox v. United States*, 156 U.S. 237 (1895), that the defendant's right to live testimony is "subject to exceptions, recognized long before the adoption of the Constitution." The Court stated further:

> Such exceptions were obviously intended to be respected. A technical adherence to the letter of a constitutional provision may occasionally be carried farther than is necessary to the just protection of the accused, and farther than the safety of the public will warrant. For instance, there could be nothing more directly contrary to the letter of the provision in question than the admission of dying declarations. They are rarely made in the presence of the accused; they are made without any opportunity for examination or cross-examination; nor is the witness brought face to face with the jury; yet from time immemorial they have been treated as competent testimony, and no one would have the hardihood at this day to question their admissibility. They are admitted not in conformity with any general rule regarding the admission of testimony, but as an exception to such rules, simply from the necessities of the case, and to prevent a manifest failure of justice.

There are three key situations in which witness testimony may be admitted at trial without the physical appearance of the witness. First, if the witness, also known as the *declarant*, is unavailable because he or she is dead, then an exception will be made. Similar exceptions are made when a witness is unavailable for other reasons, such as being in the hospital. Finally, a witness may not be required to give live testimony if his or her statements fall under one of the established hearsay exceptions, permitting introduction of those statements by a third party.

### Deceased Witness

In *Mattox*, the Supreme Court upheld the admissibility of a witness's past testimony from the defendant's first trial in the defendant's second trial because the witness died between the two trials. According to the Court, "To say that a criminal, after having once been convicted by the testimony of a certain witness, should go scot free simply because death has closed the mouth of that witness, would be carrying his constitutional protection to an unwarrantable extent." The Court also stated, in relevant part:

> The primary object of the [Confrontation Clause of the Sixth Amendment] was to prevent depositions or ex parte affidavits, such as were sometimes admitted in civil cases, being used against the prisoner in lieu of a personal examination and cross-examination of the witness in which the accused has an opportunity, not only of testing the recollection and sifting the conscience of the witness, but of compelling him to stand and face the jury in order that they may look at him, and judge by his demeanor upon the stand and the manner in which he gives his testimony whether he is worthy of belief.

## Unavailable Witness

The Supreme Court has held that an **unavailable witness**, for purposes of the Confrontation Clause, is one who permanently moves to another country (*Mancusi v. Stubbs*, 408 U.S. 204 [1972]), cannot be located after a careful search by the prosecution (*Ohio v. Roberts*, 448 U.S. 56 [1980]), or suffers from a lapse in memory (*California v. Green*, 399 U.S. 149 [1970]).

In *Motes v. United States*, 178 U.S. 458 (1900), the Court stated that it would violate the Sixth Amendment "to permit the deposition or statement of an absent witness . . . to be read at the final trial when it does not appear that the witness was absent by the suggestion, connivance, or procurement of the accused, but does appear that this absence was due to the negligence of the prosecution." In other words, if the prosecution fails to conduct a careful search for a certain witness and then claims that the witness is unavailable, then the defendant's right to live testimony will be violated.

*Motes v. United States (178 U.S. 458 [1900])*

In *Barber v. Page*, 390 U.S. 719 (1968), the Court considered whether statements by a witness who was not physically present at a preliminary hearing conformed to constitutional requirements, even though the witness was later found to be available and could have given testimony at the hearing. The Court stated that "a witness is not 'unavailable' for purposes of the exception to the confrontation requirement unless the prosecutorial authorities have made a good-faith effort to obtain his presence at trial."

In one interesting case, *Crawford v. Washington*, 541 U.S. 36 (2004), a wife did not testify at her husband's domestic violence trial because of Washington's marital privilege. Instead, the court admitted a tape-recorded statement to the effect that she was stabbed by her husband. The Supreme Court declared that the woman could not be considered unavailable and thus the defendant's right to confrontation was violated. It held in part that "[t]he Confrontation Clause commands that reliability be assessed in a particular manner: by testing in the crucible of cross-examination."

Contrast *Crawford v. Washington* with the Court's decision in *Davis v. Washington*, 547 U.S. 813 (2006). In that case, a recorded 911 call from a victim was introduced into evidence. Davis challenged the introduction of the recorded call, arguing that not being able to confront the caller violated the Sixth Amendment. The Supreme Court disagreed with his argument, holding that the confrontation clause does not apply to such statements. It went on to explain that " . . . statements are nontestimonial when made in the course of police interrogation under circumstances objectively indicating that the primary purpose of interrogation is to enable police assistance to meet an ongoing emergency." In other words, the Court held that 911 calls are not considered the same as testimony in court.

In a string of recent decisions, the Supreme Court has focused on the scope of the defendant's right to confront live witnesses:

- *Melendez-Diaz v. Massachusetts*, 557 U.S. ___ (2009). A state forensic analyst's laboratory report was testimonial and, as such, that the defendant should have been permitted to question its preparer.
- *Bullcoming v. New Mexico*, 564 U.S. ___ (2011). Confrontation was violated when prosecutors offered a crime lab report analyzing Bullcoming's blood sample and called the lab's supervisor rather than the technician who conducted the test. In other words, the

---

### DECISION-MAKING EXERCISE 14.4

#### AN UNAVAILABLE WITNESS

In the space of six months, the prosecution sent five subpoenas to a person it wished to call to testify at four separate trials. All five subpoenas were sent to the witness's residence, but the witness never appeared at trial. Can the witness be considered unavailable for confrontation purposes?

lab report could not be admitted without also calling the analyst to the witness stand for cross-examination.

- *Michigan v. Bryant*, 562 U.S. ___ (2011). A shooting victim informed police that Bryant had shot him. The victim died shortly thereafter, but the statement was introduced at trial through the testimony of the officer who heard it and used it to establish Bryant's guilt. The Court observed that the victim's statements were "not testimonial . . . because they had a 'primary purpose . . . to enable police assistance to meet an ongoing emergence.'"
- *Williams v. Illinois*, 567 U.S. ___ (2012). In a bench trial for rape, the defendant's right to confrontation was not violated when a state crime lab representative testified that the defendant's DNA profile produced by the state matched the DNA profile produced by an outside laboratory using vaginal swabs taken from the victim. The holding is distinguished from *Melendez-Diaz* and *Bullcoming* (see above) because in this case the outside laboratory's test results were not admitted into evidence. The Court held in part that "[a]n expert witness may voice an opinion based on facts concerning the events at issue even if the expert lacks first-hand knowledge of those facts."

## Hearsay and Exceptions to the Hearsay Rule

*Hearsay* is a statement made by a person *outside of court*, which is offered *in court* to prove the truth of the matter it asserts. It is often testimony given in court by someone who *heard* what someone outside of in court *said* (hence, the term *hearsay*). For example, John observed James rob the Franklin Convenience Store at gunpoint. After the incident, John told his friend Mary, "I saw James rob the Franklin Convenience Store." Mary did not observe the incident. At James' trial for armed robbery, John is unavailable to testify. The prosecution wishes to call Mary to testify that John told her that he saw James rob the store. Mary's testimony about what John said is hearsay because she is not testifying about what *she* observed, but about John's statement, out of court, of what *he* observed.

Under the rules of evidence, hearsay is generally not admissible in a criminal trial. It is regarded skeptically because if the declarant (the person who made the statements) is not available to be confronted by the defense, then there is no opportunity to question the truthfulness of his or her statements. The possibility also exists that the person communicating the declarant's statements may have misunderstood his or her intentions or forgotten exactly what he or she said.

Although hearsay is generally inadmissible, there are many **hearsay exceptions** under both state and federal rules of evidence which permit out-of-court statements made by declarants to be admitted at trial. On the surface, these exceptions seem to violate the defendant's right to confront live witnesses. But the Supreme Court, nevertheless, permits hearsay in limited circumstances. The rules of evidence regarding hearsay and its exceptions are exceedingly complex, and the reader is encouraged to consult an evidence textbook for a full review of specific exceptions to the hearsay rule. The following cases consider only two such exceptions.

*White v. Illinois*
*(502 U.S. 346 [1992])*

One pertinent case is *White v. Illinois*, 502 U.S. 346 (1992), which dealt with the admissibility of out-of-court statements made by a four-year-old girl. The prosecution argued that the statements should be admissible because two exceptions to the hearsay rule applied to her testimony. The first exception, for "spontaneous declarations" allows hearsay statements that are made in the "heat of the moment." The second exception allows hearsay statements that are made while an individual is seeking medical treatment from a doctor. The Court held that the Confrontation Clause was not violated in this instance:

> A statement that has been offered in a moment of excitement—without the opportunity to reflect on the consequences of one's exclamation—may justifiably carry more weight with a trier of fact than a similar statement made in the course of procuring medical services, where the declarant knows that a false statement may cause misdiagnosis or mistreatment, carries special guarantees of credibility that a trier of fact may not think replicated by courtroom testimony.

▼

In another case, *United States v. Inadi*, 475 U.S. 387 (1986), the Court decided on the admissibility of out-of-court statements from a co-conspirator. The Court admitted the statements, claiming that they "derive much of their value from the fact that they are made in a context very different from trial, and therefore are usually irreplaceable as substantive evidence." Stated differently, the Court thought that the out-of-court statements made by one co-conspirator to another should be admitted at trial because it would be difficult to replicate the conversation in a courtroom.

As indicated in Figure 14.3, numerous other hearsay exceptions exist, as well. Indeed, even if a relevant exception does not exist, a court may still admit the hearsay. Generally, if

---

**Present sense impression.** A statement describing or explaining an event or condition made while the declarant was perceiving the event or condition, or immediately thereafter.

**Excited utterance.** A statement relating to a startling event or condition made while the declarant was under the stress of excitement caused by the event or condition.

**Then existing mental, emotional, or physical condition.** A statement of the declarant's then existing state of mind, emotion, sensation, or physical condition (such as intent, plan, motive, design, mental feeling, pain, and bodily health), but not including a statement of memory or belief to prove the fact remembered or believed unless it relates to the execution, revocation, identification, or terms of declarant's will.

**Statements for purposes of medical diagnosis or treatment.** Statements made for purposes of medical diagnosis or treatment and describing medical history, or past or present symptoms, pain, or sensations, or the inception or general character of the cause or external source thereof insofar as reasonably pertinent to diagnosis or treatment.

**Recorded recollection.** A memorandum or record concerning a matter about which a witness once had knowledge but now has insufficient recollection to enable the witness to testify fully and accurately, shown to have been made or adopted by the witness when the matter was fresh in the witness's memory and to reflect that knowledge correctly. If admitted, the memorandum or record may be read into evidence but may not itself be received as an exhibit unless offered by an adverse party.

**Records of regularly conducted activity.** A memorandum, report, record, or data compilation, in any form, of acts, events, conditions, opinions, or diagnoses, made at or near the time by, or from information transmitted by, a person with knowledge, if kept in the course of a regularly conducted business activity, and if it was the regular practice of that business activity to make the memorandum, report, record or data compilation, all as shown by the testimony of the custodian or other qualified witness, or by certification that complies with Rule 902(11), Rule 902(12), or a statute permitting certification, unless the source of information or the method or circumstances of preparation indicate lack of trustworthiness. The term "business" as used in this paragraph includes business, institution, association, profession, occupation, and calling of every kind, whether or not conducted for profit.

**Public records and reports.** Records, reports, statements, or data compilations, in any form, of public offices or agencies, setting forth (A) the activities of the office or agency, or (B) matters observed pursuant to duty imposed by law as to which matters there was a duty to report, excluding, however, in criminal cases matters observed by police officers and other law enforcement personnel, or (C) in civil actions and proceedings and against the Government in criminal cases, factual findings resulting from an investigation made pursuant to authority granted by law, unless the sources of information or other circumstances indicate lack of trustworthiness.

**Records of vital statistics.** Records or data compilations, in any form, of births, fetal deaths, deaths, or marriages, if the report thereof was made to a public office pursuant to requirements of law.

**FIGURE 14.3 Common Hearsay Exceptions**

**Former testimony.** Testimony given as a witness at another hearing of the same or a different proceeding, or in a deposition taken in compliance with law in the course of the same or another proceeding, if the party against whom the testimony is now offered, or, in a civil action or proceeding, a predecessor in interest, had an opportunity and similar motive to develop the testimony by direct, cross, or redirect examination.

**Statement under belief of impending death.** In a prosecution for homicide or in a civil action or proceeding, a statement made by a declarant while believing that the declarant's death was imminent, concerning the cause or circumstances of what the declarant believed to be impending death.

**Statement against interest.** A statement which was at the time of its making so far contrary to the declarant's pecuniary or proprietary interest, or so far tended to subject the declarant to civil or criminal liability, or to render invalid a claim by the declarant against another, that a reasonable person in the declarant's position would not have made the statement unless believing it to be true. A statement tending to expose the declarant to criminal liability and offered to exculpate the accused is not admissible unless corroborating circumstances clearly indicate the trustworthiness of the statement.

**Statement of personal or family history.** (A) A statement concerning the declarant's own birth, adoption, marriage, divorce, legitimacy, relationship by blood, adoption, or marriage, ancestry, or other similar fact of personal or family history, even though declarant had no means of acquiring personal knowledge of the matter stated; or (B) a statement concerning the foregoing matters, and death also, of another person, if the declarant was related to the other by blood, adoption, or marriage or was so intimately associated with the other's family as to be likely to have accurate information concerning the matter declared.

*Source: Federal Rules of Evidence,* Rules 803 and 804.

**FIGURE 14.3** *Continued*

other *indicia of reliability* exist such that the accuracy and truthfulness of a hearsay statement can be judged, then it may be admissible (see *Idaho v. Wright,* 497 U.S. 805 [1990]). These indicia must, according to the Court, be "particularized guarantees of trustworthiness."

# The Defendant's Right to Challenge Witness Testimony

Part of the defendant's right to confrontation is the ability to challenge witnesses in the courtroom. This ability is manifested when each witness physically appears in court before the defendant. This type of confrontation permits questioning by the defense and is intended to submit the witness's account to scrutiny. Interestingly, though, the Supreme Court has identified at least one situation in which the defendant's right to challenge witness testimony is not compromised by the witness's absence.

Also, the Court has held that the defendant can be limited in terms of the nature of the confrontation, which is usually accomplished through questioning—specifically, *cross-examination.* Each of these limitations is discussed in a following subsection. First, the order of questioning in a typical criminal trial is considered. Then, the focus moves to when face-to-face contact is required and what Supreme Court case law addresses the defendant's right to cross-examine witnesses.

## Order and Scope of Questions

Witness testimony proceeds in several stages. That testimony is examined at each stage by a particular party to the case—the state or the defendant. And each examination is subject to limitations in terms of scope. In other words, the stages must occur sequentially, and only certain types of questions are permissible at each stage.

## A HEARSAY EXCEPTION?

Following are the actual facts from a Supreme Court case, *Idaho v. Wright*, 497 U.S. 805 (1990):

Wright was charged under Idaho law with two counts of lewd conduct with a minor—specifically, her 5½-- and 2½--year-old daughters. At the trial, it was agreed that the younger daughter was not "capable of communicating to the jury." However, the court admitted, under Idaho's residual hearsay exception, certain statements she had made to a pediatrician having extensive experience in child abuse cases. The doctor testified that the child had reluctantly answered questions about her own abuse but had spontaneously volunteered information about her sister's abuse. Wright was convicted on both counts but appealed only the conviction involving the younger child. The state supreme court reversed, finding that the admission of the doctor's testimony under the residual hearsay exception violated Wright's rights under the confrontation clause. The court noted that the child's statements did not fall within the traditional hearsay exception and lacked "particularized guarantees of trustworthiness" because the doctor had conducted the interview without procedural safeguards: He failed to videotape the interview, asked leading questions, and had a preconceived idea of what the child should be disclosing.

How should the Supreme Court decide?

---

The four stages of witness examination are (1) direct; (2) cross; (3) redirect; and (4) recross. Every witness called to the stand in a criminal case is questioned four separate times. However, because the focus here is on constitutional rights at trial, after the four types of questioning have been introduced, the focus will be mainly on the defendant's rights during cross- and recross-examination.

**Direct Examination.** The first examination of a witness is called direct examination, and it is usually conducted by the party calling the witness. The scope of direct examination is broad. In general, questions are permitted about any relevant facts that may prove or disprove an element of the offense charged.

**Cross-Examination.** The next step in examining a witness is cross-examination. It is conducted by a party other than the one who called the witness. For example, the state may call a witness in a criminal trial. Once the state's direct examination has concluded, the defense will have an opportunity to cross-examine the state's witness.

Whereas the scope of questioning in a direct examination is broad, the scope of questioning on cross-examination is limited to matters covered on direct examination. Inquiries into the credibility of the witness are also permissible. Together, these two restrictions constitute the *scope of direct rule*. This helps ensure that the opposing party (the party conducting the cross-examination) cannot use cross-examination of the witness to direct the jury's attention to other issues not raised by the party calling the witness. For example, assume that in a robbery trial, a defense witness testifies about the defendant's whereabouts on the day of the robbery. Assume further that on cross-examination, the prosecutor asks that witness whether the defendant expressed the desire to rob a bank on the day *before* the robbery. The prosecutor's question will not be permissible on cross-examination because it is beyond the scope of the original defense questioning (assuming, of course, that the defense did not ask its witness about the defendant's feelings the day before the robbery).

**Redirect Examination.** The party calling the witness conducts the redirect examination and does so *after* the cross-examination. Thus, the scope of questioning on redirect is limited to the scope of questioning on cross-examination. Again, new issues cannot be raised.

Consider another example: Suppose that on cross-examination, a burglary victim is asked about what persons have permission to enter his residence while he is away. Assume further that on redirect, the prosecutor asks the burglary victim about an incident that occurred several days prior to the burglary, in which he saw the defendant "casing" the neighborhood. The prosecutor's question is not permissible because it is beyond the scope of the cross-examination (assuming, again, that the prior incident did not come to light during the defense's cross-examination).

**Recross-Examination.**    The last stage in witness questioning is known as recross-examination. This includes any subsequent examination of a witness by a party who has previously cross-examined him or her. Recross-examination is also limited in scope to the subject matter of the examination that preceded it. That is, the party engaged in recross-examination cannot probe issues not raised during redirect examination.

Assume that an eyewitness to an accident is testifying for the plaintiff and is asked on cross-examination if she was wearing her prescription glasses at the time of the accident. If, during redirect examination, it is determined that the witness could see fine *without* her glasses, then the defense cannot question her on recross-examination about her relation to the plaintiff.

Taken together, the four stages of witness examination follow a pattern of *progressive narrowing*. That is, each subsequent examination has an increasingly narrow focus, such that there is less and less to ask the witness. In other words, the four stages of examination should clarify, rather than confuse, the witness's testimony.

## Face-to-Face Contact

*Coy v. Iowa*
*(487 U.S. 1012 [1988])*

In *Coy v. Iowa*, 487 U.S. 1012 (1988), the Supreme Court considered the constitutionality of a state law that permitted the placement of a large opaque screen between the defendant and two young girls who testified that he had sexually assaulted them. The Court declared that the statute was unconstitutional because "the Confrontation Clause guarantees the defendant a face-to-face meeting with witnesses appearing before the trier of fact."

Contrast *Coy* with *Maryland v. Craig*, 497 U.S. 836 (1990). In *Craig*, the Court considered whether a statute permitting a witness's testimony via closed-circuit television was constitutional. The statute provided for such a procedure in cases in which the judge determined that face-to-face testimony would "result in the child suffering serious emotional distress such that the child cannot reasonably communicate." The Court upheld the statute, claiming that it did not violate the Confrontation Clause. It stated that a central concern of the Confrontation Clause "is to ensure the reliability of the evidence against a criminal defendant by subjecting it to rigorous testing in the context of an adversary proceeding before the trier of fact." Further, it held that the statute in question did "not impinge upon the truth-seeking or symbolic purposes of the Confrontation Clause."

## Cross-Examining and Obtaining Evidence

The Supreme Court has considered, more than once, the constitutionality of state- and court-imposed restrictions on the defendant's right to cross-examine (and by extension, to engage in recross-examination). For instance, in *Smith v. Illinois* (390 U.S. 129 [1968]), the Court considered whether the prosecution can conceal the identity of a witness who is a police informant. The Court held that the witness's identity must be revealed because such information "opens countless avenues of in-court examination and out-of-court investigation."

In another case, *Davis v. Alaska*, 415 U.S. 308 (1974), the Court considered whether the identity of a juvenile who testifies at a criminal trial can be disguised. There, the state's lead witness in the defendant's burglary trial was a juvenile. The Court held that the juvenile's identity should have been revealed and that "the right of confrontation is paramount to the State's policy of protecting a juvenile offender."

*Chambers v. Mississippi*
*(410 U.S. 284 [1973])*

In still another case, *Chambers v. Mississippi*, 410 U.S. 284 (1973), the Court considered the constitutionality of a state statute that barred *any* cross-examination by the defense.

In that case, the defendant sought to cross-examine a witness who, on three previous occasions, had confessed to the murder with which the defendant was charged. The state did not call the witness, so the defense was forced to. However, the judge prohibited cross-examination based on the *voucher rule*, which provides that the party calling the witness vouches for (attests to) his or her credibility. According to this rule, cross-examination would be pointless because that is not typically the job of the party calling the witness. But since this case placed something of a unique twist on the voucher rule, the Supreme Court unanimously reversed the defendant's conviction. According to the Court, "The availability of the right to confront and cross-examine those who give damaging testimony against the accused has never been held to depend on whether the witness was initially put on the stand by the accused or by the state."

The Court has also considered whether the Confrontation Clause is violated when the prosecution withholds from the defense documentation of a witness's out-of-court statements. In *United States v. Bagley*, 473 U.S. 667 (1985), the Court held that the prosecution is not obligated to provide the defense with such information, unless it is exculpatory, in which case the due process clause requires disclosure. According to the Court, "[F]ailure [on the part of the prosecution] to assist the defense by disclosing information that might have been helpful in conducting . . . cross-examination . . . amounts to a constitutional violation . . . only if the evidence is material in the sense that its suppression undermines confidence in the outcome of the trial."

The defense is thus given wide latitude in terms of its authority to cross-examine. Courts cannot conceal the identity of a witness testifying against the defendant, nor can they bar cross-examination simply because the defense is calling the witness it wishes to cross-examine. Finally, the defendant's right to cross-examine rarely is violated if the prosecution fails to produce documentation of witness's out-of-court statements when they are not at all exculpatory.

While the defense is given considerable latitude in terms of confrontation, there are still some restrictions in particular types of criminal cases. The *Craig* case mentioned in the previous section restricts confrontation in cases involving child witnesses. There are also restrictions in rape cases where so-called "rape shield" laws protect victims from over-reaching questioning by the defense. Just recently, the Supreme Court upheld a rape defendant's conviction after he was denied the opportunity to present evidence of the victim's prior unsubstantiated rape allegations against him (*Nevada v. Jackson*, 569 U.S. ___ [2013]).

---

**DECISION-MAKING EXERCISE 14.6**

### THE DEFENDANT'S RIGHT TO OBTAIN EVIDENCE

Vance Lester was charged with sexual offenses against his four-year-old daughter. The matter was referred to Children's Services, the state agency charged with investigating cases of suspected child abuse. During pretrial discovery, Lester served Children's Services with a subpoena, seeking access to its records related to his alleged crime as well as earlier records related to a previous investigation into another sexual offense against his daughter. Children's Services refused to supply the requested records, claiming that they were privileged under a statute that provides that the agency's records are confidential, subject to certain exceptions. One of the exceptions specified by the statute was that Children's Services may disclose reports to a "court of competent jurisdiction pursuant to a court order." At a hearing on the matter, Lester argued that he was entitled to the information because the file might contain the names of favorable witnesses and/or exculpatory evidence. Should his argument succeed?

# ▶ The Right to Compulsory Process

*Washington v. Texas*
*(388 U.S. 14 [1967])*

The compulsory process clause of the Sixth Amendment provides that the defendant can use subpoenas to obtain witnesses, documents, and other objects that are helpful to his or her defense. The right to **compulsory process** was incorporated to the states in *Washington v. Texas*, 388 U.S. 14 (1967), in which the Supreme Court stated that compulsory process protects "[t]he right to offer the testimony of witnesses, and to compel their attendance." Further, the Court stated:

> We hold that the petitioner in this case was denied his right to have compulsory process for obtaining witnesses in his favor because the State arbitrarily denied him the right to put on the stand a witness who was physically and mentally capable of testifying to events that he had personally observed, and whose testimony would have been relevant and material to the defense. The Framers of the Constitution did not intend to commit the futile act of giving to a defendant the right to secure the attendance of witnesses whose testimony he had no right to use. The judgment of conviction must be reversed.

Several state and federal statutes govern compulsory process, as do the *Federal Rules of Criminal Procedure*. Figure 14.4 presents an example of a subpoena typically used in a criminal case.

---

AO 89 (Rev. 01/09) Subpoena to Testify at a Hearing or Trial in a Criminal Case

### UNITED STATES DISTRICT COURT
for the

| United States of America | ) | |
| v. | ) | Case No. |
| | ) | |
| _____ | ) | |
| *Defendant* | ) | |

#### SUBPOENA TO TESTIFY AT A HEARING OR TRIAL IN A CRIMINAL CASE

TO:

**YOU ARE COMMANDED** to appear in the United States district court at the time, date, and place shown below to testify in this criminal case. When you arrive, you must remain at the court until the judge or a court officer allows you to leave.

| Place of Appearance: | Courtroom No.: |
| | Date and Time: |

You must also bring with you the following documents, electronically stored information, or objects *(blank if not applicable)*:

Date: _____

*CLERK OF COURT*

_____
*Signature of Clerk or Deputy Clerk*

The name, address, e-mail, and telephone number of the attorney representing *(name of party)* _____ , who requests this subpoena, are:

Case No.

**FIGURE 14.4 Subpoena in a Criminal Case**

**PROOF OF SERVICE**

This subpoena for (*name of individual and title, if any*)
_____ was received by me on (*date*)
_____

☐ I personally served the subpoena on the individual at (*place*)
_____
_____ on (*date*) _____

☐ I left the subpoena at the individual's residence or usual place of abode with (*name*)
_____
_____ , a person of suitable age and discretion who resides there, on (*date*)
_____ , and mailed a copy to the individual's last known address; or

☐ I served the subpoena on (*name of individual*)
_____ , who is designated by law
to accept service of process on behalf of (*name of organization*)
_____
_____ on (*date*) _____ ; or

☐ I returned the subpoena unexecuted because
_____ ; or

☐ Other (*specify*)

Unless the subpoena was issued on behalf of the United States, or one of its officers
or agents, I have also tendered to the witness fees for one day's attendance, and the
mileage allowed by law, in the amount of $_____ .

My fees are $ _____ for travel and $ _____ for services,
for a total of $_____ 0.00 _____ .

I declare under penalty of perjury that this information is true.

Date: _____     _____

*Server's signature*

_____

*Printed name and title*

_____

*Server's address*

Additional information regarding attempted service, etc:

Source: Administrative Office of the U.S. Courts. Available online: http://www.uscourts.gov/forms/
AO089.pdf (accessed February 16, 2011).

**FIGURE 14.4** *Continued*

Statutes and formal rules aside, at least two Supreme Court cases have considered aspects of the defendant's right to compulsory process. In particular, questions as to constitutional rights violations have been posed in instances in which the defense has been denied the right to subpoena a witness.

For example, in *Roviaro v. United States*, 353 U.S. 53 (1957), the prosecution refused to provide the defense with the identity of a police informant. The Court recognized that the government had a significant interest in concealing the identity of the informant, mainly to further its efforts in combating the trafficking of illicit drugs. But the Court also found that the defendant's right to confrontation was denied by the prosecution's refusal to release the witness's identity. The informant was the only witness to the drug transaction for which the defendant was charged, so the defense clearly would have had a difficult time mounting an effective case without this witness.

In *United States v. Valenzuela-Bernal*, 458 U.S. 858 (1982), the defendant was charged with transporting illegal narcotics. He was arrested along with three other individuals who were unlawfully in the United States. Immigration officials concluded that two of the three aliens were not needed for the prosecution, so it deported them. The defendant then argued that his right to compulsory process was violated by the deportation. Surprisingly, the Court held that the government's interest in deporting illegal aliens and minimizing overcrowding in detention facilities outweighed the defendant's interest in mounting an effective defense. The Court concluded that the defendant did not offer a valid reason why the two deported witnesses were necessary for his defense.

## The Right to Present Evidence

The Sixth Amendment's compulsory process clause appears only to grant the defendant the right to subpoena and question witnesses. In *Washington v. Texas*, however, the Supreme Court modified the definition of compulsory process to include the right of the *defense* to present evidence. It held that compulsory process also guarantees "the right to present the defendant's version of the facts as well as the prosecution's to the jury so that it may decide where the truth lies." Several cases have since focused on the defense's ability to present its case. Some decisions have been returned in favor of the defense and others against.

### Decisions in Favor of the Defense

In *Washington v. Texas*, the Court decided on the constitutionality of a statute that prevented accomplices from testifying for each other. The statute was enacted out of fear that accomplices would give false testimony in order to benefit one another. The Court struck down the statute, stating that the defendant must be allowed to present the testimony of any witness who is capable of testifying.

In another case, *Chambers v. Mississippi*, the Court overturned the conviction of a defendant who was not allowed to put three witnesses on the stand. The defendant, Chambers, had attempted to prove that another person, MacDonald, committed the murder for which he was charged. The three people Chambers wanted to put on the stand were those to whom MacDonald had allegedly confessed. The Court felt the witnesses' testimony should have been admissible, even though it would have been considered hearsay, because MacDonald "spontaneously" confessed to each person, making it likely that these individuals' testimony would be truthful and accurate. The Court felt that "the exclusion of this critical evidence, coupled with the State's refusal to permit Chambers to cross-examine MacDonald, denied him a trial in accord with traditional and fundamental standards of due process."

*Crane v. Kentucky*
*(476 U.S. 683 [1986])*

In *Crane v. Kentucky*, 476 U.S. 683 (1986), another related case, the defendant sought to present evidence that his confession was unreliable because it had been obtained when he was young and uneducated and had been interrogated at great length. The trial court excluded this evidence and the defendant was convicted. The Supreme Court reversed that decision, however, declaring that a state may not exclude "competent, reliable evidence bearing on the credibility of a confession when such evidence is central to the defendant's claim of innocence" because "[w]hether rooted directly in the Due Process Clause . . . or in the Compulsory Process or Confrontation Clause . . . the Constitution guarantees criminal defendants a 'meaningful opportunity' to present a complete defense."

### Decisions against the Defense

*United States v. Scheffer*
*(523 U.S. 303 [1998])*

On a few occasions, the Court *has* sanctioned exclusion of certain defense evidence based on the right to compulsory process. For example, in *United States v. Scheffer*, 523 U.S. 303 (1998), the Court upheld a trial court's decision to exclude polygraph evidence presented by the defense. The Court stated, "There is simply no consensus that polygraph evidence is

### THREATENING A WITNESS

In *Webb v. Texas*, 409 U.S. 95 (1972), a man was convicted of burglary and sentenced to prison for 12 years. He appealed his conviction, claiming that the trial judge violated his Fifth Amendment constitutional right by harassing the only defense witness. The following is the judge's statement to the witness:

> Now you have been called down as a witness in this case by the Defendant. It is the Court's duty to admonish you that you don't have to testify, that anything you say can and will be used against you. If you take the witness stand and lie under oath, the Court will personally see that your case goes to the grand jury and you will be indicted for perjury and the likelihood is that you would get convicted of perjury and that it would be stacked onto what you have already got, so that is the matter you have got to make up your mind on. If you get on the witness stand and lie, it is probably going to mean several years and at least more time that you are going to have to serve. It will also be held against you in the penitentiary when you're up for parole and the Court wants you to thoroughly understand the chances you're taking by getting on that witness stand under oath. You may tell the truth and if you do, that is all right, but if you lie you can get into real trouble. The court wants you to know that. You don't owe anybody anything to testify and it must be done freely and voluntarily and with the thorough understanding that you know the hazard you are taking.

Did the judge violate the defendant's right to due process?

reliable. To this day, the scientific community remains extremely polarized about the reliability of polygraph evidence." Thus, the defense's ability to present its case can be restricted if the evidence it seeks to present cannot be considered reliable (see also *United States v. Salerno*, 505 U.S. 317 [1992]).

Another important example of Court-sanctioned restrictions on the ability of the defense to present a case is *Michigan v. Lucas*, 500 U.S. 145 (1991). The Court held that the defendant can be prevented from presenting evidence because of his or her attorney's misconduct. In this case, the trial judge in the defendant's rape trial excluded evidence about the victim's sexual history because the defendant failed to give notice of this to the prosecution within 10 days of the trial, in violation of discovery rules. A similar decision was reached in *Taylor v. Illinois*, in which the Court sanctioned a lower court's decision to deny a defense witness's testimony because of providing short notice to the prosecution, again in violation of discovery rules.

## ▶ The Right to Double-Jeopardy Protection

The constitutionally guaranteed protection against **double jeopardy** is designed to ensure that a person who has been convicted or acquitted of a crime is not tried or punished for the same offense twice. Double jeopardy occurs when, for the same offense, a person is (1) reprosecuted after acquittal; (2) reprosecuted after conviction; or (3) subjected to separate punishments for the same offense. Double jeopardy does not apply, however, to prosecutions brought by separate sovereigns. The federal government, each state government, and each Native American tribe is considered a separate sovereign.

The foundations of modern-day protection against double jeopardy can be found in early English common law. The rule of *autrefois acquit* prohibited the retrial of a defendant who was found not guilty. The rule of *autrefois convict*, on the other hand, prohibited the retrial of a defendant who *was* found guilty. These rules were adopted by the American colonies.

*Benton v. Maryland*
*(395 U.S. 784 [1969])*

Today, double-jeopardy protection is applied in every state because the Supreme Court decided, in *Benton v. Maryland*, 395 U.S. 784 (1969), that the Fifth Amendment's protection against double jeopardy is a fundamental right:

> The fundamental nature of the guarantee against double jeopardy can hardly be doubted. Its origins can be traced to Greek and Roman times, and it became established in the common law of England long before this Nation's independence. . . . As with many other elements of the common law, it was carried into the jurisprudence of this Country through the medium of Blackstone, who codified the doctrine in his Commentaries. "The plea of *autrefoits acquit*, or a former acquittal," he wrote, "is grounded on this universal maxim of the common law of England, that no man is to be brought into jeopardy of his life more than once for the same offence." . . . Today, every State incorporates some form of the prohibition in its constitution or common law. As this Court put it in *Green v. United States*, 355 U.S. 184, 187–188 (1957), "the underlying idea, one that is deeply ingrained in at least the Anglo-American system of jurisprudence, is that the State with all its resources and power should not be allowed to make repeated attempts to convict an individual for an alleged offense, thereby subjecting him to embarrassment, expense and ordeal and compelling him to live in a continuing state of anxiety and insecurity, as well as enhancing the possibility that even though innocent he may be found guilty." This underlying notion has from the very beginning been part of our constitutional tradition. Like the right to trial by jury, it is clearly "fundamental to the American scheme of justice."

## When Double-Jeopardy Protection Applies

The Fifth Amendment suggests that double jeopardy occurs when a person's "life or limb" is threatened. This language has been taken to mean that double jeopardy applies in all criminal proceedings. Determining whether a proceeding is criminal, however, is not as clear as it seems. Courts will often look to the legislature's intent in writing the statute that is the basis for prosecution. For example, in *Kansas v. Hendricks*, 521 U.S. 346 (1997), the Supreme Court found that a statute providing for a "sexual predator" proceeding, in addition to a criminal proceeding, did not place the defendant in double jeopardy because it provided for *civil* confinement. The Court stated:

*Kansas v. Hendricks*
*(521 U.S. 346 [1997])*

> Because we have determined that the Kansas Act is civil in nature, initiation of its commitment proceedings does not constitute a second prosecution. Cf. *Jones v. United States*, 463 U.S. 354, 77 L. Ed. 2d 694, 103 S. Ct. 3043 (1984) (permitting involuntary civil commitment after verdict of not guilty by reason of insanity). Moreover, as commitment under the Act is not tantamount to "punishment," Hendricks' involuntary detention does not violate the Double Jeopardy Clause, even though that confinement may follow a prison term. Indeed, in *Baxstrom v. Herold*, 383 U.S. 107, 15 L. Ed. 2d 620, 86 S. Ct. 760 (1966), we expressly recognized that civil commitment could follow the expiration of a prison term without offending double jeopardy principles. We reasoned that "there is no conceivable basis for distinguishing the commitment of a person who is nearing the end of a penal term from all other civil commitments." *Id.*, at 111–112. If an individual otherwise meets the requirements for involuntary civil commitment, the State is under no obligation to release that individual simply because the detention would follow a period of incarceration.

The courts will also examine whether the sanctions imposed are punitive in nature. In *Helvering v. Mitchell*, 303 U.S. 391 (1938), the Supreme Court upheld the constitutionality of a tax proceeding that was used to recover back taxes from a person *after* the person was acquitted on criminal charges. It declared that the proceeding was designed as a remedial sanction to reimburse the government. Because the proceeding was not considered punitive, the protection against double jeopardy did not apply. In the Court's words:

The doctrine of double jeopardy is inapplicable because the 50% addition to tax provided by § 293 (b) is not primarily punitive but is a remedial sanction imposed as a safeguard for protection of the revenue and to reimburse the Government for expense and loss resulting from the taxpayer's fraud. As such it may be enforced by a civil procedure to which the accepted rules and constitutional guaranties governing the trial of criminal prosecutions do not apply.

### The Blockburger *Rule*

A rather complicated issue in double-jeopardy jurisprudence concerns the definition of same offense. In *Blockburger v. United States*, 284 U.S. 299 (1932), the Supreme Court stated that "[w]here the same act or transaction constitutes a violation of two distinct statutory provisions, the test to be applied to determine whether there are two offenses or only one, is whether each requires proof of an additional fact which the other does not." This test came to be known as the Blockburger rule.

*Blockburger v. United States (284 U.S. 299 [1932])*

An offense is considered the "same offense" if two separate statutes that define the offense both contain elements A, B, and C. Moreover, if one crime contains elements A, B, and C and the other has elements A and B, both are considered the same offense because neither statute requires proof of a fact that the other does not. Assume, for example, that the offense of first-degree murder contains elements A (premeditated), B (deliberate), and C (killing) and that the offense of second-degree murder contains elements B (deliberate) and C (killing). Both offenses are considered the same for double-jeopardy purposes because second-degree murder does not require proof of another element that first-degree murder does not. If a person is convicted of first-degree murder, then, according to this example, he or she cannot be charged with second-degree murder.

*Separate offenses* exist when one crime contains elements A, B, and C and the other contains elements A, B, and D. Both crimes require proof of an additional element that the other does not. For example, assume the offense of joyriding contains elements A (unlawful taking), B (of an automobile), and C (the intent to *temporarily* deprive the owner of possession). Assume also that the offense of car theft contains elements A (unlawful taking), B (of an automobile), and D (the intent to *permanently* deprive the owner of possession). These are considered separate offenses because each offense requires proof of an element that the other does not. Thus, a person who is found guilty of joyriding can also be charged with the crime of car theft (see *Brown v. Ohio*, 432 U.S. 161 [1977]).

## When Double-Jeopardy Protection Does Not Apply

There are several specific situations in which double-jeopardy protection does not apply.

- Double jeopardy does not apply if the second prosecution is based on conduct committed after the first prosecution (*Diaz v. United States*, 223 U.S. 442 [1912]). The

---

**DECISION-MAKING EXERCISE 14.8**

**CASE OF DOUBLE JEOPARDY?**

In *United States v. Ursery*, 518 U.S. 267 (1996), the issue was asset forfeiture. Police had found marijuana and growing equipment when they searched the defendant's house. He was prosecuted criminally, but the federal government also sought civil forfeiture of his house, pursuant to a federal law. The defendant filed a Section 1983 lawsuit against the government, claiming that the proposed forfeiture of his house would amount to double jeopardy, a violation of the Fifth Amendment. Does civil asset forfeiture in addition to criminal prosecution place a person in double jeopardy?

defendant was convicted of assault and battery. When the victim later died, the defendant was charged with homicide. The Court stated, "The death of the injured person was the principal element of the homicide, but was no part of the assault and battery. At the time of the trial for the latter the death had not ensued, and not until it did ensue was the homicide committed. Then, and not before, was it possible to put the accused in jeopardy for that offense."

- If a defendant successfully appeals a criminal conviction or otherwise succeeds in overturning a conviction because of an error in the proceedings leading to conviction, he or she may be reprosecuted. In *United States v. Tateo*, 377 U.S. 463 (1964), the Court held:

> It would be a high price indeed for society to pay were every accused granted immunity from punishment because of any defect sufficient to constitute reversible error in the proceedings leading to conviction. From the standpoint of a defendant, it is at least doubtful that appellate courts would be as zealous as they now are in protecting against the effects of improprieties at the trial or pretrial stage if they knew that reversal of a conviction would put the accused irrevocably beyond the reach of further prosecution. In reality, therefore, the practice of retrial serves defendants' rights as well as society's interest. The underlying purpose of permitting retrial is as much furthered by application of the rule to this case as it has been in cases previously decided.

- Reprosecution is permissible if a *mistrial* occurs because of a fatal flaw in the indictment (*Illinois v. Somerville*, 410 U.S. 458 [1973]).

- If the defendant is responsible for the second prosecution, double jeopardy does not apply. In *Jeffers v. United States*, 432 U.S. 137 (1977), the defendant was indicted twice for two offenses. The state sought joinder on the charges, but the defendant successfully moved to have the charges tried separately. He was convicted in both trials but claimed that the latter conviction amounted to double jeopardy, in violation of the Fifth Amendment. The Supreme Court disagreed.

- If a case is dismissed by the judge but the defendant is not acquitted, he or she may be reprosecuted. In *United States v. Scott*, 437 U.S. 82 (1978), the Court held, in part, that "where a *defendant* successfully seeks to avoid his trial prior to its conclusion by a motion for a [dismissal], the Double Jeopardy Clause is not offended by a second prosecution. Such a motion by the defendant is deemed to be a deliberate election on his part to forgo his valued right to have his guilt or innocence determined by the first trier of fact." Note, however, that the double-jeopardy clause bars retrial following a court-directed acquittal, even if erroneous (*Evans v. Michigan*, 568 U.S. ___ [2013]).

- The defendant may be reprosecuted if the judge declares a mistrial with the defendant's consent or by the defendant's motion, provided that the prosecution does not agree to the defendant's consent or motion in bad faith, such as by intending to pursue a subsequent retrial for the purpose of subjecting the defendant to the harassment of multiple trials (*Lee v. United States*, 432 U.S. 23 [1977]; *Oregon v. Kennedy*, 456 U.S. 667 [1982]).

- If the defense plea-bargains over the prosecution's objection, double-jeopardy protection does not apply. In *Ohio v. Johnson*, 467 U.S. 493 (1984), the defendant succeeded in convincing the judge to dismiss certain charges against him, over the prosecution's objection. He was later tried on the dismissed charges, and the Court held that double-jeopardy protections did not apply. Had the prosecution acquiesced to the dismissal, the result would have been different.

- Double jeopardy does not apply when the court hearing the first offense lacks jurisdiction to try the second offense (*Fugate v. New Mexico*, 471 U.S. 1112 [1985]). The Court held that a defendant's conviction on drunk-driving charges in municipal court did not bar prosecution in a higher court for vehicular homicide tied to the same incident. It also noted that the municipal court did not have jurisdiction to try a homicide case, so double-jeopardy protections did not apply.

- A defendant can be retried for the same offense if the original trial jury was deadlocked and could not reach a unanimous verdict (*Renico v. Lett*, 559 U.S. ___ [2010]).

- The double-jeopardy clause does not prohibit the government from retrying a defendant on capital or first-degree murder charges if the jury in the defendant's first trial was deadlocked on a charge of manslaughter, resulting in a mistrial (*Blueford v. Arkansas*, 566 U.S. ___ [2012]).

## Double Jeopardy and Sentencing

Double-jeopardy protection may also apply in the context of sentencing. In some cases, a court may impose *consecutive punishments* (back-to-back punishments). For example, the defendant is sentenced to a total of 10 years for convictions on two counts that each carry a 5-year sentence. The Supreme Court has held that this determination depends on legislative intent (see *Albernaz v. United States*, 450 U.S. 333 [1981]). If the criminal law was intended to permit consecutive sentences, and the consecutive punishment is not for the same offense, as determined by the *Blockburger* test, double jeopardy is not violated.

Questions about double jeopardy have also been raised when a defendant is resentenced following some important development in the case. Increasing the sentence for the same charge (as opposed to increasing the sentence for separate charges, as in the case of cumulative punishments) after it has been imposed is permissible (1) when a conviction is reversed by an appeal (*North Carolina v. Pierce*, 395 U.S. 711 [1969]); (2) after the prosecution has appealed a sentence, provided there is legal authorization to do so (a rare occurrence) (*United States v. DiFrancesco*, 449 U.S. 117 [1980]); and (3) after discovery of a legal defect in the first sentence (see *In re Bradley*, 318 U.S. 50 [1943]).

In one interesting case, *Sattazahn v. Pennsylvania*, 537 U.S. 101 (2003), an individual was charged with capital murder, but the jury could not unanimously conclude that the death penalty was warranted. As required by a Pennsylvania statute, the judge then sentenced the offender to life in prison. The defendant was then retried and sentenced to death. He argued that the Fifth Amendment's double-jeopardy clause was violated, but the Supreme Court disagreed. The Court argued that the deadlocked jury did not amount to a "death penalty acquittal," so it saw no constitutional issues with retrying the offender.

---

### DECISION-MAKING EXERCISE 14.9

#### REPROSECUTION AFTER A MISTRIAL

In *Lee v. United States*, 432 U.S. 23 (1977), the facts were as follows:

> After the prosecutor's opening statement in petitioner's bench trial for theft in violation of the Assimilative Crimes Act and the applicable Indiana statute, petitioner's counsel moved to dismiss the information on the ground that it did not allege specific intent as required by the Indiana statute. The court tentatively denied the motion subject to further study, whereupon petitioner's counsel outlined the defense and did not object to going forward with the trial. At the close of the evidence the court, though observing that petitioner's guilt had been proved beyond any reasonable doubt, granted petitioner's motion to dismiss. Thereafter, petitioner was indicted for the same crime and convicted.

The defendant in this case claimed that the double-jeopardy clause should have barred the second trial. Is he right?

# ▶ The Entrapment Defense

A person tried for a crime may be able to assert a number of defenses to criminal liability, such as self-defense, insanity, involuntary intoxication, and others. One defense that has much of its foundation in criminal procedure is the *entrapment defense*. It is closely related to criminal procedure because it calls into question law enforcement's role in the instigation of a crime. The defendant can assert entrapment prior to trial, but because entrapment is an affirmative defense, it can easily be raised at trial.

The ability to raise the entrapment defense is often referred to as a *right* to assert an entrapment defense. It is important to note, however, that the Constitution does not provide this right. It is a right only in the sense that the Supreme Court has decided that an accused person can assert an entrapment defense.

The **entrapment defense** is based on the belief that someone should not be convicted of a crime that the government instigated. In its simplest form, the entrapment defense arises when government officials "plant the seeds" of criminal intent by coming up with the idea for the crime and inducing the defendant to engage in it. In other words, if a person commits a crime that he or she otherwise would not have committed but for the government's conduct, he or she will probably succeed with an entrapment defense.

*Sorrells v. United States*
*(287 U.S. 435 [1932])*

The first Supreme Court case recognizing the entrapment defense was *Sorrells v. United States*, 287 U.S. 435 (1932). Chief Justice Hughes stated, "We are unable to conclude that . . . [the] . . . processes of detection or enforcement should be abused by the instigation by government officials of an act on the part of persons otherwise innocent in order to lure them to its commission and to punish them." This reasoning underlies the treatment of the entrapment defense in U.S. courts to this day. The Court further stated:

> The appropriate object of this permitted activity, frequently essential to the enforcement of the law, is to reveal the criminal design; to expose the illicit traffic, the prohibited publication, the fraudulent use of the mails, the illegal conspiracy, or other offenses, and thus to disclose the would-be violators of the law. A different question is presented when the criminal design originates with the officials of the Government, and they implant in the mind of an innocent person the disposition to commit the alleged offense and induce its commission in order that they may prosecute.

Despite its apparent simplicity, the entrapment defense has been a contentious one. There has been some disagreement in the courts over the relevance of the offender's predisposition and how far the government can go in order to lure a person into criminal activity. When an entrapment decision is based on the offender's predisposition, this is known as a *subjective inquiry*. By contrast, a focus on the government conduct presumably responsible for someone's decision to commit a crime is known as an *objective inquiry*.

The American Law Institute's *Model Penal Code* takes an objective approach with regard to the entrapment defense: If the government "employ[ed] methods of persuasion or inducement which create a substantial risk that such an offense will be committed by persons other than those who are ready to commit it,"[3] then the defense is available regardless of the offender's initial willingness to offend. The Supreme Court, however, has opted to focus on the subjective predisposition of the offender instead of the government's role in instigating the crime in question (see *Hampton v. United States*, 425 U.S. 484 [1976]).

In *Sorrells*, which was decided in 1932, the defendant was charged with violating the National Prohibition Act.[4] After two unsuccessful attempts, a law enforcement agent

---

[3]American Law Institute, *Model Penal Code* 2.13(1)(b)(1985).
[4]Recall that during the Prohibition era, from 1920 to 1933, it was illegal to produce and sell alcohol in the United States.

CHAPTER 14 More Rights at Trial 430

## OUTRAGEOUS GOVERNMENT CONDUCT

In an actual case, Drug Enforcement Administration (DEA) agents sought out a convicted felon, Kubica, and offered to reduce the severity of his sentence if he agreed to cooperate with them. At the request of the DEA, Kubica contacted another man, Neville, and suggested that they set up a lab to manufacture "speed." Neville agreed, and the government supplied Kubica with glassware and a difficult-to-obtain ingredient used in the manufacture of speed. The government also made arrangements for purchasing the chemicals and even supplied an isolated farmhouse to serve as the laboratory. The laboratory was set up at the farmhouse and operated for one week. The men produced approximately six pounds of methamphetamine hydrochloride (speed). Kubica was completely in charge of the entire laboratory. At the end of the first week of lab operations, Neville left the farmhouse with the drugs in a suitcase. Kubica notified the DEA agents, who arrested Neville driving down the road. A search of the car revealed, in addition to the suitcase containing six pounds of methamphetamine hydrochloride, a Lysol can containing cocaine and some more speed. Neville was arrested, charged, and convicted. He appealed his conviction not on entrapment grounds, but by arguing that the government's outrageous conduct had violated the due process clause of the Fourteenth Amendment. What should the court decide?

convinced the defendant to sell him whiskey. Chief Justice Hughes noted that "artifice and stratagem" are permissible methods of catching criminals, so entrapment did not occur. Instead, it was the defendant's predisposition to commit the crime that was important.

In the next leading entrapment case, *Sherman v. United States*, 356 U.S. 369 (1958), the Supreme Court reached the opposite conclusion but still adhered to the predisposition test. In that case, a government informant met the defendant at a doctor's office, where both were being treated for narcotics addiction. After repeated requests by the informant, the defendant provided him with illegal narcotics. The Supreme Court reversed the defendant's conviction, noting that entrapment was "patently clear" as a matter of law. Even so, the Court also pointed out that it is difficult to judge the conduct of an informant without knowing how predisposed the offender was to act before the crime was committed.

*Sherman v. United States (356 U.S. 369 [1958])*

In *United States v. Russell*, 411 U.S. 423 (1973), the Court continued to focus on the defendant's predisposition. In *Russell*, a narcotics agent posed as a narcotics manufacturer and offered the defendant a difficult-to-obtain ingredient used to manufacture a drug. The defendant accepted and was convicted. Justice Rehnquist, the author of the majority opinion, observed that there was sufficient predisposition on the part of the defendant, so the entrapment defense did not apply.

*United States v. Russell (411 U.S. 423 [1973])*

In *Hampton v. United States*, 425 U.S. 484 (1976), the Supreme Court once again focused on the defendant's predisposition. In that case, the defendant was convicted of distributing heroin supplied to the defendant by a government informant. The Court stated that "[i]f the police engage in illegal activity in concert with a defendant beyond the scope of their duties the remedy lies, not in freeing the equally culpable defendant, but in prosecuting the police under the applicable provisions of state or federal law." In other words, it is the defendant's predisposition that matters in the context of the entrapment defense, not the government's conduct.

*Hampton v. United States (425 U.S. 484 [1976])*

To suggest that the Supreme Court has ignored the role of government conduct is not entirely true. In a concurring opinion cited in *Hampton*, Justices Powell and Blackmun argued that government behavior that "shocks the conscience" could conceivably violate due process. In their words, "[T]here is certainly a limit to allowing governmental involvement in crime. . . . It would be unthinkable . . . to permit government agents to instigate robberies and beatings merely to gather evidence to convict other members of a gang of hoodlums."

The Supreme Court has yet to affirmatively recognize a due process-based defense to government entrapment, but some lower courts have. Generally, if government officials use violence, supply contraband that is wholly unobtainable, or engage in a criminal enterprise, then the defendant in such a case will often succeed with the entrapment defense based on a due process argument.

---

# Summary

## 1. Summarize the right to a public trial.

The right to a public trial is the right to one that is open to the public. This right has been expanded to cover several pretrial proceedings, such as suppression hearings. Sometimes, the right to a public trial does not apply. If the government seeks closure, it must show (1) that there is an overriding interest, such as the protection of certain witnesses; (2) that the closure is no broader than absolutely necessary; and (3) that reasonable alternatives were considered. If the accused seeks closure of a trial, it will be permitted only if an open proceeding will compromise the ability of the jury to make a fair decision.

Attempts to close trials (and related proceedings) to the public often meet with resistance on First Amendment grounds. In response to this problem, the courts have recognized that there may be other ways to ensure an open trial that remains fair, despite media coverage. Some of these methods include (1) *voir dire* with special attention to pretrial publicity, (2) a change of venue, (3) jury sequestration, (4) gag orders on the media, and (5) gag orders on other parties.

## 2. Summarize the right to confrontation.

The right to confrontation refers to the ability of the defendant to face his or her accusers. This right is manifested in three ways: (1) by permitting the defendant to be present at trial, (2) by requiring live testimony, and (3) by allowing the defendant to challenge the government's witnesses through cross-examination.

The defendant enjoys the right not only to be physically present, but must also be mentally competent. Deciding mental competence hinges on whether the defendant is able to consult with his or her lawyer with a reasonable degree of understanding. Physical presence can be damaging to the defense, however, in cases in which the defendant does not testify or his or her being in court reminds jurors of the crime.

The defendant's right to live testimony requires that witnesses appear in person. Recordings and the like are generally not permissible, but there are exceptions: (1) if the witness is unavailable because he or she is dead; (2) if the witness is unavailable for other reasons, such as by being hospitalized or confined to an institution; and (3) if the statement made by a witness who will not provide live testimony falls under one of the established hearsay exceptions, permitting introduction of those statements by a third party.

Finally, the defendant's third guarantee for confrontation concerns the right to challenge witness testimony. The defendant can challenge witness testimony by engaging in cross-examination and recross-examination. Both forms of examination follow prosecutorial questioning and are intended to cast doubt on the witness's testimony. The Supreme Court has restricted as well as enhanced the defendant's right to challenge witness testimony. It has restricted the right insofar as witnesses are not always required to testify before the defendant, and it has enhanced the right because the defense is given wide latitude in terms of its ability to cross-examine. Further, courts and states cannot conceal the identity of a witness testifying against the defense, nor can they bar cross-examination simply because the defense is calling the witness it wishes to cross-examine.

### 3. Summarize the right to compulsory process.

Compulsory process means that the defendant is legally entitled to compel the production of witnesses. This can be accomplished via a subpoena, if the witness will not voluntarily come forward. Compulsory process also extends to the production of physical evidence. However, there are restrictions that stem from the rules of evidence.

### 4. Explain the concept of double jeopardy.

The defendant further enjoys the right to double-jeopardy protection. In general, a defendant cannot, by the same sovereign, be reprosecuted after acquittal, reprosecuted after conviction, or subjected to separate punishments for the same offense. Several exceptions to the Fifth Amendment's double-jeopardy clause exist. First, double jeopardy does not apply if the second prosecution is based on conduct committed after the first prosecution. Second, double jeopardy does not apply if the defendant is responsible for the second prosecution. Third, double jeopardy does not apply when the court hearing the first offense lacks jurisdiction to try the second offense. Fourth, if the defense plea-bargains over the prosecution's objection, double-jeopardy protection does not apply. Fifth, if a defendant successfully appeals a criminal conviction or otherwise succeeds in overturning a conviction, he or she may be reprosecuted. Sixth, if a case is dismissed by the judge but the defendant is not acquitted, the defendant may be reprosecuted. Finally, reprosecution is permissible if the dismissal occurs over the defendant's objections and is a "manifest necessity."

### 5. Outline the classifications and origins of the entrapment defense.

The entrapment defense is available in some cases where the defendant has been lured by a government official into committing a crime. While this defense is not a constitutional right, it has, nevertheless, been given a high degree of support by the Supreme Court. This defense can be asserted prior to trial—say, in a probable cause hearing or a preliminary hearing—but entrapment is also a common-law defense that can be affirmatively asserted at trial. An entrapment defense will probably succeed if the defendant can show, in general, that government officials "planted the seeds" of criminal intent and induced him or her into committing the crime in question, and the defendant would not have committed the crime without the government's conduct.

## Key Terms

| | | |
|---|---|---|
| *Blockburger* rule *427* | entrapment defense *430* | mental competence *412* |
| change of venue *408* | gag order *408* | physical presence *410* |
| compulsory process *422* | hearsay exceptions *416* | public trial *406* |
| confrontation *409* | jury sequestration *408* | same offense *427* |
| double jeopardy *425* | live testimony *414* | unavailable witness *415* |

## Key Cases

### Public Trial

- *In re Oliver*, 333 U.S. 257 (1948)
- *Waller v. Georgia*, 467 U.S. 39 (1984)
- *Sheppard v. Maxwell*, 384 U.S. 333 (1966)
- *Rideau v. Louisiana*, 373 U.S. 723 (1963)
- *Nebraska Press Ass'n v. Stuart*, 427 U.S. 539 (1976)

## Confrontation

- *Illinois v. Allen*, 397 U.S. 337 (1970)
- *Taylor v. Illinois*, 484 U.S. 400 (1988)
- *Dusky v. United States*, 362 U.S. 402 (1960)
- *Mattox v. United States*, 156 U.S. 237 (1895)
- *Motes v. United States*, 178 U.S. 458 (1900)
- *White v. Illinois*, 502 U.S. 346 (1992)
- *Coy v. Iowa*, 487 U.S. 1012 (1988)
- *Chambers v. Mississippi*, 410 U.S. 284 (1973)

## Compulsory Process

- *Washington v. Texas*, 388 U.S. 14 (1967)

- *Crane v. Kentucky*, 476 US. 683 (1986)
- *United States v. Scheffer*, 523 U.S. 303 (1998)

## Double Jeopardy

- *Benton v. Maryland*, 395 U.S. 784 (1969)
- *Kansas v. Hendricks*, 521 U.S. 346 (1997)
- *Blockburger v. United States*, 284 U.S. 299 (1932)

## Entrapment

- *Sorrells v. United States*, 287 U.S. 435 (1932)
- *Sherman v. United States*, 356 U.S. 369 (1958)
- *United States v. Russell*, 411 U.S. 423 (1973)
- *Hampton v. United States*, 425 U.S. 484 (1976)

---

# Further Exploration

1. Are the media a help or hindrance in terms of publicizing trials? What about in celebrity trials? View this video to hear the thoughts of a number of high-profile attorneys who have defended celebrities in highly publicized trials: http://www.youtube.com/watch?v=24vpKhZLr-w (accessed May 20, 2013).

2. Assume superheroes are real and that Spiderman is called to testify in court against an evil villain who has been put on trial. If he testified in costume, would this present any Confrontation Clause–related problems? Read more about costumes and confrontation here: http://lawandthemultiverse.com/2011/01/03/costumes-and-the-confrontation-clause/ (accessed May 20, 2013).

3. 18 U.S.C. 2423 criminalizes the following acts:
   a. Transportation with intent to engage in criminal sexual activity. A person who knowingly transports an individual who has not attained the age of 18 years in interstate or foreign commerce, or in any commonwealth, territory or possession of the United States, with intent that the individual engage in prostitution, or in any sexual activity for which any person can be charged with a criminal offense, shall be fined under this title and imprisoned not less than 10 years or for life.
   b. Travel with intent to engage in illicit sexual conduct. A person who travels in interstate commerce or travels into the United States, or a United States citizen or an alien admitted for permanent residence in the United States who travels in foreign commerce, for the purpose of engaging in any illicit sexual conduct with another person shall be fined under this title or imprisoned not more than 30 years, or both.

   Israel Weingarten was convicted under both statutes and appealed, claiming a double-jeopardy violation. Are these the same or different offenses for double-jeopardy purposes? See *United States v. Weingarten*, 2013 U.S. App. LEXIS 7694 (2013).

4. truTV network's *Bait Car* features would-be car thieves caught in the act. Police target criminals using cars rigged with hidden cameras and other detection and tracking devices (the "bait cars"). Viewers follow every case from theft to arrest. Does use of a bait car raise any entrapment issues? Why or why not? Does it matter that each theft is televised?

5. Read the following facts and determine whether entrapment occurred (see *United States v. Roszkowski*, 700 F.3d 50 [1st Cir. 2012]). Does it matter that the defendant was convicted of an offense besides the one he was slated to commit had the transaction been completed?

   On November 5, 2009, Roszkowski, a convicted felon, placed a phone call to Christopher Zarrella, an undercover police officer posing as a black-market arms dealer. During that conversation, which was recorded, Roszkowski sought to procure, for the stated purpose of home defense, a 12-gauge shotgun, a 9 mm handgun, and various types of ammunition, including hollow-point bullets. Roszkowski also demonstrated a substantial knowledge of firearms and ammunition during the call, and he repeatedly expressed his interest in making future purchases from Zarrella. After settling on the desired products and pricing terms, the two agreed to complete the transaction at a secluded Rhode Island park the following day.

That transaction, as evidenced by the instant appeal, did not go according to plan. As Roszkowski approached the designated exchange point, Detective Zarrella spotted a gun protruding from his front waistband. Fearing for his safety, Zarrella identified himself as a police officer and attempted, unsuccessfully, to arrest the appellant. A struggle ensued, during which Roszkowski discharged the firearm, critically injuring himself. He was quickly subdued, and a subsequent examination of his weapon, which had been manufactured in Ohio, revealed that its serial number had been removed.

Shortly thereafter, a federal grand jury in the District of Rhode Island indicted Roszkowski on one count of being a felon in possession of a firearm in violation of 18 U.S.C. § 922(g)(1), and one count of knowingly possessing a firearm with an altered serial number in violation of 18 U.S.C. § 922(k).

# Review Questions

1. Explain the term *public trial.*
2. When may the right to a public trial not apply?
3. Why is the First Amendment relevant when discussing the right to a public trial?
4. What methods are available to deal with media influence on a criminal trial?
5. In what three ways is the defendant's right to confrontation manifested?
6. Explain both elements of the defendant's right to be present. Cite pertinent cases.
7. How might the defendant's right to be present do more harm than good?
8. Explain the exceptions to the defendant's right to live testimony.
9. Explain the order and scope of questions in a criminal trial.
10. Explain both elements of the right to compulsory process.
11. Summarize two Supreme Court decisions that address compulsory process: one in favor of the defense and another against the defense.
12. When does double-jeopardy protection apply?
13. What is the *same offense* for double-jeopardy purposes?
14. When can a defendant not assert double-jeopardy protection?
15. What is the entrapment defense? When can it succeed? Can entrapment rise to the level of a due process violation? If so, how?

# Web Links and Exercises

1. Change of venue procedure: read about the requirements for a change of venue in the state of California.
URL: http://www.courts.ca.gov/documents/chgofven.pdf (accessed May 20, 2013).

2. Confrontation in the wake of *Crawford v. Washington*: What are the implications of the *Crawford* decision for domestic violence victims?
Suggested URL: http://www.law.cornell.edu/supct/html/02-9410.ZO.html (accessed May 20, 2013).

3. Questioning child witnesses: read about Virginia's procedures relating to questioning of child witnesses via closed-circuit television.
URL: http://www.dcjs.virginia.gov/juvenile/cja/protocol.cfm (accessed May 20, 2013).

4. Rape victim questioning: read about so-called "rape shield" laws.
URL: http://www.vawnet.org/Assoc_Files_VAWnet/RapeShield.pdf (accessed May 20, 2013).

5. Double jeopardy in the war on terror: read about Ehren Watada's double-jeopardy argument. He was the first commissioned U.S. soldier to refuse to go to Iraq.
URL: http://en.wikipedia.org/wiki/Ehren_Watada (accessed May 20, 2013).

6. Entrapment: read more about the history and development of the entrapment defense.
Suggested URL: http://scholarship.law.wm.edu/cgi/viewcontent.cgi?article=1621&context=facpubs (accessed May 20, 2013).

# 15 Sentencing, Appeals, and *Habeas Corpus*

## LEARNING OBJECTIVES

When you complete this chapter, you should be able to:

**1** *Explain how an appropriate sentence is determined.*

**2** *Describe the various types of appeals.*

**3** *Outline the appeal process.*

**4** *Summarize the right to, and restrictions on,* habeas corpus.

# OUTLINE

# Introduction: Closing the Door on the Criminal Process

The criminal process typically ends when the defendant is found not guilty and is released. If the accused is found guilty, a number of steps in the process may follow. First, the accused must be sentenced, which is usually accomplished in a posttrial hearing. Second, the accused can appeal his or her conviction. Finally, if the accused's appeal fails, the U.S. Constitution provides the right to *habeas corpus*, which is a method of challenging the constitutionality of one's confinement.

## ► Sentencing

After a conviction at trial, the defendant is sentenced. If the crime is a felony, sentencing usually occurs at a separate posttrial hearing. Individuals charged with misdemeanors are usually tried and sentenced in the same hearing.

When sentencing is carried out in a separate hearing, the judge will usually request a *presentence report* prior to the hearing. This report provides the judge with information concerning the defendant's pretrial record, financial characteristics, family status, employment status, and other factors that can be relevant in deciding the appropriate sentence. The time needed to complete this report is the main reason for the time lapse between trial and sentencing. The report is intended to assist the judge in reaching his or her decision and is usually completed by a probation officer retained by the court.

Several sentencing options may be available to the judge. The judge may impose a sentence and then suspend it, pending good behavior on the part of the defendant. The judge may also require the defendant to pay a fine or, in more extreme cases, to serve a term in prison. Probation or another method of supervised release is a possibility, as well. In any case, the type of sentence may depend on the judge's own goals in choosing a sentence—that is, his or her view as to the purposes of sentencing. The following section considers the leading goals of criminal sentencing.

### Types of Prison Sentences

At least four types of sentencing exist, some of which are closely related to one another.

- **Indeterminate sentencing** gives the judge the authority to set the sentence. This form of sentencing empowers the judge to set the maximum sentence—that is, up to what the legislature will allow—or the minimum sentence for the offender to serve in prison. Under this system, a parole board usually ends up deciding the actual amount of time the offender will spend in prison.

- **Determinate sentencing.** The judge is permitted to hand down a fixed sentence that cannot later be altered by a parole board. Determinate sentencing has the effect of treating all offenders similarly. It also has the effect of ensuring that criminals will be incarcerated for longer periods of time than may result under indeterminate sentencing.

- **Mandatory sentencing.** Mandatory sentencing is a form of determinate sentencing but differs insofar as it takes discretion away from the judge. "Three strikes" laws are examples of mandatory sentencing. For example, under California's "three strikes" law, if a person who has two "strikeable" felonies on his or her record commits a third felony of any type, he or she will go to prison for life. The Supreme Court has decided that such laws do not constitute cruel and unusual punishment (*Lockyer v. Andrade*, 538 U.S. 63 [2003]; *Ewing v. Andrade*, 538 U.S. 11 [2003]).

- **Sentencing guidelines.** Sentencing guidelines provide direction to the judge in determining the appropriate sentence. They are a middle ground between indeterminate and determinate methods of sentencing. As such, they serve to promote consistency in sentencing by recommending certain terms of imprisonment for a certain type of offender. Sentencing guidelines can be voluntary or involuntary, depending on state or federal law. Sentencing guidelines that must be strictly followed are known as *presumptive guidelines*.

The U.S. Sentencing Commission was created in 1984 to attempt to solve problems with sentencing in the federal courts. It put together a *sentencing grid* that federal judges use to determine appropriate sentences (see Figure 15.1). Both criminal history (the horizontal

## SENTENCE TABLE (in months of imprisonment)
### Criminal History Category (Criminal History Points)

| Offense Level | I (0 or 1) | II (2 or 3) | III (4, 5, 6) | IV (7, 8, 9) | V (10, 11, 12) | VI (13 or more) |
|---|---|---|---|---|---|---|
| 1 | 0–6 | 0–6 | 0–6 | 0–6 | 0–6 | 0–6 |
| 2 | 0–6 | 0–6 | 0–6 | 0–6 | 0–6 | 1–7 |
| 3 | 0–6 | 0–6 | 0–6 | 0–6 | 2–8 | 3–9 |
| 4 | 0–6 | 0–6 | 0–6 | 2–8 | 4–10 | 6–12 |
| 5 | 0–6 | 0–6 | 1–7 | 4–10 | 6–12 | 9–15 |
| 6 | 0–6 | 1–7 | 2–8 | 6–12 | 9–15 | 12–18 |
| 7 | 0–6 | 2–8 | 4–10 | 8–14 | 12–18 | 15–21 |
| 8 | 0–6 | 4–10 | 6–12 | 10–16 | 15–21 | 18–24 |
| 9 | 4–10 | 6–12 | 8–14 | 12–18 | 18–24 | 21–27 |
| 10 | 6–12 | 8–14 | 10–16 | 15–21 | 21–27 | 24–30 |
| 11 | 8–14 | 10–16 | 12–18 | 18–24 | 24–30 | 27–33 |
| 12 | 10–16 | 12–18 | 15–21 | 21–27 | 27–33 | 30–37 |
| 13 | 12–18 | 15–21 | 18–24 | 24–30 | 30–37 | 33–41 |
| 14 | 15–21 | 18–24 | 21–27 | 27–33 | 33–41 | 37–46 |
| 15 | 18–24 | 21–27 | 24–30 | 30–37 | 37–46 | 41–51 |
| 16 | 21–27 | 24–30 | 27–33 | 33–41 | 41–51 | 46–57 |
| 17 | 24–30 | 27–33 | 30–37 | 37–46 | 46–57 | 51–63 |
| 18 | 27–33 | 30–37 | 33–41 | 41–51 | 51–63 | 57–71 |
| 19 | 30–37 | 33–41 | 37–46 | 46–57 | 57–71 | 63–78 |
| 20 | 33–41 | 37–46 | 41–51 | 51–63 | 63–78 | 70–87 |
| 21 | 37–46 | 41–51 | 46–57 | 57–71 | 70–87 | 77–96 |
| 22 | 41–51 | 46–57 | 51–63 | 63–78 | 77–96 | 84–105 |
| 23 | 46–57 | 51–63 | 57–71 | 70–87 | 84–105 | 92–115 |
| 24 | 51–63 | 57–71 | 63–78 | 77–96 | 92–115 | 100–125 |
| 25 | 57–71 | 63–78 | 70–87 | 84–105 | 100–125 | 110–137 |
| 26 | 63–78 | 70–87 | 78–97 | 92–115 | 110–137 | 120–150 |
| 27 | 70–87 | 78–97 | 87–108 | 100–125 | 120–150 | 130–162 |
| 28 | 78–97 | 87–108 | 97–121 | 110–137 | 130–162 | 140–175 |
| 29 | 87–108 | 97–121 | 108–135 | 121–151 | 140–175 | 151–188 |
| 30 | 97–121 | 108–135 | 121–151 | 135–168 | 151–188 | 168–210 |
| 31 | 108–135 | 121–151 | 135–168 | 151–188 | 168–210 | 188–235 |
| 32 | 121–151 | 135–168 | 151–188 | 168–210 | 188–235 | 210–262 |
| 33 | 135–168 | 151–188 | 168–210 | 188–235 | 210–262 | 235–293 |
| 34 | 151–188 | 168–210 | 188–235 | 210–262 | 235–293 | 262–327 |
| 35 | 168–210 | 188–235 | 210–262 | 235–293 | 262–327 | 292–365 |
| 36 | 188–235 | 210–262 | 235–293 | 262–327 | 292–365 | 324–405 |
| 37 | 210–262 | 235–293 | 262–327 | 292–365 | 324–405 | 360–life |
| 38 | 235–293 | 262–327 | 292–365 | 324–405 | 360–life | 360–life |
| 39 | 262–327 | 292–365 | 324–405 | 360–life | 360–life | 360–life |
| 40 | 292–365 | 324–405 | 360–life | 360–life | 360–life | 360–life |
| 41 | 324–405 | 360–life | 360–life | 360–life | 360–life | 360–life |
| 42 | 360–life | 360–life | 360–life | 360–life | 360–life | 360–life |
| 43 | life | life | life | life | life | life |

Zones: Zone A (levels 1–8), Zone B (levels 9–11), Zone C (levels 12–13), Zone D (levels 14–43)

Source: U.S. Sentencing Commission, *Guidelines Manual* (Washington, DC: U.S. Sentencing Commission, 2012), http://www.ussc.gov/Guidelines/2012_Guidelines/Manual_PDF/Sentencing_Table.pdf (accessed May 23, 2013).

**FIGURE 15.1 Federal Sentencing Guidelines**

axis) and offense level (the vertical axis) are taken into account, such that a judge can set the appropriate sentence in months. Readers are encouraged to visit the U.S. Sentencing Commission's Web site to learn more about these guidelines. The link appears in the "Web Links and Exercises" section at the end of this chapter.

# Determining the Appropriate Sentence

Determining the appropriate sentence almost always involves considering both the seriousness of the offense and the offender's prior record. Other factors that are considered include the defendant's possible threat to the community and his or her degree of remorse for committing the crime. Even age, family ties, employment status, and other demographic factors can come into play. Moreover, the defendant who pleads guilty may receive a different sentence than the defendant who is found guilty in a trial. A guilty plea suggests that the defendant is willing to admit what he or she did and, as such, should be treated more leniently.

Sentencing can also be affected by the number of separate crimes growing out of a single criminal act. If, for instance, a defendant is convicted of killing another person with a handgun, he or she may be sentenced for the killing as well as for unlawful possession of a handgun, if the law permits the latter. In such a situation, the judge may sentence the defendant to consecutive or concurrent sentences. With a *concurrent sentence*, the defendant serves time for both crimes at once. *Consecutive sentences*, by contrast, are served separately, one after another. In the murder example, the defendant would serve time in prison for the killing, and then when that term was completed, he or she would begin serving the sentence for possession.

*Roberts v. United States*
*(445 U.S. 552 [1980])*

Sentencing can also be influenced by the defendant's degree of cooperation with the police. In *Roberts v. United States*, 445 U.S. 552 (1980), the Court held that the sentencing judge was permitted to consider the defendant's refusal to cooperate with the police in investigating his crime. Still other factors, such as the offender's mental status, can be considered. In fact, it has been held that a mentally ill individual can be held in custody, such as in a mental institution, for a longer term than would otherwise be imposed for the crime charged (see *Jones v. United States*, 103 S.Ct. 3043 [1983]). This often happens following an insanity plea.

Most jurisdictions have what is known as the "going rate" for a criminal offense.[1] Usually, this is an unwritten, informal agreement between members of a courtroom work group (the judge, defense attorney, and prosecutor) as to what sentence a typical case merits. Usually, if the seriousness of the offense and the offender's background characteristics are known, one can predict with a fair degree of accuracy what sentence will be imposed.

A judge's sentencing decisions can also be influenced by *victim impact statements*. For example, Proposition 8, adopted by California voters in 1982, provides that "the victim of any crime, or the next kin of the victim, . . . has the right to attend all sentencing proceedings . . . [and] to reasonably express his or her views concerning the crime, the person responsible, and the need for restitution."[2] The Supreme Court has decided that testimony in the form of a victim impact statement is admissible (*Payne v. Tennessee*, 501 U.S. 808 [1991]).

The judge is then required to take the victim's or next of kin's statement into account when deciding on a sentence for the offender.

## Death Penalty Sentencing

*Furman v. Georgia*
*(408 U.S. 238 [1972])*

The most serious punishment that can be imposed is *capital punishment*, or the death penalty. In the landmark case *Furman v. Georgia*, 408 U.S. 238 (1972), the Court held that

---

[1]S. Walker, *Sense and Nonsense about Crime and Drugs*, 5th ed. (Belmont, CA: Wadsworth, 2001), p. 41.
[2]California Penal Code, Section 1191.1 (1996).

the death penalty was carried out in the United States in a way that amounted to cruel and unusual punishment, in violation of the Eighth Amendment. Then, in 1976, the Court reinstated the death penalty in *Gregg v. Georgia*, 428 U.S. 153 (1976), holding that death is an acceptable sentence, provided the sentencing process is reasonable.

*Gregg v. Georgia*
*(428 U.S. 153 [1976])*

In the states that have not abolished the death penalty, determining whether death should be imposed is now frequently in the hands of a jury. Most state statutes call for, in essence, two proceedings. In legal terms, this is called a **bifurcated trial**. In the first proceeding, the defendant's guilt is determined, similar to a trial for a noncapital offense. Then, the jury sits for a second proceeding to determine whether a death sentence should be handed down. The importance of such a procedure is that it allows a jury of the defendant's peers, not just a judge, to determine whether capital punishment is appropriate. In addition, the jury must take into account aggravating and mitigating circumstances (*Roberts v. Louisiana*, 428 U.S. 325 [1977]). However, if aggravating or mitigating circumstances presented to the jury are later found invalid, the Eighth Amendment will not necessarily be violated if a death sentence is imposed (*Brown v. Sanders*, 546 U.S. 212 [2006]).

*Roberts v. Louisiana*
*(428 U.S. 325 [1977])*

In *Stebbing v. Maryland*, 469 U.S. 900 (1984), Justice Marshall described one state's approach to death penalty sentencing that relies on a jury's decision:

> Like most death penalty statutes, the Maryland statute begins by requiring the sentencing authority—either a judge or a jury—first to consider whether the prosecutor has proved, beyond a reasonable doubt, the existence of any of 10 statutory aggravating circumstances. . . . If the sentencer does not find at least one aggravating factor, the sentence must be life imprisonment. . . . If the sentencer finds that one or more aggravating factors exist, it then must determine whether the defendant has proven, by a preponderance of the evidence, that any of eight statutory mitigating factors exist. . . . If no mitigating factors are found, the sentencer must impose death. If, instead, the sentencer has found at least one mitigating factor, it must determine, by a preponderance of the evidence, whether the proven mitigating factors outweigh the aggravating circumstances. If they do, the sentencer must impose a life sentence. If the mitigating factors do not outweigh aggravating factors, the jury must impose a death sentence.

Whereas a jury must take aggravating and mitigating factors into consideration when determining whether a death sentence is appropriate, it is not appropriate for a judge to do so. In *Ring v. Arizona*, 122 S.Ct. 2428 (2002), the Supreme Court held that allowing a sentencing judge, without a jury, to find aggravating circumstances necessary for imposition of the death penalty violated the Sixth Amendment's jury trial provision (incidentally, judges in some states can ignore jurors' sentencing recommendations in capital cases).

The death penalty is most commonly handed down for first-degree, premeditated murder. But whether death is a permissible sentence for less serious offenses is not as certain.

## DECISION-MAKING EXERCISE 15.1

### DEATH PENALTY SENTENCING

Assume that a state law gives the trial judge authority to sentence to death a defendant convicted of a capital crime but also requires the judge to consider the jury's recommendation as to whether the death penalty should be imposed. Assume further that a man has been sentenced to death by the judge in his trial, even though the jury that convicted him recommended life in prison. The man appeals, claiming that the statute is unconstitutional because it does not specify the weight the judge must give to the jury's sentencing recommendation and thus permits the arbitrary imposition of the death penalty. He further claims that the judge should be forced to give "great weight" to the jury's recommendation. How should the appellate court rule?

For example, in *Coker v. Georgia*, 433 U.S. 584 (1977), the Court held that a sentence of death for the crime of rape against an adult woman was grossly disproportionate and in violation of the Eighth and Fourteenth Amendments to the U.S. Constitution. The Court suggested that the death penalty was not appropriate for a crime in which the offender did not take a human life. However, some states continued to allow capital punishment in cases of the rape of a *child*. But in *Kennedy v. Louisiana*, 554 U.S. 407 (2008), the Court expanded *Coker* to hold that execution may not be imposed in cases of child rape that do not result in the murder of the victim.

## Other Important Sentencing Decisions

Several other recent decisions have sought to clarify the circumstances in which death or other types of sentences can be imposed. The following are examples of these cases:

- *Woodson v. North Carolina*, 428 U.S. 280 (1976). Decided on the same day as *Gregg*, the Court held that mandatory death penalty laws—that is, those that do not take aggravating and mitigating circumstances into account—are unconstitutional.

- *Enmund v. Florida*, 458 U.S. 782 (1982). It is unconstitutional to impose death if a person participates in a felony that results in murder without considering the participant's level of intent.

- *Cabana v. Bullock*, 474 U.S. 376 (1986). The death penalty cannot be imposed on a mere accomplice, unless there is clear finding that the accomplice killed, attempted to kill, or intended to kill.

- *Ford v. Wainwright*, 477 U.S. 399 (1986). The execution of someone who is insane violates the Eighth Amendment.

- *Tison v. Arizona*, 107 S.Ct. 1714 (1987). The death penalty can be imposed in the absence of intent to kill if the defendant substantially participated in a felony likely to result in a loss of life.

- *Harmelin v. Michigan*, 501 U.S. 957 (1991). A life sentence without the possibility of parole for a first-time, nonviolent drug offender does not constitute cruel and unusual punishment.

- *Kansas v. Hendricks*, 521 U.S. 346 (1997). Civil commitment was upheld for convicted child molesters who have served their sentences under the state's Sexually Violent Predators Act.

- *Apprendi v. New Jersey*, 530 U.S. 466 (2000). Any fact, other than prior conviction, that increases the penalty for a crime beyond that allowed by statute must be submitted to a jury and proven beyond a reasonable doubt.

- *Atkins v. Virginia*, 122 S. Ct. 2242 (2002). The execution of a mentally disabled person violates the Eighth Amendment.

- *Kansas v. Crane*, 534 U.S. 407 (2002). Offenders under Kansas's Sexually Violent Predators Act cannot be civilly committed without having proof that they have serious difficulty in controlling their behavior.

- *Blakely v. Washington*, 542 U.S. 296 (2004). A fact, other than prior conviction, that increases a sentence to the maximum permitted by statute must be presented to a jury and proven beyond a reasonable doubt.

- *Roper v. Simmons*, 543 U.S. 551 (2005). The execution of offenders who committed their capital crime while under the age of 18 violates the Eighth Amendment.

- *Deck v. Missouri*, 544 U.S. 622 (2005). The Constitution forbids the use of visible shackles during a capital trial's penalty phase.

- *United States v. Booker*, 543 U.S. 220 (2005). Federal sentencing guidelines are advisory, not mandatory.

- *Oregon v. Guzek*, 546 U.S. 517 (2006). The Constitution does not permit defendants facing the death penalty to present new evidence during the sentencing phase.
- *Carey v. Musladin*, 549 U.S. 70 (2006). It was not unfairly prejudicial for trial spectators to wear buttons depicting the murder victim.
- *Rita v. United States*, 551 U.S. 338 (2007). Sentences that fall within the federal sentencing guidelines are presumptively reasonable.
- *Cunningham v. California*, 549 U.S. 270 (2007). State determinate sentencing laws violate the Sixth Amendment right to jury trial when they permit judges to impose enhanced sentences based on facts not found by a jury or admitted to by the defendant.
- *Kimbrough v. United States*, 552 U.S. 85 (2007). The federal cocaine sentencing guidelines, like other federal sentencing guidelines, are advisory.
- *Baze v. Rees*, 553 U.S. 35 (2008). A three-drug lethal-injection protocol does not violate the Eighth Amendment's prohibition of cruel and unusual punishment.
- *Graham v. Florida*, 560 U.S. ___ (2010). Juvenile offenders cannot be sentenced to life in prison for nonhomicide offenses.
- *United States v. Comstock*, 560 U.S. ___ (2010). It is constitutionally permissible for the federal government to use civil commitment to keep a "sexually dangerous person," under the Adam Walsh Child Protection and Safety Act, confined beyond the date of scheduled release.
- *Miller v. Alabama*, 567 U.S. ___ (2012). Life in prison without parole for juvenile homicide offenders is cruel and unusual punishment, in violation of the Eighth Amendment.
- *Southern Union Co. v. United States*, 567 U.S. ___ (2012). The decision in *Apprendi v. New Jersey* (see above) applies to the imposition of fines.
- *Alleyne v. United States*, 570 U.S. ___ (2013). Any element of a crime that increases the mandatory minimum punishment must be submitted to a jury and proven beyond a reasonable doubt.

## Constitutional Rights during Sentencing

A convicted offender enjoys several important constitutional rights during the sentencing process. First, the double-jeopardy provision of the Fifth Amendment, as discussed in the last chapter, applies. Further, the defendant may only be subjected to a reasonable punishment for his or her crime. Namely, the punishment should reflect the seriousness of the offense. For example, in *Solem v. Helm*, 463 U.S. 277 (1983), the Court held that a life sentence for the defendant's seventh nonviolent offense was unconstitutional. The Court stated that the defendant "received the penultimate sentence for relatively minor criminal conduct."

The defendant also has the right to participate in the sentencing process. With the possible exception of misdemeanor sentencing, which may take place out of the presence of the defendant, the defendant has the right to be present during sentencing. Also, the defendant must be advised of his or her right to appeal. In addition, the defendant has the right to have counsel present at the sentencing hearing to argue on his or her behalf. The Sixth Amendment right to counsel operates essentially the same way at sentencing as it does at trial.

The defendant also has the right to ask the sentencing judge to ignore past convictions that were obtained in violation of the right to counsel. For example, in *United States v. Tucker*, 404 U.S. 443 (1972), the Supreme Court invalidated an individual's 25-year sentence because the sentencing judge arrived at the sentence by considering the defendant's past convictions, for which he was not afforded counsel. The Court stated:

*United States v. Tucker*
*(404 U.S. 443 [1972])*

> The government is . . . on solid ground in asserting that a sentence imposed by a federal district judge, if within statutory limits, is generally not subject to review. . . . But these general propositions do not decide the case before us. For we deal here not with a sentence

imposed in the informed discretion of a trial judge, but with a sentence founded at least in part upon misinformation of constitutional magnitude. As in *Townsend v. Burke*, 334 U.S. 736, 1690, "this prisoner was sentenced on the basis of assumptions concerning his criminal record which were materially untrue." The record in the present case makes evident that the sentencing judge gave specific consideration to the respondent's previous convictions before imposing sentence upon him. Yet it is now clear that two of those convictions were wholly unconstitutional under *Gideon v. Wainwright*, 372 U.S. 335, 1963.

In summary, a defendant enjoys at least three important constitutional rights during the sentencing process: (1) protection from being tried twice for the same or similar offenses; (2) sentencing that conforms to the Eighth Amendment's proscription against cruel and unusual punishment; and (3) the right to counsel at sentencing-related hearings, regardless of his or her ability to afford representation.

# ▶ Appeals

An **appeal** is a process in which a defendant who is found guilty can challenge his or her conviction. When an appeal is filed, an appellate court, such as one of the federal circuit courts of appeal, examines a lower court's decision in order to determine whether the proper procedure was followed, or the law was correctly applied. In other words, when a defendant appeals, he or she is claiming that the court made an error regarding the law applicable to the case. Further, the appeal provides a means by which another judge or panel of judges, who were not involved in making decisions in the initial trial, will review the case and make a decision.

Although appealing convictions is an important part of the criminal process, the Supreme Court has never held that appeals, in general, are constitutionally required. That is, nowhere does the U.S. Constitution specify that a certain number of appeals will be granted to each convicted criminal. In *McKane v. Durston*, 153 U.S. 684 (1894), the Supreme Court stated, "A review by an appellate court of the final judgment in a criminal case, however grave the offense of which the accused is convicted, was not at common law, and is not now, a necessary element of due process of law."

Most appeals are made after trial is concluded, and are filed by the defense. However, in some situations, such as a ruling on a motion to suppress evidence, a decision by the court may be appealed by the defense during the trial. These types of appeals are called *interlocutory* appeals. And in some instances, the prosecution may also file an appeal.

## Types and Effects of Appeals

Although the Supreme Court has held that an appeal of one's conviction is not constitutionally guaranteed, every state and federal government has rules providing a certain number of appeals to a convicted criminal. At both the state and federal levels, a convicted criminal is usually granted at least one **direct appeal** (also known as an *appeal of right*).

An appeal of right, or direct appeal, is automatically granted to the defendant by law. That is, an appeal of right *must* be heard by an appellate court. It is not up to the appellate court to decide whether to hear such an appeal. By contrast, the appellate court can decide, at its own discretion, whether to hear a **discretionary appeal**. Also, appeals of right are limited, but discretionary appeals can be filed several times, provided they are not redundant.

When a defendant appeals a decision, there are a number of possible objectives. In the typical appeal, the defendant seeks to correct a decision by the lower court that he or she perceives to be in error. In such an instance, the appellate court will either affirm or reverse the lower court's decision. It may also remand (send back) the case for further proceedings, consistent with its opinion.

Another objective of an appeal may be a trial *de novo* in which he or she is essentially requesting a new, independent trial at the appellate level. Trials *de novo* are rare. Further, they are usually limited to appeals of decisions arising from misdemeanor courts of limited jurisdiction. A convicted felon will rarely succeed in obtaining a trial *de novo* in an appellate court because it is the primary duty of an appellate court to interpret the *law*, not the *facts*. It is the job of the trial court to determine guilt based on the facts.

It is important to remember that a successful appeal will not necessarily result in a defendant being set free. If, for example, the appellate court reviews a lower court's decision to not exclude evidence and decides that the lower court's decision should be reversed, this only means the evidence should have been excluded, not that the defendant should be acquitted. For example, in the famous *Miranda* case (*Miranda v. Arizona*, 384 U.S. 436 [1966]), the Supreme Court did not free Ernesto Miranda. Instead, it remanded his case for a new trial. He was subsequently found guilty and sentenced to more than 20 years in prison. It is, therefore, important when reading cases to understand precisely what the reviewing court is deciding. Rarely does an appellate court decide guilt; its job is to interpret the law and review the conduct of the trial court.

While appeals are pending, defendants usually begin to serve their sentences. Assume, for example, that a defendant appeals his guilty conviction on the grounds that he was denied counsel at trial. Assume further that the defendant's appeal has merit. If he was sentenced to prison following trial, he will remain there until the appeal is heard, if ever. However, for a select few convicts, the judge will issue a *stay*, which means the convicted individual will not serve time before the appeal is heard. Stays are usually granted only if the convict poses a low flight risk. Most convicted criminals are considered flight risks, and therefore stays of imprisonment are rarely granted.

## The Appellate Process

Even though an appeal of one's conviction is not constitutionally required, the Supreme Court has held, on a number of occasions, that when an appeal is permissible, the

Appeals are an integral, sometimes required part of the criminal process.

government must follow certain procedures. Specifically, the government must ensure that the defendant has (1) access to trial transcripts; (2) the right to counsel; and (3) the right to be free from government retaliation for a successful appeal. Before the defendant is afforded these rights, he or she must file a *notice of an appeal*. An example of such a notice, from the U.S. District Court for the Southern District of California, is presented in Figure 15.2.

| Print Form | Clear Form |

NAME AND ADDRESS OF ATTORNEY

_____

_____

_____

PHONE: _____

UNITED STATES DISTRICT COURT
SOUTHERN DISTRICT OF CALIFORNIA

TRIAL JUDGE _____        COURT REPORTER _____

)
)
)
)                        CIVIL NO. _____
_____ )
(Appellant/Appellee)    Plaintiff    )
)
        vs                       )
)
)                        NOTICE OF APPEAL        (Civil)
)
_____ )
(Appellant/Appellee)    Defendant

Notice if hereby given that _____

_____ Plaintiff _____ Defendant above named, hereby appeals to the United States

Court of Appeals for the:        (check appropriate box)

_____ Ninth Circuit                                _____ Federal Circuit

from the:                        (check appropriate box)

_____ Final Judgment                        _____ Order (describe)

entered in this proceeding on the _____ day of _____ .20 _____
Transcripts required _____ Yes        _____ No.
Date civil complaint filed: _____

Date: _____                        _____
                                             Signature

*Source*: U.S. District Court, Southern District of California. Available online: http://www.casd.uscourts.gov/uploads/Attorney%20Assistance/Filing%20Procedures/Forms/Civil/Post%20Judgement%20Forms/cv_apl.pdf (accessed May 23, 2013).

**FIGURE 15.2 Example of a Notice of Appeal**

▼

## Ensuring That the Defendant Has Access to Trial Transcripts

In *Griffin v. Illinois*, 351 U.S. 12 (1956), the Supreme Court reviewed an Illinois appellate procedure that required the defendant to produce transcripts of the trial—even if he or she could not afford to do so. The Court struck down this requirement, holding that the government cannot impose a restriction on the right to appeal "in a way that discriminates against some convicted defendants on account of their poverty." In a related case, *Entsminger v. Iowa*, 386 U.S. 748 (1967), the Court invalidated a state procedure that allowed defense counsel, rather than an indigent defendant, to decide whether an appeal could continue with an incomplete trial transcript. An actual trial transcript order form is shown in Figure 15.3.

*Griffin v. Illinois*
*(351 U.S. 12 [1956])*

---

### TRANSCRIPT ORDER FORM

**PART I - To be completed by appellant within 10 days of filing the notice of appeal**

Short Title: _____     District: _____

District Court Number: _____     Circuit Court Number: _____

Name of Attorney: _____

Name of Law Firm: _____

Address of Firm: _____

Telephone of Firm: _____     Attorneys for: _____

Name of Court Reporter: _____     Telephone of Reporter: _____

---

**PART II - COMPLETE SECTION A OR SECTION B**

**SECTION A - I HAVE NOT ORDERED A TRANSCRIPT BECAUSE**

     [ ] A transcript is not necessary for this appeal, or

     [ ] The necessary transcript is already on file in District Court

     [ ] The necessary transcript was ordered previously in appeal

     number _____

---

**SECTION B - I HEREBY ORDER THE FOLLOWING TRANSCRIPT:**

(Specify the date and proceeding in the space below)

Voir dire: _____;  Opening Statements _____;

Trial proceedings: _____;  Instruction Cnf: _____;

Jury Instructions: _____;  Closing Arguments: _____;

Post Trial Motions: _____;  Other Proceedings: _____.

(Attach additional pages if necessary)

     [ ] Appellant will pay the cost of the transcript.

My signature on this form is my agreement to pay for the transcript ordered on this form.

     [ ] This case is proceeding under the Criminal Justice Act.

NOTE: Leave to proceed *in forma pauperis* does not entitle appellant to a free transcript. An order of the district court allowing payment for the transcript at government expense must be obtained. See 28 U.S.C. §753(f).

**FIGURE 15.3 Example of a Trial Transcript Order Form**

**FIGURE 15.3** *Continued*

## Ensuring the Defendant's Right to Counsel during Appeals

As discussed previously, criminal defendants enjoy the Sixth Amendment right to counsel under a number of circumstances. However, the Sixth Amendment expressly states that this right only applies in *criminal prosecutions*. Even so, the Supreme Court has required that counsel be provided to indigent defendants *on appeal* as a matter of either equal protection or due process. Interestingly, though, the Court has also said that there is no right to self-representation at the appellate stage (see *Martinez v. Court of Appeal*, 528 U.S. 152 [2000]).

*Douglas v. California*
*(372 U.S. 353 [1963])*

The first case discussing the right to counsel during the appellate stage was *Douglas v. California*, 372 U.S. 353 (1963). There, the Court concluded that the government must provide an indigent defendant with counsel to assist in his or her appeals of right. The Court stated that "where the merits of the *one and only* appeal an indigent has as of right are decided without benefit of counsel . . . an unconstitutional line has been drawn between rich and poor." The Court has also held that the Constitution requires *effective* counsel for a nonindigent defendant in his or her appeals of right (see *Evitts v. Lucey*, 469 U.S. 387 [1985]).

Both *Douglas* and *Evitts* specifically held that the right to counsel applies in *appeals of right*. However, the Supreme Court has held that counsel is *not* constitutionally guaranteed in *discretionary appeals*. In *Ross v. Moffitt*, 417 U.S. 600 (1974), the Court stated:

A defendant in respondent's circumstances is not denied meaningful access to the State Supreme Court simply because the State does not appoint counsel to aid him in seeking review in that court, since at that stage, under North Carolina's multitiered appellate system, he will have, at the very least, a transcript or other record of the trial proceedings, a brief in the Court of Appeals setting forth his claims of error, and frequently an opinion by that court disposing of his case, materials which, when supplemented by any *pro se* submission that might be made, would provide the Supreme Court with an adequate basis for its decision to grant or deny review under its standards of whether the case has "significant public interest," involves "legal principles of major significance," or likely conflicts with a previous Supreme Court decision.

## Government Retaliation for Successful Defense Appeals

In several cases, the Supreme Court has dealt with retaliation by the prosecution for a successful defense appeal. The first noteworthy case in this regard was *North Carolina v. Pearce*, 395 U.S. 711 (1969). The defendant was reconvicted after a successful appeal and was actually punished more harshly the second time around. The Court concluded that due process required that the "defendant be freed of apprehension of such a retaliatory motivation on the part of the sentencing judge."

*North Carolina v. Pearce (395 U.S. 711 [1969])*

In a subsequent case, *Blackledge v. Perry*, 417 U.S. 21 (1974), the Court struck down a prosecutor's decision to increase the charge against a defendant who was convicted but appealed to a higher court for a trial *de novo*. The Court held that "upping the ante" in this fashion, simply because the defendant had exercised his right to appeal, was unconstitutional.

By contrast, there have been a few cases in which the Supreme Court has held that vindictiveness cannot be inferred from the judge's or jury's decision to increase a defendant's *sentence* following appeal. For instance, in *Colten v. Kentucky*, 407 U.S. 104 (1972), the Court held that a judge did not act vindictively by increasing the defendant's sentence following his trial *de novo*. And in a similar case, *Chaffin v. Stynchcombe*, 412 U.S. 17 (1973), the Court held that a jury's decision to increase the defendant's sentence in his trial *de novo* was constitutional.

Note that in both *Colten* and *Chaffin*, the sentencing authority was disconnected from the first trial. That is, a different judge sentenced Colten the second time, and a second jury convicted the defendant in *Chaffin* following his trial *de novo*. By contrast, in *Texas v. McCullough*, 475 U.S. 134 (1986), the same judge who presided over the defendant's first trial then decided the defendant's sentence following an appeal. The judge only *presided* over the first trial, but the first sentence was decided by the jury. The Court held that under those circumstances, the trial judge had no motivation to be vindictive. Had the judge actually handed down the defendant's sentences in both trials, the second, increased sentence probably would have been considered vindictive.

### The Defendant's Rights during the Appeals Process: A Summary

In order to make an appeal meaningful for a criminal defendant, the Supreme Court has required that three important rights be observed during this process. First, the defendant must be given access to the trial transcripts, even if he or she cannot afford them, in order to make an appeal. Second, the defendant must be given counsel during the appellate process, regardless of whether he or she can afford representation. Finally, neither the judge nor the prosecutor can act in a retaliatory fashion when the defendant decides to appeal. It is not always easy to determine what constitutes retaliation, but it is safe to say that when the judge or prosecutor has an interest in the outcome of a defendant's appeal and, consequently, increases the charge or sentence following the appeal, that action will be considered unconstitutional.

## Timing of Defense Appeals

The defense can file an appeal at one of two stages: (1) prior to adjudication—that is, prior to the reading of the verdict; or (2) following adjudication. The typical appeal is filed after adjudication, but there may be reasons to file an appeal prior to adjudication, as well.

### Appeals Prior to Adjudication

Appeals are generally governed by the **final judgment rule**, which generally limits appeals until the court hands down its final judgment as to the defendant's guilt. However, in very limited circumstances, a defendant may file an **interlocutory appeal**—an appeal filed prior to adjudication. This type of appeal is governed by a complex and confusing body of case law. In simple terms, though, an interlocutory appeal will be permitted only if it is an issue that is important enough to determine the outcome, but is not directly related to the merits of the case. That is, it must deal with a critical question, but have nothing to do with determining the defendant's guilt.

---

**DECISION-MAKING EXERCISE 15.4**

**RETALIATION FOR A SUCCESSFUL APPEAL**

Here are the facts from, *Thigpen v. Roberts*, 468 U.S. 27 (1984), as reported by the Supreme Court:

Following an accident in which he lost control of his car and collided with a pickup truck, killing a passenger in the truck, respondent was charged with four misdemeanors—reckless driving, driving while his license was revoked, driving on the wrong side of the road, and driving while intoxicated. Upon being convicted of these charges in a Mississippi Justice of the Peace Court, he appealed, and the case was transferred to the Circuit Court for a trial de novo. While the appeal was pending, he was indicted for manslaughter based on the same accident, and was convicted.

Note that the convictions were obtained by different prosecutors. Can the second prosecution be considered retaliatory?

*Cohen v. Beneficial Industrial Loan Corp.*, 337 U.S. 541 (1949), is perhaps the first noteworthy case in which the Supreme Court recognized certain interlocutory appeals, which it defined as:

*Cohen v. Beneficial Industrial Loan Corp.* (337 U.S. 541 [1949])

> a small class [of preadjudication decisions] which finally determine claims of right separable from, and collateral to, rights asserted in the action, too important to be denied review and too independent of the cause itself to require that appellate consideration be deferred until the whole case is adjudicated.

Unfortunately, this definition does not lend itself to easy interpretation. But it may be more easily understood by considering some examples of cases in which the Court applied its ruling in *Cohen*. The following two cases illustrate *successful* appeals prior to adjudication, while the subsequent cases focus on *unsuccessful* appeals.

In *Stack v. Boyle*, 342 U.S. 1 (1951), the defendant filed an interlocutory appeal arguing that bail set by the trial judge was excessive under the Eighth Amendment. The Court held that the judge's decision regarding bail could be appealed prior to final adjudication, reasoning that this matter was more or less independent of deciding the defendant's guilt. It also felt that delaying appeal until after adjudication would make it pointless, since a bail determination after a guilty verdict would have virtually no bearing on anything.

In another case, *Abney v. United States*, 431 U.S. 651 (1977), the defendant moved to dismiss an indictment on double-jeopardy grounds, and the motion was denied by the trial court. The defendant then filed an interlocutory appeal. The Supreme Court permitted the appeal, reasoning that if the protection against double jeopardy is to have any meaning, then a defendant who claims double jeopardy must be able to appeal before the second conviction is handed down. Otherwise, the appellate court would have to consider a defendant's Fifth Amendment claim in *hindsight*, which might have little impact in protecting the defendant from double jeopardy.

The decision in *Abney* can be compared to *Carroll v. United States* 354 U.S. 394 (1957), in which an interlocutory appeal was not allowed. The Court held that a defendant cannot appeal a decision on a search-and-seizure motion until after final adjudication has taken place. In other words, the Court felt that an appeal of a decision addressing evidence critical to the defendant's case is not sufficiently independent of the trial.

Similarly, in *DiBella v. United States*, 369 U.S. 121 (1962), the Court held that a judge's refusal to suppress evidence on Fourth Amendment grounds was not appealable until after trial. The Court felt that "appellate intervention makes for truncated presentation of the issue of admissibility, because the legality of the search too often cannot truly be determined until the evidence at the trial has brought all circumstances to light."

Despite the time- and resource-saving benefits of limiting interlocutory appeals, the restrictions on filing such appeals can have serious consequences for defendants. Many defendants who are found guilty on serious charges go to prison and are forced to pursue their appeals from there. Given that many appeals—especially those that ultimately reach the Supreme Court—may take several years, people who are wrongfully convicted may languish in prison for long periods. This is one of the weaknesses of the U.S. system of justice.

## Appeals after Adjudication

Compared to interlocutory appeals, appeals filed after adjudication are subject to few restrictions. Indeed, there appear to be few Supreme Court cases addressing the right to file postadjudication appeals. Nonetheless, it is important to understand that postadjudication appeals are almost limitless in terms of their possible substance. Nearly anything from the trial (as recorded in the transcripts) that the defense perceives to be in error can be appealed.

The following are constitutional issues that most commonly serve as the basis for an appeal in criminal cases:

- a plea of guilty that was unlawfully induced or not made voluntarily with understanding of the nature of the charge and the consequences of the plea;
- the use of a coerced confession;
- the use of evidence obtained pursuant to an unconstitutional search or seizure;
- the use of evidence obtained pursuant to an unlawful arrest;
- a violation of the privilege against self-incrimination;
- the failure of the prosecution to disclose to the defendant evidence favorable to him or her;
- a violation of the Fifth Amendment's double-jeopardy clause;
- action of a grand jury or petit jury that was unconstitutionally selected and impaneled;
- the denial of effective assistance of counsel;
- denial of the rights to a speedy trial and appeal.

## Appeals by Parties other than the Defense

Most appeals are filed by the defense, but in limited circumstances, the prosecution or a third party can appeal a trial court's decision. Appeals by the prosecution are rare due to the protection against double jeopardy. Third-party appeals are even more limited because decisions by the trial judge usually apply only to the parties to the case.

### Prosecution Appeals

Carroll v. United States
(354 U.S. 394 [1957])

As discussed in Chapter 14, the prosecution is usually barred from appealing a defendant's conviction because of the double-jeopardy clause of the Fifth Amendment. Trial court rulings other than those deciding the question of guilt, however, can sometimes be appealed by the prosecution. As the Supreme Court stated in *Carroll v. United States*, 354 U.S. 394 (1957), "[A]ppeals by the government in criminal cases are something unusual, exceptional, not favored. The history shows resistance of the Court to the opening of an appellate route for the Government until it was plainly provided by the Congress, and after that a close restriction of its uses to those authorized by statute." In other words, appeals by the prosecution are generally not permitted, but are possible in narrow situations authorized by state or federal law.

At the federal level, 18 U.S.C. Section 3731 allows an interlocutory appeal by the prosecution of a district court's decision to suppress or exclude evidence from trial. As discussed previously, when a judge excludes or suppresses evidence, it is usually because the police acted in violation of some constitutional provision. This is the most common basis for appeal by the prosecution, and many of the Supreme Court cases encountered in

---

**DECISION-MAKING EXERCISE 15.5**

**AN APPEAL PRIOR TO ADJUDICATION**

Jennifer Couture sued the Albuquerque Public Schools system and several of its employees for repeatedly placing her emotionally disturbed kindergartener in "time out" for acting up in class. The U.S. District Court for the District of New Mexico sided with Couture in its decision to deny qualified immunity to the school officials (see Chapter 2). The school officials are now seeking to appeal this decision. Can they? Note that there is no "final judgment" as yet.

this book and elsewhere came before the Court because the prosecution disagreed with a trial judge's decision to exclude or suppress evidence. This type of interlocutory appeal is permissible because if the defendant is acquitted at trial, the prosecution will not be able to appeal the defendant's conviction due to the double-jeopardy clause. Other prosecution appeals, besides those addressing decisions to exclude or suppress evidence, are severely restricted because of double jeopardy.

### Third-Party Appeals

Third parties—that is, parties other than the prosecution and the defense—are sometimes permitted to appeal certain types of decisions by the court. For example, in *Cobbledick v. United States*, 309 U.S. 323 (1940), the Supreme Court held that a person can appeal a court order, such as a subpoena, but only if he or she has been found in contempt of court for failing to abide by that order. The Court said that a decision to the contrary "would forever preclude review of the witness' claim, for his alternatives are to abandon the claim or languish in jail."

*Cobbledick v. United States*
*(309 U.S. 323 [1940])*

Other varieties of third-party appeals are conceivable but rare. Only when a trial judge's decision impinges on another person's rights will a third-party appeal succeed. For example, an appeal by the media to overturn a judge's gag order may be permissible on First Amendment grounds, but there appears to be no Supreme Court cases addressing this possibility. The number of third-party appeals is slight compared to the number filed by defendants.

## Reasons for Denying an Appeal

Many appellate courts have discretion over whether to hear certain types of cases that come before it. If an appeal is discretionary, it may not succeed simply because the appellate court is unwilling to hear it. However, even if the appellate court agrees to hear an appeal and agrees with the defendant's position, it may decide not to alter the defendant's conviction or sentence because the trial court's decision was a harmless error. A harmless error is a mistake at the trial level that has little practical consequence in terms of deciding whether the defendant is guilty or innocent.

### Constitutional versus Nonconstitutional Errors

Whether an error at trial is considered "harmless" depends, in part, on whether the error is constitutional or nonconstitutional. *Constitutional errors* result from constitutional rights violations, such as denying the accused the right to confront adverse witnesses at trial. *Nonconstitutional errors* do not have constitutional implications. An example of a nonconstitutional error is a trial court's decision to admit hearsay evidence. Although hearsay may be excluded under the rules of evidence, there is no constitutional prohibition against hearsay evidence in the courtroom.

In determining whether an error is harmless, the court will apply a particular analysis depending on whether the error was constitutional or nonconstitutional. In

---

**DECISION-MAKING EXERCISE 15.6**

**A PROSECUTION APPEAL**

Martin Katt was indicted for federal drug charges. He moved twice before trial and once during trial to dismiss the charges, claiming that the pre-indictment delay was unconstitutional. Once the government finished presenting its case, the court decided in Katt's favor and granted his motion for a dismissal. The government appealed the judge's decision to dismiss Katt's case. Should the prosecution's appeal be heard?

*Kotteakos v. United States*, 328 U.S. 750 (1946), the Court set the test for deciding what constitutes a nonconstitutional harmless error. In *Chapman v. California*, 386 U.S. 18 (1967), the Court set the test for a constitutional harmless error.

In *Kotteakos*, the Supreme Court held that a nonconstitutional harmless error occurs when it does not influence the jury but instead has a "very slight effect" on the outcome of the trial. In other words, "[I]f one cannot say, with fair assurance, after pondering all that happened without stripping the erroneous action from the whole, that the judgment was not substantially swayed by the error, it is impossible to conclude that substantial rights were not affected."

In *Chapman*, the Court held that the test for a constitutional harmless error requires the state to prove "beyond a reasonable doubt that the error complained of did not contribute to the verdict obtained." This test is reserved for what could be termed *modest* violations of constitutional rights. However, in situations in which a fundamental constitutional right has been violated, no harmless error test is required. Each scenario is considered in the next two subsections.

### Constitutional Harmless Error: A Review of Relevant Cases

In *Chapman,* the Court considered whether a harmless error resulted when the prosecutor's closing argument repeatedly referred to the defendant's refusal to take the stand and testify. (As discussed earlier in this text, a jury cannot draw adverse inferences from a defendant's refusal to testify.) The Court reversed the defendant's conviction, reasoning that "though the case in which this occurred presented a reasonably strong 'circumstantial web of evidence' against petitioners, it was also a case in which, absent the constitutionally forbidden comments, honest fair-minded jurors might very well have brought in not-guilty verdicts."

Similarly, in *Connecticut v. Johnson*, 460 U.S. 73 (1983), the Court held that the judge's flawed instructions to the jury regarding a certain element of the offense was not harmless error. In that case, the judge instructed the jury that it could presume intent on the part of the defendant for a specific intent crime (a crime that requires the state to prove that the defendant intended the illegal results of his or her actions). This error was considered so serious that, according to the Court, it "permitted the jury to convict respondent without ever examining the evidence concerning an element of the crime charged."

Compare the result in *Johnson* to *Milton v. Wainwright*, 407 U.S. 371 (1972). In that case, the defendant claimed that his confession should not have been admissible because it was obtained following a conversation with an undercover police officer who was posing as the defendant's fellow prisoner. The prosecution was able to prove beyond a reasonable doubt that the confession did not constitute error because three other confessions made by the defendant were admissible. In other words, the Court concluded that the confession resulting from the prison conversation was a harmless error.

### Serious Constitutional Error

In some cases, the Supreme Court has concluded that a constitutional error was so serious as to require automatic reversal of the defendant's conviction. In such a case, the prosecution is not required to prove beyond a reasonable doubt that the error is harmless. Instead, the error is automatically presumed to be harmful because of its serious nature. In fact, in *Chapman v. California*, the Court concluded that some errors may involve "rights so basic to a fair trial that their infraction can never be treated as harmless error."

The Court has stated that serious constitutional errors—those that cannot be considered harmless—arise in the following specific circumstances:

- The defendant's confession was coerced (*Payne v. Arkansas*, 356 U.S. 560 [1958]).
- The right to counsel at trial was violated (*Gideon v. Wainwright*, 372 U.S. 335 [1963]).

- The right to an impartial judge was violated (*Tumey v. Ohio*, 273 U.S. 510 [1927]).

- The right to a speedy trial was violated (*Strunk v. United States*, 412 U.S. 434 [1973]).

- The defendant was put in double jeopardy (*Price v. Georgia*, 398 U.S. 323 [1970]).

- The right to a representative jury was violated (*Taylor v. Louisiana*, 419 U.S. 522 [1975]).

## Retroactivity of Appellate Decisions

As discussed previously, cases decided by appellate courts establish precedents to guide decisions in similar cases arising in the future. But should defendants who have been convicted in prior cases be allowed to benefit from a successful appeal by another defendant? In other words, should one defendant's appeal apply only to that person or have a more sweeping effect and benefit several defendants in previous cases? This issue is often referred to as retroactivity—the extent to which a decision should be applied to prior defendants in a similar predicament.

On one level, it seems fair to treat all defendants with similar appeals, including those in prior cases, the same way. However, the consequences of doing so could be enormous. Multiple reversals, for example, could require many new trials for many defendants, imposing a serious cost on the justice system. In light of this concern, the Court has handed down several important decisions on retroactivity. In *Linkletter v. Walker*, 381 U.S. 618 (1965), the Court held that whether a constitutional ruling should be considered retroactive depends on the nature of the appeal. In *United States v. Johnson*, 457 U.S. 537 (1982), the Court held that retroactivity also depends on the *timing* of all appeals in question. In other words, all defendants who have appeals on file at the same time should benefit.

In *Stovall v. Denno*, 388 U.S. 293 (1967), the Court handed down a specific test for determining whether a decision of constitutional magnitude should be retroactive. It requires determining "(a) the purpose to be served by the new standards, (b) the extent of the reliance by law enforcement authorities on the old standards, and (c) the effect on the administration of justice of a retroactive application of the new standards." This has come to be known as the *Linkletter-Stovall test*. In *Stovall*, the Court considered whether its decision in *United States v. Wade*, 388 U.S. 218 (1967), which required counsel at postindictment, pretrial lineups, should be applied retroactively to other defendants appealing similar violations. Surprisingly, the Court held that *Wade* should *not* be retroactive, in part because law enforcement relied on previous case law that allowed lineups without the presence of counsel. In other words, under the second element of the *Linkletter-Stovall* test, law enforcement was heavily reliant on old standards before the *Wade* decision.

---

### DECISION-MAKING EXERCISE 15.7

#### A HARMLESS ERROR?

Pat Warren was tried on charges of kidnapping and transporting women across state lines for immoral purposes. The victims testified that he repeatedly raped and sodomized them. The defense attorney argued that the women consented and that they had possibly misidentified Warren. Warren did not testify. During the prosecutor's closing argument, the defense attorney objected when the prosecutor began to comment on the fact that Warren never challenged the kidnapping, the interstate transportation of the victims, or the sexual acts. The defense then moved for a mistrial, claiming that Warren's Fifth Amendment protection against self-incrimination was violated when the prosecutor said what he did to the jury. How should the appellate court decide?

The Supreme Court also felt that making *Wade* retroactive would bog down the courts with many new trials—the third element of the *Linkletter-Stovall* test. Finally, the Court felt that the purpose of *Wade* was to ensure fairness at lineups, but it also felt that its decision was not *necessary* to ensure fairness; that is, a fair lineup can be held without the assistance of counsel. In short, the Court felt that its decision in *Wade* did not serve a purpose quite as important as, say, guaranteeing the right to counsel at trial.

The Supreme Court has also refused to apply its decisions retroactively in other important cases already discussed in this text, including *Mapp v. Ohio*, 367 U.S. 643 (1961) (requiring that the exclusionary rule be recognized by the states), and *Katz v. United States*, 389 U.S. 347 (1967) (prohibiting nonconsensual electronic eavesdropping without probable cause and a warrant). By contrast, the Court *has* held that the failure to provide counsel in misdemeanor trials (see *Berry v. Cincinnati*, 414 U.S. 29 [1973]) and the failure to require unanimous verdicts in six-member juries (see *Brown v. Louisiana*, 447 U.S. 323 [1980]) *should* be retroactive.

In *Griffith v. Kentucky*, 479 U.S. 314 (1987), the Supreme Court brought further clarification to the issue of retroactivity. It held that any "new rule" it announces (one that is not based entirely on precedent, but sets a new standard for deciding similar cases) should be applied retroactively to all other cases pending review at the time. The reasoning offered by the Court in this case was far more straightforward and sensible than that applied in *Linkletter*, *Johnson*, and *Stovall*: failure to apply new constitutional decisions retroactively to other pending appeals would have the unfair consequence of benefiting only the individual whose appeal was selected for review. In other words, failure to retroactively apply new rules would be "unfair," because it would benefit only one individual, not others similarly situated.

It is important to note that *Griffith* applied to cases "pending review at that time." Cases that are pending review should be distinguished from those in which final judgments have been entered—cases where "a judgment of conviction has been rendered, the availability of appeal exhausted, and the time for a petition for *certiorari* elapsed or a petition for *certiorari* finally denied" (*Griffith*). "Pending review" means that an appeal has not yet been heard. Retroactivity does not apply to final judgments for two key reasons. One reason is that allowing new rules to be retroactive to final judgments opens the proverbial "can of worms." Justice Harlan expressed this point eloquently in *Mackey v. United States*, 401 U.S. 667 (1971):

> It is, I believe, a matter of fundamental import that there be a visible end to the litigable aspect of the criminal process. Finality in the criminal law is an end which must always be kept in plain view.

Another reason for not allowing decisions to retroactively apply to final judgments is the availability of the *habeas corpus* petition as a vehicle for challenging a conviction.

## ▶ *Habeas Corpus*

As previously noted, the most common method of challenging one's conviction is to appeal. However, filing an appeal is not the only avenue of redress for a person who is wrongfully convicted—the convicted person may also file a ***habeas corpus*** with the federal courts. This procedure is also known as a *collateral attack* and is a constitutional right.[3]

A petition for *habeas corpus* (Latin for "you have the body") plays out as follows: First, the accused individual petitions one of the federal district courts and asks the court to issue a *writ of habeas corpus*. Portions of an actual petition for *habeas corpus* form are reprinted in Figure 15.4. Then, if the court decides to issue the writ, the petitioner is brought before

---

[3]U.S. Constitution, Article I, Section 9, Clause 2.

**PETITION UNDER 28 U.S.C. § 2254 FOR WRIT OF**
***HABEAS CORPUS* BY A PERSON IN STATE CUSTODY**

| **United States District Court** | District: | |
|---|---|---|
| Name (under which you were convicted): | | Docket or Case No.: |
| Place of Confinement: | | Prisoner No.: |
| Petitioner (include the name under which you were convicted) | Respondent (authorized person having custody of petitioner) | |
| | v. | |
| The Attorney General of the State of | | |

**PETITION**

1.   **(a)** Name and location of court that entered the judgment of conviction you are challenging:


   **(b)** Criminal docket or case number (if you know):

2.   **(a)** Date of the judgment of conviction (if you know):
     **(b)** Date of sentencing:

3.   Length of sentence:

4.   In this case, were you convicted on more than one count or of more than one crime?      ☐ Yes      ☐ No

5.   Identify all crimes of which you were convicted and sentenced in this case:


6.   **(a)** What was your plea? (Check one)
        ☐ (1) Not guilty          ☐ (3) Nolo contendere (no contest)
        ☐ (2) Guilty              ☐ (4) Insanity plea

   **(b)** If you entered a guilty plea to one count or charge and a not guilty plea to another count or charge, what did you plead guilty to and what did you plead not guilty to?



   **(c)** If you went to trial, what kind of trial did you have? (Check one)
        ☐ Jury                ☐ Judge only

7.   Did you testify at a pretrial hearing, trial, or a post-trial hearing?
        ☐ Yes                ☐ No

8.   Did you appeal from the judgment of conviction?
        ☐ Yes                ☐ No

9.   If you did appeal, answer the following:
     **(a)** Name of court:
     **(b)** Docket or case number (if you know):
     **(c)** Result:
     **(d)** Date of result (if you know):

**FIGURE 15.4 Example of a Petition for a Writ of *Habeas Corpus* Form**

**(e)** Citation to the case (if you know):

**(f)** Grounds raised:

**(g)** Did you seek further review by a higher state court?　　　　❑　Yes　　　❑　No
　　　If yes, answer the following:
　　　**(1)** Name of court:
　　　**(2)** Docket or case number (if you know):
　　　**(3)** Result:

　　　**(4)** Date of result (if you know):
　　　**(5)** Citation to the case (if you know):
　　　**(6)** Grounds raised:

**(h)** Did you file a petition for certiorari in the United States Supreme Court?　　❑　Yes　　❑　No
　　　If yes, answer the following:
　　　**(1)** Docket or case number (if you know):
　　　**(2)** Result:

　　　**(3)** Date of result (if you know):
　　　**(4)** Citation to the case (if you know):

**10.** Other than the direct appeals listed above, have you previously filed any other petitions, applications, or motions concerning this judgment of conviction in any state court?　　❑　Yes　　　❑　No

**11.** If your answer to Question 10 was "Yes," give the following information:

**(a)**　**(1)** Name of court:
　　　**(2)** Docket or case number (if you know):
　　　**(3)** Date of filing (if you know):
　　　**(4)** Nature of the proceeding:
　　　**(5)** Grounds raised:

　　　**(6)** Did you receive a hearing where evidence was given on your petition, application, or motion?
　　　　　❑ Yes　　　　❑ No
　　　**(7)** Result:
　　　**(8)** Date of result (if you know):

**(b)**　If you filed any second petition, application, or motion, give the same information:
　　　**(1)** Name of court:
　　　**(2)** Docket or case number (if you know):
　　　**(3)** Date of filing (if you know):
　　　**(4)** Nature of the proceeding:
　　　**(5)** Grounds raised:

　　　**(6)** Did you receive a hearing where evidence was given on your petition, application, or motion?
　　　　　❑ Yes　　　　❑ No
　　　**(7)** Result:
　　　**(8)** Date of result (if you know):

**FIGURE 15.4** *Continued*

**(c)** If you filed any third petition, application, or motion, give the same information:
  **(1)** Name of court:
  **(2)** Docket or case number (if you know):
  **(3)** Date of filing (if you know):
  **(4)** Nature of the proceeding:
  **(5)** Grounds raised:


  **(6)** Did you receive a hearing where evidence was given on your petition, application, or motion?
    ☐ Yes          ☐ No
  **(7)** Result:
  **(8)** Date of result (if you know):

**(d)** Did you appeal to the highest state court having jurisdiction over the action taken on your petition, application, or motion?
  **(1)** First petition:          ☐ Yes          ☐ No
  **(2)** Second petition:       ☐ Yes          ☐ No
  **(3)** Third petition:          ☐ Yes          ☐ No

**(e)** If you did not appeal to the highest state court having jurisdiction, explain why you did not:

**12.** For this petition, state every ground on which you claim that you are being held in violation of the Constitution, laws, or treaties of the United States. Attach additional pages if you have more than four grounds. State the facts supporting each ground.

CAUTION: To proceed in the federal court, you must ordinarily first exhaust (use up) your available state-court remedies on each ground on which you request action by the federal court. Also, if you fail to set forth all the grounds in this petition, you may be barred from presenting additional grounds at a later date.

*Source:* Administrative Office of the U.S. Courts. Available online: http://www.uscourts.gov/forms/ao241.pdf (accessed February 16, 2011).

**FIGURE 15.4** *Continued*

the court so the constitutionality of his or her confinement can be reviewed. Technically, the opposing party in the petition is the jailer or prison official in charge of holding the petitioner, and the petition essentially argues that the petitioner is being held in violation of his or her constitutional rights.

Given that the Supreme Court hears a limited number of cases each term, it is unlikely that it will issue a writ. This leaves the defendant with the option of petitioning the federal district court. Also, it is important to remember that a *habeas corpus* petition must be limited to a constitutional claim. Finally, it is totally within the discretion of the court that is petitioned to decide whether the writ will be issued. Although the Constitution provides that the "privilege of the Writ of *Habeas Corpus* shall not be suspended," this has been interpreted to mean that a defendant can *submit habeas petitions*, not that the defendant will necessarily get his or her day in court.

Although it is difficult for a petition of *habeas corpus* to succeed before the Supreme Court, the Court has emphasized the importance of the writ. For example, in *Sanders v. United States*, 373 U.S. 1 (1963), the Court emphasized that "[c]onventional notions of finality of litigation have no place where life or liberty is at stake and infringement of constitutional rights is alleged." Similarly, in *Kaufman v. United States*, 394 U.S. 217 (1969), the Court held that the writ is necessary to provide "adequate protection of constitutional rights."

More recently, however, the Court has intimated that a *habeas corpus* review should be qualified. In particular, it has held that writs should not be liberally issued for claims arising from state courts. As the Court stated in *Stone v. Powell*, 428 U.S. 465 (1976), "Despite differences in institutional environment and the unsympathetic attitude to federal constitutional claims of some state judges in years past, we are unwilling to assume that there now exists a general lack of appropriate sensitivity to constitutional rights in the trial and appellate courts of the several States."

*Sanders v. United States*
*(373 U.S. 1 [1963])*

*Stone v. Powell*
*(428 U.S. 465 [1976])*

These conflicting perspectives have influenced a number of important Supreme Court cases addressing the constitutional right to *habeas corpus*. Recently, the Court has placed limitations on the scope of the writ. Also, the Antiterrorism and Effective Death Penalty Act of 1996 has had important effects on *habeas corpus*. The following sections focus on some of these restrictions and modifications.

## Restrictions on the Right to *Habeas Corpus*

The Supreme Court has restricted the right to *habeas corpus* in a number of ways. First, it has limited the types of claims that can succeed. Second, the Court has held that *habeas* review may not be granted if the petitioner fails to submit a claim within the time frame specified by state law. Third, it is generally necessary for a convicted individual to exhaust all state remedies before a federal *habeas* review will be granted. Finally, restrictions have been imposed in situations in which a prisoner filed multiple *habeas* petitions.

### Types of Claims for Which Writs Will Not Be Issued

Certain types of claims may not form the basis for a writ of *Habeas Corpus*. The first was announced in *Stone v. Powell*, discussed earlier. In that case, the Court held that "where the State has provided an opportunity for full and fair litigation of a Fourth Amendment claim," a federal court should not issue a writ of *habeas corpus*. The holding in *Stone* was clarified in *Jackson v. Virginia*, 443 U.S. 307 (1979), in which the Court held that "a federal *habeas corpus* court must consider not whether there was any evidence to support a state court conviction, but whether there was sufficient evidence to justify a rational trier of fact to find guilt beyond a reasonable doubt." This holding was recently revisited in *Cavazos v. Smith*, 565 U.S. ___ (2011), when the Court held that Ninth Circuit erred by reversing a conviction because it substituted its judgment for that of the trial jury in evaluating the persuasiveness of the prosecution's versus the defense's expert witnesses. In other words, it is the jury's responsibility, not the court's, to decide what conclusions can be drawn from the evidence at trial. A federal court cannot overturn a trial court verdict simply because it disagrees with it. Any attempt to do so faces a "high bar" (see *Coleman v. Johnson*, 566 U.S. ___ [2012]).

*Teague v. Lane*
*(489 U.S. 288 [1989])*

Second, the Court held in *Teague v. Lane*, 489 U.S. 288 (1989), that unless a claim is dictated by precedent, it cannot be heard on *habeas* review. In other words, if *habeas* review would result in a new rule, then review is impermissible. Only claims based on existing case law should be granted review. The Court did announce two exceptions to this rule, however. If the claim questions the jurisdiction of the trial court or is central to the accused's guilt or innocence, then it can be granted review in federal court.

*Herrera v. Collins*
*(506 U.S. 390 [1993])*

Third, *habeas* review will only be granted if it raises a federal constitutional question. In *Herrera v. Collins*, 506 U.S. 390 (1993), the petitioner claimed that his death sentence should be vacated because new evidence pointed to his innocence. The Court held that the claim could not be heard on *habeas* review because it did not raise a constitutional question. The Court explained that "[i]n light of the historical availability of new trials . . . and the contemporary practice in the States, we cannot say that Texas' refusal to entertain petitioner's newly discovered evidence eight years after his convictions transgresses a principle of fundamental fairness."

*Hill v. United States*
*(368 U.S. 424 [1962])*

Fourth, a nonconstitutional claim that does not allege that a fundamental defect took place at trial will not succeed (*Hill v. United States*, 368 U.S. 424 [1962]). The ruling is the reason why nonconstitutional claims rarely succeed. The ones that *do* succeed must argue that a serious miscarriage of justice took place at trial.

The fifth type of petition that will not be granted review is similar, in several respects, to the type considered in *Hill*, above. It is the *harmless error exception*—similar to the exception encountered in appeals. Recall that the appropriate test for determining whether

## A CONSTITUTIONAL QUESTION?

Ling Yu was convicted of first-degree murder and sentenced to death. The evidence against her consisted of the body of the victim, the murder weapon, and testimony from several witnesses that Yu spoke openly about wanting to kill the victim. Three years after her conviction, while she was awaiting execution on death row, new evidence was discovered, suggesting that Yu may not have committed the murder. The new evidence came in the form of a witness who was prepared to testify that Yu was with her in a different city on the night of the murder. Assume that Yu has exhausted all state-level appellate mechanisms, to no avail, and has decided to petition a federal district court for a writ of *habeas corpus*. Will her petition be heard?

a constitutional error is harmless is whether it is "harmless beyond a reasonable doubt" (*Chapman v. California*). By contrast, the test for nonconstitutional error is whether it has a "substantial and injurious effect or influence in determining the jury's verdict" (*Kotteakos v. United States*, 328 U.S. 750 [1946]). The Court has since held that the test announced in *Kotteakos* should be applied to *habeas corpus* petitions, as well (*Brecht v. Abrahamson*, 507 U.S. 619 [1993]; reaffirmed in *Fry v. Pliler*, 551 U.S. 112 [2007]).

Finally, in the case of petitions from state prisoners, a federal court will not issue a writ of *habeas corpus* unless it first determines that the confinement violates federal law (*Wilson v. Corcoran*, 562 U.S. ___ [2010]). In other words, *habeas corpus* is not the proper remedy for violations of state law.

## Restrictions Based on the Timing of a Claim

A *habeas corpus* petition typically must be filed within a certain specified time period after the trial or sentencing hearing. When a defendant fails to appeal or file a *habeas* petition within that period, he or she is said to have *defaulted* or given up the right to appeal or to petition for *habeas* review.

For a time, in cases of default, the Supreme Court focused on the state rule or statute that imposed the time restriction (see *Daniels v. Allen*, 344 U.S. 443 [1953]). If the statute was problematic, then review could be granted. Not satisfied with this approach, the Court then turned its attention to whether the defendant's default was intentional or accidental (*Fay v. Noia*, 372 U.S. 391 [1963]). Later cases required the defendant to demonstrate why a lack of *habeas* review, due to default, would be prejudicial to his or her case (e.g., *Davis v. United States*, 411 U.S. 233 [1973]).

The current standard for determining whether *habeas* review should be granted is known as the *actual innocence standard*. The Court described this standard in *Kuhlmann v. Wilson*, 477 U.S. 436 (1986): "[T]he prisoner must show a fair probability that, in light of all the evidence, including that alleged to have been illegally admitted (but with due regard to any unreliability of it) and evidence tenably claimed to have been wrongly excluded or to have become available only after the trial, the trier of the facts would have entertained a reasonable doubt of his guilt." In other words, when a prisoner has failed to file a *habeas* petition in a timely manner, he or she may still succeed in doing so provided that the petition sets forth sufficient facts as to his or her actual innocence.

*Kuhlmann v. Wilson (477 U.S. 436 [1986])*

Importantly, the appropriate standard of proof for granting review under this new rule is that there be a *fair probability* of the prisoner's innocence (see *Kuhlmann v. Wilson*). A higher standard has been imposed in death penalty cases, however. Specifically, in *Schlup v. Delo*, 513 U.S. 298 (1995), the Court held that in order to be granted a *habeas* review, an individual convicted of a capital crime must show that "it is more likely than not that no reasonable juror would have convicted [the petitioner]." In *House v. Bell*, 547 U.S. 518

## TIMING OF A *HABEAS CORPUS* PETITION

A man was convicted of the murder of a fellow prison inmate and sentenced to death. He claimed in a *habeas corpus* petition that a constitutional error had been committed at his trial and thus deprived the jury of critical evidence that would have established his innocence. In particular, he claimed that his defense attorney had acted ineffectively by failing to call witnesses who could testify to his innocence. The district court refused to consider the man's claim, holding that he could not satisfy the threshold showing of actual innocence. Was the district court correct in requiring this?

(2006), the Court found that a petitioner met this burden when, among other things, the petitioner provided that semen from a murder victim came from her husband, not the petitioner.

In summary, when a person is convicted of a crime, he or she is generally given a limited amount of time in which to file an appeal and/or a *habeas corpus* petition. Failure to do so in the required time period is known as *default*. In almost all cases, once a convicted individual has defaulted, he or she has no other means by which to challenge conviction. However, the Supreme Court has held that when a *habeas* petition demonstrates a fair probability of innocence, review can be granted. (See the "Appeals" section for similar restrictions on appeals.) The higher standard of "more likely than not" is required for death penalty *habeas* petitions.

### Importance of Exhausting State Remedies

Before *habeas corpus* becomes an option, a convicted criminal typically must exhaust all available state-level appeals. As the Supreme Court stated in *Ex parte Hawk*, 321 U.S. 114 (1944), "[O]rdinarily an application for habeas corpus by one detained under a state court judgment of conviction will be entertained . . . only after all state remedies available, including all appellate remedies in the state courts and in this Court by appeal or writ of certiorari, have been exhausted."

Requiring *habeas* petitioners to exhaust state-level remedies ensures that the states have the opportunity to correct federal constitutional violations. However, if a federal court sees fit to grant a *habeas* petition before a prisoner has exhausted all available state-level appeals, that is its prerogative (see *Granberry v. Greer*, 481 U.S. 129 [1987]).

A federal statute, 28 U.S.C. Section 2254(b), states that *habeas corpus* is not available to state prisoners "unless it appears that the applicant has exhausted the remedies available in the courts of the State, or that there is either an absence of available State corrective process or the existence of circumstances rendering such process ineffective to protect the rights of the prisoner." Unfortunately, the meanings of some of the terms in this statute are not entirely clear. Thus, it is useful to consider the Supreme Court's response to some pertinent questions stemming from Section 2254(b).

*Fay v. Noia, 372 U.S. (391 [1963])*

First, what is the meaning of "available state corrective process"? The Court answered this question in *Fay v. Noia*, 372 U.S. 391 (1963), in which it held that prisoners must pursue appeals through all state-level appellate courts. Further, it held that prisoners do not necessarily have to appeal all the way to a state Supreme Court to satisfy the exhaustion requirement. In other words, a prisoner *can* be said to have exhausted state-level remedies even if he or she does not appeal all the way to the state Supreme Court. However, the Supreme Court has held that a prisoner must pursue direct as well as discretionary appeals (see previous discussion on direct versus discretionary appeals). (*O'Sullivan v. Boerckel*, 526 U.S. 838 [1999]).

Section 2254(b) also mentions that state-level remedies must be pursued unless they are "ineffective." What is an *ineffective* state-level remedy? In *Duckworth v. Serrano*, 454 U.S. 1 (1981), the Court indicated that exhaustion is not necessary if there is "no opportunity to obtain redress in state court or if the corrective process is so clearly deficient as to render futile any effort to obtain relief." However, the precise meaning of this statement is unclear. For example, if a state prohibits all appeals of criminal cases (which is clearly unlikely), then that state's remedy can be considered ineffective because it is effectively absent. But it is unclear at what point state remedies are to be considered ineffective.

### Restrictions on Filing Multiple Habeas Corpus Petitions

Prisoners often file several *habeas corpus* petitions. (Some prisoners do not have much else to do while in custody.) Thus, the issue of filing multiple petitions has come before the Supreme Court more than once. In one of the more important cases, *Sanders v. United States*, the Court permitted successive petitions in which the same issues were raised. To do so, though, the petitioner must show that he or she was not given a "full or fair" hearing on the petition the first time around or that there has been "an intervening change in the law or some other justification for having failed to raise a crucial point or argument in the prior application." Later, in *Kuhlmann v. Wilson*, the Court held that successive petitions raising the same issues must be supplemented with a "colorable showing of factual innocence" (in other words, a fairly clear indication that the petitioner is possibly innocent). And in *Magwood v. Patterson*, 561 U.S. ___ (2010), the Court held that when a person is resentenced after receiving *habeas* relief, a subsequent *habeas* claim is not considered successive. The key limitation is that the second claim must raise new issues.

The Supreme Court has also decided to seriously restrict successive petitions making *different* claims. For instance, if a prisoner accidentally fails to raise a claim the first time around, it will probably not be permitted the second time. Also, a successive petition that raises different issues from the previous one should be dismissed if "the applicant has . . . on the earlier application deliberately withheld the newly asserted ground *or* otherwise abused the writ" (*McCleskey v. Zant*, 499 U.S. 467 [1991]; see also *Slack v. McDaniel*, 529 U.S. 473 [2000]).

## When a Habeas Corpus Proceeding Resembles a Trial

As previously emphasized, in most cases, an appellate court cannot decide issues of fact. Instead, it must focus on whether the law was correctly applied at the trial court level. If appellate courts were permitted to be fact finders, like trial courts, then their decisions would raise double-jeopardy problems. For example, if an appellate court acquitted a defendant because of an improperly obtained confession, then the prosecution's attempt to retry the defendant using other evidence (such as new eyewitness testimony) would be tantamount to trying the defendant twice for the same crime.

---

### DECISION-MAKING EXERCISE 15.10

#### WERE ALL STATE REMEDIES EXHAUSTED?

A man was convicted of murder in a trial court and appealed his conviction to the court of appeals, claiming that the trial judge's instructions to the jury were erroneous. The court of appeals affirmed the lower court's ruling. The man then appealed to the state supreme court. It, too, affirmed the man's conviction. He then petitioned the federal district court for a writ of *habeas corpus*, claiming that his constitutional right to due process was violated by the judge's erroneous instructions. He did not, however, raise the due process issue in any of the state-level appeals. Should his petition be heard?

However, an appellate court reviewing a *habeas corpus* petition *can* engage in fact-finding under certain limited circumstances. The leading case in this area is *Townsend v. Sain*, 372 U.S. 293 (1963). The Supreme Court identified six specific circumstances in which a *habeas* court may engage in independent fact-finding:

> (1) the merits of the factual dispute were not resolved in the state hearing; (2) the state factual determination is not fairly supported by the record as a whole; (3) the fact-finding procedure employed by the state court was not adequate to afford a full and fair hearing; (4) there is a substantial allegation of newly discovered evidence; (5) material facts were not adequately developed at the state court hearing; or (6) for any reason it appears that the state trier of fact did not afford the habeas applicant a full and fair hearing.

Importantly, a *habeas* court cannot engage in independent fact-finding if the petitioner deliberately bypasses state-level appellate mechanisms (*Keeney v. Tamayo-Reyes*, 504 U.S. 1 [1992]). In other words, the petitioner must exhaust state-level remedies before fact-finding can take place at a *habeas* proceeding. Taken together, *Townsend* and *Keeney* suggest that it is exceedingly difficult for a prisoner to succeed in having his or her guilt or innocence determined on *habeas* review.

## The Right to Counsel in the *Habeas Corpus* Context

Earlier in this chapter, it was shown that the Supreme Court has guaranteed the right to counsel in direct appeals of right but not in discretionary appeals. Since *habeas corpus* is purely discretionary, the Supreme Court has held that no right to counsel exists, unless, of course, the prisoner can afford representation (see *Ross v. Moffitt*, 417 U.S. 600 [1974]). The Court has held, however, that federal prisoners have a "constitutional right of access to the courts" (*Bounds v. Smith*, 430 U.S. 817 [1977]).

The Supreme Court has also held that a state cannot prohibit prisoners from helping each other prepare and submit *habeas corpus* petitions (*Johnson v. Avery*, 393 U.S. 483 [1969]). Moreover, the Court has held that an indigent *habeas corpus* petitioner is entitled to a free transcript of his or her trial to assist in preparing the appropriate paperwork (see *Griffin v. Illinois*).

## Retroactivity in the *Habeas Corpus* Context

Retroactivity in the *habeas corpus* context is different than it is in the appeals context. Specifically, *habeas corpus* decisions are less often made retroactive than appeals decisions. In *Teague*, discussed previously, the Court decided that only those appellate decisions that are dictated by precedent should be retroactive; that is, new rules should not be retroactive, unless one of two exceptions apply (which will be described below). Why such a strange rule? The Supreme Court has interpreted *habeas corpus* as deterring state courts from misapplying federal case law existing at the time. A new rule could have no deterrent effect because, by definition, it would not have been around long enough to serve a deterrent function.

Before discussing the exceptions, it is important to understand the term, "dictated by precedent." Decisions that are *dictated by precedent* are those to which the reviewing court has applied a previous decision. Assume, for example, that a prisoner files a *habeas* petition claiming that he was denied counsel at trial (which is highly unlikely). Relief will almost certainly be granted because precedent (the holding in *Gideon v. Wainright*) requires having counsel at trial. When the reviewing court hands down a new constitutional rule, however, there is no existing precedent that specifically governs the facts before the court, or the court is modifying or overruling old precedent. An example of a new constitutional rule would be that the Sixth Amendment requires counsel to be present at all *pre*-indictment lineups; this would be a new rule because such a rule is not in place at present.

▼

In *Teague*, the petitioner claimed that the requirement in *Taylor v. Louisiana*, 419 U.S. 522 [1975]), that a jury list represent a cross-section of the community should be applied to the jury itself. In essence, the petitioner was asking the Court to hand down a new rule because the Court also held in *Taylor* that the final jury does not need to represent a fair cross-section of the community. The Court found that neither of the two exceptions applied to petitioner Teague's claim.

New rules are not retroactive on *habeas corpus* review unless one of two exceptions is in place. First, in *Teague*, the Court held that a new rule should not be retroactive unless it places certain types of private individual conduct "beyond the power of the criminal law-making authority to proscribe." Needless to say, this language is a little cryptic. A example of this exception can be seen in *Bousley v. United States*, 523 U.S. 614 (1998). The petitioner in that case claimed that his guilty plea was involuntary because it was based on a flawed interpretation of the statute he was charged with violating. Specifically, the petitioner pled guilty to a firearms offense because he was under the impression that the statute prohibited mere *possession* of a firearm when, in fact, it prohibited *active use* of the firearm. The Court held that the claim could be heard because the petitioner was essentially convicted (through a guilty plea) for an act the statute did not define as criminal. In other words, the act in question was one that was "beyond the power of the criminal law-making authority to proscribe" (*Teague*).

Second, a "new rule" will not be retroactive to other cases pending review unless it is "implicit in the concept of ordered liberty." That is, only "watershed rules of criminal procedure," or those that are "central to an accurate determination of guilt" qualify as exceptions to the *Teague* rule.

The Court elaborated on this exception in *Sawyer v. Smith*, 497 U.S. 227 (1990), holding that a new rule is "implicit" to "ordered liberty" if it "alter[s] our understanding of the bedrock procedural elements essential to the fairness of a proceeding." The Court has yet to find a new rule that falls under this second exception. For example, in *Beard v. Banks*, 542 U.S. 406 (2004), the Court decided that its ruling in *Mills v. Maryland*, 486 U.S. 367 (1988), a case dealing with mitigating factors in capital sentencing, was a new one and therefore could not be applied retroactively. The *Mills* rule was to the effect that the Constitution's Eighth Amendment forbids states from imposing a requirement that the jury *unanimously* identify mitigating factors before such factors could figure into their death penalty decisions. The Court further noted that *Mills* did not meet either of *Teague*'s exceptions, which would have been necessary for the decision to be applied retroactively (see also *Schriro v. Summerlin*, 542 U.S. 348 [2004]).

In the recent case of *Whorton v. Bockting*, 549 U.S. 406 (2007), the Court declined to classify its decision in *Crawford v. Washington* (541 U.S. 35 [2004]—limiting hearsay evidence in domestic violence cases) as a "watershed rule." Nothing, however, prohibits states from adopting broader retroactivity standards (*Danforth v. Minnesota*, 552 U.S. ___ [2008]).

## The Antiterrorism and Effective Death Penalty Act (AEDPA) of 1996

To be sure, the *habeas corpus* process is fairly complex and often difficult to understand. It has become even more clouded in light of the **Antiterrorism and Effective Death Penalty Act** of 1996, which was passed in the wake of the infamous 1995 Oklahoma City bombing. The bombing led to numerous proposals in Congress on how to address terrorism. Early proposals called for drastic, controversial measures designed to curb the terrorist threat. Several months after the bombing, however, the legislation agreed to by both the House and the Senate was significantly less forceful. It was signed into law by then President Clinton in April 1996.

The AEDPA's supporters heralded it as a significant bipartisan achievement that would help root out terrorism. Critics of the new law claimed that it was so "watered down" that it had virtually nothing to do with combating terrorism. To some extent, the critics are probably correct. AEDPA's crowing achievement was to limit the authority of the federal courts to hear *habeas corpus* claims. Other, less litigious accomplishments are summarized in Figure 15.5.

### Restrictions on Habeas Corpus *Petitions Resulting from the AEDPA*

The first change to *habeas corpus* procedure resulting from the AEDPA is that review is permitted only when the state-level decision "(1) resulted in a decision that was contrary to, or involved an unreasonable application of, clearly established Federal law, as determined by the Supreme Court of the United States"; or (2) "resulted in a decision that was based on an unreasonable determination of the facts in light of the evidence presented in the State court proceeding" (28 U.S.C. Section 2254[d]). This set of rules can be contrasted with *Stone v. Powell*, cited earlier, in which the Supreme Court held that *habeas* review should not be granted when "the State has provided an opportunity for full and fair litigation of a Fourth Amendment claim." The AEDPA essentially limits this rule.

Second, the AEDPA alters *habeas* review in capital cases (cases in which the accused is on death row). The act provides that if a prisoner defaults and fails to submit a petition within a year, then review will only be granted when his or her failure to file a petition is "(1) the result of State action in violation of the Constitution or laws of the United States"; (2) "the result of the Supreme Court's recognition of a new Federal right that is made retroactively applicable"; or (3) "based on a factual predicate that could not have been discovered through the exercise of due diligence in time to present the claim for State or Federal post-conviction review" (28 U.S.C. Section 2264[a]). These new default rules are significantly more restrictive than those discussed earlier. In a recent decision, the Supreme Court stated that there is no extension to the one-year rule if a defendant has a petition for a writ of certiorari pending before the Supreme Court at the time (*Lawrence v. Florida*, 549 U.S. ___ [2007]; see also *Allen v. Siebert*, 552 U.S. 1 [2007]). However, in *McQuiggin v. Perkins*, 596 U.S. ___ (2013) the Court held that a defendant's actual innocence may provide an exception to the one-year rule.

The AEDPA also places restrictions on filing successive *habeas corpus* petitions. It states that a "claim presented in a second or successive *habeas corpus* application shall be dismissed" (28 U.S.C. Section 2244[b][1]). Indeed, there has already been one challenge to this part of the legislation, but the Supreme Court held that the new restriction was well within constitutional guidelines (*Felker v. Turpin*, 518 U.S. 651 [1996]).

The AEDPA further restricts filing successive petitions that raise different claims. Specifically, the legislation restricts a prisoner's different and successive claim to one that (1) "relies on a new rule of constitutional law, made retroactive to cases on collateral review by the Supreme Court, that was previously unavailable" or one for which (2) "the factual predicate could not have been discovered previously through the exercise of due diligence" and which "would be sufficient to establish by clear and convincing evidence that, but for constitutional error no reasonable factfinder would have found the applicant guilty of the underlying offense" (28 U.S.C. Section 2244[b][2]). The Court interpreted some of this confusing language in *Tyler v. Cain*, 533 U.S. 656 (2001).

Next, the AEDPA imposes strict filing deadlines for *habeas corpus* petitions. Namely, most *habeas corpus* petitions must be filed within one year from the date of the final state-level appellate judgment. For a death penalty case, the legislation is even more restrictive. It requires that a death row petition be filed within six months from the "final state court affirmance of the conviction and sentence on direct review or the expiration of the time for seeking review" (28 U.S.C. Sections 2244[d][1][A] & 2263). Both restrictions are

### Mandatory Victim Restitution

The mandatory victim restitution provisions of the bill require a federal court to impose mandatory restitution, without consideration of the defendant's ability to pay. This applies in any case in which an identifiable victim or victims suffered physical or pecuniary loss from an offense that is a crime of violence, an offense against property (including any offense committed by fraud or deceit), or a crime related to tampering with consumer products. Last year, Judge Maryanne Trump Barry (D. N.J.), chair of the Judicial Conference Committee on Criminal Law, testified before Congress on the issue of mandatory restitution, pointing out that such legislation would replace a flexible system, based on common sense and judicial discretion, with an inflexible, mandatory system that would be extremely expensive to implement.

### Closed Circuit Televised Proceedings for Victims of Crime

Another provision in the bill requires a federal trial court, in any criminal trial where the venue is changed from the state in which the case was originally brought and more than 350 miles from the location in which those proceedings originally would have taken place, to order closed circuit televising of the proceedings back to the original location. The televised coverage is to be provided for such persons the court determines have a compelling interest and who are otherwise—because of inconvenience or expense—unable to attend the trial.

The provision takes effect notwithstanding any contrary provision of the Federal Rules of Criminal Procedure, although there is a sunset mechanism. The Judicial Conference may promulgate and issue rules, or amend existing rules, to "effectuate the policy addressed by this section." Upon implementation of such rules, the closed circuit television provision ceases to be effective. The cost of such closed circuit proceedings will be paid for by appropriated funds and/or through donations.

### Other Provisions

Among other provisions in the bill are those that:

- Create an Alien Terrorist Removal Court composed of five sitting U.S. district judges designated by the Chief Justice;
- Expand the definition of an aggravated felony under which aliens may be deported, and streamline the deportation of criminal aliens after they serve their sentences;
- Create a five-member Commission on the Advancement of Federal Law Enforcement to study criminal law enforcement, the chair of which will be appointed by the Chief Justice;
- Authorize appropriations for the Judiciary of $41 million from the Crime Trust Fund from fiscal year 1997 to FY 2000 to help meet the increased demands for judicial branch activities resulting from enactment of the bill;
- Set compensation for court-appointed attorneys in capital cases at a rate of not more than $125 per hour for in-court and out-of-court time, but also authorize the Judicial Conference to increase the rate of compensation in the future under a "CPI escalator" mechanism;
- Cap fees and expenses paid for investigative and expert services in capital cases at $7,500, but provide for a waiver mechanism whereby such expenses can exceed that cap if the excess payment is certified by the court as necessary to provide fair compensation for services of an unusual character or duration and if the amount of the excess payment is approved by the chief judge of the circuit.

*Source*: "New Antiterrorism Law Contains Habeas Reform and Victim Restitution," *The Third Branch: The Newsletter of the Federal Courts* (Washington, DC: Administrative Office of the U.S. Courts, April 1996).

**FIGURE 15.5 Overview of the Antiterrorism and Effective Death Penalty Act (AEDPA) of 1996 (Unrelated to *Habeas Corpus*)**

intended to reduce the opportunities prisoners have to challenge their confinement and, in the case of death row inmates, to speed up execution. A flurry of recent Supreme Court decisions (e.g., *Jimenez v. Quarterman*, 555 U.S. 113 [2009]; *Holland v. Florida*, 560 U.S. ___ [2010]) have addressed these timing rules, but a full discussion is beyond the scope of this text.

Another AEDPA restriction on *habeas corpus*, though certainly not the last, addresses the *habeas* court's ability to engage in independent fact-finding. The legislation prohibits a *habeas* court from holding hearings to determine questions of fact unless the petitioner can make a showing of why such a review is necessary. The Supreme Court recently interpreted this requirement, making it even more restrictive (see *Williams v. Taylor*, 529 U.S. 420 [2000]).

The AEDPA imposes several other restrictions on *habeas* review that need not be addressed in depth here, although the Supreme Court is starting to address them on a fairly regular basis. For the purposes of this text, it is important to know that the AEDPA has altered *habeas corpus* procedure in many significant ways.

There is a tendency among many criminal justice critics to claim that criminals enjoy too many appeals. And while the AEDPA Act of 1996, not to mention a long line of Supreme Court cases, places significant restrictions on *habeas* review, the appellate and *habeas corpus* processes are still fundamental to the U.S. system of justice. Without them, the potential for mistakes would loom large.

# Summary

## 1. Explain how an appropriate sentence is determined.

A number of factors must guide a judge in crafting a sentence for each convicted offender. Some of these factors include, but are not limited to, the crime in question, the defendant's prior record, his or her ties to the community and family, the defendant's employment history, whether he or she was convicted for several different crimes as opposed to one specific crime, the degree of the defendant's cooperation with authorities during the investigative stage, the defendant's mental status, his or her feelings of remorse, if any, and several other pertinent factors.

Death penalty sentencing must be carried out with special care. The preferred method is to have a jury, not a judge, decide whether death is appropriate and to take into account aggravating and mitigating circumstances (see *Ring v. Arizona*, 122 S.Ct. 2428 [2002]). The death penalty is unconstitutional for young offenders but *is* sometimes appropriate for offenses other than first-degree murder. The Supreme Court has also handed down other important restrictions concerning death penalty sentencing. Excessive punishments may violate the Eighth Amendment's cruel and unusual punishment clause.

## 2. Describe the various types of appeals.

Once a sentence has been handed down, the convicted person can appeal. An appeal can also be sought prior to sentencing. This type of appeal is known as an *interlocutory appeal*. Most jurisdictions favor appeals after final adjudication, but sometimes it is necessary to appeal prior to conviction. An appeal filed prior to adjudication must be unrelated to the cause of action. An appeal filed after adjudication can be one of many varieties. Typically, the defendant is granted one appeal of right. Subsequent appeals are called discretionary appeals, because the appellate court decides if it wants to hear the appeal.

## 3. Outline the appeal process.

An appeal rarely results in the defendant going free. This point cannot be overemphasized. An appeal usually has one of two results: (1) The appellate court agrees with the trial court, in which case it affirms the lower court's decision; or (2) the appellate court reverses the trial court's decision. A reversal typically results in a new trial for the defendant, or a remand. Sometimes, a trial *de novo* is held at the appellate level, but usually only for a misdemeanor appeal.

The appellate process must be carried out such that the defendant's constitutional rights are respected. According to the Supreme Court, this means that the defendant (1) must have access to the trial transcripts; (2) must have access to counsel for appeals of right, though not necessarily for discretionary appeals; and (3) must not be retaliated against for exercising his or her right to appeal.

An appeal can also be filed by a party other than the defense, or a third party. For example, the prosecution can appeal the court's decision to exclude evidence. Another party, such as a witness, can appeal a subpoena requiring him or her to show up at court, but only if he or she is held in contempt for failing to appear.

Some appeals, though meritorious, may not succeed because they are based on harmless error. An appeal based on a nonconstitutional issue may be dismissed as harmless error if it does not influence the jury but has a very slight effect on the outcome of the trial. By contrast, to show that a constitutional error is harmless, the state must prove beyond a reasonable doubt that the error did not affect the verdict of the trial. However, in some cases, the Supreme Court has concluded that an error was so serious as to require automatic reversal of the defendant's conviction.

The last appeals issue considered in this chapter was that of retroactivity. To what extent should appellate court decisions benefit other defendants with similar appeals? The case law surrounding the issue of retroactivity is complex and confusing. But in sum, the retroactivity doctrine says that every new constitutional rule announced on direct review must be applied retroactively to other cases pending review that raise the same issue.

## 4. Summarize the right to, and restrictions on, *habeas corpus.*

*Habeas corpus* is another method for challenging one's conviction. It is also known as a collateral attack. The Supreme Court has restricted the right to *habeas* review in a number of ways. First, it has limited the types of claims that can succeed. Second, the Court has held that a *habeas corpus* review may not be granted if the petitioner fails to submit a claim within the time frame specified by state law. Third, it is generally necessary for a convicted individual to exhaust all state remedies before a federal *habeas* review will be granted. Finally, restrictions have been imposed in situations in which prisoners have filed multiple *habeas* petitions.

A *habeas corpus* proceeding can resemble a criminal trial in certain situations. In particular, a *habeas* court can engage in fact-finding (which is typically the province of the trial court). This is permissible when, for example, a factual dispute was not resolved at the state level or there is a substantial allegation of newly discovered evidence. Other such conditions have also been identified by the Supreme Court.

The Supreme Court has held that prisoners are not strictly entitled to counsel to assist in preparing their *habeas* petitions. They do, however, have constitutional access to the courts. In other words, the right to counsel is virtually nonexistent in the *habeas corpus* process, exists somewhat more so in the appellate process (mainly for direct appeals), and exists completely at trial.

Retroactivity is rare with regard to *habeas corpus* petitioners. Petitions that *do not* ask the reviewing court to hand down a new rule are retroactive. Those that *do* ask for a new rule are not retroactive unless (1) the new rule is one that involves individual conduct that cannot be prohibited by law or (2) the new rule is closely tied to the fairness of a criminal proceeding.

Finally, the Antiterrorism and Effective Death Penalty Act of 1996, passed in the wake of the Oklahoma City bombing, places significant restrictions on *habeas corpus*. The act does not completely supplant Supreme Court precedent pertaining to *habeas corpus* because the new restrictions imposed in the act rely heavily on past Supreme Court decisions.

# Key Terms

Antiterrorism and Effective Death Penalty Act *465*

appeal *444*

bifurcated trial *441*

determinate sentencing *438*

direct appeal *444*

discretionary appeal *444*

final judgment rule *450*

*habeas corpus 456*

harmless error *453*

indeterminate sentencing *438*

interlocutory appeal *450*

mandatory sentencing *438*

retroactivity *455*

sentencing guidelines *438*

# Key Cases

## Sentencing

- *Roberts v. United States*, 445 U.S. 552 (1980)
- *Furman v. Georgia*, 408 U.S. 238 (1972)
- *Gregg v. Georgia*, 428 U.S. 153 (1976)
- *Roberts v. Louisiana*, 428 U.S. 325 (1977)
- *United States v. Tucker*, 404 U.S. 443 (1972)

## Appeals

- *Griffin v. Illinois*, 351 U.S. 12 (1956)
- *Douglas v. California*, 372 U.S. 353 (1963)
- *North Carolina v. Pearce*, 395 U.S. 711 (1969)
- *Cohen v. Beneficial Industrial Loan Corp.*, 337 U.S. 541 (1949)

- *Carroll v. United States*, 354 U.S. 394 (1957)
- *Cobbledick v. United States*, 309 U.S. 323 (1940)
- *Kotteakos v. United States*, 328 U.S. 750 (1946)
- *Chapman v. California*, 386 U.S. 18 (1967)

## *Habeas Corpus*

- *Sanders v. United States*, 373 U.S. 1 (1963)
- *Stone v. Powell*, 428 U.S. 465 (1976)
- *Teague v. Lane*, 489 U.S. 288 (1989)
- *Herrera v. Collins*, 506 U.S. 390 (1993)
- *Hill v. United States*, 368 U.S. 424 (1962)
- *Kuhlmann v. Wilson*, 477 U.S. 436 (1986)
- *Fay v. Noia*, 372 U.S. 391 (1963)

# Further Exploration

1. Four broad goals of sentencing can be identified: (1) rehabilitation, or reformation; (2) retribution; (3) incapacitation; and (4) deterrence, either general or specific. Specific deterrence refers to discouraging the offender from committing additional crimes. General deterrence refers to discouraging all would-be offenders from committing crimes.

The differences among these four goals of punishment have been well-described in a famous case heard by the Pennsylvania Supreme Court, *Commonwealth v. Ritter* 13, Pa. D. & C. 285 (1930):

- As far as the principle of reformation is concerned, however important it may be in the general run of cases, it obviously has little or no application to such a case as the present. Whichever be the penalty here inflicted, the defendant will not again be in contact with society, and since secular law is concerned with one's relation to the community and not primarily with his inward moral development, the spiritual regeneration of a defendant is not, in such a case as this, a dominant factor. In other words, it would not be a practical consideration weighing in favor of life imprisonment that thereby the defendant might be susceptible of moral reformation, whereas the opportunity for this would be denied to him if the death penalty were inflicted.

- The second theory, which has been urged as a basis for the imposition of penalties, is that of retribution. This may be regarded as the doctrine of legal revenge, or punishment merely for the sake of punishment. It is to pay back the wrongdoer for his wrongdoing, to make him suffer by way of retaliation even if no benefit results thereby to himself or to others. This theory of punishment looks to the past and not to the future and rests solely upon the foundation of vindictive justice. It is this idea of punishment that generally prevails, even though those who entertain it may not be fully aware of their so doing. Historically, it may be said that the origin of all legal punishments had its root in the natural impulse of revenge. At first, this instinct was gratified by retaliatory measures on the part of the individual who suffered by the crime committed, or, in the case of murder, by his relatives. Later, the state took away the right of retaliation from individuals, and its own assumption of the function of revenge really constituted the beginning of criminal law. The entire course, however, of the refinement and humanizing of society has been in the direction of dispelling from penology any such theory. Indeed, even in classical times moralists and philosophers rejected the idea entirely. Plato puts into the mouth of Protagoras the words: "No one punishes those who have been guilty of injustice solely because they have committed injustice, unless indeed he punishes in a brutal and unreasonable manner. When any one makes use of his reason in inflicting punishment, he punishes, not on account of the fault that is past, for no one can bring it about that what has been done may not have been done, but on account of a fault to come, in order that the person punished may not again commit the fault and that his punishment may restrain from similar acts those persons who witness the punishment." . . .

- Rejecting, therefore, the theory of retribution as a proper basis upon which to impose the penalty of law, we come to the third principle which has been advocated, namely, the restraint of the wrongdoer in order to make it impossible for him to commit further crime. Here we arrive not only at a justifiable basis for action but at one which is vital to the protection of society. To permit a man of dangerous criminal tendencies to be in a position where he can give indulgence to such propensities would be a folly which no community should suffer itself to commit, any more than it should allow a wild animal to range at will in the city streets. If, therefore, there is danger that a defendant may again commit crime, society should restrain his liberty until such danger be past, and, in cases similar to the present, if reasonably necessary for that purpose, to terminate his life. Admittedly, restraint by imprisonment can never be as wholly effectual as execution, and there are, from time to time, cases where imprisonment may not be sufficient for the protection of society. It is on this ground that it is pertinent to take testimony in regard to the history of a defendant and of the circumstances attending his commission of crime. If his record shows that he is of a dangerous type, or that he habitually commits grave crimes, or that he has a homicidal tendency, or that he is hopelessly depraved, or that he has a savage nature, or that he has committed murder under circumstances of such atrocity and inhuman brutality as to make his continued existence one of likely danger to society, then, in my opinion, the sentence of death is both justifiable and advisable. The community may not be safe with such a man in existence even though he be serving a term of life imprisonment; he may again commit murder within the prison walls, or may escape and again make innocent victims his prey, or may even, by cunning simulation of repentance, obtain a pardon from governmental authorities. . . .

- This brings us to the final and what must be fairly regarded as one of the most important objectives of punishment, namely, the element of deterrence—the theory which regards the penalty as being not an end in itself but the means of attaining an end, namely, the frightening of others who might be tempted to imitate the criminal. From this angle, a penalty is a cautionary measure, aimed at the prevention of further crime in the community. There has been much controversy and an enormous amount of literature on the subject as to whether the death penalty does or does not act as a deterrent. With that controversy, we have nothing to do. As stated before, the law of Pennsylvania retains the death penalty as an optional alternative. The real question is not as to whether the death penalty is in general a deterrent, but as to the particular kinds of murder cases in which execution would or would not be most likely to effect deterrence. It becomes a problem of determining the basis upon which to make such classification.

Which goal of sentencing do you feel is most important? Explain why you think so.

2. There is much evidence of racial disparity in sentencing. See, for example, the report at this URL: http://www.sentencingproject.org/doc/publications/ rd_sentencing_review.pdf (accessed May 23, 2013). What is the nature of this disparity and why should we be concerned with it? What are the constitutional implications, if any?

3. Read more about interlocutory appeals and their many varieties here: http://digitalcommons.wcl.american. edu/cgi/viewcontent.cgi?article=1621&context=aulr (accessed May 23, 2013).

4. Here are the brief facts from retroactivity case not examined earlier in this chapter (*Butler v. McKellar*, 494 U.S. 407 [1990]):

Six weeks after Pamela Lane was murdered, petitioner Butler was arrested on an unrelated assault charge for which he retained counsel. While in custody, Butler was informed that he was a suspect in Lane's murder. After receiving *Miranda* warnings, he signed waiver of rights forms and made incriminating statements about the Lane murder during interrogation. At his capital murder trial, the court denied his motion to suppress these statements, and he was convicted and sentenced to death. After his conviction became final on direct appeal, he filed a petition for federal habeas relief, which was dismissed by the District Court. The Court of Appeals affirmed, rejecting his argument that *Edwards v. Arizona*, 451 U.S. 477, requires the police, during continuous custody, to refrain from all further questioning once an accused invokes his right to counsel on any offense. Subsequently, this Court handed down *Arizona v. Roberson*, 486 U.S. 675, which held that the Fifth Amendment bars police-initiated interrogation following a suspect's request for counsel in the context of a separate investigation. The Court of Appeals denied Butler's request for rehearing. It reasoned that he was not entitled to the retroactive benefit of *Roberson*. According to the court, the *Edwards-Roberson* limitations on police interrogation are only tangentially related to the truth-finding function. It viewed those limitations as part of the prophylactic protection of the Fifth Amendment right to counsel created to be "guidelines" for the law enforcement profession and held that Butler's interrogation, while contrary to present "guidelines," had been conducted in strict accordance with established law at the time.

What was the Court's decision? Did *Roberson* announce a new rule? If so, did it come within either of the exceptions announced in *Teague*?

# Review Questions

1. Explain the goals of sentencing.
2. Identify several criteria used in determining the appropriate sentence.
3. What constitutional rights exist during sentencing?
4. What guidelines has the Supreme Court imposed on the appellate process?
5. Summarize the relevant rules governing an appeal before and after adjudication.
6. Who else besides the defendant can appeal? For what reasons?
7. Explain the harmless error doctrine.
8. Explain the differences between constitutional and nonconstitutional errors.

9. What is retroactivity? How does it differ in the appeals process versus the *habeas corpus* process?
10. What is *habeas corpus*? From where does this right stem?
11. Summarize four restrictions on *habeas corpus* petitions.
12. When can a *habeas corpus* proceeding resemble a criminal trial?
13. Summarize the right to counsel as it applies (or does not apply) in the *habeas corpus* context.
14. Summarize the leading provisions of the Antiterrorism and Effective Death Penalty Act (AEDPA) of 1996.
15. What are some of the ways the AEDPA places restrictions on *habeas corpus*?

# Web Links and Exercises

1. U.S. Sentencing Commission: read about federal sentencing guidelines, including recent changes.
URL: http://www.ussc.gov (accessed May 23, 2013).

2. Sentencing project: read the latest in sentencing research. Is there racial disparity in sentencing? If so, what exactly is the disparity?
URL: http://www.sentencingproject.org (accessed May 23, 2013).

3. The appellate process: read about the federal appeals process in detail, particularly on page 35 at the following URL: http://www.uscourts.gov/uscourts/ FederalCourts/Publications/English.pdf (accessed May 23, 2013).

4. History of *habeas corpus*: see the timeline for *habeas corpus* and significant milestones throughout history.
URL: http://www.aclu.org/national-security/habeas-corpus-timeline (accessed May 23, 2013).

5. AEDPA: read the text of the Antiterrorism and Effective Death Penalty Act.
Suggested URL: http://thomas.loc.gov/cgi-bin/query/ z?c104:S.735.ENR: (accessed May 23, 2013).

# GLOSSARY

**18 U.S.C. Section 242.** A federal statute used to hold police officers (and other government actors) criminally liable for actions that cause violations of people's constitutional or other federally protected rights.

**18 U.S.C. Section 3501.** A federal statute enacted in the wake of the *Miranda* decision providing that any confession "shall be admissible in evidence if it is voluntarily given." The statute was deemed unconstitutional in *Dickerson v. United States* (530 U.S. 428 [2000]).

**42 U.S.C. Section 1983.** A federal statute that provides a remedy in federal court for the "deprivation of any rights . . . secured by the Constitution and laws" of the United States. Also called "Section 1983."

**absolute immunity.** A term referring to the fact that certain officials cannot ever be sued for their official decisions.

**accrediting.** It is the process by which the prosecution or defense attempts to support, bolster, or improve a witness's credibility.

**accusation rule.** The requirement that a person must first be accused (i.e., charged) for the Sixth Amendment's speedy trial provision to apply.

**ad hoc plea bargaining.** A term used to describe some of the strange concessions that defendants agree to make as part of prosecutors' decisions to secure guilty.

**administrative justification.** A standard used to support certain regulatory and special needs searches. Created by the Supreme Court, it adopts a balancing approach, weighing the privacy interests of individuals with the interests of society in preserving public safety.

**admission.** When a person can simply admit to involvement in a crime without any police encouragement.

**affirm.** An appellate court verdict that expresses agreement with a lower court's decision.

**Alford plea.** A guilty plea in which the defendant admits to the crime, but not necessarily all elements of it. An *Alford* plea does not require the defendant to allocute.

**allocution.** When the defendant explains to the judge exactly what he or she did and why. The defendant is usually required to allocate when he or she pleads guilty.

**Antiterrorism and Effective Death Penalty Act.** Federal legislation enacted in the wake of the Oklahoma City bombing in 1996. The legislation places significant restrictions on *habeas corpus*.

**apparent authority.** A person has apparent authority if the police *reasonably believe* he or she has authority to grant consent.

**appeal.** The practice of asking an appellate court to examine a lower court's decision in order to determine whether the proper procedure was followed or the correct law was applied.

**appellant.** The party that appeals; both the prosecutor and the defendant can appeal, although defense appeals are more common than prosecution appeals.

**appellee.** Sometimes called the respondent, this is the party appealed against.

**armspan rule.** Part of the search incident to arrest exception to the Fourth Amendment's warrant requirement that allows officers to search not only the suspect incident to arrest, but also his or her "grabbing area."

**arraignment.** A hearing in which the defendant is formally notified of the charge lodged against him or her. The defendant also enters one of three pleas: (1) guilty, (2) not guilty, or (3) *nolo contendere*.

**arrest warrant.** An order issued by a judge directing a law enforcement officer to arrest an individual identified as one who has committed a specific criminal offense.

**arrest.** The act of taking an individual into custody for the purpose of charging the person with a criminal offense (or, in the case of a juvenile, a delinquent act).

**articulable facts.** Events that are witnessed and can be explained. Contrast articulable facts with hunches and guesses. Articulable facts are necessary for establishing probable cause.

**automobile exception.** An exception to the Fourth Amendment's warrant requirement that permits police to search a vehicle without a warrant, so long as they have probable cause to do so.

**bail bond agent.** A professional who posts the defendant's bail in exchange for a fee.

**bail.** A process by which a defendant pays a certain amount of money in order to be released from jail prior to his or her trial date. Defendants who appear for trial receive their money back. Those who fail to appear for trial forfeit the bail amount.

**bifurcated trial.** Holding two separate proceedings in the death penalty context, one for determining guilt and another for determining the appropriate sentence (e.g., death or life in prison).

**Bivens claim.** A Section 1983 lawsuit against a federal official.

**Blockburger rule.** A rule stemming from *Blockburger v. United States* (284 U.S. 299 [1932]) that helps courts determine what constitutes the "same offense" for double-jeopardy purposes: "[w]here the same act or transaction constitutes a violation of two distinct statutory provisions, the test to be applied to determine whether there are two offenses or only one, is whether each requires proof of an additional fact which the other does not" (p. 304).

**booking.** The process by which an arrest is officially documented and the arrestee is placed into custody. During booking, the arrestee's personal items will be inventoried and he or she will be fingerprinted and/or photographed.

**bright-line decisions.** A decision in which a court hands down a *specific rule*, one subject to very little interpretation.

**case-by-case adjudication.** The reality that some cases cannot result in bright-line rules. Courts often look to the "totality of circumstances" when taking a case-by-case approach.

**chain of custody.** A chronological documentation (or paper trail) showing how seized evidence has been preserved, transferred, analyzed, and disposed of. It is mainly a record of the individuals who have had physical possession of the evidence at any point during the criminal process.

**challenges for cause.** A means of excluding prospective jurors who cannot be impartial. Prosecutors and defense attorneys have an unlimited number of challenges for cause in criminal cases.

**change of venue.** A process by which a trial is heard in another jurisdiction, perhaps in another county in the state.

**checkpoints.** Brief detentions that do not require probable cause or a warrant. Their purpose should *not* be to detect evidence of criminal conduct, such as narcotics trafficking. Examples include border checkpoints, illegal immigrant checkpoints, sobriety checkpoints, license and safety checkpoints, crime investigation checkpoints, and airport checkpoints.

**civil litigation.** The same as a lawsuit.

**civilian input.** A method of citizen input into the complaint review process in which a civilian panel receives and investigates a complaint, leaving adjudication and discipline with the department itself.

**civilian monitor.** The weakest method of citizen input that leaves investigation, adjudication, and discipline inside the department. A civilian is allowed to review the adequacy and impartiality of the process.

**civilian review.** The strongest method of citizen input in which a civilian panel investigates, adjudicates, and recommends punishment to the police chief.

**closely regulated business.** A type of business subject to warrantless, suspicionless inspections. Examples include liquor stores and firearm dealerships.

**common authority.** "mutual use of the property by persons generally having joint access or control for most purposes" (*United States v. Matlock*, 415 U.S. 164 [1974], p. 172, n. 7).

**competence.** A term that refers to a witness's ability to remember events, communicate effectively, and understand the importance of telling the truth, as well as the consequences of not doing so.

**compulsory process.** The Sixth Amendment requirement that criminal defendants enjoy the right to compel the production of witnesses and evidence. This is often accomplished via subpoena.

**concurring opinion.** At the U.S. Supreme Court level, an opinion authored by a justice in the majority that supports the majority's decision but with different legal logic. Concurring opinions are sometimes authored in lower appellate court cases.

**confession.** When a person implicates himself or herself in criminal activity following police questioning and/or interrogation.

**confrontation.** The defendant's Sixth Amendment right to be present at his or her trial, hear live testimony of adverse witnesses, and challenge such witnesses' statements in open court.

**consent search.** A search based on voluntary consent. A valid consent search permits a police officer to dispense with the Fourth Amendment's warrant and probable cause requirements.

**contempt power.** The grand jury's authority to hold people in contempt of court for failing to appear before it. Civil and criminal sanctions can be imposed.

**courts of general jurisdiction.** The main trial courts at the state level. They are usually located at the county level and are often called "superior courts."

**courts of limited jurisdiction.** Courts that have jurisdiction over relatively minor offenses and infractions. An example of a limited jurisdiction court is a traffic court.

**credibility.** A term concerned with whether the witness's testimony should be believed.

**crime control perspective.** A perspective that emphasizes the importance of controlling crime, perhaps to the detriment of civil liberties.

**criminal procedure.** A vast set of rules and guidelines that describe how suspected and accused criminals are to be handled and processed by the justice system.

**culpability.** In the Section 1983 context, the requirement that the plaintiff (i.e., the party suing) generally has to prove that the defendant officer intended for the violation to occur.

**curtilage.** The "area to which extends the intimate activity associated with the sanctity of a man's home and the privacies of life" (*Oliver v. United States*, 466 U.S. 170 [1984], p. 225).

**custody.** Typically an arrest. Custody is important in the *Miranda* context because *Miranda* warnings do not need to be read if a person is not in custody.

**damages.** Payment for injuries or perceived injuries suffered. The defendant(s) named in a civil lawsuit may be ordered to pay such damages.

**deadly force.** Force that is likely to cause death or serious bodily harm.

**defendant.** The person charged with a crime.

**deliberate elicitation.** In the Sixth Amendment right to counsel context, deliberate elicitation occurs when police officers create a situation likely to induce a suspect into making an incriminating statement.

**determinate sentencing.** A sentencing strategy that permits the judge to set the sentence, and the sentence cannot later be altered by a parole board.

**direct appeal.** An appeal that is authorized by law.

**discovery.** The process by which each party to a case learns of the evidence that the opposition will present.

**discrediting.** When the prosecution or defense attempts to attack or challenge a witness's credibility.

**discretionary appeal.** An appeal that will be heard only if the reviewing court agrees to do so.

**disparate impact.** A method of acting that treats one group in a markedly different fashion than another.

**dissent.** At the U.S. Supreme Court level, an opinion written by a justice in the minority that expresses disagreement with the majority decision. Dissenting opinions are sometimes authored in lower appellate court cases.

**distinctive group.** Historically protected groups that should not be excluded from jury service, namely women and minorities.

**distinguish.** An appellate court's decision to treat a case before it as sufficiently distinct that it cannot be decided by looking to past rulings. In other words, the set of facts is unique and never before considered by an appellate court.

**district courts.** Federal trial courts. There are 94 federal district courts in the United States, including 89 district courts in the 50 states and 1 each in Puerto Rico, the Virgin Islands, the District of Columbia, Guam, and the Northern Mariana Islands.

**double-blind lineup.** A lineup procedure in which neither the witness nor the investigator staging the lineup knows who the suspect is.

**double jeopardy.** The Fifth Amendment requirement that a person cannot be reprosecuted after acquittal, reprosecuted after conviction, or subjected to separate punishments for the same offense.

**drug and alcohol testing.** A procedure of testing for drug or alcohol use, usually via urinalysis. Employees and school students can be subjected to warrantless, suspicionless drug and alcohol testing, but hospital patients cannot—if the evidence is turned over to law enforcement authorities.

**drug courier profiling.** A crime-detection process that makes use of what is known about the likely and observable characteristics of drug couriers. Drug courier profiling usually occurs in stop-and-frisk situations.

**due process perspective.** A general concern with people's rights and liberties. The due process perspective is closely aligned with a liberal political orientation.

**due process voluntariness approach.** The requirement that any confession be voluntary under the "totality of circumstances."

**effective assistance of counsel.** The requirement that a defense attorney must effectively represent his or her client. In *Strickland v. Washington* (466 U.S. 668 [1984]), the Supreme Court held that a two-prong test must be applied in order to determine whether counsel is ineffective: "First, the defendant must show that counsel's performance was deficient. This requires showing that counsel made errors so serious that counsel was not functioning as the 'counsel' guaranteed the defendant by the Sixth Amendment. Second, the defendant must show that the deficient performance prejudiced the defense" (p. 687).

**Eighth Amendment.** Part of the U.S. Constitution, which states: "Excessive bail shall not be required, nor excessive fines imposed, nor cruel and unusual punishments inflicted."

**Electronic Communications Privacy Act.** Federal legislation enacted in 1986 that amended Title III of the Omnibus Crime Control and Safe Streets Act to include "electronic communications."

**entrapment defense.** A criminal defense based on the belief that someone should not be convicted of a crime that the government instigated. It is a defense in the criminal law sense, but it is one of the only defenses that calls into question law enforcement's role in the instigation of a crime. This is why entrapment is important in criminal procedure.

**evanescent evidence.** Evidence that is likely to disappear. An example is alcohol in a person's bloodstream.

**exceptions to the warrant requirement.** Law enforcement actions that do not require a warrant. Examples include searches incident to arrest, searches based on exigent circumstances, automobile searches, plain view searches, arrests based on exigent circumstances, and arrests in public places.

**exclusionary rule.** The Supreme Court–created rule requiring that evidence obtained in violation of the Constitution cannot be used in a criminal trial to prove guilt.

**exigent circumstances.** Emergency circumstances, including hot pursuit, the possibility of escape, or evanescent evidence. When exigent circumstances are present, the police do not need to abide by the Fourth Amendment's warrant requirement.

**extralegal remedies.** Remedies conducted outside the legal process, such as a personal vendetta.

**fair examination rule.** The requirement that a witness, including the defendant, at either a trial or a grand jury hearing can be compelled to answer questions once he or she waives Fifth Amendment protection and begins to testify.

*Federal Rules of Criminal Procedure.* The rules that govern the conduct of all criminal proceedings brought in federal courts.

**Fifth Amendment.** Part of the U.S. Constitution, which states: "No person shall be held to answer for a capital, or otherwise infamous crime, unless on a presentment or indictment of a Grand Jury, except in cases arising in the land or naval forces, or in the Militia, when in actual service in time of War or public danger; nor shall any person be subject for the same offense to be twice put in jeopardy of life or limb; nor shall be compelled in any criminal case to be a witness against himself, nor be deprived of life, liberty, or property, without due process of law; nor shall private property be taken for public use, without just compensation."

**final judgment rule.** The requirement that interlocutory appeals dealing with questions of the defendant's guilt (rather than questions of a constitutional nature) cannot be heard until after final adjudication.

**Foreign Intelligence Surveillance Act.** Federal legislation enacted in 1978 that regulates electronic surveillance as it pertains to foreign intelligence gathering.

**Foreign Intelligence Surveillance Court.** A secretive court created by the Foreign Intelligence Surveillance Act. The court reviews applications for warrants related to surveillance in national security investigations.

**formal criminal proceeding.** In the Sixth Amendment right to counsel context, either a formal charge, a preliminary hearing, indictment, information, or arraignment.

**Fourteenth Amendment.** Part of the U.S. Constitution, which states: "All persons born or naturalized in the United States, and subject to the jurisdiction thereof, are citizens of the United States and of the State wherein they reside. No State shall make or enforce any law which shall abridge the privileges or immunities of citizens of the United States, nor shall any State deprive any person of life, liberty, or property, without due process of law; nor deny to any person within its jurisdiction the equal protection of the laws."

**Fourth Amendment.** Part of the U.S. Constitution, which states: "The right of the people to be secure in their persons, houses, papers, and effects, against unreasonable searches and seizures, shall not be violated, and no Warrants shall issue, but upon probable cause, supported by Oath or affirmation and particularly describing the place to be searched, and the persons or things to be seized."

**frisk.** A superficial examination by the officer of the person's body surface or clothing to discover weapons or items that could be used to cause harm.

**"fruit of the poisonous tree" doctrine.** An extension of the exclusionary rule. The "poisonous tree" is the initial unconstitutional search or seizure. Anything obtained from the tree is considered "forbidden fruit" and is not admissible at trial.

**functional equivalent of a question.** "[A]ny words or actions on the part of the police (other than those normally attendant to arrest and custody) that the police should know are reasonably likely to elicit an incriminating response from the suspect (*Rhode Island v. Innis*, 446 U.S. 291 [1980], p. 302, n. 8).

**gag order.** A judicial order limiting what the press and/or the parties to a particular case can divulge until the proceedings are completed.

**general deterrence.** When others besides the sentenced offender are discouraged from committing additional crimes due to sentencing practices.

**"good faith" exception.** An exception to the exclusionary rule providing that when an honest mistake is made during the course of a search or seizure, any subsequently obtained evidence will be considered admissible.

**government action.** Action on the part of paid government officials, usually police officers. Government action is one of two requirements (the other being infringement on one's reasonable expectation of privacy) that must be in place for a Fourth Amendment search to occur.

**grand jury.** A body of people selected to hear evidence against an accused person (or persons) and determine whether there is sufficient evidence to bring the case to trial.

**guilty.** A plea in which the defendant claims responsibility for the crime with which he or she has been charged.

*habeas corpus.* A means of challenging the constitutionality of one's confinement, best viewed as an alternative to appealing. *Habeas corpus* is a constitutional right (Article I, Section 9, Clause 2).

**harmless error.** A mistake at the trial level that has little practical consequence in terms of deciding whether the defendant is guilty or innocent.

**hearsay exceptions.** Exceptions to the rule that hearsay is not permissible in a criminal trial. Hearsay is something that is "heard, then said." It is considered unreliable because it is filtered through a second party. An example of hearsay would be this: A witness testifies that someone else told her the defendant committed the crime. Ideally, the "someone else" would appear in court. Generally, hearsay statements such as this are not admissible. There are, however, several established exceptions to the hearsay rule (see Figure 14.2).

**hot pursuit.** An exigent circumstance that permits dispensing with the Fourth Amendment's warrant requirement. Hot pursuit applies only when the police have probable cause to believe (1) that the person they are pursuing has committed a serious offense; (2) that the person will be found on the premises the police seek to enter; and (3) that the suspect will escape or harm someone or that evidence will be lost or destroyed. Also, the pursuit must originate from a lawful vantage point and the scope and timing of the search must be reasonable.

**house.** In Fourth Amendment terms, any structure that a person uses as a residence (and frequently a business) on either a temporary or long-term basis.

**immediately apparent.** One of the requirements for a proper plain view seizure. The police must have probable cause that the item is subject to seizure.

**impartial judge.** A judge who is capable of basing his or her decisions on the law and who has no conflict of interest or pecuniary stake in the outcome of the case. There is no constitutional right to an impartial judge. This right is a Supreme Court creation.

**impartial jury.** A jury that is capable of making a decision based solely on the facts of the case.

**impeachment exception.** An exception to the exclusionary rule providing that evidence considered inadmissible at one trial can be used in later trial to impeach (i.e., cast doubt on the credibility) the defendant.

**impeachment.** The formal term for attacking a witness's credibility (similar to discrediting).

**incorporation.** The Supreme Court's practice of using the Fourteenth Amendment's due process clause, which holds that no state shall "deprive any person of life, liberty, or property, without due process of law," to make certain protections specified in the Bill of Rights applicable to the states.

**in-court showup.** A procedure in which a witness identifies the perpetrator in court. This sometimes occurs when a prosecutor asks a testifying witness to point to the perpetrator.

**independent source.** An exception to the fruit of the poisonous tree doctrine that permits the introduction of evidence if it has arrived via an independent source, such as a party disconnected from the case at hand.

**indeterminate sentencing.** A sentencing strategy that gives the judge the authority to set the sentence.

**individual liability.** In the Section 1983 context, the theory that the officer who allegedly committed the constitutional rights violation should be held liable.

**inevitable discovery.** An exception to the fruit of the poisonous tree doctrine that permits the introduction of evidence if it would have been discovered anyway.

**initial appearance.** The first appearance of an accused person before a judge. Trial may occur for misdemeanors.

**injunctive relief.** A court-ordered prohibition against a certain act or condition.

**inspection.** An exception to the Fourth Amendment's warrant requirement that permits certain authorities to inspect a closely regulated business.

**interlocutory appeal.** An appeal filed prior to adjudication.

**intermediate appellate courts.** At the state level, courts to which verdicts from courts of general jurisdiction are appealed.

**internal review.** A nonjudicial remedy in which the police investigate on their own complaints against officers.

**interrogation.** Express questioning (e.g., Where were you on the night of the crime?) or the functional equivalent of a question (see definition). The definition of interrogation is important in the *Miranda* context because *Miranda* warnings do not need to be read if a person is not technically interrogated.

**investigative detention.** Also called a stationhouse detention, a less intrusive detention than an arrest but more intrusive than a *Terry* stop. Stationhouse detentions are used in many locations for such purposes as obtaining fingerprints and photographs, ordering lineups, administering polygraph examinations, and securing other types of evidence.

**joinder.** When the prosecutor either (1) brings multiple charges against the same individual in the same trial or (2) brings charges against multiple individuals in the same trial.

**judicial activism.** The opposite of judicial restraint. A judicially active judge is one who sees his or her role as more than interpreting the Constitution. A judicially active judge avoids precedent, preferring to hand down decisions with sweeping implications for the future.

**judicial inducements.** When a judge offers something to the defendant in exchange for a guilty plea. Most judicial inducements are prohibited.

**judicial restraint.** The philosophy of limiting decisions to the facts of each case, deciding only the issue or issues that need to be resolved in a particular situation.

**jury list.** The master list from which prospective jurors are subpoenaed. Examples include lists of those with drivers' licenses or voter registration lists.

**jury panel.** The list of individuals drawn from the jury list. The jury panel consists of those individual subpoenaed for jury service.

**jury sequestration.** The process of confining jurors during a trial. Sequestered jurors usually spend nights in the same hotel together and have little to no access to press coverage of the case on which they are serving as jurors.

**justification.** Also known as cause, justification is necessary for the police to engage in actions that trigger the Fourth Amendment. Examples of justification include probable cause and reasonable suspicion.

**"knock and announce" requirement.** The requirement that, before executing an arrest or search warrant, officers identify themselves and their intentions.

**"knock and talk".** A police tactic used to obtain consent to search, in which police officers approach a home, knock on the door, and request consent to search the premises.

**lawful access.** One of the requirements for a proper plain view seizure. The police must have lawful access to the item seized.

**legal remedies.** Remedies made available by the law, by a court decision, or by a police agency policy or procedure.

**lineup.** An identification procedure in which the suspect is placed alongside several other people who resemble him or her. The intent of the procedure is to ensure that a witness or victim picks the suspect out of the lineup.

**live testimony.** The confrontation requirement that adverse witnesses provide live testimony.

**mandatory sentencing.** A sentencing strategy that takes discretion away from judges. The law, not the judge, sets the sentence.

**mediation.** A method of alternative dispute resolution in which a neutral third party renders disciplinary decisions.

**mental competence.** One of two confrontation requirements. In order to be "present at his/her trial," the defendant must be not only physically present but also mentally competent. A defendant who is not mentally competent cannot adequately confront adverse witnesses.

**Miranda warnings.** While there are some variations, the *Miranda* warnings contain four elements: (1) You have the right to remain silent; (2) anything you say can be used against you in court; (3) you have the right to talk to an attorney and to have the attorney with you during questioning; and (4) if you cannot afford an attorney, one will be provided for you.

**municipal/county liability.** In the Section 1983 context, the theory that a municipality or county should be held liable for the actions of one of its officers, such as for failure to train.

**neutral and detached magistrate.** One of the three elements of a valid warrant, any judge who does not have a conflict of interest or pecuniary interest in the outcome of a particular case or decision.

**nolo contendere.** A plea similar to guilty with a literal meaning of "I do not desire to contest the action." It resembles a guilty plea but is different in the sense that it may not be used against the defendant in any later civil litigation that arises from the acts that led to the criminal charge.

**noncriminal proceeding rule.** The rule that limits juries to criminal trials. The rule is a bit of a misnomer because civil trials are by jury. The noncriminal proceeding applies to steps of the criminal process that are not themselves considered "criminal." Examples are juvenile adjudicatory hearings and civil commitment hearings.

**nondeadly force.** Force that is unlikely to cause death or serious bodily harm.

**nonreciprocal discovery.** Discovery that benefits one side in a criminal case, but not the other. For example, the prosecution is required to share exculpatory evidence with the defendant, but there is no such requirement for the defense.

**nonstop.** A consensual encounter.

**not guilty.** A plea in which the defendant does not claim responsibility for the crime with which he or she has been charged. A not guilty plea is not the same as a plea of innocent. There is no plea of innocent.

**objective reasonableness.** When evaluating the actions of law enforcement officials, conduct that would be considered acceptable by a "reasonable person." A judge usually decides what a "reasonable person" would consider acceptable.

**ombudsman.** A term used to describe the neutral third party who conducts mediation.

**open field.** Any unoccupied or undeveloped real property falling outside the curtilage of a home (*Oliver v. United States*, 466 U.S. 170 [1984], p. 170).

**opinion.** The voice of the majority of judges in an appellate court decision. At the U.S. Supreme Court level, the opinion is the voice of at least five justices.

**papers and effects.** In Fourth Amendment terms, nearly all personal items. Business records, letters, diaries, memos, and countless other forms of tangible evidence can be defined as *papers. Effects* is the catch-all category.

**particularity.** The Fourth Amendment requirement that an arrest warrant name the person to be arrested (or provide a sufficiently detailed description) and that a search warrant describe the place to be searched and the things to be seized.

**Patriot Act.** Controversial legislation passed in the wake of the September 11, 2001, terrorist attacks on the World Trade Center towers and the Pentagon.

**peremptory challenge.** A means of excluding prospective jurors with no reason offered. Peremptory challenges are limited depending on the case type and the jurisdiction. Peremptory challenges cannot be used to excuse prospective jurors based on race.

**person inventory.** A procedure used to take record of a person's personal possessions after he or she has been lawfully arrested. Person inventories do not invoke the Fourth Amendment and do not require probable cause—but they can only occur after an a lawful arrest (i.e., one satisfying Fourth Amendment requirements).

**person.** In Fourth Amendment terms, the individual as a whole, both internally and externally. The term "person" includes words communicated that are not used for identification purposes.

**petitioner.** The name given to a convicted criminal who challenges the constitutionality of his or her confinement via a *habeas corpus* petition.

**photographic array.** A procedure in which several photographs, including one of the suspect, are shown to a witness or victim, and he or she is asked to pick out the perpetrator.

**physical evidence.** The opposite of testimonial evidence. Physical evidence can include murder weapons, documents, and even the results from police lineups.

**physical presence.** One of two confrontation requirements. In order to be "present at his/her trial," the defendant must be physically present (as opposed, for example, to appearing via closed-circuit television).

**"plain view" doctrine.** An exception to the Fourth Amendment's warrant requirement that permits police to seize certain items in plain view.

**plea bargaining.** "The defendant's agreement to plead guilty to a criminal charge with the reasonable expectation of receiving some consideration from the state."[1]

**police–probation partnerships.** A practice of teaming probation officers with police officers to do crime control or prevention. Such partnerships are controversial because police officers can effectively skirt the Fourth Amendment's requirements when they team with probation officers who have more latitude to conduct searches of probationers.

**precedent.** A rule of case law (i.e., a decision by a court) that is binding on all lower courts and the court that issued it.

**preliminary hearing.** A hearing that serves as a check on the prosecutor's charging decision. The standard of proof is probable cause, and the main inquiry in the hearing is whether there is probable cause to take the case to trial. The preliminary hearing is to be distinguished from the initial appearance, the probable cause hearing, and the pretrial release hearing. It almost always takes place after one of these hearings as well as after the charging decision.

**pretextual prosecution.** When the prosecutor lacks the evidence to charge someone with a particular crime and so charges him or her with a lesser crime.

**pretrial release.** One of several methods to release a defendant prior to his or her trial date.

**preventive detention.** The act of denying bail to certain defendants who are either dangerous or pose a high flight risk.

---

[1]H. S. Miller, W. F. McDonald, and J. A. Cramer, *Plea Bargaining in the United States* (Ann Arbor, MI: Inter University Consortium for Political and Social Research, 1978), pp. 1–2.

**pro se defense.** When a defendant waives his or her Sixth Amendment right to counsel and defends himself or herself.

**probable cause hearing.** A hearing in which a judge decides whether there was probable cause to arrest. If the arrest was with a warrant, the probable cause hearing is not necessary. Also called a *Gerstein* hearing (for the Supreme Court's decision in *Gerstein v. Pugh*).

**probable cause.** More than bare suspicion; it exists when "the facts and circumstances within [the officers'] knowledge and of which they [have] reasonably trustworthy information [are] sufficient to warrant a prudent man in believing that the [suspect] had committed or was committing an offense" (*Beck v. Ohio*, 379 U.S. 89 [1964], p. 91). In practical terms, more than 50 percent certainty. The comparable civil standard is preponderance of evidence.

**procedural due process.** Protection of significant life, liberty, or property interests, sometimes described as "procedural fairness."

**prosecutor.** The official representing the government in a criminal case.

**prosecutorial discretion.** A prosecutor's authority to decide whether to proceed with criminal charges against a particular suspect.

**prosecutorial inducements.** Offers made by the prosecution to the defendant.

**Protect America Act.** Controversial legislation enacted in August 2007 which revised the Foreign Intelligence Surveillance Act to permit *warrantless* interceptions of certain communications. It expired in February 2007.

**protective sweep.** A cursory visual inspection of those places in which a person might be hiding.

**public duty defense.** A defense that shields police officers from criminal liability when performing certain official functions, such as using deadly force.

**public trial.** A trial that is open to the public and/or complies with the Sixth Amendment's public trial provision. Courts can sometimes limit public access and the proceedings will still be considered public.

**"purged taint" exception.** An exception to the fruit of poisonous tree doctrine that permits the introduction of evidence if it has become attenuated to the extent that it dissipated the taint of the initial unconstitutional act.

**racial profiling.** The practice of stopping people based on race rather than legitimate criteria.

**real world.** A term used to describe the world in which criminal justice officials, including the police, operate on a daily basis.

**reasonable expectation of privacy.** An expectation of privacy that society (through the eyes of a judge) is prepared to accept as reasonable. For a search to occur, a reasonable expectation of privacy must be infringed upon by a government actor.

**reasonable suspicion.** Justification that falls below probable cause but above a hunch. Reasonable suspicion is Court-created justification; it is not mentioned in the Fourth Amendment. Reasonable suspicion is necessary for police to engage in stop-and-frisk activities.

**reasonableness clause.** The first part of the Fourth Amendment: "The right of the people to be secure in their persons, houses, papers, and effects, against unreasonable searches and seizures, shall not be violated . . . "

**reasonableness.** When evaluating questionable police action, it is first necessary to determine whether the Fourth Amendment applies. If it does, then we ask, Did the police act in line with Fourth Amendment requirements?; This question is concerned with the reasonableness of the action in question.

**rehabilitation.** A goal of sentencing that consists of a planned intervention intended to change behavior (e.g., drug treatment); the process of restoring a witness's credibility.

**release on recognizance (ROR).** The accused is released with the assumption that he or she will show up for scheduled court hearings.

**remand.** An appellate court verdict that sends a case back to the lower court for further action consistent with the appellate court's decision.

**remedy.** A method of rectifying wrongdoing.

**retroactivity.** The extent to which appellate court decisions should apply only to the appellant or to other similarly situated individuals.

**reverse.** An appellate court verdict that is akin to nullifying or setting aside a lower court's verdict.

**right to privacy.** A judicially created right that is found nowhere in the Constitution.

**rule of four.** The requirement that four U.S. Supreme Court justices must agree to hear a case before it goes before the full Court.

**same offense.** For double-jeopardy purposes, the same offense is one that has the same elements as another offense. For example, first- and second-degree murders are considered the "same offense" for double-jeopardy purposes. First-degree murder is defined as the premeditated deliberate killing of another person. Second-degree murder is the same offense, less the premeditation requirement. A person cannot be convicted of both offenses, otherwise a double-jeopardy violation occurs.

**school disciplinary "searches".** Though they are not "searches" in the traditional Fourth Amendment sense, school officials can search (K-12) students' possessions without a warrant or probable cause for evidence of activity in violation of school policy.

**search.** For Fourth Amendment purposes, a government action that infringes on one's reasonable expectation of privacy.

**search incident to arrest.** An exception to the Fourth Amendment's warrant requirement that allows officers to search a suspect following his or her arrest.

**search warrant.** An order issued by a judge directing a law enforcement officer to search a particular location for evidence connected with a specific criminal offense.

seizure. One of two government actions (the other being searches) restricted by the Fourth Amendment. Seizures can be of persons or property.

seizure of a person. A seizure of a person occurs when a police officer—by means of physical force or show of authority—intentionally restrains an individual's liberty in such a manner that a reasonable person would believe that he or she is not free to leave (*Terry v. Ohio*, 392 U.S. 1 [1968]; *United States v. Mendenhall*, 446 U.S. 544 [1980]).

seizure of property. A seizure of property occurs when "there is some meaningful interference with an individual's possessory interest in that property" (*United States v. Jacobsen* (466 U.S. 109 [1984]).

selective prosecution. When an individual is targeted for prosecution merely because he or she falls into a certain group (e.g., a minority group).

sentencing guidelines. State and federal rules used to set sentences based on offense severity and the offender's prior record. Sentencing guidelines achieve a balance between determinate and indeterminate sentencing.

severance. The opposite of joinder. For example, severance occurs when separate trials are held for different charges against the same defendant.

showup. An identification procedure in which the suspect is brought before the witness (or victim) alone, so the witness can be asked whether that person is the perpetrator.

"silver platter" doctrine. A practice prior to *Elkins v. United States* (364 U.S. 206 [1960]) that permitted the use of evidence in *federal* court that had been obtained illegally by *state* officials.

six-month imprisonment rule. The rule that limits jury trials to cases where more than six-months' incarceration in jail or prison is possible.

Sixth Amendment. Part of the U.S. Constitution, which states: "In all criminal prosecutions, the accused shall enjoy the right to a speedy and public trial, by an impartial jury of the State and district wherein the crime shall have been committed, which district shall have been previously ascertained by law, and to be informed of the nature and cause of the accusation; to be confronted with the witnesses against him; to have compulsory process for obtaining witnesses in his favor, and to have the Assistance of Counsel for his defence."

speedy trial. A trial that meets with the Sixth Amendment's requirement for a speedy trial. A trial is no longer "speedy" when there is intentional delay that is prejudicial to the defendant's case.

stare decisis. A Latin term that means to abide by or to adhere to decided cases. Most courts adhere to the principle of *stare decisis*.

state supreme courts. The highest courts at the state level.

statutory inducements. Statutes that offer incentives for pleading guilty.

stop. Sometimes called an "investigative stop" or an "investigative detention," a brief nonconsensual encounter between a law enforcement officer and a citizen that does not rise to the level of an arrest; the detention of a person by a law enforcement officer for the purpose of investigation.

subjective reasonableness. When evaluating the actions of law enforcement officials, conduct that would be considered reasonable by the police officer engaged in the conduct.

subpoena *ad testificandum*: A subpoena that compels a witness to appear before the grand jury.

subpoena *duces tecum*: A subpoena that compels the production of tangible evidence (e.g., a suspected murder weapon).

substantive due process. Protection from arbitrary and unreasonable action on the part of state officials.

suggestive lineup. A flawed lineup that almost ensures the victim or witness will identify the suspect. For example, if the suspect is male and the other lineup participants are female, this would be a suggestive lineup.

superior courts. The most common name for state-level courts of general jurisdiction.

supervisory liability. In the Section 1983 context, the theory that a supervisor (such as a sergeant or captain) should be held liable.

systematic exclusion. Exclusion of a distinctive group from jury service. Systematic exclusion is something more than just significant exclusion.

tainted identification. An identification that would not have taken place but for some earlier unconstitutional activity.

testimonial evidence. For Fifth Amendment purposes, "testimonial evidence" is loosely defined to include incriminating statements made at any point during the criminal justice process, whether or not the person making such statements is under oath.

theory of liability. The logic offered for who should be held accountable—and why.

theoretical world. A term used to illustrate the fact that some court decisions are divorced from reality and/or may not directly affect criminal justice officials.

Title III of the Omnibus Crime Control and Safe Streets Act. Federal legislation enacted in 1968 that set forth detailed guidelines on how authorities could intercept wire, oral, or electronic communications.

totality of circumstances. All the facts and circumstances surrounding the case. In case-by-case adjudication, these must be examined in order to determine whether a constitutional rights violation has taken place.

trespass doctrine. The practice of the U.S. Court prior to *Katz v. United States* that required a physical intrusion by authorities into a person's private property for the Fourth Amendment to be implicated.

trial *de novo*. A type of appeal in which with appellate court holds a new trial as if the prior trial never occurred.

**true bill.** The grand jury's endorsement that it found sufficient evidence to warrant a criminal charge.

**U.S. courts of appeals.** At the federal level, courts to which verdicts from the district courts are appealed.

**U.S. Supreme Court.** The highest court in the federal court system.

**unavailable witness.** For purposes of confrontation, an unavailable witness is one who permanently moves to another country, cannot be located after a careful search by the prosecution, or suffers from a lapse in memory.

**vacate.** An appellate court decision that is, for all practical purposes, the same as a reversal.

**variance.** When the prosecutor presents evidence at trial that departs significantly from that relied on by the grand jury for the purpose of issuing an indictment.

**vehicle inventory.** A procedure used to take record of a vehicle's contents after it has been lawfully impounded. Vehicle inventories do not invoke the Fourth Amendment and do not require probable cause.

**vindictive prosecution.** Prosecution based on revenge.

**voir dire.** The process of selecting jurors for service. *Voir dire* proceeds through three stages: questioning by the judge, challenges for cause, and peremptory challenges.

**warrant clause.** The second part of the Fourth Amendment: " . . . and no Warrants shall issue, but upon probable cause, supported by Oath or affirmation, and particularly describing the place to be searched, and the persons or things to be seized."

**Warren Court.** The time from 1953 to 1969, during which Earl Warren was chief justice. The Warren Court handed down a number of decisions, particularly throughout the 1960s, that provided extensive constitutional protections for criminal defendants.

**writ of certiorari.** An order by the court, requiring the lower court to send the case and a record of its proceedings to the U.S. Supreme Court for review.

# PHOTO CREDITS

# CASE INDEX

*Katz v. United States,* **389 U.S. 347 (1967),** 11, 27, 37, 70, 74, 121, 178, 456

*Kaufman v. United States,* 394 U.S. 217 (1969), 459

*Keeney v. Tamayo-Reyes,* 504 U.S. 1 (1992), 464

*Kentucky v. King,* 563 U.S. ___ (2011), 138

*Kentucky v. Stincer,* 479 U.S. 1028 (1987), 410

*Ker v. California,* 374 U.S. 23 (1963), 41, 43

*Kimbrough v. United States,* 552 U.S. 85 (2007), 443

*Kirby v. Illinois,* **406 U.S. 682 (1972),** 226, 252, 329, 334, 354

*Klopfer v. North Carolina,* 386 U.S. 213 (1967), 9

*Knowles v. Iowa,* **525 U.S. 113 (1998),** 131

*Kolender v. Lawson,* **461 U.S. 352 (1983),** 176

*Kotteakos v. United States,* **328 U.S. 750 (1946),** 453–454, 461

*Kuhlmann v. Wilson,* **477 U.S. 436 (1986),** 225, 461, 463

*Kyles v. Whitley,* **514 U.S. 419 (1995),** 298, 300

*Kyllo v. United States,* 533 U.S. 27 (2001), 12, 28, 80

# L

*La_er v. Cooper,* **566 U.S. (2012),** 340

*Lawrence v. Florida,* 549 U.S. ___ (2007), 466

*Lee v. United States,* 432 U.S. 23 (1977), 428, 429

*Leis v. Flynt,* 439 U.S. 438 (1979), 336

*Lem Woon v. Oregon,* **229 U.S. 586 (1913),** 288

*Leonard v. United States,* 378 U.S. 544 (1964), 395

*Lewis v. United States,* 518 U.S. 322 (1996), 384, 385

*Leyra v. Denno,* 347 U.S. 556 (1954), 223

*Linkletter v. Walker,* 381 U.S. 618 (1965), 455

*Lockhart v. McCree,* 476 U.S. 162 (1986), 390

*Lockyer v. Andrade,* 538 U.S. 63 (2003), 438

*Lo-Ji Sales, Inc. v. New York,* **442 U.S. 319 (1979),** 100, 102

*Lo-Ji v. State of New York,* 442 U.S. 319 (1979), 46

*Lugar v. Edmondson Oil Co.,* 457 U.S. 922 (1982), 55

*Lynch v. Baxley,* 386 F. Supp. 378 (M.D. Ala. 1974), 384

*Lynch v. United States,* 189 F.2d 476 (5th Cir. 1951), 52

*Lynumm v. Illinois,* 372 U.S. 528 (1963), 223

# M

*Mabry v. Johnson,* **467 U.S. 504 (1984),** 361

*Mackey v. United States,* 401 U.S. 667 (1971), 456

*Magwood v. Patterson,* 561 U.S. ___ (2010), 463

*Maine v. Moulton,* 474 U.S. 159 (1985), 226

*Malley v. Briggs,* **475 U.S. 335, (1986),** 59

*Malloy v. Hogan,* 378 U.S. 1 (1964), 9, 228

*Mancusi v. Stubbs,* 408 U.S. 204 (1972), 415

*Manson v. Braithwaite,* **432 U.S. 98 (1977),** 24, 253, 259

*Maples v. Thomas,* **565 U.S. (2012),** 340

*Mapp v. Ohio,* **367 U.S. 643 (1961),** 41–42, 43, 456

*Marshall v. Barlow's, Inc.,* 436 U.S. 307 (1978), 73, 91

*Marshall v. United States,* 360 U.S. 310 (1959), 407

*Martinez v. Court of Appeal,* 528 U.S. 152 (2000), 448

*Maryland v. Buie,* **494 U.S. 325 (1990),** 132, 135, 174

*Maryland v. Craig,* 497 U.S. 836 (1990), 420

*Maryland v. Garrison,* **480 U.S. 79 (1987),** 102

*Maryland v. King,* 569 U.S. ___ (2013), 278

*Maryland v. Shatzer,* **559 U.S. ___ (2010),** 240

*Maryland v. Wilson,* 519 U.S. 408 (1997), 145, 148

*Massachusetts v. Sheppard,* 468 U.S. 981 (1981), 103

*Massachusetts v. Sheppard,* 468 U.S. 981 (1984), 16, 45

*Massey v. Moore,* 348 U.S. 105 (1954), 335

*Massiah v. United States,* **377 U.S. 201 (1964),** 224

*Mathews v. Diaz,* 426 U.S. 67 (1976), 29

*Mattox v. United States,* **156 U.S. 237 (1895),** 414

*Maxwell v. City of New York,* 102 F.3d 664 (2d Cir. 1996), 204

*McCarthy v. United States,* **394 U.S. 459 (1969),** 364, 367

*McCleskey v. Kemp,* 481 U.S. 279 (1987), 147

*McCleskey v. Zant,* 499 U.S. 467 (1991), 463

*McKane v. Durston,* 153 U.S. 684 (1894), 444

*McKaskle v. Wiggins,* 465 U.S. 168 (1984), 335

*McKeiver v. Pennsylvania,* **403 U.S. 528 (1971),** 384

*McMann v. Richardson,* 397 U.S. 759 (1970), 337

*McQuiggin v. Perkins,* 596 U.S. ___ (2013), 466

*Medina v. California,* 505 U.S. 437 (1992), 412

*Melendez-Diaz v. Massachusetts,* 557 U.S. ___ (2009), 415

*Mempa v. Rhay,* 389 U.S. 128 (1967), 334

*Messerschmidt v. Millender* No. 10-704 (2012), 126

*Messerschmidt v. Millender,* 565 U.S. ___ (2012), 59

*Michigan Dept. of State Police v. Sitz,* **496 U.S. 444 (1990),** 148, 201

*Michigan v. Bryant,* 562 U.S. ___ (2011), 416

*Michigan v. Chestnut,* 486 U.S. 567 (1988), 165

*Michigan v. Clifford,* 464 U.S. 286 (1984), 91, 198

*Michigan v. DeFillippo,* 443 U.S. 31 (1979), 46

*Michigan v. Harvey,* 494 U.S. 344 (1990), 243

*Michigan v. Jackson,* 475 U.S. 625 (1986), 227

*Michigan v. Long,* 463 U.S. 1032 (1983), 145, 147, 174

*Michigan v. Lucas,* 500 U.S. 145 (1991), 295, 425

*Michigan v. Mosley,* **423 U.S. 96 (1975),** 239

*Michigan v. Summers,* **452 U.S. 692 (1981),** 106, 118

*Michigan v. Thomas,* 458 U.S. 259 (1982), 193

*Michigan v. Tucker,* 417 U.S. 433 (1974), 243

*Michigan v. Tyler,* **436 U.S. 499 (1978),** 73, 91, 197, 153

*Mickens v. Taylor,* 535 U.S. 162 (2002), 338

*Miller El v. Dretke,* 125 S.Ct. 2317 (2005), 397

*Miller v. Alabama,* 567 U.S. ___ (2012), 443

*Miller v. United States,* 404 F.2d 611 (5th Cir. 1968), 52

*Miller v. United States,* 357 U.S. 301 (1958), 110

*Mills v. District of Columbia,* 571 F.3d 1304 (D.C. Cir. 2009), 218

*Mills v. Maryland,* 486 U.S. 367 (1988), 465

*Milton v. Wainwright,* 407 U.S. 371 (1972), 454

*Mincey v. Arizona,* 437 U.S. 385 (1978), 70

*Minnesota v. Dickerson,* 508 U.S. 366 (1993), 152, 170

*Minnesota v. Murphy,* 465 U.S. 420 (1984), 231

*Minnesota v. Olson,* **495 U.S. 91 (1990),** 136

*Miranda v. Arizona,* 384 U.S. 436 (1966),

*Miranda v. Arizona,* **384 U.S. 436 (1966),** 12, 19–20, 145, 228, 247, 445

*Missouri v. Frye,* **566 U.S. (2012),** 340, 354

*Missouri v. McNeely,* 569 U.S. ___ (2013), 137

*Monell v. Department of Social Services,* **436 U.S. 658 (1978),** 57

*Monroe v. Pape,* **365 U.S. 167 (1961),** 55

*Montejo v. Louisiana,* 556 U.S. 778 (2009), 227

*Mooney v. Holohan,* **294 U.S. 103 (1935),** 297, 299

*Moore v. Illinois,* **434 U.S. 220 (1977),** 257

*Moran v. Burbine,* 475 U.S. 412 (1986), 226, 238

*Morgan v. Illinois,* 504 U.S. 719 (1992), 394

*Motes v. United States,* **178 U.S. 458 (1900),** 415

*Muehler v. Mena,* 544 U.S. 93 (2005), 118

*Mu'Min v. Virginia,* 500 U.S. 415 (1991), 394

*Muniz v. Hoffman,* 422 U.S. 454 (1975), 385

*Murphy v. Florida,* 421 U.S. 794 (1975), 408

*Murphy v. Hunt,* 455 U.S. 478 (1982), 281

*Myers v. Commonwealth,* 363 Mass. 843 (1973), 289, 290

# N

*NAACP v. Levi,* 418 F. Supp. 1109 (D.D.C. 1976), 316

*Napue v. Illinois,* **360 U.S. 264 (1959),** 297, 299

*Nardone v. United States,* 308 U.S. 338 (1939), 48

*National Treasury Employees Union v. Von Raab,* 489 U.S. 656 (1989), 91, 206

*Nebraska Press Ass'n v. Stuart,* **427 U.S. 539 (1976),** 408

Neil v. Biggers, **409 U.S. 188 (1972)**, 253, 257, 273

Nevada v. Jackson, 569 U.S. ___ (2013), 421

New Jersey v. Portash, 437 U.S. 385 (1978), 243

**New Jersey v. T.L.O., 469 U.S. 325 (1985)**, 73, 92, 203

**New York v. Belton, 453 U.S. 454 (1981)**, 133, 134, 135, 143

**New York v. Burger, 482 U.S. 691 (1987)**, 91, 92, 197, 199

New York v. Class, 475 U.S. 106 (1986), 143

**New York v. Quarles, 467 U.S. 649 (1984)**, 240

**Nix v. Williams, 467 U.S. 431 (1984)**, 50, 51

North Carolina v. Alford, 400 U.S. 25 (1970), 351, 367, 370

North Carolina v. Butler, 441 U.S. 369 (1979), 236–237

**North Carolina v. Pearce, 395 U.S. 711 (1969)**, 429, 449

## O

O'Connor v. Ortega, 480 U.S. 709 (1987), 205, 207

Ohio v. Johnson, 467 U.S. 493 (1984), 428

Ohio v. Roberts, 448 U.S. 56 (1980), 415

Ohio v. Robinette, 519 U.S. 33 (1996), 145, 210

**Oliver v. United States, 466 U.S. 170, 225 (1984)**, 77

Olmstead v. United States, 277 U.S. 438 (1928), 70

Oregon v. Elstad, 470 U.S. 298 (1985), 244

Oregon v. Guzek, 546 U.S. 517 (2006), 443

Oregon v. Hass, 420 U.S. 714 (1975), 243

Oregon v. Kennedy, 456 U.S. 667 (1982), 428

Oregon v. Mathiason, 429 U.S. 492 (1977), 231

Orozco v. Texas, 394 U.S. 324 (1969), 231

O'Sullivan v. Boerckel, 526 U.S. 838 (1999), 462

**Oyler v. Boles, 368 U.S. 448 (1968)**, 316

## P

Padilla v. Kentucky, 559 U.S. ___ (2010), 366

Pannell v. United States, 320 F.2d 698 (D.C.Cir. 1963), 282

**Papachristou v. City of Jacksonville, 405 U.S. 156 (1972)**, 176

Pate v. Robinson, 383 U.S. 375 (1966), 413

Patterson v. Illinois, 487 U.S. 285 (1988), 227

Patton v. United States, 281 U.S. 276 (1930), 386

Patton v. Yount, 467 U.S. 1025 (1984), 408

Payne v. Arkansas, 356 U.S. 560 (1958), 454

Payne v. Tennessee, 501 U.S. 808 (1991), 440

**Payton v. New York, 445 U.S. 573 (1980)**, 107, 214

Pennsylvania Board of Probation and Parole v. Scott, 524 U.S. 357 (1998), 208

Pennsylvania v. Finley, 481 U.S. 551 (1987), 334

**Pennsylvania v. Mimms, 434 U.S. 106 (1977)**, 147, 170, 174

Pennsylvania v. Ritchie, 480 U.S. 39 (1987), 298

Pennsylvania v. Scott, 524 U.S. 357 (1998), 45

People v. Banks, 50 Mich. App. 622 (1974), 266

People v. Boettner, 80 Misc.2d 3 (1974), 73

People v. Brown, 223 Cal. Rptr. 66 (Ct. App. 1986), 353

People v. Cockrell, 63 Cal. 2d 779 (1965), 331

People v. Collier (641 N.Y.S.2d 181 (App. Div. 1996), 357

People v. Mangiefico, 25 Cal.App.3d 1041 (1972), 73

People v. Thomas, 41 Ill.2d 122 (1968), 366

People v. Utica Daw's Drug Co., 16 A.D.2d 12 (1962), 317

Perry v. New Hampshire, 565 U.S. ___ (2012), 253, 274

Phillips v. State (512 S.E.2d 32 (Ga. Ct. App. 1999)), 357

Piazzola v. Watkins, 442 F.2d 284 (5th Cir. 1971), 213

Pointer v. State, 74 So.2d 615 (Ala. Ct. App. 1954), 267

Pointer v. United States, 151 U.S. 396 (1894), 398

**Powell v. Alabama, 287 U.S. 45 (1932)**, 332

Powers v. Ohio, 499 U.S. 400 (1991), 398

**Premo v. Moore, 562 U.S. (2011)**, 340

Presley v. Georgia, No. 09-5270 (2010), 406

**Preston v. United States, 376 U.S. 364 (1964)**, 131

Price v. Georgia, 398 U.S. 323 (1970), 455

Puckett v. United States, 556 U.S. ___ (2009), 361

## R

Rasul v. Bush, 542 U.S. 466 (2004), 30

Ratliff v. State (596 N.E.2d 241 (Ind. Ct. App. 1992), 357

Rawlings v. Kentucky, 448 U.S. 98 (1980), 49, 105, 131

**Reid v. Georgia, 448 U.S. 438 (1980)**, 180

Renico v. Lett, 559 U.S. ___ (2010), 429

**Rhode Island v. Innis, 446 U.S. 291 (1980)**, 233

Richards v. Wisconsin, 520 U.S. 385 (1997), 110

Richmond Newspapers, Inc. v. Virginia, 448 U.S. 555 (1980), 407

**Ricketts v. Adamson, 483 U.S. 1 (1987)**, 362

**Rideau v. Louisiana, 373 U.S. 723 (1963)**, 408

Ring v. Arizona, 122 S.Ct. 2428 (2002), 441, 468

Ristaino v. Ross, 424 U.S. 589 (1976), 394

Rita v. United States, 551 U.S. 338 (2007), 443

Rivera v. Illinois, 556 U.S. ___ (2009), 398

**Riverside County v. McLaughlin, 500 U.S. 44 (1991)**, 279

Rizzo v. Goode, **423 U.S. 362 (1976)**, 56

**Roberts v. Louisiana, 428 U.S. 325 (1977)**, 441

**Roberts v. United States, 445 U.S. 552 (1980)**, 440

Robinson, Gustafson v. Florida, 414 U.S. 260 (1973), 130

Robinson v. California, 370 U.S. 660 (1962), 9

Rochin v. California, 342 U.S. 165 (1952), 120, 138

Rogers v. Richmond, 365 U.S. 534 (1963), 223

Rolling v. State ex rel. Butterworth (741 So. 2d 627 (Fla. Dist. Ct. App. 1999), 357

**Rompilla v. Beard, 545 U.S. 374 (2005)**, 338

Roper v. Simmons, 543 U.S. 551 (2005), 442

**Rose v. Mitchell, 443 U.S. 545 (1979)**, 327

Ross v. Moffitt, 417 U.S. 600 (1974), 334, 448, 464

Ross v. Oklahoma, 487 U.S. 81 (1988), 398

Rothgery v. Gillespie County, 554 U.S. 191 (2008), 226, 278, 334

Roviaro v. United States, 353 U.S. 53 (1957), 423

Rumsfeld v. Padilla, 542 U.S. 426 (2004), 30

Ryan v. Commission on Judicial Performance, 754 P.2d 724 (Cal. 1988), 357

Ryburn v. Huff, 565 U.S. ___ (2012), 59

## S

**Sabbath v. United States, 391 U.S. 585 (1968)**, 110

Safford Unified School District v. Redding, 557 U.S. 364 (2009), 204

Salinas v. Texas, 570 U.S. ___ (2013), 230

**Samson v. California, 547 U.S. 843 (2006)**, 209

**Sanders v. United States, 373 U.S. 1 (1963)**, 459, 463

**Santobello v. New York, 404 U.S. 257 (1971)**, 353, 361

Sattazahn v. Pennsylvania, 537 U.S. 101 (2003), 429

Sawyer v. Smith, 497 U.S. 227 (1990), 465

**Schall v. Martin, 467 U.S. 253 (1984)**, 286

**Schilb v. Kuebel, 404 U.S. 357 (1971)**, 287

Schlup v. Delo, 513 U.S. 298 (1995), 461

Schmerber v. California, 384 U.S. 757 (1966), 137

**Schneckloth v. Bustamonte, 412 U.S. 218 (1973)**, 210

**Schriro v. Landrigan, 550 U.S. (2007)**, 339

Schriro v. Summerlin, 542 U.S. 348 (2004), 465

Scott v. Illinois, 440 U.S. 367 (1979), 333

**Screws v. United States, 325 U.S. 91 (1945)**, 51

See v. City of Seattle, 387 U.S. 541 (1967), 195, 198

**Segura v. United States, 468 U.S. 796 (1984)**, 50, 133, 135

Shaughnessy v. United States ex rel. Mezei, 345 U.S. 206 (1953), 30

# SUBJECT INDEX

Checkpoints, 199–203
    airport, 202–203
    border, 199
    crime investigation, 202
    illegal immigrant, 200–201
    license and safety, 201–202
    sobriety, 201
    unconstitutional, 203
Checks for identification, 177–178
Citizen complaint
    in civil lawsuit, 32, 33
    definition of, 33
    format of, 61f
    process (Claremont, CA, Police
        Department), 62f
Civil asset forfeiture, 312, 427
Civilian input, 60, 63
Civilian monitor, 63
Civilian review of law enforcement, 63
Civil litigation, 53
    stages of, 54
Civil remedies for constitutional rights
        violations, 53–59
    Bivens claims against federal officials
        and, 58
    defenses to Section 1983 civil liability and,
        54–58
    liability and, 54–55
    42 U.S.C. Section 1983 and, 54–55. See also
        42 U.S.C. Section 1983
Civil Rights Act (1964), Title VII of, 148–149
Claim, in civil lawsuit, 54
Closely regulated businesses, 196–197
Collateral attack, 44, 456
Color of law, 55–56
Common authority, 212
Competence
    of defendant, 412–413
    of witness, 266
Complaint
    citizen, in civil lawsuit, 54
    in pretrial process, 31–33
Compulsory process, right to, 422–425
    grants of immunity in, 330
    presenting evidence in, 424–425
    subpoenas in, 329–330
Concurring opinion, 21
Conditional guilty plea, 363
Confession(s)
    definition of, 222
    documenting, importance of, 244–246
    due process and, 222
    Miranda approach to, 228–242. See also
        Miranda warnings/rights
    Sixth Amendment approach to, 224–225
    various approaches, 246f
    See also Interrogations
Confrontation, right to, 409–421
    challenging testimony in, 418–421
    defendant's appearance and, 414
    defendant's presence and, 410, 411f
    definition of, 409

live testimony and, 414
    Physical presence of defendant, 410–412
Consent searches, 210–214
    drug courier profiling and, 178–180
    "knock and talk", 213–214
    scope of, limitations of, 211–212
    third-party consent for, 212–213
    voluntariness of, 210–211
Constitutional Amendments, 5f
Constitutional errors, 453–454
    serious, 454–455
Constitutional rights, 4–9
    issues of, 452
    sources of, 4–5
    violations of, 39–40, 56–58, 423, 453. See
        also specific rights, e.g. Search(es)
Contempt power, 330
Contesting guilty plea, 369–370
Contributory negligence, 379–380
Counsel
    effective assistance of, 310, 336–339, 354
    right to, 227, 252, 329, 331–339
County liability, 57
Court decisions, definition of, 4–5
Courtroom work group, 332
Courts
    appellate, intermediate, 16, 17f
    district, 16
    of general jurisdiction, 16, 17f
    of limited jurisdiction, 16, 17f
    military, 17
    relationship among, 18
    structure, state system, 17f
    superior, 16, 17f
    supreme, state, 16, 23f
Credibility of witness, 266–267
Crime control perspective, on criminal
        procedure, 15–16
Crime investigation checkpoints, 202
Criminal cases, 22–23
Criminal justice system, sequence of events, 32f
Criminal procedure, 3–34
    adjudication in, 33–34
    and Amendments
        Eighth Amendment and, 7
        Fifth Amendment and, 6
        First and, 8
        Fourteenth Amendment and, 7
        Fourth Amendment and, 6
        Sixth Amendment, 6–7
    competing concerns in, 13
    constitutional rights and, 4–9
    definition of, 4
    impact of technology, 31
    legal research and, 10, 20, 21
    overview of, 31–34
    parties involved in, 19
    post-September 11, 28, 29f
    precedent in, 4, 10–11
    pretrial phase of, 31–33. See also Pretrial
        process
    rights of relevance in, 5–7

technology, impact on, 31
    themes in, 4
    theory versus reality and, 11–12
    war on terrorism and, 28–30
Criminal proceedings
    formal, 225–226
    right to counsel in, 329
Criminal remedies for constitutional rights
        violations, 51–53, 53–59
Cross-examination of witnesses, 263, 419,
        420–421
    obtaining evidence and, 420–421
Culpability
    in constitutional rights violations, 56
    under Section 1983, 56
    theories of liability under, 56–58
Curtilage, 77–79
    definition of, 77
    open fields and, 77–79, 78f, 79f
Custody
    chain of, 300–302
    Miranda rights and, 230–232, 233f
    questioning at police station, 231
    questioning in home, 231
    questioning of juvenile, 231
    questioning of probationers, 231–232
    traffic stop, 230

## D

Damages, 53
Dangerousness, pretrial release and, 286
Deadly force, 52
    during execution of warrant, 109
    use of, 53
Death penalty cases
    challenges for cause in, 395
    sentencing in, 461
Defendant(s)
    access of, to trial transcripts, 446, 447
    allocution of, 290
    assertion of right to speedy trial by, 380
    definition of, 21, 44
    effects of plea bargaining on, 362–364
    indigent versus nonindigent, right to
        counsel of, 336
    joinder of, 320–321
    multiple, charges against multiple, 321
    multiple charges against same, 320–321
    pleas available to, 34
    presence of, at confrontation, 409–414,
        411f
    pretrial release of, 280. See also Pretrial
        release
    right of, to counsel during appeal, 448–450
    trial delay as prejudicial to, 380–381
Defense(s)
    discovery by, 295–296
    public duty, 53
Defense(s)/defense attorneys, 331–339
    appeals by, 452–453
    closure sought by, right to public trial and,
        406–407

section 1983 and, 242
substance and adequacy of, 234–235
Supreme Court and, 240–241
voluntariness of, 238
waiver of, 227, 235, 236–237, 236f, 239f
Mistrial, reprosecution after, 429
Municipal liability, 57, 58

# N

Neutral and detached magistrate in issuance of warrant, 98–101
*Nolo* contendere, 33
Nonconstitutional errors, 453–454
Noncriminal proceeding rule, 384
Nondeadly force
during execution of warrant, 112
Nonjudicial remedies for constitutional rights violations, 59–64
Nonprosecution
decision for, 310–312
reasons for, 312–315
Nonreciprocal discovery, 296–297
Nonstop, 106–107
stop distinguished from, 106f
"Not guilty" plea, 33
at arraignment, 290

# O

Objective reasonableness, 25
Fourth Amendment and, 42–43
of search of wrong residence, 112
Offender, significant, 317
Offense(s)
same, definition of, 427
Ombudsman, 60
Omnibus Crime Control and Safe Streets Act (1968), Title III of, 123–124
Open fields
curtilage and, 77–79
definition of, 77
Opinion, 21
Overview of criminal process, 31

# P

Papers and effects, 71
Parole revocation hearings, exclusionary rule and, 45
Particularity
in arrest warrants, 101
definition of, 101
in search warrants, 99f
Patriot Act (2001), 28
abolishment of constitutional protections to aliens, 29–30
aliens, impact on, 30
electronic surveillance and, 121
implications to criminal procedure, 30
significant changes of, 28–29
terrorism and domestic terrorism, 28–29
World trade center blast, 29f

Peremptory challenges in jury selection, 391, 396–399
Personal property, search and seizure of, 100
Person inventories, 193
Person(s)
definition of, 71
seizures of, 81, 82
wrong, arrest of, 112, 114
Petitioner, definition of, 21
Petty crime exception, 384–385
Photographic arrays, 251–252, 254, 258, 261–262
Physical characteristics, privacy of, 76–77
"Plain touch and feel," in stop-and-frisk, 175–176
"Plain touch/feel/smell" in "plain view" doctrine, 152
"Plain view" doctrine, 152–153
as fallback measure, 152–153
"immediately apparent" requirement of, 151
inadvertency in, 151–152
lawful access requirement of, 150
plain touch, feel, and smell in, 152
Plea bargaining, 33, 347–364
ad hoc, 356–357, 357f
arguments supporting, 350f
constitutional rights during, 353–354
definitions of, 347
effects of, 360–364
history of, 347–348
inclusion of victim, 364
judicial inducements for, 358–359
pleading guilty differentiated from, 366
procedure, 359f
process of, 353–357
prosecutor and, 310
prosecutorial inducements for, 354–356
restrictions on, 354–356
rise in, reasons for, 347–348
statutory inducements for, 357–358
U.S. Supreme Court on, 353
Pleas/pleading
at arraignment, 33, 290
guilty, 364. *See also* "Guilty" plea
"not guilty", 33, 290
sample format, 346f–347f
Police/probation partnerships, 209
Police trickery and waiver, 237–238
Precedent, 10
definition, 4
judicial restraint and, 27
Preliminary hearing (s), 33, 288–290
Pretextual prosecution, 318
Pretrial
identification procedures, 254–261
Pretrial process, 277–304, 304f
arraignment in, 33, 290
bail in, 33
booking in, 33
complaint in, 31–33

discovery in, 291–293. *See also* Discovery of evidence
grand jury in, 33
initial appearance in, 278
law enforcement in, 28
preliminary hearing in, 288
pretrial release in, 280. *See also* Pretrial release
probable cause hearing in, 278–280
treatment of detainees in, 287–288
Pretrial release, 280–288
with bail, 282–284
criteria for, 285–287
definition of, 280
hearing for, 281–282
on one's own recognizance, 284–285
preventive detention and, 285
Preventive detention, 285
Prima facia case, 33
Prison sentences
types of, 438–440
Privacy
court decisions on, 27–28
definition of, 27
physical characteristics and, 76–77
reasonable expectation of, 71, 74–75
right to, 28
Privacy doctrine, 28
Probable cause, 83–90
to arrest, 88
arrests and, 85
arrest warrants and, 97–98
components, 84f
definition of, 83
determination of, 33, 87
firsthand knowledge and, 87–88
home inspections and, 195
"immediately apparent" and, 151
informants and, 86–87
justification doctrine and, 82–83
preliminary hearing and, 289
prudent man concept and, 83
reasonable reliance on mistaken information and, 88
reasonable suspicion *vs.*, 88–90
searches and, 83–86
search warrants and, 101
third parties and, 86–87
Probable cause hearing, 278–280
Probation supervision searches, 208–209
Procedural due process, 7
Profiling
drug courier, 178–180. *See also* Drug courier profiling
racial, 146–147. *See also* Racial profiling
Property
damage to, during execution of arrest warrant, 110–111
seizures of, 81–82
Prosecutorial discretion, 310
Prosecutorial inducements, 354. *See also* Plea bargaining

constitutional protection against, 6

Sentences/sentencing, 34, 438–443
  constitutional rights during, 443–444
  death penalty, 440–442
  definition of, 438
  double jeopardy and, 429
  guidelines for, 438–439, 439f
  notions of finality of litigation, 459
  other decisions, 442–443
  plea bargaining and, 353–354
  types of, 438–440
  understanding, guilty plea and, 366

September 11 (2001). *See also* Patriot Act
    (2001)
  criminal procedures after, 28–31

Settlement, prelitigation, 54

Severance, 320

Showups, 254, 256–258, 260. *See also*
    Identification procedures

Significant offender, 317

"Silver platter" doctrine, 41

Six-month imprisonment rule, 34, 385

Sixth Amendment, 6–7, 255
  discovery and, 294–295
  implications of the Patriot Act, 29
  interrogations/confessions and, 222–223
  jury trial requirement, 29
  right to counsel and, 333–334

Slow plea of guilty, 352

Sobriety checkpoints, 201

Sovereign immunity, 53

Sovereignty, dual, in court system, 16

Speedy trial
  definition of, 376
  right to, 376–381
  violation of, 378–382

Standards of conduct
  for judges, 388–391
  for judicial employees, 313–314
  for prosecutors, 310

Standing cases, confessions and exclusionary
    rule and, 242–243

Stare decisis, 10

State constitutions, as source of rights, 5

State officials liability, 54–55

State supreme court, 16, 18

Statutes, as source of rights, 5

Statutory inducements, for plea bargaining,
    357

Stop-and-frisk, 163. *See also* Frisk(s); Stop(s)
  checks for identification, 177–178
  law on, 174–178
  plain touch and feel and, 175–176
  policy on, example of, 173f, 174
  proper seizures, example, 176f

Stop(s), 163–170
  arrest distinguished from, 104–106
  consensual encounter distinguished from,
    163, 164f
  definition of, 163–166
  duration of, 167–168
  "free to leave" and, 168

for loitering, 174
  nonstop distinguished from, 106–107
  proper, 169
  seizure of property and, 168–170
  vehicle, weapons searches and, 174

Strip and Body Cavity Search Policy, 122f

Students, drug and alcohol testing of,
    207–208

Subjective reasonableness, 24–26

Subpoena *ad testificandum,* 329

Subpoena *duces tecum,* 329–330

Substantive due process, 7, 58

Suggestive lineup, 255

Superior courts, 16–18

Supervisory liability, 56–57

Supreme court
  state, 16, 18, 21
  U.S., 15, 16

Surveillance, electronic, 121–123. *See also*
    Electronic surveillance

Suspicion, reasonable, 161–189
  stop-and-frisk and, 163

Sweeps, protective
  definition of, 174–175
  of residences, 174–175
  during searches, 133

Systematic exclusion, in jury selection,
    390–391

## T

Tainted identification, 270–271

Terrorism
  criminal procedure and, 28–31
  definition of, 29

Terrorist profiling, 183

Theory of liability, 56

Theory world, of criminal procedure, 11

Thermal imaging, 80

Third-party appeals, 453

Title III of Omnibus Crime Control and Safe
    Streets Act (1968), 121, 123–124

Title VII of Civil Rights Act of 1964, 148–149

Totality of circumstances, 24

Traffic stop, custody in, 230

Trail
  identification procedures during, 258,
    264–270

Transactional immunity, 330

Trespass doctrine, 28

Trial, 40
  bench, 34, 354, 382, 386
  bifurcated, 441
  *de novo,* 445
  right at, 376–399
  transcript of, defendant access to,
    446, 447f

True bill, 324

## U

Unavailable witness, 415–416

Unconstitutional checkpoints, 203

Undercover agents, searches and, 76

Underrepresentation, in jury selection, 390

Unreasonable, definition of, 4–5

U.S. Constitution, 5
  interpretation of, judicial restraint
    and, 27
  restrictions of, on identification
    procedures, 252–254
  rights guaranteed by, violations of, remedies
    for, 39–67. *See also* Remedies for
    constitutional violations

U.S. courts of appeals, 18f, 19f

U.S. court system, effects of plea bargaining
    on, 360–362

U.S. District Courts, 19f

U.S. Supreme Court, 14, 16, 18
  decisions of, 18, 20f
  Miranda rights and, 240–241
  personal privacy and, 27–28
  plea bargaining and, 349
  subjective *versus* objectivity of, 24–26
  faith in police and, 15

Use and derivative use immunity, 330

## V

Vacating, of lower court decisions, 21

Variance in evidence, 331

Vehicle inventories, 192–193, 194f

Vehicle search policy, 142f

Verdicts of criminal cases, 34

Vindictive prosecution, 317–319

*Voir dire* process, 391–399
  challenges for cause in, 395
  judge's questioning in, 359, 391
  peremptory challenges in, 391, 396–399
  pretrial publicity and, 407–408
  state provisions for, 392f

Voluntariness
  of confessions and admissions, 222–224,
    224f
  of guilty plea, 367
  of Miranda waiver, 238

## W

Waiver of the Sixth Amendment Right to
    Counsel (Confessions), 227

Warrant clause of Fourth Amendment, 70

Warrant(s)
  clause, 70
  components of, 98–103
  Fourth Amendment and, 98–101
  requirement for, exceptions to, 129–159.
    *See also* Exceptions to warrant
    requirement
  search. *See* Search warrants
  searches with, 97–101, 115–120
  Title III, 123–124

Warren, Earl, 27

Warren Court, 27

Witness(es)
  challenging testimony of, 414